THE GLOBAL TRADING SYSTEM
AND DEVELOPING ASIA

THE GLOBAL TRADING SYSTEM
AND DEVELOPING ASIA

Edited by

Arvind Panagariya
M.G. Quibria
Narhari Rao

Published for the Asian Development Bank
by Oxford University Press

Oxford University Press

Oxford New York
Athens Auckland Bangkok Bogota Bombay
Buenos Aires Calcutta Cape Town Dar es Salaam
Delhi Florence Hong Kong Istanbul Karachi
Kuala Lumpur Madras Madrid Melbourne
Mexico City Nairobi Paris Singapore
Taipei Tokyo Toronto

and associated companies in
Berlin Ibadan

Oxford is a trademark of Oxford University Press

First published 1997
This impression (lowest digit)
1 3 5 7 9 10 8 6 4 2

© Asian Development Bank 1997

Published for the Asian Development Bank by
Oxford University Press

British Library Cataloguing in Publication Data
available

Library of Congress Cataloging-in-Publication Data
The Global trading system and developing Asia / edited by Arvind
Panagariya, M.G. Quibria, and Narhari Rao.
p. cm.
Includes bibliographical references and index. ISBN 0-19-590502-4
1. Asia—Commerce. 2. Developing countries—Commerce. 3. Trade
blocs—Asia. 4. Trade blocs—Developing countries. 5. Uruguay
Round (1987-1994) 6. World Trade Organization. I. Panagariya,
Arvind. II. Quibria, M.G. (Muhammad Ghulam) III. Rao, Narhari.
HF3752.3.G56   1997
382' .95—dc21   97-29597
CIP

Printed in Hong Kong
Published by Oxford University Press (China) Ltd
18/F Warwick House, Taikoo Place, 979 King's Road,
Quarry Bay, Hong Kong

CONTENTS

                                                                    Page

Contents   v
Foreword   xvii
Preface   xix
List of Contributors   xxi
Abbreviations and Definitions   xxiii

Chapter One
Introduction   1
Arvind Panagariya, M.G. Quibria, and Narhari Rao

Importance of Trade in Asia   4
New Challenges: Regionalism   6
    Impact of NAFTA and the European Union on Asia   7
    Asia's Future Strategy   8
New Challenges: Environmental and Labor Standards   10
    Trade and Environment   11
    Trade and Labor Standards   14
Uruguay Round: Areas of Current Impact   16
    Textiles and Clothing   16
    Trade-Related Intellectual Property Rights   20
Nontraditional Instruments of Trade Policy   25
Uruguay Round: Areas of Future Action   33
    The General Agreement on Trade in Services   33
    Trade in Agriculture   35
Conclusion   39
References   41

Table
Table 1. Key Indicators of Asian Trade and Development   5

Part One — The New Challenge

Chapter Two
The World Trading System: The New Challenges   47
Jagdish Bhagwati

Introduction   49

Attitudes to Integration in the World Economy:

An Ironic Reversal 50

The Earlier Situation 51

The Turnaround 52

Environment and Labor Standards at the World Trade Organization 54

Environmental Standards 55

A Proposal to Extend Domestic Standards in High-Standards
Countries to Their Firms in Low-Standards Countries 58

Labor Standards and the Social Clause 62

Competition Policy 68

Regionalism Versus Multilateralism: Asia's Challenge
and Opportunity 69

References 77

Chapter Three
The New Regionalism and Asia: Impact and Options 81
Jeffrey A. Frankel and Shang-Jin Wei

The Impact of Western Free Trade Agreements on Asia 85

The Effects of NAFTA on Asia 86

The Effects of an Enlarged Free Trade Area of the
Americas 88

Effects of the European Union on Asia 89

To What Extent Do Implicit Trading Blocs Already Exist in Asia?
Estimates from the Gravity Model 91

The Gravity Model 92

Implicit and Explicit Trade Blocs in East Asia 94

Broader Asian and Pacific Groupings 96

Strategies from the Viewpoint of Asian Countries 100

Regionalism as a Possible Vehicle for External Liberalization 104

Negative Political Implications for Multilateral
Trade Liberalization 105

Positive Political Implications for Multilateral
Trade Liberalization 110

Which Effects are Likely to Dominate? 115

References 120

Comments by *Arvind Panagariya* 131

Tables
Table 1. Estimates of Regional Bloc Effects Using the
  Gravity Model Trade   99
Table 2. Openness of Subregions in Asia   116

Chapter Four
Capital Market Integration in Developing Asia   137
James Riedel

Are Capital Markets in Asia Becoming More Integrated?   139
  Net Capital Flows   140
  Foreign Direct Investment   142
  Portfolio Equity Flows   147
  Bond Flows   149
  Net Versus Gross and Large Versus Small   150
  The Law of One Price in Asian Financial Markets   152
Implications of Capital Market Integration in Asia   155
  Growth   155
  Stability   158
  Policy   159
Acknowledgments   161
References   162
Comments by *Junichi Goto*   166

Figure
Figure 1. Net Long-Term Capital Flows as Percentage of
  GNP for All LDCs, East Asia and Pacific, and South Asia   141

Tables
Table 1. Net Long-Term Capital Flows to Developing
  Countries and Selected Regions by Type of Flow   143
Table 2. Net Foreign Direct Investment Flows to Selected
  Asian Developing Countries   144
Table 3. The Source of FDI in Selected East Asian Countries,
  1986 to 1992   145
Table 4. Portfolio Equity Flows to Selected Asian
  Developing Countries   148
Table 5. Annual Average Return in Selected Asian
  Stock Markets   149

Table 6. Net Bond Flows to Selected East and
    South Asian Countries   151
Table 7. Deviations from Uncovered Interest Parity in
    Six Asian Developing Countries   153
Table 8. Real Interest Rate Differentials for Selected
    Asian Countries   154

Chapter Five
Labor Market Integration in Asia   171
  M.G. *Quibria*

Introduction   173
Labor Flows   173
    Labor Movements to West Asia: Levels and Trends   174
    Labor Movements to East Asia: Levels and Trends   175
    Prospects of Labor Market Integration in Asia   178
Implications of Labor Market Integration in Asia   179
    Labor Movement and Economic Efficiency   179
    Labor Movement and Long-Term Growth   181
    Labor Movement and Unemployment   182
Why Is Labor Movement Restricted?   184
Are Trade, Aid, and Investment Substitutes for
    International Migration?   187
The Labor Market Story Behind the Success of
    Newly Industrializing Economies   188
    Case Studies of Hong Kong and Singapore   188
    Hong Kong   189
    Singapore   190
Conclusions and Policy Implications   192
    Global Issues   193
    Regional Issues   194
References   195
Comments by *Peter J. Lloyd*   *199*

Figure
Figure 1. Unemployment and Immigration (1991)   183

Chapter Six
International Labor Standards and Trade Policy   203
Narhari Rao

Definition and Enforcement of Labor Standards   207
Some Simple Economics of Labor Standards   207
Labor Standards and the Case for Free Trade   210
The Case for Labor Standards: A Critical Evaluation   211
     The Humanitarian Argument   211
     National Welfare Argument   212
Mechanisms for Achieving Comparable Standards   215
Minimum Understanding on Labor Standards   217
Institutional Mechanism   218
Conclusion   219
References   222
Comments by *Kym Anderson*   224

Table
Table 1. Economic Growth and Earnings Growth in
     Four Newly Industrializing Economies in the 1980s   217

Chapter Seven
International Trade and the Asian Environment   229
Douglas H. Brooks

Interactions Between Trade and Environment   231
     Comparative Advantage, Environmental Endowments,
         and Property Rights   232
     Economic Growth, Trade, and the Environment   234
     The Product Life Cycle   235
     Environmental Policies, Product Standards, and
         Trade Effects   236
     International Environmental Agreements   238
     Trade Policies and Environmental Consequences   239
     Trade Liberalization and the Environment   241
     The World Trade Organization   243
Trade and Environment in Post-Uruguay Round
     Developing Asia and the Pacific   243
         Population Growth, Food, and Agriculture   243

Growth of Income   244
Growth in Trade   245
Regional Cooperation   250
Conclusions   251
Acknowledgments   252
References   254
Comments by *Ishrat Husain*   257

Figure

Figure 1. Scatter Plot of Environmentally Sensitive Share
of Exports vs GNP per Capita   249

Tables

Table 1. A Sample of International Environmental Agreements   240
Table 2. Effects of Trade Liberalization in a Small,
Open Economy and Policy Responses   242
Table 3. Average Annual Growth Rates for ADB's DMCs   246
Table 4. Export Structure of Selected Asian and
Pacific Economies   248
Table 5. Asia's Waste Imports, 1990-1993   250

Part Two — Uruguay Round: Areas of Current Action

Chapter Eight
The Impact of the Multifiber Arrangement Phaseout
on the Asian Economies   265
John Whalley

Introduction   267
The Uruguay Round Agreement and the Phaseout
of the Multifiber Arrangement   268
The Content of the Agreement   268
Assessing How the Agreement Will Operate   272
The Long-Run Effects of Eliminating the Multifiber Arrangement   275
Removal of Restraints on Trade   275
Rent Transfers   276
Degree of Restraint Implied by Quotas   277
Quality Upgrading and Product and Market Diversification   279
Quota Hopping, Foreign Investment, and

Other Related Effects   280
Internal Quota Allocation Rules   281
Implications of the Elimination of the Multifiber
     Arrangement on Asian Economies   281
       Welfare Effects of Elimination of the
         Multifiber Arrangement   282
       Long-Run Trade and Production Effects for Asian
         Economies   284
       The Special Position of the People's Republic of China   286
       Other Issues With the Asian Economies   287
Conclusion   288
Annex: Effects of Changes in Market Access in Manufactures
     Other Than Textiles and Apparel for Developing Asia   290
Acknowledgment   293
References   295
Comments by *Joseph Francois*   298

Tables

Table 1. The Uruguay Round Agreements on
     Textiles and Clothing   269
Table 2. Examples of Phased Increases in Quota Growth Rates   271
Table 3. Data on Quota Utilization Rates for
     Asian Economies in the United States, European Union,
     and Canadian Markets by Supplying Countries, 1989   278
Table 4. Estimates of General Equilibrium Welfare Effects
     of Removing Import Trade Restrictions on Textiles and
     Clothing in Developed Countries   283
Table 5. Estimates of Production and Trade Effects of
     Removing Bilateral Multifiber Arrangement Quotas
     and Tariffs on Textiles and Apparel   285
Table 6. Shares of Countries in World Exports of Clothing   287
Table 7. Hourly Wages in Apparel Industries in
     Selected Countries, 1987   289
Table A1. Pre- and Post-Uruguay Round Most-Favored
     Nation Tariff Rates on Nonagricultural Products   291

Chapter Nine
Trade-Related Intellectual Property Rights and Asian
Developing Countries: An Analytical View   305
Arvind Subramanian

Introduction   307
Origins   307
Uniqueness of Trade-Related Intellectual Property Rights   309
The TRIPs Agreement and Its Impact on Asia   310
　　Key Provisions and Legislative Changes   311
　　Copyright and Related Rights   312
　　Integrated Circuits   316
　　Trademarks and Geographical Indications   319
　　Undisclosed Information and Test Data   319
　　Anticompetitive Practices and Contractual Licenses   320
　　Enforcement   321
　　Dispute Settlement and Prevention   324
　　Transitional Arrangements   325
The Economic Impact of TRIPs   325
　　Economics of Intellectual Property Rights at the
　　　　National Level   325
　　Economics of Intellectual Property Rights at the
　　　　International Level   328
　　Research and Development and Technology Transfer Effects 329
　　The Asian Situation   330
Policy Options   339
Why Was TRIPs Successful?   341
Conclusions   342
Annex: Table 1A. Salient Features of the TRIPs Agreement   344
Acknowledgments   351
References   354
Comments by *Alan Deardorff*   357

Boxes
Box 1. Timing of Impact of the TRIPs Provisions on Pharmaceuticals 326
Box 2. Plant Variety Protection — Needless Anxiety?   337

Tables
Table 1. Key Changes to IP Regimes in Developing
　　Asian Countries Consequent Upon TRIPs Standards   313

Table 2. Membership of Asian Developing Countries
in Major IP Conventions 315
Table 3. Key Changes to IP Regimes in Developing
Asian Countries Consequent Upon TRIPs Enforcement 317
Table 4. Estimated Copyright Piracy Losses in Asian
Countries, 1994 321
Table 5. Impact of TRIPs on the Pharmaceutical
Market in Selected Asian Countries 331
Table 6. Effects of Intellectual Property Protection on FDI
and Transfer of Technology in Selected Asian Countries 335

Chapter Ten
Trade Remedies and Legal Remedies: Antidumping, Safeguards,
and Dispute Settlement After the Uruguay Round 363
Kenneth W. Abbott

Introduction 365
Antidumping Measures 367
    Practice 367
    Policy 369
    Law 376
Safeguard Measures 383
    Practice 383
    Policy 387
    Law 389
Dispute Settlement 392
    Practice 392
    Policy 393
    Law 395
Conclusion 402
Annex I: Antidumping Measures By and Against
Asian Developing Countries 404
Annex II: The Spread of Antidumping Measures 414
Annex III: WTO Disputes Involving Developing
Countries 1995/1996 416
References 421
Comments by *David Palmeter* 425

Part Three — Uruguay Round: Areas of Future Action

Chapter Eleven
World Agricultural Trade after the Uruguay Round:
Disarray Forever?   435
Ammar Siamwalla

What Was Agreed   437
    Agriculture in the General Agreement on
        Tariffs and Trade 1947   437
    Broad Outline of the New Agreement on Agriculture   438
    Fine Prints and Loopholes   442
    Sanitary and Phyto-Sanitary Measures   451
Calculations of Impact   453
    Effects on Prices: Based on Assumed Degrees
        of Liberalization   455
    Effects on Prices: Based on the Actual Results
        of the Round   460
    Effects on Price Stability   463
    Relocation of Agricultural Production   464
    Changes in Food Consumption   466
    Which Countries Gained, Which Lost, and
        By How Much?   466
Conclusions   469
Annex: A Note on the Legal Texts   471
References   473
Comments by *T.N. Srinivasan*   477

Figure
Figure 1. Nominal and Real Price Trends of Some Agricultural
    Commodities 1970-1995   447

Tables
Table 1. Changes in Tariff Escalation on Products Imported
    by Developed Economies from Developing Economies   443
Table 2. Comparison of Estimated Ad-Valorem Tariff
    Equivalent, 1986 to 1988 and Tariffs Declared in
    Country Schedules   450
Table 3. Effects of Assumed Liberalization Scenarios
    on Selected Commodity Prices   456

Table 4. Effects of Developed and Developing Countries'
Policies on World Sugar Price, 2002   460
Table 5. Effects of Actual Results of the Uruguay
Round on Selected Commodity Prices   461
Table 6. Effects of the Uruguay Round Agricultural
Trade Liberalization on Production   465
Table 7. Welfare Effects of Trade Liberalization   468

Chapter Twelve
Impact of the Uruguay Round on Asia: Trade in Services and Trade-Related Investment Measures
Patrick Low

    481

Services in the World Economy   486
The General Agreement on Trade in Services   489
Schedules of Specific Commitments   500
The Trade in Services Work Program   503
   Movement of Natural Persons   503
   Trade in Financial Services   513
   Basic Telecommunications   516
   Maritime Transport Services   518
Trade-Related Investment Measures in the Uruguay Round   520
   Investment Issues in a Broader Setting   522
Conclusions   524
Annex: Main Provisions of the General Agreement on
Trade and Services   527
References   542
Comments by *Richard H. Snape*   544

Tables
Table 1. World Growth Summary   487
Table 2. World Exports of Merchandise and
Commercial Services, 1980 to 1992   488
Table 3. Leading Exporters and Importers in World Trade
in Commercial Services, 1993   490
Table 4. Composition of Commercial Services Exports in
1980 and 1992   492
Table 5. Trade in Commercial Services for Selected Regions
and Countries, 1980 and 1992   493

Table 6. Sectoral Composition of Commercial Services
    Exports, 1982 to 1992   494
Table 7. FDI Inflows in Developing Countries and
    Other Indicators, 1986 to 1993   495
Table 8. Commitments on Services Activities by Country Group   501
Table 9. Number of Commitments on Services Activities
    of GATS Participants   502
Table 10. Specific Sectoral Commitments   504
Table 11. Commitments in Services Activities by
    Major Country Group   506

Author Index   549
Subject Index   555

FOREWORD

International trade has been the key to developing Asia's spectacular economic success in recent decades. Taking advantage of rapidly expanding markets and progressive trade liberalization in industrial economies, many of these countries launched their outward-oriented strategies as early as three decades ago and experienced unprecedented growth. But the revival of protectionism and the spread of regionalism during the 1980s and early 1990s, began to cast doubts on the ability of these countries to sustain the liberalization momentum. These doubts were reinforced by fears of the Uruguay Round's failure with the possibility of the world being divided into closed blocs.

Happily, however, the Uruguay Round was successfully completed in December 1993, with the General Agreement on Tariffs and Trade giving way to a permanent institution called the World Trade Organization (WTO). WTO, in turn, brought trade in agriculture and services into the fold of multilateral discipline for the first time. Recognizing the far-reaching importance of the Uruguay Round and the future developments likely to follow from it, in 1994, the Asian Development Bank commissioned a research study entitled, "The Emerging Trading Environment: Economic Implications for Developing Member Countries" under its regional technical assistance program. The purpose of the study was to analyze the impact of the Uruguay Round on developing Asia, and to assist the developing member countries in designing response strategies to maximize the benefits from the Round.

The study, which has been recently completed, was conducted in two parts. The first phase focused on a region-wide analysis in which thematic papers were written on the implications of the Uruguay Round agreement and of the evolving regional trade arrangements on the trade prospects of the Asian developing countries. Building on the framework provided by the papers in the first phase, the second phase undertook in-depth studies on the likely impact of the emerging global trading environment and optimal response to it in ten developing member countries, viz., Bangladesh, People's Republic of China, India, Indonesia, Republic of Korea, Malaysia, Pakistan, Philippines, Sri Lanka, and Thailand. The findings of the studies were discussed in two conferences held at the Bank's headquarters in Manila. This volume contains the papers which were presented at the first conference held on 29-30 May 1995.

The views and opinions expressed in this volume are those of the authors and do not necessarily reflect those of the Asian Development Bank or of its Board of Directors.

V. V. Desai
Director and Chief Economist
Economics and Development Resource Center

N A

B C Title: **PREFACE**

    This volume is the outcome of the Asian Development Bank Conference on The Emerging Global Trading Environment and Developing Asia held on 29-30 May 1995 at Bank Headquarters in Manila, Philippines.

    Bank President Mitsuo Sato inaugurated the conference which was attended by high-level policymakers from developing Asian and Pacific countries, academic economists, researchers, representatives from chambers of commerce and industry, staff of the Asian Development Bank, and representatives of major international development agencies. Jagdish Bhagwati, Arthur Lehman Professor of Economics at Columbia University, delivered the keynote address. A number of senior officials of the Bank chaired the sessions, namely, Vice-President Bong-Suh Lee, Vishvanath V. Desai, Paul M. Dickie, Barry Metzger, and J. Malcolm Dowling.

    The success of the conference is largely due to the cooperation and efforts of the economists of the Economics and Development Resource Center and its supporting staff, particularly Lutgarda Labios, Elizabeth Leuterio, and Patricia Baysa who provided indispensable assistance in organizing the logistics of the conference.

    The papers carried in this volume are authored by leading international experts who offer a critical assessment of the challenges posed and opportunities offered by the global trading system to developing Asian countries. The book examines the implications for Asia of the rapidly expanding preferential trade arrangements and the demands by developed countries for linking market access to labor and environmental standards. It also offers a detailed analysis of the likely impact on Asian developing countries of the Uruguay Round Agreement in areas such as textiles and clothing, agriculture, services, intellectual property rights, and administered protection.

    In preparing this book, we have benefited greatly from comments made at the conference by various individuals. In particular, we would like to acknowledge the helpful comments of Shamshad Akhtar, Frank Harrigan, Brian Hindley, Rajiv Kumar, Sudipto Mundle, and Min Tang.

    The following individuals deserve special mention for their cooperation and contributions in processing the volume. Terry Hill handled the main responsibility of copyediting the book with skill and grace and went beyond the call of her duty in nudging the volume toward completion. Cherry Lynn Zafaralla provided additional editorial assistance and efficiently managed the final stages of production. Elizabeth Leuterio and Emma Banaria provided valuable research assistance and processed voluminous correspondence, along with Ma. Luisa Sinco who assisted in the reference research and proofreading. Expert word processing assistance was rendered by Anna Liza Silverio and Patricia Baysa who conscientiously worked on several hundred pages of drafts. A team of desktop design artists namely, Ma. Lourdes Maestro who performed the layout and initial filming, Judy Yñiguez and Mercedita Cabañeros who prepared the final proofs and films, and Vicente Angeles who designed the cover, carried out the responsibility of putting the volume in its final form. Finally, despite his heavy workload, Raveendranath Rajan from the Bank's Printing section graciously processed many rounds of revisions in the layouts and films.

Arvind Panagariya
M.G. Quibria
Narhari Rao

LIST OF CONTRIBUTORS

CHAPTER WRITERS

KENNETH W. ABBOTT
Elizabeth Froeling Horner Professor of Law and Commerce
Northwestern University School of Law

JAGDISH BHAGWATI
Arthur Lehman Professor of Economics
Columbia University

DOUGLAS H. BROOKS
Economist
Economics and Development Resource Center
Asian Development Bank

JEFFREY A. FRANKEL
Professor of Economics
University of California, Berkeley

PATRICK LOW
Director
Economic Research and Analysis
World Trade Organization

ARVIND PANAGARIYA
Professor of Economics and
Co-Director, Center for International Economics
University of Maryland

M.G. QUIBRIA
Acting Assistant Chief Economist
Economics and Development Resource Center
Asian Development Bank

NARHARI RAO
Senior Economist
Economics and Development Resource Center
Asian Development Bank

JAMES RIEDEL
Professor of International Economics
The Paul H. Nitze School of Advanced International Studies
Johns Hopkins University

AMMAR SIAMWALLA
President
Thailand Development Research Institute Foundation

ARVIND SUBRAMANIAN
Senior Economist
International Monetary Fund

SHANG-JIN WEI
Associate Professor of Public Policy
John F. Kennedy School of Government
Harvard University

JOHN WHALLEY
Professor of Economics and
Director, Center for Study of International Economic Relations
University of Warwick

DISCUSSANTS

KYM ANDERSON
Professor of Economics and Director, Centre for International Economic Studies
University of Adelaide

ALAN DEARDORFF
Professor of Economics
University of Michigan

JOSEPH FRANCOIS
Professor of Economics
Tinbergen Institute, Erasmus University

JUNICHI GOTO
Professor of Economics
Kobe University

DAVID PALMETER
Partner, Graham and James LLP
Washington, D.C.

ISHRAT HUSAIN
Director, Poverty and Social Policy Department
The World Bank

PETER LLOYD
Professor of Economics and Director, Asian Business Centre
University of Melbourne

RICHARD SNAPE
Professor of Economics
Monash University

T.N. SRINIVASAN
Samuel C. Park, Jr. Professor of Economics and Director, Economic Growth Center
Yale University

ABBREVIATIONS AND DEFINITIONS

AD	antidumping
ADB	Asian Development Bank
ADC	Asian developing country
ADM	antidumping measure
AFTA	ASEAN Free Trade Area
AMS	aggregate measure of support
APEC	Asia-Pacific Economic Cooperation
ASEAN	Association of Southeast Asian Nations
BOP	balance-of-payment
CBO	Congressional Budget Office
CCII	Cross-Country Intra-Industry
CGE	computable general equilibrium
CSE	consumer subsidy equivalent
CU	customs union
CUSFTA	Canadian-United States Free Trade Agreement
DMC	developing member country
DS	dispute settlement
DSB	dispute-settlement body
EAEC	East Asian Economic Caucus
EC	European Community
EFTA	European Free Trade Area
EU	European Union
FAO	Food and Agriculture Organization
FDI	foreign direct investment
FTA	Free Trade Agreement (Area)
GATS	General Agreement on Trade in Services
GATT	General Agreement on Tariffs and Trade
GDP	gross domestic product
GNP	gross national product
HS	harmonized system
IFC	International Finance Corporation
ILO	International Labour Organisation
IP	intellectual property
IPR	intellectual property right
ITCB	International Clothing and Textile Board
LDC	less-developed country
MAI	Multilateral Agreement on Investment

MERCOSUR   Treaty Establishing the Southern Cone Common Market
MFA   Multifiber Arrangement
MFN   most-favored nation
MTN   multilateral trade negotiation
NAFTA   North American Free Trade Agreement
NGO   nongovernmental organization
NIE   newly industrializing economy
OECD   Organisation for Economic Co-operation and
              Development
PPM   processes and production method
PRC   People's Republic of China
PSE   producer subsidy equivalent
PTA   preferential trading agreement (arrangement)
R&D   research and development
S&D   special and deferential treatment
SAARC   South Asian Association for Regional Cooperation
SAPTA   South Asian Preferential Trading Area
SGM   safeguard measure
SPS   sanitary and phyto-sanitary (measures)
TAFTA   Transatlantic Free Trade Area
TRIM   trade-related investment measure
TRIP   trade-related intellectual property right
UNCTAD   United Nations Conference on Trade and Development
UPOV   International Union for the Protection of New Varieties
              of Plants
UR   Uruguay Round
US   United States of America
USITC   United States International Trade Commission
VER   voluntary export restraint
VRA   voluntary restraint agreement
WIPO   World Intellectual Property Organization
WTO   World Trade Organization

Notes: References to Taipei,China are to the island of Taiwan.
        "$" as a currency notation refers to United States of America
        dollars.
        This volume was produced before the handover of Hong Kong to
        People's Republic of China. All references herein to Hong Kong
        should be considered as referring to the Hong Kong economy
        before 1 July 1997.

1-44

CHAPTER 1
INTRODUCTION

ARVIND PANAGARIYA, M.G. QUIBRIA,
AND NARHARI RAO

In an ironic reversal of attitudes toward trade policies during the 1980s, notes Bhagwati in Chapter 2, developing countries came to appreciate the benefits of a liberal trade regime while developed countries found themselves yielding to protectionist pressures. Recognizing the high costs of protection, developing countries undertook massive trade reforms and dismantled trade barriers unilaterally. In contrast, responding to high rates of unemployment and declining wages of unskilled workers, developed countries introduced new protectionist measures including voluntary export restraints (VERs) and antidumping (AD). Also, the United States (US) abandoned a long-standing opposition to regionalism and went on to conclude preferential trading agreements (PTAs) with Israel, Canada, and Mexico.

Against this background, the successful completion of the Uruguay Round Agreement has a special significance for Asian developing countries (ADCs). Trade is the lifeblood of these economies, and a reaffirmation of the commitment to continued trade liberalization by the membership of the World Trade Organization (WTO), the successor institution to the General Agreement on Tariffs and Trade (GATT), is of utmost importance to them. The agreement will not only help contain protectionist pressures in developed countries through more stringent antidumping and safeguard requirements and an effective dispute-settlement undertaking, it will also expand market access for ADCs, particularly in the critical sector of textiles and clothing. Of course, the agreement will also bring new obligations for ADCs. Thus, like other signatories to the Uruguay Round, they must institute tighter intellectual property rights regimes and phase out trade distorting subsidies and investment measures. As negotiations for the liberalization of trade in services proceed, ADCs may also have to open their markets in services to foreign suppliers.

While offering new opportunities, the post-Uruguay Round world also presents major challenges for ADCs. Enthusiasm for *regionalism* has continued to grow. Side by side, competitive pressures have strengthened the hands of protectionists in Europe and the US. This has, in turn, led to demands in those countries for higher *environmental and labor standards* in developing countries. Proposals have been made for the introduction of trade sanctions against countries which fail to raise their environmental or labor standards. Though the issue of labor standards appears to have been effectively delegated to the International Labour Organisation (ILO) at the first WTO Ministerial Conference in Singapore in December 1996 (just ended at the time of the final revision of this chapter), one cannot yet conclude that the possibility of a link between labor standards and trade policies at a future date has disappeared altogether.

In this chapter, we discuss the main themes developed in various chapters of the volume. We begin with a discussion of the critical role international trade has played in stimulating growth in ADCs. In the next two sections we examine critically the recent challenges posed by the global trading system for developing Asia, namely, the expansion of regional arrangements and demands by developed countries for a link between environmental and labor standards on the one hand and trade policies on the other. Next we provide a critical assessment of the Uruguay Round in areas where it is already having an impact. Included in the discussion here are the agreements relating to the Multifiber Arrangement, intellectual property rights, antidumping, safeguards, and dispute-settlement understanding. In the last section we focus on areas where the Uruguay Round agreement will not have a major impact immediately but how it paves the way for such impact in the future. Thus, we discuss the General Agreement on Trade in Services (GATS) and the agreement on trade in agriculture. We conclude by addressing briefly the issues on the WTO agenda as they were emerging at the time of writing, but not covered in the volume otherwise. These include a multilateral agreement on investment and competition policy.

Importance of Trade in Asia

Since the early 1970s, ADCs have experienced a phenomenal expansion of their exports. Growth rates of exports have consistently and significantly exceeded those of the world and other developing countries. Having begun with a small share in world trade, today these countries together have become major players in the world market.

Growth in the export volume of ADCs has, on the average, been two to three times that of global exports over the last two and a half decades (see Table 1). As a result, the ADCs' share of global exports rose from about 7 percent in the early 1970s to 16 percent in the early 1990s. If Japan is included with ADCs, the share of Asian exports in global exports over this period increases from about 15 percent to 26 percent. It is also noteworthy that while the global export share of ADCs has been increasing, the average share of developing countries in world exports has remained more or less constant. If ADCs are excluded, the other developing countries as a group have experienced a sharp decline in their share of global trade. This phenomenon was most pronounced in Latin America, the Middle East, and Africa.[1] With global export shares of other developing regions declining, the share of ADC exports in total exports of developing countries more than doubled from about 26 percent in the early 1970s to 56 percent in the early 1990s, and is likely to increase further in the second half of the 1990s assuming current export trends continue.

Table 1. Key Indicators of Asian Trade and Development

Indicator	1971-1980	1981-1990	1991-1994
GDP Growth (percent)			
World	3.8	3.1	2.0
Developing countries	5.2	3.9	5.5
ADCs	6.8	7.8	7.5
Export Growth Volume (percent)			
World	5.7	4.3	4.6
Developing countries	3.5	4.2	8.3
ADCs	11.1	11.2	13.7
Share of World Exports (percent)			
Developing countries	28.5	29.0	28.7
ADCs	7.3	11.9	16.2
ADCs and Japan	14.5	21.1	25.6
Developing countries excluding ADCs	21.2	17.1	12.5
Share of Developing Country Exports (percent)			
ADCs	25.7	41.8	56.3

Sources: IMF, *World Economic Outlook*, various issues; IMF, *Direction of Trade Statistics*, various issues; and Asian Development Bank, *Asian Development Outlook 1995 and 1996* (1995).

With exports expanding rapidly, the Asian region was able to finance increasingly large volumes of imports. ADCs accounted for about 17 percent of global imports over 1990 to 1994 compared with 7 percent in the early 1970s. If Japan is included, the Asian region as a whole accounted for a little over 23 percent of global imports in 1993. With exports and imports growing more rapidly than gross domestic product (GDP), ADCs have become progressively dependent on foreign trade. In fact, the majority of ADCs has become increasingly open; the share of exports and imports as a proportion of GDP has increased in a majority of ADCs.[2] This has been most pronounced in the case of the People's Republic of China (PRC),

Hong Kong, Malaysia, Singapore, and Thailand. Among the other ADCs, Indonesia; Republic of Korea (Korea); and Taipei,China have maintained high but stable ratios of exports and imports to GDP. However, despite relatively liberal trade policies, the export orientation of the Philippine economy has not increased perceptibly, with the share of exports in GDP averaging below 20 percent so far in the 1990s. In contrast, the export orientation of the South Asian economies, with the exception of Sri Lanka, has remained low, about 10 percent or less of GDP.

New Challenges: Regionalism

Three years after the Tokyo Round, at the GATT Ministerial Meeting in November 1982, the US began efforts to start yet another round of multilateral trade negotiations. But the US was unsuccessful in persuading the European Community and developing countries to initiate such a round. This led the US to abandon steadfast opposition to regionalism and turn to PTAs as an alternative instrument for sustaining the movement toward free trade. Ambassador William Brock, the US Trade Representative at the time, believed that an ever-expanding set of free trade areas (FTAs) could achieve worldwide free trade.

This switch in tactics, completely justifiable under the circumstances, proved a turning point in the history of regionalism and launched what Bhagwati (1993) calls the Second Regionalism.[3] Negotiations were opened with Israel and Canada and FTA agreements concluded with them in 1985 and 1988, respectively. President Bush, who assumed office in 1988, continued on this path, and the North American Free Trade Agreement (NAFTA) comprising Canada, Mexico, and the US was initialed in 1992. In June 1991, Bush also announced the Enterprise of Americas Initiative under which he offered to negotiate FTAs with Latin American countries. President Clinton, who succeeded Bush in 1992, first secured the approval of the US Congress for NAFTA in December 1993, and then proceeded to flirt with the idea of FTA agreements with groups of countries in the Asia-Pacific region and Latin America. On 15 November 1994, at Bogor, Indonesia, Clinton led the 18-member Asia-Pacific Economic Cooperation (APEC) forum into signing a vaguely worded agreement for free trade by 2010 in developed and 2020 in developing member countries. On 11 December 1994, he brought all countries in the Western Hemisphere except Cuba, to Miami, to sign an agreement to form a Free Trade Area of the Americas by 2005.

Side by side with these developments, the process of widening and deepening the European Community has been moving ahead. The Community was enlarged from nine members to 12 in 1986 and to 15 in 1994. Simultaneously, plans for the creation of a Single European Market as envisaged in the Maastricht Treaty, signed in December 1991, and approved by all members in 1993, have been progressing steadily. Most recently, Klaus Kinkel of Germany has gone on to propose a Trans-Atlantic Free Trade Area.

Pursuit of regionalism in North America and Europe has, in turn, led to a dramatic pursuit of regional pacts around the world. Between 1989 and 1994, GATT was informed of as many as 33 regional agreements. Within Asia, in 1990, Prime Minister Mahathir of Malaysia announced the formation of the East Asian Economic Grouping which was later recast as the East Asian Economic Caucus (EAEC). In 1992, members of the Association of Southeast Asian Nations (ASEAN) signed an agreement to form the ASEAN Free Trade Area (AFTA) by 2007. In May 1995, South Asian countries announced plans to form a South Asian Preferential Trading Area (SAPTA).[4]

What are the challenges posed by these developments to Asia? Recognizing that the subject of regionalism is vast, we limit ourselves to answering this question in two areas: the impact of NAFTA and the European Union (EU) on Asia and Asia's future strategy.[5]

Impact of NAFTA and the European Union on Asia

So far, the impact of regionalism on Asia from its own regional arrangements has been minimal. AFTA, and prior to it ASEAN, have not resulted in major trade preferences. APEC is still a forum for consultation, and EAEC and SAPTA are yet to get off the ground. It is feared, however, that the impact on Asia of regional arrangements elsewhere in the world—particularly NAFTA and the Single Market in Europe—can be large.

In Chapter 3, Frankel and Wei provide a summary of empirical estimates from the literature. These estimates vary substantially across studies, and therefore inspire only limited confidence. According to Hufbauer and Schott (1993), NAFTA will divert from Taipei,China and Korea about $300 million of manufactured exports annually that went to the US, with machinery and transport equipment being the largest component. Kreinin (1992) and Kreinin and Plummer (1992) predict a larger diversion: 5 percent of exports to North America in the case of Korea and 4 percent in the case of ASEAN.

Hufbauer and Schott (1993) predict annual trade diversion from South Asia and East Asia excluding Korea and Taipei,China at $350 million worth of manufactures and $100 million worth of primary products. The hardest-hit sectors are machinery and transport equipment, clothing, and other consumer goods. Safadi and Yeats (1994) find the effects on South Asia to be relatively small, but in their estimates the effects are concentrated in textiles and clothing.

A major concern in Asia has been NAFTA's impact on foreign direct investment (FDI). Kreinin (1992) predicts that FDI may be diverted from ASEAN to Mexico in food, chemicals, textiles, metals, electronics, and transport sectors. McCleery (1993) predicts very large investment diversion from ASEAN: 4 to 5 percent for Indonesia, 5 to 7 percent for Malaysia, and 2 to 3 percent for Singapore. The Mexican crisis that broke out in December 1994, has changed all this, however, at least in the short run. The massive flows of investment into Mexico that preceded NAFTA have been arrested, at least temporarily, and it does not appear that the investment diversion predicted by these studies will actually materialize.

The effects of the EU on developing Asia's exports are estimated to be larger than those of NAFTA. Davenport (1991) and Page (1992) estimate that the net effects as a percentage of the region's existing exports to the EU will be -0.3 for ASEAN, -6.1 for the newly industrializing economies, and -0.3 for PRC. Kreinin and Plummer (1992) estimate diversion effects of 8 percent for ASEAN and 5 percent for Korean exports. A key reason for differences between the two sets of results is that the former allows for higher growth in the EU as a result of the single market, which partially offsets the trade diversion effect, while the latter does not.

Asia's Future Strategy

How should Asia respond to growing regionalism around the world? The first point to make, as Frankel and Wei do in Chapter 3, is that for countries with high levels of protection, the most urgent task is to carry further their unilateral liberalization. This advice is particularly applicable to countries in South Asia, though it also applies to Thailand, Indonesia, and Viet Nam. Regional integration among developing countries with high external trade barriers has been tried since the 1950s and has failed to deliver faster growth. Such integration has served primarily to extend national import substitution policies to the regional level. The option of joining a developed country regional arrangement such as the EU should also be resisted until external trade barriers have been lowered substantially. As argued by Panagariya (1996b), when an FTA is formed, the tariff revenue collected on imports from partner countries in the pre-FTA equilibrium is transferred to the partner countries' exporters. And if tariff rates are high and imports from partner countries substantial, such transfers can be considerable.

Beyond this point, what role should regionalism play in Asia? Both qualitative and quantitative analyses lead to the conclusion that subregional groupings such as AFTA and SAPTA are not particularly desirable.[6] Gains from these arrangements, if any, will come from their contribution to speeding up nondiscriminatory liberalization in member countries.

What about an Asia-wide trading bloc? Panagariya (1994) addresses this issue systematically and concludes that, the issue of desirability apart, it is an infeasible proposition. Under the current circumstances, there are barriers to such a bloc both within Asia and outside. Internally, countries in Asia—even if the bloc is limited to East Asia—are too diverse to come to an agreement. Under the current political circumstances, economies such as People's Republic of China; Japan; Korea; and Taipei,China, are unlikely to participate in a regional arrangement. Even within a small group, ASEAN's success in promoting preferential trading has been limited. Thus, excluding Singapore, which has virtually no trade barriers, intra-ASEAN trade is less than 5 percent of member countries' trade. And less than 5 percent of this trade is subject to any kind of preferences. Even if Asia could overcome internal barriers, the external barrier—opposition from the US—cannot be overcome. Countries in Asia depend heavily for their exports on the US and are unlikely to risk participating in a bloc opposed by it.[7]

This naturally brings us to the possibility of an APEC-wide FTA, which, under the current membership of APEC, would include all the major countries in East Asia, Australia, New Zealand, NAFTA members, and Chile.[8] Because APEC countries constitute a large economic space, an APEC-wide FTA is likely to lead to a net trade creation.[9] According to some simulation, all members would benefit while the main outside entity, the EU, would lose. It has also been argued that an APEC FTA would give its members a strategic advantage in future multilateral negotiations.

While these arguments have some value, this approach also brings dangers. First, there is a strong possibility that an APEC FTA will be dominated by the US. Because the US is also pursuing an FTA with its Latin American neighbors, it is not clear how it would balance the interests of Asia with those of Latin America. Second, because the arrangement would be an FTA and not a customs union (CU), it is not clear how much extra leverage it would give member countries in a multilateral bargain. Member countries would still have to be represented individually at multilateral negotiations and would have to bargain for their individual as opposed to collective interests. Third, creation of an APEC FTA along with the expansion of NAFTA into a Western Hemispheric FTA contains all ingredients for dividing the world into three major trading blocs. These blocs have as much potential for triggering trade wars as for facilitating multilateral negotiations. Even if blocs did not turn pernicious, they could become a hindrance to further multilateral liberalization for reasons discussed earlier. Finally, there is the "innocent bystander" problem. Countries likely to be left out of all of these blocs, primarily those in South Asia and Africa, could find their trade opportunities drastically reduced.

Bhagwati advocates in Chapter 2 a proactive role by Asian members of APEC in seeking an agreement that APEC will not be converted into a preferential FTA and ensuring that multilateral free trade, not preferential free trade, will constitute the centerpiece of the newly emerging world trading system. For this, Japan will have to play a leadership role in the architecture of the new world trading system. The US and the EU are at present preoccupied with preferential arrangements, and without Asia's proactive role, multilateralism runs the risk of being pushed into the background.

New Challenges: Environmental and Labor Standards

Though international environmental agreements and arguments in favor of using trade policy to counter "unfair" competitive advantage arising out of lower labor standards have been around for almost a century, demands for linking market access to environmental and labor standards have never been expressed as forcefully as today. In Chapter 2, Bhagwati offers several reasons for this development. First, persistent unemployment in Europe and a decline in real wages of the unskilled in the US have given way to the fear that free trade with labor-abundant developing countries perils the fortunes of the unskilled in the North. Second, the increased globalization of the world economy and the fierce competition it has brought about have led to increased sensitivity to any policy or institution of a trading partner that seems to give it an edge. Third, some environmental and labor groups in "higher" standards countries fear that free trade with "lower" standards countries will generate pressures for lowering their own standards. Finally, the environmental and especially labor groups, feel a sense of transborder moral obligation to human beings abroad.

Trade and Environment

Today, environmental cleanup is a major challenge facing virtually all Asian countries. Pollution of water, air, and soil and the depletion of forests are major problems these countries must confront in the forthcoming decades. There can be little disagreement on this. The same is not true, however, when it comes to the choice of instruments for cleaning up the environment. Differences of opinion exist on whether trade policies should be employed to foster a cleaner environment. The differences are particularly pronounced in the international arena, where developed countries advocate trade sanctions against a trading partner who fails to enforce a minimal environmental standard, while developing countries oppose sanctions.

To understand whether or not a link between environmental standards and trade policy is justified, we must distinguish between *national* and *transnational* environmental pollution. When pollution affects primarily the population of the country where it originates, it is national in nature. Pollution that originates in one country but affects the pollution levels of another is transnational. Transnational pollution may, in turn, be bilateral, regional, or global. In the following, we present a critical analysis of the link between trade policy and the environment in the case of each type of pollution.

National Pollution

A majority of pollution problems in developing Asia are national in nature. The first question we may ask is whether a country should restrict its own imports or exports to reduce environmental pollution. For example, to reduce auto emissions, should a country raise tariffs on auto and gasoline imports? The answer is in the negative: the most efficient policy to reduce auto emissions is to tax auto emissions directly. Current GATT/ WTO rules are in conformity with this prescription in the sense that they do not allow increased trade restriction to promote a cleaner environment.

The demand by Northern countries for trade sanctions to enforce higher labor standards in Southern countries is backed by two arguments. First, working like subsidies, cross-country, intra-industry differences in environmental standards give lower-standards countries an "unfair" competitive advantage and should be subject to countervailing duties. Second, free trade with lower-standards countries can lead to a "race to the bottom" and a progressive lowering of standards in higher-standards countries. Let us examine each of these arguments.

11

A key limitation of the first argument is that there is no reason to believe that lower environmental standards in a country are intended to gain unfair competitive advantage. Cross-country intra-industry differences in environmental standards are likely to arise purely from differences in trade-offs between aggregate pollution and income at different levels of income. In the words of Bhagwati in Chapter 2, "...richer Americans prefer to save dolphins from purse seine nets whereas poorer Mexicans prefer...to raise the productivity of fishing...by using such nets." Countries are also likely to have differences in priorities on which kind of pollution to attack. ADCs will want to worry more about clean water, while richer countries will focus on clean air.

As for the second argument, it is based on the possibility that in today's world of highly mobile capital, countries with higher environmental standards will lose "capital and jobs" to countries with lower standards. This may, in turn, trigger a "race to the bottom" where all countries will lower standards in order to attract capital and jobs.[10] There may then be a case for setting, at the least, minimum floors to the standards.

This argument, though valid in principle, rests on two assumptions: capital is responsive to the differences in environmental standards; and different countries engage in competitive lowering of environmental standards to attract capital. The first assumption does not stand up to a careful empirical scrutiny.[11] In Chapter 7, Brooks concludes:

> Evidence of firms or industries migrating to overseas locations with lower environmental standards remains largely anecdotal . . . .On the other hand, there is solid evidence that the bulk of foreign direct investment has been targeted to countries with higher environmental standards, suggesting that the low relative costs of compliance with environmental regulations and higher benefits of more skilled workers and more developed infrastructure and markets in those countries outweigh the production cost benefits of lax environmental standards.

No empirical evidence is available for or against the second assumption. But the likelihood that countries systematically lower environmental standards to compete for capital is very low. Such competition typically takes place through tax breaks, which may result in a "race to the bottom" in taxation of foreign capital.

The inevitable conclusion from discussions in Chapters 2 and 7 is that the *economic* case for eco-dumping duties on the basis of either "unfair trade" or "race to the bottom" is not persuasive. Bhagwati concludes,

"The 'fixing' of WTO for environmental issues, therefore, should not proceed along the lines of legitimating eco-dumping."

Transnational Pollution

Transnational pollution requires a cooperative solution at the international level. The natural vehicle to achieve this cooperation is an international agreement or treaty. Though the 1987 Montreal Protocol on Substances that Deplete the Ozone Layer is the best-known example, international environmental agreements cover a wide range of subjects and have existed at least since the beginning of this century. Most recently, in August 1995, countries adopted a global accord to regulate fishing on the high seas. A long, albeit partial list of international environmental agreements is provided by Brooks in Chapter 7.

An essential problem international treaties face is that, because of the public-good nature of environmental protection, nations have an incentive for a free ride. Because the benefits of reductions by complying members in fishing or carbon dioxide emissions become automatically available to others, countries have an incentive not to comply with international agreements. This naturally brings into the picture trade sanctions as an instrument to secure compliance.

The trade policy question WTO confronts, then, is whether to legitimize trade sanctions on WTO members who try to "free ride" a treaty concluded by a plurality of the membership. The answer would seem to be in the affirmative, but the issue is more complex, for it is entirely possible that the provisions of the treaty themselves are not legitimate in the eyes of the countries accused of free riding. In Chapter 2, Bhagwati argues,

> ... these nations have to be satisfied that the agreement being pressed
> on them is efficient and, especially, that it is equitable in burden-
> sharing. Otherwise, nothing prevents the politically powerful (the
> rich nations) from devising a treaty that puts an inequitable burden
> on the politically weak (the poor nations), and then using the cloak
> of a 'multilateral' agreement and a new GATT/WTO-legitimacy to
> impose that burden with the aid of trade sanctions with a clear
> conscience.

To ensure that the solution to global warming is efficient and equitable, Bhagwati favors pollution permits that are marketable at the world level. Under this scheme, any country wishing to emit greenhouse gases would have to buy a permit from a worldwide quota. This would ensure efficiency. To ensure equity, the proceeds from permits could be used according to some multilaterally agreed upon criteria for such purposes as refugee resettlement and United Nations peacekeeping operations.

Trade and Labor Standards

As Rao notes in Chapter 6, there is considerable ambiguity in the definitions of labor standards. The US Department of Labor emphasizes freedom of association, the right of labor to organize and bargain collectively, prohibition of forced labor, minimum age of employment, and acceptable conditions of work. The European Union's "Social Charter" lists a broader set of labor rights, including the right to vocational training and the protection of elderly and disabled persons. ILO has more than 170 conventions, evolved over a period of 75 years, covering a wide range of labor standards. Enforcement of labor standards is up to national governments. Only those standards for which national laws exist can be enforced.

Some Simple Economics of Labor Standards

The basic economics of labor standards is not very different from that of environmental standards. Drawing on the rapidly growing literature, Rao identifies five propositions. First, contrary to what some proponents of higher labor standards claim, a rise in labor standards need not raise a country's welfare. In particular, if the initial labor standards are above what the society considers to be optimum, raising them further will lower welfare. Second, optimum standards themselves depend on other variables in the economy. For example, in a country with poor facilities for education and low income, the optimum minimum age of employment will be lower than in a rich country with ample opportunities for education. Third, a rise in one labor standard can well lead to a decline in another labor standard. For instance, if a country raises the minimum wage, to remain competitive, firms may lower safety standards. Thus, raising labor standards in an overall sense is a tricky issue. Fourth, within the Heckscher-Ohlin model, the terms of trade and welfare effects of raising labor standards in labor-abundant countries are likely to be negative on labor-scarce countries. A higher labor standard such as an increase in the minimum working age lowers labor supply and hence the supply of labor-abundant exports. This, in turn, worsens the terms of trade and welfare of labor-scarce countries which import labor-intensive goods. Finally, the inclusion of labor standards among the choice variables does not undermine the case for free trade. As long as labor standards are chosen optimally, free trade remains globally welfare-superior to restricted trade.

A Critical Evaluation of the Case for Labor Standards

The case for raising labor standards is made on either moral or national welfare grounds. Here we focus on the latter only. As Rao notes, the case is made on the basis of either "unfair" trade or "race to the bottom." With respect to the former, one can essentially invoke the critique offered above in the context of national environmental standards. With respect to the latter, there is no systematic evidence supporting the view that the decline in wages of the unskilled in the US and high unemployment in Europe have been caused by freer trade with labor-abundant countries or by migration of capital to developing countries in response to lower labor standards there. Technological change, which may have favored skilled over unskilled labor, is perhaps the more likely explanation for the decline in the unskilled wage. If free trade were the main culprit for the wage decline, at least the relative price of labor-intensive goods should have declined in the US. Available evidence shows that the opposite is true. Similarly, migration of capital in response to wage differences is also unlikely, as several studies have shown that once we adjust for productivity differences, wages in developing countries are not significantly different from those in developed countries.

Policy Options

A defensible case for developed-country demands for higher labor standards in developing countries has not been made so far. Yet, political pressures for action exist. Bhagwati, while rejecting unequivocally the idea of a social clause in WTO, offers four solutions. First, those wishing to improve a given set of labor standards can employ instrumentalities such as nongovernmental organization-led educational activities in favor of their positions. If the ideas being proposed are good, they are likely to be accepted without coercion. One can also add private boycotts, available under national and international law, to the arsenal. Second, assisted by these methods of suasion, a multilateral consensus must be achieved on a carefully defined labor standard and formally agreed to by ILO in the light of modern thinking in economics. Third, in extraordinary cases, international processes are available for even coercive corrective multilateral action. For example, under the United Nations embargo procedures, which take precedence over GATT and other treaties, South Africa was subject to an international embargo despite its membership in GATT. Finally, nations that feel that their moral views must be respected at any cost can also take corrective actions under the existing GATT/WTO procedures. Thus, if the US wishes not to import carpets made with child labor in India and Pakistan, it can do so unilaterally by making a compensatory offer of an alternative trade concession or accepting retaliation by the offended parties in the form of withdrawal of an equivalent trade concession. The compensatory concession or retaliation by the partner can be viewed essentially as the cost of spreading one's virtue to other countries.

Rao draws attention to the fact that, in the long run, economic growth in the poor countries will be the most effective and noncontroversial way to raise labor standards there. "Empirical evidence suggests that economic growth increases both employment and real wages; and rising real wages in turn raise labor standards. This is borne out in the detailed study by Gary Fields (1995)..."

Uruguay Round: Areas of Current Impact

Though the Uruguay Round Agreement deals with a wide variety of topics and consists of as many as 18 separate agreements, from the viewpoint of ADCs, six areas are of special significance: textiles and clothing; trade-related intellectual property rights (TRIPs); new instruments of trade policy including antidumping, safeguards, and the dispute-settlement mechanism; agriculture; services; and trade-related investment measures. In the first three of these areas, the Agreement will have profound effects in the coming years. In the remaining three areas, the immediate effect will be modest, but the Agreement sets the stage for future negotiations for liberalization. We begin by offering a critical analysis of the Agreement on textiles and clothing.

Textiles and Clothing

Approximately half of the world trade in textiles and clothing is governed today by MFA, a global VER consisting of 3,000 bilateral quotas distinguished by countries and products and administered by exporting countries. It restricts imports into developed countries including the US, EU, Australia, and Canada from developing countries and Japan. MFA applies to cloth and clothing made from cotton, wool, and synthetic fibers, and hence the term "multifiber."

The Textiles and Clothing Agreement of the Uruguay Round pro-
poses to phase out MFA and to return textiles and clothing to full GATT/
WTO discipline in ten years. This is of immense significance for ADCs,
which account for more than 40 percent of the world exports of clothing.
For many ADCs, textiles and clothing account for as much as one quarter
of their manufactured exports. In contrast to many Latin American and
African countries whose exports of textiles and clothing are either unconstrained or subject to nonbinding quotas, most ADCs face binding quotas.
Therefore, among exporters, they have the most to gain from the MFA
phaseout.

How Will the Phaseout Work?

The Textiles and Clothing Agreement consists of nine Articles and
an Annex and is applicable to all WTO members, irrespective of whether
they are signatories to MFA. The Annex sets out textiles and apparel products to be integrated into GATT/WTO. There are 800 Harmonized System tariff lines listed in the Annex. Liberalization will proceed on two tracks:
abolition of quotas and faster growth of quotas not abolished.

Abolition of quotas is to be done in four stages. Stage One liberalization took place in the first half of 1995, when products accounting for
16 percent of the restraining country's imports in 1990 were freed up from
the quota restriction. Stage Two will be implemented in the first half of
1998 when quotas on products accounting for another 17 percent of 1990
MFA imports will be abolished. In Stage Three, to be implemented in the
first half of 2002, products accounting for yet another 18 percent of 1990
imports will be integrated into GATT/WTO. Stage Four liberalization takes
place on 1 January 2005, when all MFA quotas will be abolished. On that
date, trade in textiles will come to be governed by the same rules as trade
in other manufactures.

Because quotas on a large number of products will remain in existence during the ten-year transition period, liberalization will proceed along
a second track by expanding the quotas at a rate faster than that laid out
in the original bilateral agreement. The Uruguay Round Agreement boosts
the original MFA growth rate by 16 percent in Stage One (the first three
years of the phase-out period), 25 percent in Stage Two (the next four
years), and 27 percent in Stage Three (the last three years). Thus, if the
quota for a product would have grown annually at 3 percent under the
original bilateral MFA, it will now grow at 3.48 percent during the first
three years, 4.35 percent during the following four years, and 5.52 percent
during the remaining three years.

Though the phaseout is a vast improvement over MFA, as Whalley points out in Chapter 8, there are several reasons why liberalization *during the ten-year transition* will be limited. First, products accounting for 49 percent of MFA imports in 1990 will simply not be liberalized until 1 January 2005. Thus, the phaseout is back-loaded. Second, because importing countries choose which products will go first and which ones later, they can avoid effective liberalization through this channel almost until the end. The Annex to the Agreement, which lists products to be integrated includes many tariff lines that are not currently restricted under MFA. But these can be, in-deed, have been, reintegrated into GATT/WTO in the early phases to satisfy the requirements of the phaseout. Third, the impact of accelerated growth in quotas will also be limited because the most binding quotas are likely to have a very low established growth rate, about 1 percent. Even after all three acceleration factors have been applied, the growth rate will be below 2 percent. Finally, safeguards provisions may lead to a backsliding even when some liberalization takes place. The Agreement permits safeguard actions for three years if liberalization results in damage to domestic indus-try.[12] Taking these and other factors into account, Whalley sums up the situation as follows:

> Given the complexity of, and differences among, the MFA classi-fication systems in the importing countries, it is difficult to make clear judgments about either the speed or coverage of integration under the program, except to say that all products will be integrated into GATT after ten years. But because a significant number of MFA quotas are nonbinding, and the initial quota growth rates for the more sensitive products are restrictively low, the fear is that much of the effective long-run adjustment needed to eliminate MFA will be delayed until the tenth year of the phaseout.

Finally, it deserves noting that the Uruguay Round does not imply free trade in textiles and clothing at the end of the ten-year transition period. Tariffs, which are high at present, will remain in place unless fur-ther action is taken. The Agreement permits safeguard actions for three years. Therefore, any safeguard actions taken in the last two years of the phaseout could still be in force in 2005. Moreover, like other manufac-tures, textiles and clothing will be subject to antidumping.

Economic Impact

Given all the complications during transition and the strong likelihood that much of the liberalization will take place on 1 January 2005, the payoff on speculating on transitional effects is low. Not surprisingly, most studies have focused on estimating the impact of a complete removal of MFA. Though the effects of the phaseout will be along several dimensions, including foreign direct investment and product quality, the greatest attention has been paid to static welfare effects.

Static welfare can be judged in terms of (i) global efficiency; (ii) gains to importing countries; and (iii) gains to exporting countries. Each of the last two of these effects can be further divided into gains to consumers and producers. In Panagariya, Quibria, and Rao (1996), there is a detailed analysis of these effects. Here we simply note that the MFA phaseout will lower the price in the importing countries and, thus, benefit the consumers and hurt producers there. Because the phaseout will bring the internal price in these countries closer to the external price and also improve their terms of trade by transferring quota rents to their consumers, the net effect on them is almost guaranteed to be positive. The exporting countries can, in principle, gain or lose from the phaseout. They will gain from improved market access, but lose on account of the transfer of quota rents to importing countries' consumers. Consumers in the exporting countries will, of course, lose due to the increase in the price resulting from larger exports.

These basic conclusions can be modified on account of factors such as quality upgrading under MFA, the impact of the phaseout on investment, and the presence of tariffs which will remain in force even after the MFA phaseout. Simulation models that try to get at quantitative estimates of the effects of MFA removal rarely take all these modifications into account. According to the analysis above, the welfare effects of MFA removal alone are positive on importing countries and ambiguous on exporting countries. But because quotas on Asian exporters are binding, while those on Latin American and African exporters are not, studies uniformly show Asia benefiting from the removal of MFA. But within Asia, there are both winners and losers. A representative study by Trela and Whalley (1990) has the US, EU, and Canada as importers and 34 developing economies as exporters. There are 14 textiles and apparel items and a residual other good. The model is calibrated to 1986 data on production, consumption, and trade. Two counterfactual experiments are of interest: (i) both MFA quotas and tariffs are removed; and (ii) only MFA quotas are removed. In case (i), global gains as measured by equivalent variation are $23.4 billion, with

$15.3 billion accruing to developed countries, $5.4 billion to Asia, and the rest to other developing economies. PRC is the largest winner in Asia with $1.8 billion. Hong Kong, Macao, and Singapore lose. In case (ii), global gains decline to $21.9 billion, of which $19 billion accrues to developed countries. Gains to developing economies and Asia are dramatically lower than in case (i). Asia gains just $1.3 billion. This comparison shows the crucial importance to ADCs of tariff liberalization in textiles and clothing in developed countries.

Policy Response

What should be the policy response of Asian countries? There are three broad areas that require attention. First, Asia is by far the largest player in the world textiles and clothing market. And though market shares may shift among Asian countries as just noted, overall Asia will remain dominant in the years to come. Therefore, it is critical that the proposed MFA phaseout does not slide back. This means close monitoring of the process of liberalization itself, including the products that are liberalized at various stages and quota expansion. More importantly, as imports into developed country markets expand, pressures for the use of transitional safeguard and eventually antidumping actions will rise. Countries in Asia must resist these pressures through an active presence at WTO and recourse to its dispute-settlement process (see below under "New Instruments of Protection") to ensure that these measures are not substitutes for MFA quotas. Second, ADCs should also exert pressure for further reductions in tariffs on textiles and clothing in developed countries. As Whalley's calculations in Chapter 8 illustrate, the extra gains from tariff liberalization to Asia are even more than from the removal of MFA. In future market-access negotiations, developing Asia should continue to push in this area.

The final area where attention is needed is policies of exporting countries themselves. Low wage countries such as Bangladesh, India, and Pakistan stand to benefit greatly from the MFA phaseout. This means getting the internal trade and investment policies right. The precise nature of these policies depends on specific circumstances of the countries and will require detailed analyses at the country level.

Trade-Related Intellectual Property Rights

The TRIPs agreement has been one of the most contentious parts of the Uruguay Round Agreement in Asia. Though the introduction of intellectual property (IP) rights will generate both positive and negative effects on developing countries, the net effect will very likely be negative because of the increased prices of patented products, particularly in the area of pharmaceuticals. That said, it must be noted that in public debate in some countries, for example, India, losses were greatly exaggerated and gains understated.

In the following, we discuss the economic impact of the TRIPs agreement on Asia and policy options available to the countries in this area. We choose not to discuss the provisions of the agreement except in the area of enforcement. As for other provisions, we merely note that the TRIPs agreement is wide-ranging and covers virtually all areas of intellectual property including patents, copyright and related rights, trademarks and geographic indications, layout designs of integrated circuits, industrial designs, and protection of undisclosed information (trade secrets). The agreement is built upon existing international conventions negotiated under the auspices of the World Intellectual Property Organization. The relevant conventions are the Berne Convention on copyright, the Paris Convention on patents, and the Washington Treaty on Intellectual Property in Respect of Integrated Circuits. In addition to requiring compliance with the substantive provisions of these conventions, the agreement specifies standards to define key issues of protection in each area. The agreement includes commitments on national enforcement procedures as well as effective multilateral procedures for settlement of disputes. As Subramanian notes in Chapter 9, "The post-TRIPs world can proclaim levels of IP protection in developing countries comparable to, and in some cases exceeding those, in industrial countries prior to the Round."

There is a long transition period over which the TRIPs agreement is to be implemented. National treatment and the most-favored nation (MFN) provision were to come into force beginning 1 January 1996. Provision on enforcement, introduction of plant variety protection, and protection of biotechnological *processes* will have to be implemented by 1 January 2000 by developing countries and 1 January 2006 by the least-developed countries. Patent protection for biotechnological *products* will have to be implemented by 2005. In the important area of pharmaceuticals, the transitional provisions are complex. But, in short, business will be as usual (in other words, no impact) until 1 January 2005. Implementation will begin to have an impact starting 1 January 2005. Any drugs that are already on the market before 1 January 2005 will not be subject to patents.

21

Enforcement Provisions

The important but tricky issue of enforcement of TRIPs is discussed in Part III of the agreement. The broad objective of the enforcement provision of the agreement is to ensure effective national enforcement of IP laws without the procedure becoming abusive. The main point to note here is that the primary responsibility for initiating action for enforcement falls on the *private* right holders, not the country. The country's responsibility is to put in place procedures and remedies that will enable the right holder to initiate enforcement action in case of infringement. This means that the mere fact of infringement of IP rights does not make a country susceptible to multilateral trade sanctions. The country can be challenged by WTO only if it can be shown that it has failed to fulfill its obligations under the TRIPs agreement.

Countries have two types of obligation: on procedures and outcomes. The former includes judicial, administrative, and criminal procedures. These will not require major changes in existing laws. The more difficult issue concerns outcomes. As Subramanian notes in Chapter 9,

> Article 41.1 of the TRIPs agreement specifies that enforcement must be expeditious, while Article 41.5 states that the TRIPs agreement '. . .does not create any obligation to put in place a judicial system for the enforcement of IP rights distinct from that for the enforcement of law in general, nor does it affect the capacity of Members to enforce their laws in general.' The key question that arises, in my view, is whether the standards of performance required of national courts and customs are *absolute* or *relative*. Frankly, the TRIPs agreement does not provide a clear answer. . . .

Subramanian goes on to explain the point with the help of an example. Suppose it takes ten years for an IP case to move through national courts in India. Would that be regarded as ineffective enforcement and therefore subject to the WTO process? Would India's case be weakened by the fact that the equivalent figure for the US or EU is two years? Or could it invoke the fact that a developing country cannot be held to the standards of developed countries? Answers to these questions are not clear and may have to await future deliberations at WTO. If dispute-settlement panels decide to hold countries to some absolute standards, a disparity will arise in a country's legal system because IP cases will be processed faster, and hence become a privilege.

Part III also deals with the issue of dispute-settlement procedures. The strengthened WTO dispute-settlement procedures (see below) will apply to the TRIPs agreement. On the one hand, this means that countries that fail to meet their obligations can be subject to trade sanctions by offended countries. On the other, it will help contain unilateral sanctions such as those imposed by the US under its Special 301 provision of the Trade Act of 1988. Offended countries must seek the redress of TRIPs violations by their trading partners through the dispute-settlement procedure.

Economic Impact[13]

On the one hand, the grant of an IP right helps generate innovations, but on the other, it raises the price of the resulting product to the consumer. The society must weigh these two interests to arrive at the *optimal length* of IP protection. The optimal length will vary by product, but for administrative convenience, the actual length of patents is uniform.

In the *international* context, if innovators are concentrated in the North, the South has little incentive to provide IP protection. A conflict between the two sides is then likely to follow with the North demanding TRIPs and the South objecting to it. The conflict is made particularly complicated by the nonrivalry property of knowledge: the use of knowledge by the South does not reduce its availability to the North.

From the viewpoint of ADCs, the effect of the TRIPs agreement can be divided into four categories. First, TRIPs will lead to monopoly pricing of products that could be sold previously at a fraction of the cost by imitators. This effect could give rise to large losses in sectors such as pharmaceuticals and chemicals, where reverse engineering is relatively easy. Second, if TRIPs leads to new innovations, which in turn result in higher consumption of products in Asia, Asia will benefit. For example, IP protection may lead to more research on tropical diseases. This gain will accrue regardless of who innovates. Third, if TRIPs also gives rise to innovations by Asian firms, the firms will profit from selling the resulting product globally. These profits constitute a part of Asian gains. An example is computer software from India and Pakistan. Finally, the presence of IP protection may influence the location of research and development (R&D) activity itself. Systematic evidence on this effect is not available.

Developing countries are likely to lose most in pharmaceutical and chemical sectors in the post-TRIPs world. This is because of increased prices of drugs and chemicals which will no longer be subject to imitation. Using a simple, partial equilibrium model, Subramanian estimates that, assuming the elasticity of demand to be 0.75, starting in 2015 when the full impact will be felt, annual real income losses in the pharmaceuticals sector could range between $315 million and $1.3 billion for India, $33 million to $133 million for Indonesia, $46 million to $186 million for Pakistan, $59 million to $237 million for the Philippines, and $47 million to $189 million for Thailand.

TRIPs may bring some gains in the area of agriculture. This sector is increasingly witnessing a privatization of R&D efforts. There is also evidence from the US that R&D in agriculture responds positively to IP rights protection. In Asia currently, R&D is concentrated in hybrids, which are difficult to duplicate. If IP rights protection is introduced, R&D will rise in other varieties as well.

There has been a great deal of confusion regarding the potentially harmful effects of TRIPs on farmers' rights to retain grain from harvest to be used as seed, across-the-fence sales, and experimental research using protected seeds. As Box 2 in Chapter 9 by Subramanian explains, these concerns are unfounded.

Finally, for some countries such as India, gains may also arise from *exports* of IP-based products. India is an exporter of computer software, films, and audio and video recordings. There will be gains in these areas from royalties as well as increased R&D.

Policy Option

In areas such as pharmaceuticals, where countries expect to lose from TRIPs, Subramanian suggests three policy actions. First, the TRIPs agreement does not prevent the use of price controls. Indeed, price controls exist in many developed countries with strong IP rights regimes. In Europe, which has a nearly harmonized patent regime, the average price of patented drugs can vary by a factor of 3:1, due largely to price controls. Second, the TRIPs agreement has severely limited the use of compulsory licensing (which was, for example, the preferred tool in Canada for regulating drug prices) by imposing two stringent requirements: (i) the country must demonstrate that the patentee has refused to make available a voluntary license on reasonable commercial terms and conditions; and (ii) adequate compensation must be paid to the patentee. These conditions can be waived, however, if it can be shown that the IP rights holder's actions have resulted in an anticompetitive practice. ADCs can, in their national competition laws, specify standards of abuse, encompassing such outcomes as high prices. In the event that these standards are violated, compulsory licensing could be used to redress the abuse and bring prices down to a reasonable level. Finally, under TRIPs, governments retain the possibility of allowing parallel imports. If a patent holder acts as a discriminating monopolist, charging a higher price in one market and a lower one in another, the higher-price country can import from the lower-price country. Though on average, prices charged by a discriminating monopolist will be lower in ADCs than in developed countries, there may be variation within Asia. Countries may be able to take advantage of this price differential by going to the lowest source of supply.

Nontraditional Instruments of Trade Policy

With the decline of tariffs and quotas, the use of nontraditional instruments of protection, principally antidumping and safeguards, has been on the rise. In addition, the WTO dispute-settlement process which is considerably tighter than its predecessor under GATT, promises to become an effective instrument of containing protectionist actions taken in violation of GATT/WTO.

Antidumping

There has been an explosion of AD proceedings in recent years. According to Abbott in Chapter 10, the number of outstanding AD measures in the US rose from 112 in 1985, to 198 in 1989, and 236 in 1992. Until recently, only the EU, US, Canada, and Australia, regularly used AD measures. Japan has used its AD laws only a handful of times. Among developing Asian countries, Korea has been the only consistent practitioner of AD over the past ten years, though India has begun to appear with some regularity. Recently, Taipei,China and Thailand have also taken AD actions. Interestingly, a significant proportion of Asian AD actions have been taken against other Asian countries.

ADCs have been frequent targets of Western AD actions. The economies most frequently subject to antidumping proceedings are the People's Republic of China; Korea; Taipei,China; and Thailand. But India, Indonesia, Malaysia, Philippines, and others have also been targeted. AD measures against ADCs have constituted some 30 percent of the total AD cases in developed countries since 1985.

AD measures are permitted by GATT under its Article VI, which defines dumping as having occurred if the product of a country is sold in another country at less than its normal value. Normal value is, in turn, defined as the price at which the product is sold in the domestic market. If the latter is not available, normal value is defined as the highest export price in any third country or the cost of production of the product in the country of origin plus a reasonable addition for selling cost and profit. Article VI allows AD duties provided the effect of dumping is to cause or threaten material injury to the established domestic industry. The duty is not to exceed the difference between the normal price and the price at which the product is sold in the country where dumping occurs.

Beyond these general guidelines, Article VI does not provide any detail on how a particular price is to be calculated (for example, should it be the average of various transactions prices within a specified period?), the determination of material injury, or the procedure to be followed in imposing AD measures. The Tokyo Round Antidumping Code made some progress in this direction but did not go far enough and, moreover, was signed by only 35 countries until as late as 1990. The Uruguay Round Antidumping Measures (ADM) Code goes much further and will be adhered to by all members of WTO.

Provisions of the ADM Code

In Chapter 10, Abbott notes that the Uruguay Round ADM Code introduces several features restraining protectionist elements of AD but, in many cases, these are weakened by additional provisions. There are seven main features that deserve mentioning. First, the US and EU have for years compared the prices charged in individual export transactions with the average home market price to determine the existence of dumping. This practice is biased in favor of a finding. The ADM Code now requires that export prices be compared on either an "average-to-average or transaction-to-transaction" basis. As a result, the US has adopted the average-to-average comparisons in the majority of cases. Second, the ADM Code also restrains the methodology for calculating "constructed value," which has been used in the US as a measure of normal value, which is compared with the export price to establish the existence of dumping. In the past, calculations of constructed value could be inflated by adding 10 percent of overhead cost and 8 percent profit to direct costs of labor and material. This biased the system in favor of a finding. The new Code requires that overhead and profit be based on actual data. Third, Article VI requires an injury test for the "industry" but does not define industry. As a result, in practice, when individual firms or trade associations file AD petitions, it is presumed that they are acting on behalf of an "industry." Under the ADM Code, a determination must now be made, though, in Abbott's view, the test is relatively lax. The test requires that the petition must be "supported" by producers (i) accounting for 25 percent of the total production of "like products;" and (ii) representing more than 50 percent of the production of those firms expressing a position, pro or con, on the petition. Fourth, in the US, AD duties stay in force for years. The ADM Code introduces a sunset clause under which such duties are to be generally terminated after five years. Unfortunately, the clause is weakened by the provision that if the authorities determine that the expiration will lead to further dumping and material injury, they can extend the measures beyond five years—apparently indefinitely. Fifth, in the US, a dumping margin in excess of 0.5 percent of the export price was sufficient for a finding. The ADM Code raises this margin to 2 percent. Finally, if the volume of dumped imports from a country is less than 3 percent of the total imports of like products, AD proceedings must be terminated. This restraint is weakened, however, by the additional provision that if dumped imports from several countries together account for more than 7 percent of total imports, the 3 percent rule does not apply.

Economic Effects

Economists have long believed that, except in the case when dumping is predatory and leads to the replacement of competitive firms by a monopoly or oligopoly, it is beneficial to the country in which it takes place. The logic is simple: a country benefits from the low price of imports and the high price of exports. Because in today's world many firms from many countries compete against one another in any given market, the existence of predatory dumping is nearly impossible to find. Therefore, economists almost always regard AD as pure protection.

It may seem that AD duties generate revenues that may be a source of improved welfare. This is unlikely to be true, however, since the effect of ADM is to *raise* the border price rather than lower it. Therefore, while a tariff can improve a country's terms of trade, an AD duty is likely to do the opposite. The price to the buyer in the importing country rises by more than the AD duty per unit.

From the seller's viewpoint, the increase in the border price, constituting an improvement in the terms of trade, may seem to be a good thing. But because the duty is discriminatory and other exporters are present in the market, the seller subject to ADM can be priced out of the market. Thus, because of what may be called "trade diversion" to a higher-cost source, the welfare effect of AD actions are likely to be harmful for both exporting and importing countries.

Policy Options

Noting that AD actions are costly to the countries imposing these measures, Abbott does not favor their introduction in ADCs. He goes on to note, however, that if domestic pressures in ADCs are going to require the adoption of ADM in any case, a strategic approach may be worth considering. In his words,

> Strategically, the wisest course for developing countries might be to mimic the laws of the US, the EU, and other users within these areas. This approach would have two benefits. First, if elements of the new laws were challenged as inconsistent with the Code, the same challenges would lie against the laws of those other countries. Litigation by one country would effectively liberalize the laws of many. Second, even if the new laws were not challenged or were upheld, the resulting symmetry would set the stage for negotiated liberalization.

Safeguard Measures

GATT Article XIX provides an explicit "escape clause" remedy for industries that incur serious economic costs because of liberalization of markets. If, as a result of the obligation incurred by a country under GATT, including tariff concessions, there is such a large increase in imports that it threatens serious injury to domestic producers of like products, the country can suspend the obligation in whole or in part. Article XIX is consistent with the use of quantitative restrictions.

Formal safeguard measures have not been employed frequently, however, because of the availability of other instruments (for example, tariffs and quotas in developing countries and ADM in developed countries). What have been used are "gray area measures" such as VERs. This is one of the areas the newly created Safeguard Measures (SGM) Code attempts to address.

Main Provisions of the Safeguard Measures Code

There are five important changes the new SGM Code makes. First and most important, the SGM Code abolishes the use of VERs. Existing VERs are to be phased out over four years. For the future, the Code explicitly states that a WTO member state "shall not seek, take or maintain any voluntary export restraints, orderly market arrangement, or any other similar measures on the import side." But the only way to enforce this provision is through a challenge by the "victim" in WTO, which, given that the "victim" is the initiator, is unlikely. Because of this problem, it is difficult to predict whether the Code will actually be successful in banishing VERs.

Second, with respect to formal SGMs (as opposed to VERs which are informal measures), the SGM Code limits the duration of SGMs to four years. If it is determined, however, that protection is necessary and there is evidence that the industry is adjusting rather than simply enjoying its protection status, they can be extended for another four years.

Third, the original Article XIX provides for either compensation to affected exporting countries or, if an agreement on compensation cannot be reached, suspension of offsetting concessions granted to the nations imposing SGMs. SGMs are also to be applied on an MFN basis. These and other requirements introduced by the new SGM Code make the use of the safeguard mechanism unattractive, especially because the AD mechanism is available. Therefore, the SGM Code drafters decided to eliminate the provision of retaliation for the first three years provided the measure is taken in response to an absolute increase in imports and in accordance with other provisions of the Code. With no threat of retaliation, it is then unlikely that any country will offer compensation.

Fourth, exports of a developing country are exempt from SGM as long as they constitute less than 3 percent of the total imports of the products in question. The exemption does not apply, however, if cumulative exports of such countries exceed 9 percent of the total imports.

Finally, developing countries can use SGMs for ten years. But because they are not exempt from retaliation in the absence of compensation beyond the three-year period, this provision does not help make safeguard actions more attractive than AD measures. There is a provision in the SGM Code, however, that allows developing countries to reuse SGMs more frequently. According to Abbott, this provision "could provide a way to minimize compensation."

Economic Effects and Policy Options

The economic rationale behind SGMs is clearly much more sensible than that behind AD measures. Safeguard measures are intended to minimize the costs of adjustment to a more liberal trading environment. And they are correctly intended to be temporary. They are to be levied on an MFN basis and as such do not discriminate across different sources of supply. Most important, they do not have the perverse effect of *worsening* the importing country's terms of trade.

Given these benefits, it stands to reason that when there is a choice between SGM and AD actions, the former should be the preferred instrument. A disadvantage of safeguard measures under the old regime was compensation or, in its absence, retaliation. The new SGM Code has, however, solved that problem by dropping retaliation for the first three years. Moreover, because developing countries are allowed to reuse SGMs more frequently, they may be able to extend that period, coming close to the five-year limit (under normal circumstances) for AD actions. Indeed, even if the option to reuse safeguards turns out to be difficult, given other advantages, ADCs should consider this option more seriously than has been the case so far.

Dispute Settlement

Under the dispute-settlement (DS) provision, created originally by GATT Article XXIII and strengthened in 1979, 1989, and 1994, members agreed to discuss trade problems at meetings of the GATT Council of Representatives, and to submit their disputes to GATT panels. In the earlier years, the DS procedure was used infrequently, and it was feared during the 1970s that it might collapse out of disuse. But partly because of steady strengthening and partly because of intensification of disputes, the mechanism has been used more frequently in recent years. From two or three cases per year during 1983 to1986, the number jumped to eight in 1987, and 17 in 1988. Significantly, developing countries, including those in Asia, have been absent from the DS system, especially as complainants. For example, during the five years from 1985 to 1989, there were only five cases against developing countries, of which three were essentially the same (the Korean beef case), brought by different complainants. None at all was brought by developing countries.

Provisions of the Understanding on Dispute Settlement

The UR Understanding on Rules and Procedures Governing the Settlement of Disputes creates a powerful rules-oriented DS system roughly akin to domestic legal systems. The system is in the spirit of civil litigation. A country that feels wronged by another country's violation of one of the UR agreements must initiate a proceeding by a request to the WTO Dispute-Settlement Body (DSB), the General Council. Unless formation of a panel is rejected by consensus of DSB, which includes the complainant, a DS panel is created. Because the panel must be created by the second meeting of DSB at which the matter appears on the agenda, there is no fear of delay. Time limits also apply to the later stages of the proceedings.

If the panel finds that a violation has taken place, it is to "recommend" that the country concerned bring the offending measure into compliance. The primary objective of the procedure is to secure removal of offending measures. Any sanctions are viewed as a means to this end. The new GATT/WTO DS system also has a standing Appellate Body to which panel decisions can be appealed. The Appellate Body can affirm, reverse, or modify panel decisions. If it determines that a violation has occurred, it, too, must recommend the removal of the offending measure.

Panel and Appellate Body decisions, which are advisory to DSB, are automatically adopted by the latter unless there exists a consensus for rejection. A "reasonable period of time" for compliance is established. The time period is suggested by the party subject to the decision but approved by the complainant, DSB, or an arbitrator. If the decision has not been implemented within the "reasonable time," the complainant country may initiate negotiation for trade compensation. If compensation is not agreed upon within 20 days, the complainant country may ask for authorization to suspend an equivalent level of concessions. Approval for such suspensions is automatic unless there is consensus in DSB against it. The understanding limits the suspension of concessions to economic sectors related to the one in which the violation occurred.

Special Provision for Developing Countries

The agreement includes several special provisions to assist developing countries, especially as complainants, and to protect least-developed countries. First, when a developing country is the complainant, it is guaranteed at least one developing country member on the dispute panel. Second, WTO is required to make available the assistance of a legal expert from the WTO technical cooperation service to a developing country complainant. Third, DSB is required to consider additional measures to encourage the implementation of decisions when the complainant is a developing country. Finally, all members are to "exercise due restraint" in bringing cases against and seeking compensation from least-developed countries.

The new system does not, however, respond to the long-time developing country demand for more public-oriented procedures; and it does not overcome all the practical problems faced by developing countries contemplating WTO litigation. A key problem is that, even when the DS process leads to a ruling that permits retaliation by a developing country,

31

the retaliation may be meaningless when undertaken against an economically powerful country.

Provisions Regarding Unilateral Actions and Safeguard and Antidumping Measures

A special provision in the Understanding entitled "Strengthening of the Multilateral System" deals with challenges by one member to policies of other member countries. The context to this provision is provided by the Section 301 actions taken unilaterally by the US against several countries over the last two decades. Though the primary target of such actions has been Japan, many Asian developing countries including PRC, India, and Korea have also been subject to them. According to the Understanding, member states are prohibited from determining the existence of a violation except through the DS process.

Regarding safeguards, the main weakness to which there is no apparent solution, is that the Understanding leaves open the possibility of VERs when there is no complainant to challenge them. A purely private interest DS system in which proceedings can begin only when someone files a complaint, cannot solve this problem. Abbott suggests that this is an area in which further strengthening may be required, either by providing for the initiation of DS proceedings against VERs by the WTO Secretariat, or by more aggressive review or political pressure by the SGM Committee.

The DS system is also weak in the area of antidumping. In response to US demands, the Understanding requires a unique "standard of review" to be applied to DS panels reviewing national ADMs. A DS panel may review the facts determined by national AD authorities, but the review must be limited to whether they properly established those facts and whether their evaluation of facts was unbiased and objective. If these standards are met, the panel may not reach a different factual determination. Unlike the ADM Code, which creates objective rules on AD measures, the standard review opens the door for national discretion in the application of those rules.

Economic Impact and Policy Options

The impact of the DS Understanding is far-reaching. Good policies cannot yield results unless they are enforced. And, despite the weaknesses pointed out by Abbott in the areas of Safeguards and AD, the new DS procedures will go a long way toward creating a powerful enforcement mechanism. This is particularly so in comparison with the lax DS procedures implemented in the past.

From a policy perspective, it stands to reason that developing Asia should make more active use of the DS system than it has in the past. As noted above, developing countries have simply not been complainants at GATT despite the fact that they were subject to unilateral actions and AD measures. To change this, developing Asian countries will surely need to invest in the training of personnel, gathering information, and creating institutions capable of making a country's case to WTO in the event of violations by other countries.

Uruguay Round: Areas of Future Action

The General Agreement on Trade in Services

The key feature of services which made a simple extension of GATT to trade in services infeasible and necessitated the creation of the General Agreement on Trade in Services is the manner in which services are delivered. Article I of GATS identifies four different modes of delivery of services: arms-length delivery (such as electronic mail and on-line data transmission), movement of buyer to the location of delivery (tourism), commercial presence (financial services), and movement of the provider to the place of delivery (construction and consulting services).

For each of these modes of delivery, the international movement of services cannot be regulated through traditional border measures such as tariffs and quotas. Even services delivered by the arms-length mode cannot be examined at the border for customs purposes. Therefore, the method of restriction and hence discrimination against foreign sources of supply depends on the specific mode of delivery and other features of the industry. Symmetrically, the liberalization of trade in services requires a removal of "regulations" which discriminate against foreign sources of supply. Free trade in services essentially boils down to conferring "national status" on foreign suppliers. Of course, because the regulations designed to discriminate against and among foreign sources are themselves complex and vary by industry, liberalization in this area is a more complex affair than that in goods.

By including the "commercial presence" and "movement of natural persons" modes of delivery, GATS has effectively brought capital and labor mobility, into WTO. Once a country commits to giving foreign suppliers national status and unbound market access in a service sector requiring commercial presence, it effectively opens the sector to foreign investment. Thus, GATS and the multilateral investment code, to be studied by WTO under the agreement reached at the first WTO Ministerial Conference in Singapore in December 1996, are intimately linked.

A detailed description of GATS is provided by Low in Chapter 12. Rather than repeat the detailed provisons of the Agreement, we note that it is composed of three main components: (i) a framework agreement that provides a set of general principles and rules that apply to all trade in services as defined in Article I; (ii) the sectoral annexes defining specific commitments with regard to specific sectors each country is willing to subject to nongeneral obligations; and (iii) national schedules of specific commitments regarding market access and national treatment that apply to a subset of services on a sector-by-sector and country-by-country basis.

The most important operational tool of liberalization under GATS is the national schedule of specific commitments. Each country lists in its schedule the sectors and subsectors in which it is willing to offer market access and limitations by subsectors imposed on such access. If a sector is not listed, the country has made no commitment whatsoever for market access in that sector. On the other hand, if a sector or subsector is listed with no qualifications, that sector or subsector effectively becomes subject to complete free trade in the country.

Except in four sectors, Schedules of commitments were finalized at the time of the signing of the Uruguay Round (December 1993). In four sectors, Movement of Natural Persons, Financial Services, Maritime Transport Services, and Basic Telecommunications, Ministerial Decisions of 15 December 1993, required that negotiations continue beyond the Uruguay Round. In the area of financial services, the US withdrew from negotiations in June 1995, and decided to go the reciprocity route rather than commit itself to an MFN treatment. At the initiative of the EU, negotiations continued and an interim agreement was reached by the end of July 1995. The agreement is to last until the beginning of November 1997. Specific commitments can then be modified between 1 November 1997 and 31 December 1997. This means that negotiations will continue in this sector with a view to improving the commitments and bringing the US back into the fold.

In the area of the Movement of Natural Persons, negotiations have been completed and the date for acceptance of revised Schedules was set for 30 November 1996. In Maritime Transport, negotiations were suspended and a decision made to resume negotiations with the new comprehensive round under Article XIX of GATS. For Communications, the deadline has been set for 30 November 1997.

By all accounts, trade liberalization in services has been modest so far. The important achievement of the Uruguay Round in this area has been to establish for the first time a set of rules and disciplines regulating access to services trade. In addition, the built-in agenda in GATS requires that a round of negotiations in services trade be launched by the year 2000. The built-in agenda also requires negotiations on rules in certain areas left open by GATS. These include government procurement, emergency safe-guards, and subsidies.

Trade in Agriculture

Trade in agriculture has traditionally been excluded from key GATT disciplines as applicable to trade policies in industrial products. In the original GATT Agreement, while Article XI imposed a general prohibi-tion on quantitative restrictions on trade, paragraph 2(c) allowed import restrictions on agriculture and fisheries products. Similarly, primary products were exempt from the subsidies discipline under Article XVI. Over time, large distortions built up in the agriculture sectors of both the US and the EU affecting not merely the volume but also the pattern of trade. Thus, in Chapter 11, Siamwalla observes, ". . . the European Community for example, was able to move through a highly protectionist regime, from importing cereals to exporting them, from importing sugar to exporting it. . .indeed becoming the largest sugar exporter." GATT (1994) echoes the same sentiment when it reports the estimated annual cost of domestic support measured for the agriculture sector at $173 billion in industrial economies and $24 billion in developing economies over 1986 to 1988.

Provisions of the Agreement on Agriculture

At the time the UR negotiations began, hopes were high that con-siderable progress would be made in dismantling the trade barriers in the agriculture sector of the industrialized countries. Though the actual achieve-ment was far short of the initial expectations, as in the case of services, the Agreement on Agriculture laid down the foundation for future liberaliza-tion. The salient features of the agreement are listed below.

Market Access and Tariffication

The Agreement requires that for all agricultural commodities, exist-ing nontariff measures be converted into the tariff rate equivalent and added to the existing tariffs and "bound" at the resulting rate. The combined (unweighted) average tariff would then be cut from this level, in equal installments, by 36 percent over six years in developed countries and 24 percent over ten years in developing countries. The agreement gives flexibility to countries in cutting tariffs across commodities as long as each tariff is cut by at least 15 percent by developed and 10 percent by developing countries.[14] For commodities whose imports have faced prohibitive trade barriers, the participating countries have agreed to a "minimum access" commitment, which will initially permit import quotas equal to 3 percent of domestic consumption in developed and 2 percent in developing countries. These percentages are to rise to 5 percent in developed countries at the end of six years and 4 percent in ten years in developing countries.

To fulfill the quota commitment, a two-tier tariff policy has been adopted. A lower tariff rate (maximum of about 32 percent of the bound tariff rates) will be set for the quota imports while the higher "bound" rate will be applicable for the rest of imports. While the minimum access quotas are supposed to be nondiscriminatory, in practice a good deal of flexibility has been built into the agreement. For example, the sugar quota of the EU to the Lomé Convention countries, the US sugar import quota, and the US meat import law were converted into a quota-tariff system with the quota countries retaining their shares and the importing country able to fulfill its obligation of minimum market access.

Export Subsidies

Export subsidies are defined to include outlay in the budget for payments that are contingent on export performance. These include payments to exporters of any proceeds that arise as a result of government action such as subsidies on marketing costs, internal transport and freight charges, and sales by the government of its own stocks at prices below the comparable price for domestic products.

Over the years, agricultural subsidies had become a major policy instrument for distorting international trade in this sector. The surplus agricultural production that resulted on account of high protection and support schemes was exported to the world markets with sizeable subsidies. There was no limit to the extent of export subsidies in the pre-UR regime which contributed to unpredictability of trading in these commodities and severely restricted competitive international trade. The extent of subsidized international trade in agricultural products was significant and Ingco (1995) notes that during the base period (1986 to 1990) nearly half of world wheat trade was subsidized. Her computations indicate that, "In

1986-1990, the European Union subsidized more than 95 percent of its exports of wheat and butter, more than 90 percent of cheese exports, 40 percent of its sugar exports, and more than 30 percent of its milk powder exports. US-subsidized exports were largest in butter (94 percent), wheat (55 percent), non-fat dairy milk (40 percent) and cheese (23 percent)." Under the UR agreement, export subsidy *expenditure* will be reduced from the 1986 to 1990 level by 36 percent (24 percent) over six years (ten years) in equal annual installments. In addition, the *volume* of subsidized exports is to be cut by 21 percent (14 percent) over six years (10 years). The envisaged cuts in subsidies will be applied at the four-digit harmonized tariff system.[15]

The Agreement, however, prohibits escalation of subsidies and also the extension of export subsidies to products not previously subsidized. Food aid is, however, exempt from subsidy reduction requirements. The agreement also excludes export credits, credit guarantees, and insurance programs from the scheme, as these are subject to further negotiations. Export subsidies in violation of these provisions can be countervailed if injury to the domestic producer can be established.

Domestic Support

The Uruguay Round agreement also seeks to reduce the total domestic support extended to the agriculture sector in a country. Domestic support measures relate mainly to market support prices— in other words, any policy measure that enables producers to receive a higher price than the prevailing world price, including activities that involve transfers from consumers and in the case of developing countries, to subsidies extended to inputs used in agricultural production.[16]

The manner in which total domestic support to agriculture will be reduced is as follows. For all agricultural commodities the total domestic support extended in the base year (1986 to 1988) will be computed and aggregated. The latter, termed the "Aggregate Measure of Support" (AMS), will be capped and reduced by 20 percent over a six-year period. It is, however, noteworthy that the reduction in AMS applies at an aggregate level and not to individual commodities. This gives countries considerable flexibility in choosing the level of support they wish to extend to any particular commodity as long as the obligations toward the overall ceilings are met. Moreover, cuts in tariffs and export subsidies also count toward the 20 percent AMS reduction, diluting the effectiveness of this measure.

Economic Impact of the Agreement on Agriculture

The Agreement has achieved considerably less than what was expected when the UR trade negotiations began. Import liberalization resulting from agreed tariff cuts is likely to be limited because the tariff reductions envisaged are small and the impact of even these minimal tariff cuts may be diluted. Countries have agreed to "unweighted" average tariff reduction of 36 percent over six years with a commitment to cut each tariff line by at least 15 percent over the six-year period. This gives them considerable discretion in deciding tariff cuts across commodities which makes Siamwalla observe that ". . .the outcome would inevitably be that the cuts in tariffs on products imported in significant quantities will be closer to the 15 (10) percent level than the 36 (24) percent level." (The figures in parentheses refer to expectations for the developing countries.) Further, the "minimum access commitment" may not prove to be effective because countries can easily use special safeguard provisions to shield domestic producers from foreign competition.[17]

The choice of the base period for determining tariff cuts and tariff-binding offers that countries have made will have even more serious implications for limiting trade liberalization in the sector. World prices of agricultural commodities were at their lowest in the mid-1980s, and hence the level of protection and support measures to the agriculture sector in the industrial countries were at their highest levels in the post-World War II period. Protection levels have subsequently come down in several countries as world prices have picked up in recent years. Using 1986 to 1988 as the base years for calculating the tariff equivalent of nontariff barriers and in computing AMS, clearly reduces the amount of liberalization that would be achieved, even if we ignore the fact that the Agreement itself offers only modest reduction in protection and support levels.

Even more significant is the fact that countries have indulged in "dirty tariffication;" in other words, the tariff bindings offered for individual commodities in the country schedules *exceed* the implicit tariffs in the base period 1986 to 1988, computed by comparing the domestic and international prices in the base period. The careful research of Ingco (1995) bears testimony to extensive "dirty tariffication" by both developed and developing countries, thus providing them higher protection in the post-UR period than that prevailing in the base period. Thus, while the Agreement does bring the sector under WTO rules and discipline, the actual trade liberalization on account of it will be minimal. Inclusion of agriculture under the WTO umbrella, of course, has long-term implications for trade liberalization. It is likely that liberalization in this sector would be more widespread and meaningful in the subsequent rounds of trade negotiations.

Conclusion

In December 1996, the first WTO Ministerial Conference took place in Singapore. With it, the agenda for future trade talks has been further reshaped. While the pressure for a link between trade policies and environmental and labor standards appears to have receded, the issues of a multilateral investment code and competition policy have come to the fore-front. Both of these issues are critical from the viewpoint of developing Asian countries. As large recipients of foreign capital, these countries have a deep interest in ensuring that the code governing the flow of investments guards the interests of host countries and not just the source countries and multinationals. Similarly, competition policy, if it is adopted at a future date, should pay attention to not just those practices which impair market access in developing countries, but also government policies such as antidumping which discourage competition and market access in developed countries. Asian developing countries will want to make sure that negotiations in these areas do not produce an agreement which leads to a redistribution of the gains from past and future liberalization away from them.

A key issue which will need to be resolved in this area is whether the members choose to follow the TRIPs model whereby they agree on a code and then implement it, or they adopt the GATS approach under which a broad set of rules will be agreed to and then countries will list the sectors in which they wish to introduce those rules. Of course, future discussions will also have to work out the relationship between multilateral investment policy and competition policy, and between each of these policies and GATS.

A possible strategy Asian developing countries may wish to follow is to link the investment agreement to the movement of natural persons. This was implicitly done in GATS and can be done in future negotiations as well. Getting developed countries to give improved access to their markets in the services in which developing Asian countries have a comparative advantage should be the concession Asian developing countries insist on if they are to give free access to their markets for services which require commercial presence and are, thus, clearly related to investment flows.

Notes

[1] Part of the reason for the declining export shares of Africa, the Middle East, and Latin America is that their average export unit values have dropped continuously since the early 1980s because of the concentration of primary products in their total exports. Since the export composition of Asia is predominantly in manufactured goods, the average export unit value did not drop so sharply. See International Monetary Fund (1994).

[2] Increased "openness" of ADCs to foreign trade has been matched by a marked increase of external financial flows (mainly private) to them. ADCs currently account for about 48 percent of total net external inflows to all developing countries. The Asian economies are thus getting progressively integrated into the global economy both in the goods and money markets. See Asian Development Bank (1995).

[3] The First Regionalism was launched with the creation of the European Economic Community.

[4] It is important to point out that apart from the European Union, NAFTA, and MERCOSUR (which establishes a customs union among Brazil, Argentina, Paraguay, and Uruguay), few regional arrangements are effective FTAs or customs unions. Even NAFTA is just beginning its implementation. AFTA members have taken a largely unilateral, nondiscriminatory approach to liberalization and, as such, cannot be characterized as a true preferential trading area.

[5] For a relatively up-to-date introduction to the subject, see de Melo and Panagariya (1992). A critical overview of the subject is provided in Bhagwati and Panagariya (1996).

[6] Panagariya (1994) and DeRosa (1993) provide qualitative and quantitative analyses of AFTA, respectively. Srinivasan and Canonero (1995) do the same for SAPTA.

[7] There have also been proposals for Asia-wide, nondiscriminatory liberalization. Though such liberalization is unlikely to be opposed by the US, it is sure to be opposed by Asian countries themselves. For one thing, it would worsen the region's terms of trade vis-à-vis outside countries. Moreover, liberalization by Japan would reduce the margin of preference enjoyed by developing East Asian countries under the Generalized System of Preferences.

[8] For a skeptical view of an APEC FTA, see Panagariya (1997).

[9] For Computable General Equilibrium models supporting this conclusion, see Lewis, Robinson, and Wang (1995).

[10] Purely on theoretical grounds, there is no necessity for such a race and one cannot even rule out the possibility of a "race to the top." See Wilson (1996).

[11] Levinson (1996) examines the available evidence systematically and finds, at best, weak support for the assumption.

[12] There are two limitations on the use of safeguards actions. First, safeguards are not to reduce imports below the level attained in the preceding 12 months. Second, if a safeguard measure remains in force for more than a year, it must allow

at least 6 percent growth annually in the subsequent two years. Of course, it must be phased out at the end of three years.

[13] For a detailed analysis of the economics of TRIPs, see Panagariya (1996a).

[14] The least-developed countries are expected to bind their tariffs but do not have any obligations for liberalizing trade in agricultural commodities.

[15] The subsidy agreement allows some flexibility in the choice of the base period to US and EU producers of wheat and EU producers of beef. Because exports of these commodities were higher in 1991/92 compared with the base period (1986 to 1990), it would have amounted to larger cuts in export subsidies in the initial years. In order to smooth the subsidy cuts over the six-year period, the agreement allows the base period in the case of EU and US wheat to be 1991/92 and in the case of EU beef to be 1986 to 1992. The change in the base period has led to peculiar anomalies whereby the ceiling for subsidized exports of EU wheat and wheat flour has been set at 19.1 million metric tons even though the base quantity from which the total reduction is calculated is 17 million metric tons. See Schott (1994).

[16] The developing countries have been exempted from reduction commitments on input subsidies that are provided to "low income or resource-poor producers."

[17] Siamwalla correctly questions the logic of the safeguards provisions, considering that they are in addition to the two-tier tariff protection, which should give countries adequate protection against import surges or price declines. The case becomes even weaker when account is taken of the "dirty tariffication" in which countries have indulged (see later in the text).

References

Asian Development Bank, 1995. *Asian Development Outlook 1995 and 1996*. Hong Kong: Oxford University Press for the Asian Development Bank.

Bhagwati, J., 1993. "Regionalism vs. Multilateralism: An Overview." In J. de Melo and A. Panagariya, eds., *New Dimensions in Regional Integration*. Cambridge: Cambridge University Press.

Bhagwati, J., and A. Panagariya, 1996. "Preferential Trading Areas and Multilateralism: Strangers, Friends or Foes?" In J. Bhagwati and A. Panagariya, eds., *The Economics of Preferential Trade Agreements*. Washington, D. C.: AEI Press.

Davenport, M. with S. Page, 1991. *Europe 1992 and the Developing World*. London.

de Melo, J., and A. Panagariya, 1992. *The New Regionalism in Trade Policy*. Washington, D. C.: World Bank.

DeRosa, D., 1993. "Regional Trading Arrangements Among Developing Countries: The ASEAN Example." International Food Policy Research Institute, Washington, D. C. Mimeographed.

Fields, G., 1995. "Changing Labour Market Conditions and Economic Development in Hong Kong, Singapore and Taiwan." *World Bank Economic Review* 8(3):395-414.

General Agreement on Tariffs and Trade (GATT), 1994. "Market Access for Goods and Services: Overview of the Results." In *The Results of the Uruguay Round of Multilateral Trade Negotiations*. Mimeographed.

Hufbauer, G., and J. Schott, 1993. "Regionalism in North America." In K. Ohno, ed., *Regional Integration and Its Impact on Developing Countries*. Tokyo: Institute of Developing Economies.

Ingco, M. D., 1995. "Agricultural Trade Liberalization in the Uruguay Round: One Step Forward, One Step Back?" World Bank, Washington, D. C. Mimeographed.

International Monetary Fund, various years. *Direction of Trade Statistics*. Washington, D. C.

———, 1994. *International Financial Statistics Yearbook 1994*. Washington, D.C.

———, various years. *World Economic Outlook*. Washington, D. C.

Kreinin M., 1992. "Multinationalism, Regionalism, and Their Implications for Asia." Paper presented at the Conference on Global Interdependence and Asia-Pacific Cooperation, 8-10 June 1992, Hong Kong.

Kreinin, M., and M. Plummer, 1992. "Effects of Economic Integration in the Industrial Countries on ASEAN and the Asian NIEs." *World Development* 20(9):1345-66.

Levinson, A., 1996. "Environmental Regulations and Industry Location: International and Domestic Evidence." In J. Bhagwati and R. Hudec, eds., *Fair Trade and Harmonization: Prerequisites for Free Trade?* Cambridge: MIT Press.

Lewis, J., S. Robinson, and Z. Wang, 1995. "Beyond the Uruguay Round: The Implications of an Asian Free Trade Area." *China Economic Review* 6(1): 35-90.

McCleery, R., 1993. "Modelling NAFTA: Macroeconomic Effects." In K. Ohno, ed., *Regional Integration and Its Impact on Developing Countries.* Tokyo: Institute of Developing Economies.

Page, S., 1992. Some Implications of Europe 1992 for Developing Countries. OECD Development Centre Technical Paper No. 60. Paris.

Panagariya, A., 1994. "East Asia and the New Regionalism." *World Economy* 17(6):817-39.

_____, 1996a. "Some Economic Aspects of the TRIPs Agreement." University of Maryland, College Park. Mimeographed.

_____, 1996b. "The Free Trade Area of the Americas: Good for Latin America?" *World Economy* 19(5):485-515.

_____, 1997. "APEC and the United States," In J. Piggott and A. Woodland, eds., *International Trade Policy and the Pacific Rim.* U.K.: MacMillan Publishing Co. Forthcoming.

Panagariya, A., M. G. Quibria, and N. Rao, 1996. The Emerging Global Trading Environment and Developing Asia. Economic Staff Paper Number 55. Asian Development Bank, Manila.

Safadi, R., and A. Yeats, 1994. "NAFTA: Its Effect on South Asia." *Journal of Asian Economics* 5(2): 197-216.

Schott, J. J., 1994. *The Uruguay Round: An Assessment.* Washington, D. C.: Institute for International Economics.

Srinivasan, T. N., and G. Canonero, 1995. "Preferential Trading Arrangements in South Asia: Theory, Empirics and Policy." Mimeographed.

Trela, I., and J. Whalley, 1990. "Global Effects of Developed Country Trade Restrictions on Textiles and Apparel." *Economics Journal* 100:1190-205 (December).

Wilson, J., 1996. "Capital Mobility and Environmental Standards: Is There a Theoretical Basis for a Race to the Bottom?" In J. Bhagwati and R. Hudec, eds., *Fair Trade and Harmonization: Prerequisites for Free Trade?* Cambridge: MIT Press.

PART 1

THE NEW CHALLENGE

PART I

THE NEW CHALLENGE

Chapter 2
The World Trading System:
The New Challenges

Jagdish Bhagwati
Columbia University

Introduction*

T he Uruguay Round has finally ended. The General Agreement on Tariffs and Trade (GATT) is now dead,[1] as my good friend Lester Thurow proclaimed in Davos some years ago, but not for the reasons of impotence, impracticality, and irrelevance that he claimed (and which I decried in my Harry Johnson Lecture in London in 1990 by noting that, if this was so, the frenzied activity of nonmember countries to get into GATT and of several lobbies to include their agenda into GATT certainly showed that necrophilia had broken out) (Bhagwati 1991b). It is dead simply because it has been replaced by the new World Trade Organization (WTO). We should proclaim, as with the monarchic succession in Great Britain: The GATT is dead; long live WTO.

Indeed, the trading system is now pregnant with a host of questions and challenges. At WTO itself, the remaining tasks on the Uruguay Round's agenda must be completed, though they will be settled in due course, one way or another, as was the financial services pact, despite the opposition of the United States (US) to the pact's most favored nation (MFN) provisions, which then led to the European Union (EU) initiative to close the deal. Then, Mr. Renato Ruggiero, the first Director-General of WTO, will have to confront and guide to benign conclusion several new questions; the new issues of the Uruguay Round, such as services and intellectual property protection are now old issues, of course.

The new issues include, in particular, the interface between trade and the environment, and the demands to include a social clause in WTO to make WTO-sanctioned access to one's markets conditional on acceptance of certain labor standards. These issues cut across all trading nations, of course, but they arise principally due to concerns about lower standards in the developing countries and their feared adverse effects on the developed countries. Hence, they reflect North-South concerns and are also leading to a *North-South* rift at WTO, with much public opinion and many policy makers in the North pushing for WTO to include the acceptance of higher standards as a precondition for freeing trade and for continued market access, while several of the governments of the South are

---

*This is the original text of the Keynote Address delivered at the Asian Development Bank Conference on Emerging Global Trading Environment and Developing Asia held on 29-30 May 1995 in Manila, Philippines. Only the style has been formatted to conform with the other chapters of this volume.

concerned that these demands, if conceded, will create obstacles to free trade and to their exports.

Sadly, just when all countries, whether developed or developing, have unified behind the passage of the Uruguay Round, a divide is opening up, predominantly (but not exclusively) in North-South terms.

By contrast, the new issue of Competition Policy derives mainly from *North-North* competitive concerns, especially the conflictual relations between the US and Japan, and less so between the US and EU.

At the same time, the world is suffering from an explosion of preferential trading arrangements (PTAs), in the shape of free trade areas (FTAs) of different shapes and configurations, posing a threat to the multilateral trading system that is ill-understood. This epidemic could well devour Asia-Pacific Economic Cooperation (APEC) if the United States gains the primary role in shaping APEC since this country is currently infatuated with PTAs and has been known to flirt with the notion of turning APEC into an FTA. If APEC does indeed so succumb, then PTAs will succeed in continuing to decimate the importance and effectiveness of WTO's guiding principle of nondiscrimination.

I intend to address these issues today, putting before you my ideas and arguing in turn that the Asian members of APEC, all in turn members of the Asian Development Bank, can be expected to share them. Indeed, for that reason, I would urge them to take the leadership on them at APEC and at WTO.

Attitudes to Integration in the World Economy: An Ironic Reversal

Permit me to begin, however, with the phenomenon of the increased trade and investment flows, and the opportunities from it that characterize the world economy and the problems that it is feared to pose to trading nations.

Economists are generally likely to see the increasingly interdependent world, with its growing exchange of goods and services and flows of funds to where the returns are expected to be higher, as one that is gaining in prosperity as it is exploiting the opportunities to trade and to invest that have been provided by the postwar dismantling of trade barriers and obstacles to investment flows. This is the conventional "mutual-gain" or "nonzero-sum" game view of the situation. I would argue that it is also the appropriate one.

It is also a view that many developing countries that were skeptical about, even hostile to, this *benign-impact* view of the interaction between themselves and the world economy at the beginning of the postwar period, and indeed through much of it, have now embraced. But I must point to an irony: where the developing countries (the South) were skeptical of the benign-impact view, and the developed countries (the North) were confident of it, today the situation is the other way around.

The Earlier Situation

Thus, if you look back at the 1950s and 1960s, the contrast between the developing countries (the South) and the developed countries (the North) was striking and made the South strongly pessimistic about the effects of integration into the world economy while the North was firmly optimistic instead.

The South generally subscribed not to the liberal, mutual-gain, benign-impact view, but to *malign-neglect* and even *malign-intent* views of trade and investment interactions with the world economy.[2] It was feared that "integration into the world economy would lead to disintegration of the domestic economy." While the malign-neglect view is manifest most clearly in the famous *dependencia* theory that President-elect Cardoso of Brazil formulated in his radical youth as Latin America's foremost sociologist, the malign-impact view was most vividly embodied in the concept and theory of *neocolonialism*.

Trade thus had to be protected; investment inflows had to be drastically regulated and curtailed. The inward-oriented, import-substituting strategy was the order of the day almost everywhere. Only the Far Eastern economies, starting mainly in the early 1960s, shifted dramatically to an outward-oriented policy posture. The results, attributable principally to this contrast in orientation to the world economy, but partly also to initial advantages such as inherited land reforms and high literacy rates, were to produce the most remarkable growth experiences of this century. But at the time, the developing countries were certainly in an inward, cautious mode about embracing the world economy.

By contrast, the developed countries, the North, moved steadily forward with dismantling trade barriers through the GATT Rounds, with firm commitment to multilateralism as well, subscribing essentially to the principles of multilateral free trade and of freer investment flows as the central guiding principles for a liberal, international economic order that would assure economic prosperity for all participating nations.[3]

The Turnaround

Today, however, the situation is almost reversed. The fears of integration into the world economy are being heard, not from the developing countries which see great good from it as they have extensively undertaken what GATT calls "autonomous" reductions in their trade barriers, such as unilateral reductions outside the GATT context of reciprocal reductions.

Of course, not all these reductions, and increased openness to inward foreign direct investment (FDI), have resulted from changed convictions in favor of the liberal international economic order and its benefits to oneself, though the failure of policies based on the old pro-inward orientation views and the contrasting success of the Far Eastern countries following the pro-outward orientation views have certainly played an important role, especially in Latin America and Asia. But some measure of the shift must also be ascribed to necessity resulting from the conditionality imposed by the World Bank and, at times, by the International Monetary Fund, as several debt crisis-afflicted countries flocked to these institutions for support in the 1980s, and equally from their own perceived need to restore their external viability by liberal domestic and international policies designed to reassure and attract FDI. (Where the trade liberalization has been a result of conditionality imposed by the Bretton Woods institutions, it is, of course, misleading to call it "autonomous." For the reciprocity then, while not within trade, is between trade and aid.)[4]

But if the South has moved to regard integration into the world economy as an opportunity rather than a peril, it is the North that is now fearful. In particular, the fear has grown after the experience with the decline in the real wages of the unskilled in the United States and with their employment in Europe in the 1970s and 1980s, that by trading with the South with its abundance of unskilled labor, the North will find its own unskilled at risk.[5] The demand for protection that follows is then not the old and defunct "pauper-labor" argument which asserted falsely that trade between the South and the North could not be beneficial. Rather, it is the theoretically more defensible, income-distributional argument that trade with countries with paupers will produce paupers in our midst, that trade with the poor countries will produce more poor at home.

Now, it is indeed true that the real wages of the unskilled have fallen significantly in the United States during the previous two decades. In 1973, the "real hourly earnings of nonsupervisory workers measured in 1982 dollars were $8.55. By 1992, they had actually *declined* to $7.43, a level that had been achieved in the late 1960s. Had earnings increased at their earlier pace, they would have risen by 40 percent to over $12.00" (Lawrence 1994). The experience in Europe has generally been similar in spirit, with the more "inflexible" labor markets implying that the adverse impact has been on jobs rather than on real wages (Organisation for Economic Co-operation and Development [OECD]1993).

But the key question is whether the cause of this phenomenon is trade with the South, as unions and many politicians feel, or rapid, modern information-based technical change that is increasingly substituting unskilled labor with computers that need skilled rather than unskilled labor. As always, there is debate among economists about the evidence. But my own view, as that also of the trade economists Paul Krugman and Robert Lawrence, is that the evidence for linking trade with the South to the observed distress among the unskilled to date is extremely thin, at best. In fact, the main study by labor experts that first suggested otherwise has been shown to be methodologically unsound in not appreciating that if real wages were to fall for unskilled labor due to trade with the South, the argument being based on the well-known Stolper-Samuelson theorem of trade theory, then the domestic goods prices of the unskilled labor-intensive goods in the countries of the North would have to have fallen (Bhagwati 1991a). But subsequent examination of the data on domestic prices of goods shows that the opposite happened to be true during the relevant period of the 1980s and beyond, for the United States and for Germany and Japan.[6][7]

Thus, the case for the thesis that trade with the poor countries is creating paupers in our midst is essentially unproven, though one cannot rule out that further and better empirical analysis will show that there is some truth in it. On the other hand, there is a substantial consensus currently that technical change has indeed immiserized our proletariat.

Nonetheless, the fear still persists that trade is a major threat to the unskilled. In Europe, there has thus been talk of the difficulty of competing with "Asiatic ants;" such talk leads to talk of protectionism, in turn.

Alongside with this is the fear that multinationals will move out to take advantage of the cheaper labor in the poor countries, as trade becomes freer, thus adding to the pressure that trade alone, with each nation's capital at home, brings on the real wages of the unskilled. Of course, this too, is fear without any foundation in serious economic analysis of the empirical reality that I am aware of. But it has even greater political salience since the loss of jobs to trade is less easily focused on specific competing countries and their characteristics than when a factory shuts down and opens in a foreign country instead. As it happens, I suspect that, at least in the United States, the flow of capital also is in the wrong direction from the viewpoint of those who are gripped by such fear. For, during the 1980s, the United

States surely received more FDI than it sent out elsewhere, both absolutely and relative to the 1950s and 1960s. Besides, if foreign savings are considered instead, the 1980s saw an influx, corresponding to the current account deficit that has bedeviled US-Japan trade relations for sure.

Environment and Labor Standards at the World Trade Organization

Recent years have witnessed also the move to center stage of demands in the US and in Europe for inclusion of environmental and labor standards in WTO, requiring that either they be moved up in the developing countries or else the developed countries should be allowed to countervail the "implied subsidy" represented by these lower standards. Proposals for such legislation have already been introduced in the US Congress, as in Congressman Gephardt's so-called "blue" and "green" bill which would authorize the administration to impose "eco-dumping" duties against lower environmental or *green* standards abroad and "social dumping" duties against lower labor or *blue*-collar worker standards abroad.

The demands for imposing environmental and labor standards on the poor countries reflect several factors.[8] Let me mention just a few of the more compelling ones. First, the fears concerning the effect of trade with the South on real wages of the unskilled in the North that I just discussed, seem to me to be the most potent in this regard. They have prompted the threatened workers and unions to seek all kinds of ways in which the costs of production in the South can be raised. The push for higher environmental and labor standards, which would appear to raise foreign costs of production, certainly derives its political passion and salience from this desire.

Second, the fierce competition as the world economy gets increasingly globalized has, in any event, led to increased sensitivity to any domestic policy or institution abroad that seems to give one's foreign rivals an extra edge. If then a country's producers have lower environmental and labor regulatory burdens, that is objected to as "unfair."

Third, protectionists see great value in invoking "unfairness" of trade as an argument for getting protection. It is likely to be more successful than simply claiming that you cannot hack it and therefore need protection. This has made the diversity of burdens for an industry among different countries appear illegitimate, making demands to reduce it look like a reasonable alternative to overt protectionism.

Fourth, some in the environmental and labor movements worry about the effect that competition with "lower standards" countries will have on their own standards. If trade shifts activity to where the costs are lower because of lower standards, and if additionally capital and jobs move away to exploit lower standards abroad, then the countries with higher standards may be forced to lower their own.

Fifth, aside from these economic and political concerns focused on their own society, the environmental, and especially labor lobbies have moral concerns. They feel a sense of transborder moral obligation to human beings abroad. They would like child labor to cease abroad because they worry about children abroad; they do not want Mexicans to suffer from lower environmental standards; and so on.

These arguments cover a broad spectrum and are typically jumbled together in popular and political discourse. But they must be kept sharply distinct in our reflections and analysis if we are to arrive at proper policy judgments, as I hope to do now. Let me begin with environmental questions and then turn to labor issues, keeping in mind the proposals that are currently in the political arena.

Environmental Standards

Why should one object to differences in different nations' environmental standards in regard to such domestic pollution in the same industry (what I call cross-country intra-industry [CCII] differences in standards), typically in the shape of pollution tax rates? Note that we are talking here about purely *domestic* environmental problems (for example, a country is polluting its own lakes), not about the environmental problems that arise when one's pollution creates *transborder* externalities, as with global warming, ozone layer depletion, and acid rain (which raise problems about WTO of a different, and more compelling nature, as I discuss below).

Indefensible Demands for Eco-Dumping

In fact, for an economist, the basic presumption instead is that different countries, even if they accept the same "polluter pays" principle, *will have legitimate diversity of CCII environmental taxes and standards* for environmental problems which create purely domestic pollution. This diversity will follow from differences in trade-offs between aggregate pollution and income at different levels of income, as when richer Americans prefer to save dolphins from purse-seine nets, whereas poorer Mexicans prefer to put people first and want to raise the productivity of fishing, and hence accelerate the amelioration of Mexican poverty by using such nets. Again, countries will have natural differences in the priorities attached to which kind of pollution to attack, arising from differences of historical and other circumstances. Mexicans will want to worry more about clean water, as dysentery is a greater problem, than Americans who will want to attach greater priority to spending pollution dollars on clean air. Differences in technological know-how and in endowments can also lead to CCII diversity in pollution tax rates.

The notion, therefore, that the diversity of CCII pollution standards and taxes is illegitimate and constitutes "unfair trade" or "unfair competition," to be eliminated or countervailed by eco-dumping duties, is itself illegitimate. It is incorrect, indeed illogical, to assert that competing with foreign firms that do not bear equal pollution tax burdens is unfair.

I would add two more observations. First, we should recognize that if we lose competitive advantage because we put a larger negative value on a certain kind of pollution whereas others do not, is simply the flip side of the differential valuations. To object to that implication of the differential valuation is to object to the differential valuation itself, and hence to our own larger negative valuation. To see this clearly, think only of a closed economy without trade. If we were to tax pollution by an industry in such an economy, its implication would be precisely that this industry would shrink. It would lose competitive advantage vis-à-vis other industries in our own country. To object to that shrinking is to object to the negative valuation being put on the pollution. There is, therefore, nothing "unfair" from this perspective, if our industry shrinks because we impose higher standards such as pollution taxes on our industry, while others who value that pollution less, choose lower standards such as pollution taxes.

Second, it is worth noting that the attribution of competitive disadvantage to differential pollution tax burdens in the fashion of CCII comparisons for individual industries confuses absolute with comparative advantage. Thus, for instance, in a two-industry world, if both industries abroad have lower pollution tax rates than at home, both will not contract at home. Rather, the industry with the *comparatively* higher tax rate will. The noise that each industry makes on the basis of CCII comparisons, aggregated to total noise by all industries, is then likely to exaggerate seriously the effect of different environmental valuations and CCII differences on the competitiveness of industries in higher-standards nations.

But one more worry needs to be laid at rest if the demands for upward harmonization of standards or eco-dumping duties in lieu thereof are to be effectively dismissed. This is the worry that free trade with countries with lower standards will force down one's higher standards. The most potent of these worries arises from the fear that "capital and jobs" will move to countries with lower standards, triggering a "race to the bottom" (or more accurately a race toward the bottom), where countries lower their standards in an interjurisdictional contest, below what some or all would like, in order to attract capital and jobs.[9] So, the solution would lie then in coordinating the standards-setting among the nations engaged in freer trade and investment. In turn, this may, but is most unlikely to require harmonization among countries to the higher standards though even then, not necessarily at those in place, or perhaps there might be improvement in welfare from simply setting minimum floors to the standards.

This is undoubtedly a theoretically valid argument. The key question for policy, however, is whether the empirical evidence shows, as required by the argument, that (i) capital is in fact responsive to the differences in environmental standards; and (ii) different countries or jurisdictions actually play the game then of competitive lowering of standards to attract capital. Without both these phenomena holding in a significant fashion in reality, the "race to the bottom" would be a theoretical curiosity.

As it happens, systematic evidence is available for the former proposition alone, but the finding is that the proposition is not supported by the studies to date. There is very weak evidence, at best, in favor of interjurisdictional mobility in response to CCII differences in environmental standards.[10] There are, in fact, many ways to explain this lack of responsiveness: (i) the differences in standards may not be significant and are outweighed by other factors that affect locational decisions; (ii) exploiting differences in standards may not be a good strategy relative to not exploiting them; and (iii) lower standards may paradoxically even repel, instead of attract, FDI.[11]

While we do not have similar evidence on the latter proposition, it is hardly likely that, as a systematic tendency, countries would be actually lowering environmental standards in order to attract capital. As it happens, countries, and even state governments in federal countries (for example, President Bill Clinton, while still Governor of Arkansas), typically play the game of attracting capital to their jurisdictions. But this game is almost universally played, not by inviting firms to pollute freely, but instead through tax breaks and holidays, land grants at throwaway prices, and so on, resulting most likely in a "race to the bottom" on business tax rates which wind up below their optimal levels. It is, therefore, not surprising that there is little systematic evidence of governments lowering environmental standards in order to attract scarce capital. Contrary to the fears of the environmental groups, "the race to the bottom" on environmental standards, therefore, seems to be an unlikely phenomenon in the real world.

I would then conclude that both the "unfair trade" and the "race to the bottom" arguments for harmonizing CCII standards or else legalizing eco-dumping duties at WTO are therefore lacking in rationale. The former is theoretically illogical and the latter is empirically unsupported. In addition, such GATT-WTO legalization of eco-dumping will facilitate protectionism without doubt. Antidumping processes have become the favored tool of protectionists today. Is there any doubt that their extension to eco-dumping (and equally to social dumping), where the "implied subsidy" through lower standards must be inevitably "constructed" by national agencies such as the Environmental Protection Agency in the same jurisdiction as the complainant industry, will lead to the same results, even more surely?

The "fixing" of WTO for environmental issues, therefore, should not proceed along the lines of legitimating eco-dumping.[12] However, the political salience of such demands remains a major problem. One may well then ask if there are any "second-best" approaches, short of the eco-dumping and CCII harmonization proposals, that may address some of the political concerns, at least economic cost.

A Proposal to Extend Domestic Standards in High-Standards Countries to Their Firms in Low-Standards Countries[13]

The political salience of the harmful demands for eco-dumping duties and CCII harmonization is greatest when *plants are closed* by one's own multinationals and shifted to other countries. The actual shifting of location, and the associated loss of jobs in that plant, magnify greatly the fear of the "race to the bottom" and of the "impossibility" of competing against low-standards countries. Similarly, when investment by one's own firms is seen to go to specific countries which happen to have lower standards, the resentment gets to be focused readily against those countries and their standards. However, when jobs are lost simply because of *trade* competition, it is much harder to locate one's resentment and fear on one specific foreign country and its policies as a source of unfair competition.[14] Hence, a second-best proposal could well be to address this particular fear, however unfounded, of outmigration of plants and investment by one's firms abroad to low-standards countries.

The proposal is to adapt the so-called Sullivan Principles approach to the problem at hand. Under Sullivan, US firms in South Africa were urged to adopt US practices, not the South African apartheid ways, in their operations. If this principle that the US firms in Mexico be subject to US environmental policies (choosing the desired ones from the many that obtain across different states in this federal country) were adopted by

US legislation, that would automatically remove whatever incentive there was to remove because of environmental burden differences (Bhagwati 1993a).

This proposal that one's firms abroad behave as if they were at home (do in Rome as you do in New York, not as Romans do), can be either legislated unilaterally by any high-standards country or by a multilateral binding treaty among different high-standards countries. Again, it may be reduced to an exhortation, just as Sullivan Principles were, by single countries in isolation, or by several as through a nonbinding but ethos-defining and policy-encouraging Organisation for Economic Co-operation and Development Code. The disadvantage of this proposal, of course, is that it does violate the "diversity-is-legitimate" rule (whose desirability was discussed by me). Investment flows, like investment of one's own funds and production and trade therefrom, should reflect this diversity. It reduces, therefore, the efficiency gains from a freer flow of cross-country investments today. But if environmental tax burden differences are not all that different, or do not figure prominently in firms' locational decisions, as the empirical literature (that I just cited) seems to stress, the efficiency costs of this proposal could also be minimal while the gains in allaying fears and, therefore, moderating the demand for bad proposals could be very large indeed.

Yet another objection may focus on intra-OECD differences in high standards. Because there are differences among the OECD countries in CCII environmental tax burdens in specific industries for specific pollution, this proposal would lead to "horizontal inequity" among the OECD firms in third countries. If the British burden is higher than the French, British firms would face a bigger burden in Mexico than the French firms. But then such differences already exist among firms abroad since tax practices among the OECD countries on taxation of firms abroad are not harmonized in many respects. Interestingly, the problem of horizontal equity has come up in relation also to the demands of the poor countries (that often find it difficult to enforce import restrictions effectively) that the domestic restrictions on hazardous products be automatically extended to exports by every country. That would put firms in the countries with greater restrictions at an economic disadvantage. But agreement has now been reached to disregard the problem.

Other problems may arise: (i) monitoring of one's firms in a foreign country may be difficult; and (ii) the countries with lower standards may object on grounds of "national sovereignty." Neither argument seems compelling. It is unlikely that a developing country would object to foreign firms doing better by its citizens in regard to environmental standards that it itself cannot afford to impose, given its own priorities, on its own firms. Equally, it would then assist in monitoring the foreign firms.

Transborder Externalities: Global Pollution and the World Trade Organization

The preceding analysis considered the trade issues which arise between countries even when the environmental problems are purely domestic in their scope. They can arise, of course, even when these problems involve transborder spillovers or externalities. However, the latter are generally more complex. Let me consider only the problems that arise when the problem is not just *bilateral* (as with say, acid rain, where the US and Canada were involved) or regional, but truly *global*.

The chief policy questions concerning trade policy when global pollution problems are involved instead, as with ozone layer depletion and global warming, relate to the cooperative solution-oriented, multilateral treaties that are sought to address them. They are essentially tied into noncompliance ("defection") by members and "free riding" by nonmembers. Because the obligations accepted by members of such a treaty typically relate to targeted actions (such as reducing chloro-fluorocarbons or carbon dioxide emissions) that are a public good (in particular, that the benefits are nonexcludable, so that if I incur the cost and do something, I cannot exclude you from benefiting from it), the use of trade sanctions to secure and enforce compliance inevitably turns up on the agenda.

At the same time, the problem is compounded because the agreement itself has to be legitimate in the eyes of those accused of free riding. Before those pejorative epithets are applied and punishment prescribed in the form of trade sanctions legitimated at GATT/WTO, these nations have to be satisfied that the agreement being pressed on them is efficient and, especially, that it is equitable in burden sharing. Otherwise, nothing prevents the politically powerful (the rich nations) from devising a treaty that puts an inequitable burden on the politically weak (the poor nations), and then using the cloak of a "multilateral" agreement and a new GATT/WTO legitimacy to impose that burden with the aid of trade sanctions with a clear conscience.

This is why the policy demand, often made, to alter GATT/WTO to legitimate trade sanctions on contracting parties who remain outside of a treaty, whenever a plurilateral treaty on a global environmental problem dictates it, is unlikely to be accepted by the poor nations without safeguards to prevent unjust impositions. The spokesmen of the poor countries have been more or less explicit on this issue, with justification. These concerns have also been recognized by the rich nations.

Thus, at the Rio Conference in 1992, the Framework Convention on Climate Change set explicit goals under which several rich nations agreed to emission level reduction targets (returning, more or less, to 1990 levels), whereas the commitments of the poor countries were contingent on the rich nations footing the bill.

Ultimately, burden sharing by different formulas related to past emissions, current income, current population, and so on, are inherently arbitrary; they also distribute burdens without regard to efficiency. Economists will argue for burden sharing dictated by cost-minimization across countries, for the earth as a whole. If Brazilian rain forests must be saved to minimize the cost of a targeted reduction in carbon dioxide emissions in the world, while the US keeps guzzling gas because it is too expensive to cut that down, then so be it. But then this efficient "cooperative" solution must not leave Brazil footing the bill. Efficient solutions, with compensation and equitable distribution of the gains from the efficient solution, make economic sense.

A step toward them is the idea of having a market in permits at the world level. No country may emit carbon dioxide without having bought the necessary permit from a worldwide quota. That would ensure efficiency,[15] whereas the distribution of the proceeds from the sold permits would require a decision reflecting some multilaterally agreed ethical or equity criteria (the proceeds may be used for refugee resettlement, United Nations peacekeeping operations, aid dispensed to poor nations by the United Nations Development Programme, or the World Health Organization fight against AIDS). This type of agreement would have the legitimacy that could then provide the legitimacy in turn for a WTO rule that permits the use of trade sanctions against free riders.

Conclusion

I would then conclude that statesmanship and the safeguarding of the world trading system require that the popular and populist pressures in the developed countries to clutter up WTO with eco-dumping type of preconditions for market access be deflected into attention to the principal global pollution problems facing us today and to the problem of making WTO user-friendly toward equitable, efficiently designed, and multilaterally agreed solutions to them.

Equally, I believe that the eco-dumping variety of demands can be directly defanged by agreeing on OECD-wide codes that urge, preferably require, these countries to get their multinational investments in the developing countries to abide by home-country standards rather than by host-country standards.

Labor Standards and the Social Clause

The question of labor standards, and making them into prerequisites for market access by introducing a social clause in WTO, has both parallels and contrasts to the environmental questions that I just discussed.

The contrast is that labor standards have nothing equivalent to *transborder* environmental externalities. One's labor standards are purely *domestic* in scope. In that regard, the demands for "social dumping" for lower labor standards that parallel the demands for eco-dumping have the same rationale, and hence must be rejected for the same reasons.

But a different aspect to the whole question results from the fact that labor standards, unlike most environmental standards, are seen in moral terms. Thus, for example, central to United States thinking on the question of the Social Clause is the notion that competitive advantage can be morally "illegitimate." In particular, it is argued that if labor standards elsewhere are different and unacceptable morally, then the resulting competition is morally illegitimate and "unfair." One may, therefore, reject such trade, even though it is beneficial to one's nation; or one may alternatively veto it because it is unfair to have one's industry or its labor force be subjected to competition that is "unfair."

Now, when this argument is made about a practice such as slavery (defined strictly as the practice of owning and transacting in human beings, as for centuries before the Abolitionists triumphed), there will be nearly universal agreement that if slavery produces competitive advantage, that advantage is illegitimate and ought to be rejected.

Thus, we have here a "values"-related argument for suspending another country's trading rights or access to our markets, in a sense similar to (but far more compelling than) the case when the United States sought to suspend Mexico's tuna trading rights because of its use of purse-seine nets.[16] The insertion of a social clause for labor standards into WTO can then be seen as a way of legitimating an exception to the sensible GATT/WTO rule that prohibits the suspension (without compensation) of a contracting party's trading rights concerning a product simply on the ground that, for reasons of morality unilaterally asserted by another contracting party, the process by which that product is produced is considered illegitimate, and hence unacceptable.

The real problem with the argument, however, is that universally condemned practices such as slavery are rare indeed. True, the International Labour Organisation (ILO) has many Conventions that many nations have signed. But many have been signed simply because, in effect, they are not binding. Equally, the United States itself has signed no more than a tiny fraction of these Conventions in any case; I am afraid that this is true also of non-ILO Conventions such as the Convention on the Rights of the Child adopted by the United Nations General Assembly in November 1989, and entered into force in September 1990.[17] The question whether a substantive consensus on anything except well-meaning and broad principles without consequences for trade access in case of noncompliance can be obtained, is therefore highly dubious.

Indeed, the reality is that diversity of labor practices and standards is widespread in practice and reflects, not necessarily venality and wickedness, but rather diversity of cultural values, economic conditions, and analytical beliefs and theories concerning the economic (and therefore moral) consequences of specific labor standards. The notion that labor standards can be universalized, like human rights such as liberty and habeas corpus, simply by calling them "labor rights," ignores the fact that this easy equation between culture-specific labor standards and universal human rights will have a difficult time surviving deeper scrutiny.

Take the United States itself and one sees immediately that its easy presumption that it is only providing "moral leadership" on the question vis-à-vis developing countries, is hard to sustain when its own violations would surely qualify for trade sanctions in an impartial tribunal. Thus, for instance, worker participation in decision making on the plant, a measure of true economic democracy much more pertinent than the unionization of labor, is far more widespread in Europe than in North America. Would we then condemn North America to denial of trading rights by the Europeans? Migrant labor is ill-treated to the level of brutality and slavery in US agriculture due to grossly inadequate and corrupt enforcement, if investigative television shows on US television programs are a guide; does this mean that other nations should prohibit the import of US agricultural products? Sweatshops exploiting female immigrants in textiles with long hours and below-minimum wages are endemic in the textile industry, as documented amply by several civil liberties groups. Indeed, in August 1995, the discovery of a garment factory in California run with about 70 illegal female migrants who were virtually imprisoned and worked as slaves, with major retailers as its clients, created waves in the US media, leading to official admissions of widespread abuse of minimum-wage, overtime, health, and safety regulations throughout the garment industry as also of a colossal lack of enforcement.[18] Should the right of the United States to export any textiles then not be suspended by other countries as much as many in the United States seek to suspend the imports of textiles from others because of the use of child labor?

Even the right to organize trade unions may be considered to be inadequate in the US if we go by "results," as the US favors in judging Japan. Less than 12 percent of the US labor force in the private sector today is unionized. Indeed, it is no secret that unions are actively discouraged in several ways in the United States. For instance, strikes are circumscribed; indeed, in essential industries they are restricted, the definition of such industries reflecting economic structure and political realities, making each country's definition only culture-specific, and hence open to objection by others. Should other countries have then suspended US flights because President Reagan had broken the Air Traffic Controllers' strike? Then again, countries differ on whether secondary boycotts and replacement workers are permitted. Should those that restrain the ability of unions to strike by prohibiting secondary boycotts (as the US generally does, with limited exclusions) and permitting the hire of replacement workers (as the US has done until President Clinton's recent executive action) be subjected to trade sanctions by those many nations that do not and feel strongly about these practices as amounting to the emasculation of the workers' right to strike and hence as a direct attack on the workers' right to form trade unions and press workers' rights effectively in the market place?

Lest you think that the question of child labor is an easy one, let me remind you that even this raises complex questions as indeed recognized by ILO, though not in many of the arguments heard in the United States today. The use of child labor, as such, is surely not the issue. Few children grow up even in the US without working as babysitters or delivering newspapers; many are even paid by parents for housework in the home. The pertinent social question, familiar to anyone with even a nodding acquaintance with Chadwick, Engels, and Dickens, and the appalling conditions afflicting children at work in England's factories in the early Industrial Revolution, is rather whether children at work are protected from hazardous and oppressive working conditions.[19]

Whether child labor should be altogether prohibited in a poor country is a matter on which views legitimately differ. Many feel that children's work is unavoidable in the face of poverty and that the alternative to it is starvation which is a greater calamity, and that eliminating child labor would then be like voting to eliminate abortion without worrying about the needs of the children that are then born.

I am not surprised, therefore, that the ILO Conventions on child labor have been ratified by less than a third of the membership. Much of this reflects an appreciation of genuine difficulties, not an outbreak of moral defectiveness, in making the transition to a child labor-free economy. Similarly, the recent Convention on the Rights of the Child, adopted by the United Nations General Assembly in November 1989, and entering into force in September 1990, and which is more directly under human rights auspices, does *not* proscribe child labor under its Article 32. Instead it allows the minimum age of labor to be set differentially by different countries and requires that children's work should be regulated (a provision that makes no sense if children are not to be allowed to work).

Then again, insisting on the "positive rights"-related right to unionize to demand higher wages, for instance, as against the "negative rights"-related right of freedom to associate for political activity, for example, can also be morally obtuse. In practice, such a right could imply higher wages for the "insiders" who have jobs, at the expense of the unemployed "outsiders." Besides, the unions in developing countries with large populations and much poverty are likely to be in the urban-industrial activities, with the industrial proletariat among the better-off sections of the population, whereas the real poverty is among the nonunionized, landless labor. Raising the wages of the former will generally hurt, in the opinion of many developing country economists, the prospects of rapid accumulation and growth which alone can pull more of the landless labor eventually into gainful employment. If so, the imposition of the culture-specific developed country union views on poor countries about the rights of unions to push for higher wages will resolve current equity and intergenerational equity problems in ways that are morally unacceptable to these countries, and correctly so. Indeed, these demands, while advanced by groups that arrogate moral high ground to themselves, are then to be judged as themselves morally deficient, at best, and morally wicked, at worst.

One is then led to conclude that the idea of the Social Clause in WTO is rooted generally in an ill-considered rejection of the general legitimacy of diversity of labor standards and practices across countries. The alleged claim for the universality of labor standards is (except for a rare few cases such as slavery) generally unpersuasive.

The developing countries cannot then be blamed for worrying that the recent escalation of support for such a clause in WTO in major OECD countries derives instead from the desire of labor unions to protect their jobs by protecting the industries that face competition from the poor countries. They fear that moral arguments are produced to justify restrictions on such trade since they are so effective in the public domain. In short, the "white man's burden" is being exploited to secure the "white man's gain." Or, to use another metaphor, "blue protectionism" is breaking out, masking behind a moral face.

Indeed, this fearful conclusion is reinforced by the fact that none of the major OECD countries pushing for such a social clause expects to be the defendants, instead of the plaintiffs, in social clause-generated trade access cases. This is for three reasons. First, the standards (such as prohibition of child labor) to be included in the Social Clause to date are invariably presented as those that the developing countries are guilty of violating, when some transgressions thereof are to be found in the developed countries themselves. Thus, according to a report in *The Financial Times*, a standard example used by the labor movement to garner support for better safety standards is a disastrous fire in a toy factory in Bangkok, Thailand, where many died because exits were shut and unusable. Yet, a similar fire with big fatalities had broken out also in North Carolina, in the United States, in a chicken plant around the same time, with exits being closed again to prevent theft.[20] Yet, the public focus of the agitation was on the poor, not the rich, country.

Second, the choice of standards chosen for attention and sanctions at WTO is also clearly biased against the poor countries in the sense that none of the problems where some of the developed countries would be manifestly found in significant violation, such as worker participation in management, union rights, and rights of migrants and immigrants, is meant to be included in the Social Clause. The stones are to be (properly) thrown at the poor countries' glass houses by rich countries that (improperly) build fortresses around their own. Symmetry of obligations simply does not exist in the Social Clause, as contemplated currently, in terms of the coverage of the standards.

Third, there is the question of standing. Since only governments can bring action against governments for dispute settlement at WTO, major powers such as the United States can expect asymmetry of actions. Few countries would be willing to take the US or EU to court. If the OECD governments that push for a social clause at WTO were truly actuated by moral concerns, urged on them by morally driven nongovernment organizations (NGOs), they would grant standing to NGOs on this issue. In fact, it is revealing that, in the matter of the International Covenant on Civil and Political Rights, a properly designated Human Rights Covenant to be sure, the United States is among the nonsignatories to the Optional Protocol that gives standing to individuals to bring complaints about violations of any of the rights set forth in the Covenant before the Human

Rights Committee (set up under Part IV of the Covenant), after exhausting all available domestic remedies.

If not social clause, what else? If this analysis is correct, then the idea of a social clause in WTO is not appealing; and the developing countries' opposition to its enactment is justified. We would not be justified then in condemning their objections and unwillingness to go along with our demands as depravity and "rejectionism."

But if a social clause does not make good sense, is everything lost for those in both developed and developing countries who genuinely wish to advance their own views of what are "good" labor standards? Evidently not. It is surely open to them to use other instrumentalities such as NGO-led educational activities to secure a consensus in favor of their positions. In fact, if ideas are good, they should spread without coercion. The Spanish Inquisition should not be necessary to spread Christianity; indeed, the Pope has no troops. Mahatma Gandhi's splendid idea of nonviolent agitation spread, and was picked up by Martin Luther King, not because Gandhi worked on the Indian government to threaten retribution against others otherwise; it happened to be just morally compelling.

I would add that one also has the possibility of recourse to private boycotts, available under national and international law; they are an occasionally effective instrument. They constitute a well-recognized method of protest and consensus-creation in favor of one's moral positions.

With the assistance of such methods of suasion, our objective should then be to achieve a multilateral consensus on the moral and economic legitimacy of carefully defined labor standards. Such a consensus can be reached and formally agreed to in light of modern thinking in economics and of the accumulated experience of developmental and labor issues to date, and with the clear understanding that we are not just passing resolutions. ILO is clearly the institution that is best equipped to create such a consensus, not GATT/WTO, just as multilateral trade negotiations are conducted at GATT, not at ILO.

In turn, the annual ILO monitoring of compliance with ILO conventions is an impartial and multilateral process, undertaken with the aid of eminent jurists across the world. Such a process, with changes for standing and for transparency, should be the appropriate forum for the annual review of compliance by nation states of such newly clarified and multilaterally agreed standards. Such monitoring, the opprobrium of public exposure, and the effective strengthening therewith of NGOs in the offending countries (many of which are now democratic and permissive of NGO activity), will often be large enough forces to prod these countries into corrective action.

In extraordinary cases where the violations are such that the moral sense of the world community is outraged, the existing international processes are available to undertake even coercive, corrective, multilateral sanctions against specific countries and to suspend their entire trading rights.

Thus, for instance, under United Nations embargo procedures, which take precedence over GATT and other treaties, South Africa's GATT membership proved no barrier to the embargo against it precisely because the world was virtually united in its opposition to apartheid. Even outside of the United Nations, the GATT waiver procedure has permitted two thirds of the contracting parties to suspend any GATT member's trading rights, altogether or for specific goods and now, services; WTO similarly permits waivers with appropriate majorities.

I must add one final thought to assure those who feel that their own moral view must be respected and their actions taken to conform to that view, even if others cannot be persuaded to see things that way. Even they need not worry under current international procedures. Thus, suppose that (say) United States or French public opinion on an issue (as in the tuna-dolphin case for the former and the beef hormone case for the latter) forces the government to undertake a unilateral suspension of another GATT member's trading rights. There is nothing in GATT, nor will there be anything in WTO, which will then compel the overturning of such unilateral action. The offending contracting party (the one undertaking the unilateral action) can persist in a violation while making a compensatory offer of an alternative trade concession, or the offended party can retaliate by withdrawing an equivalent trade concession.

Thus, unless one resents having to pay for one's virtue (because the claim is that "our labor standard is morally superior"), this is a perfectly sensible solution even to politically unavoidable unilateralism. Do not import glass bangles made with child labor in Pakistan or India, but make some other compensatory trade concession. And remember that the grant of an alternative trade concession (or tariff retaliation) makes some other activity than the offending one more attractive, thus helping one to shrink the offending activity. That surely should be a matter for approbation rather than "knee-jerk" dismissal.

Competition Policy

So far, I have discussed issues that touch primarily on the North-South questions as they are emerging in the new world economy of freer trade and investment, cautioning against the proposals to modify WTO to sanction and legitimate eco-dumping, social dumping, and the inclusion of a social clause in WTO.

But the enhanced integration of the world economy, and the sensitivity to "unfair trade" of all varieties, have prompted increased friction and demands for harmonization of policies among the developed countries as well.

The principal area in which demands for such (predominantly) North-North harmonization are emerging is competition policy. The main impetus behind the emergence of this demand has been the suspicion that the *keiretsu* and the *retail distribution* systems of Japan lead to impaired market access, in effect "nullifying and impairing" the value of Japan's trade concessions.

It is important to observe, however, that these problems are not endemic only to Japan. For example, thanks to the dramatic US-Japan car dispute and the United States objection to Japan's single-agency system of car dealerships, we have recently been reminded that EU also provides exemption from its competition directives to its auto industry so as to permit exclusive dealerships, and has just renewed it. Besides, the *keiretsu* system, again a target of US criticisms, is now widely recognized to be an efficient system and its side effects on market access may be no more than those accruing from the vertical integration that is more widely practiced in the United States and works against outside suppliers more directly. WTO will have to move in the direction of bringing these questions into its purview fairly soon as they are now beginning to prompt unilateral approaches and solutions.

My view is that while we do this, it is possible even under current GATT rules, to use Article XXIII 1(b) on nonviolation to bring *some* competition, policy-related questions before GATT and to develop jurisprudence that will reflect some minimal "norms" that are commonly shared. Unfortunately, the opportunity to do so in the US-Japan car dispute was missed by the United States, which instead took the route of unilateral threats with negligible results. The Japanese inspection system for afterparts could certainly have been targeted for a WTO Dispute-Settlement Panel, for nullification and impairment under Article 23(1)(b), citing Technical Barriers to Trade and Article 20 violations.[21]

Regionalism Versus Multilateralism: Asia's Challenge and Opportunity

I must conclude now with thoughts on the one overriding phenomenon in the world economy today: the proliferation of inherently preferential free trade areas, and hence the issue of how we view them. Do they detract from, or add to, multilateral free trade; or, as I remarked several years ago (Bhagwati 1995b), are they building blocks or stumbling blocks to the ultimate goal of a world trading system ensuring freer trade to all?[22] These issues have become central today with Mr. Klaus Kinkel of Germany proposing the Transatlantic Free Trade Area (TAFTA) with the demands within the US to turn APEC into an FTA, with the US intention to expand the North American Free Trade Agreement (NAFTA) to Chile and other South American countries and even beyond, and with the formation of MERCOSUR, the Treaty Establishing the Southern Cone Common Market, and other prospective interdeveloping country FTAs. As I argued in my Harry Johnson Lecture in 1991, this Second Regionalism (as distinct from the aborted First Regionalism constituted by the extensive flirtation with FTAs in response to the formation of the European Community in 1957), is here to stay.[23]

In my view, there are only two compelling arguments for giving up the nondiscrimination implied in all-embracing multilateralism in trade:

- that a smaller group of countries wants to develop a Common Market. In this case, not just trade, but also investment and migration barriers are eventually eliminated just as in a federal state, and the full economic and political advantages of such integration follow; and

- that it is not possible to move to fully multilateral free trade for all through multilateral trade negotiations (MTN), at GATT or now WTO, so that the only feasible way to continue reducing trade barriers is to go down the route of open-ended, easy-to-join preferential FTAs among as many willing nations as you can find.

The former argument underlay the European initiative for the Common Market. The latter argument provided a key motivation for the United States, a keen opponent of PTAs and an avid supporter of multilateralism throughout the postwar period, to shift course and to embrace PTAs by initiating the Canada-US Free Trade Agreement (CUSFTA) in 1983. The failure to secure agreement from Europe and the developing countries to start a new round of MTN at the GATT Ministerial in November 1982, led Ambassador William Brock to this approach; and the intention then was certainly to use an ever-expanding set of FTAs, with the United States acting as both catalyst and nucleus, to achieve the worldwide free trade that could not be reached via GATT any more.

With Secretary James Baker, this open-ended approach, where the United States-centered FTAs would be open to any nation anywhere (they were informally discussed with Egypt and the Association of Southeast Asian Nations [ASEAN] at the time), became captured by the proponents of "regionalism" who linked it instead, and constrained it, to the Americas, as part of President Bush's Initiative for the Americas. Thus grew the fears that the world was dividing into three blocs: the EU, the Americas, and possibly a Japan-centered Asian bloc.

In the event, the US expanded CUSFTA to NAFTA, and is now poised to go down the FTA route more energetically, promising to take Chile and then other South American nations on board. While the idea of regionalism is not dead, the Washington policy makers, in response to criticisms including mine,[24] have occasionally expressed the view that the earlier open-ended, nonregional FTAs approach will be adopted instead. Thus, President Bush, in a major speech in Detroit at the end of the Presidential campaign, promised that he would extend NAFTA to Eastern European nations and to the Far East. And recently, the Clinton administration has tentatively explored the possibility of extending NAFTA to the Republic of Korea and Singapore.

But we must ask if this infatuation with FTAs, including the pressure being exerted by many in the United States to move APEC in the direction of an FTA, is desirable when the multilateral trading system has already been jump-started with the impending ratification of the Uruguay Round and the birth of WTO? Would it not be wiser for the world's only remaining superpower, and currently also its most robust economy, to take again the leadership role on multilateral free trade and to focus on converting NAFTA into a Common Market instead of seeking to extend it to more members and, given the inherently preferential nature of such free FTAs, spreading what can be properly considered to be a stain on the now-realistic vision of a nondiscriminatory world trading system?

I believe that this analysis and judgment are shared by many in academic circles and also by some policy makers everywhere. They certainly seem to provide an opening for a leadership role for Japan in her own region, at APEC and at WTO. It seems wholly appropriate for me to suggest what the Asian members of APEC might do to turn the clock in favor of multilateralism and away from regionalism.

It is important at the outset to remember that Japan and the Far Eastern super performers, known often as "the new Japans," have produced supreme examples for the rest of the world by transforming their nations into world class economies in just one generation of phenomenal growth. Many talk in economics of the "Japanese miracle." I sometimes wonder if ours is after all not truly a "dismal science" if, every time an economy does strikingly well, we call it a miracle!

True, many seek in this outstanding success the validity of their own pet policy prescriptions. And, indeed, few things can be explained in terms of a single cause. But, I think there is broad agreement among most economists today that Japan and the new Japans have done tremendously well by going for outward-oriented trade policies and then again for world, rather than only regional or subregional, markets.[25]

Thus, preferential free trade areas where you set your sights low by thinking only of FTA-limited markets, instead of rooting for the world's markets (as would be the case if trade barriers were lowered worldwide), has characterized this area. Even ASEAN, a grouping of political significance, had no economic dimension of substance for much of its life. Multilateralism came naturally with these attitudes. It may be argued that these attitudes were strengthened in turn with economic success whereas pro-FTA attitudes have often been associated, as often noted by Martin Wolf, with economic weakness. Imperial Preference went with Britain's fear of the newly emerging competition from Germany and the United States, whereas the NAFTA debate betrayed a similar desire of many business groups and politicians to keep Mexico's markets for themselves instead of sharing them with Japan and the European Union.

But, while we may debate the many reasons for these Asian nations' desire to go for the world's, rather than just regional and subregional, markets, it surely provides them with a potential leadership role in world trade policy.

The post-Uruguay agenda at WTO will inevitably involve our looking again at Article XXIV in a much more careful way than has been done to date. But more than that, the new Director-General of WTO will have to provide leadership that seeks to shape the emerging picture of exploding preferential trade groupings and to confront its impact on WTO-centered multilateralism, instead of simply accepting their emergence as a foregone political reality. Indeed, this is exactly what Mr. Ruggiero did in a *Financial Times* interview with the paper's World Trade Editor, decrying the Kinkel initiative for TAFTA and arguing for a return to MTN at WTO.

However, the role of countries such as Japan, and the Asian nations, which have generally and indeed properly kept away from preferential trade arrangements like FTAs, in providing support to the WTO leadership will be essential.

I strongly believe that Japan, and indeed the other Asian members of APEC, can play a useful role at APEC itself by opposing its being turned into yet another FTA. APEC can set an example by rejecting such a model and using the arrangement rather as a way of coordinating policies in the region on questions such as an Investment Code and, equally important, on the new issues before WTO (such as the Social Clause) that I have discussed in this lecture. My informed guess is that, on those issues as well, Japan and the Asian nations have much to offer that is closer to what I have suggested.

APEC, since it straddles part of Asia and part of the Americas, may well be the place for these remarkable Asian nations to bring their friends across the common ocean to greater wisdom on these new issues and thus to assist the development of WTO, and of the world trading system, in more appropriate directions.

It may be thought that, after the Indonesian meeting of APEC where free trade within APEC was embraced as a goal for 2020, this is a lost cause. But it is not. While free trade is a goal for 2020, it is clouded in fundamental ambiguity and cannot be seen with 20/20 vision. Is this free trade for APEC members to be for the members only, or is it to be on an MFN basis? If the former, then the only way for this to happen consistent with WTO, is for APEC to seek to be an FTA and to get Article XXIV exemption from MFN requirements, with all the damage that yet another gigantic FTA would impose on the multilateral trading system. If the latter, then there are distinct problems. It is hard to imagine that APEC countries would make more than token MFN reductions in their trade barriers without reciprocal concessions by non-APEC members. The matter cannot long be left in ambiguity.

At annual APEC meetings, Asian member countries, particularly Japan, have the opportunity to mobilize their diplomatic skills and energies to remove this ambiguity in favor of multilateralism and against the FTA approach. I suggest they do so by considering the following:

◆ seek agreement among the Asian APEC members (including prospective new Asian members such as India) that APEC would not become a preferential FTA, while ensuring that the American members of APEC led by the United States are confronted clearly on the broader issue of the utmost importance, such as whether multilateral free trade, not a spaghetti bowl of preferential free trade areas, is to be the centerpiece of the newly emerging world trading system;

- ◆ at the same time, embrace an APEC agenda that includes coordination of policies and positions at WTO and the new Round on matters such as the wisdom of inclusion at all of labor standards and the optimal nature of the inclusion of environmental matters in WTO; and

- ◆ transform President Suharto's call for free trade in the APEC region by 2020 explicitly into a concerted effort to achieve this goal by a succession of, not APEC-alone liberalizations, but a succession of focused APEC initiatives, in conjunction with G-7 (whose non-European members are members of APEC), to launch *multilateral* trade negotiations to reduce trade barriers worldwide on a *nondiscriminatory* MFN basis.

This can be Asia's, and indeed Japan's, central contribution to the design of the new world trading system, in keeping with Asia's commitment in the postwar period to a nonregional, nonpreferential approach to world trade and her profound skepticism of the illogical and misguided political demands to make "fair trade" in environmental and labor standards a precondition for freeing trade.

Whether Asia, particularly Japan, can rise to the leadership role that is required now on these central questions of the design of the new world trading system, undertaking a proactive policy, or whether she will continue to play a reactive role that leaves leadership, and hence the architecture of the new world trading system entirely to others, is the key issue now. If the architecture of the new world trading system is left exclusively to the United States (which is obsessed with FTAs) and the European Union (which, too, has proliferated all kinds of preferential arrangements with other countries not in the core of the Common Market), it is certain that the dilution of the multilateral trading regime by the spaghetti bowl of preferential trading arrangements will be our fate. So will the intrusion into WTO of labor and environmental standards as preconditions for, and indeed barriers to, free trade.

Notes

[1] Technically, of course, it is dying rather than dead. The last rites have been administered, however.

[2] These different economic-philosophical positions are discussed in depth in Bhagwati (1977: Ch. 1).

[3] See, for example, Jagdish Bhagwati (1988, 1991b) on the issue of multilateralism.

[4] Thus, genuine "convictions-led," autonomous trade liberalization, reflecting changed belief in the virtues of freer trade, is less than what is commonly asserted. But it does exist. It is also characterizing the trend to deregulation and openness that we are witnessing today in countries such as Japan, which see themselves as falling behind the United States if they do not also deregulate and open their markets in modern sectors such as telecommunications and finance where the US has moved ahead of its competitors by deregulating ahead of the curve. Such liberalization then, is resulting from the US example, not from US demands for reciprocity.

[5] The evidence in support of this phenomenon in the 1980s, both for the US and for several other countries, is reviewed and synthesized nicely by Marvin Kosters in Chapter 1, Bhagwati and Kosters (1994).

[6] The basic empirical work is by Robert Lawrence and Matthew Slaughter. It is reviewed in Bhagwati and Dehejia (1994). A subsequent empirical study by Jeffrey Sachs and Howard Schatz (1994) claims to overturn the Lawrence-Slaughter findings by taking out computers (a procedure that is debatable at best). Even then the coefficient with the changed sign is both small and statistically insignificant. So, while Noam Chomsky has educated us that two negatives add up to a positive in every language, it is wrong to claim that the two negatives of a statistically insignificant and small parameter of the required sign add up to a positive support for the thesis that trade has been depressing the real wages of the unskilled! I have dealt with this question in depth in my latest paper on the subject (Bhagwati 1996).

[7] The work of Adrian Wood (1994) argues in support of the "trade hurting real wages of the unskilled" thesis, but his arguments have been effectively criticized by Lawrence (1994). See also the review of the theory and evidence in Jagdish Bhagwati (1995a).

[8] I have dealt with these factors systematically in my extended analysis in Chapter 1 of Volume 1 of the 2-volume set of studies in Bhagwati and Hudec (1996). Volume 1 is on *Economic Analysis* and Volume 2 is on *Legal Analysis* and both are the product of a substantial Ford Foundation-financed project under the auspices of the American Society of International Law in Washington, D.C.

[9] John Wilson (1996) demonstrates that there can even be a "race to the top." This possibility is disregarded in the analysis above, as in the public discourse.

[10] The evidence was systematically reviewed and assessed in 1994 by Arik Levinson. See Levinson (1996).

[11] These factors were analyzed by Jagdish Bhagwati and T. N. Srinivasan in 1994 (Bhagwati and Srinivasan 1996). Their analysis is based on Levinson (1996).

[12] There are other issues. One main class relates to the current GATT restrictions, as reflected in recent GATT Panel findings as in the two dolphin-tuna cases involving the US on "values"-inspired restrictions on imports of products using processes that are unacceptable, which will have to be clarified and will be the subject of new negotiations. My own views on the best solution to this class of problems, as also to the other main class of problems raised by environmentalists who fear that it is too easy for countries to challenge the higher standards which they have enacted in their own countries (an issue that was at the heart of the latest GATT Panel finding, mostly in US favor, in the EU-US case on differentially punitive US taxes and standards on higher gasoline usage cars) are developed at length in Bhagwati and Srinivasan (1996); unfortunately I have no time to address them today.

[13] This proposal can be implemented unilaterally by countries or preferably through an OECD Code.

[14] This, of course, does not apply equally to trade in highly differentiated products like autos where one can get fixated on specific countries, such as Japan.

[15] This efficiency is only in the sense of cost minimization. The number of permits may, however, be too small or too large, and getting it right by letting nonusers also bid (and then destroy permits) is bedeviled by free-rider problems.

[16] First I talk of the US suspending Mexico's trade rights since the GATT Panel in the dolphin-tuna case upheld these rights for Mexico. If it had not, I should be talking simply of the US denying market access to Mexico.

[17] In fact, the Preamble to that Convention considers that "the child should be...brought up...in the spirit of peace, dignity. . .," a spirit that is wholly lacking in the inner cities of the US where, according to recent estimates and findings by agencies such as the Children's Defense Fund, millions of children live under hazardous conditions. This is, of course, a question that has not been raised by the proponents of the Social Clause at WTO as one that ought to be included as among the prerequisites for permitting market access by countries guilty of such violations of the spirit urged by the Convention. The attention is rather on what are thought to be developing country failings, as I discuss in the text below.

[18] See, for example, the revealing interview with Secretary of Labor, Robert Reich in the *New York Times*, the "Week in Review" section, 20 August 1995.

[19] As I have noted, the Convention on the Rights of the Child does not prohibit child labor at all; its language in Article 32 is accommodating to having children work.

[20] See the report in the *New York Times* (3 September 1991). The fire in a plant of Imperial Food Products in Hamlet, North Carolina, killed 25 and hurt 55. Several doors had been blocked to prevent employees from stealing chicken parts. There had been no inspection in 11 years.

[21] Article 20 violations could have been argued on the ground that, while the US accepted the Japanese standard of safety, even if excessive, the inspection system in place was maximally, rather than minimally trade-disruptive. The US, of course,

had no interest in going to WTO on this or other issues, having determined to use unilateral methods to achieve its goals. For a detailed analysis of the car dispute, see Bhagwati (1995b).

[22] Subsequent to delivering this lecture in Manila, I have developed further some of the analytical arguments in a pamphlet, jointly authored with Anne Krueger. See Bhagwati and Krueger (1995).

[23] In Jagdish Bhagwati (1991b), I consider the reasons why the First Regionalism failed and why the Second Regionalism would endure.

[24] In Jagdish Bhagwati (1993b), I advocated there the position taken above, that the best course was to return now to multilateralism and to give up on further FTAs, but that if FTAs were to be pursued, then nonregional FTAs were better than regional ones because, among other reasons, the regional approach would be more likely to promote fragmentation of the world economy into preferential blocs.

[25] In regard to imports, there has certainly been "controlled openness" in Japan; and the role of protection in her development, as of the other Far Eastern nations, is more complex than made out by ideologues on the side of either free trade or protection.

References

Bhagwati, J, ed., 1977. *The New International Economic Order: The North-South Debate*. Cambridge, Massachusetts: MIT Press.

_____, 1988. "Protectionism". Bertil Ohlin Lectures. Cambridge, Massachusetts: MIT Press.

_____, 1991a. Free Traders and Free Immigrationists: Strangers or Friends? Working Paper No. 20. Russell Sage Foundation, New York.

_____, 1991b. *The World Trading System at Risk*. Princeton, New Jersey: Princeton University Press.

_____, 1993a. "American Rules, Mexican Jobs." *New York Times*. 24 March.

_____, 1993b. "President Clinton's Trading Choices: Beyond NAFTA What?" *Foreign Policy* (Summer).

_____, 1995a. "Trade and Wages: Choosing Among Alternative Explanations." *Federal Reserve Bank of New York Economic Policy Review* (January).

_____, 1995b. "The US-Japan Car Dispute: The Causes and Consequences of U.S. Trade Action." The American Enterprise Institute, Washington, D.C. Mimeographed.

_____, 1996. "Trade and Wages: A Malign Relationship?" In S. Collins, ed., *Imports, Exports and the American Worker*. Washington, D.C.: The Brookings Institution.

Bhagwati, J., and R. Hudec, eds., 1996. *Fair Trade and Harmonization: Prerequisites for Free Trade?* Cambridge, Massachusetts: MIT Press.

Bhagwati, J., and M. Kosters, eds., 1994. *Trade and Wages: Leveling Wages Down?* Washington, D.C.: The American Enterprise Institute.

Bhagwati, J., and V. Dehejia, 1994. "Freer Trade and Wages of the Unskilled-Is Marx Striking Again?" In J. Bhagwati and M. Kosters, eds., *Trade and Wages: Leveling Wages Down?* Washington, D.C.: The American Enterprise Institute.

Bhagwati, J., and A. Kreuger, 1995. *The Dangerous Drift to Preferential Trading Arrangments*. Washington, D.C.: The American Enterprise Institute.

Bhagwati, J., and T. N. Srinivasan, 1996. "Trade and the Environment: Does Environmental Diversity Detract from the Case for Free Trade?" In J. Bhagwati and R. Hudec, eds., *Fair Trade and Harmonization: Prerequisites for Free Trade?* Cambridge, Massachusetts: MIT Press.

Lawrence, R., 1994. Trade, Multinationals and Labor. Working Paper No. 4836. National Bureau of Economic Research, Cambridge, Massachusetts.

Levinson, A., 1996. "Environmental Regulations and Industry Location: International and Domestic Evidence." In J. Bhagwati and R. Hudec, eds., *Fair Trade and Harmonization: Prerequisites for Free Trade?* Cambridge, Massachusetts: MIT Press.

New York Times, 1991. 3 September.

_____, 1995. 20 August.

Organisation for Economic Co-operation and Development, 1993. *Employment Outlook*. Paris.

Sachs, J., and H. Schatz, 1994. "Trade and Jobs in US Manufacturing." *Brookings Papers*.

Wilson, J., 1996. "Capital Mobility and Environmental Standards: Is There a Theoretical Basis for a Race to the Bottom?" In J. Bhagwati and R. Hudec, eds., *Fair Trade and Harmonization: Prerequisites for Free Trade?* Cambridge, Massachusetts: MIT Press.

Wood, A., 1994. *North-South Trade, Employment and Inequality*. Oxford: Clarendon Press.

CHAPTER 3
THE NEW REGIONALISM AND ASIA: IMPACT AND OPTIONS

JEFFREY A. FRANKEL
DEPARTMENT OF ECONOMICS
UNIVERSITY OF CALIFORNIA, BERKELEY

AND

SHANG-JIN WEI
JOHN F. KENNEDY SCHOOL OF GOVERNMENT
HARVARD UNIVERSITY

The fever of regional trading arrangements has taken hold.[1] One might date the beginning of the recent trend to 1986/87, when the members of the European Community (EC) hatched their plans for a Single Market by 1992. Or, on the reasoning that serious steps toward regional integration were not a new development in the case of the EC, one might instead identify the watershed as the years 1988/89. This is when the United States agreed to and implemented the Free Trade Agreement with Canada; it thereby abandoned 40 years of opposition in principle to regional initiatives on the view that they detracted from multilateral liberalization.[2] Or one might date the recent surge in activity to 1990 to1992. These were the years when a new customs union was agreed in the eastern half of South America (MERCOSUR), the Andes countries agreed to form a serious Free Trade Area, and the Association of Southeast Asian Nations (ASEAN) countries agreed in principle on an ASEAN Free Trade Area (AFTA). Since historical protectionist tendencies in all three regions had previously stymied proposals for regional integration, the spread of serious regional arrangements to these areas was noteworthy.

Subsequently, the order of the day seems to be geographic enlargement of existing trading arrangements. The European Union (EU) in 1994 took in three new members, to reach a membership of 15. The United States (US) has begun discussions with Chile, regarding the possibility of it joining the North American Free Trade Area (NAFTA). A hemisphere-wide trading bloc, under the (not very elegant) name Free Trade Area of the Americas, was envisioned at the Miami Summit in November 1994. Mercosur and the Andes group are both steaming ahead, and Brazil has thoughts of combining the two into a South American Free Trade Area before bargaining with the North Americans on hemispheric arrangements.

Formal regional arrangements are much less common in Asia. The most important plans are perhaps the ones in ASEAN. It was founded in 1967 for political purposes, and declared a preferential trading arrangement (PTA) in 1977, which amounted to little. As recently as 1989, the fraction of goods eligible for regional preferences was only on the order of 3 percent. The ASEAN FTA agreed upon in January 1992, sounds more serious, calling for the reduction of tariffs and nontariff barriers in phases from 1993 to 2008 (DeRosa 1993a, b, c; Jackson 1991; Panagariya 1994; and Jaggi 1995).

Seven countries of the Indian subcontinent formed the South Asian Association for Regional Cooperation (SAARC) ten years ago. The members are India, Pakistan, Bangladesh, Sri Lanka, Nepal, Bhutan, and the Maldives. Their past talks had been even more fruitless than ASEAN's. In May 1995, however, the members agreed to put a preferential trading arrangement into place on 8 December. How much substance there will be in this PTA remains to be seen.

When Americans and others worry about a trading bloc forming in Asia, it is generally not ASEAN that concerns them, and still less SAARC. Rather it is the possibility of an East Asia bloc. One version would be the East Asian Economic Group proposed by Malaysian Prime Minister Mahatir, more recently toned down to a proposed East Asian Economic Caucus (EAEC). Another version would be a bloc created by Japan. The "yen bloc" hypothesis is discussed further below.[3]

In the Pacific, the bilateral Australia-New Zealand Closer Economic Relationship agreed in 1983, is noteworthy, particularly in that it represents much deeper integration than most FTAs. The Australians were also active in starting the Asia-Pacific Economic Cooperation (APEC) forum in 1989, in an effort to make sure they were not excluded from the rapidly growing East Asian economy. There was a danger that APEC would come to be viewed as a vacuous talk-shop. The US was finally galvanized into action by the prospect of regional blocs forming in Asia and the Pacific without its participation. In 1993, the Clinton Administration decided to throw its weight behind APEC, taking advantage of the occasion of US government chairmanship to upgrade the meeting of ministers that had been scheduled in Seattle into a high profile Leaders' Meeting. The "vision" of a future Pacific Community, which was proposed at that time by the advisory Eminent Persons' Group, was largely adopted by the APEC leaders at their 1994 meeting in Bogor, Indonesia. It struck some as too ambitious. Nevertheless, many APEC members welcomed the renewed US emphasis on the region.

In this chapter we review the recent regional initiatives, focusing in particular on their impact on Asia. We begin by discussing what simulation models predict as the direct implications for Asia of FTAs and other arrangements in the Western Hemisphere, notably NAFTA and its possible enlargement, and in Europe, notably the EU. Then we apply the gravity model of bilateral trade to test for bloc effects in such groupings as ASEAN, East Asia, and all of Asia, for data up to 1992. We test nested or concentric groupings, to determine the appropriate places to "draw the line." Next we consider the strategic question, from the viewpoint of an individual Asian country, whether to pursue unilateral, subregional, panregional, or multilateral routes to enhanced trade. Multilateral liberalization is much more advantageous than regional agreements. To the extent that domestic politics prevents unilateral liberalization and international politics prevents multilateral liberalization, regional arrangements may have some advantages. The advantages are particularly clear if the regional initiatives help to build political momentum, both domestically and internationally, for unilateral and multilateral liberalization. The last part of the chapter reviews many political economy arguments: first those that suggest that regionalism undermines support for more generalized liberalization and then those that say that regional initiatives help build political momentum for global liberalization. We return to the gravity model for a verdict on which category of political economy forces appear to have been dominant among the trading blocs of 1970 to1992. The conclusion is that regionalism has in the recent experiences been politically consistent with general openness, particularly in the case of East Asia and the European Community.

The Impact of Western Free Trade Agreements on Asia

We begin by noting that a belief in free trade, which most economists share, does not necessarily imply a belief in Free Trade Areas. Removing trade barriers within a group of countries is on the one hand good in that it eliminates some distortions, particularly those between the goods of the members. But it is, on the other hand, bad in that it creates new distortions, those between the goods of the members and goods of nonmembers. It is good in that it creates trade within the grouping, but it can be bad in that it diverts trade away from nonmembers.

Because of this possible conflict between trade creation and trade diversion, different standard models do not give unambiguous answers on the desirability of a world in which all countries are grouped into trading blocs. The models tend to agree, however, that the formation of a trading bloc can have harmful effects on the countries that are unfortunate enough to be left out of it. Even if the bloc members leave their tariffs and other trade barriers unchanged vis-à-vis outsiders (and under Article XXIV of the General Agreement on Trade and Tariffs [GATT], the average tariff level of the members of a customs union cannot be raised), there will nevertheless be some diversion of trade away from the nonmembers, toward bloc members. The fall in demand for the products of the nonmembers will worsen the terms of trade they receive for their goods, unless the bloc in question is so small that its effects on world markets can be ignored. This section reviews some of the projected effects from recent regional trading initiatives in the West.

The Effects of NAFTA on Asia

Studies of the Canadian-US FTA (CUSFTA) show a decline in trade with third countries in general (Cox and Harris 1992, Braga et al. 1994). The developing countries of Asia potentially have more to lose from NAFTA, in the form of the possible loss of the US market in labor-intensive manufactured goods to Mexican producers.

We begin with the effects on the two larger newly industrializing economies (NIEs). Noland (1994) estimates that NAFTA could divert trade from the Republic of Korea (Korea) equal to 1 to 3 percent of total Korean exports by the end of the decade, and that similar trade diversion could be experienced by exporters in other Asian countries. Almost two thirds of this estimated impact is in the textile spinning and weaving sector where quotas under the Multifiber Arrangement (MFA) currently apply. Hufbauer and Schott (1993) predict that NAFTA will divert from Taipei,China and Korea only $300 million of manufactured exports that previously went to the US, with machinery and transport equipment the largest component on a base year of 1990. Estimates by Kreinen (1992:17) and Kreinen and Plummer (1992) predict that diversion out of the US market caused by the elimination of intra-North American tariffs will impact exports from Korea by 5 percent, measured as the adverse effect on their terms of trade. (Hufbauer and Schott note the importance of using actual applied tariff rates in the analysis, which include any existing preferences, rather than most-favored nation [MFN] rates. This is one reason their results imply less trade diversion than Kreinen and Plummer's.)

The range of estimates for effects on Southeast and South Asia is similar. The Hufbauer-Schott estimates predict that South and East Asian developing countries, excluding Korea and Taipei,China, will lose only $350 million in manufactures, with machinery and transport equipment again the hardest hit sector, but clothing and other consumer goods also adversely affected. These countries will also lose an estimated $100 million of primary products.[4] Safadi and Yeats (1993) examine the effects of NAFTA specifically on the South Asian countries. They find that trade diversion of exports is heavily concentrated in textiles and apparel, though the aggregate effect on South Asia would be small. Industrialized countries pledged under the Uruguay Round to phase out their textile quotas; but the scheduled phaseout is sufficiently long-lived and back-loaded that NAFTA makes a significant difference to worldwide textile trade in the meantime. The Kreinen-Plummer estimates predict that the elimination of intra-North American tariffs will cause a deterioration of the terms of trade for the ASEAN countries by 4 percent.

These estimated effects are not trivial, but are not particularly large either, especially the Hufbauer-Schott estimates. In part, this is because US tariffs were already very low to begin with and were already slightly lower against some Mexican goods than against imports from industrialized countries, under the Generalized System of Preferences. On these grounds, one might argue that the scope for both trade creation and trade diversion in the US market was limited.

As is widely recognized, however, the major barriers remaining in the US, as in other industrialized countries, are not tariffs, but nontariff barriers and administrative protection, such as antidumping duties. Canada and Mexico are to a greater extent exempt from much US protection under NAFTA (though the US refused to exempt them from antidumping actions); indeed, this was the major attraction of FTA from their viewpoint. Thus concerns about diversion of trade away from East Asia, where these trade barriers are often applied, are quite relevant. The manipulation of rules of origin, so as to extend existing US protection to the Mexican market, may in particular hit Japanese auto producers and other Asian exporters (Krueger 1993).

The rapid growth in US-Mexican trade in 1993/94, across the border in both directions, initially seemed to be consistent with these concerns. There has not been time, however, to assess the amount of trade creation versus trade diversion in these early results.

At the time of the NAFTA agreement, another major concern on the part of the Asian countries was the diversion of investment from themselves to Mexico. This concern was most relevant for the case of access to capital from US investors, as CUSFTA and NAFTA included provisions to make within-bloc investors welcome. The concern particularly applies to flows of foreign direct investment (FDI), as opposed to flows of portfolio capital, on the grounds that the latter are more fungible across countries.[5] Kreinen (1992) predicts that FDI may be diverted from ASEAN to Mexico in the food, chemical, textile, metals, and electronics sectors, and from Korea to Mexico in the chemical, machinery, electronics, and transport equipment sectors. McCleery (1993:319, 325-9) argues that investment diversion is the most important impact of NAFTA on Asia, with a bigger adverse effect than trade diversion. His (probably overstated) scenarios have Indonesia losing 4 to 5 percent of investment to NAFTA, which contributes to a 2.2 percent fall in gross domestic product (GDP); Malaysia losing 5 to 7 percent of its investment, which causes a 1.4 percent drop in GDP; Singapore losing 2 to 3 percent of its investment, which causes a 1.3 decline in GDP; and Thailand losing 4 to 5 percent of its investment, for a 1.0 percent drop in GDP. The effects in other countries considered are not so great as in the ASEAN cases; Hong Kong comes the closest.

US investment, direct as well as portfolio investment, in Mexico started to grow even before NAFTA, but grew especially rapidly in 1993/94. There was, moreover, the possibility that enhanced trade and liberalization generally in Mexico would touch off a growth boom there, and attract capital also from Japan and elsewhere in addition to attracting investors in the US. Of course, a growth boom in Mexico or in other NAFTA member countries would have led to increased imports from Asia and elsewhere. These are the dynamic effects of FTAs, to which proponents often appeal when they wish to argue that FTAs will have large benefits for everyone.

The Mexican crisis that broke in December 1994, changed everything, at least in the short run. The large and growing trade deficit that Mexico ran in 1993 and 1994 was reversed at least in part in 1995 and 1996, because the private capital flows to support it dried up in February 1994, and the central bank's reserves virtually ran out in December. The unexpectedly large peso devaluation that took place at that time became the principal instrument of this adjustment. An effect of North American economic integration will now be that the US experiences a larger share of the decline in Mexican demand for goods and Asia experiences a smaller share of that decline, ironically, than would have taken place in the absence of NAFTA.[6] A partial revaluation of the Mexican peso in 1996 helped to limit the decline in its demand for imported goods. Given the small size of Mexico, however, this effect on Asia is small.

Another implication of the December 1994 crisis is that less capital will be flowing into Mexico for the next few years. Some of it may flow to the Asian emerging markets instead, as they came through the crisis relatively intact. Nevertheless the worldwide contagion effect of the Mexican crisis was sufficiently great that we will probably see somewhat less capital going to all emerging markets for a while, as compared to the boom years of 1991 to 1993.

The Effects of an Enlarged Free Trade Area of the Americas

Anticipating the Miami Summit, Hufbauer and Schott (1994:163-4) made estimates of the effects of a hemisphere-wide FTA. They calculate by commodity groups how much of the increased US imports from the rest of the hemisphere would represent diversion of trade that would otherwise come from other countries. Their estimates indicate East Asia experiencing diversion of $7.3 billion of exports annually by 2002, equal to 2.6 percent of projected East Asian exports to the US. Over 40 percent of this diversion is concentrated in the textiles and apparel sectors ($3.4 billion). The next largest categories affected are leather products (diversion of $0.9 billion), primary metals ($0.6 billion), and amusement and sporting goods ($0.4 billion). They show South Asia suffering diversion of about $3.2 billion by 2002, or 2.8 percent of its projected exports to the US market. The two sectors that experience the most diversion are textiles and apparel ($1.2 billion) and food products ($1 billion).

These numbers, while calculated to be somewhat biased upward, represent a small effect. One reason already noted is that US tariff barriers are already low, and will be even lower after the Uruguay Round: they will be below 3 percent by the year 2000. The estimates do not include the loss of exports to Latin America. If tariffs in Latin America were currently as high as they were ten years ago, the trade diversion there might be substantial. But tariffs in these countries have already come down a lot, and will probably come down a lot more. This fact, together with the fact that the Latin American market is not as large as the US, implies that trade diversion should not be that large, as long as the elasticity of demand for the East and Southeast Asian products is not particularly high.

Effects of the European Union on Asia

Studies of the earlier stages of regional integration in Europe, such as research by Kreinen (1972, 1982) on the formation of the European Community and on its enlargement, found trade-creation five to seven times larger than trade diversion.

The relatively few studies of the effects of 1990s European integration on outside countries tend to predict small gains for East Asian developing countries and Australia/New Zealand, though some find negative effects on Japan from diversion of skill-intensive manufactured products (Anderson 1993; Stoeckl, Pearce, and Banks 1990; Greenaway 1991; and Haaland and Norman 1992). The Japanese auto industry has been particularly hit by the spread of import quotas from France and Italy to other EU members after 1992, and the application of local content requirements. The EC has also used rules of origin against Japanese makers of photocopiers, electric scales, electric typewriters, and semiconductors (Gundlach et al. 1993:208).

Gundlach et al. (1993:212-19) summarize some recent studies of the effect of the 1992 Single Market. Within the category of primary commodities, very little trade diversion is expected, because EC countries do not produce them or close substitutes. Koekoek, Kuyvenhoven, and

Molle (1990), Matthews and MacAleese (1990), and Page (1992) conclude that the effect on developing countries' commodity exports should be positive (though small), because of the greater demand arising from faster European growth.

Despite the past importance of commodity exports in Southeast Asia, manufactured goods now constitute 86 percent of exports from East and Southeast Asia to the EU. Here there is more scope for trade diversion, particularly at the hands of producers in Spain, Portugal, and Greece. Davenport (1990), using low estimates of the elasticity of EC import demand with respect to European income, estimates that negative effects from trade diversion will be large enough to cancel out the positive effects from faster European growth.

Davenport (1991) and Page (1992) estimate that the total net trade effects of EC 1992, as percentages of each region's existing exports to the EC, will be -0.3 for ASEAN, -6.1 for the Asian NIEs, and -0.3 percent for South Asia and the People's Republic of China (PRC). Kreinen and Plummer (1992) estimate diversion effects of 8 percent for ASEAN exports and 5 percent for Korean exports. Gundlach, et al. (1993:218) are more optimistic. They argue that the Single Market is likely to open up substantial new export opportunities that outweigh trade diversion. The argument is that EU productivity gains are not likely to be concentrated in those manufacturing industries where European firms have already lost competitiveness to Asians in the past, and that Asian producers can exploit their proven ability to adapt to new patterns of demand for goods and services in the EU.[7]

The 1994 enlargement of the EU to take in Austria, Finland, and Sweden, formerly members of the European Free Trade Area (EFTA), should impact skill-intensive Japan more than the other East Asian countries. If there is in the future another enlargement to include the poorer Czech and Slovak Republics, Poland, and Hungary, trade diversion should be felt more by the labor-intensive East Asian developing countries. This would be a repeat of the earlier assimilation of Spain, Portugal, and Greece into what was then the nine-member European Economic Community.

The studies cited above follow studies of the effects on income within Europe in that they allow dynamic effects on European growth. This approach tends to yield a rosier outlook for everyone. The dynamic effects, in contrast to earlier static (and generally small) estimates, are maximized under the assumption that the investment rate will be stimulated. The classic references, the Cecchini Report (1988) and Baldwin (1989), estimated that EC gross national product (GNP) by the end of the century would go up on the order of 2.5 to 6.5 percent as the result of the 1992 Single Market. This higher European income would raise imports from all trading partners. If the elasticity of import demand is about 2, then exports from Asia to Europe would go up at least 5 percent. This effect is to be netted against the negative effects of trade diversion.

The grounds for the dynamic estimates are unusually uncertain however. Kreinen (1992:17) and Kreinen and Plummer (1992), who do not allow for dynamic effects, predict that trade diversion from the European integration would reduce exports from ASEAN and Korea by 8 percent and 5 percent, respectively. Again, only tariffs are included. The estimated effect on ASEAN is greater for European integration than for North American integration, in part because the European tariffs are higher than US tariffs.

To What Extent Do Implicit Trading Blocs Already Exist in Asia? Estimates from the Gravity Model

Most of the estimates cited above are ex ante projections, derived from feeding into econometric models the assumption that a given formally announced Free Trade Area would, in fact, entail the removal of all tariffs among its members. Based on past history, there are grounds for suspicion that formal proclamations of FTAs are not always followed by full implementation. In the 1960s and 1970s, announced groupings that did not turn out to lead up to their advanced billing were numerous. Besides ASEAN, they included the Latin American Free Trade Area and the Economic Community of West African States (launched in 1975), and many others. There is often a failure to translate generalities into specifics, to keep to timetables, or to enforce agreements. The question therefore arises: How can we tell that the more recent round of regional trading arrangements is indeed more serious?

If some suspect that formal arrangements do not always lead to meaningful trade blocs, others suspect that important de facto trade blocs can arise even in the absence of de jure trading arrangements. It is often noted that the economies of Asia and the Pacific, despite their rapidly increasing pace of interaction, have adopted fewer explicit public mechanisms of integration or cooperation. Only the Australia-New Zealand Closer Economic Relationship is a formal, deep arrangement to foster integration. It even prevents the two members from bringing antidumping actions against each other, and substitutes an integrated competition policy. As already noted, SAARC and even AFTA have not yet really gotten off the ground, and the larger EAEC is presently at most a caucus.

Yet reports abound that an East Asia bloc is forming, centered on Japan. Sometimes the emerging grouping is called a "yen bloc" especially when it is seen as including the growing financial and monetary influence of Japan in the region. Those seeing a yen bloc do not claim that Japan maintains formal discriminatory trading arrangements with East Asian countries. They claim that Japan is bringing about a bloc using means that are indirect, invisible, and implicit, rather than direct, visible, or explicit. They have in mind Japan's use of foreign direct investment and overseas development assistance to redirect the Asian trade flows toward itself.[8] To test the hypothesis that such a bloc is forming, it clearly will not do to look at explicit preferential tariffs on the part of Japan, since the proponents of the bloc hypothesis concede that this is not the instrument.

The Gravity Model

The key to detecting and quantifying a possible intraregional trade bias is to establish a "norm" of bilateral trade volume based on economic, geographic, and cultural factors. A useful framework for this purpose is the gravity model.[9] Once the norm has been established by the gravity model, a dummy variable can then be added to represent when both countries in a given pair belong to the same regional grouping. One can check how the level of trade and time trend in, for example, East Asia compares with that in other groupings.

The dependent variable in our gravity estimation is the bilateral volume of total trade, exports plus imports (in logarithmic form). The two most important factors in explaining bilateral trade flows are the geographic distance between the two countries, and their economic size. These factors are the essence of the gravity model and are the source of the name, by analogy, to the formula for gravitational attraction between two heavenly bodies.

It has been frequently observed that the magnitude of intraregional trade within such groupings as the EU and East Asia is disproportionately high. It is plausible that a large part of the apparent bias toward intraregional trade is due to simple geographic proximity. Most obviously, proximity reduces shipping costs; it also reduces other costs associated with time lags such as interest charges, spoilage, and obsolescence, and costs associated with what Linneman called psychic distance such as ignorance of foreign customs and tastes. Indeed Krugman (1991b) and Summers (1991) assert that most of the observed tendency for countries to trade disproportionately with their intraregional neighbors is due to proximity. Krugman uses this proposition to argue that the three trading blocs are welfare-improving "natural" groupings (as distinct from "unnatural" trading arrangements between distant trading partners such as the United Kingdom and a Commonwealth member). The argument is that natural intracontinental trade blocs are likely to be more trade-creating than trade-diverting, because transportation and other distance-related costs inhibit trade between continents anyway, so that there is less trade to be diverted.

Theoretical models and empirical studies alike surprisingly often neglect to take into account distance and transportation costs. Our measure is the log of distance between the two major cities (usually the capitals) of the respective countries.[10] We also add a dummy "adjacent" variable to indicate when two countries share a common land border.

Entering GNPs in product form is empirically well established in bilateral trade regressions. It can be easily justified by the modern theory of trade under imperfect competition. Intuitively, one will choose to trade more with a larger country than a smaller country, because it has more varieties to offer, and consumers like variety. There are reasons to believe that GNP per capita also has a positive effect, for a given size: as countries become more developed, they tend to specialize more and to trade more; also, more developed countries have better ports and communication systems that facilitate goods trade.

A common language can facilitate trade partly because it directly reduces transaction (translation) costs and partly because it enhances exporters' and importers' understanding of each other's culture and legal system, which indirectly promotes trade. To capture this effect, we also include a dummy that takes the value of one if the country pair in question shares a common language or has a previous colonial connection. We consider nine languages: English, French, German, Spanish, Portuguese, Dutch, Arabic, Chinese, and Japanese.

A representative specification is:

$$\log(T_{ij}) = \alpha + \beta_1 \log(GNP_i \, GNP_j) + \beta_2 \log(GNP/pop_i \, GNP/pop_j)$$
(1)

$$+ \beta_3 \log(DISTANCE) + \beta_4 (ADJACENT) + \beta_5 (LANGUAGE).$$

$$+ \gamma_1 (W.\,Europe_{ij}) + \gamma_2 (W.\,Hemisphere_{ij}) + \gamma_3 (E.\,ASIA_{ij}) + u_{ij}.$$

The last five explanatory factors are dummy variables. *W. Europe* (Western Europe), *W. Hemisphere* (Western Hemisphere), and *E. ASIA* (East Asia) are examples of the dummy variables we use when testing the effects of membership in a common regional grouping. They are defined as 1 for a given pair when both countries are members of that grouping, and 0 otherwise. We use the technique of Ordinary Least Squares regression, which is capable of testing the effect of each independent variable while holding constant the effects of the others.

Our data set covers 63 countries (or 1,953 country pairs) for 1970, 1980, and 1990 (and 1992 later in the chapter as well). The source is the United Nations trade matrix for 1970 and 1980, and the International Monetary Fund's *Direction of Trade Statistics* for 1990 (and 1992).

We employ the panel regression technique that allows for year-specific intercepts. Unlike usual panel regressions, we do not include country pair dummies unless there is a specific reason for doing so, because the loss in degrees of freedom would undermine our effort in detecting possible intraregional biases.

Implicit and Explicit Trade Blocs in East Asia

As our first application (beyond our earlier studies [Frankel 1991, 1993; Frankel and Wei 1994a, 1995; and Frankel, Wei, and Stein 1994][11]), we carry out a full examination of possible blocs in Asia-Pacific. Specifically, by bringing South Asia and Middle East Asian economies into our analysis, we examine to what degree Asia and its subregions are integrated in terms of goods trade. We consider a sequence of nested country groupings in Asia: ASEAN, East Asia, East and South Asia, and the whole of Asia. For a complete list of countries in various groups that are in our sample, readers are referred to the list that follows Table 1. In all of our estimations, we control for possible bloc effects in the Western Hemisphere and Western Europe. As our previous work has shown, both groupings exhibit intraregional bias.

First, in Table 1 we note that our control variables behave very much the same way as in our previous studies. The coefficient on GNP is 0.7 and statistically significant, indicating that larger economies trade more, but trade increases less than proportionally as GNP expands. Per capita GNP also has a positive and statistically significant coefficient: richer economies trade more.

As predicted, geography matters as well. Distance has an economically and statistically large effect on trade: as distance increases by 1 percent, trade declines by 0.5 percent. The significance of the "adjacency" dummy shows that two countries with a common land border have a larger amount of trade than two otherwise identical countries. A common language or past colonial connection facilitates trade. In our estimation, this brings in 50 percent more trade than otherwise.

Trade in both the Western Hemisphere and Western Europe exhibits intraregional biases. However, as in our previous studies, the relative magnitude of bloc variables is different from conclusions that others have reached based on simple magnitudes of intraregional trade. The latter do not attempt to take into account the factors of the gravity model. For example, once we take into account the contributions of economic size, level of development, geography, and linguistics, the intraregional bias turns out to be higher in the Western Hemisphere than in Western Europe.[12]

Now we come to the central issue of this section of the chapter, the degree of integration within Asia. In Column 1 of Table 1, we append a dummy ASEAN-Bloc to denote trade among members of the Association of Southeast Asian Nations. The dummy is extraordinarily large and statistically significant. Interpreted literally, two ASEAN economies trade 600 percent $[=\exp(1.97)\text{-}1]$ more than two otherwise identical economies.[13]

We know that Singapore plays an entrepot role: its imports and exports are more than 100 percent of GDP. It is possible that the apparent intra-ASEAN bias is partly or wholly a reflection of the extreme openness of Singapore. To examine this, we add a Singapore dummy (any bilateral trade involving Singapore) to the regression in Column 1. (The results of this test are not reported, to save space.) The Singapore dummy does indeed have a positive and very significant coefficient (1.51 with a standard error of 0.09). The coefficient on the ASEAN dummy is reduced to 1.40 but remains quantitatively large and statistically significant (with a standard error of 0.16). This suggests that Singapore's extreme openness does not explain all of the apparent inward bias among the ASEAN countries.

It is possible that *all* East Asian economies tend to concentrate their trade with each other, and ASEAN countries are not special in this regard. To examine this possibility, we add an East Asia dummy to the regression. Indeed, the new dummy has a positive and statistically significant coefficient: two East Asian economies trade 700 percent $[=\exp(2.12)\text{-}1]$ more than two random economies in the world. Once we take this into account, ASEAN economies no longer exhibit an abnormal amount of trade among themselves relative to their East Asian neighbors.

Again, we may control for the extreme openness of Singapore, and now also Hong Kong, which has a similar role as entrepot. We add two dummies to represent bilateral trade pairs that involve Hong Kong and Singapore, respectively (not reported). The coefficients for Hong Kong and Singapore are 0.87 and 1.40, respectively, both significant at the 1 percent level. After controlling for the openness of these two city economies, the East Asia dummy continues to have a large and significant coefficient (1.70 with a standard error of 0.10).

We have tried testing whether some linguistic links are stronger than others. As of 1990, two Chinese-speaking countries appeared to trade an estimated four and a half times as much as other similarly situated countries. The apparent magnitude of the Chinese language term raises the possibility that the influence of the Chinese Diaspora is a dominant source of East Asian intraregional trade. There is an important possible objection that must be registered however. PRC-Taipei,China trade does not appear in the statistics, because it is officially nonexistent. Such trade is, in reality, thought to be large and rapidly growing, and heavily to take the form of trade routed indirectly through Hong Kong. If PRC-Taipei,China trade is routed through Hong Kong (or Singapore), then it is counted twice in our data, and thus may be exaggerating the estimate of the influence of the Chinese variable. We have attempted to correct for this double-counting of PRC-Taipei,China trade. The governments of Taipei,China and PRC report estimates of their true bilateral trade. To err on the side of caution, we took the larger of the estimates, and treated it as if it were all counted twice in the form of Hong Kong trade. We re-ran the gravity estimates with trade among "the three Chinas" adjusted in this way. The independent Chinese-language effect is no longer significantly stronger than other linguistic links around the world.

Broader Asian and Pacific Groupings

South Asians wonder if they should not be included in Asia. The habit of speaking of "Asia-East-of-Burma" as a separate region called East Asia, almost as a separate continent, has not always prevailed. It has become standard only in the last few decades, in response to the superior growth performance of most of these countries.[14] In the third column, we consider South and East Asia collectively as one candidate trading group. The coefficient for the East-and-South Asia group is 0.65 and significant, indicating two countries in this group trade 90 percent [=exp(0.65)-1] more than a random pair of otherwise identical countries. If we add the Hong Kong and Singapore dummies to the regression, the coefficients on East Asia and East-and-South Asia dummies remain quantitatively large (1.36 and 0.37, respectively) and statistically significant.

In our sample, the term "South Asia" refers to two countries, India and Pakistan. One conjectures that the trade between these two countries is negatively impacted by their historical animosity. The last column of Table 1 shows that this is indeed the case: their trade is 70 percent lower than two otherwise identical economies.[15] This finding suggests that the positive coefficient on the East-and-South Asia bloc in column 3 mainly reflects higher-than-average trade between East and South Asian economies.

Unfortunately, Bangladesh, Sri Lanka, and Nepal are not in our sample of available bilateral trade data. But Srinivasan and Canonero (1995:29) do have data on trade between these countries and other major trading partners. They note that Bangladesh and Sri Lanka trade very little within the South Asia region. Much of Nepal's trade is with India; but then Nepal has few alternative routes to the outside world. It seems possible that the "negative bloc" effect reported in the table for South Asia would generalize, even if all the members were represented.

A few of the most eminent international trade economists are skeptical of the notion of natural trading blocs. Specifically, Bhagwati (1992, 1993a) is suspicious of the claim that proximity is an important determinant of trade. He asserts that the high levels of intraregional trade that are already observed in such areas as Europe must be the result of FTAs and other preferential trading arrangements that are already in place.[16] The issue becomes an important one for policy when other economists, such as Krugman and Summers, argue that proximity does promote trade, and propose that regional trading arrangements be pursued on the grounds that it is *natural* for neighbors to trade with each other.[17] The gravity equation estimates convinced many of us sometime ago that distance is, in fact, a very important determinant of trade. But special historical attractions or repulsions also matter, independently of distance. In South Asia, it is in fact true that neighbors do not necessarily trade more with each other. Historical enmity has reduced trade between India and Pakistan, as is seen in the last column of Table 1. Perhaps the root of Jagdish Bhagwati's skepticism regarding the role of proximity in trade is that he has been unduly influenced by this one observation.[18]

To repeat, the gravity model clearly shows that proximity is in general an important determinant of bilateral trade around the world, notwithstanding exceptions like India-Pakistan and other cases. Ideally, one would use a dummy variable to represent all pairs with a recent history of strong political or military conflict, especially including embargoes and boycotts. This variable would, in essence, be the antithesis of the dummy variable for linguistic and colonial links. The distance and adjacency effects are so strong however, that they show up as highly significant statistically even when no account is taken of the antagonist pairs.

The next question to arise is whether the right place to draw the line dividing up Asia, if not between Myanmar and Thailand, is between Pakistan and Iran. In column 4, we include in the regression the whole of the continent of Asia (adding Asian countries in the Middle East to the above list) as a potential bloc. Two results are noteworthy. First, East Asian economies continue to show certain inward bias among themselves. Second, even after controlling for a special East Asia effect, Asian economies as a group appear to trade more among themselves than one would expect based on their economic and geographic characteristics. There is no reason to draw a line between South Asia and the Middle East. Part of the pan-Asia trade concentration undoubtedly has to do with the fact that many Asian economies have to import a substantial amount of oil from the Middle East. Adding the Hong Kong and Singapore dummies does not change the qualitative features of the picture (not reported here).

We complete our investigation by considering all members of the APEC forum as another potential bloc. We use the criterion of membership as it was up to 1992, not including Mexico or other new members of APEC. The result is reported in Column 5 of Table 1. We can make several observations regarding this most comprehensive regression. First, of all possible implicit trade blocs in Asia-Pacific, the one that shows the strongest intraregional bias is, in fact, the APEC group that includes the US as its member. Two APEC members trade 200 percent $[=\exp(1.14)\text{-}1]$ more than two otherwise identical economies. The US fear that it may be excluded by trade integration among East Asian economies is largely unfounded. Second, once we have controlled for an APEC effect, the coefficient on the East Asia bloc is greatly reduced and becomes only marginally significant at the 10 percent level. This suggests that East Asian economies, though trading a lot among themselves, do not trade substantially more than other APEC countries. Evidently there is an independent Pacific effect that can be represented either by an East Asia bloc or an APEC bloc. Third, even after we have controlled for an APEC effect, there continues to be a pan-Asia bloc that exhibits a strong inward trade bias. Again, controlling for the openness of Hong Kong and Singapore does not alter the basic picture. In that case, the coefficients on East Asia, Asia, and APEC blocs are 0.30, 0.38 and 1.06, respectively.[19]

Table 1: Estimates of Regional Bloc Effects Using the Gravity Model Trade

Dependent Variable: Trade $_{ij}$				Sample: 1970-1990		
Intercept	-9.045** (0.292)	-9.766** (0.280)	-9.875** (0.280)	-10.029* (0.280)	-9.478** (0.281)	-9.754** (0.280)
1980 Dummy	-0.987** (0.052)	-1.003** (0.051)	-1.016** (0.051)	-1.02** (0.051)	-0.97** (0.051)	-1.001** (0.051)
1990 Dummy	-1.257** (0.059)	-1.276** (0.059)	-1.292** (0.059)	-1.298** (0.059)	-1.234** (0.059)	-1.273** (0.058)
GNP	0.74** (0.010)	0.728** (0.010)	0.723** (0.010)	0.723** (0.010)	0.710** (0.010)	0.728 (0.010)
per-capita GNP	0.204** (0.013)	0.222** (0.013)	0.232** (0.013)	0.234** (0.013)	0.227** (0.013)	0.220** (0.013)
Distance	-0.581** (0.025)	-0.504** (0.024)	-0.498** (0.024)	-0.487** (0.024)	-0.513** (0.024)	-0.504** (0.024)
Adjacency	0.607** (0.100)	0.721** (0.096)	0.711** (0.096)	0.710** (0.097)	0.681** (0.097)	0.737** (0.096)
Language	0.508** (0.540)	0.474** (0.052)	0.460** (0.052)	0.472** (0.052)	0.383** (0.051)	0.477** (0.052)
WHem Bloc	0.232** (0.086)	0.319** (0.085)	0.346** (0.086)	0.373** (0.086)	0.408** (0.086)	0.312** (0.085)
WEurope BLoc	0.086 (0.063)	0.216** (0.062)	0.215** (0.062)	0.253** (0.062)	0.272** (0.062)	0.215** (0.062)
ASEAN Bloc	1.972** (0.215)	-0.002 (0.234)	0.009 (0.233)	0.019 (0.233)	-0.019 (0.232)	-0.008 (0.234)
EastAsia Bloc		2.124** (0.099)	1.497** (0.194)	1.499** (0.193)	0.349# (0.209)	2.121** (0.099)
E&SAsia Bloc			0.654 (0.174)	0.202 (0.222)	0.216 (0.222)	
Asia Bloc				0.482** (0.141)	0.503** (0.141)	
APEC Bloc					1.140** (0.076)	
SAsia Bloc						-1.436** (0.240)
# of OBS.	4555	4555	4555	4555	4555	4555
Std. Err of Reg	1.184	1.15	1.148	1.144	1.13	1.149
ADJ R2	0.744	0.76	0.759	0.761	0.767	0.759

Notes:

1. **, *, # denotes significance at the 99%, 95%, and 90% levels, respectively.
2. All variables except dummy variables are in logs.
3. Data cover 1970, 1980, and 1990.

Table 1 (cont'd.)
Definitions of Regional Dummy Variables

WHem Bloc   Canada, United States, Argentina, Brazil, Chile,
             Colombia, Ecuador, Mexico, Peru, Venezuela,
             Bolivia, Uruguay, Paraguay

WEurope Bloc France, Germany, Italy, United Kingdom, Austria,
             Belgium, Denmark, Finland, Netherlands, Norway,
             Sweden, Switzerland, Greece, Iceland, Ireland,
             Portugal, Spain

ASEAN Bloc   Indonesia, Malaysia, Philippines, Singapore,
             Thailand

EastAsia Bloc ASEANBloc, Japan, Taipei,China, Hong Kong,
             Republic of Korea, People's Republic of China

E&SAsia Bloc EastAsiaBloc, India, Pakistan

Asia Bloc   EastAsiaBloc, India, Pakistan, Turkey, Israel, Iran,
             Kuwait, Saudi Arabia

APEC Bloc   EastAsiaBloc, Canada, United States, Australia,
             New Zealand

SAsian Bloc India, Pakistan

Strategies from the Viewpoint of Asian Countries

Individual countries need to choose on what level to seek integration, or what priorities to give to the different levels: unilateral liberalization;[20] integration with a small group of immediate neighbors in such groupings as ASEAN and SAARC, or even EAEC integration in a Pacific-wide grouping (APEC); or, at the highest level, multilateral negotiations through the World Trade Organization (WTO).

It is worth restating the point that integration in general is to be desired. Isolation on the Myanmar model, or less extreme (but messier) versions on the Indian model, are no longer a viable option for a country that wishes to grow. The literature on the connection between trade and growth is huge, even if one stays within the Asian context. To summarize briefly, econometric estimates of cross-country growth equations show that trade, while ranking behind such determinants of growth as rates of saving and education, is nevertheless important.[21] Critics question how one can be sure, when looking at the correlations, that trade causes growth, rather than growth causing trade, or both responding to some third variable such as investment or good macroeconomic policies. This is the problem of simultaneous causality.[22] One way to get around the simultaneity problem is to focus on the variation in trade that can be attributed to the exogenous determinants of the gravity model: distance from one's trading partners, common borders, common languages, and the size of one's trading partners. This exogenous component of trade turns out to be an even stronger correlate of growth than in the simple tests that do not correct for simultaneity. In other words, trade is indeed a determinant of growth.[23]

For those countries that historically have had high trade barriers, and have had domestic economies that are highly directed and distorted as well, there is little reason not to begin the process of liberalization unilaterally (with the help of the multilateral development banks, of course). This advice is most relevant for South Asia and Indochina, though tariffs remain very high in such supposedly trade-oriented economies as Indonesia. Unilateral liberalization is also desirable for other countries as well. But issues of strategy in dealing with one's trading partners arise in addition. Unilateral liberalization might be viewed as a necessary prelude to multilateral negotiations in that the large industrialized countries are unlikely to wish to bargain with a nonmarket economy.[24] This leaves the question whether to pursue local regional FTAs like AFTA and SAARC versus larger blocs like APEC, or whether to eschew regionalism entirely for the sake of multilateralism.

The ultimate goal should be worldwide liberalization, in which the industrialized countries agree to curtail their restrictive practices at the same time as the developing countries liberalize. The most relevant restrictive practices of the industrialized countries are agriculture quotas and textile quotas, which the Uruguay Round is supposed to phase out, voluntary export restraints, the misleadingly named antidumping duties, and other aspects of managed trade.

Economists continue to believe that worldwide free trade is the first-best strategy. New economic theories have ultimately done little to change the bottom line. New economic arguments are made that in the presence of imperfect competition, increasing returns to scale, and endogenous technology, an individual country can theoretically raise economic welfare by imposing just the right tariffs or subsidies. But the introduction of imperfect competition does at least as much to strengthen the arguments for free trade as to weaken them. In most of these models, intervention works only if the foreign country fails to retaliate. In reality, countries do retaliate, and emulate. An equilibrium in which all countries are effectively prevented from intervening, such as by means of GATT or the World Trade Organization, is better for all than the noncooperative equilibrium in which everyone intervenes.

Model simulations support the idea that the strategy of forming regional FTAs is not as desirable, from the viewpoint of Asian countries, as pursuing free trade itself. Various authors have looked at various possible FTAs in Asia.

What would be the effects of the ASEAN Free Trade Area, if it came to full fruition? DeRosa (1993b:5-6; 1993c) uses a Computable General Equilibrium (CGE) model to find that an AFTA would be trade-creating, expanding intrabloc trade as much as 21 percent. But MFN liberalization on the part of ASEAN members (even nonreciprocal) would raise trade by three times as much. The problem with purely intraregional liberalization is that the Southeast Asian countries mostly produce the same sorts of things; it is necessary to promote trade with outsiders, especially developing countries, to get larger welfare gains. "Overall, the findings. . .cast substantial doubt on the desirability of pursuing regional economic arrangements. . ."

Srinivasan and Canonero (1993, 1995) look at possibilities for South Asia. They use a more stylized model, along the lines of the gravity equation in the preceding section, but broken down by commodity. They add explicit measures of tariffs in the gravity equation, and use those coefficients to infer what would be the effect of various changes in trading arrangements. For all countries in the region, the most important effects come in the sector of textile fibers and manufactures, particularly textile yarn and clothing. They find that SAARC would promote trade substantially for the smaller members. Bangladesh's estimated new trade within the region would amount to a very large 21 percent of GNP, more than doubling its current level of total trade. Nepal's estimated new trade amounts to an even larger (proportionately) 56 percent of GNP, almost three times its current level of total trade. For these countries, the benefits of regional integration are likely to be large, because their initial levels of trade are small, and India and Pakistan are large enough partners to make a big difference to them.

For the two larger countries themselves, SAARC would not do as much. Srinivasan and Canonero find that integrating with Europe or with the US would be far more attractive to India and Pakistan than regional integration. An FTA with the EU would raise India's bilateral trade by an amount equal to 30 percent of GNP, twice its current total trade. It would raise Pakistan's trade with the EU also by 30 percent of GNP, 95 percent of its current total trade. Like Panagariya (1994) and DeRosa (1993b, 1993c), Srinivasan and Canonero (1995:32) conclude, assuming recipro-cal liberalization with Europe and the US is not an option, that coordi-nated liberalization of countries within an Asian region on an uncondi-tional MFN basis is probably preferable to the formation of a discrimina-tory FTA within that region.

Brown, Deardorff, and Stern (1995) study the implication of an East Asian FTA linking Japan with major NIEs. They find welfare gains ranging from 0.2 percent to 1.2 percent of GDP. They find that excluded countries or regions gain as well, positive spillovers arising from realization of scale economies and increased product varieties. But the welfare gains to the East Asian bloc is greater when it is assumed that the US joins in.

What would be the effects of a full-fledged Asia or Pacific trading bloc? Lewis, Robinson, and Wang (1995) use a CGE model to estimate the effects of an APEC Free Trade Area. They find that there would be some trade diversion, away from the EU, in particular, but a lot of trade creation. They conclude that all countries gain (except for the EU, which loses slightly). They also find that omitting one region, whether PRC, the ASEAN 4, or the US, would hurt the excluded countries, and lower the gains for the members as well. The loss is particularly great if the US is excluded, as it would be under an Asia-only FTA. Gains for everyone are much greater if the EU is included in the liberalization, as under multilateral agreements. Results in Martin, Petri, and Yanagishima (1995) and Martin and Yanagishima (1994) are similar: positive welfare gains from regional liber-alization that are relatively small in most cases, but larger for more inclu-sive and nondiscriminatory liberalization.

From the viewpoint of Asian or Pacific countries, there is an argu-ment for forming an Asian or Pacific grouping to safeguard their interests in the global process. Whether it is a caucus or a customs union, a regional grouping has some potential advantages: it can help its members speak with one voice in global negotiations, it can pose a threat to other coun-tries that they will be left out if they do not "play ball," and, as a fallback in case global progress is stymied, it can constitute an area in which gains from reciprocal liberalization and economies of scale can be achieved even without other countries.

Unsurprisingly, there are fears among Asian developing countries that an Asia bloc would be dominated by Japan, and other fears that an APEC bloc would be dominated by the US. Here such subgroupings as ASEAN and SAARC might play a role. Currently the individual members of these clubs have very little bargaining power vis-à-vis the world's two biggest economies. But a more unified and integrated ASEAN, perhaps even with a common external tariff and speaking with a common voice, would command more attention. The idea for Southeast Asian countries would be to use AFTA as leverage to be taken more seriously in APEC, and to use APEC as leverage at the global level. The game is a tricky one.[25]

The danger, of course, is that the world ends up split into a number of warring trade blocs. The formation of blocs in the 1930s was associated with a sharp fall in worldwide trade and with the Great Depression. The postwar multilateral trading system founded on GATT was associated with a dramatic increase in the volume of world trade and with worldwide economic growth. It is thus natural to worry that the reemergence of regional blocs might lead to a resumption of less satisfactory growth performance like that of the 1930s and be harmful for economic welfare. In the remainder of the chapter, we examine whether regional trading arrangements are likely to help build political momentum for global liberalization, or whether they are more likely to detract from multilateral efforts.

Regionalism as a Possible Vehicle for External Liberalization

Although the multilateral system has made large strides toward freer trade, most recently in the form of the successful conclusion of the Uruguay Round negotiations in December 1993, political constraints inevitably prevent the immediate attainment of the economist's nirvana. Since influential producer interest groups in each country typically stand to lose from free trade, full unilateral liberalization rarely occurs, and the world must instead await the outcome of step-by-step multilateral negotiations. In these negotiations, countries trade concessions with each other in such a way that at each step the percentage of the population that stands to gain is sufficiently high to overcome the political opposition.

In this light, the case in favor of regional trading arrangements is a second-best argument that takes as given the impossibility of further MFN liberalization. The uninitiated might assume that free-trade economists would, under these circumstances, necessarily support FTAs. But from the standpoint of static economic welfare, trade economists are in fact ambivalent about the desirability of FTAs, as noted earlier.[26] So long as tariffs and other barriers against third countries remain in place, the elimination of barriers between two FTA members can as easily intensify distortions as eliminate them.[27]

As already noted, the classical distinction is between the harmful trade-diverting effects of FTAs and their beneficial trade-creating effects. Although modern theories of trade have gone beyond the diversion/creation distinction, it is still a useful intuitive guide to likely welfare effects.[28] Grossman and Helpman (1993), for example, find in a median-voter model that a free trade area is most likely to be adopted when trade diversion outweighs trade creation, which unfortunately is also when it is most likely to reduce aggregate welfare.

Negative Political Implications for Multilateral Trade Liberalization

There is a variety of arguments as to how the adoption of a regional trading area might undermine movement toward unilateral or multilateral liberalization for political reasons; these fall under the headings "incentive to protect," manipulation of the process by special interests, scarce negotiator resources, and political dead end. We consider these antiregionalization arguments first, before considering some arguments that go the other way.

Blocs' Incentive to Protect

The standard experiment presumes that the level of trade barriers against outsiders remains unchanged when a customs union is established. However, Krugman (1991a) shows how, in a world consisting of a few large blocs, each unit will have more monopoly power, and thus will be more tempted to seek to shift the terms of trade in its favor by raising tariffs against the other blocs. This is the "incentive to protect." This temptation will be minimized in a world of many small trading blocs, or in a world of MFN, with each country its own bloc. A world of a few large blocs is thus one in which the noncooperative equilibrium features a higher level of interbloc tariffs and a lower level of economic welfare. In Krugman's simulation, three turns out to be the worst number of blocs to have.[29] Haveman (1992) gets essentially the same result, with expected world welfare minimized in a world of only two customs unions, using a model where trade arises from comparative advantage rather than from product differentiation (following the Deardorff-Stern critique of Krugman). Froot and Yoffie

(1993) point out some implications of foreign direct investment for blocs' incentive to protect.

The Krugman model assumes that members of a trade bloc set their external tariffs together; that is, that the arrangement is a customs union. The "incentive to protect" story would be different for a standard FTA, in which each country is able to set its tariffs with respect to nonmembers independently. Sinclair and Vines (1994) argue that in the FTA case, there is actually an incentive for each country to *reduce* its external tariffs, just the opposite of the customs union case. Panagariya and Findlay (1994) assume that protection is the endogenous outcome of lobbying, and derive the opposite results regarding the FTA/customs union comparison from Sinclair and Vines: the lobby chooses a lower external tariff under a customs union than under an FTA. The customs union is more effective at diluting the power of interest groups.

In reality, governments in one sense are less capable of national economic optimization than the Krugman model presupposes, and in another sense they are more capable. In both respects, large trading blocs are less vulnerable to the incentive to raise tariffs against each other than under Krugman's assumptions. Governments are less capable of optimization, in that maximum exploitation of the terms of trade through imposition of the "optimum tariff," is in practice one of the less prevalent determinants of trade policy. More commonly seen are arguments regarding infant industries, protecting the scarce factor of production, increasing employment, and adjustment costs. Governments are *more* capable of optimization in that they have already instituted the cooperative international regime of GATT, as Bergsten (1991) pointed out in his comment on Krugman (1991b). Article XXIV of GATT explicitly rules out Krugman's concern. This provision allows deviations from the MFN principle only for FTAs or customs unions that do not raise the average level of their tariffs against nonmembers.

There are several reasons to worry that blocs' "incentive to protect" survives despite the existence of Article XXIV. First, and most obviously, Article XXIV is often disregarded, as Bhagwati (1992) reminds us. Second, as Bagwell and Staiger (1993:fn 25) point out, exacerbation of the incentive to protect in customs unions can take the form of "gray area" measures when explicit tariff increases are ruled out. Third, one hopes that the multilateral process is on a path whereby worldwide tariff rates are gradually reduced through negotiation, and that this path is the relevant benchmark, not unchanging tariffs. Bond and Syropoulos (1994) show that arriving at the cooperative equilibrium of an agreement for interbloc liberalization in a repeated game, which is seen as GATT's role to facilitate, becomes more difficult as the size of the blocs, and therefore their monopoly power, rises.

Manipulation by Special Interests

The special interests argument points out that the process of instituting a regional trading arrangement features abundant opportunities for trade sensitive industries to manipulate the process, particularly those sectors that might be adversely affected. Examples abound. First, Wonnacott and Lutz (1989:65-6) emphasize that negotiators frequently seek to exclude from regional FTAs precisely those of their sectors that would be most threatened by welfare enhancing trade creation. The members of ASEAN, for example, have until now exempted almost all the important sectors from the system of preferences that they are supposed to grant each other (Panagariya 1994:828-9). Grossman and Helpman (1993:34-43) have used their median-voter model to understand how the possibility of such industry exclusions increases the chances of FTAs being adopted. This was the primary reason for another restriction that GATT Article XXIV places on FTAs, that "substantially all" barriers within the region be removed. In practice, FTAs have tended to comply less than completely with this provision. Examples include the European Economic Community's exclusion of agriculture and, in practice, steel, and many other goods.

Second, Anne Krueger (1993, 1995) emphasizes the exploitation of rules of origin. An FTA, unlike a customs union, does not involve the setting of common external tariffs. Rules of origin are a mechanism by which a country can prevent imports coming in from nonmembers, transshipped via the FTA partner, in those sectors where the partner has lower tariffs. Krueger (1993) and Krishna and Krueger (1993) show how individual industries in the FTA negotiation can enhance the extent of protection they receive when their governments use rules of origin to enable them to capture their FTA-partner's market in addition to their own, thus diverting trade from foreign suppliers. Krueger (1995) argues that customs unions are Pareto-superior to FTAs because they have no rules of origin that can be exploited in this way. Nagaoka (1994) develops a model in which the government is committed to preserve a given "strategic" monopolistic industry, for example, by manipulating rules of origin. He finds some effects whereby regional integration can reduce the incentive for protection for that industry, and thereby accelerate liberalization vis-à-vis the rest of the world, but also finds that the formation of a customs union can exacerbate the incentive to protect.

Bhagwati (1993a:30-1, 1995:22) and Panagariya (1995:16-21) point out that large countries like the US may use their overwhelming bargaining power within regional groupings to obtain from small countries distorting concessions that they might not obtain in more balanced multilateral negotiations. Perroni and Whalley (1994) point out that small countries have been the supplicants in recent regional agreements, and show how large countries have all the bargaining power on their side.

Scarce Negotiator Resources

The scarce-negotiator-resources argument points out that negotiations are not without cost. If they were, then the world would have achieved free trade by now. If the US Special Trade Representative is spending all the time—and spending all the White House's political capital with Congress—on a regional agreement such as NAFTA, there is presumably less time or capital left over to spend on multilateral negotiations, such as the Uruguay Round. As with the incentive-to-protect argument, regional trading arrangements may set back the process of negotiating worldwide trade liberalization under GATT.

Firms' Support for FTAs May Be a Political Dead End

Regional initiatives might prevent multilateral initiatives when the sequence of decisions matters. The forces in favor of liberalization might win over protectionists if the only choice is between the status quo and multilateral liberalization, but when offered the option of a regional free trade area, the political process might then take the regional route to the exclusion of the multilateral route. Bhagwati (1993a:28-9) worries that people in business and bureaucrats, after having achieved regional integration, might then find the effort involved in multilateral negotiation too difficult. "Lobbying support and political energies can readily be diverted to preferential trading arrangements such as FTAs. . .That deprives the multilateral system of the support it needs to survive, let alone be conducive to further trade liberalization" (Bhagwati, 1993b:162).

Krueger (1995:22-4) shares these concerns, and argues that the diversion of political energies is likely to be worse in the case of FTAs than in the case of customs unions. She reasons from two propositions: (i) once trade diversion has taken place as the result of any preferential arrangement, the newly established firms producing for the partner country's market will oppose moves away from the new status quo toward global free trade; and (ii) trade diversion is more likely to occur under an FTA than a customs union, due to the arguments explained above regarding rules of origin. It then follows that it will be harder to muster the political support to move from an FTA to multilateral free trade than it would be from a customs union.

A few authors have sought to model issues of sequence. Krishna (1995) assumes that a country will accept proposed changes in trade policy if its firms see a net increase in their profits (in all markets) from the change. She then derives two conclusions: (i) preferential arrangements that are more trade-diverting are more likely to be supported by member countries, because the gains by firms are at the expense of nonmembers; and (ii) preferential arrangements that divert trade will reduce the incentives to seek multilateral liberalization. The end result is that multilateral agreements that otherwise are attainable might be precluded, once countries start down the FTA path. The argument is similar to Krueger's except that it does not rely on rules of origin.

Levy (1993) offers what might be called a median-voter dead end model, in which a bilateral free trade agreement can undermine support for multilateral liberalization because it is a dead end in the political process. As in Grossman and Helpman (1993), it is assumed that trade policy is determined by the median voter. Trade itself is determined in some sectors by differences in factor endowments, and in others by considerations of imperfect substitutes (which are the rationale behind the gravity model's basic proportionality between trade and country size). As others have argued, the intra-industry sort of trade that is generated in imperfect substitutes is easier to accept politically than the factor-endowment kind of trade. The reason is that adjustment to import competition requires workers only to move from the assembly line for one product variety to the assembly line for another variety of the same product. Trade based on differences in factor endowments is much more difficult to accept politically, because it requires workers in previously protected industries to move to different industries and at lower wages, as in the case of capital-intensive industrialized countries.

Levy argues that policy toward trade is thus always a tradeoff between the gains afforded by increased varieties and the losses inflicted by a fall in the relative price of the product that is intensive in the scarce factor (labor, in the case of industrialized countries). If liberalization is not attainable, it is because the losses from factor-endowment trade dominate. If a vote is held first on whether to join a bilateral free trade area, it is more likely to pass when the potential partner has similar factor endowments. It is easier politically to achieve a EU than a NAFTA or APEC. The reason is that the gains from increased trade in imperfect substitutes will be large, while the losses from a fall in the relative price of labor-intensive products will be small. But if a vote is then held on multilateral liberalization, it will fail. Those key sectors that stand to profit from trade in imperfect substitutes will already have reaped those gains, and there will be fewer political forces to countervail the sectors that lose from the additional factor-endowment trade. In this way regional free trade agreements undermine political support for multilateral liberalization in this model.

In sum, there is no shortage of models and arguments in which regional trading arrangements can undermine multilateral liberalization, or, to use the terminology of Lawrence (1991), in which trade blocs can operate as stumbling blocks rather than building blocks.

Positive Political Implications for Multilateral Trade Liberalization

Other arguments go the other way. They offer the hope that the adoption of a regional trading area might undermine protectionism and reinforce movement toward liberalization more generally. The arguments concern locking-in unilateral liberalization, the efficiency of negotiating with larger units, mobilization of regional solidarity, building export constituencies to create domestic political momentum, and competitive liberalization.

Locking In and Mobilizing Regional Solidarity

In the late 1980s, Mexican President Salinas reversed a half-century of Mexican protectionism and imposed sweeping unilateral liberalization measures. Future presidents of Mexico might seek to reverse this liberalization. Thus, a good argument for NAFTA was that it locked in the Salinas reforms in a manner that would be difficult to reverse in the future (Lawrence 1991). Panagariya (1995:22-6) and others respond that tariff bindings under GATT are better devices for locking in reforms than are regional agreements.

Elsewhere, such as in Andean Pact countries, leaders have used popular support for regional solidarity to achieve liberalization that would be politically impossible if pursued unilaterally. De Melo, Panagariya, and Rodrik (1993: Section 3) model the process whereby governments can adopt rules or institutions in a regional grouping to insulate themselves from pressure by private sector lobbies for intervention on their behalf.

Efficiency of Negotiating with Larger Units

Within the context of multilateral negotiations, it is awkward to negotiate separately with over 100 small countries. Some authors have argued that the costs of negotiations go up with the number of countries involved, so that it is easier for a group of countries to negotiate a customs union first; with a common external trade policy, they can then enter multilateral negotiations as a group (Deardorff and Stern 1994, Krugman 1993, and Summers 1991).[30] Others question the practicality of the small numbers claim (Bhagwati 1993a, Winters 1993, and Panagariya 1994: 830-1). This is thought to increase the efficiency of the negotiations, and to make a satisfactory worldwide agreement more likely. The EU is certainly the most important example of this. Other groupings, such as ASEAN and SAARC, have also been urged to integrate regionally, so as to be able to talk with the larger powers.

Building Export Constituencies to Create Domestic Political Momentum

Wei and Frankel (1994) have made a primitive start at modeling an argument regarding political constituencies. We consider the problem of building export constituencies in a system, like Grossman-Helpman, where a country chooses its trade policies by majority vote. The hypothesis is that, under certain conditions, leaders might not be able to obtain a majority vote in favor of multilateral liberalization, much less unilateral liberalization, and yet might be able to obtain a majority vote in favor of regional liberalization, which, when completed, then shifts the economic incentives so as to produce a majority in favor of wider liberalization.

This model is inspired by Fernandez and Rodrik (1991), who consider a nonregional situation where the majority in a country would vote against unilateral liberalization, even though a majority would ex post gain from it economically. Divide the population into three groups: those who know they would gain from liberalization because they are confident of their ability to compete on world markets; those who will eventually gain from liberalization because they will turn out to be competitive on world markets but do not know this ex ante; and those who will lose from liberalization because of new import competition but do not know this ex ante. If the two thirds of the population who are uncertain have as little as a 49 percent chance of gaining, all of this group, a majority of the entire population, will oppose liberalization ex ante, even though a majority of the population gains ex post (2/3 x .49, plus the 1/3 who are sure gainers). The interesting aspect of the model is that if the leaders are somehow able to push liberalization through anyway and a new vote is taken after the uncertainty is resolved, a majority will then vote in favor of maintaining the new liberalized status quo. In essence, the act of liberalization itself builds a constituency for liberalization, as those who are good at exporting discover their previously unknown talents. Similar conclusions could be reached in a model where capital and labor moved from previously pro-tected sectors to new trade-oriented sectors, though the status quo bias in this case would hold for reforms that did not benefit a majority in addition to those that did.

In the Wei-Frankel (1994) version, political leaders may be able to obtain a majority vote in favor of regional liberalization because fewer sectors are adversely affected. More firms then discover their export potential, making it possible to obtain a majority support for previously unattainable MFN liberalization. The story is thus a counter-example to the overly strong claim of Levy (1993) that "bilateral free trade agreements can never in-crease political support for multilateral free trade."

Competitive Liberalization

In an important analysis of the political economy of regional blocs, Oye (1992) argues that the expected costs of exclusion from groupings change the political dynamics, by strengthening the antiprotectionist con-stituencies domestically, so as to draw countries into multilateral negotia-tions. Whereas many authors might read the recent experience as one in which regionalism helps build support for multilateral liberalization, Oye finds that this was also true of the 1930s experience.

"Competitive liberalization" refers to building political momentum for liberalization among countries, rather than domestically (Bergsten 1995). An illustration is President Clinton's "Triple Play" of late 1993 (Bergsten 1994:18-20 and Kahler 1994:19, 25). By upgrading the Seattle meeting of APEC ministers that had been scheduled for November 1993, into a high-profile Leaders' Meeting, he signaled to the Europeans that if they contin-ued to allow French farmers to hold up the Uruguay Round, other coun-tries might proceed without them. This message carried credibility because of its fortunate timing, coming as it did on the heels of the hard-fought approval of NAFTA in the US Congress. Thus, the NAFTA outcome demonstrated the political will necessary for meaningful agreements, while the APEC meeting demonstrated the possibility that agreements would cover a fraction of the world economy that was sufficiently large and dynamic to give the Europeans cause for worry at the prospect of being left out. German policy makers have reportedly confirmed that this was part of their motive for concluding the Uruguay Round in December. In this episode at least, it appears that regional initiatives helped bring about multilateral agreement.

Of course, the game need not always come out so well. The trouble with making credible threats is that sometimes they must be carried out. The process that is traditionally feared is *competitive regionalization*, where the formation of one regional grouping puts pressure on other countries to form a bloc of their own, rather than to liberalize unilaterally or multilaterally. The worst situation for a country is to be one of the few that does not belong to any bloc, because the terms of trade then turn against it. For this reason, there is a danger that the world will become stuck in a Nash noncooperative equilibrium of several continental FTAs: each continent forms an FTA because, given that the next continent is doing so, it will be hurt if it does not respond in kind. In the resulting equilibrium, all are worse off than they were under the status quo of MFN; hence, the argument for discouraging FTAs in GATT in the first place, as under Article XXIV. Furthermore, even if continents are allowed to choose the level of intrabloc preference to maximize their individual welfares, rather than being constrained to go all the way to FTAs, in equilibrium, they will still choose a level of preference that is so high as to leave everyone worse off. This is the "incentive to protect" argument we have already seen. These points are shown in a model with intercontinental transport costs by Stein (1994:83-93).[31]

On the other hand, since the ultimate goal is worldwide free trade, it is not clear that the ultimate political economy dynamic is bad. Worldwide economic welfare is so reduced by a noncooperative equilibrium of four continental FTAs, that it may then become politically possible for them to agree multilaterally to remove the barriers that remain between them and go to worldwide free trade. This would seem to follow if the obstacle to a move from MFN to worldwide free trade is a moderate fixed resource cost to negotiations, say 1 percent of GDP, to buy off producers that stand to lose. The leap to free trade would be all the more likely to follow if the resource cost to negotiation increases with the number of distinct entities involved.

What happens if the first bloc allows other countries to join? This is one possible interpretation of the phrase "open regionalism." A number of authors have shown that nonmember countries will, one by one find it in their interest to join a given FTA.[32] As the bloc expands, its members gain progressively, as the terms of trade are shifted further and further in their favor. Those that continue to be left out, lose progressively. In the model of Deardorff and Stern (1994), the bloc continues to grow until it encompasses the whole world, the happy outcome of global free trade. Their model, however, assumes that the bloc at each stage places prohibitive tariffs on outsiders, a rather extreme assumption.

Saxonhouse (1993) and Stein (1994) consider the same problem, while allowing trade with nonmembers. They find that when the bloc reaches a certain size (20 out of 30 members in Saxonhouse, and 16 out of 30 in Stein), it will choose not to accept any new members, because its own welfare starts to decline after that. What makes this story especially alarming from the viewpoint of ultimate multilateral liberalization is that the single bloc is truly a dead end: welfare of the bloc members is higher than it would be under worldwide free trade, so that they have an incentive to reject multilateral liberalization that they did not have when the alternative was MFN. (At this unhappy dead end point, worldwide welfare is close to its minimum, the very low welfare of the nonmembers outweighing the high welfare of the members.)

At some point, the nonmembers will presumably wise up and form a bloc of their own. But given two competing blocs, the incentive for individual countries will be to join the larger of the two to share in its monopoly power. A world of two equal size blocs is unstable (Bond and Syropoulos, 1994). A simulation in Stein (1994:99-102) shows that the stable equilibrium has 26 out of 30 countries in one large bloc, and 4 in the other. Again, the large bloc has no incentive to take mercy on those excluded.

Stein (1994:103-5) has a proposed solution to this difficulty: that Article XXIV be amended to state that preferences within a bloc cannot go beyond a specified low level (22 percent is the magic limit, in his simulation). We have already seen in Frankel, Wei, and Stein (1994) that such a restriction, the opposite of the current Article XXIV requirement for 100 percent preferences, would be welfare-improving in a world of equal size continental blocs. The same is true when there are no intercontinental transport costs and there is a temptation for countries to join the larger of two blocs. The equilibrium still features one large bloc (24 countries) and one small (6 countries). But with the limit on the margin of preferences in place, the large bloc has nothing to lose by moving to worldwide free trade, so that the happy outcome is still ultimately attainable. Of course, the members of the large bloc would vote against such a rule in GATT. However, if the issue is decided before any single incipient grouping is large enough to know that it will be the dominant bloc, then everything will work out for free trade.

Which Effects Are Likely to Dominate?

In short, there are a variety of possible channels of political causation running from regionalism to multilateralism, some positive and some negative. How can one get an idea as to which effects dominate in practice? The gravity framework presented above offers a way of shedding some light on the net effect of political interactions like the ones described, as they have actually played themselves out over the last 25 years. For each grouping that is believed to have undertaken regionalization, a dummy variable is added for "openness." This dummy variable indicates when at least one country of the pair is a member of the grouping in question, not necessarily both countries.

If tariffs and other barriers against imports from nonmembers remain unchanged when a given regional grouping is formed, then the coefficient on the openness variable should be negative, indicating trade diversion. Trade creation is indicated by a positive coefficient on the standard bloc variable (the dummy variable indicating when both countries in the pair are members of the grouping in question). If trade diversion is large enough relative to trade creation, then FTA may reduce economic welfare. If trade diversion is small, FTA is likely to improve welfare. A third possibility is that adoption of a regional FTA is associated with political momentum in favor of more widespread liberalization, for any of the reasons enumerated in the preceding subsection. In this case, the best outcome from the standpoint of economic welfare, the coefficient on the openness variable would be positive rather than negative.

Table 2 supplements Table 1 by adding to the gravity equation variables to test the openness of six groups. East Asia and Western Europe both show highly significant openness with respect to the rest of the world. When East Asia is divided into ASEAN countries and others, both show highly significant openness (as reported in Table 2). These results are similar to those of Dhar and Panagariya (1995), who use the gravity model to find that East Asian countries are open with respect to outside countries, contrary to the usual view. They also find that North America and the EU are characterized by greater intraregional trade bias than East Asia. When Western Europe is divided into the European Community countries and others (the old EFTA), it is the EC that shows positive openness.[33] The Western Hemisphere shows no significant openness effect in Table 2.[34]

The openness coefficient is insignificant for Asia as a whole: the openness of the East Asian countries has already been captured by the East Asia variables. Finally, South Asia is the one grouping that shows up with a significant negative openness coefficient: India and Pakistan are

115

Table 2: Openness of Subregions in Asia

Dependent Variable: Trade $_{ij}$	1970-1992
Intercept	-8.926**
	(0.276)
1980 Dummy	-0.946**
	(0.052)
1990 Dummy	-1.236**
	(0.060)
1992 Dummy	-1.551**
	(0.064)
GNP	0.752**
	(0.009)
per-capita GNP	0.178**
	(0.013)
Distance	-0.629**
	(0.026)
Adjacency	0.617**
	(0.082)
Language	0.519**
	(0.044)
WHem Bloc	0.648**
	(0.080)
WEurope Bloc	0.228**
	(0.056)
East Asia Bloc	-0.049
	(0.145)
Asia Bloc	0.569**
	(0.112)
APEC Bloc	1.097**
	(0.071)
WEurope[1]	0.281**
	(0.046)
WHem[1]	-0.011
	(0.045)
ASEAN[1]	0.378**
	(0.070)
East Asia-ASEAN[1]	0.410**
	(0.067)
Asia 1	0.093
	(0.059)
SAsia 1	-206**
	(0.086)
# of OBS.	6102
Std. Err of Reg	1.144
ADJ R^2	0.776

relatively closed to trade with the rest of the world. This is not an example of a trade-diverting bloc. India and Pakistan are a sort of "antibloc." Because they also have an unusually low level of trade with each other, their low level of trade with the rest of the world is perfectly consistent with the general pattern evident in the table. That pattern is that when groups of countries integrate their economies with each other, they also tend to reduce their barriers to outsiders. The liberalization vis-à-vis outsiders is not as great as the liberalization within the bloc, but it is not necessary that it be so. In other words, our results suggest that the third possibility enumerated above is the relevant one. These countries have tended to open up with respect to all trading partners at the same time that they have opened up with respect to other members of their own grouping. This conclusion matches that of a recent report from the WTO Secretariat (1995), to the effect that the recent regional arrangements among its members have not been fortresses, but to the contrary, have sometimes helped to promote freer trade worldwide.

Thus, the tentative verdict seems to be that the net political effect of the removal of regional barriers has tended to support liberalization with respect to nonmembers as well, and that the effect of further liberalization has been more than enough to offset any trade diversion resulting directly from the original regional arrangements themselves. From the economists' viewpoint, this verdict is an encouraging one.

Notes

[1] Introductions to this subject include Bhagwati (1993a); Bliss (1994); De la Torre and Kelly (1992); Fieleke (1992); de Melo, Panagariya, and Rodrik (1993); Schott (1991); and WTO Secretariat (1995).

[2] For example, Schott (1989), Kahler (1994:13), Krueger (1995:1, 23-4), Panagariya (1995:15), and Saxonhouse (1995).

[3] Earlier research of ours had looked at the yen bloc hypothesis extensively, and had given other references: Frankel (1991, 1993) and Frankel and Wei (1994, 1995).

[4] GATT (1992), "International Trade 90-91," as cited by Hufbauer and Schott (1993).

[5] Portfolio capital has more of a bilateral and regional dimension than is generally realized, however, so that it does not necessarily follow that East Asians can without cost make up for diminished US portfolio investments by borrowing elsewhere instead.

[6] This is not to say that the US should view NAFTA as having been a mistake in light of the Mexican crisis. The standard argument in favor of NAFTA, that it helped to lock in the recent beneficial Mexican trade liberalization, has already shown its virtue in this crisis.

[7] They cite Verbiest and Tang (1991), Page (1992), and Dicke and Langhammer (1991).

[8] Examples include Arase (1991), Dornbusch (1989), Encarnation (1992), Kwan (1994), and Thurow (1992:16, 65), among many others. For various perspectives on the hypothesis, see papers in Frankel and Kahler (1993).

[9] References with more of a European emphasis include Linneman (1966), Hamilton and Winters (1992), and Wang and Winters (1991).

[10] We have also tried our tests with a more thorough measure of distance that takes into account land and sea routes, the data generously supplied by Wang and Winters (1991). The results tend to be similar (Frankel, Wei, and Stein 1994).

[11] The chief extensions of the econometrics in the present paper are the tests for various Asian groupings, the tests for openness versus trade diversion, and the updating of results through 1992.

[12] If we estimate the bias in the EC alone, it shows a higher inward bias than Western Europe considered as a whole.

[13] Hamilton and Winters (1992) also find a strong effect for ASEAN, without testing for broader Asian effects at the same time.

[14] Easterly (1993) and Easterly, Kremer, Pritchett, and Summers (1993) see the drawing of the line that separates East Asia from the rest of Asia as having been endogenous.

[15] Dhar and Panagariya (1995:12-13) find a negative effect for India-PRC trade as well as India-Pakistan trade.

[16] Panagariya (1995:9-10) echoes Bhagwati's suspicions. He attacks Summers' argument that an FTA among natural bloc partners is less likely to be trade diverting, with "natural" defined by a low level of trade with countries outside the group. To the extent that a low observed level of trade reflects natural barriers, such as distance, the model in Frankel, Stein, and Wei (1994) supports Summers and Krugman.

[17] Frankel, Stein, and Wei (1994) derive the idea of an *optimal degree* of regionalization that can be justified by natural geographic factors. Although the approach builds on that of Krugman, the conclusion is that the world trading system is currently becoming more regionalized than can be justified, that it has entered what we call the *supernatural* zone.

[18] Here is Bhagwati (1992:544-5) attacking the proposition that geographically proximate FTAs (natural blocs, in Krugman's language) are better than far-flung ones (unnatural ones): "If I had access to captive research assistance and funds, I could examine whether, for all conceivable combinations of countries and distances among them, and for several different time periods, the premise is valid (that proximate countries have higher proportions of trade than countries farther apart). As I do not, I must rely on casual empiricism and a priori

arguments. Compare for instance the trade through the 1960s between India and Pakistan with that between India and the UK or the USSR. The former trade has been smaller than the latter. Borders can breed hostility and undermine trade. . . .Again, even if the premise is statistically valid for any set of observations, it may be a result of trade diversion itself: proximity may have led to preferential grant of concessions. . ." We believe that our statistical results using the gravity model show that the premise regarding proximity is indeed true, even when one also holds constant for existing preferential trading arrangements, and notwithstanding such special cases as stunted India-Pakistan trade.

[19] The regression results are not reported here, to save space.

[20] Such economies as Singapore and Hong Kong have already pursued the road of unilateral liberalization much more fully than other economies located anywhere in the world.

[21] Examples include Feder (1982) and Edwards (1993:9-11).

[22] For example, Rodrik (1994), Bradford and Chakwin (1993), and Sala-i-Martin (1991).

[23] Frankel, Romer, and Cyrus (1995) elaborate on the idea, present the results, and give many citations to the extensive literature.

[24] Hufbauer and Schott give Latin American countries scores on various economic and political criteria, to evaluate whether they are ready to join an FTA with North America. (Panagariya 1995:32-4) argues that a high tariff country like India must reduce its tariffs before hoping to join a major FTA; otherwise the partners' producers will simply come in and reap the benefit of India's high tariffs.)

[25] See Petri (1992) for some political and economic considerations. DeRosa (1993b) and Panagariya (1994: 825-6) argue that ASEAN countries would be better off liberalizing unilaterally or multilaterally than via an AFTA.

[26] Since the phrase "Free Trade Areas" contains the magic words "free trade," the general assumption is that economists must be in favor of them. Indeed many mainstream US economists signed a public letter of support for NAFTA, and virtually none publicly opposed it. Those who rejected their advice most often did so under a misunderstanding regarding both the case for Free Trade Areas and the case for free trade: that they rely on either a naive assumption that other countries will reduce their barriers as much as the domestic country (the US), or on a naive willingness to incur domestic costs for the sake of the trading partners' gain.

[27] On the grounds of such trade diversion effects, and other considerations discussed below, Bhagwati, Krueger, and Panagariya generally oppose regional trading arrangements. Bhagwati (1995:11) and Panagariya (1995:20, fn 8) have confessed that they were prepared to oppose NAFTA publicly, if asked. They are now skeptical of other ongoing initiatives, including APEC.

[28] Stein and Frankel (1994) show in a model of imperfect competition that a simulation comparison of the magnitudes of trade creation and trade diversion provides the right answer to the question whether FTAs raise the welfare of the representative consumer, under many plausible parameter values, though not all.

[29] We have already noted that, even when interbloc tariff rates are held constant, the distortions created by free trade areas can reduce world welfare. But preferential trading areas drawn along continental boundaries can *raise* welfare, if the degree of preferences does not exceed a specific natural level justified by intercontinental transport costs (Krugman, 1991b; Frankel, Stein, and Wei 1994; and Stein, 1994:84-93). If the margin of preference is so great as to reduce welfare, we call this a "supernatural" trade bloc. Full-fledged FTAs are likely to be supernatural.

[30] Kahler (1994, 1995:125-7) suggests that negotiations among a small number of regional neighbors may allow more efficient treatment of new individual issue areas than do global negotiations.

[31] In a simulation, the status quo of MFN features worldwide welfare that falls short of free trade by only about 0.5 per cent of GNP (which may not be enough to overcome negotiating costs). Each continent in sequence has an incentive to form an FTA, raising its welfare but lowering that of all the other continents, until all four have done so. In that noncooperative equilibrium, the loss relative to global free trade is about 2.5 per cent.

[32] See Bond and Syropoulos (1994), Deardorff and Stern (1994), Saxonhouse (1993) and Stein (1994), each with somewhat different specifications of the model.

[33] EFTA members show up with a negative openness coefficient, indicating that the grouping is actually trade-diverting. It does not show a significant bloc effect. These results are reported in Frankel, Wei, and Stein (1994).

[34] This result, which pools data from 1970 to 1992, masks a pattern of some significant negative openness coefficients in 1965 to 1975, followed by significant positive coefficients in 1985 and 1990, as Latin America entered its era of benign FTAs. Estimates on subregional FTAs show this pattern for MERCOSUR in particular (Frankel, Wei, and Stein 1994).

References

Anderson, K., 1993. "European Integration in the 1990s: Implications for World Trade and for Australia." In D.G. Mayes, ed., *External Implications of European Integration*. London: Harvester Wheatsheaf.

Arase, D., 1991. "US and ASEAN Perceptions of Japan's Role in the Asian-Pacific Region." In H. Kendall and C. Joewono, eds., *Japan, ASEAN and the United States*. Berkeley: University of California, Institute for East Asian Studies.

Bagwell, K., and R. Staiger, 1993. Multilateral Cooperation During the Formation of Customs Unions. NBER Working Paper No. 4543. Cambridge, Massachusetts.

Baldwin, R., 1989. "Economic Growth Effects of 1992." *Economic Policy* (October):248-281.

Bergsten, C. Fred, 1991. "Commentary: The Move Toward Free Trade Zones." In *Policy Implications of Trade and Currency Zones*. Wyoming: Federal Reserve Bank of Kansas City.

_____, 1994. "Sunrise in Seattle." *International Economic Insights*. 5(1).

_____, 1995. "Competitive Liberalization." Institute for International Economics.

Bhagwati, J., 1992. "Regionalism vs. Multilateralism." *The World Economy* 15(5):535-6.

_____, 1993a. "Regionalism and Multilateralism: An Overview." In J. de Melo and A. Panagariya, eds., *New Dimensions in Regional Integration*. New York: Cambridge University Press.

_____, 1993b. "Beyond NAFTA: Clinton's Trading Choices." *Foreign Policy* (Summer): 155-62.

_____, 1995. "President Clinton's Trade Policy: Is it Really a Triumph?" Presented at the American Economics Association meeting, January, Washington, D.C.

Bliss, C., 1994. *Economic Theory and Policy for Trading Blocks*. Manchester and New York: Manchester University Press.

Bond, E., and C. Syropoulos, 1994. Trading Blocs and the Sustainability of Inter-Regional Cooperation. Discussion Paper 93-17. Department of Economics, University of Birmingham.

Bradford, C., Jr., and N. Chakwin, 1993. Alternative Explanation of the Trade-Output Correlation in the East Asian Economies. Technical Papers No. 87. OECD Development Centre, Paris.

Braga, C. A. Primo, R. Safafdi, and A. Yeats, 1994. NAFTA's Implications for East Asian Exports. Policy Research Working Paper No. 1351. World Bank.

Brown, D., A. Deardorff, and R. Stern, 1995. "Computational Analysis of the Economic Effects of an East Asian Preferential Trading Bloc." University of Michigan.

Cecchini, P., 1988. *1992, The European Challenge: The Benefits of a Single Market*. London: Aldershot and Hants Publishers.

Cox, D., and R. Harris, 1992. "North American Free Trade and Its Implications for Canada: Results from a CGE Model of North American Trade." *World Economy* 15(1):31-44.

Davenport, M., 1990. "The External Policy of the Community and Its Effects Upon the Manufactured Exports of the Developing Countries." *Journal of Common Market Studies* 29(2):181-200.

Davenport, M., with S. Page, 1991. *Europe: 1992 and the Developing World*. London.

Deardorff, A., and R. Stern, 1994. "Multilateral Trade Negotiations and Preferential Trading Arrangements." In A. Deardorff and R. Stern, eds., *Analytical and Negotiating Issues in the Global Trading System*. Ann Arbor: University of Michigan Press.

de la Torre, A., and M. Kelly, 1992. Regional Trading Arrangements. Occasional Paper No. 93. International Monetary Fund, Washington, D.C.

de Melo, J., A. Panagariya, and D. Rodrik, 1993. "Regional Integration: An Analytical and Empirical Overview." In J. de Melo and A. Panagariya, *New Dimensions in Regional Integration*. New York: Cambridge University Press.

DeRosa, D., 1993a. "Sources of Comparative Advantage in the International Trade of the ASEAN Countries." *ASEAN Economic Bulletin* 10(1):41.

_____, 1993b. "The ASEAN Free Trade Area Plan and Intra-Regional Trade in Developing Asia." International Food Policy Research Institute, Washington, D.C.

_____, 1993c. "Regional Trading Arrangements Among Developing Countries: The ASEAN Example." International Food Policy Research Institute, Washington, D.C.

Dhar, S., and A. Panagariya, 1995. Is East Asia Less Open Than North America and the EEC? — No. Policy Research Working Paper Series No. 1370. World Bank. Revised.

Dicke, H., and R. Langhammer, 1991. "The Institutional Framework and External Dimension of the EC Internal Market." In S. Young and M. Kang, eds., *The Single European Market and Its Implications for Korea as an NIE*. Seoul: Korea Development Institute, Friedrich-Ebert Foundation.

Dornbusch, R., 1989. "The Dollar in the 1990s: Competitiveness and the Challenges of New Economic Blocs." In *Monetary Policy Issues in the 1990s*. Federal Reserve Bank of Kansas City.

Easterly, W., 1993. "Explaining Miracles: Growth Regressions Meet the Gang of Four." Paper presented at the Fourth Annual NBER East Asian Seminar on Economics, June, San Francisco.

Easterly, W., M. Kremer, L. Pritchett, and L. Summers, 1993. Good Policy or Good Luck? Country Growth Performance and Temporary Shocks. NBER Working Paper No. 4474. National Bureau of Economic Research, Cambridge, Massachusetts.

Edwards, S. 1993. Trade Policy, Exchange Rates and Growth. NBER Working Paper No. 4511. National Bureau of Economic Research, Cambridge, Massachusetts.

Encarnation, D., 1992. *Rivals Beyond Trade: America Versus Japan in Global Competition*. Ithaca and London: Cornell University Press.

Feder, G., 1982. "On Exports and Economic Growth." *Journal of Development Economics* 12(1):59-73.

Fernandez, R., and D. Rodrik, 1991. Resistance to Reform: Status Quo Bias in the Presence of Individual-Specific Uncertainty. NBER Working Paper No. 3269; *American Economic Review* 81(5):1146-55.

123

Fieleke, N., 1992. "One Trading World, or Many: The Issue of Regional Trading Blocs." *New England Economic Review* (3 May-20 June). Federal Reserve Bank of Boston.

Frankel, J., 1991. "Is a Yen Bloc Forming in Pacific Asia?" In R. O'Brien, ed., *Finance and the International Economy*. The AMEX Bank Review Prize Essays. United Kingdom: Oxford University Press.

_____, 1993. "Is Japan Creating a Yen Bloc in East Asia and the Pacific?" In J. Frankel and M. Kahler, eds., *Regionalism and Rivalry: Japan and the US in Pacific Asia*. Chicago: University of Chicago Press. Reprinted in P. Drysdale and R. Garnaut, eds., *Asia Pacific Regionalism: Readings in International Economic Relations*. Australia: Harper Educational Publishers.

Frankel, J., and M. Kahler, eds., 1993. *Regionalism and Rivalry: Japan and the US in Pacific Asia*. Chicago: University of Chicago Press.

_____, 1995. "Is a Yen Bloc Emerging?" Paper presented at the Joint US-Korea Academic Symposium, 7-9 September 1994, University of California, Berkeley. In R. Rich, ed., *Economic Cooperation and Challenges in the Pacific*. Washington, D.C.: Korea Economic Institute of America.

Frankel, J., and S. J. Wei, 1994. "Yen Bloc or Dollar Bloc? Exchange Rate Policies of the East Asian Economies." In T. Ito and A. Krueger, eds., *Third Annual East Asian Seminar on Economics*. Chicago: University of Chicago Press.

Frankel, J., D. Romer, and T. Cyrus, 1995. "Trade and Growth in East Asian Countries: Cause and Effect?" American Economic Association meetings, 6 January, Washington, D.C.

Frankel, J., E. Stein, and S. J. Wei, 1994. Trading Blocs and the Americas: The Natural, the Unnatural, and the Super-Natural. Working Paper C94-034. University of California at Berkeley.

Frankel, J., S. J. Wei, and E. Stein, 1994. APEC and Regional Trading Arrangements in the Pacific. Asia-Pacific Economic Cooperation Working Paper Series No. 94-1. Institute for International Economics, Washington, D.C.

Froot, K., and D. Yoffie, 1993. "Strategic Trade Policies in a Tripolar World." In J. Frankel and M. Kahler, eds., *Regionalism and Rivalry: Japan and the US in Pacific Asia*. Chicago: University of Chicago Press.

Greenaway, D., 1991. *Implications of the EC 1992 Programme for Outside Countries*. New York: United Nations.

Grossman, G., and E. Helpman, 1993. The Politics of Free Trade Agreements. NBER Working Paper No. 4597, Cambridge, Massachusetts.

Gundlach, E., U. Hiemenz, R. Langhammer, and P. Nunnenkamp, 1993. "Regional Integration in Europe and Its Impact on Developing Countries." In K. Ohno, ed., *Regional Integration and Its Impact on Developing Countries*. Tokyo: Institute of Developing Economies.

Haaland, J. I., and V. D. Norman, 1992. Global Production Effects of European Integration. Discussion Paper No. 669. Centre for Economic Policy Research, Paris.

Hamilton, C., and L. Alan Winters, 1992. "Opening Up International Trade in Eastern Europe." *Economic Policy* 77-116.

Haveman, J., 1992. *On the Consequences of Recent Changes in the Global Trading Environment*. Ph.D. thesis. University of Michigan.

Hufbauer, G., and J. Schott, 1993. "Regionalism in North America." In K. Ohno, ed., *Regional Integration and Its Impact on Developing Countries*. Tokyo: Institute of Developing Economies.

_____, 1994. *Western Hemisphere Economic Integration*. Washington, D.C.: Institute for International Economics.

International Monetary Fund, various years. *Direction of Trade Statistics*. Washington, D.C.

Jackson, T., 1991. "A Game Model of ASEAN Trade Liberalization." *Open Economies Review* 2(3):237-54.

Jaggi, G., 1995. Association of Southeast Asian Nations (ASEAN) and ASEAN Free Trade Area (AFTA). Asia-Pacific Economic Cooperation Working Paper Series No. 95-4. Institute for International Economics, Washington, D.C.

Kahler, M., 1994. "Regional Futures and Transatlantic Economic Relations." Council on Foreign Relations, New York.

_____, 1995. *International Institutions and the Political Economy of Integration*. Washington, D.C.: The Brookings Institution.

Koekoek, A., A. Kuyvenhoven, and W. Molle, 1990. "Europe 1992 and the Developing Countries: An Overview." *Journal of Common Market Studies* 29(2):111-32.

Kreinen, M., 1972. "Effects of the EEC on Imports of Manufactures." *Economic Journal* 82(327):897-920.

_____, 1982. "Effect of EC Enlargement on Trade in Manufactures." *Kyklos.*

_____, 1992. "Multinationalism, Regionalism, and Their Implications for Asia." Paper presented at the Conference on Global Interdependence and Asia-Pacific Cooperation, 8-10 June, Hong Kong.

Kreinen, M., and M. Plummer, 1992. "Effects of Economics Integration in the Industrial Countries on ASEAN and the Asian NIEs." *World Development* 20(9):1345-66.

Krishna, K., and A. Krueger, 1993. "Implementing Free Trade Areas: Rules of Origin and Hidden Protection." In J. Levinsohn, A. Deardorff, and R. Stern, eds., *New Directions in Trade Theory*. Ann Arbor: University of Michigan Press.

Krishna, P., 1995. "Regionalism and Multilateralism: A Political Economy Approach." Revised version of paper presented at the Universities Research Conference on International Trade Rules and Regulations, December 1993, Columbia University.

Krueger, A., 1993. Rules of Origin as Protectionist Devices. NBER Working Paper No. 4352. Forthcoming in J. Melvin, J. Moore, and R. Reisman, eds., *International Trade and Trade Policy*. Cambridge, MA: MIT Press.

_____, 1995. Free Trade Agreements Versus Customs Unions. NBER Working Paper No. 5084. Cambridge, Massachusetts.

Krugman, P., 1991a. "Is Bilateralism Bad?" In E.Helpman and A.Razin, eds., *International Trade and Trade Policy*. Cambridge: MIT Press.

_____, 1991b. "The Move Toward Free Trade Zones." In *Policy Implications of Trade and Currency Zones*. Wyoming: Federal Reserve Bank of Kansas City.

_____, 1993. "Regionalism vs. Multilateralism: Analytical Notes." In J. de Melo and A. Panagariya, *New Dimensions in Regional Integration*. New York: Cambridge University Press.

Kwan, C. H., 1994. *Economic Interdependence in the Asia-Pacific Region: Towards a Yen Bloc*. Routledge: London and New York.

Lawrence, R., 1991. "Emerging Regional Arrangements: Building Blocks or Stumbling Blocks?" In R. O'Brien, ed., *Finance and the International Economy*. The AMEX Bank Review Prize Essays. United Kingdom: Oxford University Press.

Levy, P., 1993. A Political Economic Analysis of Free Trade Agreements. Center for Economic Policy Research Publication No. 347. Stanford University.

Lewis, J., S. Robinson, and Z. Wang, 1995. "Beyond the Uruguay Round: The Implications of an Asian Free Trade Area." International Food Policy Research Institute, Washington, D.C.

Linneman, H., 1966. *An Econometric Study of International Trade Flows*. Amsterdam: North-Holland.

Martin, W., P. Petri, and K. Yanagishima, 1995. "Concerted Trade Liberalization and Economic Development in the Asia-Pacific Region." In *Asia-Pacific Economic Modeling Review*. Washington, D.C.: World Bank. Forthcoming.

Martin, W., and K. Yanagishima, 1994. "Charting the Pacific: An Empirical Assessment of Integration Initiatives." *The International Trade Journal* VIII(4) (Winter).

Matthews, A., and D. MacAleese, 1990. "LDC Primary Exports to the EC: Prospects Post-1992." *Journal of Common Market Studies* 29(2):157-80.

McCleery, R., 1993. "Modeling NAFTA: Macroeconomic Effects." In K. Ohno, ed., *Regional Integration and Its Impact on Developing Countries*. Tokyo: Institute of Developing Economies.

Nagaoka, S., 1994. "Does Regional Integration Promote Global Liberalization? A Case of Endogenous Protection." *Journal of the Japanese and International Economies* 8(4):551-64.

Noland, M., 1994. "Asia and the NAFTA." In Y. S. Kim and K. S. Oh eds., *The US-Korea Economic Partnership*. Aldershot, U.K. and Brookfield, Vermont: Ashgate Publishers.

Oye, K., 1992. *Economic Discrimination and Political Exchange: World Political Economy in the 1930s and 1980s*. Princeton, NJ: Princeton University Press.

Page, S., 1992. Some Implications of Europe 1992 for Developing Countries. Technical Papers No. 60. OECD Development Centre, Paris.

Panagariya, A., 1994. "East Asia and the New Regionalism." *The World Economy* 17(6):817-39.

_____, 1995. "The Free Trade Area of the Americas: Good for Latin America?" Center for International Economics, University of Maryland.

Panagariya, A., and R. Findlay, 1994. A Political-Economy Analysis of Free Trade Areas and Customs Unions. Working Papers in International Economics 2. University of Maryland.

Perroni, C., and J. Whalley, 1994. The New Regionalism: Trade Liberalization or Insurance? NBER Working Paper No. 4626. Cambridge, Massachusetts.

Petri, P., 1992. "One Bloc, Two Blocs or None? Political-Economic Factors in Pacific Trade Policy." In K. Okuzumi, K. Calder, and G. Gong, eds., *The US-Japan Economic Relationship in East and Southeast*

Asia: A Policy Framework for Asia-Pacific Economic Cooperation. Significant Issues Series. Center for Strategic and International Studies, Washington, D.C.

Rodrik, D., 1994. Getting Interventions Right: How South Korea and Taiwan Grew Rich. NBER Working Paper No. 4964. Cambridge, Massachusetts.

Safadi, R., and A. Yeats, 1993. The North American Free Trade Agreement: Its Effect on South Asia. Journal of Asian Economics 5(2):197-216.

Sala-i-Martin, X., 1991. "Comment." NBER Macroeconomics Annual 6:368-78.

Saxonhouse, G., 1993. "Pricing Strategies and Trading Blocs in East Asia." In J. Frankel and M. Kahler, eds., Regionalism and Rivalry: Japan and the US in Pacific Asia. Chicago: University of Chicago Press.

_____, 1995. "Regionalism in Asia." Paper presented at the Conference on Regionalism, American Enterprise Institute, 13 June, Washington, D.C.

Schott, J., 1989. Free Trade Areas and US Trade Policy. Washington, D.C.: Institute for International Economics.

_____, 1991. "Regional Trading Blocs." The World Economy.

Sinclair, P., and D. Vines, 1994. "Do Fewer, Larger Trade Blocs Imply Greater Protection? The Good News and the Bad News about Regional Trading Blocs." University of Birmingham and Oxford University.

Srinivasan, T. N., and G. Canonero, 1993. "Preferential Trading Arrangements: Estimating the Effects on South Asia Countries."

_____, 1995. "Preferential Trading Arrangements in South Asia: Theory, Empirics and Policy."

Stein, E., 1994. Essays on the Welfare Implications of Trading Blocs with Transport Costs and on Political Cycles of Inflation. Ph.D. thesis. University of California, Berkeley.

Stein, E., and J. Frankel, 1994. The Welfare Implications of Continental Trading Blocs in a Model with Transport Costs. Pacific Basin Working Paper Series No. PB94-03. Federal Reserve Bank of San Francisco.

Stoeckl, A., D. Pearce, and G. Banks, 1990. *Western Trading Blocs: Game, Set or Match for Asia Pacific and the World Economy*. Canberra: Centre for International Economics.

Summers, L., 1991. "Regionalism and the World Trading System." In *Policy Implications of Trade and Currency Zones*. Wyoming: Federal Reserve Bank of Kansas City.

Thurow, L., 1992. *The Coming Economic Battle Among Japan, Europe and America*. New York: William Morrow.

Verbiest, J. P., and M. Tang, 1991. The Completion of the Single European Community Market in 1992: A Tentative Assessment of Its Impact on Asian Developing Countries. Economic Staff Papers 48. Asian Development Bank, Manila.

Wang, Z. K., and L. Alan Winters, 1991. The Trading Potential of Eastern Europe. Centre for Economic Policy Research Discussion Paper No. 610. London, UK.

Wei, S. J., and J. Frankel, 1994. "Can Regional Blocs be Stepping Stones to Global Free Trade?" Institute for International Economics, Washington, D.C.

Winters, A., "The European Community: A Case of Successful Integration?" In J. de Melo and A. Panagariya, eds., *New Dimensions in Regional Integration*. New York: Cambridge University Press.

Wonnacott, P., and M. Lutz, 1989. "Is There a Case for Free Trade Areas?" In J. Schott, ed., *Free Trade Areas and US Trade Policy*. Washington, D.C.: Institute for International Economics.

World Trade Organization Secretariat, 1995. *Regionalism and the World Trading System*. World Trade Organization, Geneva.

Comments on "The New Regionalism and Asia: Impact and Options"

by

Arvind Panagariya

This chapter pulls together a very large body of the recent literature on regional integration. Anyone interested in wishing to catch up with the ongoing debate on this subject can do so by simply reading this single chapter. Though the authors have a particular view on the subject, they have articulated the positions of other contributors to the debate with remarkable care. On top of all this, the chapter contains a good deal of new, original research. So while I will take issue with a number of the authors' conclusions, I wish to state at the outset that these are merely differences of opinion rather than criticisms of the chapter.

It has become fashionable to equate free trade areas with free trade. During the debate on the North America Free Trade Agreement (NAFTA) at least in the United States (US), this confusion became so rampant that any opposition to NAFTA was viewed as opposition to free trade. Yet, nothing could be farther from the truth. Free trade areas promote free trade with one or two union members but indirectly raise barriers against more than 150 countries outside the union.

By the end of 1994, the General Agreement on Tariffs and Trade (GATT) had been notified of 108 regional arrangements, 33 of them during 1989 to 1994 alone. Today, virtually every member country of the World Trade Organization (WTO) has one or more regional arrangements under its belt. If regional arrangements were promoting free trade as their proponents argue, by now our task of trade liberalization should have been over. At a minimum, the 33 regional arrangements in the last five years should have contributed significantly to the opening of the world markets. But none of that has happened. The major accomplishments in the area of trade liberalization have been unilateral liberalization in the 1980s and multilateral accord known as the Uruguay Round in the 1990s.

Starting with the tariffs that are less than 20 percent in Mexico and around 5 percent in the US and Canada, it took NAFTA more than a thousand pages to declare free trade among just three countries. By comparison, the multilateral process has brought together many, many more countries at the negotiating table. A staggering 121 countries participated in the Uruguay Round. And, with far shorter documents than NAFTA —the Uruguay Round Agreement is only 500 pages long —GATT has led to a very substantial trade liberalization, particularly in developed countries. Since the beginning of its journey in 1947, GATT has secured overall reductions in tariffs on manufactures from about 40 percent to 5 percent. This figure is expected to fall down to 3 percent after the implementation of the Uruguay Round. Side by side with the multilateral process, nondiscriminatory, unilateral liberalization has contributed in a big way to the opening of developing country markets. Thanks to this process, nontariff barriers have virtually disappeared from a large number of developing countries and tariff levels have come down at an astronomical pace.

Though the chapter offers a very careful and detailed treatment of the pros and cons of regional arrangements of various types, it does not seem to confront one central issue of interest to Asia: Does regional integration hold promise in Asia? I will argue that the answer to this question is in the negative. To explain why, let me begin by noting that the definition of a regional approach in the context of Asia is tricky. There is a strong tendency on the part of many authors to confuse the integration of the East Asian economy through market, particularly direct foreign investment, as regional integration. In spirit, this integration is no different than the integration of the economies of the US and Canada through cross investments prior to the Canada-US Free Trade Agreement. Being nondiscriminatory, this integration is in line with the multilateral process. Hence, when I say that regionalism does not have a bright future in Asia, I am not referring to this type of market-driven, nondiscriminatory integration which should and will flourish. (Some observers see a grand design by Japan to use foreign investment to form a bloc. These observers should look back at the concentration of the US investments in Canada in the1960s and 1970s and ask themselves if there was a grand design by the US to form a bloc in North America then.)

According to the traditional definition, regional integration means discriminatory liberalization as has been the case with the European Community (EC), NAFTA, MERCOSUR, and a host of other arrangements. It is this regional integration which, at least in the current political and economic environment, has little future in Asia. Allow me to elaborate.

First of all, the past experience with regionalism in Asia is not very encouraging. The only serious regional grouping in Asia — ASEAN or the Association of Southeast Asian Nations — was founded in August 1967. The ASEAN membership includes Brunei, Indonesia, Malaysia, Philippines, Singapore, and Thailand. Of these, Brunei is very small and Singapore has virtual free trade. Therefore, the scope for expansion of preferential trade is limited to the remaining four countries called the ASEAN 4. Intra-trade among the ASEAN 4 as a proportion of their total trade has hovered around 4 percent during the1980s and early 1990s. Moreover, though a central goal of ASEAN has been to promote preferential trading, only a minuscule part of this trade is covered by preferences. For example, in 1987, 20 years after ASEAN was founded, a paltry 1.4 percent of Indonesia's exports to ASEAN received any tariff preferences at all.

In January 1992, the NAFTA movement swung the ASEAN members into action. The result was an agreement to create the ASEAN Free Trade Area or AFTA by the year 2007. Yet, in July 1992, when Indonesia announced preferential tariff reductions on 250 items, 90 percent of these were on different types of batik cloth produced in Indonesia only. Prior to that, items such as snow plows had adorned the lists of tariff preferences.

The battle over tariff preferences is complicated by the fact that Singapore has no tariffs to remove and Malaysia has very few. In this situation, preferential liberalization is asymmetric: while Indonesia and Thailand can *give* preferential access to Singapore and Malaysia, they do not *receive* any tariff preference. If liberalization was nondiscriminatory this would not be a problem: benefits of liberalization will accrue to countries undertaking liberalization. But when liberalization is discriminatory, there is a strong presumption that the outcome will be mercantilist. A country will lose from its own preferential liberalization and benefit from a similar liberalization by its partner. The simple logic behind this conclusion is that when liberalization is discriminatory, the tariff revenue collected prior to liberalization ends up in the pockets of partner-country exporters.

The conflict arising out of the asymmetric situations of Indonesia and Singapore is captured well in the following statement by a former foreign minister of Indonesia delivered at the twenty-fifth anniversary celebration of ASEAN and reported in the *Financial Times*, 26 January 1993:

> Singapore and Malaysia are always telling us to lower tariffs and duties and let their goods into the country. But, in return, how about the free movement of labor? We will take your goods if you take our surplus labor supply. When they hear this and think about all those Indonesians coming to work in their countries, then they say, 'wait a minute, maybe it's not such a good idea'.

Even if the internal difficulties in promoting regional integration schemes can be overcome, Asia faces formidable external constraints when it comes to a discriminatory regional trading bloc. To promote regionalism seriously in Asia, Japan must play the same central role as that played by the US in the Western Hemisphere. Under the current circumstances, that is unlikely. Due to the existence of bilateral trade imbalance with the US, Japan has been a constant target of Section 301 and Super 301 actions. Even the threat of participation in a discriminatory trading bloc by Japan is frowned upon by Washington, D.C. This was demonstrated graphically when the Malaysian Prime Minister Mahathir announced the formation of the East Asian Economic Group and, under intense pressure from the White House, Japan "chose" to stay out of such a group. Though Japan's role and relationship with the US is at a critical juncture right now and may be changing quite rapidly, with one third of its exports going to the latter, Japan is unlikely to participate in a bloc opposed by the US.

This brings us to the possibility of pursuing a regional approach which includes the US. For geopolitical reasons, the US is committed more strongly to its neighbors to the south than to Asia. Thus, even though the US trades more heavily with Asia than Latin America, it is unlikely to entertain regional arrangements with the former before doing so with the latter. Indeed, in discussions for reauthorization of the fast-track authority to negotiate further free trade agreements (FTAs), the focus has been exclusively on Latin American countries such as Chile and members of MERCOSUR.

This commitment of the US to Latin America implies that the regional route is open to Asia only if the entire Asia-Pacific region negotiates together. Not surprisingly, within less than two years' time, we have seen the Asia-Pacific Economic Cooperation forum or APEC rise from nothing to a forum at which no less than the heads of states of the member countries come together annually to discuss future trade liberalization.

The APEC summits have led to a great deal of optimism for the regional approach in some quarters. Indeed, at the end of the meeting in Jakarta, an agreement was signed by APEC members to establish a free trade area by the year 2020. But the agreement is very likely a delaying tactic by the US while it expands NAFTA into a Western Hemispheric FTA. In terms of concrete action, the proposal to start the first free trade agreements even as far into the future as the year 2000 got nowhere. Barriers on the Asian side notwithstanding, such a commitment on the part of the US would have surely been a virtual impossibility. The difficulties facing the US are captured well by the late, astute columnist Hobart Rowen in November 1994, in the *Washington Post*:

> For the moment, there is little to indicate that the American public, almost torn apart by the prospect of free trade with tiny Mexico, is ready to endorse free trade with the huge potential productive

power of low-income countries in Asia. For a while, APEC is likely to remain a paper organization, and its free-trade goals a vision — worthwhile but still only a dream.

To conclude, let me state my position explicitly. Paraphrasing Larry Summers, economists should support all lateral approaches to liberalization — unilateral, bilateral, plurilateral and multilateral — provided they are nondiscriminatory and, hence, grounded in the MFN principle. Bilateralism of the last half of the nineteenth century was nondiscriminatory and open. Not surprisingly, it rapidly led to an open world trading system. Unfortunately, the current bilateralism and regionalism is discriminatory and closed. As such, it only promises to fragment rather than unite the world trading system. We should abandon it.

References

Financial Times, 1993. 26 January.

Washington Post, 1994. Column of Hobart Rowen. November.

CHAPTER 4
CAPITAL MARKET INTEGRATION
IN DEVELOPING ASIA

JAMES RIEDEL
THE PAUL H. NITZE SCHOOL OF ADVANCED INTERNATIONAL STUDIES
JOHNS HOPKINS UNIVERSITY

A re capital markets in Asia becoming more integrated with each other and with world capital markets and, if so, what is driving the process? What are the implications of capital market integration for economic growth and stability in the region? Is a policy response required and, if so, what should it be? These are wide-ranging and very complicated questions, any one of which, if examined thoroughly, would be beyond the scope of this chapter. Nevertheless, we attempt tentative answers to each one.

Are Capital Markets in Asia Becoming More Integrated?

A country is integrated into world capital markets if (i) capital is free to move into and out of the country and (ii) if the country's assets are substitutes for those of other countries. Because most developing countries, including those in Asia, impose some restrictions on capital mobility, and because none can claim that all of its assets are perfect substitutes for those of other countries, capital market integration is a matter of degree.

Conceptually, the purest measure of the degree of capital market integration is the extent to which the law of one price holds in international capital markets. Unfortunately, it is difficult to apply this measure empirically because the relevant prices (the expected returns to assets in different countries) are not directly observable. Information on ex post returns is not even available for some important types of assets, such as for foreign direct investments (FDI). Where ex post returns are available, as, for example, in the case of interest-earning financial assets, testing the law of one price in financial markets requires testing a joint hypothesis about how subjective expectations of future returns are formed, which makes matters very complicated indeed (Frankel 1989; Montiel 1994:331-50).

A much simpler, but conceptually inferior measure of the degree of capital market integration is changes in the magnitude of capital flows. The shortcoming of this measure is that capital market integration is an ex ante concept, while the magnitude of capital flows (or stocks) is an ex post measure. A zero capital flow is consistent with perfect capital market integration if expected returns are continuously equal and there are no disturbances in capital markets. However, because there are disturbances in the real world, and it is through capital flows that differences in expected returns between integrated capital markets are arbitraged away, one can reasonably expect that countries with a high degree of capital market integration will experience international capital flows. Furthermore, if there are changes in the degree of openness to capital flows, as we know have occurred in developing countries in recent years, they should be reflected in changes in the magnitude of international capital flows. It is useful, therefore, to begin an analysis of the degree of capital market integration with an examination of the magnitude of capital flows in the Asian countries. Subsequently we will review the evidence, such as it is, on how well the law of one price holds in Asian capital markets.

In examining the magnitude of international capital flows, one can look at either net or gross flows. Both are relevant to the issues at hand. Net flows measure the transfer of resources into or out of a country through international capital markets, as well as the change in a country's net asset position, both of which are important in assessing the growth and stability implications of international capital flows. Gross flows, on the other hand, are probably a better general indicator of the level of capital mobility, since the netting of inflows and outflows can obscure the magnitude of inflows in either direction. For most of the developing countries considered here, however, the net and gross measures of capital flows are broadly similar, since the capital flows are largely in one direction.[1]

Net Capital Flows

It is hard to avoid being overwhelmed by the data on capital flows; their quality may be low, but their quantity is enormous. To make the problem manageable, it is necessary to limit the countries considered to only the most important economies in the region, and whenever possible to aggregate them into regional groups. In what follows, the focus is on four South Asian countries (Bangladesh, India, Pakistan, and Sri Lanka), and six East Asian countries (two in the northeast: the Republic of Korea [Korea] and the People's Republic of China [PRC]; and four in the southeast: Indonesia, Malaysia, Philippines, and Thailand). Hong Kong; Singapore; and Taipei,China come into the story mainly as sources of foreign capital flows to the other Asian developing countries.

To put things into perspective, it is useful to begin by comparing total (public and private) net capital flows to Asia with those to all developing countries, each in relation to its respective gross national product (GNP). This is done in Figure 1, which indicates a significant rise in the net flow of capital to all developing countries, and especially to the East Asian countries in the 1990s. The 1970s also witnessed the rise in net capital flows to developing countries, only to be reversed in the 1980s as the debt crisis spread in Africa and Latin America. The Asian countries mostly avoided the debt crisis, and experienced no reversal in the ratio of net capital inflows to GNP in the 1980s. Since 1990, however, capital flows to East Asia have soared, more than doubling as a percent of GNP. In South Asia, aggregate net capital flows have remained fairly constant as a percentage of GNP.

The divergence between the East Asian and South Asian countries in terms of their participation in international capital markets is even more striking when considering the composition of capital flows, which are presented in Table 1.

Figure 1. Net Long-Term Capital Flows as Percentage of GNP for All LDCs,* East Asia and Pacific, and South Asia

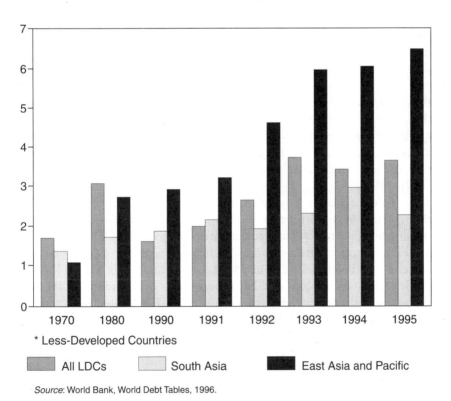

* Less-Developed Countries

▨ All LDCs   ▨ South Asia   ■ East Asia and Pacific

Source: World Bank, World Debt Tables, 1996.

Private capital flows to the East Asian developing countries in the 1990s, were eight to ten times greater than to the South Asian countries. From 1991 to 1994, the East Asian countries absorbed about 92 percent of total private debt flows (commercial bank flows, bonds, and other private debt flows), 97 percent of FDI flows, and 91 percent of portfolio equity flows to Asia. As Table 1 shows, by far the most important type of private capital flow to East Asia since the mid-1980s, has been FDI, followed in importance by portfolio equity flows and bond issues.

Foreign Direct Investment

In the 1990s, the East Asian countries absorbed about 65 percent of the total net FDI in developing countries. As Table 2 shows, about 90 percent of it went to four countries: PRC, Indonesia, Malaysia, and Thailand. In 1993, PRC alone accounted for about 40 percent of net FDI in developing countries.

To appreciate the relative importance of these flows to the host countries, it is useful to express them as percentages of GNP. As Table 2 shows, FDI played no appreciable role in the South Asian countries, with the minor exception of Sri Lanka, where it has risen in the last two years to almost 2 percent of GNP. Liberalization in India since 1991 has led to a significant increase in FDI approvals, but the actual amounts invested remain minuscule in relation to the Indian GNP (United Nations [UN] 1994:41).

In the four major recipient countries of East Asia, FDI flows, although large in comparison to the flows to other countries, are relatively small in relation to the recipient countries' economies. Only in Malaysia has FDI in recent years risen to a significant proportion of GNP (about 8 percent) and investment (about 25 percent). The level of FDI in PRC in 1993, at almost 7 percent of GNP, is also exceptional. Indeed, in relation to the size of the regional economies in which FDI is located (for example, Guangdong and Fujian), its role is, of course, far greater. Even at the national level, however, FDI in PRC in 1993, accounted for about 15 percent of gross domestic investment and about 30 percent of exports (UN 1994:68).[2]

The source of FDI in East Asia is, as Table 3 shows, predominantly from within the region itself, Hong Kong and Taipei,China together accounting for about 45 percent of FDI in the major recipient countries. These two sources which really cannot be separated, because a significant amount of Taipei,China investment is channeled through Hong Kong, account for almost 70 percent of FDI in PRC.[3] Behind the East Asian newly industrializing economies (NIEs), Japan ranks as the second largest

Table 1. Net Long-Term Capital Flows to Developing Countries and Selected Regions by Type of Flow
($ million)

	1970	1980	1990	1991	1992	1993	1994	1995
All Less Developed Countries								
Net Capital Flows	9,160	75,137	72,540	89,504	123,365	177,928	174,932	198,580
Official Flows	3,394	21,848	28,523	27,990	23,090	23,644	16,144	31,417
Private Flows	5,766	53,288	44,017	61,514	100,275	154,285	158,788	167,164
Bonds			2,960	12,833	13,178	38,342	32,163	
Commercial Banks	2,344	34,827	1,721	2,475	13,757	-4,867	9,167	33,391
FDI	2,268	5,098	25,009	34,978	46,610	68,261	80,120	90,346
Portfolio Equity	0	0	3,743	7,552	14,057	45,616	34,894	22,001
Other Private	1,154	13,363	10,584	3,676	12,673	6,933	2,444	21,426
East Asia and Pacific								
Net Capital Flows	1,444	11,957	26,529	32,434	51,035	70,889	82,308	105,343
Official Flows	614	3,040	6,103	6,298	6,349	8,011	5,019	7,254
Private Flows	830	8,917	20,427	26,135	44,686	62,878	77,289	98,089
Bonds			243	3,312	2,832	8,485	13,200	
Commercial Banks	447	5,249	4,666	5,951	8,808	-3,895	3,385	23,203
FDI	267	1,318	10,968	13,890	21,668	37,872	43,037	53,703
Portfolio Equity	0	0	2,268	1,049	5,102	18,107	12,613	12,230
Other Private	116	2,350	2,282	1,933	6,276	2,309	5,054	8,953
South Asia								
Net Capital Flows	1,074	3,741	6,958	7,499	6,752	7,857	11,259	9,642
Official Flows	995	2,503	4,587	5,351	3,908	3,217	3,843	3,625
Private Flows	80	1,238	2,371	2,148	2,844	4,638	7,416	6,017
Bonds			304	1,400	-211	451	176	
Commercial Banks	3	952	1,699	218	1,757	844	-645	2,271
FDI	69	185	464	456	624	841	1,242	2,046
Portfolio Equity	0	0	105	23	380	2,025	6,222	1,430
Other Private	8	101	-201	51	294	477	421	270

Notes: * 1995 is preliminary.
** Net Capital Flows are defined as Net Resource Flows less Grants.
*** Regional aggregates of the World Bank, rather than the selected East and South Asian countries which appear in the tables below.

Source: World Bank, 1996.

Table 2. Net Foreign Direct Investment Flows to Selected Asian Developing Countries
($ million and as percentage of GNP)

	1970	1980	1990	1991	1992	1993	1994
FDI in $ millions							
East Asia (6)	261	1,204	10,675	13,584	21,187	37,602	42,693
Republic of Korea	66	6	788	1,180	727	588	809
PRC	0	0	3,487	4,366	11,156	27,515	33,787
Indonesia	83	180	1,093	1,482	1,777	2,004	2,109
Malaysia	94	934	2,333	3,998	5,183	5,006	4,348
Philippines	-25	-106	530	544	228	763	1,000
Thailand	43	190	2,444	2,014	2,116	1,726	640
South Asia (4)	69	185	452	447	613	828	1,227
Bangladesh	0	0	3	1	4	14	11
India	46	79	162	141	151	273	620
Pakistan	23	63	244	257	335	346	430
Sri Lanka	0	43	43	48	123	195	166
FDI as percent of GNP							
East Asia (6)	0.2	0.3	1.2	1.4	2.0	3.3	3.2
Republic of Korea	0.7	0.0	0.3	0.4	0.2	0.2	0.2
PRC	0.0	0.0	1.0	1.2	2.7	6.4	6.5
Indonesia	0.9	0.2	1.0	1.2	1.3	1.3	1.3
Malaysia	2.3	4.0	5.7	9.0	9.4	8.3	6.5
Philippines	-0.4	-0.3	1.2	1.2	0.4	1.4	1.5
Thailand	0.6	0.6	2.9	2.1	1.9	1.4	0.5
South Asia (4)	0.1	0.1	0.1	0.1	0.2	0.2	0.3
Bangladesh	0.0	0.0	0.0	0.0	0.0	0.1	0.0
India	0.1	0.0	0.1	0.1	0.1	0.1	0.2
Pakistan	0.2	0.3	0.6	0.6	0.7	0.7	0.8
Sri Lanka	0.0	1.1	0.5	0.5	1.3	1.9	1.4

Source: World Bank, 1996.

Table 3. The Source of FDI in Selected East Asian Countries,
1986 to 1992
($ million and percent)

	PRC	Indonesia	Malaysia	Philippines	Thailand	Total
NIEs	21,123	1,573	4,123	580	3,565	30,964
	(70.9)	(25.2)	(29.8)	(17.9)	(35.4)	(49.0)
Taipei,China	1,903	501	3,086	87	828	6,405
	(6.4)	(8.0)	(22.3)	(2.7)	(8.2)	(10.1)
Hong Kong	18,719	478	433	338	1,720	21,686
	(62.8)	(7.6)	(3.1)	(10.4)	(17.1)	(34.3)
Singapore	378	239	940	48	954	2,558
	(1.3)	(3.8)	(6.8)	(1.5	(9.5)	(4.1)
Korea	123	355	755	108	64	2,558
	(0.4)	(5.7)	(5.5)	(3.3)	(0.6)	(4.1)
Japan	3,042	1,102	3,065	855	3,586	11,650
	(10.2)	(17.6)	(22.2)	(26.4)	(35.6)	(18.4)
United States	2,390	428	1,499	1,193	1,373	6,884
	(8.0)	(6.8)	(10.8)	(36.9)	(13.6)	(10.9)
Europe	1,316	1,009	2,711	378	1,108	6,522
	(4.4)	(16.1)	(19.6)	(11.0)	(11.0)	(10.3)
Total	29,785	6,250	13,822	3,235	10,071	63,163
	(100.0)	(100.0)	(100.0)	(100.0)	(100.0)	(100.0)

Note: The values for total FDI are taken from the International Monetary Fund *Balance of Payment Statistics Yearbook*. The shares of source countries are derived from recipient country data.

Source: Kawaguchi, 1994:4.

investor in the region, its investments spread more or less equally between PRC, Malaysia, and Thailand, with Indonesia joining the other countries in the Association of Southeast Asian Nations (ASEAN) in terms of importance as a destination for Japanese investment only in the 1990s.

FDI can be classified into three broad categories according to its main purpose: (i) to exploit a natural resource abundance; (ii) to circumvent trade barriers in order to serve the host country market; and (iii) to take advantage of relatively low labor costs to produce for export. Indonesia and Malaysia in particular, have attracted FDI of the first variety. PRC is currently attracting a substantial amount of foreign investment of the second variety, especially from Japan, the United States (US), and Europe. However, even in PRC, Indonesia, and Malaysia, the most rapidly expanding form of FDI, especially that originating from within the region, is the export-oriented variety.

The surge since the mid-1980s in export-oriented FDI in PRC and Southeast Asia by firms, many of them small or medium-sized, from Japan, Taipei,China, and Hong Kong, is explained by a convergence of several conducive push-and-pull factors. On the push side, the loss of international competitiveness of export-oriented firms in Japan and the newly industrializing countries of Hong Kong; Korea; Singapore; and Taipei,China, due to rising real wages and currency appreciation, was especially important. On the pull side, a key inducement was trade policy reforms, which got under way and were accelerated in the 1980s in PRC and Southeast Asia, allowing exporters to have freer access to imported capital goods and imported inputs. Thus, the opportunity was created for firms in Northeast Asia, which were losing international competitiveness at home, to shift their operations to Southeast Asia, where they could continue to profit from their acquired know-how of producing and exporting labor-intensive manufactures.

The fact that much of FDI in East Asia is motivated by a reduction in trade barriers in the host countries, rather than by increasing trade barriers as was the case for much of FDI in developing countries in the 1960s and 1970s, has profound implications for the costs and benefits of FDI for the recipient country. As is well known, FDI in highly protected economies is likely to be immiserizing, since protection distorts the market rate of return earned by foreign investors (Brecher and Diaz-Alejandro 1977:317-22). Some empirical support for this proposition is offered in a recent study (Fry 1993) of FDI from 1966 to 1988 in 16 developing countries, including eight of the ten Asian countries considered here (Bangladesh and PRC excluded). Outside of Southeast Asia (Southeast Asia is defined to include Indonesia, Korea, Malaysia, Philippines, and Thailand), the study found that FDI lowered the rate of investment and growth, while in Southeast Asia it raised both. The author concluded from that evidence that, "The superior efficiency of foreign direct investment in Southeast Asian economies reflects not only less distorted financial conditions than in other parts of the developing world but also less distorted trading systems" (Fry 1993:57).

The positive growth effects of export-oriented FDI in East Asia have been shown in a number of firm surveys to derive less from their financial contribution to raising level investment than from the infusion of technology and international business know-how that accompanies export-oriented FDI. A recent survey of 122 Taipei,China small to medium size firms operating in Malaysia, found that a large part of their invested capital was in fact raised in the domestic capital market (Ariff and Tho 1994). The main benefit of Taipei,China FDI to the local economy, aside from creating employment and generating export earnings, was found to be the commercial linkages that grew up between the Taipei,China firms and local (Bumiputra as well as Malaysian Chinese) firms in Malaysia, which replicated to a large extent the complex networks of small and medium-size firms that characterize the manufacturing sector in Taipei,China (Ariff and Tho 1994). The contribution of export-oriented investment by Hong Kong and Taipei,China firms in PRC is reportedly similar, deriving far more from the manufacturing and international business know-how they bring than from the financial inflow associated with their investments (Sung 1994).

Portfolio Equity Flows

While FDI has been the largest flow of private capital to developing countries in recent years, portfolio equity flows have been the most rapidly growing, rising from $3.8 billion in 1990 to almost $47 billion in 1993, or about 30 percent of total private capital flows to developing countries. The Asian countries accounted for about 45 percent of the total portfolio equity flow to developing countries in 1993, with all but a small fraction of the remainder going to Latin America.

The geographic distribution of portfolio equity investment in Asia, shown in Table 4, is rather different from that of FDI, favoring not so much the largest, low wage country (PRC), but instead the higher income and more financially developed ones (Korea, Malaysia, and Thailand). Moreover, the main source of portfolio equity capital, unlike FDI, is the US and European countries, Japan and other Asian countries having so far participated only modestly (World Bank 1994).

Of the $47 billion in portfolio equity investment in developing countries in 1993, about $35 billion took the form of the direct equity purchases in developing country stock markets, with the remaining $11 billion taking the form of equity placements in international capital markets via (US and global) depository receipts, international tranches of new placements in domestic stock markets, and by placing issues in foreign stock markets (World Bank 1994). The latter has been the principal channel of portfolio capital flow to PRC, as some nine PRC companies were listed on the Hong Kong Stock Exchange in 1993 (Khan 1994:18). In the other

Asian countries, however, where restrictions on foreign ownership are fewer and where liberalization of capital account transcriptions has proceeded further, direct foreign purchases in local stock markets are the main form of equity inflows. It is estimated, for example, that in 1993, foreign net purchases of local stocks was about $5.5 billion in Korea, $3.7 billion in Malaysia, $2.5 billion in Thailand, and about $1.5 billion in India (World Bank 1994:15).

Table 4. Portfolio Equity Flows to Selected Asian Developing Countries
($ million)

	1990	1991	1992	1993	1994
East Asia (6)	1,572	1,039	5,080	18,042	12,301
Korea	518	345	3,045	6,029	2,525
PRC	0	653	1,194	2,278	3,915
Indonesia	312	0	119	1,836	3,672
Malaysia	293	0	385	3,700	1,320
Philippines	0	0	333	1,082	1,407
Thailand	449	41	4	3,117	-538
South Asia (4)	105	23	380	2,025	6,223
Bangladesh	0	0	0	0	47
India	105	0	241	1,840	4,729
Pakistan	0	23	139	185	1,335
Sri Lanka	0	0	0	0	112

Source: World Bank, 1996.

The attraction of Asian stocks to foreign investors is, of course, their relatively high returns, as shown in Table 5. On the other hand, as the standard deviations of these returns indicate, Asian stock markets are volatile, as are the international inflows into and out of them. Indeed, portfolio equity flows are sensitive not only to changing market conditions in the recipient countries, but also to changing conditions in the capital exporting countries. The recession and precipitous fall in interest rates in the US in the early 1990s, for example, played an important part in the rapid rise in portfolio equity flows to the emerging markets (Calvo, et al. 1992). In the Asian emerging markets, however, the evidence suggests that domestic, country-specific factors are three to four times more important than in Latin America, where flows appear to be far more heavily influenced by conditions in US capital markets (Chuchan, Claessens, and Mamingi 1993). Thus, with the economic growth strong and interest rates rising in the US in 1994, the flow of portfolio equity capital to Latin America took an abrupt decline and the flow to Asia leveled off at the amount recorded in 1993.

Table 5. Annual Average Return in Selected Asian Stock Markets
($ for the period December 1988 to December 1993)

	Annualized Mean Return	Standard Deviation of Annualized Return	Correlation with S&P 500*
East Asia			
PRC	34.08	48.50	0.15
Indonesia	14.28	36.30	0.15
Korea	13.44	29.20	-0.16
Malaysia	30.00	23.73	0.41
Philippines	33.72	40.43	0.37
Thailand	39.84	32.84	0.33
South Asia			
India	28.92	33.19	-0.14
Pakistan	61.08	44.89	0.22
Sri Lanka	62.88	25.88	-0.01
US S&P 500	14.40	13.03	1.00

Note: Based on the International Finance Corporation (IFC) Investible Indexes, which measure the returns that foreign portfolio investors might receive from investing in stocks that were legally and practically available to them.

* Standard and Poor's composite index (S&P).

Source: International Finance Corporation (IFC), 1994:102.

Bond Flows

Bond placements in international markets by Asian developing countries have also grown rapidly since 1989, and have become a significant source of external finance. Before 1989, bonds issued by developing countries were mainly the result of debt conversions negotiated between commercial bank creditors and developing country debtors (Gooptu 1993:13). With the normalization of relations between many developing

149

country debtors and their creditors, and a general improvement in creditworthiness in developing countries, the bond market was opened up to developing countries in the 1990s. In addition, the stock market booms in the emerging markets also played a role, as firms found that they could raise capital by issuing bonds convertible into equities (Khan 1994:12). As with the surge in portfolio equity investment, declining US interest rates and the worldwide recession in 1992 and 1993 were important in raising the relative attractiveness of developing country bond issues.

The geographic distribution of net bond flows to Asia is shown in Table 6.[4] The pattern is not significantly different from that of portfolio equity investment, although the Asian share of flow to developing countries is considerably smaller than in the case of equities. Indeed, the volume of bonds issued by Mexican private and state-owned enterprises since 1990 has been as great as for all of Asia, this in spite of the fact that the yield spread on Asian bonds is significantly lower (97 basis points in 1993) than on Mexican ones (200 basis points for public borrowers and 350 for private borrowers in 1993) (Khan 1994).

The figures reported in Table 6 refer to foreign currency bonds issued by Asian developing countries, 85 percent of which are in US dollars and mainly placed in the Euro bond market. In addition to these flows, however, there have been significant direct purchases of local currency fixed-income securities in the capital markets of developing countries, although reliable statistics on these flows are not available. Estimates are, however, that as of May 1994, foreigners held $32 billion (or 32 percent) of Mexican government short- and medium-term securities (*cetes* and *ajustobonus*). In Asia, foreigners have not yet been given as much access to local fixed-income securities markets as in Latin America. Nevertheless, it is estimated that foreigners purchased the equivalent of $5 billion (or 20 percent of the outstanding stock) of ringgit bonds in Malaysia and $1.5 billion (or 245 percent) of baht securities in Thailand in 1993 (World Bank 1994:14).

Net Versus Gross and Large Versus Small

On the basis of observed changes in the magnitude of net capital flows to Asian developing countries, the degree of capital market integration appears to have increased in the 1990s. A similar conclusion emerges from the data on the magnitude gross flows since the net and gross flows are broadly similar, the credits in the capital account of the balance-of-payments generally totaling about four times the debits.[5]

Table 6. Net Bond Flows to Selected East and South Asian Countries
($ million)

	1990	1991	1992	1993	1994
East Asia (6)	-372	1,460	2,047	8,679	12,981
Korea	168	2,722	2,560	3,694	4,157
PRC	-48	24	-3	2,238	2,876
Indonesia	-588	-1,475	-632	197	269
Malaysia	-212	143	-374	44	976
Philippines	395	124	-52	734	927
Thailand	-87	-78	548	1,772	3,776
South Asia (4)	304	1,400	-211	451	176
Bangladesh	0	0	0	0	0
India	304	1,400	-211	451	-19
Pakistan	0	0	0	0	195
Sri Lanka	0	0	0	0	0

Note: Net Bond Flows are from private creditors including both publicly guaranteed and nonguaranteed flows.

Source: World Bank, 1996.

It is easier, however, to conclude from the flow of data that capital market integration is increasing, than to say anything precise about its level. Montiel (1994:323) compared gross capital flows to gross trade flows in 88 developing countries and upon finding that gross trade flows (exports plus imports) were, in the 1980s, on average four times greater than gross capital flows, concluded that, "By this measure, then, developing countries would seem to be much less open financially than they are commercially."

Aside from the fact that the measurement of gross capital flows is less precise than gross trade flows (because of the netting-out problem mentioned in note 6), it is not clear what the basis is of Montiel's conclusion. It seems to presume that a perfectly integrated economy would engage in equal amounts of international trade in goods and assets, but there is no basis (of which the author is aware) for such a presumption. Indeed, if developing countries follow the conventional rule of thumb of limiting the stock of external liabilities to two times exports, then gross capital flows are almost bound to be less than half of gross trade flows.[6] Nevertheless, Montiel's overall conclusion based on flow data, that "...the overwhelming majority of countries in the sample exhibit at least an intermediate degree of integration with external markets..." sounds reasonable, but is hard to validate or refute.[7] It is worth noting, however, that even in the advanced industrial countries, the stock of external assets and liabilities is generally no more than about 10 percent that of domestic assets and liabilities (Golub 1990:424-39).

The Law of One Price in Asian Financial Markets

What the flow of data indicates about the degree, or at least about changes in the degree, of capital market integration in Asian developing countries is broadly confirmed by the scant evidence available on the law of one price in Asian financial markets. What evidence there is relates only to interest-earning financial assets, which, as noted above, are not the most important type of capital flow to Asia. It is useful, nevertheless, to review the evidence on nominal and real interest rate parity that is available.

Interest rate differentials can be decomposed into three components: (i) a country risk premium; (ii) a currency risk premium; and (iii) the expected rate of currency depreciation. These correspond to the three bracketed terms on the right-hand side of the following identity:

$$i - i^* = (i - i^* - fd) + (fd - \widehat{S}^c) + (\widehat{S}^c)$$

where i and i* are the nominal interest rates at home and abroad, fd is the rate of discount on forward exchange, and $\widehat{S}^c$ is the expected rate of depreciation of the home currency. An analogous decomposition for real interest rate differentials (r - r*) is obtained by subtracting the difference between the expected rate of inflation at home and abroad $\pi^c - \pi^{*c}$ from both sides of the above identity:

$$r - r^* = (i - i^* - fd) + (fd - \widehat{S}^c) + (\widehat{S}^c + \pi^c - \pi^{*c})$$

The last term on the right-hand side is the expected rate of real devaluation ($\widehat{s}^c = \widehat{S}^c + \pi^c - \pi^{*c}$) or deviations from relative purchasing-power parity.

The removal of barriers to international capital flows would be expected to reduce the country risk premium, as measured by the covered interest differential. Indeed, Frankel and Chinn (1993:27, 28) report a statistically significant decline in covered interest differentials for Australia and New Zealand following the lifting of capital controls in those countries. Unfortunately, the nonexistence of forward exchange markets in the

Asian developing countries considered here, with the exception of Malaysia, precludes a similar analysis for those countries. In the case of Malaysia, however, Frankel and Chinn found no significant decline in covered interest differential over the period 1988 to 1992 in spite of its measure to liberalize the capital account.

Because forward exchange markets are absent in most of the Asian developing countries, the best that one can do is analyze country risk and currency risk premia combined, by estimating uncovered differentials $(i - i^* - \widehat{S}^c)$. This was done recently by Montiel (1994) for 48 developing countries over the period 1985 to 1990. Using short-term deposit rates or six-month treasury bill rates and invoking expectations to justify using the ex post rate of devaluation for the expected rate, Montiel found uncovered interest rate differentials significantly different from zero in 32 of 48 countries for which he could obtain data. Montiel's sample contained six of the ten Asian countries considered here, the results for which are shown in Table 7. The uncovered interest rate differentials were significantly different from zero for four of the six, and in all cases deviations from the mean uncovered differential were serially correlated, which also invalidate the joint hypotheses of uncovered interest parity and rational expectations (Montiel 1994:334).

Another approach to testing the law of one price in Asian capital markets is to assume that the expected rate of devaluation is stationary and then proceed directly to analyze the co-movement between domestic and international interest rates. Glick and Moreno (1994) use bivariate vector autoregressions to analyze whether changes in US nominal interest rates lead to changes in nominal rates in selected Asian countries. They

Table 7. Deviations from Uncovered Interest Parity
in Six Asian Developing Countries
(percent)

	Mean Deviation $(i - i^* - \widehat{S}^c)$	Standard Error	Ratio of Mean Deviation to Mean Uncovered Interest Parity
Indonesia	-6.10	4.16	1.00
Korea	0.76	2.22	1.00
Malaysia	-4.29	1.09	0.79
Philippines	3.55	1.37	0.59
Thailand	4.14	0.70	0.94
Sri Lanka	-3.67	1.27	1.11

Source: Montiel, 1994:336-7

find a relatively strong effect in Hong Kong, Singapore, and Thailand, but a relatively weak effect in Indonesia, Korea, Malaysia, and the Philippines. The only possible surprise in these results was the relatively weak linkage in Indonesia and Malaysia, since neither has many restrictions on capital mobility. The explanation that is offered for Indonesia was that while its markets are open, its assets are poor substitutes for those in the international market. In the case of Malaysia, a weak linkage to external capital markets was found, but to the Japanese market rather than to the US market.

A similar study by Chinn and Frankel (1994) examines linkages between real interest rates in selected Asian countries on the one hand, and the US and Japan, on the other. They report that substantial real interest rate differentials exist (see Table 8), but point out that it would be inappropriate to infer anything about the degree of integration, because the differing risk attributes of internationally traded financial assets are unknown.[8] Using Johansen's multivariate cointegration technique on quarterly interbank interest rate data, they find, however, that a linkage does exist between real interest rates in Hong Kong; Thailand; and Taipei,China and those in the US and Japan. Real interest rates in Indonesia, Korea, and Malaysia, on the other hand, were found to be linked only to the Japanese rates.

Table 8. Real Interest Rate Differentials for Selected Asian Countries (percent)

	Local versus United States	Local versus Japan
Indonesia	-6.39	-6.96
Korea	-5.43	-6.00
Malaysia	-0.23	-0.82
Thailand	-3.53	-4.01
Hong Kong	3.57	2.99
Taipei,China	-0.22	-0.80

Source: Chinn and Frankel, 1994:18.

Implications of Capital Market Integration in Asia

Growth

Will the integration of the Asian developing countries into world capital markets significantly increase per capita income and support higher rates of economic growth? The answer, of course, depends on what the causes of poverty and the determinants of growth are. If one holds with traditional development economics that low per capita income is the consequence of the relative scarcity of capital, and that the rate of economic growth depends primarily on the rate of capital accumulation, then recent trends in capital flows would be seen to make a potentially important contribution to both the level and the rate of growth of income. Unfortunately, this once-popular view of the development problem has been rather thoroughly demolished by the weight of empirical evidence against it.

The idea that differences in per capita income are due to differences in the per capita stock of capital, and that the key to growth is capital accumulation, rests fundamentally on the assumption that countries operate on the same production function (Lucas 1990:92-6; Krugman 1993:11-23). If this were the case, per capita income differences of the order observed between developed and developing countries would imply enormous differences in rates of return to investment, and hence enormous potential benefits from increased capital market integration to both capital importing and capital exporting countries.[9]

If international capital mobility is ruled out for whatever reason, these same benefits can be captured through international trade, in which goods embodying the relatively abundant factor (relatively intensively) are exchanged for goods embodying the relatively scarce factor (relatively intensively). Exploiting the differences in relative factor prices through trade would, of course, have the same effect as through factor mobility, which is to arbitrage the differences away. The fact that international trade has not equalized factor prices internationally, even between countries with few restrictions on trade, indicates that the fundamental assumption that countries operate on the same production function is invalid. If it is not so much differences in capital per worker that account for differences in real wages internationally, but rather differences in technology (or human capital), then the potential contribution to growth of increased capital market integration is likely to be modest, unless it is found that foreign capital contributes directly to raising the level of technology (of human capital) in capital importing developing countries.

155

The conventional neoclassical growth model, and the growth accounting framework that derived from it, have viewed capital accumulation and technical change as separate from one another. As is well known, in the neoclassical model the growth or per capita income in the long run, steady state depends entirely on the rate of technical change. Even in the short run, before diminishing returns set in, the contribution of capital accumulation is small compared to the other sources of growth. Thus, in this framework, even a rather substantial inflow of foreign capital, say on the order of 10 percent of GNP, adds only about one percentage point to the rate of growth.[10] Thus, Krugman (1993:15) for example, concludes that, "...it falls far short of the crucial importance that attracting capital flows is generally given in much current discussion."

The neoclassical model has, however, been criticized in recent years precisely because of its treatment of technical change as exogenous and separate from investment. Following Romer (1986:1002-37) and Lucas (1990:92-6), a plethora of growth models has been introduced in which technology is redefined as another form of reproducible capital, sometimes termed the stock knowledge, sometimes the stock of human capital. In such models, the return to investment, broadly defined, is constant because of the external effects of the accumulation of knowledge or human capital.[11]

A similar but more intuitively appealing "endogenous" growth model is developed by Scott (1989), who challenges any distinction between expenditures for imitation such as capital accumulation in the neoclassical model, and on innovation such as research and development spending more in some endogenous growth models. Firms grow, he asserts, by "changing economic arrangements," all of which changes are costly. The cost of change, in terms of consumption foregone, is investment. What is called technical change is just one of the ways in which economic arrangements are changed, and like all the others involves a cost, or in other words, investment. Thus technical change and investment are part and parcel of the same thing. What determines growth, therefore, is how much a country sacrifices (saves and invests) to change economic arrangements, and the environment in which investment decisions are made. In Scott's model, as in other endogenous growth models, the potential contribution of foreign capital inflows is, therefore, potentially much greater.[12]

There is, however, a "Catch-22;" for if the return to cumulative investment does not fall as the capital-labor ratio rises, then there is no reason to presume that with the elimination of barriers to international capital mobility, capital will necessarily flow from rich to poor countries. Indeed, it may flow in the reverse direction if returns are higher in rich than in poor countries, as was the case in the nineteenth century, for example, when capital flowed in substantial amounts from Europe to the countries of recent settlement whose per capita incomes were higher than in the capital exporting countries. Certainly, one observes in the recent flows to developing countries generally, and to Asian developing countries in particular, that foreign capital is attracted not by low wages but by economic dynamism. It is worth noting in this regard that while Taipei,China has established itself as the single largest direct investor in several East Asian countries in recent years, its direct investments in the US and western Europe far exceeded those in East Asia.[13]

If it is accepted that the effect of foreign capital inflows on economic growth derives less from its contribution to savings and more from its contribution to changing technology and raising the productivity investment, then it is apparent that the various forms of foreign capital inflow have quite different effects on growth. Direct investment certainly has a more direct effect on the level of technology and business know-how in capital importing countries than do portfolio flows. Furthermore, it is likely that portfolio flows contribute, dollar for dollar, even less to gross savings than direct investment, since the likelihood of consuming rather than investing portfolio inflows is much greater than in the case of direct investment.

Even though portfolio capital flows do not bring technology with them, they may indirectly contribute to raising intrinsic productivity if they permit policy makers to undertake reforms which would not otherwise be politically feasible without foreign financial assistance (Baldwin 1993:24). There are two ways in which they may do this. First, a foreign capital inflow can ease the pain of adjustment by allowing a country to raise investment without sacrificing current consumption. Secondly, a foreign capital inflow can serve as a "vote of confidence" or "seal of approval," raising the credibility of a reform program, which can help to lower the costs of adjustment and increase the likelihood of success of the reform program. It is on this premise that the structural adjustment and stabilization programs of the World Bank and International Monetary Fund rest. Unfortunately, the validity of this premise is somewhat in doubt, as often countries use foreign capital inflows as a means of avoiding adjustment rather than to facilitate it. Indeed, in what is one of the most remarkable economic turnarounds in history, in Viet Nam since 1989, it was the withdrawal of foreign financial assistance from the former Soviet Union that motivated economic reform and raised the rate of growth (Riedel 1991).

Stability

The implications of increased capital market integration for economic stability in developing countries have commanded priority attention ever since the financial crisis erupted in Mexico in December 1994. Certainly the Mexican experience illustrates the difficulty of preventing real currency appreciation, and with it a loss of international competitiveness, in the face of a large autonomous capital inflow. An attempt can be made to prevent real appreciation through sterilized intervention, but in order for that to work, sterilized intervention should be accompanied by an appropriate level of fiscal contraction. If sterilized intervention is not accompanied by fiscal contraction, the difference between domestic and foreign rates will not diminish, and may even widen, encouraging further capital inflow and pushing the country toward a potential crisis. If the flow of foreign capital is reversed for whatever reason, internal or external, sterilized intervention will require the central bank to draw down the stock of reserves it built up during the previous period of capital inflow, and at the same time buy back the domestic assets. Unfortunately, the symmetry of this operation can easily break down, because if there is truly a run on the currency, no amount of reserves is likely to be enough. Indeed, the failure of the central bank to allow the currency to devalue early on only feeds expectations of a subsequent devaluation and accelerates the outflow, as occurred in Mexico.

If policy makers have a strong commitment to supporting the traded goods sector of their economies, as most of the East Asian developing countries clearly do, having successfully relied on export-oriented industrialization as their principal strategy for growth, precipitous inflows of foreign capital pose a serious challenge. The threat to an export-oriented growth strategy from a significant inflow of foreign capital is, of course, far greater if the inflow is portfolio capital rather than FDI. Indeed, if the financial inflow accompanying FDI is intended to finance imports of machinery and equipment or other imported material inputs, there may be no pressure on the currency to appreciate. Moreover, since a large proportion of FDI in East Asia is export-oriented, it has served to enhance rather than to undermine international competitiveness. In addition, FDI is, of course, much less able to take flight if circumstances change. Thus, the threat to exchange rate and price level stability that rises from increasing international capital mobility is related mainly to portfolio flows.

Because sterilized intervention is unlikely to succeed if portfolio capital inflows persist, a country which attaches high priority to a real exchange rate target may choose to de-integrate from international capital markets by imposing capital controls, if not permanently, then at least temporarily. This was the reaction of the authorities in Malaysia in January 1994, for example, when they imposed ceilings on the external liabilities of banks, banned sales of short-term instruments to foreigners, and restricted ringgit deposits of foreign institutions to noninterest-bearing accounts to stem a speculative inflow (Woo and Hirayama 1994). Instead of appreciating as speculators anticipated, these measures caused the currency to depreciate, resulting in substantial losses to speculators. Once the upward pressure on the ringgit eased and the furor over the government's measures subsided, the restrictions were lifted (by August 1994) and currency gradually rose to the level at which it stood before the crisis erupted. Thus, eventually the fundamentals favoring appreciation of the ringgit won out; nonetheless, the government of Malaysia did successfully avoid overshooting the required appreciation, which might have resulted if speculators had been given free rein.

The fundamental incompatibility between high capital mobility, a managed exchange rate, and monetary autonomy has been called the "triad of incompatibilities" by Fischer and Reisen (1993), who suggest that the "impossible" is possible in Southeast Asia, where large inflows of foreign capital have generally been accompanied by stable nominal exchange rates and low inflation. However, the recent events in Malaysia described above, contradict this sanguine view (Woo and Hirayama 1994); Malaysia faced the same hard choices faced by any country integrated into international financial markets. It chose to abandon capital mobility while Mexico sacrificed international competitiveness. The other of the Asian developing countries have not yet been forced to choose between the triad of incompatibilities because the dominant form of capital inflow has been, until recently, FDI. So far they have been able to maintain exchange rate stability and monetary autonomy (Glick and Moreno 1994).[14] However, if portfolio inflows continue to grow as they have the last two or three years, they, too, will be forced to make the same hard choices.

Policy

Should capital market integration be promoted or resisted? The case against it rests mainly on the premise that capital flows are, or often can be, destabilizing, and that the costs associated with instability exceed whatever benefits otherwise derive from free capital mobility. Though instability arises from capital flows that are speculative, speculative flows are not necessarily destabilizing. Indeed, speculative capital flows that force authorities to abandon an exchange rate that is inconsistent with fundamentals are stabilizing, and it is the authorities' policies which, in these circumstances, are destabilizing (Corden 1994:296). In other words, capital market integration imposes discipline on policy makers, which can be a potentially important benefit of capital market integration.

What if countries use their access to international capital markets to borrow unwisely, as many apparently did from 1975 to 1982? If the borrowing is by the private sector, the problem should be self-correcting, as unwise borrowers generally can be counted on to put themselves out of business. The same cannot be said of governments that borrow abroad to finance unwise expenditures. However, if being denied access to external borrowing does not mitigate government profligacy, then it may make little difference whether a government raises funds by borrowing in international capital markets or by crowding out domestic investment. Restricting access to international capital markets is clearly a second-best (or worse) way of restraining government spending.

The dominant flow of capital to Asia in recent years has, of course, been FDI, for which concerns about destabilizing speculation and imprudent public sector borrowing are not relevant. There are, however, policy issues related to the control of FDI. Among the more prevalent controls are restrictions on foreign equity participation, local-content requirements, and mandates of minimum export volume. An attempt was made to negotiate agreements on these types of controls in the General Agreement on Tariffs and Trade (GATT) Uruguay Round, but it did not succeed beyond an agreement to ban local-content requirements on grounds of their inconsistency with GATT rules. In the meantime, however, Asian developing countries have been unilaterally liberalizing their policy toward FDI, by lifting restrictions on entry and establishment and on ownership and control (Low and Subramanian 1995:10). Nevertheless, some still argue for a multilateral agreement on rules governing FDI comparable to the GATT rules on trade (Low and Subramanian 1995:10). The case for such an agreement, which applies also to GATT, is that it gives countries an excuse for doing what is already in their own best interest. Asian developing countries, however, have not needed such an excuse, and have proceeded unilaterally to lower trade barriers and simultaneously liberalize foreign investment policy.

The fact that capital market integration in Asian developing countries in the 1990s was a consequence of broad based economic reforms, especially in the trade and financial sectors, is critically important. It is these reforms which give reason for confidence that the economic crises which followed increased capital market integration in the 1970s in many countries will not be repeated in the 1990s. Deepening and strengthening the process of economic liberalization ongoing in the Asian developing countries is essential for minimizing the risks and maximizing the benefits from increased international capital market integration.

Acknowledgments

The author is indebted to Mr. Charles Chang for research assistance, to Mrs. Flora Paoli for editorial assistance, and to Dr. M. G. Quibria, Professor Junichi Goto, and Professor Jaime Marquez for helpful comments and suggestions.

Notes

[1] The source of data on net is the World Bank's *World Debt Tables*, 1996, which reports long-term net flows, conveniently broken down into the major types of public and private flows. The data on gross are taken from the International Monetary Fund, Balance-of-Payment Statistics (computer files), and are aggregated differently from the World Bank's net flow data. The two sets of data are not, therefore, strictly comparable.

[2] The figures on FDI in PRC are inflated by some unknown amount due to "round-tripping" investment, in which investment capital which originates in PRC flows to Hong Kong and then re-enters PRC as foreign direct investment in order to take advantage of the favorable tax treatment and other preferences which are given to foreign investment.

[3] The caveat in the previous footnote applies here as well.

[4] The difference between net and gross is still minor because the average maturity of the bonds issued since 1990 is five to eight years.

[5] The measure of gross flows in International Monetary Fund statistics is very imprecise. Many lines in the capital account are reported in net terms only, and the coverage varies widely from country to country.

[6] The external debt (D) to export (X) ratio is constant if $rD=(rX/X)\cdot(D/X)\cdot X$. Since exports are no more (and generally are less) than one half of gross trade and net capital inflows are no less (and generally are more) than one half of gross capital flows, with export growth at 20 percent and the debt-export ratio at two, the gross capital flows are no more than 40 percent of gross trade flows.

[7] Among the exceptions with unusually low ratios of gross capital flows to gross trade flows were the four South Asian countries and Indonesia.

[8] The point is also made that real interest rate differentials may reflect differentials in productivity growth in tradables and nontradables which lead to changes in relative purchasing-power-parity (Chinn and Frankel 1994:8).

[9] For example, Lucas (1990:92) notes that with per capita income in the US 15 times that of India, even after adjusting for purchasing-power-parity, the rate of return in the US would be 58 times higher than in India if the two countries shared the same production function.

[10] As Krugman (1993:14) explains, if the capital share of value added is .33 and the capital-output ratio is three, a one percentage point increase in the rate of investment adds one ninth of a percentage point to the rate of growth.

[11] If we begin with a constant returns to scale production function, $Q = A\,K^{(1-\lambda)}L^{\lambda}$, in which there is diminishing returns to capital (K) and labor (L), and then in the spirit of Romer (1986) assume that the level of knowledge (A) depends on the stock of capital according to $A=K^{\lambda}$, then we get $Q=K{\cdot}L^{\lambda}$, which makes the marginal product of capital constant. Note, if labor earns a positive return, private rate of return to capital will be less than the social rate of return (Bertola 1993:1184-99).

[12] For example, if the elasticity of output with respect to capital is 1.0 instead of 0.33, as in the neoclassical model, the growth effect of net capital inflow is three times greater.

[13] Taipei,China direct investment (approvals) in the US, Europe, and Japan from 1959 to 1992, amounted to $3.8 billion, or two thirds of the total (*Taiwan Statistical Data Book* 1994:248).

[14] Woo and Hirayama (1994) note one instance in Singapore and one in Indonesia where runs on the currency required sacrificing one of the triad of incompatibilities.

References

Ariff, M., and N. S. Tho, 1994. "Taiwanese Investment in Malaysia: Profile and Performance." Chung-Hua Institution for Economic Research, Taipei, Taiwan.

Baldwin, R., 1993. "Comment." In A. Giovannini, ed., *Finance and Development: Issues and Experience*. Cambridge: Cambridge University Press.

Bertola, G., 1993. "Factor Shares and Savings in Endogenous Growth." *American Economic Review* 83(5).

Brecher, R. A., and C. F. Diaz-Alejandro, 1977. "Tariffs, Foreign Capital and Immiserizing Growth." *Journal of International Economics* 7(4):317-22.

Calvo, G. A., L. Leiderman, and C. Reinhart, 1992. Capital Flows to Latin America: The 1970s and 1990s. IMF Working Paper WP/92/85. Washington, D.C.

Chinn, M. D., and J. A. Frankel, 1994. The Relative Influence of US and Japan on Real Interest Rates Around the Pacific Rim. Working Paper 248. Department of Economics, University of California, Santa Cruz.

Chuchan, P., S. Claessens, and N. Mamingi, 1993. Equity and Bond Flows to Asia and Latin America, The Role of Global and Country Factors. WPS 1160. World Bank, Washington D.C.

Corden, W. M., 1994. *Economic Policy, Exchange Rates and the International System.* Chicago: University of Chicago Press.

Fischer, B., and H. Reisen, 1993. *Liberalizing Capital Flows in Developing Countries: Pitfalls, Prerequisites and Perspectives.* OECD Center Studies, Paris.

Frankel, J. A., 1989. Qualifying International Capital Mobility in the 1980s. Working Paper No. 2856. National Bureau of Economic Research, Cambridge, Massachusetts.

Frankel, J. A., and M. D. Chinn, 1993. Financial Links Around the Pacific Rim: 1982-1992. Working Paper PB93-08. Center for Pacific Basin Monetary and Economic Studies, Federal Reserve Bank of San Francisco.

Fry, M. J., 1993. *Foreign Direct Investment in Southeast Asia: Differential Impacts.* ASEAN Economic Research Unit, Institute of Southeast Asian Studies.

Glick, R., and R. Moreno, 1994. Capital Flows and Monetary Policy in East Asia. Working Paper No. PB94-08. Center for Pacific Basin Monetary and Economic Studies, Federal Reserve Bank of San Francisco.

Golub, S. S., 1990. "International Capital Mobility: Net Vs. Gross Stocks and Flows." *Journal of International Money and Finance* 9(4): 424-39.

Gooptu, S., 1993. Portfolio Investment Flows to Emerging Markets. WPS No. 1117. International Economics Department, World Bank, Washington, D.C.

International Finance Corporation (IFC), 1994. *Emerging Stock Markets Factbook*. Washington, D.C.

Kawaguchi, O., 1994. Foreign Direct Investment in East Asia: Trends, Determinants and Policy Implications. Report No. IDP-139. World Bank, Washington, D.C.

Khan, M., 1994. "Portfolio Capital Flows to the Developing Country Members of APEC." International Monetary Fund. Unpublished.

Krugman, P., 1993. "International Finance and Economic Development." In A. Giovannini, ed., *Finance and Development: Issues and Experiences*. Cambridge: Cambridge University Press.

Low, P., and A. Subramanian, 1995. "TRIMS in the Uruguay Round: An Unfinished Business?" Paper presented at the World Bank Conference on The Uruguay Round and the Developing Countries, 26-27 January.

Lucas, R. E. Jr., 1990. "Why Doesn't Capital Flow from Rich to Poor Countries?" *American Economic Review Papers and Proceedings* 80(2):92-6.

Montiel, P. J., 1994. "Capital Mobility in Developing Countries: Some Measurement Issues and Empirical Estimates." *The World Bank Economic Review* 8(3):311-50.

Riedel, J., 1991. "Intra-Asian Trade and Foreign Direct Investment." *Asian Development Review* 9(1):111-46.

Romer, P., 1986. "Increasing Returns and Long Run Growth." *Journal of Political Economy* 94(5):1002-37.

Scott, M. F. G., 1989. *A New View of Economic Growth*. Oxford: Oxford University Press.

Sung, Y. W., 1994. "Subregional Economic Integration: Hong Kong, Taiwan, South China and Beyond." Paper presented at the 21st Pacific Trade and Development Conference on Corporate Links and Direct Foreign Investment in Asia and the Pacific, Chinese University of Hong Kong.

Taiwan Statistical Data Book, 1994. Taipei,China.

United Nations (UN), 1994. *World Investment Report 1994: Transnational Corporations, Employment, and the Workplace*. New York.

Woo, W. T., and K. Hirayama, 1994. "Monetary Autonomy in the Presence of Capital Flows: and Never the Twain Shall Meet?" In T. Ito and A. Krueger, eds., *Financial Integration in East Asia*. Chicago: University of Chicago Press.

World Bank, 1994. *World Debt Tables: External Finance for Developing Countries 1994-95*. Washington, D.C.

_____, 1996. *World Debt Tables.Washington, D.C.*

$166 - 69$

Comments on "Capital Market Integration in Developing Asia"

by

Junichi Goto

079
016
$F21$
$F32$

T his chapter examines many data on capital market integration in Asia, and also discusses the implications of such an integration on the growth and stability of Asian economies.

My comments concern three points. The first point relates to the author's conclusion on the *superiority of foreign direct investment over portfolio* investment from the viewpoint of the host country's interests. In section II, Professor Riedel strongly suggested that foreign direct investment (FDI) is better than portfolio investment because FDI brings with it technology transfer, and because it is more stabilizing due to the difficulty of capital flight. In principle, I am ready to agree with the author's conclusion that FDI is better than portfolio investment. But, I think, for the fairness of the argument, the possible disadvantage of FDI should be also mentioned. One such disadvantage is the problem of foreign control of the economy. As the history of the Middle East before the first oil crisis and experiences in many less-developed countries suggest, foreign companies sometimes become so dominant that the national economy, or at least an important part of the production activity, can be effectively controlled by the foreign companies which have brought FDI to the host country. Furthermore, since the decision of FDI is usually made by the foreign private companies, their fundamental motivation is, of course, to earn profit for themselves, rather than to contribute to the economic development of the host country. On the other hand, if the government borrows money from abroad, it can spend the money in order to enhance the long-term economic development of the country. So, if we can trust our own government more than the foreign private firms, portfolio investment can be more beneficial to the host country economy than FDI. Although Professor Riedel seems to be skeptical, Japanese experiences suggest that we can trust our own government at least more than foreign private companies. In short, although I generally agree with the author's judgment on the superiority of FDI, I think that some caveats should also be mentioned for the fairness of the argument.

My second comment concerns another economic implication of the increase in the degree of capital market integration in Asia. Integration of capital markets can constitute an economic precondition for a stronger form of integration, namely a currency union, or at least for trying to fix the exchange rates among currencies in Asia. But will increased capital market integration indeed push Asian countries to form a currency union, as Europe is now moving toward? Although the argument is a little bit technical, assuming the majority here are economists, I would like to elaborate this point in order to extend Professor Riedel's analysis of the impact of capital markets integration in Asia. As Mundell (1961) started with an analysis of the "optimum currency area," there are several criteria about preconditions for a currency union: (i) degree of openness of the economy emphasized by McKinnon (1963); (ii) a synchronization of real shocks (or IS shocks) emphasized by Mundell (1961); and (iii) degree of factor market integration emphasized by Mundell (1961) and Ingram (1973). These points are discussed below.

First of all, as McKinnon pointed out, when the degree of oneness of the economy is high, it is easier to participate in a currency union, because the merit of an autonomous monetary policy will be small, due to the fact that the wage level will be immediately adjusted to the international level. When we look at the actual data on the share of exports in GNP in many Asian countries, we can conclude, generally speaking, that the economies of Asian countries are very open, with Singapore as a good example. And therefore currency unification is easier than otherwise.

As to the second criterion, the degree of synchronization of real shock, if, for instance, all ASEAN countries are under the same or very similar real shocks, the need to conduct a different monetary policy is small. In a paper with Hamada (1994) which compares the degree of the synchronization of real shocks among Asian developing with that among EC and G7 countries, we found that, surprisingly, the degree of synchronization of real shocks among East or Southeast Asian countries is higher than that for the EC or G7. This high degree of synchronization of real disturbances also suggests that an economic precondition for currency integration in Asia is met.

The third criterion is the degree of factor market integration within the region. If production factors move quickly from, say, the Philippines to Malaysia, then unemployment in the Philippines would be a lesser concern to the monetary policymaker than otherwise, and therefore, the need for the independent monetary policy is also smaller than otherwise. On these points, Professor Riedel found that capital market integration in Asia is increasing. And, there is also some evidence of an increase in labor mobility in the Asian region, a typical example of which would be a recent surge in the inflow of migrant workers from Asian less developed countries to Japan. According to the criteria for an optimal currency area emphasized by Mundell, increased integration of the factor market in Asia suggests a high precondition for a currency union, or at least for a coordination of exchange rates in the Asia region. It would have been helpful if the author had included something about the future prospect for currency union in the Asian region in view of his finding of increased capital market integration in Asia.

My third comment relates to the author's point that Taipei,China direct investment in the United States (US) is an example of capital flows in a reverse direction resulting from high returns to capital in the US. But, I am wondering whether such an investment flow into the US is largely due to the trade restriction or the threat of it by the US. According to the Japanese experience, the huge increase in direct investment into the US is largely because the Japanese makers of automobiles or color televisions built a factory in the US for the purpose of quota-jumping.

Finally, I would like to touch upon the recent increase in the degree of capital market integration between Japan and other Asian countries, because it is very important in the Asian capital market although Professor Riedel did not discuss this in great detail. The outflow of Japanese foreign direct investment dramatically increased after the middle of the 1980s when the trade friction with the US became serious and the Japanese yen dramatically appreciated. But due to serious recession in the Japanese economy, Japanese FDI nose-dived after 1990. For example, from 1990 to 1994, the annual flow of Japanese FDI to the US and Europe *declined* by 37 percent and 57 percent, respectively. In contrast to these declines, Japanese FDI to the Asian region increased by 38 percent. And, when we include the active reinvestment of the Japanese affiliates in the Asian host countries, the difference is all the more striking. Furthermore, it should be noted that the reverse flow (the inflow of foreign direct investment into Japan from Asian countries like Korea; Singapore; and Taipei,China) has dramatically increased in recent years. For example, in 1993, the value of FDI from Asian countries more than doubled to become close to 20 percent of the total inflow of FDI into Japan.

Thus, in addition to the fact that the capital market of Asian developing countries has become more and more integrated with each other, these Asian countries and Japan have also strengthened ties in the capital market.

References

Goto, J., and K. Hamada, 1994. "Economic Preconditions for Asian Regional Integration." In T. Ito and A. Krueger, eds., *Macroeconomic Linkage: Saving Exchange Rates, and Capital Flows*. Chicago: University of Chicago Press.

Ingram, J., 1973. *The Case for European Monetary Integration*. Princeton, N. J.: Princeton University Press.

McKinnon, R., 1963. "Optimum Currency Area." *American Economic Review* 53:717-24.

Mundell, R., 1961. "The Theory of Optimum Areas." *American Economic Review* 51:657-64.

F22 O15
F16 O19
J61

CHAPTER 5
LABOR MARKET INTEGRATION IN ASIA

M.G. QUIBRIA
ECONOMICS AND DEVELOPMENT RESOURCE CENTER
ASIAN DEVELOPMENT BANK

Introduction

The degree of integration between labor markets varies along a continuum from being highly segmented to being highly integrated with each other. Two labor markets are said to be completely segmented if changes and disturbances in one market do not have any impact on the outcomes of the other. On the other hand, two labor markets may be so closely integrated that changes and disturbances in one market have a substantial and immediate impact on the other. The most important precondition for the integration of two labor markets is the freer movement of labor between the two markets. Most countries, including those in Asia, impose various kinds of restrictive measures on labor flows; the issue of labor market integration is, therefore, strictly a matter of degree, as is the case with capital market integration.

The simplest economic indicator of the extent of labor market integration is provided by the degree of convergence in the real earnings of labor across countries. However, data on real wages which are comparable across countries, are not readily available. To calculate real wages which are comparable across countries, one needs to convert nominal wage data by their respective purchasing-power-parity exchange rates. Given the lack of available data on real wages for Asian developing countries, a proxy measure is provided by per capita income in purchasing-power-parity terms across countries. A causal examination of such data does not indicate a convergence toward one real (welfare) price for labor across countries. On the contrary, due to divergent economic performances of countries, real returns to labor have varied considerably across countries.[1] The other indicator of labor market integration is the magnitude of labor movement. Countries integrated with each other are likely to experience a significant volume of labor movement, given that the countries are at various stages of economic development and experience different rates of growth. This aspect of labor market integration is addressed at length in this chapter.

Labor Flows

Labor migration from Asia to Europe and America has been a long-standing phenomenon. Labor movement from Asia, particularly from the People's Republic of China (PRC) and Japan, to the United States goes back to as early as the late nineteenth century. From South Asia to Europe, particularly to the United Kingdom, the labor movement dates back at least to the early 1950s. Despite this historical antecedent, the magnitude of international migration to destinations outside Asia has recently been exceeded by that within Asia.

The labor movement within Asia has a number of characteristics that differentiate it from the traditional migration that takes place between developed and developing countries. First, as the various surveys of return-migrants of labor-sending countries indicate, labor movement within Asia is predominantly short term, typically from two to five years. This temporary labor migration is to be distinguished from permanent labor migration that characterizes a large volume of migration between developing and developed countries. Second, labor migration within Asia encompasses predominantly unskilled and semiskilled labor, while that between developed and developing countries includes a large volume of skilled labor, a phenomenon which has been widely labeled as "the brain drain." Finally, international migration in Asia has produced a degree of flexibility in the Asian labor markets unavailable in most of the western developed countries. Indeed, much of the economic dynamism displayed by the newly industrializing economies (NIEs) can be traced to the labor market flexibility exhibited by these economies (Fields 1994).

Labor Movements to West Asia: Levels and Trends

The process of large labor movement from South and Southeast Asia to West Asia began in the aftermath of the first oil shock in 1973. With the increase in oil revenues, West Asian oil-exporting countries decided to embark on a massive program of infrastructure development. Given the small population base, the low labor force participation ratio, and the limited availability of skills, the West Asian countries had to rely largely on a migrant labor force for the implementation of this effort. On the other hand, most South and Southeast Asian countries, with a large population base, a generally high labor force participation rate, and a lower level of per capita income, were well positioned to supply the required labor.

In comparison to the heyday of the Middle Eastern economic boom, there has been in recent years a slowdown in the demand for, and consequently a reduction in the outflow of, labor from South and Southeast Asia to West Asia. This slowdown in labor demand is partly due to the completion or near-completion of major infrastructure projects in West Asia, and partly due to a decline in oil revenues brought about by the fall in oil prices. The Gulf War, which has sapped much of the economic dynamism from West Asia, provided a further setback to the process.

While it is well known that there is a large number of workers from South and Southeast Asia in West Asia, the exact number is not known.

In addition to a lack of reliable data as to the entry and exit of legal workers, the problem is further compounded by the presence of illegal and clandestine migrants. As Shah (1993) suggests, in 1985, the total stock of South Asian workers exceeded two million and that of Southeast Asia one million.

The national composition of migrant workers has undergone significant changes over the years. Immediately after the 1973 Middle East War, India and Pakistan were the first among the non-Arab countries to send their workers to West Asia, subsequently followed by Bangladesh, the Philippines, Republic of Korea (Korea), and Thailand. As Shah (1993) notes, while in 1975, Indonesia, Philippines, Korea, and Thailand constituted about 2 percent of the annual flows of legal migrant workers from South and Southeast Asia to West Asia, their shares increased rapidly to account for 54 percent of all workers in 1980. Notwithstanding fluctuations in their shares, these countries continued to account for more than 50 percent of workers in 1989. In contrast, Shah (1993) notes, the share of India and Pakistan, which accounted for 97 percent of the flow of migrant workers in 1975, declined to less than 30 percent in 1989. However, Bangladesh and Sri Lanka improved their shares significantly, from less than 1 percent in 1975 to 22 percent in 1989.

Labor Movement to East Asia: Levels and Trends

Labor movement to East Asia did not start in any significant way until the late 1980s. By that time, Japan and the NIEs had achieved considerably higher per capita incomes in relation to their neighboring countries. In the decade of the 1980s, while the world economy performed in a lackluster fashion, Japan grew at a rate exceeding 4 percent and the NIEs at rates between 6 and 10 percent. This high growth in East Asia led to a dual disequilibrium: a serious shortage of workers and a large surplus in the current accounts. To address this dual disequilibrium problem, Japan and the NIEs had two policy options: to increase domestic investment and allow movement of foreign workers to meet the resulting increased demands for labor; and to increase foreign investment and thereby reduce the demand for imported labor.

While these capital-surplus economies have extensively utilized the second option of foreign investment, there are limits beyond which this option cannot be pursued. First, there are certain nontraded service industries, some of which are labor-intensive, that cannot be relocated. Second, some of these countries need to expand, or at the very least maintain, the existing physical infrastructure facilities, a task that includes

175

activities which are labor-intensive in nature. Finally, there are some industries that are strategically important from a country's economic, social, and political perspectives. For the above reasons, the capital-surplus East Asian economies have used a judicious combination of both options, foreign investment and labor import.

As in the case with labor movement to West Asia, it is difficult to arrive at any precise number as to the magnitude of migrant workers in East Asia. The estimation problem is compounded by a higher degree of illegal and clandestine labor movement to East Asia. The following provides a rough estimate of the magnitudes involved.

Japan faces a serious shortage of workers in construction, shipbuilding, and certain types of manufacturing. To address this shortage, the country has in recent years relaxed its immigration laws with respect to workers of Japanese descent and admitted 30,000 to 50,000 Brazilians and Peruvians into the country (Shah 1993). In addition, there has been some relaxation in the admission of legal workers of certain categories from other countries. The majority of legal migrant workers are female entertainers, variously estimated at between 50,000 and 100,000. While the number of illegal workers is difficult to estimate, according to one estimate (Mori 1991), there were at the end of 1990, about 273,000 illegal workers in Japan composed predominantly of women from Philippines and Thailand, who worked as entertainers, and men from Bangladesh, PRC, Korea, and Pakistan who worked in shipyards and industrial plants. However, despite a significant increase in their numbers, migrant workers continue to constitute a small proportion of the labor force in Japan.

In Singapore, a significant proportion of the work force, estimated at between 9 and 14 percent, is made up of foreign workers (Shah 1993). While traditionally Malaysia (especially Johore) constituted the most important source of this supply, recent years have seen some diversification of these sources. New sources of supply include Bangladesh, India, Indonesia, Philippines, and Thailand. The majority of migrant workers are unskilled, although the share of skilled migrant workers has been on the rise, reflecting changes in government policies.

While Korea was an important source of migrant workers to West Asia during the 1970s and early 1980s, it has become insignificant in the 1990s. The total stock of Korean migrant workers to West Asia has now fallen to less than 10,000 in the 1990s, from its peak of more than 150,000 in the early 1980s (Shah 1993). This trend reflects the effects of both an increasing competition from the cheaper labor-exporting countries of South and Southeast Asia and improved economic conditions in Korea that have diminished the incentives to migrate.

As Korea does not allow easy entry of unskilled workers into the country, most foreign workers in Korea are therefore illegal. The number of such foreign workers has been variously estimated at between 2,000 and 25,000, which is a minuscule part of the total labor force. The illegal workers who come from countries such as Bangladesh, Pakistan, Philippines, and Thailand, are employed as language teachers, maids, and construction and garment workers.

Hong Kong's migrant labor force has come primarily from PRC. However, the flow of migrant workers to Hong Kong has decreased from about 79,000 in 1976 to 1981, to about 25,000 in 1981 to 1986, reflecting the relocation of many Hong Kong industries to southern PRC (Shah 1993). According to some estimates, about three million PRC workers were employed in 1992 in the Pearl River Delta area in businesses and industries owned by Hong Kong interests. There has been some recent inflow of labor, although mostly illegal, to Hong Kong from the subcontinent.

Taipei,China, whose gross domestic product has grown at an average rate of 7 percent in the last 25 years but whose population growth has fallen sharply to about 1 percent per annum, faces a serious tightening of its labor market. In addition, the country has recently embarked on an ambitious infrastructure development program, which has led to a further exacerbation of the labor market tightening problem. While estimates of foreign workers vary between 20,000 and 300,000, Tsay (1992), who has made the most systematic study of the problem, argues that an estimate of 40,000 is more realistic. Most foreign workers, who come from PRC, Malaysia, Philippines, and Thailand, are employed in construction and service industries.

Malaysia has experienced simultaneous inflows and outflows of workers. As Shah (1993) notes, the vast majority of the migrants to Malaysia are Indonesians who constitute half of Sabah's population of about 70,000, and contribute another 350,000 to the work force of Peninsular Malaysia. Malaysia has also received a significant inflow of workers from Bangladesh and Philippines. On the other hand, Malaysia has seen some outflow of workers to Singapore; Taipei,China; and West Asia, as well as to the western countries.

In sum, despite considerable legal and political restrictions, there has been some measure of labor movement across Asia in response to a wide divergence in economic conditions. While this labor movement reflects some degree of labor market integration, the economic pressure for a greater degree of labor market integration will not ebb unless there is a convergence of economic conditions across countries.

Prospects of Labor Market Integration in Asia

The future trend of labor movements to West Asia will depend on the economic prospects of these countries, which are in turn inextricably linked to oil prices and oil exports. In the present international economic and political environment, it appears that (real) oil prices are going to remain stable or experience a decline in the short to medium term. Therefore, it is highly unlikely that the West Asian economies will experience an economic boom of the type witnessed in the 1970s. Nevertheless, given their present economic and demographic conditions, the West Asian economies will have to rely considerably on migrant labor from South and Southeast Asia in the near future.

For most West Asian countries, there is likely to be a change in the nature of demand from unskilled and semiskilled to more skilled and professional workers as major infrastructure projects are completed. However, both Kuwait and Iraq need to undertake varying amounts of reconstruction work to restore their infrastructures to the pre-Gulf War level. Given its present political and economic difficulties, it will be impossible for Iraq to generate sufficient revenues to start a significant reconstruction effort, hence absorb any inflow of foreign labor in the near future. Kuwait, which has implemented a major phase of the reconstruction work, requires a substantial inflow of migrant workers to sustain the economy.[2] However, the government of Kuwait has expressed its plan to reduce the country's dependence on foreign labor in postwar Kuwait.

Will the volume of labor movement in East Asia gain more prominence in the future? The answer to this question depends to a large extent on whether these countries can sustain their present growth momentum. This growth momentum, which stems largely from their success in foreign trade and foreign investment, will depend largely on the openness in the trade and investment regime, as well as the growth prospects of the world.[3] There has been a general slowdown in the growth of the United States and western European countries that absorb the large part of exports from Japan and the Asian NIEs. This slowdown of growth of industrialized countries will affect adversely the growth in Japan and the NIEs. However, in recent years, domestic demand as well as intra-Asian trade has come to play an important role in determining the growth performance of these countries. At the time of this writing, Japan has just come out of the worst recession of the postwar period, though the economic performance of the NIEs has remained buoyant. In short, even if Japan and the NIEs would experience a slowdown over the long run in their growth, their short- and medium-term prospects still remain bright. To sustain their growth momentum, the NIEs will require a larger inflow of foreign labor.[4] This economic calculus has led the NIEs to foster some measure of linkage, if not integration, with the labor markets of South and Southeast Asia, a connection which is likely to be further strengthened in the future.

As has been argued elsewhere (Quibria 1994), the inducement for labor movement is a function of real income in the home country. It is now widely acknowledged that the sustained rapid growth of Japan and the NIEs was due largely to their success in pursuing an outward-oriented strategy of development and attracting a considerable amount of foreign investment. Inspired by the success of Asian NIEs, most countries in Southeast Asia have instituted measures of external and internal liberalization to increase exports and induce foreign investment (Asian Development Bank 1990, 1991). Similarly, South Asian countries which have been traditionally inward-looking, have in recent years undertaken significant economic reforms. A greater success in promoting trade and attracting foreign investment will accelerate economic growth in South and Southeast Asian countries and lead to eventual stemming of the outflow of labor.

Implications of Labor Market Integration in Asia

Due to the lack of sufficient empirical studies, the discussion of the implications of labor migration for economic efficiency, long-term growth, and unemployment focuses on theoretical aspects. The few empirical studies that are available relate to western, developed countries. Nevertheless, it is hoped that the studies provide insights which are also valid for Asian countries.

Labor Movement and Economic Efficiency

As is well established in international trade theory, free trade between countries leads to enhanced economic welfare for the countries that engage in such trade; similarly, there is a well-established, but not always well-highlighted, proposition with regard to international factor mobility, including international labor mobility. The essence of the proposition is that, "Trade in factors is in purely economic terms very much like trade in goods, occurring for much the same reasons and producing similar results" (Krugman and Obstfeld 1994:155). Like free trade, free mobility of labor improves the efficiency of the global economic system, and both the home and host countries benefit.

179

How much in efficiency gains does a freer movement of labor generate for the world economy? By applying the framework of a computable general equilibrium model, Hamilton and Whalley (1984:74-5) provide a quantitative answer to this issue.

> [There are] large potential worldwide efficiency gains from moving toward a worldwide labor market free of immigration controls. Gains to the world economy in many of the unadjusted cases exceed existing worldwide GNP; in the adjusted case gains are smaller but still large. Thus, while the main conclusion of this paper may not be surprising, it is the potential quantitative size of the effects involved [that] is striking...The calculations reported here suggest that gains from liberalized labor mobility are likely to dominate developing country gains from nonmigration initiatives.

In other words, Hamilton and Whalley's calculations suggest that labor movement from poor to rich countries, even under relatively conservative assumptions, could double world income, and that efficiency gains from a marginal increase in labor mobility are likely to outweigh the corresponding efficiency gains from either trade or investment liberalization.

The foregoing calculations regarding the efficiency gains from labor movement assume that labor movement augments only the host country's labor endowment. A number of recent studies (for example, Helpman and Krugman 1985) argue that an increase in trade generates increasing returns to the economy. Immigration, in a likewise manner, expands the size of the market and brings about increasing returns to scale. In particular, immigration

> can introduce new interactions among workers and firms, so that both workers and firms might 'pickup' knowledge without paying for it. As a result, even though the production technology at the firm level has constant returns to scale, the external effects resulting from immigration might lead to increasing returns on the aggregate (Borjas 1995:11).

The impact of the external effects of immigration is to shift the marginal productivity of the labor curve upward and increase the size of the immigration surplus substantially. There is no precise empirical estimate of the size of external effects. However, for an illustrative calculation of the immigration surplus for the United States economy that incorporates the existence of the external effects, see Borjas (1995). In sum, the above discussion suggests that labor market liberalization can lead to substantial efficiency gains for countries engaging in such liberalization. The Asian economies, which are at various stages of economic development and characterized by various degrees of tightness in their labor markets, can therefore benefit from greater integration of their labor markets.

The models we have discussed so far do not admit to any unemployment. But how does the presence of unemployment affect the efficiency result described above? Unemployment may emerge for many different reasons. If unemployment arises due to downward inflexibility of union wages, than labor migration may further increase unemployment. However, this is not the only outcome that migration leads to. In the face of rising unemployment, the union may also choose to lower wages in return for higher employment (Zimmermann 1995a). Migration can thus act as a countervailing power against trade unions which appears consistent with the experiences of Singapore and Hong Kong, and contribute to greater labor market flexibility in the economy.

The issue of equilibrium unemployment has been highlighted in the efficiency wage model of Shapiro and Stiglitz (1984). In this model, firms cannot observe the work efforts of the workers, and to ensure that workers do not shirk, the firms need to devise an incentive mechanism. Equilibrium unemployment becomes a disciplinary device in this framework, as workers who are found shirking are discharged from employment. In equilibrium, the wage rate is negatively related to the employment rate. In this framework, an increase in the supply of foreign labor increases the size of the labor force; the firms lower the wage rate and raise the employment level. Once again, migration, by bringing about a greater flexibility in the economy, creates efficiency gains.

In sum, the above discussion suggests that a freer labor movement across countries contributes to increased global economic efficiency. This result, which is valid in the context of full employment economies, also applies in the presence of unemployment.

Labor Movement and Long-Term Growth

There has been a surge of interest in growth theory in recent years. In light of the recent advances in growth theory, is there any definitive conclusion one can draw on the impact of labor movement on economic growth? While the recent theoretical advances in growth theory provide some insights into the relationship between migration and growth, the empirical studies in this regard are rather sparse.

If the Solow growth model (1956) is modified to incorporate human capital, in addition to physical capital and labor, and if it is assumed that the economy in question is closed, then Barro and Sala-i-Martin (1995) show that the critical factor determining the impact of immigration is whether the migrants bring enough human capital to offset their dilution of the physical capital in the host country. If immigrants bring little or no human capital, this leads to a situation akin to fast population growth, which causes a slowdown in per capita income growth. If immigrants bring in human capital which exceeds the average for the domestic population, this will speed up per capita income growth.

A recent empirical study by Barro and Sala-i-Martin (1992) for Japan and the United States, which regressed growth in per capita income on the level of per capita income and migrations for Japanese and American regions for different time periods, found that the addition of the migration variable raises the convergence coefficient and yields a positive coefficient for migration. This study suggests a positive, though weak, relationship between growth and migration. The extension of this empirical study for a number of industrial economies by Barro and Sala-i-Martin (1995) corroborates the convergence result, though not necessarily the migration-growth relationship. However, given the state of empirical knowledge at this stage, the above results should perhaps be considered as suggestive rather than conclusive.

Labor Movement and Unemployment

It is often argued that labor movement between countries leads to lower wages and higher unemployment for the host country. This is likely to be the case if foreign workers are substitutable for domestic workers. Then a greater supply of foreign workers due to migration would lead to a fall in the wage level in the host country. However, if the wages are inflexible due to the presence of trade unions, an influx of labor will lead to a higher unemployment level.

However, the impact of migration can also be very different from what is described above. The inputs of the foreign workers may be complements to native workers in production and thus labor migration may lead to higher productivity and higher wages for the native workers. Migration of labor may also help to erode the union power and contribute toward a more efficient functioning of the labor market.

The relationship between immigration and unemployment has been the subject of a good deal of empirical literature. Figure 1, which is reproduced from Zimmermann (1995a), depicts the relationship between the unemployment rate and the share of foreign population in a number of advanced industrial countries. This simple graph does not show any

Figure 1. Unemployment and Immigration (1991)
(percent)

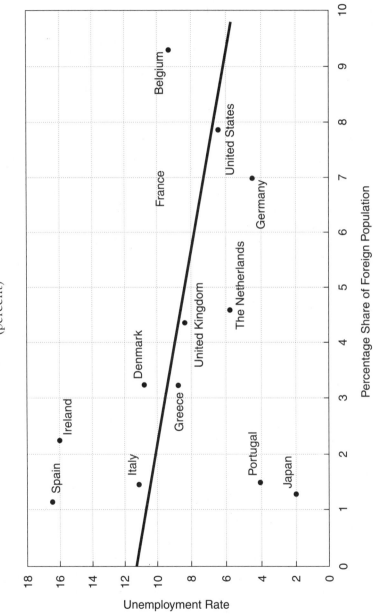

Source: Zimmermann, 1995a.

trade-off between unemployment and migration. However, such a simple statistical analysis, as Zimmermann was quick to note, should be viewed with caution as there is a simultaneity problem here: while unemployment may be caused by the presence of migrants, migrants are also attracted by countries with low unemployment rates.

More sophisticated empirical work has failed to find any relationship between migration and unemployment. Simon (1995:344), who has reviewed the recent United States studies, concludes that, "there is a solid body of careful empirical studies, using a variety of data sources and methods, that shows that immigrants into the United States do not raise the rate of native unemployment." A similar review of the European studies by Zimmermann (1995b) finds no evidence of increased unemployment being caused by immigrants.

In sum, there is no compelling empirical evidence that suggests that migration leads to greater unemployment. On the contrary, there is a body of careful studies from advanced industrial nations that suggests that no such causal relationship exists. However, there is to date no study from Asian countries addressed to this issue.

Why is Labor Movement Restricted?

Despite the widespread acceptance among economists that a freer movement of factors, including labor, enhances the economic efficiency and the growth potential of the world economy, why is there such a maze of restrictions on labor movement? There are three possible explanations for this anomaly.

First, any economic policy, trade and migration policies included, generates winners and losers in society. Whether a particular policy in a democratic society gets adopted depends on the relative political strengths of the winners and losers. For example, in the case of free trade, the winners include many consumers who are often loosely organized and the losers are the less numerous producers and workers in import-competing industries who are politically more organized and articulate. Yet in a democratic setting, the losers often succeed, despite their numerical weakness, to block free trade legislation. However, in the case of migration policy, the winners are often the capitalists, landowners, and skilled workers, and the losers are the unskilled workers. As Freeman (1995:886-7) has described:

> Immigration politics in liberal democracies exhibits an expansionary
> bias. Popular opinion is typically restrictionist, but not well

articulated. Organized opinion, reflecting the distribution of the costs and the benefits of immigration, is more favorable. Organized opinion has more impact on policy because vote-maximizing politicians find it in their electoral interest to cater to it. The normal clientilistic politics of immigration nonetheless tends to evolve into a more open interest-group politics within particular immigration cycles.

He further noted (1995:888):

Immigration politics is made in the context of a dense web of organized groups whose orientations are overwhelmingly admissionist and it is to these groups, reasonably enough, that politicians attend. The most active and influential private sector players are employers, ethnic advocacy groups, and civil and human rights organizations. The most significant counterpoint to this consensus has traditionally been labor unions, but they have generally come to support immigration, resigning themselves to defensive rather than restrictive measures such as employer sanctions against hiring illegal workers and labor certification procedures tying the composition of inflows to employment sectors where demand is high.

However, immigration politics is cyclical. Economic recessions, unanticipated inflows of asylum seekers, and rising tides of illegal entries tend to make migration a hot issue in the national agenda and reverse the expansionist bias in policy. In short, restrictions on labor movement are largely reflective of the political economy of the host country and its changing configuration. Immigration policies go through cycles depending on the economic conditions and social mood prevailing in the country.

Second, migration may be politically unattractive to a country because of noneconomic reasons, such as racism or bigotry. It is interesting that the most liberal democracy in the world, the United States, which in general has maintained a liberal migration policy, had also been subject to

. . .occasional agitations against immigrants or free immigration, as when the aptly titled Know-Nothing Party arose in response to Irish immigration and even managed to elect six governors and seventy-five Congressman in 1854; Chinese immigration was made illegal in 1882 under the Chinese Exclusion Act; and in 1907, as the economist observer of today's practices in regard to VERs [voluntary export restraints] on Japanese and other exports of goods will be amused to hear, President Theodore Roosevelt had even entered into a so-called Gentleman's Agreement with Japan to limit immigration of Japanese laborers! But the truly restrictive and comprehensive legislation enacting immigration restrictions come with the 1921 Emergency Quota Law, which ended the era of an essentially unrestricted immigration and the 1924 National Origins Act, under which discriminatory national and racial quotas were adopted. This initiated the phrase of 'ethnic screening with numerical limits,' which was to yield with the 1950s the current phrase, described as 'familial screening with numerical limits,' as a result of the 1965 act that eliminated the racial and origin quotas and permitted open access to all races within quotas set by functional and familial considerations (Bhagwati 1983:46).

Third, it is argued that there are valid economic reasons for restricting labor movement for reasons of externality (Sala-i-Martin 1995). Two types of externalities have been cited. The first type refers to an externality that stems from the congestion in the use of public goods. Assume that output in a country is produced with three inputs: private capital, labor, and a public good. The public good is subject to congestion, or the greater the number of people using this good, the less use for it. Suppose the output Y for firm i is given by $Y_i = A \ (K_i^a \ L_i^{1-a}) \ (G/L)^b$, where K_i and L_i are capital and labor used by firm i, G is the supply of public good and L is the total number of people in the economy. Note that this economy exhibits constant returns to scale in its private inputs; and finally an increase in total population reduces the productivity of the public good as well as the private inputs. In this economy, as it can be easily seen, an increase in the total population due to migration may increase or decrease the demand for labor, depending on the level of congestion on the public good. Note that the result depends on the importance of the public good and how severely it is affected by congestion. The second type of externality, emphasized in the so-called new growth theory, refers to human capital externality. Suppose there is an externality from the average stock of human capital. If there is an increase in the supply of highly skilled people due to migration, then the average level of human capital and the productivity of everyone in the economy goes up. However, an increase in the supply of semiskilled people lowers the level of average human capital in the economy and everyone's productivity. Migration of semiskilled people reduces the average wage level and per capita output, therefore adversely affecting the earnings of the native population.

The above "externality" arguments, as rightly noted by Sala-i-Martin (1995), are not really arguments against migration. The first-best solution to the first problem is not to prohibit labor movement but to simply charge migrants a fee for the use of public goods in the host country. In the second instance, the migrants should be charged for the exact amount of externality. In either case, the first-best solutions to these problems are definitely not prohibiting migration.

In sum, restrictions on labor movement are largely inspired by political and social considerations. The case for prohibiting labor movement on economic grounds does not stand close scrutiny.

Are Trade, Aid, and Investment Substitutes for International Migration?[5]

In an autarkic situation, different economies are characterized by different commodity and factor prices. A relevant policy question with regard to migration is whether trade in goods can narrow or eliminate the wage differentials that exist between countries, thereby reducing the incentives for labor movement. In short, is trade in goods a substitute for or complement to labor mobility? This issue has been discussed, among others, by Markusen (1983), Wong (1986), Razin and Sadka (1993), and Ethier (1995).

The putative conclusion of the standard trade theory is that trade and migration are substitutes. The Heckscher-Ohlin proposition in international trade theory states that in the absence of international factor mobility, each country exports the good which is intensive in its abundant factor. Trade between countries equalizes not only commodity prices but factor prices across countries. Therefore, when free trade exists, it eliminates the incentives for factors to move across countries. However, if there is no trade between countries, but factors are allowed to move freely, then labor will move from the labor-abundant to the labor-scarce country, and capital will move from the capital-abundant to the capital-poor country. The Stolper-Samuelson theorem suggests that commodity prices will be equalized across countries, assuming that the same technology prevails across countries. Thus, with either commodity trade and no labor mobility, or no commodity trade but perfect labor mobility, the same outcome with respect to commodity and factor prices will emerge. Thus, free trade in commodities and free mobility of factors are perfect substitutes. The classic statement of this proposition is to be found in Mundell (1957).

However, trade theory has identified a number of conditions and circumstances where migration and trade may be complements, at least in the short run. We briefly note three such cases. First, if countries are identical in terms of relative endowments but differ in terms of technologies, for example, one country is more productive than the other in the production of a particular commodity, then the post-trade factor price ratios between countries may diverge further as compared to the pretrade situation. If factor mobility is allowed, capital and labor will move in the opposite direction and factor mobility and commodity trade will complement each other. Second, the existence of external economies may also lead to a complementary relation between trade and factor mobility. If countries differ in absolute size but possess identical relative factor endowments, then the large country will export the good in the production of which it has external economies.

Finally, Schiff (1994) has provided yet another instance of migration and trade being complements. He argues that migration costs, along with the existence of imperfect capital markets, constitute a constraint on labor mobility. The costs of migration for legal migrants include transportation, living expenses until employment becomes available in the host country, and, for illegal migrants, additional payments to intermediaries for information and other services. In the context of the Heckscher-Ohlin framework, Schiff argues that trade liberalization, foreign aid, and remittances in a labor-abundant country, by increasing labor income and the workers' ability to incur the cost of migration, lead to greater outward migration. Schiff notes that trade liberalization may result in higher migration also through intrahousehold transfer of income. As trade liberalization takes place, the industries to flourish first are those that make intensive use of female labor. In most developing countries, the textile, garment, light electronics, and agriculture processing industries use disproportionately large numbers of women compared to men. In these countries, savings by women have been used to finance the migration of men.

The Labor Market Story Behind the Success of the Newly Industrializing Economies

Case Studies of Hong Kong and Singapore

It is now widely accepted that a large part of the economic success of the NIEs in Asia can be attributed to their labor market institutions. A critical feature of the labor markets of these economies has been their

188

flexibility. The characteristic of a flexible economy is that it operates on or near the production possibility frontier: its resources are fully or nearly fully utilized and all profit opportunities are captured without undue time lag. A flexible economy responds quickly to exogenous changes in prices and technologies while an inflexible economy operates largely inside its production possibility frontier, wastes resources, and fails to capture profitable opportunities. In the following, we discuss briefly the issue of the labor market flexibility of Hong Kong and Singapore. The data and analysis for Hong Kong are drawn from Young (undated), while those for Singapore are from Lim, Fong, and Findlay (1993).

Hong Kong

Young (undated:45) has documented that Hong Kong has enjoyed an unusual degree of labor market flexibility.

> Hong Kong's labor force is very weakly unionized. . . . Hong Kong has had an unusual record of industrial peace. . . . Among the seven economies for which data are available across the entire 1968-1976 period, Hong Kong had by far the least number of working days lost per 1,000 employees due to industrial disputes. . . .Hong Kong usually lost less working days per 1,000 employees than the Federal Republic of Germany and Sweden, both of which had unusual records of industrial peace.

It may be noted that the manufacturing sector, which is usually the bastion of most labor union activities, is the least-unionized of all sectors in Hong Kong. Politically, there is considerable fragmentation in the labor movement on the basis of crafts, industries, occupations, employers, and geographical location. This fragmentation is also reflected in the very limited union membership growth in Hong Kong.

Hong Kong has received a large volume of migrants from PRC. In the initial wave between 1945 and 1947, Hong Kong received 1.2 million migrants from PRC. In the second wave between 1949 and 1950, about 340,000 were received and about 270,000 returned to the mainland the following year. The third wave occurred between 1961 and 1962, following the disasters of the Great Leap Forward, when 130,000 came from PRC. The fourth wave came in the aftermath of the Cultural Revolution when 150,000 Chinese emigrated to Hong Kong in 1973/74. From 1978 to 1980, with the fall of the Gang of Four, again 400,000 Chinese entered Hong Kong. Not all inflows of migrants to Hong Kong were, however, exogenously induced. In fact, as Young (undated) notes, Hong Kong also encouraged substantial illegal migration until the 1980s.

This continuous flow of migration, both in quantity and quality, played a significant part in shaping the labor market flexibility of Hong Kong. As reported by Young, various surveys of immigrant and nonimmigrant groups in Hong Kong indicate that the immigrant population is extremely politically apathetic. Indeed, available quantitative estimates show that there is a significant negative correlation between the proportions of migrant populations in different sectors and the degree and militancy of union organizations.

Though the presence of immigrants may not have been the principal determinant of the relative lack of unionization in Hong Kong, it definitely has played an important role. Young (undated:58) notes:

> . . .To provide a complete explanation of Hong Kong's overall low level of unionization and, particularly, the political and economic quiescence of Hong Kong's blue collar unions that contrasts so strongly with the well-organized militancy of the white collar unions, we point to the large number of immigrants in the economy as a whole and their particular concentration in the weakly unionized sectors.

In essence, migration has worked out as a disciplinary device for the trade unions, thereby maintaining labor market flexibility which has been at the core of the manufacturing success of Hong Kong.

However, in the 1980s, Hong Kong was faced with a difficult economic decision: to allow migration of a larger volume of workers and further congest its already crowded public goods but maintain the real wage rate advantage that is necessary for the persistence of its comparative advantage in manufacturing; or to relocate its manufacturing in PRC (which had become politically feasible by then) and reduce the flow of migration to Hong Kong. At the same time, Hong Kong still needs to import considerable numbers of foreign workers to work for its service as well as infrastructure industries.

Singapore

The experience of Singapore is in many ways similar to that of Hong Kong. In 1972, the government set up a tripartite National Wages Council to formulate annual wage guidelines, to determine public sector wages and to influence wage settlements in the private sector. Between 1972 and 1978, the government adopted a policy to promote "orderly" wage increases to maintain international competitiveness in labor-intensive manufacturing, to arrest worsening wage shortages, and to reduce increased dependence on foreign labor. In 1979, the government responded to the labor shortage problem by instituting a "high wage" policy to "restore to market levels" and encourage capital-labor substitution and technological upgrading, and reduce dependence on foreign labor. The result was a rapid acceleration of wage costs in Singapore, which reduced its international competitiveness in relation to other NIEs. The recession that followed 1985, led to a decline in manufactured exports and employment. In 1987, the National Wages Council committee recommended wage reforms that included annual rather than three-year collective agreements, a variable bonus, and other measures.

Wage policy is one way the government has influenced the labor market in Singapore. The other and equally important component of Singapore's labor market strategy has been the admission of foreign labor. In 1968, the government relaxed immigration rules to recruit workers from Malaysia and by 1972, foreign workers accounted for 8 percent of the domestic work force. The number of foreign workers declined in 1974/75 when the recession hit, but the number rose steadily in the late 1980s when workers from nontraditional sources such as Indonesia, Philippines, Thailand, and the subcontinent, began to be recruited. As a consequence of this effort, the proportion of foreign workers reached 11 percent of the labor force by 1980. In 1981, the government imposed special employer levies on foreign workers to discourage their employment. Yet the size of the foreign labor force did not decline because of the construction boom that took place in the early 1980s.

With the severe recession of 1985/86, tens of thousands of foreign workers were laid off and sent home. But to preserve its comparative advantage in labor-intensive industries, the government did not tighten its policy on foreign labor imports. Rather, the government decided to continue to allow entry of a revolving pool of foreign workers on short-term work permits. Indeed, "labor short" employers in the electronics export industry were not only allowed, but also encouraged, to import workers. Needless to emphasize, the country has always permitted liberal importation of skilled foreign workers.

In the late 1980s, it became increasingly evident that the country would have difficulty in maintaining its labor-intensive manufacturing base, unless it continued to import large volumes of foreign workers. The present policy seems to be both to relocate its manufacturing industries across the border in the so-called growth triangle area and to import labor on a short-term basis.

As the experiences of Singapore and Hong Kong indicate, judicious importation of foreign labor has played an important part in the labor market strategies of these economies. Both economies have strategically used labor importation as a device to discipline workers, and avoided the undesirable economic consequences of labor market inflexibility.

Conclusions and Policy Implications

There are a number of issues relating to international labor migration and labor market integration in Asia. Some of the important conclusions of this chapter include the following.

◆ Asian economies over the years have experienced a limited degree of labor market integration through international migration across countries. In that process, East and West Asian countries have been the net recipients of the migrant workers who moved from the rest of developing Asia.

◆ Freer movement of workers across countries contributes to increased global efficiency. This result is valid not only for full employment economies, but also for economies characterized by some measure of unemployment. There is no presumption in economic theory that labor movement necessarily leads to lower long-term growth. The outcome appears to depend to a large extent on the average skills level of the migrants. Similarly, there is no empirical evidence to prove that there is a causal relationship between migration and unemployment.

◆ Despite the beneficial effects of migration, labor movement is restricted across countries. This has to do with partly political-economic factors, partly social reasons such as racism and bigotry, and partly various types of externality, such as congestion of public goods. The case for prohibiting labor movement on economic grounds does not stand close scrutiny.

◆ While trade, aid, and investment are generally substitutes for international migration, there are circumstances and conditions that make migration and trade complements, at least in the short run. In these circumstances, trade might induce rather than inhibit migration.

♦ The important lesson that emerges from the success of Hong Kong and Singapore is that these economies exhibited a high degree of labor market flexibility, which was greatly facilitated by the presence of a large inflow of foreign workers.

Global Issues

As labor movement is both a global and a regional phenomenon, it would be misleading to discuss migration policies only in the regional context. As the earlier discussion indicates, under most common economic circumstances, trade and migration tend to be substitutes, a fact which has also been borne out by the experiences of outward-oriented East Asian economies. If for political and social reasons international labor movement needs to be restricted, then it is important that the world trading environment be kept as free as possible. The conclusion of the Uruguay Round of multilateral trading agreement is an important step in this regard. Nevertheless, there are areas where the threat of protectionism still persists.[6] The textile and garments trade, where the developing countries have a major stake, is largely dominated by a quota system in the form of the Multifiber Arrangement (MFA). While MFA is scheduled to be phased out by 2005, developing countries fear that MFA may be replaced by antidumping measures. Likewise, it is widely perceived in developing countries that the initiative to impose "labor standards" is an indirect way of imposing protectionism. "Labor standards" are viewed as an instrument both to nullify the comparative advantage of the poor countries in labor-intensive commodities and services, and to protect the sunset industries in the industrialized countries. Finally, the emergence of various preferential trading blocks, to the extent that they are discriminatory and exclude the poorer developing countries, is considered a threat to the evolution of a freer world trade system. If the above issues are not satisfactorily resolved and a freer trading system established where poor countries can gainfully participate and benefit, the tide of migration will not ebb.

As noted earlier, trade can be a complement to labor mobility and thereby generate greater incentives for labor migration. This complementarity can occur if the high-wage country has a productivity advantage over the low-wage country in some key industries due to, for example, the existence of a superior infrastructure such as roads and highways, ports, and telecommunications. If the immigration policy of advanced countries becomes increasingly restrictive, then foreign aid should be directed to building such infrastructure in poor countries. Foreign direct investment can contribute toward raising productivity and diffusing

193

technology. However, to attract foreign private investment, developing countries themselves can help by fostering an environment conducive to foreign investment.

Regional Issues

In the greater economic integration as well as income convergence of Asian countries, labor movement can play an important part in generating greater economic efficiency, maintaining the comparative advantage in labor-intensive manufacturing, and nurturing labor market flexibility.

For continued economic dynamism of Asian economies into the twenty-first century, it is essential that Asian economic integration be maintained and fostered. The countries should further open up their economies on a nondiscriminatory basis to facilitate greater trade between countries. This trade is not meant to replace more efficient global trade by less efficient regional trade, which should equally reflect comparative advantages and gains from trade. That is, trade should follow the dictates of the market and not the dictates of the government. For a smoother flow of capital, both the host and home governments should ensure that there are no unnecessary restrictions. Similarly, there should be efforts by both the home and the host countries to ensure that labor mobility, which can be mutually beneficial, is not unnecessarily encumbered by myriads of rules and restrictions. This is neither to suggest the right of immigration nor the curtailment of the rights of the governments to issue visas, but to liberalize mutually beneficial labor movement. Much of the economic dynamism of the capital-surplus, fast-growing Asian economies is related to labor market flexibility ensured by freer mobility of labor. Should the rapidly growing Asian economies forget this lesson and act in a myopic manner as many developed countries do, they may soon find themselves bereft of their economic dynamism and suffer from the same kind of economic sclerosis that the lack of labor market flexibility entails.[7]

Notes

[1] There has been a marked increase in income inequality in per capita incomes (in purchasing-power-parity terms) among South, Southeast, and East Asian countries. Preliminary estimates by the author indicate that for 18 countries of the region for which data were readily available (including Japan and the NIEs),

the coefficient of variations in per capita incomes increased from 71.3 in 1965 to 89.6 in 1993.

[2] The composition of the migrant work force in Kuwait has somewhat shifted from the prewar workforce of Kuwait. In view of the political role played by Yemen, Jordan, and the Palestinians during the Gulf War, workers from these countries faced some degree of discrimination in postwar Kuwait.

[3] In evaluating trends in world trade, the postwar period can be divided into two subperiods: before and after the first oil shock, 1948 to 1973 and 1974 to 1990, respectively. For the first period, the annual rate of growth of real exports was 7 percent per annum, which exceeded the trend rate of growth of real output of 5 percent. In the post-first oil shock period, the annual rate of growth of real exports was around 4.5 percent per annum (Greenway 1990).

[4] This is not to deny that the capital-surplus economies will invest some of their surpluses in other countries and there will be an effort to upgrade the technology so that the need for labor import is minimized. Despite these efforts, however, there will still be a need for import of a substantial amount of labor on two counts: to build and maintain physical infrastructure, and to staff labor-intensive, nontraded service industries. However, in the longer run, this demand for foreign workers will be further augmented for reasons of demography that will lead to the aging of the population.

[5] This discussion draws on Quibria (1996).

[6] For a comprehensive discussion of the post-Uruguay Round issues and their implications for developing countries, see Srinivasan (1996).

[7] If one believes in the recent findings of growth accounting of the East Asian economies, most of Asian growth can be explained by factor augmentation. If that is the case and if the East Asian economies have to maintain their present growth trend, an important instrument is likely to be the augmentation of domestic labor supply through freer mobility of labor. For a sample of these growth-accounting studies, see Lau and Kim (1994) and Young (1992, 1994, 1995).

References

Asian Development Bank, 1990. *The Middle East Crisis: Potential Implications for the Economies of the Bank's DMCs*. Manila.

_____, 1991. *Asian Development Outlook 1991*. Manila.

Barro, R. J., and X. Sala-i-Martin, 1992. "Regional Growth and Migration: A Japan-United States Comparison." *Journal of the Japanese and International Economy* 6(4):312-46.

_____, 1995. *Economic Growth*. New York: McGraw Hill, Inc.

Bhagwati, J. N., 1983. "The Economic Analysis of International Migration." In R. E. Feenstra, ed., *International Factor Mobility: Essays in International Economic Theory*. Vol II. Cambridge, MA: MIT Press.

Borjas, G. J., 1995. "The Economic Benefits from Immigration." *The Journal of Economic Perspectives* 9(2):3-22.

Ethier, W. J., 1995. "Theories About Trade Liberalization and Migration: Substitutes or Complements?" Department of Economics, University of Pennsylvania. Mimeographed.

Fields, G. S., 1994. "Changing Labor Market Conditions and Economic Development in Hong Kong, the Republic of Korea, Singapore, and Taiwan." *The World Bank Economic Review* 8(3):395-414.

Freeman, G. P., 1995. "Modes of Immigration Politics in Liberal Democratic States." *International Migration Review* 29 (3,4):881-902.

Greenway, D., 1990. "Multilateralism and Bilateralism in Trade Policy: Editorial Note." *Economic Journal* 100(403):1286-7.

Hamilton, B., and J. Whalley, 1984. "Efficiency and Distributional Implications of Global Restrictions on Labor Mobility." *Journal of Development Economics* 14:61-75.

Helpman, E., and P. Krugman, 1985. *Market Structure and Foreign Trade*. Cambridge, MA: MIT Press.

Krugman, P., and M. Obstfeld, 1994. *International Economics: Theory and Policy*. New York: Harper Collins College Publishers.

Lau, L., and J. I. Kim, 1994. "The Sources of Growth of the East Asian Newly Industrialized Countries." *Journal of the Japanese and International Economies* 8:235-71.

Lim, L., P. Fong, and R. Findlay, 1993. "Singapore." In R. Findlay and S. Wellizc, eds., *The Political Economy of Poverty, Equity and Growth: Five Small Open Economies*. New York and Oxford: Oxford University Press.

Markusen, J. R., 1983. "Factor Movements and Commodity Trade as Complements." *Journal of International Economics* 14:341-56.

Mori, H., 1991. "Structural Change in Contemporary Japanese Labor Market and Immigrant Workers." Paper presented at the Second Japan ASEAN Forum on International Migration in East Asia, 26-27 September, Tokyo.

Mundell, R. A., 1957. "International Trade and Factor Mobility." *American Economic Review* 47:321-37.

Quibria, M. G., 1994. "International Migration in Asia: Facts, Issues and Policies." *Journal of Behavioral and Social Sciences* 4:1-20.

_____, 1996. "Migration, Remittances and Trade: With Special Reference to Asian Developing Economies." In P. Lloyd and L. Williams, eds., *International Trade and Migration in the APEC Region*. Melbourne and Oxford: Oxford University Press. Forthcoming.

Razin, A., and E. Sadka, 1993. Interactions Between International Migration and International Trade: Positive and Normative Aspects. Working Paper No. 4-93. Foerder Institute of Economic Research, Tel Aviv University.

Sala-i-Martin, X., 1995. Comment on "European Migration: Push and Pull." Proceedings of the World Bank Annual Conference on Development Economics 1994, Supplement to the *World Bank Economic Review and the World Bank Research Observer*.

Schiff, M., 1994. How Trade, Aid and Remittances Affect International Migration. World Bank Policy Research Working Paper 1376. Washington, D.C.

Shah, N., 1993, "Migration Between Asian Countries and Its Likely Future." Paper presented at the Expert Group Meeting on Population Distribution and Migration, 18-22 January, Santa Cruz, Bolivia.

Shapiro, C., and J. Stiglitz, 1984. "Equilibrium Unemployment as a Discipline Device." *American Economic Review* 74:433-44.

Simon, J., 1995. Comment on "European Migration: Push and Pull." Proceedings of the World Bank Annual Conference on Development Economics 1994, Supplement to the *World Bank Economic Review and the World Bank Research Observer*.

Solow, R., 1956. "A Contribution to the Theory of Economic Growth." *Quarterly Journal of Economics* 70:65-94.

Srinivasan, T. N., 1996. "Post Uruguay Round Issues for Asian Developing Member Countries." Economics and Development Resource Center, Asian Development Bank. Mimeographed.

Tsay, C., 1992. "Clandestine Labor Migration to Taiwan." *Asian and Pacific Migration Journal* 1(3-4):637-55.

Wong, K. Y., 1986. "Are International Trade and Factor Mobility Substitutes?" *Journal of International Economics*. 21:5-43.

Young, A., undated. "The Political Economy of Poverty, Equity and Growth: Hong Kong." Department of Economics, Columbia University. Unpublished manuscript.

_____, 1992. "A Tale of Two Cities: Factor Accumulation and Technical Change in Hong Kong and Singapore." In O. Blanchard and S. Fischer, eds., *NBER Macroeconomics Annual 1992*. Cambridge, MA: MIT Press.

_____, 1994. "Lessons from the East Asian NIEs: A Contrarian View." *European Economic Review Papers and Proceedings* 38:964-73.

_____, 1995. "The Tyranny of Numbers: Confronting the Statistical Realities of the East Asian Growth Experience." *Quarterly Journal of Economics* 110(3):641-80.

Zimmermann, K. F., 1995a. "Tackling the European Migration Problem." *The Journal of Economic Perspectives* 9(2):45-62.

_____, 1995b. "European Migration: Push and Pull." Proceedings of the World Bank Annual Conference on Development Economics 1994, Supplement to the *World Bank Economic Review and the World Bank Research Observer*.

Comments on "Labor Market Integration in Asia"

by

Peter J. Lloyd

his chapter presents a comprehensive and well-argued view of the
labor markets in Asia. It focuses on the issues relating to the effects
of international movements of labor on the integration of labor
markets across countries. This focus brings out the effects on the regional
economy as a system, whereas the traditional focus on the welfare of the
host country and, less commonly, the source country, misses the system-
wide effects.

There is, as Quibria notes, a much higher level of movement of
labor into and from the countries of the region than in the past, and most
of this is now intra-Asian rather than emigration to the high income countries of North America and Europe. One can also note that the pattern of
movements is continuing to change rapidly. In East Asia there are now at
least seven countries which are primarily importers rather than exporters
of labor; these are the People's Republic of China (PRC); Hong Kong; Japan;
Korea; Malaysia; Singapore; Taipei,China; and Thailand. This list is
remarkable. Less than a decade ago, Korea and Thailand were major
exporters of labor to the Middle East, Japan, and other countries. Malaysia
is experiencing a great increase in the demand for foreign labor as domestic
real wages rise sharply and employers seek to keep down wage costs.

These new destination countries, with the exception of Japan and
Singapore, have to devise policies for the restriction and selection of
immigrant workers. Immigration in all of these Asian countries has been
strictly controlled and very selective. There is evidence of a strong convergence of immigration policies for all seven countries toward a set of policies which has been dubbed the 3-S strategy by Freeman and Mo (1996).
These countries are seeking *skilled* workers to take up *short-term* employment in *specific* sectors. The emphasis on skilled workers generally fits the
policies of the major source countries, such as the PRC, Indonesia, and
Philippines, which are also seeking to promote the emigration of more
skilled contract workers. However, it does not match the aspirations of the
poor and unskilled workers in the source countries. There is a large flow
into most of these destination countries of illegal workers. Most illegal

workers are unskilled, and, by the nature of these flows, nonspecific, and many seek to be long term. Hence, there are emerging problems of enforcement of these policies.

One interesting question, which is not addressed in the chapter, is why there are labor shortages in these countries if their labor markets are so flexible. Part of the answer is that some immigrant labor supplies skills and other characteristics which are not available from the domestic force, at least in the short run when the human capital is fixed. Another part of the answer is that employers are seeking to avoid the costs of adjustments to rising costs of labor by hiring from abroad; for example, in the construction industry. In other cases, foreign workers are employed to do jobs which domestic workers are increasingly unwilling to do, the so-called 3-D (dirty, dangerous, and demanding) jobs.

Immigration policy is an important part of national development policy. By emphasizing skilled workers in the selection of legal entrants, Asian countries have reinforced the policies of upgrading labor skills and moving employment into sunrise industries in which they are competitive, rather than seeking to prop up more labor-intensive industries in which they are losing competitiveness. Construction industries are a permitted exception for the importation of unskilled or semiskilled labor as it is difficult to substitute for labor in these activities and they are essential to the expansion of the productive capacity of the economies.

The chapter has a good discussion of the integration of labor markets, which results from the movement of labor from low productivity jobs in the source countries to higher productivity jobs in the destination countries. This is partly a matter of factor proportions which change the marginal productivities of factors and partly of other gains in productivity. In respect of these other gains, I would emphasize the kind of effect which occurs in the classical model of international trade, rather than increasing returns to scale. In this model, the moving factor labor takes on the efficiency of workers in the country in which the work is located because of "atmospheric" factors (know-how, work organization, and so on.)

The effects of labor migration should be viewed in the broader context of other changes in these economies. Here the most notable is the rapid expansion of international trade in goods and services due to the liberalization of restrictions on this trade. Quibria notes the recent literature which suggests that unproduced factors, including labor, may be complements rather than substitutes for the movement internationally of produce goods and services, especially if the technologies are different across countries. Some types of labor movement are plainly complementary with trade in goods and services; for example, imports of expatriate labor into managerial and skilled labor positions facilitate the establishment of new foreign enterprises and new technologies, most of which in Asia are export-oriented. Hence, in such cases, the liberalization of trade in goods and services has increased the demand for the international movements of labor, not reduced it.

International movements of labor should also be viewed alongside the international movements of capital which are occurring in the region. Foreign direct investment alone has been increasing over the last decade or so at about four times the rate of increase in international trade in goods and services for the world as a whole and considerably faster in Asia. Just over half of stock of foreign direct investment (FDI) in Asia has come from other Asian countries, chiefly Japan but increasingly the Asian newly industrializing economies, and most of it has been invested in export activities. Thus, the primary moving force in raising factor productivities and real incomes in Asia has been the rapid growth of exports and the development of new exports, and associated with this, the flows of FDI. The flows of labor have responded to the new income opportunities which these changes have brought.

The importance of these links between trade in goods and services, FDI, and in labor is that the integration of markets is not a process of integration in each market separately. Markets are linked through input-output relations. Hence, the liberalization of trade in goods and services will have the effect of integrating the factor markets, too, if the conditions which produce factor price equalization hold — or of causing a divergence in factor prices, if they do not hold. Taking a general equilibrium view of these economies, it seems that the labor market integration has been small relative to that in capital and commodity markets and it is these markets, rather than the labor markets, which are primarily bringing about a greater integration in the open economies of Asia.

Reference

Freeman, G. P., and J. Mo, 1996. "Japan and the Asian NICs as New Countries of Destination." In P. J. Lloyd and L. Williams, eds., *International Trade and Migration in the APEC Region*. Melbourne: Oxford University Press.

CHAPTER 6
INTERNATIONAL LABOR STANDARDS
AND TRADE POLICY

NARHARI RAO
ECONOMICS AND DEVELOPMENT RESOURCE CENTER
ASIAN DEVELOPMENT BANK

Demands to link international labor standards with trade policy are not new. Arguments in favor of using trade policy instruments to counter "unfair" competitive advantage on account of lower labor standards in partner countries have been made intermittently for almost a century (Charnovitz 1987). No systematic actions have been taken, however, in terms of either harmonization of labor standards across countries or reaching a multilateral agreement on minimum standards. More important, there are only a few examples of trade policy actions to counter low labor standards in a partner country. Based on history, it is perhaps fair to say that so far there has been "more talk and little action." The natural question then is what has changed in recent years to ignite the present round of debate?

An answer to this question is offered by changes in the economic conditions in developed countries and in the international economic climate during the 1980s and early 1990s. A high rate of unemployment in several European countries, especially among unskilled workers, and a decline in real wages of this category of labor in the United States (US) have generated pressures for remedial action. Based on what may be described at best as casual evidence, the political leadership has, in turn, found it convenient to attribute the decline in the demand for unskilled labor to "cheap" imports from developing countries. It has been further argued that such imports are "cheap" not necessarily because developing countries have comparative advantage in their production, but because they are manufactured utilizing unacceptably low labor standards. Since standards are higher in the richer countries, the cost of production is correspondingly higher, which means that their producers face "unfair" competition on account of "social dumping" from the poorer countries. This diagnosis has led developed country leadership to consider higher labor standards in developing countries' export industries as the solution to stagnant or declining wages and employment in their own economies.[1]

The US had insisted as early as 1986 that the subject of labor standards be included in the Preparatory Committee of the General Agreement on Tariffs and Trade (GATT) for the new round of trade negotiations. The initiative failed, however, and the subject was not included in the Ministerial Round that initiated the Uruguay Round[2] (Charnovitz 1987). The issue was revived during the North America Free Trade Agreement (NAFTA) negotiations and the US labor lobby was partially successful this time. Mexico had to enter into a supplementary agreement on labor standards in order to placate a hostile US Congress into approving the agreement. Meanwhile, the European Union (EU) member governments (excluding Britain) approved an elaborate social charter of voluntary workers' rights.

The success in obtaining an agreement on labor standards with Mexico and the adoption of the "Social Charter" in Europe paved the way for a renewal of the debate on labor standards in the closing stages of the Uruguay Round. The US and France demanded that a social clause be included in the mandate of the World Trade Organization (WTO). Though the initiative failed, it was agreed that the issue could be discussed by the preparatory committee of WTO.

The developing countries, especially the successful East Asian economies, are understandably disturbed by these developments. Most of these economies have been following an export promotion strategy, and their economic success to a large extent has been dependent on rapid export growth of manufactured products. In many instances, controls on their trade and payments regimes have been unilaterally dismantled and their economies have become progressively outward-oriented. In conjunction with other reforms, the outward-oriented strategy has also helped these economies attract large amounts of external resources, a significant proportion of which in recent years has been in the form of foreign direct investment. Against this background, any move to reduce export competitiveness by externally imposed standards is bound to be resisted. Labor standards have thus become a North-South issue with potentially dangerous implications for global trade liberalization.

Because the threat of trade sanctions on grounds of social dumping is real, the merits of the case for harmonization of standards across countries and its feasibility have recently been subject to scrutiny by trade theorists, labor market specialists, lawyers, and political scientists. Furthermore, since the issue has moral and humanitarian dimensions, views of political philosophers have also been brought to bear on it. This has, in turn, led to an improvement in our understanding of the economics and politics of the link between labor standards and trade policy.[3]

In this chapter, an attempt has been made to summarize the current debate on labor standards and their interaction with trade policy. The discussion is organized around five main questions. First, what constitutes labor standards and how are they enforced? Second, what is the welfare economics of labor standards in an open economy? Third, does the diversity of labor standards undermine the case for free trade? Fourth, what minimum understanding should the international community aim at in order to avoid trade-related disputes? Finally, if harmonization must be achieved, what are the right mechanisms for it, and what should be the institutional mechanism for achieving it?

Definition and Enforcement of Labor Standards

There is considerable ambiguity regarding which aspects of working conditions should be included in labor standards and what their minimum levels should be. As a part of its definition, the US Department of Labor emphasizes freedom of association, the right of labor to organize and bargain collectively, prohibition of forced labor, minimum age for employment, and setting acceptable conditions of work. The last of these is defined to include a decent standard of living for workers and their families, a work week not exceeding 48 hours, specified annual paid holiday, and minimum conditions for the protection of the safety and health of workers.[4] The European Union's "Social Charter" lists an even broader set of labor rights which include the right to vocational training and protection of elderly and disabled persons. The International Labour Organisation (ILO) has 174 Conventions covering a wide range of labor standards. These Conventions have evolved over the last 75 years through a multilateral process and have been voluntarily ratified by individual member states' legislatures.

Enforcement of labor standards is up to national governments. The standards for which national laws exist can be enforced through normal legislative process. But there is no equivalent process for the enforcement of ILO conventions. Historically, these have not been enforced through international threats of sanctions; rather, the motivating factor is persuasion and conviction among member states that the Conventions are worth enforcing to protect the interests of workers. The GATT's articles in general do not specify minimum labor standards as a precondition for conducting multilateral free trade. The only exception is Article XX (e) which permits import prohibition of goods made by prison labor. Even this limited application of labor standards in the GATT Agreement has a built-in protection for the most-favored nation (MFN) principle so that such restrictions "are not applied in a manner which would constitute a means of arbitrary or unjustifiable discrimination between countries when the same conditions prevail, or as a disguised restriction in international trade."

Some Simple Economics of Labor Standards

A rise in labor standards can affect production structure, and hence the volume and pattern of trade, primarily through two mechanisms. First, it can lower the supply of factors of production. For example, if the hours of labor are reduced or child labor is eliminated, labor supply falls. Similarly, higher occupational safety standards may require the use of capital for safer machines, for example, which may leave less capital for other production activity. Second, higher labor standards may lead to increased production costs. This is true of minimum wage laws, collective bargaining, and health regulations.

In dealing with the basic economics of labor standards, we will attempt to answer four questions.[5] First, does an improvement in labor standards raise a country's welfare? Second, is there an *economic* case for harmonization of labor standards internationally? Third, when there are multiple labor standards such as safety and child labor, and their choice is endogenous, can we raise one labor standard without affecting the other adversely? Finally, what is the effect of raising labor standards on the terms of trade? Because changes in the terms of trade redistribute incomes between countries, such effects can be important.

Answers to these questions depend critically on the type of model one chooses, initial conditions, and the nature of labor standard. Rather than launch into a detailed taxonomy of models and outcomes, it suffices to state that answers to these questions suggest that the arguments in favor of higher labor standards in developing countries do not necessarily follow from sound economic analysis. Regarding the first question, it is obvious that the answer depends on whether the initial level of labor standard is above or below the optimum. By definition, a rise in labor standards will increase or reduce welfare if the initial standard is below or above what the society regards as optimum. Any case for a rise in labor standard must therefore be based on the presumption that its initial level is below society's optimum. If there are externalities in the choice of labor standards in the sense that benefits of the standard are not fully internalized by those choosing the standard, the market may underprovide the standard and the case for welfare-improving intervention may exist. For instance, if the society views child labor as a social evil but firms hiring children do not, the market will produce an outcome in which children will be employed. Then, the introduction of laws against child labor will improve social welfare.

It is important to note, however, that the presence of externalities provides a case for intervention by the country's national government only, and cannot form the basis of intervention by another country's government. In order to establish an economic case for intervention by another country's government, we need a negative *transnational* externality. We have an exact parallel with environmental standards. As is well understood in the literature on that subject, pollution which is national in character does not provide an economic basis for intervention by another country; only transnational pollution offers the basis for intervention by another affected country. The same holds true for labor standards.

Next, let us examine the *economic* case for international harmonization. Once again, as with pollution, there is no reason for optimal labor standards to be identical across countries. In a country with low incomes and insufficient infrastructure for education, optimum minimum age of employment will be much lower than in a rich country with ample educational facilities. The same goes for the minimum wage. In a different but related context, a dramatic example is that of the poverty line. The poverty line varies vastly across countries according to the level of incomes, even after we adjust for international differences in price levels.

Turning to the third question raised above, suppose the government decides to raise the minimum age for workers. This will lower the supply of labor and raise the wage rate. It is then entirely possible that in order to remain competitive, firms will react by lowering the safety standards.[6] The point is that even when there is consensus on raising standards, the matter is not a straightforward one in that a partial approach may not yield an unambiguous, overall improvement in labor standards.

Finally, let us turn to the terms-of-trade effects. Once again, no generalizations are possible. Brown et al. (1996) analyze the terms-of-trade effects within the Heckscher-Ohlin model. In this model, if the impact of the standard is to reduce labor supply, regardless of where such a standard is introduced, the terms of trade of countries which are labor-abundant relative to the world will improve, and those of other countries will worsen. At constant terms of trade, a reduction in labor supply lowers the world output of the labor intensive good via the Rybczynski effect. This reduction in output raises the world price of the product. Because labor-abundant countries export the labor-intensive good, their terms of trade improve. The implication of this model is that capital-abundant countries will want low labor standards.[7] For labor-abundant countries, the answer is not clear-cut because the higher labor standard is also accompanied by a part of the labor force being forced out of employment. The terms of trade improve but real income may still fall due to the reduction in labor force.

More interesting terms-of-trade effects arise when we consider labor standards which are sector-specific. For instance, the use of child labor may be concentrated in certain sectors such as agriculture. An increase in the minimum age in this case will improve the country's terms of trade if the affected sector exports its product, and worsen them if it imports the product.

The above summary of some of the main results of the current theoretical literature on labor standards yields no general conclusions regarding the effects of labor standards on either welfare or terms of trade, and the results are dependent on the particular specification of the model. Summarizing the analysis of Brown et al. (1996), Srinivasan (1995) correctly notes,

> . . .the analysis of Brown, et al., confirms that the consequences of imposing labor standards are complex depending on the technology of production of goods *and* standards and whether or not standards are endogenous and, if they are, whether or not there is a market failure in that the equilibrium level determined by the market is socially optimal. Even if it is not, intervention need not correct the failure. As such, their analysis calls for extreme caution in advocating a social clause.

Labor Standards and the Case for Free Trade

Let us next turn to the question, does the inclusion of labor standards among choice variables weaken the case for free trade? Bhagwati and Srinivasan (1996) and Srinivasan (1995) consider this question in detail. The latter also develops a series of formal models to demonstrate that (i) endogeneity of labor standards does not detract from the case for free trade; and (ii) diversity of labor standards across nations is consistent with Pareto efficiency and free trade. Indeed, Srinivasan goes a step further and shows that even if the socially desirable labor standards, independent of how they are derived, are higher than those obtaining at a market equilibrium, and if the objective is global welfare maximization, the case for free trade is not diluted. As long as international income transfers are feasible, Pareto efficiency with the socially desired labor standards requires free trade. The simple point is that as long as the optimal conditions for labor standards are satisfied, there is no reason to distort the goods market. And if global welfare is the objective, Pareto efficiency requires that the marginal rate of substitution between each pair of goods for all consumers be equated to the marginal rate of transformation between the same pair of goods across all producers. This condition, in turn, requires that consumers and producers everywhere must face the same prices (free trade). It is only when Pareto-efficiency conditions for labor standards break down that global welfare will improve by a movement away from free trade.

The Case for Labor Standards: A Critical Evaluation

Keeping the above premises in mind, the following discussion will attempt to evaluate the various arguments for a rise in labor standards in the developing countries. The discussion can be organized conveniently around two broad topics: (i) the humanitarian argument and (ii) the national welfare argument.

The Humanitarian Argument

According to this argument, labor standards are a common-property resource. Welfare of a country's citizens depends not merely on labor standards within the country, but also those in other countries. Then if other countries, for whatever reason, adopt labor standards that are too low, this country may be justified in taking actions necessary to persuade the former to raise their labor standards. One such action may be trade policy sanctions.

There are many problems with this argument. To begin with, we may question whether labor standards are really a common property resource. Do the citizens of one country really care so much about what goes on in another country as may appear from public pronouncements? Bhagwati (1995), who offers a powerful critique of this argument, invokes Adam Smith thus,

> Let us suppose that the great empire of China, with its myriads of inhabitants, was swallowed up by an earthquake and let us consider how a man of humanity in Europe, who had no sort of connection with that part of the world, would be affected upon receiving intelligence of this dreadful calamity. He would, I imagine, first of all express very strongly his sorrow for the misfortune of that unhappy people, he would make many melancholy reflections upon the precariousness of human life . . . . And when all this fine philosophy was over, . . .he would pursue his business or pleasure. . .with the same ease and tranquillity as if no such accident had happened.

> The most frivolous disaster which could befall himself would occasion a more real disturbance. If he was to lose his little finger to-morrow, he would not sleep to-night; but provided he never saw them, he would snore with the most profound security over the ruin of a hundred million of his brethren.

The point which emerges from these passages is that in public pronounce-ments, concerns about labor standards in other countries are probably over-stated.

For a moment, suppose we take these concerns on their face value. Assume further that the market generates a suboptimal level of labor stan-dards in a country. Is another country then justified in imposing trade sanc-tions aimed at raising labor standards? The answer is in the negative. The first issue is that, as Srinivasan (1995) points out, trade sanctions are not the first-best instrument and will fail to yield a Pareto efficient outcome. To achieve a Pareto-efficient outcome, one must find the source of the market failure and attack it directly. If that is done, free trade need not be tampered with.

But even if we admit that the first-best action is not possible, who should bear the cost of raising the suboptimal labor standards? If developed country demands are made on moral grounds as assumed, those countries should be willing to compensate the country being subjected to such de-mands for the lost output from higher standards. Thus, for instance, when the US adopted a set of labor standards, the accompanying loss of output was viewed as an acceptable cost of achieving a desirable social objective. If it is now felt that the social objective of the US extends to seeing the same standards established in the rest of the world, then clearly the US should be willing to bear the cost of the lost output in the countries adopting higher standards. In the absence of such willingness, it is difficult to take seriously the moral basis of the demand for higher standards.

National Welfare Argument

A large number of arguments for the link between trade policy and labor standards are driven by national considerations and are, deep down, arguments for protection. One such argument is that lower standards in the exporting countries (primarily low-income countries) give them a competi-tive edge, especially in products that use unskilled labor. Hence, the argu-ment goes, that workers in the import competing sectors of high-standards countries need protection to prevent unemployment and to bring the affected sector on a "level playing field." This can be achieved either by insisting that higher standards be adopted in low-standards countries, failing which, imports from low-standards countries should be restricted.[8] Apart from finding an instant remedy to the existing unemployment, restricting imports from low-standards countries are also seen as a solution to a wider set of problems that could arise from inaction. One such problem is that investment (mainly by multinational corporations) would be attracted by the lower-standards developing countries because of lower cost of production. The outward flow of capital would create further loss of jobs in the high-standards countries. Indeed, according to some analysts, this phenomenon is already taking place on a significant scale. The following quote from an article published in *Foreign Affairs* is a telling example (Collingsworth, Williams Gould, and Harvey 1994):

> The reality is plain enough. Nike is making its famously expensive athletic shoes in Indonesia, where its women workers labor long hours for a meager $38 a month. WalMart, K-Mart, and Sears, the great American retail icons, are having their shirts made in Bangladesh by culturally passive Islamic women toiling 60 hours a week and making less than $30 a month. The companies sell the shirts in the US at US prices. The labor cost per shirt is roughly four cents. The multinationals assert the need to lower costs in order to remain competitive, but their main competitors are all there in Bangladesh as well, enjoying the same windfall profits of cheap labor.

Needless to add, such assertions are made without any attempt at quantification (barring causal empiricism), the main purpose being not to analyze a problem, but to suggest sensational and appealing solutions.

Another fear often expressed by high-standards countries is that competitive pressure emanating on account of free trade with low-standards countries would force labor-intensive industries to lower their own standards, a phenomenon referred to as "race to the bottom." According to this argument, labor in rich countries would also become poor through a destructive downward bidding spiral.

There is a broad consensus among economists that attempts to establish linkages between labor standards and trade policy, represents an ominous trend toward rationalizing protectionist motives. There is further cause for concern that the labor standards controversy is being stirred up so soon after the conclusion of the tedious and procrastinated negotiations of the Uruguay Round. Jagdish Bhagwati's paper (1995) in Chapter 2 of this book has examined many of these issues. In broad terms, competition from developing countries' exports and the consequent threat to jobs have been grossly overplayed in the industrialized countries. Real wages of unskilled workers have been declining steadily in developed countries for almost two decades due mainly to rapid technological change. Low wage competition from developing countries is probably only a marginal contribution to this phenomenon. Using the Stolper-Samuelson result, Bhagwati has analyzed the effects of these two distinct causes by posing the question: if competition from developing-country exports was responsible for declining real wages of unskilled labor, then the prices of labor-intensive goods should have fallen. US data provide little support for this hypothesis (Lawrence and Slaughter 1993; Bhagwati and Dahejia 1994).

Furthermore, there is little systematic evidence that foreign direct investment in developing countries is being attracted primarily by lower labor standards. This is not surprising because several studies have pointed out that, adjusting for productivity of labor, real wages are not significantly lower than in developed countries. There could also be other locational disadvantages such as inadequate infrastructure, which could outweigh the advantage on account of divergence in standards. Nor is there any compelling evidence that industrialized countries are being forced to lower their standards because of competitive pressures from imports produced under conditions of lower labor standards.[9]

Developing countries view attempts to link labor standards and trade policy with considerable suspicion and no different from disguised protectionism. The views of Prime Minister Mahathir (1994) of Malaysia probably sum up the feelings of several developing countries on this issue:

> Western governments openly propose to eliminate the competitive edge of East Asia. The recent proposal for a worldwide minimum wage is a blatant example. Westerners know that this is the sole comparative advantage of the developing countries. All other comparative advantages (technology, capital, rich domestic markets, legal frameworks, management and marketing networks) are with the developed states. It is obvious that the professed concern about workers' welfare is motivated by selfish interest. Sanctimonious pronouncements on humanitarian, democratic and environmental issues are likely to be motivated by a similar selfish desire to put as many obstacles as possible in the way of anyone attempting to catch up and compete with the West.

Developing countries also feel that given their state of development, demands for raising labor standards amount to an unnecessary intrusion in their internal affairs and questions their national sovereignty in a blatantly crude manner. On some of the specific issues raised in the debate, developing countries assert that the often repeated allegation that they are exploiting "child labor" to gain a competitive edge is misplaced, and the allegation reflects an inadequate understanding of their problems. According to their view, "child labor" is, of course, not desirable and should be discouraged. But economic necessities force parents to utilize the labor of children and the issue should be viewed sympathetically, especially since the alternative to using child labor is exacerbation of poverty and hunger.

The developing countries are also unconvinced that the demand for freedom of workers to form labor unions and engage in collective bargaining is of particular relevance in their current stage of development. They argue that much of the labor in a majority of developing countries is employed in rural, agricultural activities or in the urban, informal sector where unionization has little relevance. Furthermore, past experience suggests that in countries where the freedom to unionize has been permitted and exercised such as in India, the labor unions have tended to promote the interests of a minority of privileged workers who are employed in the formal sector, ignoring a vast majority of unprivileged workers in the informal sector (Srinivasan 1995; Fields 1994).

Mechanisms for Achieving Comparable Standards

Given that imposition of higher labor standards on developing countries has the potential of creating a major North-South rift, what are the mechanisms by which labor standards in the poorer countries can be raised? Several suggestions have been made, some of which are appealing, but not easily applicable. Two such suggestions are (i) the higher-standards countries should compensate the lower-standards countries if they want higher standards imposed (Srinivasan, 1995), and (ii) the higher-standards countries should permit free immigration so that "people everywhere seek the best possible labor standards wherever in the world they may be found" (Fields 1994).[10] Appealing as these suggestions are on rational and ethical grounds, they are clearly unrealistic in the current international environment.[11] Indeed if such solutions were even remotely feasible it would not be necessary to debate the issue of linkages between labor standards and trade policy.

Another suggestion made by Jagdish Bhagwati relates to applying the "Sullivan Principles" to US multinationals in their operations in developing countries. Under this approach, the US should legislate that their multinationals apply the same environmental and labor standards as they do in their home operations or to put it in his own words, "Do in Rome as you do in New York–not as Romans do." Even if we ignore the problems

215

of implementing the proposal, what would the proposal achieve? Actually very little, except to partially convince the powerful lobbies in the US that investment is not being "sucked" into the developing countries on account of lower cost considerations. But would it not amount to accepting intellectual defeat from the proponents whose views are not particularly rational?[12] Even on the face of it, such a proposal would further distort the labor markets in developing countries and impose work ethics which are culturally alien and incompatible with the stage of development (like an eight-hour work day and a forty-hour work week), especially if people are willing to work harder to improve their economic circumstances. More importantly, unless the agreement is rigidly implemented both by the industrialized countries as a group (since imposing it, only the US multinationals would put them at a competitive disadvantage) and by the recipient developing countries, the proposal is unlikely to be workable. In addition, there would be an incentive for some of the poorer countries to be lax on implementation and a competitive downward spiral to bid for investment would soon create a situation where the proposal loses much of its appeal.

There is another indirect way of bridging the intercountry gap in labor standards via methods that accelerate and sustain economic growth in the poorer countries. Empirical evidence suggests that economic growth increases both employment and real wages; and rising real wages in turn raise labor standards. This is borne out in the detailed study of Gary Fields (1995) on the close linkage between real wages and growth of real per capita gross national product (GNP) in Hong Kong; Korea; Singapore; and Taipei,China. As shown in Table 1 below, once these economies had attained nearly full employment, real labor earnings grew at least as fast as real per capita GNP. Gary Fields thus observes that the experience of these economies shows that "growth raised labor standards: real minimum wages were increased, unemployment insurance systems were instituted, social protection systems were created and collective bargaining grew in importance." This phenomenon is, however, not confined to Asian economies. A study by the Organisation for Economic Co-operation and Development (1994) also confirms that total wage and nonwage benefits are closely related to per capita GDP (expressed in dollar purchasing-power-parity) for the European countries.

Even though the evidence is compelling that rising per capita incomes and labor standards are correlated, and that as the divergence of per capita incomes between countries is narrowed, so will intercountry labor standards, it does little to address the problems that arise in the interim period when the poorer countries are trying to catch up with the richer countries and free trade is an essential factor facilitating the process. So, is there any mechanism which can resolve the labor standards "problem" in the interim period? The answer is unfortunately no. The only approach that can be adopted is that the richer countries attempt to mold public opinion along rational lines by explaining to the labor unions that technical innovations in their own economies are largely responsible for unemployment and declining real wages of unskilled labor. Restricting trade with the poorer countries is not a solution as it will only end up making both sets of countries worse off. In tandem with influencing public opinion, the industrialized countries could also adopt measures to train the existing labor force so that they can be absorbed in expanding high-technology industries. While all this sounds fine on paper, the actual obstacles of putting these proposals into practice are bound to be difficult. Labor standards controversies could persist.

Table 1. Economic Growth and Earnings Growth in Four Newly Industrializing Economies in the 1980s

		Growth of Real GNP or GDP Per Capita (percent)	Growth of Real Earnings (percent)
Republic of Korea	1980-1990	+121.8[1]	+115.8[3]
Taipei,China	1980-1990	+88.0[1]	+102.7[4]
Hong Kong	1980-1990	+64.2[2]	+60.0[4]
Singapore	1980-1990	+77.5[2]	+79.8[5]

[1] GNP Growth
[2] GDP Growth
[3] Mining and Manufacturing
[4] Manufacturing
[5] All Industries

Source: G. Fields, 1995.

Minimum Understanding on Labor Standards

Because harmonization of labor standards is neither feasible nor desirable, and attempting to narrow diversity through trade policy measures is inappropriate, is there any minimum understanding possible between the rich and poor countries on this issue so that the existing tensions are eased? A minimum understanding should be such that it is acceptable to all parties (and hence scope for a multilateral agreement), feasible to implement, and does not attempt to use trade policy measures to ensure enforcement except in extreme situations.

In an effort to resolve the current labor standards controversy, Gary Fields (1994) draws a distinction between "labor rights" and "labor standards." According to this distinction, basic labor rights are akin to fundamental human rights and should therefore be enforceable in every country. Such a list could conceivably include a minimum set of workers' rights such as (i) slavery and or indentured labor should be banned; (ii) labor should be exposed to unsafe or unhealthy working conditions only with the full knowledge of the risks involved; (iii) child labor should be dissuaded contingent on family financial circumstances; and (iv) labor should have the freedom of association in the workplace and the right to organize and bargain collectively with employers.

Beyond these basic labor rights there should be no attempts at imposing harmonization in labor standards across countries. Even achieving a consensus on these basic rights may be difficult. Further, there are less chances of these "basic rights" being universally accepted and implemented if they are forced upon the poorer countries. In addition, in so far as possible, countries unable to adhere to labor rights should not be penalized through trade sanctions. Rather, the approach should be to build international consensus in favor of universal labor rights and, persuasion, as opposed to trade sanctions, should be used to change the undesirable practices of certain countries. Of course, in extreme circumstances, where a country's political leadership uses force to flagrantly deny labor their basic rights, the international community can galvanize together and, through an appropriate multilateral forum, impose trade sanctions.[13]

Institutional Mechanism

Since trade policy is not the appropriate manner in dealing with diversity in labor standards, then clearly WTO is not the appropriate organization to multilaterally impose minimum labor rights. If labor-related issues do come under the jurisdiction of WTO, as has been recently demanded by the US and France, then that will clearly amount to endorsing the linkage between trade policy and labor standards. In such an event, it is more than likely that the avenues for protectionism would once again be open for abuse.

To enforce the minimum labor rights through a consensus approach, the appropriate institution would be ILO. According to Srinivasan (1995), ILO may even be able to get broad-based support for this activity because

> ... the consensus approach of the ILO and its consultative and assistance (technical and other) mechanisms that attempt to persuade and help national governments enforce standards are likely to make a resisting government lose support of their [sic] own citizens. On the other hand, the sanctions imposed with the sledge-hammer of a social clause in the WTO are likely to unite the same citizens behind their governments in resisting what would be seen as foreign bullying.

Conclusion

The main results from the theoretical literature on labor standards can be summarized as follows:

- ◆ A priori, we cannot say that an improvement in labor standards in a country will improve welfare in that country.

- ◆ Diverse labor standards across countries are entirely consistent with global welfare maximization even when no intercountry transfers of income are possible. Indeed, in the presence of international diversity in income levels, diversity in labor standards is likely to be necessary to achieve a Pareto optimum.

- ◆ An improvement in labor standards along one dimension can very well be accompanied by a deterioration in labor standards along another dimension. For example, an increase in the minimum age for work which raises the wage levels can lead to a reduction in the safety standards chosen by firms. Thus, even if a consensus is evolved regarding minimum labor standards along some dimensions, implementation along those dimensions can be accompanied by a deterioration of labor standards along other dimensions.

- ◆ The terms-of-trade effects of higher labor standards are ambiguous in general. But if such a change is favorable to the developing countries, the presumption is that it will worsen for the devel-

219

oped countries. The effect of such a change on the overall welfare will be negative on developed countries and ambiguous on developing countries.

- The inclusion of labor standards into the analysis does not undermine the case for free trade.

Given these conclusions, it should come as no surprise that the economic basis for developed country demands for higher labor standards in developing countries is not convincing. The humanitarian case is revealed to be weak in that none of the countries demanding higher labor standards is willing to compensate the countries on whom such demands are being made for their losses.

In view of the fact that the terms-of-trade effects of higher labor standards in developing countries on developed countries are likely to be negative, the effect on their national welfare will also be negative. Therefore, the demand for higher labor standards cannot be justified even on grounds of maximizing national welfare. This leaves internal income distribution as the primary culprit for developed country demands. For instance, within the Heckscher-Ohlin model, higher labor standards reduce the supply of labor intensive goods, raise their prices, and hence benefit workers. Labor standards which turn out to be sector specific, benefit developed country producers in those sectors at the expense of developing country exporters within the same sectors.

Theoretical arguments apart, harmonization of labor standards across countries is neither feasible nor practical. The only practical solution is that countries voluntarily agree on a minimum code of "labor rights" which can be enforced by ILO through a process of multilateral negotiations, using persuasion, as opposed to threats of trade sanctions. Labor standards raise a complex web of controversies and it is unlikely that the underlying issues would be resolved in the near future. What is important, however, is that labor standards and trade policy measures should be kept apart in policy debates.

Notes

[1] That politicians are under pressure on such issues is evident from the side agreement that President Clinton had to negotiate on labor standards and environment before the US Congress ratified NAFTA. Similarly, the European Union's "Social Charter" endorsed by all members, except Britain, contains a 47-measure implementation program. In order to impose higher labor standards on the poorest members, the EU's "Structural and Cohesion Fund" transfers compensatory money to Ireland, Spain, Portugal, and Greece (Steil 1994).

[2] Some authors have argued that the US multinationals are the main culprits as "they successfully blunted attempts to include meaningful labor standards in NAFTA and prevent the inclusion of any social clause" in GATT and the European Community Charter (Collingsworth, Gould, and Harvey 1994).

[3] Major research projects are under way, for example the Bhagwati-Hudec Ford Foundation-financed project (Bhagwati and Hudec 1996) on the analytical problems raised by the growing demands to remove domestic standards differences prior to freeing trade among nations.

[4] The US position has not been consistent on specification of minimum labor standards. For example, in the past, the US has maintained that "unfair" labor standards in the export industries abroad nullify or impair the benefits of trade under GATT. However, "unfair" in this context has been defined as maintenance of labor standards below which the productivity of the industry or economy would justify (Charnovitz 1987). Even if we ignore that measurement problem, implementing such a demand would inevitably introduce considerable amount of arbitrariness. Furthermore, the proposition seems to suggest that diversity in standards is both natural and acceptable. Yet the current US position appears to suggest harmonization of standards across countries.

[5] This section draws on Brown et al. (1996), who, in turn, draw heavily on Alam (1992).

[6] Brown et al. (1996) make this point formally.

[7] Interestingly, this result is exactly opposite of what the capital abundant (industrialized) countries are wanting.

[8] Import restrictions can be in the form of tariffs or quotas, fines as in the NAFTA agreement, or denial of Generalized System of Preferences. In extreme cases, trade sanctions could also be used against countries, such as against the erstwhile apartheid regime in South Africa.

[9] Proponents of harmonization of standards who base their arguments that trade and investment will shift to low labor standards countries often tend to confuse between absolute and comparative advantage. The theory of comparative advantage would suggest that not all industries will be relocated from high- to low-standards countries.

[10] The impracticality of these suggestions in the current international economic climate should be evident from the fact that most OECD countries are cutting down on external aid budgets and are simultaneously tightening immigration laws.

[11] It could be argued that compensation may not be unrealistic; after all, the EU's richer countries compensate their poorer partners. In theory, it is possible that richer countries could compensate developing countries to pull up their labor standards. But this has not even been promised to Mexico for joining NAFTA.

[12] Bhagwati accepts that this proposal violates the principle that "diversity is legitimate."

[13] The effectiveness of trade sanctions has, however, been questioned (see Hafbauer, Schott, and Eliott 1990).

References

Alam, A., 1992. "Labor Standards and Comparative Advantage." Unpublished doctoral dissertation. Columbia University.

Anderson, Kym, 1996. "The Entwining of Trade Policy with Environmental and Labor Standards." In W. Martin and A. Winters, eds., *The Uruguay Round and the Developing Economies*. Cambridge, Great Britain: Cambridge University Press.

Bhagwati, J., 1995. "The World Trading Systems: The New Challenges." Keynote Address delivered at the Asian Development Bank Conference on Emerging Global Trading Environment and Developing Asia, May, Manila.

Bhagwati, J., and V. Dahejia, 1994. "Freer Trade and Wages of the Unskilled: Is Marx Striking Again?" In J. Bhagwati and M. Kasters, eds., *Trade and Wages: Leveling Wages Down?* Washington, D.C.: American Enterprise Institute.

Bhagwati, J., and R. Hudec, eds., 1996. *Fair Trade and Harmonization: Prerequisites for Free Trade?* Vols. 1 and 2. Cambridge, Massachusetts: MIT Press.

Bhagwati, J. N., and T. N. Srinivasan, 1996. "Trade and the Environment: Does Environmental Diversity Detract from the Case for Free Trade?" In J. Bhagwati and R. Hudec, eds., *Fair Trade and Harmonization: Prerequisites for Free Trade?* Cambridge, Massachusetts: MIT Press.

Brown, D. K., A. V. Deardorff, and R. M. Stern, 1996. "International Labor Standards and Trade: A Theoretical Analysis." In J. Bhagwati and R. Hudec, eds., *Fair Trade and Harmonization: Prerequisites for Free Trade?* Cambridge, Massachusetts: MIT Press.

Charnovitz, S., 1987. "The Influence of International Labor Standards on the World Trading Regime: A Historical Overview." *International Labor Review* 126(5):565-84.

Collingsworth, T., T. Williams Gould, and P. J. Harvey, 1994. "Time for a Global New Deal." *Foreign Affairs* 73(1):8-13.

Fields, G. S., 1994. "Labor Standards and International Trade." Paper prepared for the Informal OECD Trade Committee Meeting on Trade and Labor Standards, September, The Hague.

———, 1995. "Changing Labor Market Conditions and Economic Development in Hong Kong, Korea, Singapore and Taiwan." *World Bank Economic Review* 8(3):395-414.

Hafbauer, G. G., J. J. Schott, and K. A. Eliott, 1990. *Economic Sanctions Reconsidered.* Washington, D.C.: Institute for International Economies.

Lawrence, R. Z., and M. J. Slaughter, 1993. "International Trade and American Wages in the 1980s: Giant Sucking Sound or Small Hiccup?" *Brookings Papers* (Microeconomics) 2:161-210.

Mahathir bin Mohammed, 1994. "East Asia Will Find its Own Road to Democracy." *International Herald Tribune*, 17 May.

Organisation for Economic Co-operation and Development, 1994. *Employment Outlook.* Paris.

Steil, B., 1994. "Social Correctness is the New Protectionism." *Foreign Affairs* (January/February):14-20.

Srinivasan, T. N., 1995. "International Trade and Labor Standards." Yale University.

224-27

Comments on "International Labor Standards and Trade Policy"

by

Kym Anderson

D
r. Rao's survey of this issue has the clear bottom line that there is an even more tenuous connection between trade policy and labor standards than there is between trade and the environment. There are numerous similarities between the two sets of issues, but also some important differences.

The chapter begins by asking what is driving the debate and why have labor standards surfaced again at this time. As to the first question, Dr. Rao makes clear that the issue is mostly driven by competitiveness concerns of those producers in high-wage industrial countries whose industries are intensive in the use of low-skill workers, for it tends to be in those industries where high labor standards raise costs of production most. Owners of firms in such industries in high-standard countries see themselves as having three options: they could lobby against such standards at home, they could demand protection from imports from lower-standard countries, and/or they could lobby for higher labor standards abroad. That implies a country's choice of labor standards is not independent of the standards chosen by other countries, nor is the country's trade policy independent of its labor standards.

Why has the issue suddenly arisen? Dr. Rao suggests it is because of poor labor market performance in the US and the EU, especially for low-skilled workers. He also notes that it has cropped up before when the global trading system has been in the news, for example at the end of the Tokyo Round; the end of the Uruguay Round is just another opportunity for labor advocates (bolstered by the success of getting labor standards into the North American Free Trade Agreement [NAFTA]) and the European Union's Social Clause to voice their views again at a multilateral level. An additional reason is that as traditional barriers to trade and investment (including transportation and communication costs) fall over time, firms and especially employees/unions perceive lower labor standards abroad as becoming relatively more important determinants of cost differences across plant locations. A further reason associated with lower costs of international communication is that information for nongovernmental organizations on labor standards abroad is becoming ever-more available. Both of these reasons ensure that the concerns about labor standards abroad are likely to continue to grow over time, other things being equal. To what extent is there a parallel claim with the trade/environment issue that international spillovers exist which justify labor standards being on the World Trade Organization agenda? Most would say not at all, because they do not perceive any physical spillovers of the CFC or carbon type that may justify intervention (in those cases to reduce ozone depletion or global warming, respectively). Dr. Rao mentions in his chapter, but gives little credence to, the possibility of a parallel in the form of humanitarian concerns stretching beyond national borders (what might be called "psychological spillovers"). A person may be upset that someone in another country is working under poor conditions, or that politicians in that other country are not putting their people's wishes for higher labor standards into law, for example.

Even so, Dr. Rao makes the point that there are only very limited circumstances in which multilateral trade measures are worthy of consideration as sticks or carrots for encouraging other countries to raise their standards. One such circumstance might be when a country adopts attitudes to people that are abhorrent to the rest of the world (for example, slavery or apartheid). Another might be if there comes a point where a significant negotiating party refuses to sign a trade agreement without such provisions, as happened with the NAFTA negotiations. Is it possible that no lower-cost way other than trade may be available to those countries with humanitarian concerns and wishing to influence the labor policies of low-standard countries? It seems unlikely, given the nontrade options available. These include firms, under pressure from consumers and shareholders, choosing to boycott products from producers with low labor standards; the International Labour Organisation persuading signatories to its conventions to comply to at least minimum standards; and the Organisation for Economic Co-operation and Development promoting its code of employment behavior among multinational corporations. Even if all those options achieved little, still no action is warranted if trade sanctions were more costly to the rest of the world than the psychological benefit they would provide to the proponents of higher standards. And even if the costs were less than the value of the benefits, there is the distributional question of who should bear the cost.

Dr. Rao suggests it should be those pushing for higher standards, but that begs the practical question of how and from whom to collect and how and to whom to distribute such compensation, as only a small group in each set of countries is directly affected. A far better option would seem to be to put more effort into persuading people in high-standard countries that this issue is little more than traditional protectionism made more socially respectable by dressing it in humanitarian garb. That could involve pointing out that forcing higher standards on poorer countries simply drives labor in those countries from the formal to the informal sector. For example, children are more inclined to turn to stealing or begging and young women to prostitution or earlier marriage if paid employment is denied them. And we know from Harris-Todaro theory that unemployment may rise if there is a rise in only the formal sector's real wage (incorporating the value of higher labor standards). Further-more, if the import competition from labor intensive manufacturers in developing countries has relatively little to do with the poor labor market performance for low-skill workers in industrial countries, then protect-ing the latter from such competition would do little to improve the lot of those workers, notwithstanding the factor-price equalization and Stolper-Samuelson theorems. According to Dr. Rao, those workers are doing poorly mainly because of labor-saving technological change which is lowering the demand for low-skilled workers. One might add that the demand for high-skill workers is rising rapidly. In fact, business schools are referring to gold-collar workers (as compared with blue- or white-collar workers). Who are these gold-collar workers? They are people whose skill is to make good use of new opportunities, of disequilibria in markets. And the new opportunities currently before us have to do with the information and communication revolutions. People who can efficiently keep abreast of those developments and make profitable use of this ever-cheaper information are going to be highly rewarded. This is not to deny that many people are taking steps to build their human capital stocks; rather, it is suggesting the demand for such skills has been growing faster than the supply. That skill upgrading means that while it may be true that the relative wage of low-skill workers remains low in the US, it is also true that many people are shifting themselves out of that category and becoming higher-skilled workers through get-ting more education and training. Pressing these points more forcefully in industrial countries should help diffuse the focus on trade policy as a remedy for sluggishness in labor market adjustment.

Finally, what does this chapter imply for our future research agenda? It would be helpful if we had empirical evidence of the extent to which economic growth and trade liberalization in developing Asia have been accompanied by rising labor standards. That would expose the folly of suggesting trade barriers as a remedy for raising labor standards, for it would be clear that exactly the opposite is needed to improve labor standards in developing countries, namely, better access to industrial country markets.

CHAPTER 7
INTERNATIONAL TRADE AND THE
ASIAN ENVIRONMENT

DOUGLAS H. BROOKS
ECONOMICS AND DEVELOPMENT RESOURCE CENTER
ASIAN DEVELOPMENT BANK

The Asian environment sustains more than half of the world's population, the majority of its poor population who depend on the rural environment for their survival, and a large share of the world's biodiversity. In recent years, Asian trade has expanded more rapidly than that in any other region. This rapid growth in trade, which is expected to continue in the post-Uruguay Round trading environment, affects and is affected by the natural environment. Improved understanding of these interactions can help in formulation of better policies that influence trade and the environment.

This chapter briefly considers the justifications for linking trade and environmental policy, and discusses concerns in both developing and developed countries of environmental policy effects on trade as well as concerns that developing countries are particularly vulnerable to trade effects on the environment. It then examines the situation in developing Asia today and the outlook for greater interaction of trade and the environment in developing Asia.

Interactions Between Trade and Environment

International environmental concerns generally relate to externalities in production, consumption, shipping and handling, or waste disposal of traded goods. To internalize the externalities, the solution preferred on efficiency grounds is to target the source of the externality, such as through the "polluter pays" principle.[1] Trade policy serves as a relatively inefficient method of accounting for environmental externalities, yet a large number of individuals and organizations advocate links between trade and environmental policies. The result is often an odd alliance of liberal environmentalists, interested in preserving natural habitats, and conservative business people with protectionist commercial interests.

Advocates of using trade policy for environmental aims, at least those advocates with environmental rather than protectionist goals, frequently expect the gains from environmental quality improvements to outweigh the costs in terms of foregone gains from trade. Inefficiency in targeting trade instruments on activities affecting the environment suggests this expectation is unrealistic, yet the practice persists. Environmentalists advocate trade and environmental policy linkages primarily for three reasons: (i) poorly defined property rights may lead to suboptimal use and trade of environmentally intensive resources; (ii) difficulties exist in targeting foreign sources of negative externalities with domestic policies; and

231

(iii) there is no suitable alternative forum in which to argue for international environmental action.

In addition, there are fears that developing countries are particularly vulnerable to environmental effects of trade through influences of economic growth, concentration of production on environmentally intensive products or methods, and the migration of polluting industries or technologies from more developed to less-developed countries where environmental standards are likely to be more lax. It is interesting to note that this latter argument is the reverse of that considered in labor discussions, in which more developed countries fear the loss of employment from emigration of labor-intensive industries to less-developed, lower-wage destinations.

There is also concern in both more developed and less-developed economies about the effects of environmental policies on trade, although for different reasons. In less-developed economies this concern is usually directed toward perceived green protectionism among more developed countries in which ostensibly environmentally directed standards are used as a form of nontariff barrier to trade. In more developed economies, there is fear of green protectionism among developed competitors, and fears of eco-dumping, or a "race-to-the-bottom" in environmental standards on the part of developing competitors.[2] Despite vocal lobbies and vigorous political activity warning of environmental dangers of trade, there is more anecdotal than strong evidence that multinational corporations relocate production activity to follow lower environmental standards, or that these standards have influenced competitiveness. In fact, most foreign direct investment remains targeted on more developed countries with relatively higher environmental standards.

Comparative Advantage, Environmental Endowments, and Property Rights

A country's comparative advantage in environmentally intensive goods depends on, among other factors, its natural resource endowments, climate, distance to neighboring countries, and length of shared borders. It also depends on the density, health, wealth, demographic structure, and preferences of its population, including their valuation of environmental resources and amenities, their willingness and ability to pay for conservation, and their tolerance of pollution. Exploitation of natural resources may be sustainable such as in eco-tourism and logging carefully coordinated with reforestation, or unsustainable such as when reducing stocks of endangered species and rampant deforestation. Exploitation depends on how property rights are assigned, the level and pace of society's economic and

technological development, and possible profit margins and social preferences concerning the environment.

Changes in the environment can also influence trade patterns. Trade
raises welfare only when the gains from trade more than compensate for
environmental degradation. Conversely, potential environmental policies
should balance environmental improvements against reductions in the gains
from trade at the margin. Even if all environmental costs could be properly
assessed and internalized, there would still be connections between trade
and the environment. There is trade in endangered species, trade in toxic
waste, and trade in other environmentally hazardous products.

Investigating openness to trade and environmental quality, Lucas
(1994) found that total toxic emission release-intensity rises significantly
as export propensity rises, irrespective of population size. This also holds
true for volatile organic compound air pollutants and carbon monoxide
emissions. On the other hand, suspended water pollutants, suspended and
fine air particulates, and nitrogen dioxide emissions all decline significantly
as export propensity rises, irrespective of population size. Bioaccumulative
metals, sulfur dioxide, and lead released into the atmosphere were found
to decline with export intensity for countries with small populations and
rise for those with larger populations. In the Philippines it has been found
that the major environmental offenders are the government, households,
forestry, and agriculture, and not the industrial sector (Intal and Quintos
1994). These results emphasize the complex interactions of related scientific
and economic principles, and the dangers of expecting simple relationships
between trade and the environment.

Whether or not less-developed countries have a comparative
advantage in environmentally intensive exports is a subject of considerable
debate. In this regard, the delineation of property rights affecting differences
between apparent and actual comparative advantages and gains from trade
may play an important role. Chichilnisky (1994) has shown in a two-country
model that even identically endowed economies can find reasons to trade
if one country has poorly defined property rights. In the presence of
decreasing returns to scale, that country will produce and export
environmentally intensive goods at a price below marginal social cost since
full production costs are not internalized. It will therefore tend to overuse
the environment and worsen resource misallocation, with trade leading to
price equalization with one country overproducing and the other
overconsuming relative to what is Pareto optimal.[3]

More complete assignment of property rights will help in internalizing
environmental costs, although the internalization may itself be costly. When
property rights are incompletely assigned and trade policies are

implemented, there is potential for rent-seeking and associated income transfers, with likely regressive consequences.

Economic Growth, Trade, and the Environment

Richly endowed countries can raise their incomes, and usually do so with assistance from gains from trade. A graph positing a measure of environmental degradation per unit of output as the dependent variable and income per capita as the independent variable exhibits an "inverted U" shape, with environmental quality per unit of output deteriorating to a per capita income level of roughly $5,000, and then improving again (Radetzki 1992). Factors explaining this relationship are the high-income elasticity of demand for environmental quality, shifts in the composition of economic activity from predominantly primary sector through manufacturing to service sectors, and extension of property rights.

Lucas (1994) finds a similar "inverted U" pattern in relation to unit of gross national product (GNP) for emission intensities of total toxic releases, bioaccumulative metals, suspended water pollutants, and volatile, organic compound air pollutants, with varying turning points of income all significantly above $5,000. He finds the opposite pattern for nitrogen dioxide emissions, and consistently negative relationships between income per capita and carbon monoxide emissions, suspended particles in the air, sulfur dioxide emissions, and releases of lead into the atmosphere. Thus, trade may have indirect effects on the environment through income growth that are not monotonic.

While toxic intensity of manufacturing *per unit* of GNP may eventually decline, total pollution is likely to continue rising. Hettige, et al. (1992) found no "inverted U" for pollutant intensity per unit of industrial output, and their results indicate that "pollution intensity of manufacturing output rises steadily with income, at most tapering off somewhat at very high incomes." They also found that toxic intensity in less developed country manufacturing grew most quickly after the advent of stricter Organisation for Economic Co-operation and Development (OECD) environmental regulations, consistent with an industrial displacement effect on dirtier industries.

Using a simple, static two-country model of North-South trade in which income-induced differences in environmental policy create incentives to trade and environmental quality, is considered a normal good. Copeland and Taylor (1994) demonstrate that the country with higher income will adopt greater environmental protection measures and specialize in producing goods with relatively lower pollution intensity. Free trade is seen to increase world pollution, but to increase welfare when the pattern of specialization is based solely on differences in environmental policy. In a finding supportive of international aid, unilateral transfers from North to South are found to reduce world pollution levels by narrowing the income differential.

With the high growth rates that have come to be considered common in Asia, economies may reach a stage of improving environmental quality sooner than they would with slower growth. This is not to suggest that economic growth alone will be sufficient to protect the environment and guarantee achievement of elusive sustainable development. However, when the environment is viewed as a resource in future production, pollution can decline during economic growth since the environment has an opportunity cost in future production (Lopez 1992).

The Product Life Cycle

Besides the indirect effects of trade on the environment through general income growth resulting from gains from trade, there are four basic avenues in the life cycle of traded products for environmental degradation to arise through international trade. These are through the production, including resource extraction, shipping or handling, consumption, and waste recycling or disposal of the product. That a traded product may have effects on the environment at more than one stage of its existence argues strongly for a life-cycle approach to management of environmental consequences.

First, in the production process, there may be environmental danger from traded goods in their processes and production methods (PPMs). OECD (1994) distinguishes between product-related PPMs, where the environmental danger is through consumption externalities which are rare in the environmental realm, and nonproduct-related PPMs. While, in general, the General Agreement on Tariffs and Trade (GATT), now succeeded by the World Trade Organization (WTO), has argued that trade policies should not distinguish between identical products, even if they were made differently,[4] there has been growing pressure from environmentalists and, in some cases from green protectionists, to limit trade with PPM standards. Probably the most publicized case relating to PPMs has been the United States-Mexico tuna-dolphin dispute.[5]

Second, there may be environmental danger in shipping or handling traded goods. This may occur either through danger from the products themselves, or from efforts to facilitate their shipping and handling. Protests from environmental groups and a number of Pacific and Caribbean countries concerned over dangers from a shipment of highly radioactive waste from

France to Japan highlighted this issue in early 1995 (*Reuters* 1995b). Vaughan (1994:129) notes that, "In total, some 100,000 transborder shipments of hazardous wastes take place every year, and the numbers continue to increase." Concerns have also been raised about the environmental effects of infrastructure projects designed to facilitate trade.

Third, there may be environmental danger in consumption of the product. For example, consumption of endangered species may reduce the world's store of biodiversity. Consumption of food products treated with toxic chemicals may endanger consumers. Pesticides, whose use has been banned in producing countries as environmentally dangerous, are still shipped to other countries where priorities, as reflected in policies, are different.

Fourth, environmental danger can result from the release or disposal of the waste produced by consumption of a product. For example, consumption (use) of refrigerants that release chlorofluorocarbons into the atmosphere may damage the world's ozone layer. Improper use or disposal of fertilizers, pesticides, herbicides, engine oil, and nuclear fuel can also have obvious negative environmental impacts.

Environmental Policies, Product Standards, and Trade Effects

Environmental policies influence the product life cycle of internationally traded goods by changing production or disposal costs, changing the relative resource endowments that contribute to comparative advantage, or by affecting the transaction costs involved in trade. "Subject to the requirement that such measures are not applied in a manner which would constitute a means of arbitrary or unjustifiable discrimination between countries where the same conditions prevail, or a disguised restriction on international trade," environmental policies are in conformity with GATT when they are "necessary for the protection of human, animal, or plant life or health" (Article XXb), or "relating to the conservation of exhaustible natural resources if such measures are made effective in conjunction with restrictions on domestic production or consumption" (Article XXg). Environmental subsidies are excluded from the list of actionable subsidies in the GATT subsidies code, increasing their attraction for environmentalists and protectionists.

The reluctance of developing countries to implement environmental controls is not surprising. In addition to difficulties in planning, implementing, monitoring, and enforcing such controls, and often entrenched interest groups with close connections to, or in some cases more power than, the government, there is fear of inhibiting competitiveness. A pollution tax levied on production of a pollution-intensive commodity raises its relative price and reduces the country's comparative advantage in production of that good. Further, if capital is internationally mobile and the country is poorly endowed with assimilative environmental capacity, environmental policies that raise firms' production costs can lead to capital being transferred from an environmentally disadvantaged country to an environmentally richer country (Siebert 1985). On the other hand, effective environmental policies implemented in a coordinated manner by developing countries could improve their terms of trade since the demand by wealthier consumers for their exports is relatively price-inelastic (Repetto 1995).

Product standards are increasingly being considered as environmental instruments. Such standards, whether on product content such as Alar pesticide residues on apples, or PPMs as in the case of tuna caught in a dolphin-friendly manner, can reduce trade opportunities by acting as nontariff trade barriers, particularly if they discriminate between domestically produced and imported goods. While GATT regulations do not permit such discrimination, or disguised protectionist measures, product standards are often formulated in a manner that permits easier conformation by domestic industries than foreign competitors. For example, recycling requirements on packaging materials in Europe for environmental aims may reduce the opportunities for producers of jute bags in Bangladesh, even though the jute bags may be more environment-friendly than European-produced and recycled alternatives.

Two agreements were reached in the Uruguay Round of GATT negotiations which place greater limits on the ability of governments to set product standards and have implications for traded goods. The Agreement on Technical Barriers to Trade applies a "least-trade restrictive" or "no more trade restrictive than necessary to fulfill a legitimate objective" test to national regulations. The Agreement on Sanitary and Phytosanitary Measures applies to food and plant and animal products and favors those measures "significantly less restrictive to trade." Efforts are also currently under way at the International Standards Organization to set guidelines aimed at standardizing requirements for the growing proliferation of eco-labels (*Business News Advisory* 1995).

Evidence of firms or industries migrating to overseas locations with lower environmental standards remains largely anecdotal. Despite substantial evidence that the balance of global *production* in pollution-intensive industries is shifting to developing countries, there is little evidence that environmental regulations have influenced competitiveness (Beghin, et al. 1994b). Tobey (1990) examined effects on trade and found "the

237

stringent environmental regulations imposed on industries in the late 1960s and early 1970s by most industrialized countries have not measurably affected international trade patterns in the most polluting industries." On the other hand, there is solid evidence that the bulk of foreign direct investment has been targeted to countries with higher environmental standards, suggesting that the low relative costs of compliance with environmental regulations and higher benefits of more skilled workers and more developed infrastructure and markets in those countries outweigh the production cost benefits of lax environmental standards.

International Environmental Agreements

For political reasons and for want of better information on resource values and ecological interactions, environmental policies tend more often to take the form of regulation than of market incentives. In the absence of what environmentalists consider adequate national environmental policies, there is a tendency to look for international regulation as a means of protecting the environment. Trade provisions have played three roles in international environmental agreements. They have been used to (i) enforce agreements through the threat of trade sanctions; (ii) persuade nonparticipants to accede to an agreement;[6] and (iii) set environmental conditions on traded products or PPMs.

International environmental agreements cover a wide range of subjects and are not a new phenomenon, although their number has grown rapidly in the past few decades. Although there are international agreements covering some environmentally sensitive areas, there is no organization to set *and enforce* regulations covering cross-border environmental effects the way that national governments can protect their domestic environments.[7] Consequently, environmentalists try to use what *is* available, such as GATT or WTO, to protect the environment. As the primary agreement/ organization governing world trade, GATT/WTO is the natural focus of efforts to change world trade rules. OECD also has a Trade and Environment Committee, the United Nations Conference on Trade and Development has convened an Ad Hoc Working Group on Trade, Environment, and Development, and there are sector-specific organizations, such as the International Tropical Timber Organization, considering trade and environmental issues.[8]

One reason why many countries support discussion of the trade and environment nexus in GATT and WTO has been noted by Hewison (1994:69):

For the most part, the United States has traditionally been the nation proposing or taking trade measures to enforce environmental agreements. This is due primarily to its large domestic market, the significance of that market for the exports of most other nations, and the role the United States plays as *'global police officer'* particularly over marine mammal issues. But the United States is incapable of taking trade measures against itself, and it is difficult to recall any examples of any other nation taking trade sanctions against the United States. In general, the effective use of trade measures for environmental purposes may remain the province of large countries such as the United States, the European Community and Japan.

Trade Policies and Environmental Consequences

Economic theory suggests that trade measures are second-best responses to environmental issues, which could be better handled through internalizing all costs and possibly reaching a consensus on guidelines for environmental standards, at least for those with international implications. This overlooks the limits on scientific information about many environmental interactions, difficulties in valuing resources and amenities, and difficulties in enforcing international agreements.[9] The latter point was highlighted by the developed countries' pressure at the Berlin conference in April 1995, to relax their targets for reducing output of greenhouse gases agreed to as recently as the 1992 United Nations Conference on Environment and Development. Recent improvements have been made in applying the "polluter pays" principle, in contingent valuation techniques, and in the development of satellite national income accounts to incorporate effects of changes in natural resource stocks. However, there is still a lack of adequate knowledge, especially empirical evidence, and appropriate mechanisms for fully separating environmental from trade issues in analysis.

Under standard assumptions of perfect competition, free trade is a globally Pareto optimal outcome in the presence of environmental externalities if appropriate policies internalize the externalities (Bhagwati and Srinivasan 1996). International trade increases competitive pressures for efficient resource and energy use. The same is true for political accountability, as there are many examples of the state being the worst polluter and flouting its own environmental regulations. Government underpricing of natural resource extraction and poor implementation of environmental protection measures have led to resource mining beyond sustainable levels

239

Table 1. A Sample of International Environmental Agreements

1911	Convention for the Preservation and Protection of Fur Seals
1931	Convention on the Regulation of Whaling
1956	Plant Protection Agreement for the Southeast Asia and Pacific Region
1959	Antarctic Treaty
1972	Convention for the Conservation of Antarctic Seals
1973	Convention on International Trade in Endangered Species
1980	Convention on the Conservation of Antarctic Marine Living Resources
1985	ASEAN Agreement on the Conservation of Nature and Natural Resources
1985	International Code of Conduct on the Distribution and Use of Pesticides
1987	Montreal Protocol on Substances that Deplete the Ozone Layer
1989	Wellington Convention for the Prohibition of Fishing with Long Driftnets in the South Pacific
1989	Basel Convention on Transboundary Movement of Hazardous Wastes
1992	Convention on Climate Change
1992	Convention on Biodiversity
1994	Convention on Desertification

United Nations Resolutions on Driftnet Fishing (Resolution 44/225, 1989; Resolution 45/197, 1990; Resolution 46/215, 1991; Resolution 47/443, 1992; Resolution 48/445, 1993) in a number of countries, including the Philippines (Intal and Quintos 1994).

Trade Liberalization and the Environment

The Uruguay Round of GATT negotiations moved the international trading system closer to full trade liberalization. The new World Trade Organization will continue to advocate greater trade liberalization. The environmental effects of trade liberalization may be direct, through trade in goods and services with environmental externalities, or indirect, as greater gains from trade foster growth with both positive and negative influences on the environment. In the absence of policies to internalize negative environmental externalities in production or consumption of traded goods, trade liberalization may worsen the environment.

Trade liberalization will have varying direct effects in a small, open economy depending on whether the goods affected are imports and import substitutes or exports, and whether the negative environmental externality occurs in production or consumption of the good. The environmental welfare effects and appropriate policy responses can be classified as in the chart below, derived from Anderson (1992).

While the East Asian "miracle" economies have highlighted the advantages of export growth, some other Asian economies remain enamored of import substitution and drives for self-sufficiency, at probable environmental risk. Toxic intensity of manufacturing is slow-growing or declining in outward-oriented economies and increasing more rapidly in inward-oriented economies (Hettige, et al. 1992). Especially, toxic intensity of less-developed country manufacturing output rises with trade protection for chemicals production, the most intensely toxic manufacturing sector.

In recent decades there has been a shift from command-and-control environmental measures to more market incentives. To achieve pollution abatement, a Pigouvian effluent tax is generally the most efficient policy instrument, followed by production or consumption taxes. Any of these is preferable to tariffs in a first-best world (Beghin et al. 1994a). In the second-best world in which we live, trade policy interventions, alone or in concert with environmental taxes, can increase welfare in some cases but generalizations are not feasible (Beghin et al. 1994b).

Trade liberalization under the auspices of WTO and in accordance with the Uruguay Round agreements will be gradual in some sectors, such as the phasing out of the Multifiber Arrangement for textiles. In theory, the reduction of protectionism in developed countries can be expected to

Table 2. Effects of Trade Liberalization in a Small,
Open Economy and Policy Responses

Location of Negative Externality	Importable Goods	Exportable Goods
Production	Positive for welfare and environment if trade liberalization leads to increased reliance on imports (*appropriate production tax*)	Negative for environment if trade liberalization leads to increased export and production – see if efficiency effects of liberalized tade outweigh externality effects on environ- ment (*appropriate production tax, whether for domestic or export market*)
Consumption	Negative for environment if trade liberalization leads to greater consumption and imports (*appropriate consumption tax, whether domestic or imported product*)	Positive for environment if trade liberalization leads to greater exports and lower domestic consumption (*appropriate consumption tax*)

eventually ease some environmental pressures in developing countries by allowing them to shift production and exports away from natural resource-based commodities and toward labor-intensive manufactured goods and downstream processing activities. However, higher environmental standards in the developed countries may have an opposite effect as discussed above, strengthening the comparative advantage of some developing countries in pollution-intensive activities. Similarly, reduction in agricultural protectionism among the developed countries may ease environmental problems related to intensive agriculture in those countries and increase intensification in the developing world. Whether that intensification eases pressures of extensive agriculture on marginal lands and forests will be an empirical question. The complexity of these interactions also suggests the need for more general equilibrium modeling of trade and the environment.

The World Trade Organization

WTO and its Committee on Trade and Environment provide the principal international forum for discussing and resolving international trade and environment issues at present. WTO allows trade interventions for environmental purposes, provided the interventions are nondiscriminatory, nonprotectionist, conform with national treatment, and restrict trade the least of available instruments.

A number of trade and environment issues remain unresolved and subject to further discussion and negotiation in WTO. Prominent among these are the unilateral use of trade measures for environmental purposes, trade implications of product standards and eco-labeling, separating green protectionism from protective environmentalism, and ensuring consistency of international environmental agreements with international trade agreements.[10] Further efforts to promote open debate and to build technical, analytical, and negotiating capacity among the economies of the Asia and Pacific region remain an important challenge, both for the sake of international trade and for the Asian and global environment.

Trade and Environment in Post-Uruguay Round Developing Asia and the Pacific

So far, this chapter has discussed the principles relating trade and the environment. We now turn to the evolving situation in Asia and the Pacific. In this context there are a number of key issues which affect the trade and environment nexus.

Population Growth, Food, and Agriculture

The Asian Development Bank's (ADB) developing member countries (DMCs) account for slightly more than half of the world's population, and the bulk of its poor population. Despite declining rates of fertility and poverty, two factors often with negative implications for the environment, from 1990 to 2010, these countries will add almost a billion new consumers to those already straining the earth's carrying capacity. Even by 2010, over half of their economically active population will still be involved in agriculture, implying further intensification of land and water use, with more mineral fertilizers and pesticides. Asia is already the region with the lowest per capita freshwater availability in the world and the shortage is expected to worsen, even as demand for the outputs of irrigated agriculture increases. Asia is also the region that has experienced the greatest amount of soil degradation (Food and Agriculture Organization [FAO] 1993). Both domestic and international demands for agriculture products in Asia can be expected to increase pressure on the environment and increase agricultural trade while stimulating demand for, and trade in, more environmentally friendly agricultural technologies. At the same time, to the extent that warming of the global climate raises sea level, the amount of arable land available for growing export crops may be reduced, or at least redistributed among nations.

Property rights are poorly defined in many areas of Asia and the Pacific. Inconsistencies in the treatment of squatters in the forests of Thailand have exacerbated deforestation both in that country, and through trade, in its neighbors (*Reuters* 1995e). Rapid deforestation has led to bans on log exports from Cambodia, Indonesia, the Philippines, Thailand, and Vanuatu, supporting a shift to higher value-added exports of wood products from those countries. Land reform remains a critical issue to be addressed in the development of the Philippines. Pacific island nations have had to reduce fish exports as drift-net techniques reduced stocks, and to reduce certain mineral exports as those stocks were depleted.

Rising land valuations may induce resolution of property right disputes and reduce the tragedy of the commons, but rarely without controversy or conflict. Confrontation over the Spratley Islands, arguments over water flows to the Aral Sea, and the 1995 seizing of Japanese fishing boats in the Pacific by the United States make clear that it is not only domestic, but also international property rights that are unsettled. As populations grow and the demand for scarce resources increases, tensions over the assignment of some property rights can be expected to increase.

Growth of Income

Gross domestic product (GDP) among ADB's DMCs grew at an average annual rate of 8 percent during the 1980s. From 1990 to 1994, average annual growth in GDP ranged from 6.2 to 8.2 percent. Even on a per capita basis, average annual DMC growth in GDP from 1990 to 1994 remained between 4.6 and 6.7 percent, and economic growth in the region is likely to remain strong. Whether or not we agree with those in developing countries who argue for development first and worries about the environment later, in practice this is often what occurs. At such rapid growth rates in the face of continuing poverty, there often seems to be little time for environmental considerations, suggesting in particular that greater attention should be paid to which environmental effects are likely to be permanent and which may respond to remedial actions.

If the finding discussed above concerning the "inverted U" of environmental degradation per unit of output peaking at about per capita income of $5,000 has any predictive value, it suggests that most of Asia and the Pacific can expect things to get worse environmentally at an increasing rate before the degradation slows. Among ADB's 35 DMCs, only the newly industrializing economies such as Hong Kong; the Republic of Korea (Korea); Singapore; and Taipei,China, had per capita GNP in 1993 above $5,000. Of the rest, only Malaysia had income above $3,000, at $3,160.

At low levels of per capita income, countries often rely on inefficient technology. For example, with its high reliance on coal for fuel, in 1987 the People's Republic of China (PRC) had fossil fuel carbon emissions per capita only one ninth the level of those in the United States, but had more than seven times the number of grams of carbon emissions per dollar of GNP (Whalley 1991). While total emissions in PRC were less than half those in the United States, the potential for rapid growth in PRC emissions with rapid income growth has alarmed environmentalists concerned about global warming. While the evidence indicates greater use of cleaner technologies with increased expenditures on pollution abatement and rising preference for environmental quality at higher-income levels, every country faces different dynamics of economic growth and environmental change along the way, calling for greater domestic assessment and analysis. Corrective action has already begun in some Asian economies with relatively higher income per capita, as utilities in Korea and Taipei,China have switched to burning fuel oil containing 1.5 percent sulfur or less, and in Bangkok to 2 percent or less, while most refineries in the region still produce high (3.5-4 percent) fuel oil (Reuters 1995a).

Growth in Trade

As shown in the table below, average growth in trade has been even stronger than growth in income. During the 15-year period from 1979 through 1993, developing Asia's exports increased more than fivefold, measured by value, and more than doubled as a share of total world exports, rising from 8.1 to 17.5 percent. Over the same period, intra-Asian trade, excluding that with Japan, increased more than eightfold and rose from 21

Table 3. Average Annual Growth Rates for ADB's DMCs
(percent per annum)

Variable	Year					
	1989	1990	1991	1992	1993	1994
GDP	6.3	6.2	6.4	7.5	7.9	8.2
GDP per capita	4.2	4.6	4.9	6.0	6.3	6.7
Merchandise Exports	11.5	10.8	14.0	13.2	11.0	16.6
Merchandise Imports	12.7	12.3	13.8	13.6	13.1	16.8

Source: Asian Development Bank, 1995.

percent of developing Asia's exports to 35 percent. With Japan included, by 1994, roughly half of Asia's exports were intraregional exports.

This trend toward greater trade, and in particular greater intra-Asian trade, is likely to continue, with consequences for the Asian environment. Greater market integration and trade liberalization facilitate technology transfer,[11] specialization on the basis of comparative advantage, and improved resource pricing and management. The environmental impact may come at different stages in the product life cycle as discussed above, or from infrastructure development to facilitate the increasing trade, as at the new Chek Lap Kok Airport in Hong Kong, the new bridge over the Jamuna River in Bangladesh, or development of the Subic Bay duty-free zone in the Philippines.

While it is difficult to assess the environmental impact of all individual trade transactions, some inferences can be drawn from the composition of trade. In Asia's merchandise trade, over 80 percent of exports are manufactured goods. Agricultural and mining outputs are each less than 10 percent of exports for the region as a whole, although they are substantially more for some individual countries. In 1992, almost 40 percent of Asia's manufactured exports were traded within Asia itself. The same is true for 60 percent of agricultural exports and over 80 percent of mining products. On what is perhaps a bright note for the Asia and Pacific environment,[12] a study of the region's revealed comparative advantage (Evans and Walsh 1994) found that it is greatest in (in order) (i) office and telecommunications equipment; (ii) clothing; and (iii) textiles. The region's greatest-revealed comparative disadvantages are in chemicals and mining products, two areas where production often has serious negative effects on the environment.

The percentage shares of some categories of exports commonly assumed to be "environmentally sensitive," or likely to have negative impacts on the environment in their production or extraction are presented in Table 4 for a number of Asian and Pacific economies. The environmentally sensitive exports are taken to be those of agricultural raw materials, fuels, ores and metals, and chemical products. These broad export categories include some environmentally benign products, but also miss some with potential for environmental damage, such as processed food products and manufactured goods whose production involves malignant by-products such as Nepali carpets manufactured for export with dyes that pollute local water courses.

The table highlights the diversity in export structure among the region's economies and the high share of environmentally sensitive exports in some individual countries. Agricultural raw materials are important exports in several countries such as Lao PDR, Myanmar, and the Solomon Islands where deforestation has been a growing concern. Oil and natural gas account for more than five sixths of exports from Brunei Darussalam. Ores and metals are particularly significant exports for some Pacific island countries. Chemical products are more important in those economies which are either more developed or larger (such as PRC and India), where more advanced technology or standards can be expected.[13]

A simple, cross-sectional scatter plot of the "economically sensitive shares of exports" versus GNP per capita is presented in Figure 1 for those countries for which GNP data were available in purchasing-power parity terms. It offers weak support for the argument that poorer countries in Asia will concentrate on "dirtier" exports. The correlation coefficient for the data presented is -0.06, and the negative relationship depends heavily on the outliers Lao PDR, Papua New Guinea, and Indonesia. If a conforming income estimate was available for Brunei Darussalam, this wealthy oil exporter would appear above the upper-right section of the current chart, weakening the present negative correlation even further.

Imports can also have significant environmental consequences. Low-wage labor, useful in recycling industries, can make developing countries attractive destinations for waste from higher-wage countries. Africa and Latin America officially banned trade in waste in 1991, but Asia remains a major importer in the trade (see Table 6).

Asia has recently experienced a rapid expansion and integration of its capital markets both with others in the region and with global markets.[14] Globalization of international capital markets facilitates trade, but "it also

Table 4. Export Structure of Selected Asian and Pacific Economies

Country	Year	Total Value of Exports ($ million)	Percentage Share in Exports of				Environmentally Sensitive Share of Exports
			Agricultural Raw Materials	Fuels	Ores and Metals	Chemical Products	
Afghanistan	1990	235.0	14.7	47.6	-	0.1	62.4
Australia	1992	38,044.8	9.5	20.1	15.7	2.9	48.2
Bangladesh	1992	1,902.8	5.7	0.4	-	0.8	6.9
Brunei							
Darussalam	1989	2,160.0	-	84.0	0.1	-	84.1
PRC	1992	84,940.0	2.3	5.5	1.7	5.2	14.7
Cook Islands	1980	4.1	10.2	-	24.3	0.8	35.3
Fiji	1992	341.3	2.0	-	0.2	0.9	3.1
French Polynesia	1991	142.6	2.7	-	-	3.6	6.3
Hong Kong	1992	119,566.5	1.5	0.7	1.1	5.9	9.2
India	1992	17,911.0	1.6	2.8	4.3	7.1	15.8
Indonesia	1992	33,815.5	4.6	33.3	4.2	2.3	44.4
Japan	1992	339,491.3	0.5	0.5	0.9	5.5	7.4
Kiribati	1985	4.2	-	-	-	-	-
Korea,							
Republic of	1992	76,394.2	1.2	2.2	0.8	5.9	10.1
Lao PDR	1980	23.6	38.6	-	22.5	-	61.1
Macau	1992	1,749.1	1.3	-	0.1	1.4	2.8
Malaysia	1991	34,375.0	11.3	15.5	1.5	1.8	30.1
Myanmar	1991	412.0	28.9	1.5	5.1	0.2	35.7
Nepal	1991	273.1	15.7	-	-	-	15.7
New Caledonia	1991	444.0	0.2	0.2	30.4	0.9	31.7
New Zealand	1992	9,338.2	16.8	2.6	4.6	5.8	29.8
Pakistan	1992	7,264.2	9.7	1.2	0.2	0.4	11.5
Papua							
New Guinea	1990	1,141.0	13.9	0.1	41.3	0.3	55.6
Philippines	1992	9,789.6	1.5	2.4	5.8	2.7	12.4
Samoa	1990	9.0	1.1	-	-	-	1.1
Singapore	1992	63,385.5	1.8	13.0	1.6	6.5	22.9
Solomon Islands	1991	76.9	43.8	-	-	-	43.8
Sri Lanka	1992	2,486.9	4.2	-	0.8	1.5	6.5
Taipei,China	1992	81,337.4	1.5	0.7	1.0	4.6	7.8
Thailand	1991	28,324.0	4.5	1.0	0.7	2.5	8.7
Tonga	1991	13.8	-	-	-	-	-
Vanuatu	1991	19.7	8.6	3.0	-	-	11.6

Source: United Nations Conference on Trade and Development, Handbook of International Trade and Development Statistics 1993 (1994).

Figure 1. Scatter Plot of Environmentally Sensitive Share of Exports vs GNP per Capita

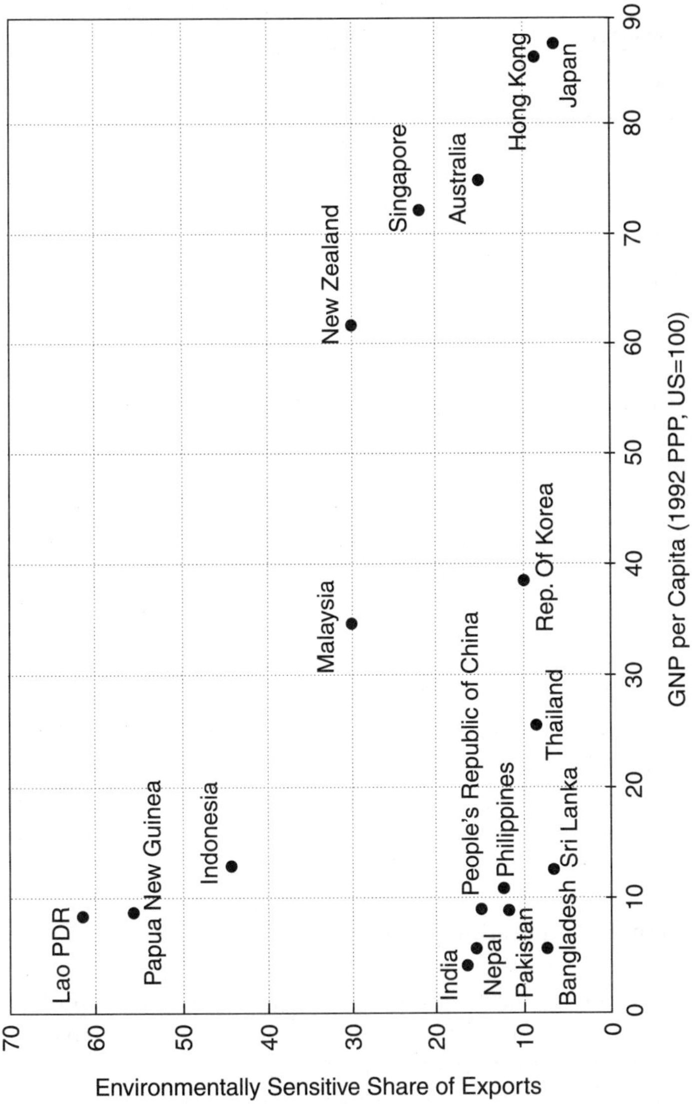

Table 5. Asia's Waste Imports, 1990-1993
(metric ton)

Importer	Copper	Other Nonferrous Metals	Plastic
Bangladesh	3,130	–	16
China, People's Republic of	6,600	120,630	1,849
Hong Kong*	2,582	–	71,529
India	5,980	90	11,951
Indonesia	103	–	7,327
Korea, Republic of	4,670	2,634	74
Malaysia	–	–	522
Pakistan	–	–	38
Philippines	50	–	7,236
Singapore	–	–	381
Sri Lanka	–	–	432
Taipei,China	4,770	–	317
Thailand	–	–	90

Note: List is not complete. Data are based on shipments known to have occurred.
* Most waste shipments to Hong Kong are transhipped to PRC.

Source: Greenpeace, 1995.

magnifies the external damage arising from pollution taxes which are too low. Thus, although the relation between trade and pollution policy is complex, the cost of doing nothing will likely increase as markets become more integrated" (Copeland 1994:64). Also, as noted above, global integration of capital markets may lead to the transfer of capital from environmentally poorer to richer countries.

Regional Cooperation

Over the last two decades, as the economic interdependence of developing economies in the Asia and Pacific region has increased, so have their efforts toward regional and subregional cooperation, particularly in areas of trade. This is evident in the Asia-Pacific Economic Cooperation (APEC) forum's plans for trade liberalization among developed members by 2010 and by developing members by 2020,[15] the Association of Southeast Asian Nations (ASEAN) Free Trade Area currently under implementation, and recent plans for a preferential trading arrangement among members of the South Asian Association for Regional Cooperation. With more limited trade plans, there are the South Pacific Forum, South Pacific Commission, Southern China Growth Triangle, Singapore-Johor-Riau Growth Triangle, Tumen River Area Development, Indonesia-Malaysia-Thailand Growth Triangle, Brunei-Indonesia-Malaysia-Philippines East ASEAN Growth Area, and the Greater Mekong Subregion. These cooperative efforts aim at promoting intraregional trade and investment, and more efficient resource use, with hopefully beneficial environmental consequences. They also provide fora for discussing and planning cooperative efforts for sustainable use of the environment.

Most of the cooperative efforts to liberalize Asian trade involve gradual liberalization. Consequently, we can expect to experience a gradual contraction of output in protected industries and expansion in others with uncertain environmental consequences in the interim. Simulation results for the Philippines indicate that trade liberalization would increase the national pollution intensity of production by reallocating output toward logging, mining, and agriculture, and within manufacturing, toward more pollution-intensive industries such as food processing, beverages, and wood products (Intal and Quintos 1994).

That trade policies can have unintended environmental consequences, even when applied for environmental purposes, argues for their careful consideration. Export restrictions to favor local wood processors in Indonesia have been found to promote more intensive use of logs in production due to a lowering of the domestic price for timber, resulting in greater environmental degradation than a tax on all timber at the logging stage would have (Braga 1992). In this manner recent proposals among richer, tropical timber-importing countries to limit imports of tropical wood products to "save the rain forests" could actually lead to increased deforestation.

Conclusions

The linkages between trade and the environment remain complex, but our understanding of that complexity is increasing. In Asia and the Pacific, rapid growth in income and trade, and slower but steady growth in population, is increasing pressure on the environment. Efforts to conserve or enhance the environment are having increasing effects on production techniques and trade composition, levels, and patterns. Gradual trade liberalization in a second-best world does not guarantee welfare improvement in the absence of adequate environmental policies.

Complementary investments in institutional capacity-building and infrastructure will be necessary to ensure the effectiveness of environmental policies and to limit environmental damage from trade policies. From an economic perspective, not enough analysis has been undertaken to assess the full costs and benefits of environmental changes, although the work on satellite national accounts to include changes in resource values and increasing applications of the "polluter pays" principle are positive steps. So, too, is the recent proposal to apply contingent valuation techniques to determine how much people in developed countries would be willing to transfer to poorer countries to turn endangered tropical rain forests into protected national parks (*Reuters* 1995c).

Reform of environmental or trade policies in one country can affect the environment and trade of another, suggesting that considerations of trade policy should be undertaken in conjunction with considerations of environmental policy, which may be unlikely unless WTO dispute-settlement panel procedures complement their emphasis on trade expertise with equal attention to environmental expertise. Trade can endanger or enhance environmental quality. In the rush for higher income, which in the Asian context is generally coexistent with greater trade, the contributions of the environment to welfare, and to trade itself must be remembered, particularly in policy-making. Cooperation and coordination of Asian and Pacific developing countries in establishing environmental policies, taking trade effects into account, is likely to be their best option for sustaining increases in welfare in a region where economies and ecosystems are heavily interdependent.

Acknowledgments

The author is grateful for comments and suggestions from Jagdish Bhagwati, Ishrat Husain, and John Whalley. Charissa Castillo provided valuable research assistance. The author claims sole ownership of property rights for remaining errors.

Notes

[1] This principle, under which producers pay the difference between social and private marginal costs, effectively allocates environmental property rights to consumers and was adopted by the OECD countries in 1972.

[2] Little consideration has so far been given to a potential "race-to-the-top" as environmental groups argue for standards at least as strict as those of neighboring countries.

[3] The model thus demonstrates a case of market failure where trade may be immiserizing.

[4] In Article XX(e) GATT exceptionally allows for PPM-based trade measures "relating to the products of prison labor."

[5] In this case, the United States banned imports of Mexican tuna on the grounds that methods in which the tuna were caught endangered dolphins swimming together with the tuna in the eastern Pacific. A GATT dispute-settlement panel ruled against the ban on the grounds that it constituted a unilateral trade action applied extraterritorially.

[6] In an unusual development, the Montreal Protocol on Substances that Deplete the Ozone Layer permits the imposition of limited trade sanctions to encourage accession to the accord.

[7] For a proposal to create such a global environmental organization, see Esty (1994).

[8] One major international service sector with a direct interest in the environment is tourism. In line with Agenda 21 resulting from the 1992 United Nations Conference on Environment and Development, the World Travel & Tourism Council, World Tourism Organization, and the Earth Council have jointly issued "Agenda 21 for the Travel & Tourism Industry: Towards Environmentally Sustainable Development."

[9] It is also *not* to suggest that a harmonization of environmental standards would be appropriate in a world of varying environmental endowments, preferences, and assimilative capacities among countries.

[10] For a more complete list, see Anderson (1993).

[11] See, for example, *Reuters* (1995d).

[12] As used here, the Asia and Pacific region does not encompass Russia or those countries on the eastern edge of the Pacific Ocean.

[13] Note that technology and standards may not be sufficient to protect the environment if enforcement and precautions are weak, as evidenced by the 1984 chemical plant gas leak in Bhopal, India, which killed over 2,500 people and injured more than 200,000.

[14] For a fuller discussion, see "Resource Mobilization for Development in Asia" and "The Financial Sector and Asian Development: Historical Experiences and Prospects" in ADB (1995).

[15] The linkage between trade and the environment was identified as a "key facilitation issue" in the Second Report of the Eminent Persons Group, Achieving the APEC Vision: Free and Open Trade in the Asia-Pacific, Singapore: APEC, August 1994.

References

Anderson, K., 1992. "Welfare Analytics of Trade and Environment Policies." In K. Anderson and J. Blackhurst, eds., *The Greening of World Trade Issues*. London: Harvester-Wheatsheaf.

_____, 1993. A Plain-Language Guide to the Agendas of OECD and GATT Working Groups on Trade and Environment Issues. Policy Discussion Paper No. 93/10. University of Adelaide Centre for International Economic Studies.

Asian Development Bank, 1995. *Asian Development Outlook 1995 and 1996*. Hong Kong: Oxford University Press.

Beghin, J., D. Roland-Holst, and D. van der Mensbrugghe, 1994a. Trade and Pollution Linkages: Piecemeal Reform and Optimal Intervention. OECD Development Centre Technical Papers No. 99. Paris.

_____, 1994b. "A Survey of the Trade and Environment Nexus: Global Dimensions." *OECD Economic Studies* 23:167-92.

Bhagwati, J., and T. N. Srinivasan, 1996. "Trade and the Environment: Does Environmental Diversity Detract from the Case for Free Trade?" In J. Bhagwati and R. Hudec, eds., *Fair Trade and Harmonization: Prerequisites for Free Trade?* Cambridge, Massachusetts: MIT Press.

Braga, C. A. P., 1992. "Tropical Forests and Trade Policy: The Case of Indonesia and Brazil." In P. Low, ed., *International Trade and the Environment*. Washington, D.C.: World Bank.

Business News Advisory, 1995. "New ISO Standards Said to Provide Test for Systems to Detect, Prevent Violations." 16 May. Washington.

Chichilnisky, G., 1994. "North-South Trade and the Global Environment." *American Economic Review* 84(4):851-74.

Copeland, B. R., 1994. "International Trade and the Environment: Policy Reform in a Polluted Small Open Economy." *Journal of Environmental Economics and Management* 26:44-65.

Copeland, B. R., and M. Scott Taylor, 1994. "North-South Trade and the Environment." *Quarterly Journal of Economics* 109:755-87.

Esty, D. C., 1994. *Greening the GATT: Trade, Environment and the Future.* Washington, D.C.: Institute for International Economics.

Evans, P., and J. Walsh, 1994. "The EIU Guide to the New GATT." London: The Economist Intelligence Unit.

Food and Agriculture Organization of the United Nations (FAO), 1993. *Agriculture: Towards 2010.* Rome.

Greenpeace, 1995. "China Becomes Dump Site for the World's Garbage." *Asian Wall Street Journal,* 4 October.

Hettige, H., R. E. B. Lucas, and D. Wheeler, 1992. "The Toxic Intensity of Industrial Production: Global Patterns, Trends and Trade Policy." *American Economic Review* 82(2):478-81.

Hewison, G., 1994. "The Case of Driftnet Fishing." In Organisation for Economic Co-operation and Development (OECD), *Trade and Environment: Processes and Production Methods.* Paris: OECD.

Intal, P., Jr., and P. Quintos, 1994. "Adjusting to the New Trade and Environment Paradigm: The Case of the Philippines." Paper presented at the Symposium in Honor of Dr. Gelia Castillo, Quezon City, 27-28 September, Manila.

Lopez, R., 1992. "The Environment as a Factor of Production: The Economic Growth and Trade Policy Linkages." In P. Low, ed., *International Trade and Environment.* Washington, D.C.: World Bank.

Lucas, R. E. B., 1994. International Environmental Indicators: Trade, Income and Endowments. Institute for Economic Development Discussion Paper No. 46. Washington, D.C.

Organisation for Economic Co-operation and Development, 1994. *Trade and Environment: Processes and Production Methods.* Paris: OECD.

255

Radetzki, M., 1992. "Economic Growth and Environment." In P. Low, ed., *International Trade and Environment*. Washington, D.C.: World Bank.

Repetto, R., 1995. "Trade and Sustainable Development." In M.G. Quibria, ed., *Critical Issues in Asian Development: Theories, Experiences and Policies*. Hong Kong: Oxford University Press.

Reuters, 1995a. "*Asia's Green Concerns Come with Higher Oil Costs.*" 26 January. Singapore.

_____, 1995b. "Japan Nuclear Waste Shipment Stirs Wide Concern." 30 January. Tokyo.

_____, 1995c. "Economists Plan to Evaluate World's Rainforests." 18 April. Sydney.

_____, 1995d. "India, U.S. Sign Pact to Boost Green Business." 18 April. New Delhi.

_____, 1995e. "Cambodian Premier Calls on Thais to Help Log Ban." 1 May. Phnom Penh.

Siebert, H., 1985. "Spatial Aspects of Environmental Economics." In A.V. Kneese and J. L. Sweeney, eds., *Handbook of Natural Resource and Energy Economics*. New York: North-Holland.

Tobey, J. A., 1990. "The Effects of Domestic Environmental Policies on Patterns of World Trade: An Empirical Test." *Kyklos* 43(2):191-209.

United Nations Conference on Trade and Development, 1994. *Handbook of International Trade and Development Statistics 1993*. New York.

Vaughan, S., 1994. "PMS and International Environmental Agreements." In Organisation for Economic Co-operation and Development, *Trade and Environment: Processes and Production Methods*. Paris: OECD.

Comments on "International Trade and the Asian Environment"[1]

by

Ishrat Husain

019 F13
013 Q20
E1 F18

The chapter presented by Douglas Brooks makes an important contribution to the growing literature on trade and environment. His chapter makes an advance in this debate in two ways. First, it clarifies the issues that are germane to the Asian countries. The table he presents to illustrate the effects of trade liberalization in a small, open economy and policy responses according to the source of negative externality is very helpful. Second, it assembles empirical evidence on the environmentally sensitive exports from Asia. With few exceptions such as Brunei, Lao PDR, and Papua New Guinea, their share is less than one half or lower in most cases. Mr. Brook's instincts in this chapter are quite right, his insights are instructive, and there are very few points with which I would quibble. However, I found the chapter to be too tentative and cautious in its tone and approach and the important messages and conclusions were buried in details and did not spring out at the reader.

What I will attempt to do, therefore, is to pick out the central messages of the chapter, supplement them with other pieces of evidence, and present to you my own interpretation of the current state of knowledge in this important topic with special reference to Asian countries.

Trade and Environment

I would divide my comments in four parts. First, I would argue that environmental protection should not be considered in isolation but in the broader context of sustainable development. Second, I believe that the argument that there should be uniform environmental standards across all the 180 developing or developed countries of the world is unpersuasive. Third, while the Asian countries should improve environmental quality and tackle looming environmental problems, trade policy is not the right instrument to achieve this objective. Finally, the dominant preference shown by some government and environmental NGOs for relying heavily, and in some cases exclusively, on direct controls rather than market-based approaches to resolve the environmental problems is misplaced.

Let me elaborate upon each of these:

- Environmental protection should be a legitimate objective of domestic public policy not as an isolated single dimensional goal, but in the broader context of sustainable development that takes into account the fuller interactions between various forms of capital — physical capital, natural capital, human capital, and social capital. The scope of substitutability among various types of capital in production process needs to be explored. For example, is it feasible that increased investments in human capital could offset the growth-inhibiting effect of the imposition of pollution abatement and control requirements on physical capital? Are the countries with highly developed social capital able to recognize the input use of natural capital per unit of output? To make this concept operationally valid, it is important that the definition of national welfare that is proxied at present by GNP should be further refined to take into account the depletion of natural capital in the production process. Net national product resulting from this modification should be used as the true indicator of national welfare. The use of satellite accounts in the System of National Accounts of the United Nations is the step in the right direction, but natural resource accounting adopted by countries such as Norway, provides an encouraging direction. The difficult valuation questions still loom.

- The growing empirical evidence shows that, if properly managed and supported by appropriate institutional changes, there are hardly any trade-offs between growth and environmental protection. In fact, much knowledge has been gained to influence and alter public policies to achieve the win-win situation and avoid the trade-offs and deleterious effects of economic growth. It is now generally agreed that increasing levels of economic activity are linked to improved environmental conditions. High-income elasticity of demand for environment quality, compositional shifts toward cleaner environment activities at higher-income levels, and extension of property rights combined with the development of policies to deal with global common externalities in more developed economies are the key factors explaining this relationship. There is empirical evidence to support the observation that the pollution intensity of economic activity tends to decline as incomes rise. The hypothesis of the inverted U-shape curve relating environment and growth has been tested and found to exist. I will argue that in the case of Asia there are enormous problems of environmental quality which should be dealt with vigorously in their own right as a tenet of domestic policy, but there is no justification for using threats or sanctions by industrial countries to restrict trade to achieve this objective. This misappropriation of trade policy, which masquerades as environmental policy, is the wrong way to go about. Since trade itself is nearly the source of an environmental problem, there is not much sense in using trade policy to address such problems. Moreover, trade measures can be shown to be unambiguously inferior to other policies where the environment objective is to preserve a natural source. The only exception is where there are significant spillovers. In such cases, the right course of action is to provide incentives to developing countries to minimize the adverse effects of these spillovers rather than use sanctions and dumping duties on exports from their countries.

◆   The strong preference of many OECD governments and environmentalists for direct environmental controls over market-based approaches is also, in my view, misplaced. The efficiency argument, in itself, is highly powerful to respond to the concerns of the environmentalists, and any deviation from the least-cost solution to address environmental externalities is fraught with serious difficulties in macroeconomic management. The welfare costs to the society of ignoring these least-cost solutions using prices, taxes, and tradeable permits could be significant. In East Asia, for example, the work done at the World Bank suggests the removal of remaining subsidies for environmentally damaging activities, particularly water use and forestry, the clarification of property rights, particularly of land in ecologically vulnerable areas, and most importantly, the imposition of taxes on polluting activities which can contribute toward reaching sufficient outcome.

Underpricing of natural resources such as water, energy, and forest products results in extensive environmental damage by encouraging the oversupply and overuse of the natural resources in question. Inadequate stumpage fees for timber harvested in public forests has led to wasteful exploitation and ecological losses. In Indonesia, if the government's rent capture on forestry products was increased from the present 30 percent to its full potential, revenues equivalent to an additional 8 to 12 percent of total government revenue would be generated. In Malaysia, doubling the price of gasoline and diesel fuel, an increase commensurate with the estimated health costs associated with the use of these fuels, would raise revenues equivalent to about 10 percent of current government's expenditure.

The proposal in industrialized countries for an import embargo on tropical hardwoods does not make sense. It has been demonstrated that an import prohibition would depress the price of the product, thereby assigning a lower value to forests, and encouraging less careful management of the resource and providing greater incentives to convert forest lands to other uses.

For example, the export restrictions on logs in Indonesia have led to additional environmental degradation upon the Indonesian wet tropical forest compared to what a proper tax on all timber at the logging stage would have done. From an environmental perspective, the discrimination in favor of local wood processors resulting from export restrictions led to a more intensive use of the logs industry. The removal of tariff escalation practiced by industrial countries along the wood processing chain would add to an efficient, less environmentally degrading use of tropical wood.

Conclusion

Where does all this lead us in regard to the future prospects of East Asian countries pursuing environment-friendly policies? In the case of Asian countries, it is my contention that outward orientation of their economies, large inflows of foreign direct investment, the compositional change in industrial structure, reduced poverty, and rising consciousness about protecting the environment make these countries more amenable toward adoption of environment-friendly policies.

- First, the empirical investigation of Lucas et al. (1992) of 95 developing countries reveals that the fast growing, more open economies became significantly less pollution-intensive in the 1970s and 1980s. These economies experienced essentially pollution-neutral structural change in the 1970s and a significant shift toward a less pollution-intensive structure in the 1980s. Wheeler and Martin (1992) show, with the example of the wood and pulp industry, that the more open an economy is, the more rapidly clean technology is adopted and diffused.

- Second, East Asian countries that have open trade regimes have also attracted more FDI, and due to the technological and other economic and noneconomic factors, foreign investment has been associated with environmentally cleaner techniques of production. These factors are the fear of liability in relation to environmental accidents, the desire to protect a firm's reputation, the costs of unbundling technology, green consumerism in export markets, anticipation of future environmental regulation, and the relatively high cost of retrofitting capital equipment.

- Third, in East Asia, there is not much acute economic stress which can be a source of cumulative causation where poverty, high fertility rates, and environmental degradation feed upon one another. Most of these countries have reduced fertility rates and absolute poverty significantly, which have been found to contribute to environmental degradation in developing countries.

- Fourth, there is a structural change taking place in Asian countries away from natural resources and agriculture-based exports to more labor-intensive, information-intensive industries and services which are cleaner environmentally. Even for capital-intensive or dirtier industries, the new vintage capital that embodies cleaner technologies developed in industrial countries where environmental standards are more stringent would reduce the pollution intensity of manufacturing production but also absolute pollution levels over time as this capital stock expands.

- Fifth, in the initial stages of development, factor accumulation such as physical capital investment explains much of the growth, but at later stages, technological factors and productivity growth are the main explanatory factors. Recent evidence from Indonesia for the period 1985 to 1992 points in this direction. The de-emphasis on capital accumulation in the growth process would also lead to reduced pollution intensity.

Notes

[1] The views expressed in this paper are those of the author and should not be attributed to the World Bank.

References

Lucas, R. E. B., D. Wheeler, and H. Hettige, 1992. "Economic Development, Environmental Regulation and the International Migration of Toxic Industrial Pollution: 1960-1988." In P. Low, ed., International Trade and Development. Washington, D.C.: World Bank.

Wheeler, D., and P. Martin, 1992. "Prices, Policies and International Diffusion of Clean Technology: The Case of Wood Pulp Production." In P. Low, ed., International Trade and Development. Washington, D.C.: World Bank.

PART 2

URUGUAY ROUND:
AREAS OF CURRENT ACTION

Chapter 8
The Impact of the Multifiber Arrangement Phaseout on the Asian Economies

John Whalley
Center for Study of International Economic Relations
University of Warwick

Introduction

In the 1994 final decisions of the Uruguay Round, a ten-year phaseout was agreed for the Multifiber Arrangement (MFA), the multilaterally agreed set of trade restrictions which, since 1974, has restrained world trade in textiles and apparel. The avowed aim of these decisions is to fully reintegrate trade in textiles and apparel into the trade disciplines of the General Agreement on Tariffs and Trade (GATT), now the World Trade Organization (WTO), through this ten-year phaseout. This chapter attempts to assess the potential implications of this process for the Asian economies both in the short and longer runs, drawing on existing quantitative literature and other related studies.

This chapter argues that as the restrained exporters of textiles and apparel, the Asian countries have the most to gain among the developing countries, in contrast to the Latin and Central American countries and countries in Africa, many of whom are either unrestrained or have low-quota utilization rates. Indeed, at first sight the textiles and apparel sector seems to be one of the relatively few Uruguay Round issues clearly dividing the Asian countries from other developing countries; constrained countries in Asia would seem to gain from the phaseout, while unconstrained countries in Latin and Central America would seem to lose.

Having said this, however, there are a number of further subtleties involved with this broad picture, as well as sharp differences among the Asian countries. One is that original MFA countries, such as Hong Kong; the Republic of Korea (Korea); and Taipei,China, now have higher wage rates and considerably larger quotas than on entry, and, so it is alleged, have a protected position relative to the newer, low-wage entrants to MFA, such as Bangladesh and Pakistan. Redistribution, so it is alleged, between higher-wage, earlier entrants and lower-wage later entrants will result from an elimination of MFA.

Another subtlety is that MFA has also generated its own responses to the constraints it has spawned, including investment flowing from constrained countries, such as Taipei,China and Korea, to lower wage, unconstrained (or higher quota growth) countries elsewhere, as well as in the region. Terminating MFA could reverse these investment flows. Yet another issue is the special position of the People's Republic of China (PRC) which has, in recent years, become the largest exporter of apparel to both the European Union (EU) and the United States (US), and now faces the added complication of not being a member of the new WTO which has replaced GATT. PRC could thus face new country-specific selective safeguards upon the eventual termination of MFA.

A final issue is the timing of liberalization during the phaseout. Both early removal of products from MFA coverage, and acceleration of MFA quota growth rates of various points in the phaseout will be involved. For reasons more fully discussed later in the chapter, it seems likely that quota restraints facing Asian exporters will be the last to be eliminated. Thus, what substantive liberalization there is in the transitional process will likely benefit regions other than Asia.

All of these features and more, thus potentially divide the Asian countries, while as a bloc their long-run gain from eliminating MFA seems clear. The picture this chapter paints, therefore, is one of regional long-run gain in aggregate for Asia from phased MFA elimination, but with a range of complicating factors which make the outcome for individual countries within the region less clear.

The Uruguay Round Agreement and the Phaseout of the Multifiber Arrangement[1]

The Content of the Agreement

As Table 1 indicates, the final decisions in the Uruguay Round commit both importing and exporting countries to a gradual phaseout of MFA, and an associated reintegration of the textiles and apparel sector back under the normal disciplines of GATT/WTO. As agreed, the phaseout is to take place in four stages beginning January 1995, and occur over a ten-year transitional period. The relevant text of the Agreement consists of nine Articles and an Annex, is applicable to all WTO members including both MFA and non-MFA signatories,[2] and covers all trade in textiles and apparel. All MFA restrictions affecting GATT contracting parties and in place on the day before the entry into force of the Agreement are covered, and they can only be maintained until either the restrictions are removed, or the products integrated are into GATT. The clear bottom line is that at the end of the transition period, all restrictions will be terminated, and there will be no extension of the Agreement (Article 9).[3]

The textile and apparel products to be covered are set out in a detailed Annex to the Agreement. This lists approximately 800 Harmonized System (HS) tariff lines, which define the universe of textile and apparel products to be reintegrated into GATT, and also provides the basis for product integration into GATT which is to occur in the transition period. All items defined by HS codes at the six-digit level within Chapters 50 to 63 of the HS are included, which importantly also covers several products

Table 1. The Uruguay Round Agreements on Textiles and Clothing

---

1. **Basic Commitment**
   To return textiles and clothing to full GATT/WTO disciplines in ten years, by 2005

2. **Transitional Arrangements**
   Accelerated Growth Rate Factors for MFA Quotas
   > Stage 1. (January 1995) MFA growth rates all increased by 16 percent
   > Stage 2. (June 1998) MFA growth rates all increased further by 25 percent
   > Stage 3. (January 2002) MFA growth rates all increased further by 27 percent

   Product Integration
   > Stage 1. (June 1995) All countries to integrate 16 percent of products listed in Annex in Agreement into GATT/WTO
   > Stage 2. (June 1998) All countries to integrate a further 17 percent of products into GATT/WTO
   > Stage 3. (June 2002) All countries to integrate a further 18 percent of products into GATT/WTO

   Special Selective Safeguards
   > New trade restrictions allowed in transitional period where damage to domestic industry occurs attributable to agreement
   > Safeguards degressive (three years)
   > Safeguards also not to reduce trade below previous 12-month level
   > Certain products exempt from safeguards action

   Treatment of Least-Developed
   > Special treatment in growth factors for small suppliers
   > Special treatment for least-developed under special safeguards

3. **Developing Country Concerns**
   Transitional arrangements will do little to achieve integration into GATT/WTO
   Most adjustment in importing countries postponed until tenth-year
   Doubts over political commitment to implement tenth year measures

Regime to follow after transitional period may not be free trade; antidumping is a concern.

---

not currently subject to restraint, plus various textile and apparel products in Chapters 30 to 49 and 64 to 96 which are currently included in the MFA commodity systems of only some of the restraining countries. The Annex also sets out those products that may be subject to a special safeguard mechanism for importers under the Agreement over the transitional period. Actions under the safeguard provisions are to be taken on particular products, not on the basis of HS lines per se.

As Table 1 indicates, the integration into GATT/WTO of the products covered in the Annex is to be achieved in four stages. Stage One, beginning on 1 January 1995, requires contracting parties to integrate products listed in the Annex and accounting for not less than 16 percent of their total volume of imports in 1990. A further (minimum) 17 percent of 1990 imports is to be integrated at the start of Stage Two (1 January 1998), and an additional (minimum) 18 percent to follow at the start of Stage Three (1 January 2002). This leaves 49 percent of products to be integrated on the last day of the Agreement on 1 January 2005.

In this process, each importing country is free to choose the products to be integrated at each stage, the only constraint being that they must include some products from a specified list of categories: tops and yarns, fabrics, made-up textile products, and apparel. The Agreement gives no instruction as to how many products from each category are to be integrated at each stage. Countries are free to make these decisions unilaterally, and hence importing countries have substantial discretion in how they integrate their MFA trade restraints into normal GATT disciplines over the transition period.

Besides the products to be integrated at each stage of the Agreement, progressively higher-quota growth rates across stages will apply so as to also speed integration for remaining products. In Stage One, individual country growth rate quotas will be 16 percent higher than the growth rates established in preceding MFA bilateral agreements. In Stage Two, these growth rate quotas will be increased by a further 25 percent annually, and in Stage Three, they will be increased by a further 27 percent annually. See Table 2 for an illustration of how these stages are to work. This growth-on-growth approach tends to favor countries with high existing growth rate quotas, although the phase-out agreement also has provisions for a special treatment of small suppliers.[4]

The Agreement allows for special transitional safeguards in the sector, beyond those already allowable under GATT Article 19. These new safeguards permit importing countries to impose new trade restrictions when imports of a textile or apparel product cause serious damage, and the damage is attributed to the agreement. Such safeguards actions are to be applied

Table 2. Examples of Phased Increases in Quota Growth Rates

Stage of Integration	Year	Growth Factor to be Applied to MFA Growth Rate Quotas	Established Growth Rate* 3 percent	Base Quota: 100	Established Growth Rate* 5 percent	Base Quota: 100	Established Growth Rate* 6 percent	Base Quota: 100
Stage I	1	16%	3.48	103.4	5.8	105.8	6.96	107.0
	2		3.48	107.0	5.8	112.9	6.96	114.4
	3		3.48	110.8	5.8	119.5	6.96	122.4
Stage II	4	25%	4.35	115.5	7.25	128.2	8.70	133.0
	5		4.35	120.5	7.25	137.5	8.70	144.5
	6		4.35	125.7	7.25	147.4	8.70	157.1
	7		4.35	131.2	7.25	158.1	8.70	170.8
Stage III	8	27%	5.52	138.4	9.21	172.7	11.05	189.7
	9		5.52	146.1	9.21	188.6	11.05	210.6
	10		5.52	154.1	9.21	205.9	11.05	233.9

* This is the assumed growth rate carried over from the former MFA bilateral restraints.

Source: Trela, 1994. Based on United Nations Conference on Trade and Development (UNCTAD), 1994, Table 9.

selectively against particular exporters, but only on products covered by the Annex to the Agreement. They are not to be applied against certain products such as traditional folklore handicrafts, pure silk products, handloom fabrics, products of cottage industries, or historically traded textile products. Least-developed countries, small suppliers, wool-producing countries, and outward processing trade are to be accorded special treatment in the transitional safeguards, though the Agreement does not spell out its form in detail.

There are, however, clear restrictions which apply to these safeguards. One is that if these safeguards are used, they are not to reduce trade below the actual level of imports over the previous 12-month period for the country taking the action. Also, such measures can only be maintained for three years, and if a safeguard measure remains in force for more than a year, it must subsequently provide for quota growth of at least 6 percent annually.

Finally, the Agreement provides that flexibility provisions (swing, carry over, and carry forward) will be the same during the transitional period as under the previous MFA regime. These can be applied both to restrictions still in place, and to transitional safeguard measures. Countries that keep restrictions are prevented from setting limits on the combined use of swing, carryover, and carryforward. The Agreement also contains anticircumvention measures to deal with transhipment, rerouting, false declaration of country or place of origin, and falsification of official documents.

Assessing How the Agreement Will Operate

The Agreement in Textiles and Clothing is surprisingly complex, raising a number of issues as to how the Agreement will operate in practice, and how quickly and in what ways substantive liberalization under it will occur.

Perhaps the most important and the least uncertain feature of the Agreement is that it is not renewable, and thus MFA will cease to operate at its conclusion. But under it, all existing MFA restrictions will also be maintained until restrained products are reintegrated into GATT/WTO. And while existing restrictions are being phased out, new restrictions can be imposed under the transitional safeguard mechanism, with the criteria and procedures governing such actions bearing a strong resemblance to the market disruption provisions of MFA. They can also be applied against non-MFA signatories. Thus, despite the phaseout, the Agreement still represents a further extension of MFA over the transitional period.

One concern of developing countries is that if safeguards actions are invoked, they could have the effect of rolling back liberalization within the transition period. Another is that, by a variety of technical devices in applying the phaseout, effective adjustment could well be delayed until the end of the ten-year transitional period, and political pressures could well mount in importing countries for a further protective regime to replace MFA. Indeed, there is already major concern over the possibility of significantly increased use of dumping actions by developed countries in this sector, following its reintegration into GATT/WTO.

Exactly how much adjustment will occur before the end of ten years through the acceleration in quota growth rate is a key question. The Agreement provides for an elevation of growth factors in existing growth rate quotas, a potentially important element of liberalization compared to the previous MFA regime. But these acceleration factors will only have an impact if the growth rates carried over from the former MFA are significant, and the quotas which they represent are binding. The growth acceleration factors agreed for the three phases in the transition period are 16, 25, and 27 percent, respectively. Under these factors, an initial annual growth rate of 6 percent would increase to 11.05 in the third stage (see Table 2), or by a total of 134 percent over 10 years, potentially making some quotas nonbinding even before integration into GATT. But for a 1 percent quota growth rate, the annual growth rate under these acceleration provisions would never exceed 2 percent. Because the most sensitive products will likely be in this latter group and among the last to be integrated, given that the process for eliminating all quotas is backloaded with 49 percent of quotas remaining at the end of the period, the natural conclusion is that the majority of the binding protection in textiles and apparel will likely remain until the end of the transition period. And, if transitional safeguards further constrain annual import growth of products still subject to MFA restraints during the transition period, the level of protection remaining in the final stage could well be even larger.

Another issue is how the product phaseout will work over the various stages of the agreement. As importing countries are free to choose the products they will integrate at each stage of the transitional period,[5] they will likely choose unrestricted products to integrate in the early stages. The products identified in the Annex to the Agreement cover a number of tariff lines not currently restricted under MFA; but this does not prevent them being selected by importing countries for reintegration into GATT/WTO in the early phases. According to the International Textile and Clothing Board (1994) estimates, more than one third of the total volume of textile and apparel imports into the EU and the US are now unrestricted, reflecting in part large volumes of interdeveloped country trade. This feature will thus enable restraining countries if they so desire, to effectively delay the end of binding MFA restrictions until the beginning of the third stage, or in seven years. Even then the dismantling of MFA restrictions may not imply much meaningful trade liberalization if the most trade-restricted items are left until the final stage.

Indeed, the initial integration lists which have been submitted by the US and the EU suggest that the first stage of product integration will do little for developing country access to developed country markets. None of the products the US will be integrating in the first stage was covered by US quantitative restrictions in place in 1990, the most recent year for which comprehensive data are available. Moreover, there are no MFA categories included in the product list. While the integration list of the EU includes several MFA categories (69, 75, 85, 94, 134, 148A, and 153), none of these included any bilateral quota binding in 1990. Hence, as things now stand, the first stage of integration will most likely not have any meaningful impact on trade in textile and apparel products; and there are doubts about subsequent stages.

There is a range of additional complications in understanding how these arrangements will work. One is that both Canada and the US list products that they will be integrating in the first stage in terms of HS codes at a ten-digit level, despite the fact that the products covered by the Agreement and listed in the Annex use six-digit HS codes. By specifying products at the ten-digit level in this way, these countries have increased the number of items within the range of products covered by the Agreement, even though the import volumes remain the same. As a result, they have more unrestricted products to choose from, and hence more discretion in structuring their liberalization during the transition period. By contrast, other MFA-importing countries such as the EU, Austria, Finland, and Norway, have notified the products they will be integrating in the first stage using six-digit HS codes, as listed in the Annex.[6]

Furthermore, the selection of products from each of the four groups of tops and yarns, fabrics, made-up textile products, and clothing in each phase is left to the discretion of the importing countries, and hence the extent of integration is spread unevenly across these categories. The EU, for instance, will integrate products from each of the above groups, but from some countries it is as little as 3.1 percent of the trade volume of products listed in the Annex.

Given the complexity of, and differences among, the MFA classification systems in the importing countries, it is difficult to make clear judgments about either the speed or coverage of integration under the program, except to say that all products will be integrated into GATT after ten years. But because a significant number of MFA quotas are nonbinding, and the initial quota growth rates for the more sensitive products are restrictively low, the fear is that much of the effective long-run adjustment needed to eliminate MFA will be delayed until the tenth year of the phase-out. An additional concern for developing countries is that the phaseout of MFA will eventually trigger new trade restricting actions in importing countries, potentially removing some of the benefits of MFA liberalization.[7]

The Long-Run Effects of Eliminating the Multifiber Arrangement

Prior to discussing the effects of phased MFA elimination under the Uruguay Round Agreement on the Asian economies, it may be helpful to discuss some of the more significant effects MFA is believed to have on trade, production, and consumption in both importing and exporting countries, as well as some of its unintended effects, such as quality upgrading and quota-hopping investment among MFA exporters.[8] The gains for the Asian economies which will likely follow from the elimination of MFA after ten years all reflect an unwinding of these various effects. It is also perhaps worth flagging at this stage that model-based analyses tend to show the majority of benefits from the elimination of MFA as occurring on the consumption side in developed countries, rather than accruing to developing countries. This is, in part, because of the elimination of the rent transfer to exporters which accompanies the bilateral export quota arrangements used in this MFA.

Removal of Restraints on Trade

A central effect which, by universal agreement, can be attributed to MFA is that it has restrained exports of textiles and apparel from developing countries to developed countries. Most studies have found the decline in exports for developing countries due to MFA to be substantial. The United Nations Conference on Trade and Development (UNCTAD) (1986) estimated that complete nondiscriminatory liberalization involving both tariffs and the MFA quotas could increase developing country exports of clothing by 135 percent and textiles by 78 percent. A similar study by Kirmani et al. (1984) suggested that developing country exports to the major Organisation for Economic Co-operation and Development (OECD) countries could increase by 82 percent for textiles and 93 percent for clothing, if both MFA quotas and developed country tariffs were removed. Another study by the US International Trade Commission (USITC) (1989) estimated that the value of exports of constrained suppliers to the US would rise by 20 percent for textiles and 36 percent for clothing.

Trela and Whalley (1990), using a global general equilibrium model, in contrast to previous partial equilibrium exercises, estimate that individual developing countries could increase their exports by several hundred percent if both quota and tariff restrictions were removed. Their results show exports from developing countries increasing by more than imports would increase in the US, Canada, and the European Community because of the reduction in interdeveloped country trade. For example, their results suggested that imports by the US, Canada, and the European Community would increase by 305 percent, 200 percent, and 190 percent, respectively.

Rent Transfers

Another long-run effect of MFA elimination will be the termination of rent transfers between importing and exporting countries. These rents arise due to the export quotas in MFA, because exporters sell their restricted export volumes at higher domestic prices. MFA elimination will lower prices in importing countries, and eliminate these rent transfers. Some authors have suggested that these rent transfers may more than have compensated developing countries in the past for the restrictions placed on their market access.

Various attempts have been made to estimate the magnitude of transferred rents due to trade restrictions affecting textiles and apparel. A study by USITC (1989) estimates the quota premium on clothing products at 16.8 percent. Kumar and Khanna (1990) put Indian export tariff equivalents in 1989, averaged over product categories, from 14 percent in Canada to 42 percent in Ireland. A study by Chaudhry and Hamid (1988) estimated quota premiums for Pakistan which ranged from about 50 percent for cloth, to about 80 percent for cotton knitwear. Yet another study by Hamilton (1988) estimated that imported tariff equivalents of voluntary export restraints on clothing from Hong Kong in the EU over the period 1980 to 1984 were about 14 percent; in the US, these same premia were about 28 percent. Similarly, Morkre (1984) found that for nine major clothing product categories, the average quota premium for US imports from Hong Kong in 1980 amounted to 23 percent. An earlier editorial in *Textile Asia* (1976), published in Hong Kong, claimed quota premia accounted for 15 to 25 percent of export value.

Two important features of these quota premia are that they increase with tariff liberalization, because tariff cuts reduce the differential between the domestic market price in the importing country, and the net of duty price received by exporters; and the impact of MFA elimination on them depends partly on relative country size. If the importing country is small, domestic prices will equal export supply prices on MFA elimination, but if the importing country is large, smaller price changes will apply.

Degree of Restraint Implied by Quotas

The extent to which MFA actually restrains trade, despite the studies cited above, is also an issue. At issue is the degree of restrictiveness of quotas, or the extent of quota utilization. Rapid import growth in some OECD countries of textile and apparel products from developing countries has led some to query the extent to which MFA actually restricts textile and apparel exports from individual developing countries. Others argue that were it not for MFA restraints, even more rapid trade growth would occur.

Data from the World Bank data base on MFA, and reproduced here as Table 3, emphasize how sharp this debate is. In this data, quota utilization rates are reported for individual supplying countries, covering both textiles and clothing, and averaged across both importing countries and product categories. While these utilization rates are generally below 100 percent, they are also volatile and, for any given supplying country, show a wide variation across countries. They also differ across individual textile and clothing product categories. For example, in 1989, Bangladesh's utilization rates of Canadian quota ranged from 38 percent in outerwear to 97 percent in the category of shorts, pants, and overalls. This reflects in part, by exporters, the use of MFA flexibility provisions to respond to changing market conditions and shifts in fashion.[9]

Even these data, however, only provide inconclusive evidence as to the degree of restrictiveness of MFA quotas, because there are many reasons why seemingly binding quotas can in fact be nonbinding. One may be the way quota is allocated among importers. Some quotas in the EU, for instance, are allocated between importing countries on the basis of historical market shares, regardless of the geographic distribution of demands within the EU. Hence, demand for, say, winter coats may be unmet in some of the EU countries because quotas are binding, while quotas remain unused in other countries and are not allowed to be reallocated between countries. It can also be the case that there are aggregate quotas for, say, shirts which are less than the sum of the subaggregate quotas for, say, particular types

Table 3. Data on Quota Utilization Rates for Asian Economies in the
United States, European Union, and Canadian Markets
By Supplying Countries, 1989
(rates expressed as actual imports as a percent of quota available)

	Importing Country		
1. Asian Exporting Countries	United States	European Union	Canada
Bangladesh	89.8	n/a	69.3
China, People's Republic of	92.6	77.8	71.9
Hong Kong	87.9	88.2	92.7
India	72.8	71.4	85.9
Indonesia	95.1	81.9	90.9
Korea, Republic of	84.7	66.1	76.1
Macao	53.4	91.8	77.1
Malaysia	42.9	65.8	79.8
Pakistan	80.6	119.5	94.7
Philippines	83.1	65.5	53.3
Singapore	60.0	52.0	73.0
Sri Lanka	n/a	56.1	65.2
Thailand	89.1	93.2	87.1
2. Other Exporting Countries			
Argentina	n/a	34.7	n/a
Brazil	58.7	60.3	83.7
Colombia	25.9	n/a	n/a
Costa Rica	72.5	n/a	n/a
Czechoslovakia	n/a	60.1	76.8
Dominican Republic	n/a	n/a	86.9
Egypt	32.1	n/a	n/a
El Salvador	66.3	n/a	n/a
Guatemala	95.0	n/a	n/a
Hungary	47.4	44.4	98.9
Jamaica	51.0	n/a	n/a
Mexico	41.3	n/a	n/a
Peru	49.5	100.1	n/a
Poland	10.3	63.2	41.1
Romania	10.1	38.9	45.0
Turkey	n/a	n/a	84.4
Uruguay	n/a	n/a	61.9
Yugoslavia	35.7	64.3	n/a

Note: n/a: not available, usually because no bilateral agreement was in operation.

Source: Trela, 1994. Calculated from the World Bank computer files on MFA.

of shirts. Thus, quotas may not appear to be binding at subaggregate levels, while they might be binding at the aggregate level.[10] Also, some quotas are issued on a monthly basis at an even rate throughout the year; quotas in summer months for winter coats, for instance, can go unfulfilled giving the appearance of unutilized quotas in annual data.

Despite these debates over what is a binding quota, the rapid market penetration by developing countries of developed country textiles and clothing markets over the last 15 years suggests that many MFA restraints have indeed been relatively ineffective. Data from UNCTAD (1994) show that, for the period 1980 to 1992, clothing imports by developed countries have grown at relatively rapid rates, on average 10.2 percent annually, which is well above the notional 6 percent target originally incorporated in MFA. Textile imports, on the other hand, have risen relatively slowly, with the exception of a surge in 1984 and, to a lesser extent, 1986. For the whole period 1980 to 1992, textile imports have grown at an average rate of around 6.0 percent.

But while the market penetration of developing countries in textiles and especially apparel has been substantial, without MFA, exports of textiles and apparel from developing to developed countries would likely have been larger. As noted above, this is in part because the restrictive effects of MFA may be partially offset through various adjustments to basic quotas using MFA flexibility provisions; and flexibility provisions can create the appearance of laxness in restraints today while implying tighter restraints tomorrow. Much of the increase in clothing imports by the US in 1983/84, as Cline (1987) suggests, can be attributed to the flexibility provisions in MFA. These allowed exporters to take advantage of the overvalued dollar and the strong US recovery from recession in 1982. Flexibility provisions were also the main reason for the import surges in Canada in 1983/84. But flexibility through carrybackwards can mean more binding quotas subsequently.

Quality Upgrading and Product and Market Diversification

Another feature of MFA is that it generates its own offsetting features to its protective intent. One way this occurs is through quality upgrading, reflecting the feature that MFA restricts growth rates of export quantities rather than values (that is, by weight, number of pieces, or surface area). When faced with a volume restriction on their exports, producers can expand the value of sales by moving upmarket into higher quality lines within quota categories. This has been true of Hong Kong; Korea; and Taipei,China, which have succeeded in progressively establishing a stronger reputation for quality fabrics and sophisticated fashion the more they have exported. Lower-income countries have also engaged in quality upgrading. There has been substantial new investment in Bangladesh in recent years, for example, both within and out of quota-controlled categories. The intent is to improve productivity, design, and quality characteristics, and to build up local value-added and backward linkages to create a local fabrics industry.

Product diversification is another way exporting countries try to offset the effects of MFA quota restrictions. This has involved particular exporters moving into new, uncontrolled products, as well as using new products and fibers. For example, Rhee (1990) reported that as a result of efforts to diversify its products, Bangladesh is now exporting in 35 separate categories of clothing covering items made with cotton, wool, and man-made fibers.

Diversifying trade to nonquota markets is yet another response to MFA. In India, efforts to diversify exports away from quota-restricted markets are taken into account under the country's internal quota-distribution system. Consequently, and as Cable (1990) reports, Indian fabric exporters have started selling to Russia. Large export orders have also been secured in Japan by the Pakistan textile industry and in Japan, Russia, and the Gulf States by Sri Lankan exporters. In Bangladesh, efforts are under way recently to develop export sales to Russia, Japan, Australia, and the Middle East, in addition to countries in Europe.

Quota Hopping, Foreign Investment, and Other Related Effects

Yet another response to trade restraints under MFA has been geographical diversification in the form of "quota hopping," or investment flowing from heavily restricted to more lightly restricted countries. The increase in foreign investment activities of Hong Kong clothing industries in lower-wage, less quota-restricted countries, for example, can be partly viewed as such a response to Hong Kong's own quota limitations. Hong Kong investment occurred first in Macao in the mid-1970s, then in Sri Lanka and Indonesia in the late 1970s, and more recently in PRC, the Philippines, Jamaica, Costa Rica, the Dominican Republic, Panama, Maldives, Mauritius, and Bangladesh (Cable 1990). Another example is businessmen from Korea who ventured into Bangladesh in the late 1970s and early 1980s, not only to transfer physical capital, but also production technology and marketing and managerial know-how. This effort was motivated by a wish to evade quotas and develop an integrated buying and distribution operation, so as to expand the international market for their fabrics and machinery.

Internal Quota Allocation Rules

Finally, MFA has spawned a variety of internal quota allocation schemes within exporting countries. Under MFA, exporting countries have responsibility for administering the licensing system. Faced with this, individual developing countries have set up various quota allocation procedures (Trela and Whalley 1993). These allocation systems often involve reallocation of quota to the same firm each year, and other elements of rigidity. These features can lead to substantial economic inefficiency, and some argue they may have had equally adverse effects on developing countries as MFA itself.

Not permitting trade in licenses protects existing firms against more efficient producers and new domestic competition. The use of past performance criteria in allocating quota volumes can result in firms producing at suboptimal scale. Also, eligibility criteria, such as shipment to third-country (nonquota-restricted) markets, may have the effect of causing some of the rents derivable from ownership of quota to be dissipated. If full transferability were allowed, some firms might simply sell their allocation of licenses or even close down, but the firms which bought the licenses could then operate at a more efficient scale.

In recent work, Trela and Whalley (1993) have used their global general equilibrium model referred to earlier to estimate the effects of MFA restrictions on developing countries, incorporating the additional effects associated with internal quota allocation schemes as commonly used in the exporting countries. The theme that emerges strongly from their analysis is that gains to developing countries from an elimination of MFA quotas are substantially larger in a model which captures the effects of these internal quota allocation schemes than in a similar model in which they are absent. In addition, several countries who are losers from an MFA removal in a model without internal quota allocation schemes, emerge as gainers in a model which incorporates them.

Implications of the Elimination of the Multifiber Arrangement on Asian Economies

Having set out the main features of the Uruguay Round Agreement regarding textiles and apparel, and the various effects attributable to MFA, it remains to provide an assessment of the implications of MFA removal for Asia. As noted in the introduction, the bloc-wide assessment of the longer-term implications for Asia seems both clear and ambiguous:

281

because constrained textile and apparel exporters are in Asia including South Asia, while unconstrained exporters dominate in Latin and Central America, Asia as a region would clearly seem to benefit from an elimination of MFA. But on the other hand, the diversity among the Asian economies makes generalization based on a bloc-wide pattern difficult. In addition, in the short run and during the transitional ten-year period, it seems likely that the more severely restrained products and countries will be the last to be removed from restraint, implying, de facto, that Asian exporters will likely remain under restraint longer than those from other regions.

Quantifying exactly these effects is difficult, because there are estimates of only a few of the effects from MFA that are listed above. Most studies concentrate on the trade and welfare effects of MFA elimination, and do not take into account quality upgrading, quota hopping, and investment, or other effects. Strong assumptions are also made as to what degree of quota utilization represents a binding trade restriction; and also which countries have binding quotas.

Welfare Effects of Elimination of the Multifiber Arrangement

The potential long-run welfare effects of the Asian economies that might follow from MFA elimination can, in part, be gauged from the general equilibrium study of the global effects of textile and apparel trade restrictions by Trela and Whalley (1990) mentioned earlier. In this model, bilateral trade restrictions covering textile and clothing exports between three major importing regions, the EU, the US, and Canada, and 34 developing country exporters are captured within a structure calibrated to 1986 global data on production, consumption, and trade, and covering 14 textile and apparel items and residual other goods. Constant Elasticity of Substitution and Constant Elasticity of Transformation functions characterize production and demands in each region, with literature-based and central case elasticities used.

Welfare effects on developing countries from MFA elimination in this model can be either positive or negative because they gain from improved market access, but lose from the removal of rent transfers. Importantly, because developing countries are small relative to large, developed country importers, rent-transfer effects are not as large in this model as often assumed under price-taking importing country behavior. If quotas are nonbinding for particular exporting countries, then these countries will lose from MFA elimination as additional previously restricted suppliers penetrate industrial country markets.

This model also ignores quality upgrading, which can be a significant effect, and quota hopping, circumvention, and other issues. It also ignores rent sharing due to monopolistic retailers in developed countries, as stressed by Krishna and Tan (1992).

Table 4 reports welfare impacts in terms of Hicksian equivalent variations for two different counter-factual experiments with the model. The first column reports results where both MFA quotas and developed-country

Table 4. Estimates of General Equilibrium Welfare Effects of Removing Import Trade Restrictions on Textiles and Clothing in Developed Countries

	Case 1	Case 2
	Country Welfare Gain or Loss in Terms of Hicksian Equivalent Variations ($ billion 1986)	Country Welfare Gain or Loss in Terms of Hicksian Equivalent Variations ($ billion 1986)
Asian Countries		
Bangladesh	0.237	0.188
China, People's Republic of	1.827	0.944
Hong Kong	-0.519	-1.080
India	0.077	-0.071
Indonesia	0.610	0.361
Korea, Republic of	1.579	0.779
Macao	-0.030	-0.089
Malaysia	0.217	0.143
Nepal	0.028	0.017
Pakistan	0.008	-0.016
Philippines	0.127	0.003
Singapore	-0.012	-0.084
Sri Lanka	0.048	-0.015
Taipei,China	1.193	0.308
Thailand	0.025	-0.048
All Asia	5.415	1.318
All Other Developing Countries	2.663	1.616
United States	12.309	15.038
Canada	0.831	0.928
European Union	2.215	3.039
All Other Developing Countries	2.663	1.616
All Countries	23.435	21.941

Note: Case 1: Removal of bilateral MFA quotas and developed country tariffs on textiles and clothing.
Case 2: Removal of bilateral MFA quotas, but not tariffs.

Source: Trela and Whalley, 1990. Tables 3 and 4.

tariffs on textiles and clothing are abolished. The second column reports results where only MFA quotas are abolished, with the tariffs left in place.

In the first case, global gains are $23.4 billion, of which $15.3 billion accrues to the developed countries, and only $8.1 billion to the developing countries: $5.4 billion accrues to Asia, with PRC the largest gainer at $1.8 billion. Hong Kong loses due to high-wage rates, as do Macao and Singapore. All the other Asian countries appear as gainers, with the next largest gains accruing to Taipei,China and Korea. These latter gains, in part, reflect the use of 1986 data by Trela and Whalley, rather than more current data. However, overall these results seem consistent with the intuition offered earlier, that among the developing country exporters, it is exporting countries in Asia who have potentially the most to gain from a long-term elimination of MFA.

In the second case, global gains are slightly smaller at $21.9 billion, but gains to developed countries are higher at $19.0 billion, with gains to developing countries smaller at $2.9 billion. Gains to the Asian economies are sharply lower at $1.3 billion. This pattern of difference between the two sets of results reflects the feature that the presence of tariffs reduces rent transfers to textile and apparel exporters.

Two more recent studies (Harrison et al. 1995, Hertel et al. 1995) also show the large majority of benefits from MFA elimination accruing to consumers on the demand-side in the importing, industrialized economies. The results in Harrison et al. suggest that PRC will gain over $2 billion a year, and Indonesia, Malaysia, Philippines, and Thailand, members of the Association of Southeast Asian Nations (ASEAN), will gain nearly $3 billion annually. The results in Hertel et al. imply larger gains when considering elimination of restrictions in the year 2005, because with growth in the underlying real economy, the severity of restrictions increases over time, even with the phaseout arrangement in place.

Long-Run Trade and Production Effects for Asian Economies

The trade and production effects following elimination of MFA are reported by Trela and Whalley, and are summarized in Table 5. These results also show a significant positive impact on performance for the Asian exporters, and associated negative impacts on production in the developed countries. Thus, in the case of Indonesia and Malaysia, more than 50 percent increases in the production of textiles and clothing result from the abolition of MFA. Increases of 38 percent for Bangladesh, 44 percent for Sri Lanka, 38 percent for Singapore, and 25 percent for the Philippines also occur. A smaller impact occurs for the larger producers: 11 percent for

PRC and 8 percent for India. There are also increases in production for Hong Kong, and hence, the argument that MFA is a "zero-sum" game which protects high-cost suppliers at the expense of low-cost suppliers, is cast in doubt because of the pattern of production shown.

Because under MFA elimination producers at the margin receive prices on exports equal to the domestic prices in the importing country, the elimination of transferred rents means that prices in importing countries are producers' prices net of tariffs. But because marginal sales from quota-constrained suppliers are onto domestic markets, the effect of eliminating MFA restraints is that production rises. In contrast, there are falls in production in the importing countries as protection is withdrawn. In the US, Canada, and the EU, on average the effect is around 18 percent. Along

Table 5. Estimates of Production and Trade Effects of Removing Bilateral Multifiber Arrangement Quotas and Tariffs on Textiles and Apparel

	Change in Value of Production of Textiles and Apparel (percent)	Change in Value of Imports and Exports of Textiles and Apparel (percent)
Asian Countries		
Bangladesh	38.19	141.00
China, People's Republic of	11.26	433.57
Hong Kong	15.86	66.15
India	8.20	197.78
Indonesia	54.19	461.01
Korea, Republic of	34.60	314.88
Macao	3.29	25.60
Malaysia	53.13	274.82
Mauritius	24.11	101.48
Nepal	12.24	161.13
Pakistan	13.24	23.29
Philippines	25.83	183.14
Singapore	37.82	122.30
Sri Lanka	44.92	105.34
Taipei,China	27.59	223.97
Thailand	24.74	54.01
United States	-25.14	305.49
Canada	-18.58	200.17
European Union	-12.42	190.16

Source: Trela and Whalley, 1990.

with these changes in production come large changes in trade with increases in import volumes (300 percent in the US) and large increases in export volumes in some of the larger exporters, including Indonesia, PRC, and Malaysia.

The Special Position of the People's Republic of China

All in all, under elimination of MFA the prospect for the Asian exporting countries is one of large increases in trade volumes and correspondingly large adjustments in the importing countries. But in the discussion of the impact of MFA elimination on the Asian economies, it is important to keep in mind that PRC occupies a special position in such an assessment.

PRC has recently surged substantially in this sector (see Table 6). The potential for further large surges is there; and PRC is still not a member of GATT/WTO. PRC's potential in textiles and clothing is currently so large that under an MFA elimination, some have speculated that PRC could rapidly become the dominant supplier in the global textile and apparel market. Since the mid-1980s, Chinese exports of textiles and clothing have grown progressively to the point that PRC now accounts for the largest shipments of any developing country exporter into the markets of the EU and the US, displacing Hong Kong; Korea; and Taipei,China. The share of Chinese exports in the world trade of textiles and apparel has more than doubled between 1985 and 1991, whereas the share of exports from Hong Kong and Korea has been falling also. Generally, trade among the developed countries has been falling.

This all suggests that PRC will increasingly be a focal point for pressure for trade protection in apparel as has been evident in bilateral US-PRC trade relations. In being outside of WTO pending admission through accession, the position of PRC is especially difficult. Without membership in WTO, PRC would suffer no special protection against the use of selective safeguards continuing after the transitional period following the termination of MFA. Indeed, special safeguards actions could, in principle, be applied unilaterally against PRC even in the transitional period, although in reality this is unlikely as the Uruguay Round Agreement in textiles and apparel covers non-GATT signatories. The potential impact of MFA elimination on PRC becomes especially severe if this country remains outside the framework of GATT, with special selective safeguards applied against PRC after the transitional period. On the other hand, with no selective safeguards, there is the issue of whether PRC will come to dominate the global industry.

Other Issues With the Asian Economies

It is also the case that for the Asian economies there are a number of other effects associated with their participation in MFA which needs to enter any evaluation of the effects on them of MFA elimination. It is the Asian economies, for instance, that have seen the most-pronounced quota hopping and investment effects from MFA quotas, particularly in the case of Hong Kong; Korea; and Taipei,China, from which there has been extensive outflow of investment in the textiles and apparel sector. Hence, one effect from the elimination of MFA, and not captured in the calculations mentioned above, will be a slow repatriation of capital which has left higher-wage countries in response to MFA interventions by the exporting countries.

Quality upgrading has also been a response by Asian clothing suppliers to MFA trade restrictions, to the point that higher cost Asian suppliers such as Hong Kong; Korea; and Taipei,China now generally occupy the highest-quality segments of the apparel market, in part because of these quota-driven pressures. Because the outcome in the presence of MFA restrictions already reflects substitution effects across qualities, unwinding

Table 6. Shares of Countries in World Exports of Clothing
(percent)

	1980	1992	1980-1992	1991	1992
PRC	4.0	12.8	21	27	36
Hong Kong	11.5	7.6	12	17	12
Italy	11.3	9.4	9	-1	4
Germany	7.1	6.4	9	6	12
Korea, Republic of	7.3	5.2	7	-6	-9
France	5.7	4.0	7	2	10
United States	3.1	3.2	11	29	27
Turkey	0.3	3.2	33	4	20
Taipei,China	6.0	3.1	4	12	-8
Portugal	1.6	3.1	17	3	12
Thailand	0.7	2.9	25	30	3
United Kingdom	4.6	2.8	6	12	8
Indonesia	0.2	2.4	34	38	40
India	1.5	2.4	15	0	23
Netherlands	2.2	2.1	10	12	10
Others	33.1	29.5			

Source: GATT, 1993. Table III.42:70.

these trade restrictions will probably have larger welfare effects than current estimates imply, because quality response has already taken place in response to the trade restrictions imposed on them.[11] The elimination of MFA restrictions will have the effect of unwinding these responses, including quota hopping. Hence, a realignment of the cross-country investment profile within the global textiles and apparel industry may take place, having an impact on the allocation of production between higher-income and lower-income countries.

A further complication is that the cost situation in the key Asian exporting economies is only known with uncertainty. At the point of the launch of the negotiations in the Uruguay Round, when a commitment to phase out MFA was jointly made, it became clear that several developing countries were opposed on the grounds that they did not consider themselves to be cost competitive with other developing countries. This was also true of some of the lower-income developing countries.

The difficulty is that after more than 25 years of restraints on exports of textiles and apparel globally, it is not clear to individual countries whom they are competitive with, and hence their concern over the impact of liberalization. Many of these concerns have been evident among the higher-cost Asian economies, but at the same time these economies have generally supported the elimination of MFA on grounds that a systemic commitment to return the trading system to clear multilateral disciplines is consistent with their wider interest in a multilateral rules-based trading system. But difficulties in determining individual country gains and losses are amplified by this clouded picture on relative competitiveness.

A recent United Nations Industrial Development Organization (1990) report provides estimates of hourly wage rates in the apparel industry across selected countries for 1987, indicating, not surprisingly, that the wage-rate differentials are large. These are shown in Table 7. These will have narrowed somewhat since 1987, but they indicate that the intercountry effects within Asia of MFA elimination could be large. At the same time, the share of exports accounted for by textiles and apparel of the higher-wage Asian economies is beginning to fall, a feature which would soften the adjustments involved.

Conclusion

This chapter discusses the impact on the Asian economies of the ten-year phased elimination of MFA under the Uruguay Round Agreement. It sets out the complexities associated with the ten-year transitional process

Table 7. Hourly Wages in Apparel Industries in Selected Countries, 1987

Country or Area	Basic Wage ($)	Fringe Benefits and Other Costs as Percentage of Basic Rate	Effective Wage ($)
PRC	0.23	25	0.29
Hong Kong	2.65	14	1.88
Korea, Republic of	1.78	45	2.50
Taipei,China	2.20	47	3.23
United States	5.47	31	7.17

Source: United Nations Industrial Development Organization, 1990:40.

in the Agreement, and emphasizes how during the phaseout, it seems likely that relatively little liberalization will occur because of the ways in which the products are sequentially taken out of coverage of MFA, and various growth rate factors are applied to MFA quotas to accelerate the liberalization process. It also emphasizes how likely it is that, in being the most severely restrained, Asian products and exporters will probably also be the last to emerge from restraint. The argument on the phaseout, therefore, is that MFA will likely remain largely in place over the ten-year transitional period, and will only disappear at the end of the tenth year.

The effects on Asian countries are therefore best gauged in terms of the potential long-run effects. Among the developing countries, the Asian countries are perhaps the best placed compared to any other developing countries to gain from MFA elimination. This is partly because of the degree of binding of the trade restrictions which they face; and the fact that as a bloc they will clearly gain relative to other developing country exporters, many of whom face nonbinding quotas.

Having said this, however, the differences between the Asian economies are so clear in terms of level of development and wage-rate differentials, and length of membership to MFA (and hence the size of quota to which growth rates have been subsequently applied), that some redistribution between countries seems inevitable. Relative losers would seem to be Hong Kong, and to a lesser extent, Korea and Taipei,China. PRC is in a somewhat peculiar position. Even though textile and apparel exports are rapidly growing, PRC is potentially subject to special, selective safeguards because of it being outside WTO as MFA terminates. Other lower-income economies that are now showing substantial growth in their textile and clothing export volumes, including India and Pakistan, would seem to be among the clear gainers.

Annex

EFFECTS OF CHANGES IN MARKET ACCESS IN MANUFACTURES OTHER THAN TEXTILES AND APPAREL FOR DEVELOPING ASIA

Beyond the effects of liberalization in textiles and apparel from the Uruguay Round discussed in the main body of this paper, a number of other elements in the decisions from the Round clearly affect the market access situation for the Asian economies in other manufactured exports.

Tariff Reductions

In the tariff area, the Round has yielded significant percentage reductions by the industrial countries, although these apply on a relatively low base in most cases, except for a few items with significant tariffs, such as apparel. Early in the Round it was agreed that tariffs on industrial products could be reduced by at least one third, but the cuts achieved are slightly larger averaging around 35 percent, with slightly higher cuts than this in the smaller OECD countries. In some sectors, tariffs have been eliminated in the developed world, including in steel, pharmaceuticals, and wood products. While the cuts involved in industrial countries are modest, as far as the Asian economies are concerned, immediate trade impacts will flow from these reductions in tariffs. The pre- and post-Round tariffs by product for aggregated categories are reproduced here as Table A1 and taken from Francois, McDonald, and Nordstrom (1994). There is also a series of other issues in the tariff area, which applies less to Asia than to other lower-income developing economies, including erosion of preference margins under such arrangements, such as Lomé. Another aspect of the decisions in this area from the Round is the substantial expansion in tariff bindings for the developing countries.

Other Changes

Beyond the tariff area there are other changes in key areas which impinge on the market access of the Asian economies. These affect access less directly, and rather change the risk of truncated market access in the future. The important changes occur in the broad area of trade rules, one of which is the agreement on antidumping. The Uruguay Round agreements

Table A1. Pre- and Post-Uruguay Round
Most-Favored Nation Tariff Rates on Nonagricultural Products

Product	Australia and New Zealand			Canada			United States			Japan		
	Old Level	New Level	Percent Cut	Old Level	New Level	Percent Cut	Old Level	New Level	Percent Cut	Old Level	New Level	Percent Cut
Fishery Products	0.7	0.5	28.3	3.2	2.1	34.4	1.2	0.9	20.6	5.7	4.1	28.6
Forestry Products	0.2	0.2	0	0	0	34.3	0.3	0	100	0	0	30.2
Mining	1.5	1.1	31.5	2.6	1.3	49.3	1.3	0.8	36.4	1.3	0.6	56.3
Textiles	24.6	14.5	41.1	18.6	11.7	36.8	10.5	7.5	29	7.4	6	19.5
Clothing	50.5	34.8	31	22.9	16.6	27.7	16.7	15.2	9.1	13	10.2	21.9
Primary Steel	9.7	1.6	83.5	7.4	0.4	95.2	4.5	0.2	95.2	3.9	0.6	84.6
Primary Nonferrous Metals	11.2	6.4	42.8	4.9	2.7	44.4	2.9	2.6	7.2	4.1	2.4	41.7
Fabricated Metal Products	17.1	12.7	25.9	9.7	6	37.8	4.7	2.8	41.1	3.4	0.9	74.3
Chemicals and Rubber	11.9	7.5	37	10.3	5.3	48.4	5	3	39.7	4.1	1.6	60.9
Transport Equipment	25.7	19.4	24.8	8.1	5.4	34.1	4.8	4.6	4.5	1.5	0	100
Other Manufactures	11.6	7.6	34.5	6.3	2.9	54.3	3.5	1.5	56.5	2	0.9	52.1
Trade-Weighted Average	14.2	9.5	32.9	7.4	4.2	43.9	4.6	3.2	30.1	4.4	2.7	38.2

Table A1. Pre- and Post-Uruguay Round
Most-Favored Nation Tariff Rates on Nonagricultural Products (cont'd.)

Product	European Union			European Free Trade Area			Developing/Transitional Economies		
	Old Level	New Level	Percent Cut	Old Level	New Level	Percent Cut	Old Level	New Level	Percent Cut
Fishery Products	12.9	10.7	17.4	1.7	1.4	17.9	35.2	8.1	76.9
Forestry Products	0	0	100	0.2	0.1	48	0.1	0.1	14.3
Mining	1.1	0.8	27.3	1	0.8	23.2	11.5	9.5	17.6
Textiles	9	6.8	25	12.2	8	34.3	30.3	20.3	33
Clothing	12.6	10.9	13.2	17	11.4	33.1	14.6	10.8	25.9
Primary Steel	5.3	0.5	90.8	4.1	0.6	85.7	8.7	6.1	30.7
Primary Nonferrous Metals	7.2	5.9	17.9	4	2.9	26.4	2.7	2.1	20.7
Fabricated Metal Products	5.7	3.1	46.4	5.3	3	43.1	8.5	6.9	18.9
Chemicals and Rubber	7.7	4.2	44.8	5.8	3	48.9	19.1	13.2	30.7
Transport Equipment	6.9	6	13	7.5	6.3	16.2	27.2	17.3	36.6
Other Manufactures	5.5	2.5	54.7	4.3	2.3	46.9	18	13.3	26.1
Trade-Weighted Average	5.3	3.2	39.7	6.2	3.9	36.4	13.5	9.8	27.4

Source: Francois, McDonald, and Nordstrom, 1994.

in this area deal with the procedures and the application of rules for methods of determination of dumping; the criteria to be used in determining whether dumped products cause injury; and the procedures to be followed to initiate antidumping investigations. The revisions made to the antidumping code in the Round generally tighten the application of antidumping rules.

Another relevant agreement is that on subsidies and countervailing measures. Here the agreement establishes different categories of subsidies: prohibited subsidies, including subsidies contingent on export performance; actionable subsidies, including subsidies which cause adverse effects on members; and nonactionable subsidies, including subsidies for industrial research and regional assistance.

The agreement on safeguards is also a key element of the Uruguay Round decisions in the trade rules area for the Asian economies, because it is in the agreement on safeguards that a four-year commitment to a phaseout of voluntary export restraints is to be found. See the more extended discussion in Low and Yeats (1995). In addition, there are other important elements to the agreement, which include a limited redefinition of nondiscrimination to include a new, if limited form of selectivity through quota modulation. In addition, safeguards are made very clearly time-digressive for the first time.

All in all, these changes materially affect market access for manufactured products other than clothing and textiles for the developing Asian economies. While not perhaps representing major change in the system itself, long-term impacts will follow from all of these changes, even if their precise quantitative importance remains to be determined.

Acknowledgment

An earlier draft of this chapter was prepared for a conference on "The Impact of the Uruguay Round on Asia" held at the Asian Development Bank, Manila, 29-31 May 1995. It draws on collaboration and joint work over the years on various pieces of research work on trade in textiles and clothing executed jointly with Irene Trela of the University of Western Ontario.

Notes

[1] This subsection draws on the description of the Uruguay Round decisions covering textiles and apparel in Trela (1994).

[2] MFA restrictions applied by GATT-contracting parties against noncontracting parties are also covered.

[3] The agreement also covers non-MFA restrictions affecting textiles and apparel products, including all unilateral restrictions, bilateral arrangements, and other measures having a similar effect. The agreement is that all GATT-inconsistent, non-MFA restrictions are to be brought into conformity with GATT within one year following the entry into force of the Agreement, or phased out progressively during the transition period (2005).

[4] These are suppliers whose restrictions represent 1.2 percent or less of the total volume of restrictions applied by any importing country as of 31 December 1991. These suppliers are to be granted yet further improvements in access for their exports during the transition period by advancing one stage of the growth rates (their growth rates will be increased at the beginning of each stage by 25, 27, and 27 percent, respectively). Small suppliers of textiles and apparel include the following: Colombia, Macao, and Uruguay, in their exports to Canada; Peru and Sri Lanka, in their exports to the European communities; Sri Lanka, in its exports to Finland; and Argentina, Costa Rica, Jamaica, Macao, Peru, Uruguay, and Yugoslavia, in their exports to the US. These reflect ITCB estimates, and are based on specific limits in the bilateral agreements under MFA (GATT 1994:Table 10).

[5] The only constraint being that they include products from each of the following categories: tops and yarns, fabrics, made-up textile products, and clothing.

[6] However, the EU's integration list includes some items which constitute only a fraction of the full HS item at the six-digit level the EU uses when computing the amount of imports integrated. For this reason, the amount of trade actually integrated by the EU at each stage will, in reality, be less than what is specified in the Agreement.

[7] Developing countries are also concerned about the continuation of high tariffs and tariff peaks. The Uruguay Round will cut developed-country tariffs by an average of 38 percent, but more limited cuts were agreed for textiles and clothing, where the reductions average only 22 percent. This sector also remains subject to numerous tariff peaks. For example, the share of developed-country imports of textiles and apparel subject to tariff peaks will be reduced from 38 percent to 28 percent only (OECD 1994).

[8] Also see the recent discussion of these and other effects in Faini, de Melo, and Takacs (1995).

[9] These flexibility provisions include "swing" provisions which allow an exporting country to shift some portion of an underutilized quota to a product category where the quota is binding, and an allowance for a country to "carry

over" unfilled quota balances from the previous year or to "carry forward" from the following year's quota.

[10] Chaudry and Hamid (1988), for example, found that in 1983 "the overall US quota for Pakistan was less than the aggregate category-wide quotas by 13.4 percent. Thus, though a category-wide quota may be available, increased export sales may become impossible because of aggregate quota limitations."

[11] Also see the discussion of welfare effects of quality upgrading in Hutton and Whalley (1994).

References

Cable, V., 1990. "Adjusting to Textile and Clothing Quotas: A Summary of Some Commonwealth Countries' Experiences as a Pointer to the Future." In C. Hamilton, ed., *Textiles Trade and the Developing Countries: Eliminating the Multifiber Arrangement in the 1990s*. Washington: World Bank.

Chaudhry, S. A. and J. Hamid, 1988. "Foreign Trade Barriers to Exports: Pakistan." In *Foreign Trade Barriers and Export Growth*. Manila: Asian Development Bank.

Cline, W. R., 1987. *The Future of World Trade in Textiles and Apparel*. 2nd ed. Washington: Institute for International Economics.

Faini, R., J. De Melo, and W. Takacs, 1995. "A Primer on the MFA Maze." *The World Economy* 18(1):113-135.

Francois, M., and Nordstrom, 1994. "The Uruguay Round: A Critical Assessment." Geneva. Mimeographed.

General Agreement on Tariffs and Trade (GATT), 1993. *International Trade Statistics, 1993*. Geneva.

_____, 1994. *International Trade Statistics, 1994*. Geneva.

Hamilton, C., 1988. "Restrictiveness and International Transmission of the 'New Protectionism'." In R. Baldwin, C. Hamilton, and A. Sapir, eds., *Issues in US-EC Trade Relations*. National Bureau of Economic Research and University of Chicago Press.

Harrison, G. W., T. F. Rutherford, and D.G. Tarr, 1995. "Quantifying the Uruguay Round." Paper presented at the World Bank Conference on The Uruguay Round and Developing Economies, 26-27 January, Washington, D.C.

Hertel, T., W. Martin, K. Yanagashima, and B. Dimaranan, 1995. "Liberalizing Manufactures Trade in a Changing World Economy." Paper presented at the World Bank Conference on The Uruguay Round and Developing Economies, 26-27 January, Washington, D.C.

Hutton, E. and J. Whalley, 1994. Reference Point Dependence For Specification Bias From Quality Upgrading. Working Paper Series No. 4816. National Bureau of Economic Research, Cambridge, Massachusetts.

International Textiles and Clothing Bureau (ITCB), 1994. CR/XIX/ARQ:3 (3 June).

Kirmani, N., P. Molajani, and T. Mayer, 1984. "Effects of Increased Market Access on Exports of Developing Countries." International Monetary Fund, Washington, D.C.

Krishna, K., and L. H. Tan, 1992. "Rent Sharing in the Multi-Fibre Arrangement: Evidence from US-Hong Kong Trade in Apparel." Policy Research Working Paper No. 1003. World Bank.

Kumar, K., and Sri Ram Khanna, 1990. "India, the Multi-Fibre Arrangement and the Uruguay Round." In C. Hamilton, ed., *Textiles, Trade and the Developing Countries: Eliminating the Multi-fibre Arrangement in the 1990s*. Washington, D.C.: World Bank.

Low, P., and A. Yeats, 1995. "Non-Tariff Measures and the Uruguay Round." *The World Economy* 18(1):51-70.

Morkre, M. E., 1984. "Import Quotas on Textiles: The Welfare Effects of US Restrictions on Hong Kong." Bureau of Economics Staff Report to the Federal Trade Commission. Washington, D.C.

Organisation for Economic Co-operation and Development (OECD), 1994. *A Preliminary Assessment of the Impact of the Uruguay Round on Developing Countries*. Paris.

Rhee, Y. W., 1990. "The Catalyst Model of Development: Lessons From Bangladesh's Success with Garment Exports." *World Development* 18:333-46.

Textile Asia, 1976. April.

Trela, I., 1994. "Textiles and Clothing in the Uruguay Round." Draft paper prepared for an UNCTAD-Ford Foundation Project. University of Western Ontario.

Trela, I., and J. Whalley, 1990. "Global Effects of Developed Country Trade Restrictions on Textiles and Apparel." *Economics Journal* 100:1190-1205.

_____, 1993. "Internal Quota Allocation Schemes and the Costs of the MFA." Centre for the Study of International Economic Relations, University of Western Ontario. London, Canada and the *Review of International Economics* 3(3).

United Nations Conference on Trade and Development (UNCTAD), 1986. *Protectionism and Structural Adjustment*. New York.

_____, 1994. *The Outcome of the Uruguay Round: An Initial Assessment.* New York.

United Nations Industrial Development Organization, 1990. *Industry and Development, Global Report 1989/90.* New York.

United States International Trade Commission (USITC), 1989. *The Economic Effects of Significant US Import Restraints.* ITC Publication 2222.

Comments on "The Impact of the Multifiber Arrangement
Phaseout on the Asian Economies"

by

Joseph Francois

What are the implications of the Agreement on Textiles and
Clothing for Asian developing economies? The chapter by
Whalley highlights a number of important points in this regard.
These include the uneven nature of accelerated quota-growth rates under
the Agreement, the scope for application of special safeguards, the importance of quota rents to the whole process of Multifiber Arrangement (MFA)
dismantlement, the pace of the proposed phaseout, and the quantitative
implications of the phaseout. In my comments, I will first expand on two
of these — safeguards and the pace of phaseout — examining their implications for the odds for the success of the planned phaseout. I will then
turn to a brief discussion of the likely pattern of structural adjustment that
would follow from a successful phaseout.

The MFA — To Be Phased Out or Renamed?

Whalley emphasizes the "long-run" impact of liberalization. This
may be appropriate not only because adjustment will take many years, but
perhaps also because the phaseout may also take longer than the ten years
envisioned in the Agreement on Textiles and Clothing. The Agreement
contains provisions for "special safeguards," in addition to Article 19
safeguards. A number of economists have focused on these as a potential
source of friction. Whalley argues that special safeguards may also offer yet
another opportunity to backload the MFA phaseout, beyond the
backloading explicitly contained in the Agreement. While Whalley ex-
presses concern about special safeguards, I would argue that we should
look one step further, at the potential application of other contingent
measures, especially Article VI of the General Agreement on Tariffs and
Trade (GATT) (antidumping) and the Agreement on Subsidies and
Countervailing Measures. Recall that, under the MFA regime, there had
been an implicit understanding that, as long as exporters played the game
of restrictive quotas, they would not be subjected to antidumping or

countervailing duty measures. Like the participants in the now-expired United States steel-quota regime, participants in MFA had to weigh the costs and benefits of participation in the regime against the threat of contingent protection. The result has been a relatively stable arrangement for existing exporters, with provisions for bringing new exporters and products into the fold as they emerge, and with the carrot and stick of quota rents and threatened contingent protection to keep the exporters in line.

The game will be quite different, in a world without MFA-type quota arrangements. The result will be pressure for protection in the currently restricted Organisation for Economic Co-operation and Development markets, with a high probability that we will observe a wave of petitions for import relief under either general World Trade Organization (WTO)-sanctioned Article 19 safeguard mechanisms, or under antidumping and countervailing duty mechanisms. Such an outcome could lead to comparable (or worse) restrictions than those we have under the current regime. At a minimum, exporters would face much more uncertainty about market-access conditions. Critical differences would be the recapture of the current quota rents by the importing countries through contingent import duties, and the increased uncertainty about market access that follows from threats of contingent protection. Even under the alternative of general safeguards, under the new GATT 1994 Agreement on Safeguards (Article II Section 1(b) footnote 3), there is a scope for import quotas "administered by the exporting Member." The possibility, at least, exists for a GATT-legal regime made up of a mix of selective tariffs viewed as legal under GATT antidumping and countervailing duty codes, combined with new quotas implemented under the Agreement on Safeguards. Depending on how the sunset provisions of the contingent protection rules operate in practice, we could see individual products and exporters, over time, cycling between the various options offered under the contingent protection menu.

This is rather a bleak picture, and certainly not the one envisioned by the negotiators on the Agreement on Textiles and Clothing. How likely is it that we will actually see such an outcome, with new duties and quotas replacing the old regime? This depends critically on the pace of the phaseout, and the seriousness with which the parties to the Agreement work to implement the spirit of the Agreement. This is also why we should be worried about warnings on backloading. By design, even with genuine liberalization through the phaseout period, a substantial share of textile and clothing trade (49 percent to be exact) has been saved for coverage by the Agreement on Textiles and Clothing until the very end of the phaseout period. As Whalley has pointed out, even with accelerated quota rates, sensitive products, which are often characterized by low-benchmark growth rates, are likely to remain quite restricted under the Agreement even at the end of the ten-year period. There is even scope, with disingenuous scheduling of products in the early phase of the Agreement (as in fact occurred in the first phase), to backload almost all of the product graduation, for genuinely restricted products, until the last phase of the ten-year phaseout period. In the parlance of contingent protection injury tests, this implies a "surge" or potential surge in imports. Such a surge would surely be sufficient to justify positive injury findings under contingent protection rules. This would, in turn, justify the application of contingent duties in the eyes of WTO.

Applied analysis of the MFA phaseout provides yet another reason to worry about backloading and deferred liberalization. In their computable generalized equilibrium-based research on the Uruguay Round, Hertel et al. (1996) have found that underlying growth trends in Asia imply that, as currently administered, the quota regime for textiles and clothing will be much more restrictive than it is today. This is because of expected supply-side growth over the next ten years. This finding adds yet more weight to the notion that a delayed liberalization may prove to be an impossible liberalization.

The pitfalls flagged by Whalley, combined with the added risks of the backloading implementation I have listed above, all point to the need for active management. The Agreement on Textiles and Clothing, as it stands, will not work unless there is genuine cooperation between importing and exporting interests, leading to genuine liberalization through the full implementation period. Such cooperation must go beyond the letter of the Agreement. Unfortunately, without such cooperation, there is a scope within the current Agreement for importing-country governments to delay most of the actual liberalization until the end of the implementation period, when the backloaded liberalization becomes a problem for a new generation of politicians, while still meeting the technical requirements of the Agreement. This would lead us directly to another in the long chain of "temporary" crises that has led us through 35 years of temporary measures in the textile and clothing trade: the Short-Term Arrangement Regarding International Trade in Cotton Textiles; the Long-Term Arrangement; the Multifiber Arrangement; and the Agreement on Textiles and Clothing.

What Kind of Adjustment Does the Uruguay Round Imply for Asia?

Whalley's voluminous research output on MFA has been critical to our understanding of MFA, and the insights from this paper on the firm foundation of this past body of research. In addition to Whalley's own research (see, for example, Trela and Whalley 1990), other recent work on the Uruguay Round results (Hertel et al. 1996, Francois et al. 1996) reinforces his conclusions about adjustment. These studies find that the impact of real liberalization in textiles and clothing trade across Asia will clearly be uneven. This is because the incidence of MFA quotas, in terms of restrictiveness, is much stronger on developing South Asia than on East Asia (see table below). Hence, we should expect strong pressure for a re-allocation of exports within developing Asia. In particular—and depending critically on the People's Republic of China (PRC) WTO membership

Export Tax Equivalents of MFA Quotas

	European Union	United States	Canada
Republic of Korea	10.09	9.85	9.63
	19.37	23.33	19.54
Indonesia	17.46	11.95	17.50
	48.37	46.74	41.13
Malaysia	11.70	9.50	15.17
	32.40	37.40	35.66
Philippines	10.03	8.57	11.52
	27.79	33.52	27.08
Singapore	10.10	7.93	11.89
	27.98	31.01	27.94
Thailand	12.85	9.07	13.71
	35.58	35.46	32.23
India and Pakistan	27.35	18.41	23.21
	36.11	40.32	42.00
PRC	27.35	18.14	23.21
	36.11	40.32	42.00

Note: First row is for textiles, the second for clothing.
Source: Hertel et al. 1996: Table 3.7

we should expect a shift from exporters like Hong Kong; the Republic of Korea (Korea); and Taipei,China, and toward countries like PRC, India, and Pakistan. This, in turn, carries implications for other markets. For example, if Korea is squeezed even further out of textiles, then those resources are likely to shift up the product chain into other sectors where Korea has a demonstrated comparative advantage (like steel and electronics).

The shifting patterns of production and trade that will follow textile and clothing liberalization will be affected by other aspects of the Uruguay Round as well. Prior to the Uruguay Round, the countries with the greatest concentration of their exports in MFA-constrained items faced the highest weight-average trade barriers in developed country markets. For example, because over 40 percent of South Asian merchandise exports (valued free on board) are in textiles and wearing apparel, this grouping has faced the highest import barriers in developed country markets. While East Asia faces similar (though lower) barriers for textile and clothing exports, these products account for "only" about 16 percent of total merchandise exports. PRC, with roughly 26 percent of its merchandise exports in textiles and clothing, faces weight-average trade barriers somewhere between those of East Asia and South Asia. Because other developing-country regions are much less dependent on textiles and apparel exports, the impact of removing MFA will be much more limited. Developing countries in Africa have the lowest export share for textiles and clothing and the highest for raw materials, and also face the lowest rate of aggregate protection in developed country markets. In contrast, developing Asia faces the highest-average tariffs because of the importance of manufactures, including consumer electronics, textiles, and apparel, in its exports. Because these rates will be coming down (in conjunction with the MFA phaseout and other Uruguay Round commitments), the most significant improvements in market access will therefore be realized by developing economies in Asia. This improvement, which is in no way limited to textiles and clothing, will be reinforced by the continued trend of reduction in applied tariff rates within developing East Asia. We may, therefore, see dramatic shifts in regional trade and production patterns over the next ten years, in textiles and clothing, and also in machinery, equipment, and chemicals. An important area of research, on a country level, therefore relates to the national adjustment processes that are likely to follow not only from the (eventual) elimination of textile and clothing restrictions, but also from the concurrent scheduled reduction of tariffs in other sectors.

References

Francois, J. F., B. J. Mc Donald, and H. Nordstrom., 1996. "The Uruguay Round: A Numerically-based Qualitative Assessment." In W. Martin and A. Winters, eds., *The Uruguay Round and the Developing Countries*. Cambridge: Cambridge University Press.

Hertel, T.W., W. Martin, K. Yanagishima, and B. Dimaranan, 1996. "Liberalizing Manufactures Trade in a Changing World Economy." In W. Martin and A. Winters, eds., *The Uruguay Round and the Developing Countries*. Cambridge: Cambridge University Press.

Trela, I., and J. Whalley, 1990. "Global Effects of Developed Country Trade Restrictions on Textiles and Apparel." *Economic Journal* 100:1190-1205.

CHAPTER 9

TRADE-RELATED INTELLECTUAL PROPERTY
RIGHTS AND ASIAN DEVELOPING
COUNTRIES: AN ANALYTICAL VIEW

ARVIND SUBRAMANIAN
INTERNATIONAL MONETARY FUND

Introduction

The Uruguay Round agreement on the trade-related aspects of intellectual property rights (TRIPs), including trade in counterfeit goods (General Agreement on Tariffs and Trade [GATT] 1994), represents one of the major accomplishments of the Uruguay Round, not least because it will entail major changes in national policies around the world — in developing and industrial countries alike — in the different fields of intellectual property (IP). The post-TRIPs world can proclaim levels of IP protection in developing countries comparable to, and in some cases, exceeding those, in industrial countries prior to the Round. In conjunction with the traditional area of trade in goods, and the other new area of trade in services, TRIPs will constitute one of the three main pillars on which the new edifice of the World Trade Organization (WTO) will rest. The objective of this chapter is to evaluate the TRIPs agreement from a general perspective as well as from that of Asian developing countries.

Origins

Globalization and a general disenchantment with *dirigiste* economic policies, two of the more-enduring clichés of the world economy in the last two decades, have also embraced the arena of IP rights. The growth rate of trade in high-technology products, which increased from less than $10 billion in 1965, to about $740 billion in 1992, outstripped that of total trade. Its share in total trade rose dramatically from 11 percent in 1965 to 23 percent in 1992 (Braga 1995). Another indicator — receipts from and payments for international IP transactions in Organisation for Economic Co-operation and Development (OECD) countries, which increased from $3.5 billion in 1970 to $51.2 billion in 1990 (a near fifteenfold growth), points to a similar importance for IP-based economic activity.

From the comfortable vantage point of the post-Uruguay Round, it is easy to overlook the other driving force behind the TRIPs initiative. A constellation of factors in the early 1980s, including the tight monetary, policy-induced recession, the rising dollar, and the emergence of large trade deficits in the United States (US), fed protectionist sentiment and led to growing doubts about US competitiveness, captured in Bhagwati's apt phrase "the diminished giant syndrome." TRIPs became a natural rallying point for advancing the trade policy interests of the US. At the level of substance, the shifting pattern of comparative advantage pointed to greater specialization away from traditional manufacturing, where Japan and the

307

newly industrializing economies of East Asia started to acquire preeminence, toward sectors that were intensive in knowledge, research and development (R&D), and hence IP-intensive. At the level of rhetoric, concerns in the field of IP could be articulated in the same terms as, and with less defensiveness than, perceived grievances in other areas of trade policy that led to unfairness claims in trade policy.[1] Inadequate IP protection translated into the Lockean natural rights idiom of the violation of the rights of US creators by "pirates" and "thieves."[2] Thus, competitiveness concerns were combined with righteous indignation to produce a persuasive call for "leveling the playing field" by requiring countries to raise their levels of IP protection.

Intellectual property had featured prominently in bilateral initiatives, notably those undertaken by the US. During the 1980s and 1990s, the continued maintenance of the generalized system of preferences benefits was contingent upon beneficiaries increasing their level of IP protection. The basis for action against weak IP protection was significantly strengthened under Section 301 of the US Trade Acts of 1984 and 1988 (the latter even created a new Section 301 variant aimed exclusively at IP-related cases) which authorized, even mandated, action, including trade sanctions, against countries with inadequate IP protection. Between 1975, when the first action under Section 301 was initiated, and 1993, 11 out of a total of 92 cases (including cases under special 301 and super 301) were related to IP. Between 1990 and 1993, however, 7 out of 15 Section 301 cases were in the area of IP. The countries against which IP-related Section 301 action has been taken are Argentina (1988); Brazil (1985, 1987, 1993); the People's Republic of China (PRC) (1991); India (1992); Republic of Korea (Korea) (1985); Taipei,China (1992); and Thailand (1990, 1991, 1992).

TRIPs was not the first multilateral attempt at addressing IP issues; indeed, it was a response to an earlier failure to secure higher IP protection in the World Intellectual Property Organization (WIPO). Years of deliberation had resulted in IP agreements, which, particularly in the area of patent protection, had produced "weak" agreements that essentially preserved the right of countries to determine nationally their IP regime. Underlying this perceived failure in WIPO was a tacit admission that at least within the field of IP, there was little possibility of striking mutually beneficial deals between major importers and exporters of IP-intensive goods. In other words, some countries did not on balance perceive increased IP protection to be in their interest. The *demandeurs* of the TRIPs initiative recognized that countervailing "concessions" might have to be offered to induce countries to increase IP protection. The Uruguay Round, a negotiation involving many subjects, afforded just such an opportunity, with the prospect of greater liberalization in textiles and agriculture providing the inducement for countries to adopt stronger IP laws.

But in many ways the appearance of IP in the multilateral trade arena was also a logical consequence of globalization. Clearly, IP had become an important element in commercial relations between countries, in establishing the conditions of international competition between increasingly globalized enterprises that was in many ways the *raison d'être* of the Uruguay Round when it was launched in 1986. A multilateral approach embodied in the TRIPs initiative was thus a natural way of coping with the tensions emanating from the globalization of IP-based economic activity.

Finally, the other attraction of the multilateral system in situating the TRIPs initiative was its dispute-settlement system. Hitherto, multilateral procedures for settling disputes in the area of IP were either nonexistent or, as in the case of WIPO, seen to be ineffective. The GATT dispute-settlement system, strengthened by the new Uruguay Round rules, offered a viable alternative to unilateral and bilateral methods for settling disputes that held promise for both the *demandeurs* and the weaker countries from whom higher IP protection was being sought.[3]

Uniqueness of Trade-Related Intellectual Property Rights

From the perspective of the multilateral trade system, the TRIPs initiative and outcome are unique in a number of ways. First, in a mundane sense, TRIPs represents the first and only comprehensive international agreement that covers all the main areas of IP,[4] and includes elaborately specified commitments on *national* enforcement procedures, as well as effective multilateral procedures for the settlement of disputes.

Second, it is arguable whether commitments in certain sectors under TRIPs will necessarily serve to enhance global efficiency. This issue is discussed in greater detail below. If the effects of higher IP protection by some countries in inducing additional R&D is weak — and the evidence is not compelling one way or the other — TRIPs will predominantly be a distributive issue to the first order, involving a transfer of rents away from consumers and firms in technology-importing countries to firms in technology-exporting countries (Rodrik 1994). In contrast, in most other areas in goods and services, a move toward global free trade increases efficiency and improves individual countries' and *global* welfare (subject of course to caveats where terms-of-trade effects are important). Any departure from liberalization is countenanced on a temporary, exceptional basis under strict conditions, as the necessary price to be paid for otherwise genuflecting at the altar of overall global efficiency. In TRIPs, unlike in other areas, it is not entirely clear whether global efficiency, the benchmark for assessment, would be achieved.

Third, TRIPs is the only area in the new WTO which does not contain any special and differential treatment (S&D) for developing countries to reduce the substantive obligations that need to be undertaken. The only nod in the direction of S&D is in relation to timing and some provision for technical assistance, whereby developing countries can delay the implementation of the new obligations without diluting them. By contrast, in trade in goods and services, S&D (relating to the substantive obligations rather than timing), although diminished since the Uruguay Round, endures in several areas, including tariff cuts, liberalization in agriculture, government procurement, market liberalization in agriculture, and so on. There is some irony in the fact that whereas developing countries appear to have been "let off" in areas of liberalization where they had most to gain, most was sought of them where outcomes were either mixed or even negative in their consequences.

Fourth, and related to the earlier point, TRIPs represent a watershed in the evolution of the GATT system in that for the first time countries have been required to *harmonize* in a comprehensive manner *domestic* policy instruments. In other areas, including services, GATT/WTO rules constitute negative obligations, enjoining countries *not* to use domestic policy instruments in a manner that discriminates either between foreign sources of supply, or between a domestic and foreign source of supply; but they essentially preserve countries' freedom to determine how to use these instruments. On the other hand, the TRIPs agreement contains positive obligations, requiring countries not just to avoid discrimination but to pursue certain IP policies in accordance with international norms. On a continuum, harmonization represents a higher degree of cooperation than an international framework that merely requires the avoidance of discrimination. Thus, TRIPs has clearly advanced the momentum of multilateral economic cooperation, prefiguring more intensified initiatives in the future in more areas than was hitherto thought either possible or desirable.

The TRIPs Agreement and Its Impact on Asia

Despite its very broad coverage, the TRIPs agreement has remarkable economy of expression, achieved in large part because it incorporates by reference rather than repetition the text and obligations of four existing international agreements on IP.[5] The important features of the TRIPs agreement are described in Table 1A in the Annex.

Key Provisions and Legislative Changes

General Obligations

The most important general obligation under the TRIPs agreement is national treatment, which requires all members to treat nationals of other countries no less favorably than their own nationals on all IP matters — standards, enforcement, and acquisition — subject to certain exceptions (Article 3). However, this obligation is not likely to require legislative changes, as most countries already grant national treatment in their domestic laws. The second general obligation, an innovation in the field of IP, is that of most-favored nation (MFN) treatment (Article 4). This requires countries to treat nationals of any one country no less favorably than nationals of another country. MFN has limited significance in the IP area as it is irrelevant once national treatment is granted. MFN becomes operative only when a country is treating nationals of another country more favorably than its own nationals; in such an event MFN becomes necessary to prevent discrimination between foreigners.[6] The final general obligation, exhaustion or the permissibility of parallel imports, is noteworthy for its absence despite the *demandeurs'* keen desire to see this provision included (Article 6).[7] The TRIPs agreement neither requires nor prevents countries from specifying what national regime should prevail on exhaustion (see the section on Policy Options for a discussion of this provision).

Patents

Perhaps the most difficult issue in the negotiations was the demand to provide protection for pharmaceutical products. It was in this sector that patent regimes differed most starkly, with several developing countries providing very little or virtually no protection for pharmaceutical products, while industrial countries had strong patent regimes and were seeking to further strengthen them by increasing the term of protection (Nogues 1990).

Under TRIPs, no field of technology can be excluded from patent protection, effectively disallowing any exemption for pharmaceuticals from protection (Article 27.1). Further, all countries would have to provide a minimum term of protection of 20 years (Article 33). There is also a tight nondiscrimination provision (Article 27.1) that would have important economic implications: it would disallow discrimination in the grant of protection (such as certain features of the US first-to-invent system); it would prevent more permissive rules for compulsory licensing in the pharmaceutical sector; and finally, it would prevent countries from requiring, under the threat of compulsory licensing, that a patentee should "work" the invention locally. The latter amounts to a requirement that demand in a market be met by local production rather than through imports. Finally, while TRIPs does not specify when a compulsory license may be granted except to disallow compulsory licenses for nonworking, some important conditions are laid down that must be fulfilled when a license is granted (Article 31). Notable among these are the requirements to establish that normal channels of obtaining a voluntary license have proved unsuccessful (Article 31.[b]) and that the patentee be provided adequate compensation for a compulsory license (Article 31.[h]).

Table 1 illustrates the impact that the TRIPs provisions relating to the standards of IP protection will have on Asia. Several countries, including India, Bangladesh, and Pakistan, will have to amend their national laws to introduce patent protection for pharmaceutical and chemical products. Although this list appears small, it must be remembered that a number of countries, including Indonesia, Philippines, and Thailand, changed their laws and/or administrative regulations in the early 1900s, pursuant to bilateral initiatives, but in anticipation of the TRIPs agreement. A number of countries, including Malaysia, Pakistan, Sri Lanka, and Viet Nam, will have to increase the term of patent protection.

As Table 2 indicates, virtually no Asian developing country is a member of the International Convention for the Protection of New Varieties of Plants (UPOV Convention); thus, nearly all Asian countries will have to introduce some kind of protection for plant varieties and seeds to be in conformity with TRIPs. Even in countries considered to have strong patent protection such as Singapore and Malaysia, the TRIPs provisions on compulsory licensing could require legislative changes. In nearly all other countries, compulsory licensing provisions will require important changes to eliminate the "working requirement" (for example, India and Indonesia), and to change compulsory licensing provisions that are more permissive for the pharmaceutical sector (for example, Indonesia, Malaysia, Philippines, and Thailand).

Copyright and Related Rights

Copyright protects the artistic and literary works of *authors*, which includes authors of books, music, and films. It protects the expression of

Table 1. Key Changes to IP Regimes in Developing Asian Countries
Consequent Upon TRIPs Standards

Key Changes	Countries that Need to Make Changes
I. Patents	
Introduce pharmaceutical product protection	India, Indonesia, Pakistan, Bangladesh
Introduce plant variety protection	Nearly all countries
Increase patent term	Malaysia, Pakistan, Philippines, Sri Lanka, India, Indonesia, Korea, Malaysia, Viet Nam
Eliminate compulsory licensing for nonworking/other restrictive compulsory licensing	India, Indonesia, Malaysia, Singapore, Thailand, Philippines[1]
Introduce Product and Process Rights	Indonesia, Philippines
II. Copyright and Related Rights	
Introduce protection of computer programs	Thailand, Viet Nam
Establish TRIPs-consistent term of copyright protection	Indonesia, Viet Nam
Introduce rental rights	India, Indonesia, Thailand, Viet Nam
Increase term of protection for sound recordings to 50 years	Nearly all countries
Introduce Rome Convention standards	Malaysia, Singapore, Thailand, Viet Nam (?)
III. Integrated Circuits	
Introduce protection	Nearly all countries with the exception of Korea

313

Table 1. Key Changes to IP Regimes in Developing Asian Countries
Consequent Upon TRIPs Standards *(cont'd.)*

Key Changes	Countries that Need to Make Changes
IV. Trademarks and Geographical Indications	
Eliminate restrictions on use of foreign trademarks	India, Malaysia
Introduce protection of service marks as trademarks	India, Malaysia, Pakistan
Introduce protection of geographical indications	India (?), Indonesia, Singapore (?), Taipei,China (?), Thailand (?)
Introduce protection of well-known trademarks	Viet Nam
Protect combination of colors as trademarks	PRC, Hong Kong, India, Indonesia, Korea, Viet Nam, Malaysia, Philippines, Singapore, Thailand, Taipei,China
V. Industrial Designs	
Introduce protection	Indonesia
Establish appropriate term of protection	Indonesia, Philippines
VI. Undisclosed Information and Test Data	
Introduce protection of undisclosed information and/or test data	Indonesia, Philippines, Thailand, Viet Nam (?)

---

[1] Singapore's Patent Act of 1968 permits the government to buy patented products from any source (including unauthorized producers) for use in government medical facilities without legal infringement of the patent. Indonesia's Patent Law has a provision for unauthorized importation of 50 selected products.

Source: Ogawa, 1994.

Table 2: Membership of Asian Developing Countries
in Major IP Conventions

Country	Rome Convention	UPOV[1] (1978)	Paris Convention	Berne Convention
Bangladesh	no	no	yes	no
Brunei	no	no	no	no
PRC	no	no	yes	yes
Fiji	yes	no	no	yes [2]
Hong Kong	no	no	no	no
India	no	no	no	yes
Indonesia	no	no	no	no
Korea, Rep. of	no	?	yes	no
Macao	no	no	no	no
Malaysia	no	no	yes	yes
Maldives	no	no	no	no
Myanmar	no	no	no	no
Pakistan	no	no	no	yes [2]
Philippines	yes	no	yes	yes [2]
Singapore	no	no	no	no
Sri Lanka	no	no	yes	yes [2]
Thailand	no	?	no	yes [2]
Viet Nam	no	no	no	yes

[1] International Convention for the Protection of New Varieties of Plants.

[2] These countries are not signatories to the Paris Act of the Convention which contains important provisions, for example, the application of the 50-year term of protection for cinematographic works.

Source: WIPO, 1994.

ideas rather than the ideas themselves. The Berne Convention is the most important agreement in this area and contains high standards of protection, including a broad definition of authorship and a term of protection equal to the lifetime of the author plus 50 years. Related rights protect the output of phonogram producers, as in the music industry, of performers, and of broadcasting organizations; protection for such rights is embodied in the Rome Convention.[8]

The TRIPs provisions on copyright and related rights will require adherence by all TRIPs signatories to the Berne Convention,[9] except for its provision on "moral rights" (Article 9; see Table 1A in the Annex). In addition, countries will have to protect computer programs and databases as literary works, establishing an international consensus in this regard

315

(Article 10). TRIPs will require the introduction of an exclusive rental right, the right to prevent unauthorized rentals, for computer programs and sound recordings, and a conditional rental right for films, where commercial rental of films leads to widespread copying, impairing the economic benefits that accrue to the right holder (Article 11). TRIPs will require the introduction of performers' rights, which is more limited than that found in the Rome Convention (Article 14); however, a significant addition will be the extension of the term of protection of sound recordings from 20 to 50 years (Article 14.5).

Table 3 shows the immediate impact of the TRIPs agreement in requiring a number of important Asian countries that are not members of the Berne Convention, including Hong Kong, Indonesia, Korea, and Singapore, to comply with its substantive provisions. Some countries, such as Pakistan, Philippines, Sri Lanka, and Thailand, though members of the Berne Convention, are not signatories to its most recent version (the 1971 Paris Act) which contains important additional provisions relating to the term of protection of cinematographic works. Changes in their national legislation will therefore be required. The provisions on computer programs will affect Thailand and Viet Nam, those on the introduction of rental rights will affect, in addition, India, Indonesia, and other South Asian countries. Nearly all countries will need to amend their laws to increase the term of protection for sound recordings to 50 years. While Table 2 shows that very few Asian countries are members of the Rome Convention, most countries nevertheless accord protection in their national laws to performers. Changes will, however, be necessitated to national laws in Malaysia, Singapore, Thailand, and Viet Nam.

Integrated Circuits

Protection for semiconductor chips, the basic building block of the modern electronics industry, is currently absent in most countries with the exception of Korea. Thus, nearly all Asian countries will need to introduce laws to grant protection not just in accordance with the provisions of the unratified Washington Treaty (Article 35), but to go further in some important respects. These include increasing the term of protection for chips to ten years (Article 38), specifying that protection extends to chips and products incorporating them (Article 36), tightening the conditions of compulsory licensing in conformity with TRIPs (Article 37.2), and specifying that an "innocent infringer," though free from liability, will nevertheless have to pay royalty on the stock that he has, after he has received notice of the infringement (Article 37.1).

Table 3. Key Changes to IP Regimes in Developing Asian Countries Consequent Upon TRIPs Enforcement

Provision	TRIPs Conditions Basically Met	TRIPs Conditions Not Met, but Other Measures Provided, or Amendment Under Consideration	TRIPs Conditions Not Met	Uncertain
General Procedure/Remedies				
Means to Protect Confidential Information			PRC	Hong Kong; India; Indonesia; Korea; Malaysia; Philippines; Singapore; Thailand; Taipei,China; Viet Nam
Availability of Injunctions	All countries			Viet Nam
Availability of Damages	All countries			Viet Nam
Availability of Other Remedies	Nearly all countries			Indonesia
Right to Seek Information	All countries			
Availability of Criminal Procedures for Trademark, Counterfeiting, and Copyright Piracy				

Table 3. Key Changes to IP Regimes in Developing Asian Countries Consequent Upon TRIPs Enforcement (cont'd.)

Provision	TRIPs Conditions Basically Met	TRIPs Conditions Not Met, but Other Measures Provided, or Amendment Under Consideration	TRIPs Conditions Not Met	Uncertain
Border Measures				
Suspension of Release of Goods by Customs	Hong Kong, India, Singapore, Thailand	PRC; Malaysia; Philippines; Taipei,China	Indonesia, Korea	Viet Nam
Availability of Ex-Officio Action	Hong Kong; India; Taipei,China	PRC		Philippines, Singapore, Thailand, Viet Nam
Right to Require Security	Malaysia	PRC	Indonesia, Korea	Hong Kong; India; Philippines; Singapore; Taipei,China; Thailand; Viet Nam
Right to Seek Indemnification of the Importer		PRC, Malaysia	Indonesia, Korea	Hong Kong; India; Philippines; Singapore; Taipei,China; Thailand; Viet Nam
Availability of Remedies	Hong Kong; India; Malaysia; Taipei,China	PRC	Indonesia, Korea	Philippines, Singapore, Thailand, Viet Nam

Source: Ogawa, 1994.

Trademarks and Geographical Indications

This was not an area where there were fundamental problems, but there were some minor difficulties. All countries accept, at least in principle, the desirability of protecting consumers from deception, the basic function of the trading system.[10] The TRIPs agreement represents the first full set of key standards that include the definition of the rights that must flow from a trademark (Article 16); specification of a minimum period (seven years) of protection that is renewable indefinitely (Article 18); and the minimum period of nonuse (three years) that might give rise to cancellation of trademark registration (Article 19). Two key provisions include the obligation to protect service marks as trademarks (Article 16.2), which will require changes in trademark legislation in India, Pakistan, and Malaysia; and the elimination of the requirement that a foreign trademark should be used only when linked with local trademarks (Article 20). The latter condition, which was imposed in countries such as India, aimed at preventing the alleged exploitation of foreign brand names by requiring them to be indigenized.

Another area where differences were to be found on the North-North axis was geographical indications. The basic difficulties concerned the protection of wines and spirits, especially between certain continental European countries (France, Spain, and Portugal) and those countries which had been colonized by Europeans, such as the US, Canada, Australia, Argentina, and Chile, where the names of European wines and spirits had become commonly used.

The basic obligation is to provide means for interested parties to prevent use which might mislead the public as to the true origin of a product, or might constitute an act of unfair competition (Article 22). However, for wines and spirits, protection must be provided against use even where the public is not being misled (Article 23). To give an example, the label "Scotch" accompanied by an indication that the whisky's provenance was the Fiji Islands would be considered an infringement even if that were the true geographical origin of the whisky.[11]

The extent to which Asian developing countries will be affected by the TRIPs provisions is unclear, but changes in legislation would appear necessary in India; Indonesia; Singapore; Taipei,China; and Thailand.

Undisclosed Information and Test Data

Prior to TRIPs, there were no clear international rules concerning the protection of undisclosed information or trade secrets; a good example of a trade secret is the formula for producing Coca-Cola. Developing countries were reluctant to recognize or concede the principle that trade secrets were an intellectual property right (IPR); in their view, trade secrets did not fulfill one of the prerequisites of an IPR, namely, the obligation on the part of the right holder to disclose the "secret." In practice, the TRIPs agreement will pose less difficulties because the main obligation is only to prevent the acquisition, use, or disclosure of information in a manner contrary to honest commercial practices (Article 39). This feature is found, in one form or another, in most countries' laws on unfair competition. However, in Asia, it is likely that additional legislative changes could be necessary in Indonesia, Philippines, Thailand, and Viet Nam.

The differences between trade secret protection and patent protection are twofold: (i) the former does not prevent persons from independently developing or lawfully obtaining the same information; and (ii) trade secrets protection is not limited in time. It continues as long as the conditions for protection still apply, namely, that the information that is sought to be protected is secret, has commercial value because it is secret, and has been subject to reasonable steps to keep it secret.

Anticompetitive Practices and Contractual Licenses

Developing countries' wariness of IP protection stemmed from the belief that monopolistic control over technology, facilitated by IP protection, would increase the price of and limit access to foreign technology, thereby impeding its transfer and diffusion in favor of developing countries. On this view, strong IP protection strengthened the hands of foreign technology owners in negotiations with developing-country users over voluntary licenses. One way of redressing this monopoly power would be to prohibit certain practices that were the most egregious manifestations of monopoly control over technology. The TRIPs agreement reflects developing countries' concerns by (i) recognizing the right they have always had to specify in their domestic legislation and anticompetitive licensing practices or conditions that constitute an abusive use of IPRs (Article 40.2); (ii) recognizing the right to take remedial measures against anticompetitive practices which, however, need to be consistent with the TRIPs provisions, notably those on compulsory licensing; and (iii) obliging countries to consult with each other and exchange information to facilitate the enforcement of national laws against companies whose activities straddle borders (Articles 40.3 and 40.4).

Enforcement

Many of the grievances of the major *demandeurs* pertained to the weak enforcement of IP protection in East Asian countries, including PRC; Indonesia; Philippines; Singapore; Taipei,China; and Thailand. According to figures produced by an industry group, annual losses due to copyright piracy in Asia, emanating predominantly from inadequate national enforcement of IP laws, are alleged to exceed $2 billion (see Table 4). Losses are estimated to be greatest in PRC; Thailand; India; and Taipei,China. Greater attention is also warranted because the TRIPs provisions on enforcement have been less-understood, giving rise to some confusion and perhaps even needless anxiety in terms of what they entail for member countries' obligations under WTO.

Table 4. Estimated Copyright Piracy Losses in Asian Countries, 1994
($ million)

Country	Motion Pictures	Records and Music	Computer Programs	Books	Total
PRC	50	345	351	120	866
Indonesia	10	12	92	40	154
India	40	40	57	25	162
Korea, Rep. of	20	3	313	20	356
Philippines	20	4	25	70	119
Pakistan	21	5	6	30	62
Taipei,China	21	6	152	10	189
Thailand	26	12	100	30	168
Hong Kong	7	35	87	2	131
Singapore	1	3	33	2	39
Total	216	465	1,216	349	2,246

Source: International Intellectual Property Alliance, 1995.

Inadequate national enforcement of IP creates the same economic effects on market structure and prices as low standards of protection. To a right holder, there is arguably little difference between not having a law requiring, say, protection of sound recordings, and having one that is then honored more in the breach than in the observance. Indeed, the IP issue made its first appearance on the multilateral arena primarily as an enforcement issue. Attempts to marshal a consensus in favor of an

Anticounterfeiting Code in the early 1980s, the progenitor of the more wide-ranging TRIPs initiative, were intended to improve the enforcement by customs of goods that were already violating national laws on IP. Over time, it was claimed that inadequate enforcement, especially of copyright and trademark laws, created losses amounting to billions of dollars (United States International Trade Commission 1988; see Table 4.)

While inadequate enforcement and low standards of IP protection are similar in terms of their economic effects, there is at least one significant difference between the two. A country that is not enforcing its laws invites more opprobrium than a country that does not have these laws in the first place. According to some trade negotiators, adopting a strategy of "weak laws and strong enforcement" rather than the converse was a more viable and effective bargaining position. The latter course of action raises questions whether the country is acting in good faith, leaving it more exposed to retaliatory action, which even if illegal in a strictly technical sense, would nevertheless carry tacit legitimacy. Hence, effective enforcement of IP laws will be essential to a country's standing in the multilateral trading system.

The TRIPs provisions on enforcement are unique in that they represent the first set of comprehensive, multilateral rules not just in the area of IP, but in any area. A major problem in designing such rules was the need to make them sufficiently specific to make commitments clear, rendering them justifiable later under multilateral dispute-settlement procedures, while at the same time maintaining sufficient generality to make them consistent with vastly different legal systems. The alternative of common rules and procedures was simply inadmissible as it would imply harmonization, for the sake of IP alone, of such diverse legal systems as the common law system of the Commonwealth, and its US variant, and the civil law systems of much of continental Europe and their adaptations in Latin America.[12]

Negotiations on enforcement also had to contend with the nervousness of many countries, already reluctant to raise IP standards, about accepting international responsibility for the performance of their customs, administrative law, and above all, their judicial authorities. This perceived extension of the long arm of international law was viewed as an unacceptable undermining of national sovereignty.

The broad objectives of the TRIPs enforcement provisions embodied in Article 41 were twofold: to provide for the effective national enforcement of IP laws, while ensuring that enforcement did not become abusive or overzealous, turning into an instrument of protection through harassment of legitimate trade.

The most important point to note about enforcement is that the basic responsibility or obligation of countries under the TRIPs agreement is not to themselves take action to prevent infringing activity, but to put in place the procedures and remedies that would enable right holders to do so. Hence, the primary responsibility for initiating action aimed at enforcement is still left to *private* right holders. The popular portrayal that the mere fact of infringing activity in a country makes that country susceptible to multilateral trade sanctions is simply wrong. Thailand will no more be likely to be retaliated against for its *Lacoste*-hawking street sellers than the US for the vendors of dubious wares that one may routinely encounter in a short walk from many metro stations in Washington, D.C. A country can be successfully challenged in WTO for infringing activity within its borders only if it can be shown that it has not fulfilled its obligation under the TRIPs agreement. What are these obligations?

The TRIPs agreement's provisions on enforcement contain two types of obligations: those on *procedures* and those on *outcomes*. The former include judicial, administrative, and criminal procedures, and related remedies that must be available under national law (both internally and at the border), to right holders to prevent infringing activity and to obtain redress in the event that such activity is taking place. These procedures and remedies are too technical to merit an elaborate discussion here and are described in Table 1A in the Annex. In general, as Table 3 suggests, the TRIPs provisions are not likely to be unduly burdensome for Asian developing countries as no major changes to existing laws or regulations will be necessary pursuant to TRIPs, except with respect to border enforcement measures in Indonesia and Korea. There is some uncertainty whether other countries such as Singapore; Taipei,China; Thailand; and Viet Nam may have to change specific, possibly minor, aspects of their border enforcement measures.

However, the more interesting and difficult issue concerns the implied obligations on outcomes. Article 41.1 of the TRIPs agreement specifies that enforcement must be expeditious, while Article 41.5 states that the TRIPs agreement "does not create any obligation to put in place a judicial system for the enforcement of IP rights distinct from that for the enforcement of law in general, nor does it affect the capacity of Members to enforce their law in general." The key question that arises is whether the standards of performance required of national courts and customs are *absolute* or *relative*. Frankly, the TRIPs agreement does not provide a clear answer, making it part of the constructive ambiguity that allows important international agreements to be negotiated.

If, on average, it takes ten years for an IP case to move through national courts say, in India, would that constitute inexpedient, and therefore ineffective enforcement for which India could be prosecuted in WTO by its trading partners? Would India's case be weakened by the fact that the equivalent figure is two years in the US and the European Union? Or could it invoke the fact that as a developing country, with limited administrative resources and capabilities, it cannot be held to the same standards as Article 41.1 appears to support? It was understood in the negotiations that, if such an issue came up before a WTO panel, it would be reasonable to expect it to take into account the objective constraints facing a country in deciding whether it had met the obligations to provide effective and expeditious means of enforcement. However, if a panel interpreted the TRIPs provisions as implicitly mandating absolute standards of performance, countries would simply have to devote extra administrative and financial resources to fulfill international requirements. A consequence could be a disparity in a country's domestic legal system because IP cases would be processed faster, owing to international obligations, than cases in other areas. Why should IP be so privileged? Would such precedence be consistent with national priorities for the judicial system? These are uncharted waters as far as WTO goes, and a further clarification of the real commitments entailed by the TRIPs enforcement might have to await future deliberations in WTO.

Dispute Settlement and Prevention

The new strengthened WTO dispute-settlement procedures that have emerged from the Uruguay Round will apply to the TRIPs agreement. These procedures will be faster because of strict time limits, and will provide for greater automaticity in the adoption of panel verdicts and their implementation because the ability of the country that has been ruled against to block the process has been eliminated. There is also provision for cross-retaliation, subject to certain conditions. A country could suspend benefits in the area of goods for violation of TRIPs obligations, provided multilateral authorization could be obtained.

Crucially, the TRIPs agreement and the WTO dispute-settlement procedures would constrain the future use of unilateral measures. When members seek redress of a violation of a TRIPs or Uruguay Round obligation, or of any impediment to the attainment of the *objective* of the TRIPs agreement, they must have recourse to and abide by *multilateral* dispute-settlement procedures. Any ruling or determination to retaliate must be made in accordance with those procedures. Thus the commitment to eschew

Section 301-type *unilateral* actions would appear to be broad as it potentially encompasses not only the TRIPs provisions themselves, but also matters related to the objectives of TRIPs.

Transitional Arrangements

Beginning 1 January 1996, Asian developing and least-developed countries were expected to implement the national treatment and MFN provisions. Other provisions of the agreement, including those on enforcement, introduction of plant variety protection, and protection for biotechnological *processes*, will have to be implemented by 1 January 2000 in the case of developing countries, and 2006 in the case of the least-developed Asian countries. Patent protection for biotechnological products will have to be implemented by 2005. In the critical area of pharmaceuticals, the transitional provisions are complex (see Box 1).

The Economic Impact of TRIPs

The previous section spelled out the impact of the TRIPs agreement in terms of the legislative and other changes that would have to be effected in the national IP regimes of Asian countries. This section examines the likely *economic* impact of the TRIPs agreement.[13]

Economics of Intellectual Property Rights at the National Level

The rationale for a system of IPRs, particularly patents, has to do with the "public good" nature of knowledge. Once created, the benefits from it can be relatively easily appropriated by agents other than the creator. This in turn can blunt the incentive to undertake the effort to create the knowledge in the first place, leading to an underproduction of knowledge from society's point of view. IPRs, therefore, represent an arrangement whereby society mitigates the appropriability problem and reduces the divergence between the private and social returns to knowledge creation. Although IPRs create a static distortion by rendering the market more monopolistic, it is assumed that the dynamic benefits from the incentives to R&D creation will offset the static efficiency losses.

Box 1. Timing of Impact of the TRIPs Provisions on Pharmaceuticals

One of the most controversial topics in the TRIPs negotiations was the protection of pharmaceutical products, hitherto exempt from protection in several Asian countries (see Table 1A in the Annex). This subject roused impassioned debate because of the perception that patent protection would have a significant and adverse impact on the price and availability of drugs, and hence upon public health and life. However, it is important to understand *when* the economic effects, be they positive or negative, are likely to be felt under the TRIPs agreement, especially since the general impression seems to be that legislative changes and economic impacts will occur immediately.

Although developing countries appear to have a ten-year transition period for the introduction of pharmaceutical patent protection (Article 65.4), the effective period of transition will be determined by the combination of Articles 65 and 70.8. The latter effectively requires all patent applications filed after 1 January 1994,[1] to be granted protection. The chart below explains how these complicated transition provisions apply.

All patent applications for pharmaceutical products filed after 1 January 1995, will have to be put into a "black box" by countries that did not earlier grant pharmaceutical product protection. By 2005, countries will have had to pass legislation that would allow patents to be granted for such black box applications. However, no commercial benefits would have been lost during the ten-year interval because the products for which patents had been granted in industrial countries, but which were in the black box in developing countries, would have been going through the process of obtaining regulatory approval prior to commercial marketing. This process is estimated to take an average of 10 to 12 years for new chemical entities, giving each patent a commercial life of eight to ten years.

This means that the patent applications that went into the black box in 1995 in say, Indonesia, would emerge in 2005; in 2005 the Indonesian patent authorities would have to examine these applications under the new TRIPs-consistent laws; concurrently, the drug would also be ready for commercial marketing in Indonesia.

As the chart shows, no patented drugs would be on the Indonesian market until 2005 and hence *no economic* impact of the TRIPs agreement would be felt until ten years after the agreement. *In other words, drugs that enter the market over the next ten years, and certainly drugs already on the market, will be unaffected by the TRIPs agreement.*[2] If 100 of the applications in 1995 were to be granted patents

---

[1] Although the agreement requires patent applications made after 1 January 1995, to be accorded patent protection, patents filed in industrial countries after 1 January 1994, could in effect be eligible for protection because of the operation of the provision relating to the "priority date" of an application.

[2] The one significant caveat to this is that if regulatory approval for a drug takes less than ten years, countries will still have to protect that drug by granting an exclusive marketing right (a patent by another name) until such time as they can receive formal patents (Article 70.9). Such drugs will enjoy a commercial patented life greater than ten years, depending on how quickly they obtain regulatory approval.

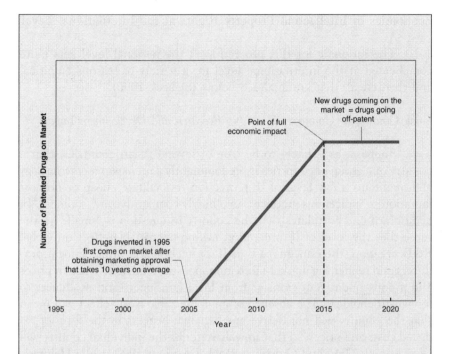

New drugs coming on the market = drugs going off-patent

Point of full economic impact

Number of Patented Drugs on Market

Drugs invented in 1995 first come on market after obtaining marketing approval that takes 10 years on average

1995 2000 2005 2010 2015 2020

Year

in 2005, these 100 patented drugs would be on the market in 2005. Assuming a uniform rate of successful drug patents, the number of drugs on the market by the year 2006 would be 200 (the 100 granted patents in 2005 plus the 100 in 2006), 300 in 2007, and so on. After 2015, the number of patented drugs on the market would be constant because the number of new drugs coming on to the market would be balanced by those going off-patent after the expiration of their 20-year patent term. *Thus only in 2015, 20 years after WTO enters into force, will countries such as Indonesia and India have a full roster of patented drugs comparable with that in countries that currently provide patent protection.* The comparable impact in the textiles agreement, namely, the elimination of all bilateral quotas, would be felt in 2005, ten years after the entry into force of WTO.

Economics of Intellectual Property Rights at the International Level

The rationale for IPR protection at the national level gets more complicated at the international level for a variety of reasons empirical and theoretical, that are analyzed below (Siebeck 1990).

Small Country or Countries Case: No Research and Development Impact

Suppose, as is likely to be true of several Asian countries, that a country or a group of countries is predominantly a *net importer of technology* and maintains a low level of IP protection to facilitate cheap or no-cost imitation by indigenous producers in a highly competitive environment. In addition, if one postulates that the country in question is "small," in the sense that the level of IP protection has no appreciable effect on global R&D creation, then an increase in IP protection will displace local producers and render the market more monopolistic, leading to a rise in prices and a consequent rent transfer from local consumers and producers to foreign titleholders. The absence of an appreciable R&D effect will mean that the country will not derive any dynamic benefits in the form of reduced costs and prices, so that in welfare terms the individual country will be worse off (Chin and Grossman 1990; Deardorff 1990, 1992; Helpman 1993; Maskus 1990). Interestingly, in this situation global welfare is also likely to deteriorate because there are no dynamic benefits to offset the static efficiency losses.

Imitation Plus Large-Country Effect

On the other hand, in a country or a group of countries that is sufficiently large, the level of IP protection could have a significant effect on R&D. An example of this could relate to the development of drugs for the treatment of diseases specific to developing countries, or technologies, such as seeds and chemicals, designed for agriculture in developing countries. The possibilities of ex post copying, in the absence of IP protection, could dent the incentive to undertake R&D. This is essentially the case examined in Diwan and Rodric (1991), who show that if the R&D inducement effect is sufficiently strong, higher IP protection could lead to gains for individual countries and for the world.

Technology-Transfer Effect

Where an invitation can be copied easily, for example, through reverse engineering, it cannot be plausibly argued that patent protection is necessary for the transfer of technology (Subramanian 1990). Therefore, in sectors such as pharmaceuticals, where the technology is easily obtained through copying, this argument is less relevant. Where, however, the assistance of the inventor is required, there may well be cases where patent protection creates the conditions for a voluntary transfer of technology which might not exist in the absence of a patent regime. The patent enables its owner to control the diffusion of the related secret know-how required to utilize the invention protected by the patent. In the absence of the patent, there would be little legal means of preventing persons, once trained in the use of the know-how, from setting up competing units, leading possibly to an uncontrolled diffusion of the technology. While ex post such diffusion might be in the national interest, the risk of such diffusion would deter the technology owner, forestalling the technology transfer in the first place. Thus the country could lose out on the benefits to employment, skills, and growth, by not providing a climate conducive for the transfer of technology or foreign direct investment (Maskus and Konan 1994).

Research and Development and Technology Transfer Effects

Before analyzing the likely economic impact on Asian countries, it is necessary to clarify the types of R&D effects that are important for evaluating putative gains and losses. In principle, there are three distinct R&D effects: know-what, know-who, and know-where, that could be occasioned by TRIPs. Know-what effects relate to whether higher IP protection would lead to greater R&D *on products consumed* (actual or potential) by developing countries (or on processes used in the production of products consumed in developing countries). For example, will higher pharmaceutical protection accorded by developing countries lead to greater R&D on the range of diseases typically found in developing countries?

Know-how effects relate to whether higher IP protection will lead to greater R&D *by indigenous firms;* and know-where effects relate to whether protection will lead to a shift in the *location* of R&D investment in favor of developing countries. These three effects affect the welfare calculus of higher IP protection in different ways. Know-what effects affect costs, prices, and product variety, thereby affecting consumer welfare. Know-who effects determine who, foreigners or domestic nationals, would appropriate the

rents from successful R&D activity; and know-where effects have implications for the rent effects (if R&D takes place locally, rents can be taxed
by the country), but arguably also for the extent of diffusion of technology.

The Asian Situation

The economic effects on certain sectors in Asia can be examined in
terms of the factors outlined above.

Pharmaceutical and Chemicals

One of the most significant areas of impact of the TRIPs agreement
will be the pharmaceuticals sector. Research shows that proprietary rights
in the form of patent protection are most important in the case of pharmaceuticals in ensuring that the returns from R&D are appropriated by
the inventor because of the relative ease of copying (Levin et al. 1987;
Mansfield 1986, 1994; Mansfield et al. 1981). In other sectors there are
natural factors such as lead time, secrecy, increasing returns to scale, and
marketing that can help prevent imitation by competitors. In the case of
pharmaceuticals, legal protection is relatively crucial in ensuring that competitors do not dilute the competitive edge of the firms that have undertaken the R&D by cheaply or without cost, imitating the invention.

Among the Asian countries, India, Indonesia, Pakistan, Philippines,
Thailand, and Indonesia have made or will need to make changes requiring protection of pharmaceutical products. Table 5 presents the *annual* price,
welfare, and profit effects consequent upon the TRIPs agreement for these
countries.[14] (As explained in Box 1, these effects will only be felt 20 years
hence; in view of the arbitrariness of the assumptions, these effects should
be viewed as illustrative, suggesting broad indications rather than measuring precise outcomes.) This table only captures the static effects. Three
features are evident from the table. First, that in each of these countries
the effects on price and welfare are negative. Second, however, the magnitude of the negative effects is *extremely sensitive* to assumptions made
about the underlying market structure and demand elasticities. For example,
the welfare loss for India can range from about $315 million to $1.3 billion, for Indonesia from $33 million to $133 million, for Pakistan from $46
million to $186 million, for the Philippines from $59 million to $237 million,
and for Thailand from $47 million to $189 million.

Two parameters in particular alter drastically the nature of the
conclusions. The first is the proportion of drugs in the future that will be
patented. This is, of course, something that is impossible to predict since

Table 5. Impact of TRIPs on the Pharmaceutical Market in Selected Asian Countries
($ million, unless otherwise stated)

	India			Indonesia			Pakistan			Philippines			Thailand		
	e=-.75	e=-1	e=-2	e=-.75	e=-1	e=-2	e=-.75	e=-1	e=-2	e=-.75	e=-1	e=-2	e=-.75	e=-1	e=-2
SCENARIO I[1]															
Average Price Rise															
patented drugs	67.0%	50.0%	25.0%	67.0%	50.0%	25.0%	67.0%	50.0%	25.0%	67.0%	50.0%	25.0%	67.0%	50.0%	25.0%
all drugs	10.1%	7.5%	3.8%	10.1%	7.5%	3.8%	10.1%	7.5%	3.8%	10.1%	7.5%	3.8%	10.1%	7.5%	3.8%
Welfare Loss	315	236	118	33	25	12	46	35	17	59	44	22	47	35	18
Profit Transfer to Foreign Firms	210	158	79	22	17	8	31	23	12	39	30	15	32	24	12
SCENARIO II[2]															
Average Price Rise															
patented drugs	67.0%	50.0%	25.0%	67.0%	50.0%	25.0%	67.0%	50.0%	25.0%	67.0%	50.0%	25.0%	67.0%	50.0%	25.0%
all drugs	40.2%	30.0%	15.0%	40.2%	30.0%	15.0%	40.2%	30.0%	15.0%	40.2%	30.0%	15.0%	40.2%	30.0%	15.0%
Welfare Loss	1,261	945	473	133	100	50	186	139	70	237	178	89	189	142	71
Profit Transfer to Foreign Firms	839	630	315	89	67	33	124	93	46	158	119	59	126	95	47

	India			Indonesia			Pakistan			Philippines			Thailand		
	e=-2.5	e=-3	e=-5	e=-2.5	e=-3	e=-5	e=-2.5	e=-3	e=-5	e=-2.5	e=-3	e=-5	e=-2.5	e=-3	e=-5
SCENARIO III[3]															
Average Price Rise															
patented drugs	10.0%	8.0%	5.0%	10.0%	8.0%	5.0%	10.0%	8.0%	5.0%	10.0%	8.0%	5.0%	10.0%	8.0%	5.0%
all drugs	1.5%	1.2%	.8%	1.5%	1.2%	.8%	1.5%	1.2%	.8%	1.5%	1.2%	.8%	1.5%	1.2%	.8%
Welfare Loss	162	132	8	17	14	8	24	20	12	31	25	15	24	20	12
Profit Transfer to Foreign Firms	101	82	5	11	9	5	15	12	7	19	16	9	15	12	7

Table 5. Impact of TRIPs on the Pharmaceutical Market in Selected Asian Countries
($ million, unless otherwise stated) *(cont'd.)*

	India			Indonesia			Pakistan			Philippines			Thailand		
	e=-2.5	e=-3	e=-5	e=-2.5	e=-3	e=-5	e=-2.5	e=-3	e=-5	e=-2.5	e=-3	e=-5	e=-2.5	e=-3	e=-5
SCENARIO IV[3]															
Average Price Rise															
patented drugs	10.0%	8.0%	5.0%	10.0%	8.0%	5.0%	10.0%	8.0%	5.0%	10.0%	8.0%	5.0%	10.0%	8.0%	5.0%
all drugs	6.0%	4.8%	3.0%	6.0%	4.8%	3.0%	6.0%	4.8%	3.0%	6.0%	4.8%	3.0%	6.0%	4.8%	3.0%
Welfare Loss	649	530	312	69	56	33	96	78	46	122	100	59	98	80	47
Profit Transfer to Foreign Firms	403	330	21	43	35	21	59	49	29	76	62	37	61	50	29
Memorandum Item															
Annual sales of pharmaceutical products[4]	4,200			444			619			790			631		

[1] Estimates are based on the following data on pharmaceutical sales: India, Indonesia = total sales; Pakistan = sales in pharmacies only. Philippines and Thailand = sales in pharmacies and hospitals. "e" refers to the price elasticity of market demand; in the case of a duopoly this translates into different perceived elasticities for individual duopolists. All numbers other than those for the price increases are in constant $ million at 1994 prices (1988 prices for India). In all scenarios, marginal costs remain the same in pre- and post-patent situations. The theoretical models used for deriving these numbers are described in Subramanian (1994).

[2] Share of patented drugs = 15% in Scenario I and 60% in Scenario II. In both scenarios pre-TRIPs market is perfectly competitive, and post-TRIPs is a foreign monopoly.

[3] Share of patented drugs = 15% in Scenario III and 60% in Scenario IV. In both scenarios, pre-TRIPs market comprises two duopolists, one foreign and one domestic, and the post-TRIPs market comprises foreign monopolists.

[4] Figures refer to 1994, except for India for which they refer to 1988.

it will depend on the nature and rapidity of R&D over the coming years. However, if the present serves as a guide to the future, it is interesting to note that according to data presented by the pharmaceutical industry (Gadbaw and Richards 1988), almost 60 percent of current sales of drugs in developing countries would have been patentable had these countries granted patent protection. If this is so, the effects are large, as scenarios I and III in Table 5 show. On the other hand, a more careful analysis undertaken for India by Wattal (1995) indicates that only 16 percent of the total current sales of the top 500 products would have been patentable. If this proportion is used for the sample Asian countries, the effects diminish significantly (scenarios II and IV in Table 5). Thus, if higher prices are a concern, the drug price index as a whole will increase between 3 percent and 40 percent if industry data are proved correct, but only between 0.8 percent and 10 percent under the alternative scenario (see Table 5).

The results are also sensitive to how competitive the market is assumed to be and what policies are followed after the TRIPs agreement. For example, in the limiting case where the pre-patent situation is perfectly competitive and the post-TRIPs regime is a perfect monopoly, the results are extreme (see scenarios I and II in Table 5). This represents an upper bound to the economic impacts. If, on the other hand, the pre-patent situation is a duopoly with one foreign and one domestic producer, and the post-TRIPs regime is a monopoly with one foreign producer, the impacts become less adverse as scenarios III and IV demonstrate (this is the model analyzed in Chin and Grossman 1990).[15]

The third feature about the results is that no matter what the assumption, welfare losses to individual countries outweigh the gains to pharmaceutical producers. Thus, if pharmaceutical producers have been correct in their claims of large-scale "losses," pharmaceutical technology-importing countries will probably be justified in fearing equivalent, even larger, welfare losses; conversely, if Asian developing countries are persuaded that the losses will be minor, claims of losses by industrial country pharmaceutical producers should be correspondingly moderated.

But these calculations potentially ignore important dynamic benefits stemming from TRIPs-induced R&D effects. The evidence on these R&D effects is unfortunately neither extensive nor systematic. A number of studies do, however, show that IP protection is important in R&D decisions in the pharmaceutical and chemical sectors, but less so in other sectors (Levin et al. 1987; Mansfield 1986, 1994). But the question of whether individual developing countries, or even developing countries as a whole, accounting for a fraction (between 15 and 20 percent) of total worldwide drug sales, are important enough to induce welfare enhancing R&D is open. In the future, however, developing countries are likely to account for a large share of sales, and R&D effects could become quite important. But it should be noted that a global welfare increase would require not only a positive R&D effect, but one of sufficient magnitude to offset the static losses from increased market imperfection. An illustrative calculation suggests that the R&D response induced by developing countries granting higher protection should reduce the marginal costs of production by about 60 percent for individual countries to gain overall.[16] How plausible such patent protection-induced R&D and cost reduction effects are, remains open and merits further empirical examination.

Table 6 presents some new data (Mansfield 1994) for Asian developing countries on the know-where effects and the transfer of technology effects put together. These data, based on surveys of patent attorneys and executives of major US manufacturing firms, reveal a few interesting patterns. First, foreign firms' decisions to set up plants or to transfer technology are conditioned by the level of IP protection only in the pharmaceutical and chemical sectors. Second, the choice between modes of supplying a market, either through foreign direct investment or licensing, is not significantly affected by the type of sector or the extent of IP protection. Third, the level of IP protection has a greater bearing on firms' decisions on the location of R&D activity than on the location of other activities such as manufacturing, sales, and marketing.

Agriculture

The attitude of Asian countries toward IP protection may need to be qualitatively different in relation to plant variety protection (see Box 2 for a discussion of developing countries' concern in relation to the TRIPs provisions on plant variety protection) than in the pharmaceutical sector. This is because in several of these countries, the know-what, know-where, and especially, the know-who effects are increasingly going to be more favorable than in the pharmaceutical industries. This is most clearly illustrated in relation to agriculture, which is increasingly witnessing a privatization of R&D effort.

While data on agricultural research in the private sector are scanty, the limited evidence available shows that IPRs are potentially important for R&D activity. This evidence comes in two forms. In the US, studies show that the US Plant Variety Protection Act had a positive impact on private plant-breeding research (Pray and Echeverria 1991). More significantly, it has been observed that private R&D in agriculture in Asian

334

Table 6. Effects of Intellectual Property Protection on FDI and
Transfer of Technology in Selected Asian Countries

A. Percentage of firms reporting that IP protection too weak to permit investment in joint ventures with local partners

	Chemicals and Pharmaceuticals	Transportation Equipment	Electrical Equipment	Food	Metals	Machinery	Mean
Hong Kong	21	20	38	12	0	23	19
India	80	40	39	38	20	48	44
Indonesia	50	40	29	25	0	25	28
Philippines	43	40	31	12	0	18	24
Singapore	20	40	24	12	20	0	19
Korea, Rep. of	33	20	21	12	25	26	23
Taipei,China	27	40	41	25	20	17	28
Thailand	43	80	21	12	0	20	29
Mean (Asia)	40	40	31	19	11	22	27
Mean (all)	37	30	28	16	7	21	23

B. Percentage of firms reporting that IP protection too weak to permit transfer of newest or most effective technology to wholly owned subsidiaries

	Chemicals and Pharmaceuticals	Transportation Equipment	Electrical Equipment	Food	Metals	Machinery	Mean
Hong Kong	21	20	38	12	0	14	18
India	81	40	38	38	20	41	43
Indonesia	40	20	31	25	0	23	23
Philippines	47	40	28	12	0	17	24
Singapore	12	40	21	12	0	0	14

Table 6. Effects of Intellectual Property Protection on FDI and Transfer of Technology in Selected Asian Countries (cont'd.)

	Chemicals and Pharmaceuticals	Transportation Equipment	Electrical Equipment	Food	Metals	Machinery	Mean
Korea, Rep. of	31	20	28	12	40	22	26
Taipei,China	19	40	41	25	0	35	27
Thailand	60	80	31	12	0	14	33
Mean (Asia)	39	38	32	19	8	21	26
Mean (all)	38	28	25	15	5	20	22

C. Percentage of firms reporting that IP protection too weak to permit transfer of newest technology to unrelated firms

	Chemicals and Pharmaceuticals	Transportation Equipment	Electrical Equipment	Food	Metals	Machinery	Mean
Hong Kong	33	20	38	12	0	14	20
India	81	40	38	38	20	50	45
Indonesia	73	20	33	25	0	37	31
Philippines	47	40	34	12	0	24	26
Singapore	25	40	24	12	20	0	20
Korea, Rep. of	38	20	34	12	40	29	29
Taipei,China	44	40	55	25	20	36	37
Thailand	73	80	36	12	0	25	38
Mean (Asia)	52	38	37	19	13	27	31
Mean (all)	50	28	30	17	8	28	27

Source: Mansfield, 1994.

Box 2: Plant Variety Protection — Needless Anxiety?

The TRIPs provisions on the protection of plant varieties and seeds have raised concerns about their possible detrimental impact on the development of agriculture, which still accounts for a high share of gross domestic product in several Asian developing countries. Farmers, who have led the chorus of opposition against these TRIPS provisions, perceive their very livelihood as being threatened, believing that the agreement would create monopolies of seed creators (usually foreign) and raise significantly the costs of production in agriculture by doing the following:

- bringing under protection existing seed varieties and genetic material;

- preventing farmers from retaining their seeds from the current harvest for re-sowing the following season (the so-called "farmer's privilege");

- preventing farmers from selling small quantities of retained seeds (across-the-fence sales); and

- preventing the experimental or research use of protected seeds without the authorization of the creator of the seed variety.

How valid are these concerns?

It should be noted that the TRIPs provisions on plant varieties offer countries the option of choosing either a system of patent protection (which is likely to be stronger than the alternatives in terms of favoring creators) or a *sui generis* method, or a combination of the two. The only requirement of the *sui generis* method of protection is that it be "effective;" this term has been intentionally cloaked in constructive ambiguity, although it is understood that such a system should not in practice deviate too far from the provisions of the international convention for the protection of new varieties of plants (the UPOV Convention). However, countries retain the freedom to choose the weaker version of UPOV (the 1978 agreement) over its stronger revision (the 1991 agreement).

In relation to farmers' concerns, the following should be noted. First, plant variety protection would only apply to *new* subject matter, that is, matter created five years after the entry into force of the agreement for developing countries (the year 2000), and 11 years in the case of the least-developed countries (2006). Matter in the public domain — existing seeds and other material — would not have to be protected.

Second, as regards "farmers' privilege," both UPOV 1978 and UPOV 1991 explicitly recognize the right of countries to allow their farmers to retain seeds from their harvest for further sowing on their land. Indeed, this is a widespread practice in several industrial countries.

Third, "across-the-fence" sales of seeds would probably be technically inconsistent with both UPOV versions, unless they were considered to be covered by

---

Box 2. Plant Variety Protection — Needless Anxiety? *(cont'd.)*

the exception for private, noncommercial purposes. In practice, such sales occur all around the world, and it would in all probability not be feasible or economic for right holders to take action against such commercially insignificant activity.

Fourth, as regards the concerns about technology diffusion, the UPOV Convention explicitly states that the right holder should not prevent use of protected matter for experimental purposes — the so-called breeders' exemption. However, under UPOV 1991, if a seed is "essentially derived" from a protected seed, the commercial sale of the former cannot be effected without the consent of the creator of the latter. UPOV 1978 does not impose even this constraint.

Thus, many of the specific concerns of farmers are probably not well founded, being based on an inaccurate reading of the text of the agreement. The overall welfare implications of TRIPs on agriculture for Asian countries might even be positive in the medium term, as discussed in the text.

---

developing countries is almost exclusively concentrated on breeding hybrids rather than other varieties. Hybrids have the advantage of being difficult to duplicate, thereby helping to ensure a market because farmers must buy seed every year from the hybrid developer to get maximum yields.

Another key difference is that unlike in the area of industrial products, *Asian developing countries themselves have — at least potentially — a strong R&D capability in the agriculture sector.* According to the available evidence, locally owned companies account for over 60 percent of the current private sector agricultural R&D effort in Asian developing countries. Furthermore, the scope for further indigenous private sector effort is suggested by the current small size of private R&D effort in developing countries (1 percent of total R&D) compared to about 60 percent in developed countries. Thus, not only do developing country-consumers stand to benefit from higher IP protection because of the fillip to R&D activity on products of interest to developing countries, but local producers and R&D creators can also expect to benefit by appropriating the rents from their efforts. And based on the current pattern of location of R&D activity in agriculture, the know-where effects are also likely to be favorable. Thus, for Asian countries, the economics of IP protection in the area of agriculture and seed technology could be favorable in the medium term, unlike the consequences in other areas such as pharmaceuticals.

Software, Films, Sound Recordings

In the cases of pharmaceuticals, chemicals, and agriculture described above, Asian developing countries were predominantly net importers of IP-based products. However, in some industries Asian countries are net exporters of IP-based products or close to being so. For example, India, and to some extent, Pakistan, are large exporters of computer software (to industrial and developing countries), movies and audio and video cassettes (to the Middle East and other countries where the Diaspora is spread). In these cases, greater IP protection confers unambiguous welfare benefits. Static gains are realized because higher IP protection transfers rents to nationals of these countries who create the IP-based product (this is the obverse of the pharmaceutical case considered above); higher global IP protection amounts to a favorable terms-of-trade shock for a net exporter. Dynamic effects are also likely to be beneficial because the rents from the additional R&D that is induced will be appropriated by nationals of these countries who are likely to undertake R&D. This effect is similar to that in the field of agriculture discussed above.

Policy Options

The policies adopted by countries in the aftermath of TRIPs should be guided by their assessment of the likely net benefits and costs. If the assessment is negative or mixed, countries can consider the policy options outlined below, aimed at mitigating any adverse impacts. However, such options would not be appropriate if the assessment were positive. When a country has expectations of sizable dynamic gains, any attempt at minimizing adverse impacts could, in fact, reduce the chances of any real gains. This is because the policies designed to minimize adverse effects are also likely to reduce profits, and hence the incentives for R&D and the transfer of technology. In other words, countries cannot have their cake and eat it, too.

Against the background of the earlier discussion, it is clear that there are some areas, notably in relation to pharmaceuticals, where opinion can be genuinely divided on the merits of higher IP protection. But even in these areas, the TRIPs agreement does not foreclose the entire range of policy options that can be deployed by countries to mitigate the agreement's possible adverse impacts.

First, the TRIPs agreement would not prevent the use of price controls by TRIPs signatories. Indeed, price control regimes coexist with strong patent regimes in many developed countries. Even in Europe, which has a nearly harmonized patent regime, the average price of patented drugs can vary by a factor of 3.1, owing largely to price controls and other government policies related to health care, such as reimbursement under social security regimes. If higher drug prices are a source of concern, the European model of price controls could serve as an example.

Second, while the TRIPs agreement has significantly limited the use of compulsory licensing (which was, for example, the preferred tool in Canada for regulating drug prices), countries retain some margin of maneuver in using this form of regulatory control. Two of the stringent conditions attached to compulsory licensing are the need to demonstrate that the patent owner has refused to make available a voluntary license on reasonable commercial terms and conditions, and the criterion of adequate compensation. It should be noted that both can be waived if it can be shown that an IPR holder's actions have resulted in an anticompetitive practice. Hence, developing countries can, in their national competition laws, specify standards of abuse, encompassing such outcomes as high prices. Further, countries retain enough latitude in determining where these standards could be set, for example, the point at which a price would constitute an abuse of the patent right. In the event that these standards are flouted, compulsory licensing could be used to redress the abuse and bring prices down to reasonable levels.[17]

Finally, one feature of the TRIPs agreement is noteworthy for its absence. Despite serious efforts, the *demandeurs* were unable to include in the agreement a prohibition on *exhaustion*. At stake in this issue was whether right holders could prevent parallel imports and sustain discriminating prices between markets. In other words, the prohibition of exhaustion would have permitted the patent holder to behave like a discriminating monopolist. The absence of such a prohibition means that, at least in larger developing-country markets, governments retain the possibility of allowing parallel imports that would exert incipient pressure on prices and prevent them from reaching levels that a discriminating monopolist would have been able to maintain.

But these are all essentially damage-limitation exercises. There does exist an area where Asian developing countries could proactively use the IP system to harness important economic and environmental benefits. In mind here are the genetic resources found so abundantly in Asia. In the recent past, developing countries have advanced the notion of farmers' rights, and their right to remuneration for the use of endoplasm, seeds, and other genetic material used by foreign companies in the pharmaceutical and biotechnology sectors. These calls are usually founded on equity grounds, invoking appeals to fairness. In an ironic reversal of the rhetoric of the 1980s when developing countries were accused of "piracy," it is now the industrialized countries that stand accused of "biopiracy." A study argues that the use of genetic resources by industrial country firms and research organizations results in "losses" that amount to $5.1 billion in pharmaceuticals, and $302 million in chemicals.[18]

It can be argued on global efficiency grounds (Subramanian 1992, Sedjo 1992) that proprietary rights should be granted to individuals and communities that expend valuable time and effort in maintaining and preserving the genetic resources found in developing countries; that in the absence of such rights there will be a potentially large market failure leading to a socially wasteful depletion of biodiversity and genetic resources; and that granting proprietary rights for such resources would represent a market-based mechanism of international cooperation to address the problem. However, there are several unresolved issues that need to be addressed to operationalize this idea to which developing countries should devote greater attention.[19] This would be an area where the new climate in favor of IP protection could be used to their benefit.[20]

Why was TRIPs Successful?

Despite all the fuss and early anxiety — and it is no secret that the negotiations were rife with conflict — the negotiators produced a comprehensive agreement on IP with very high standards of protection, providing for the first time detailed rules for national enforcement procedures. This invites the question as to why it happened at all. It is instructive to examine the factors that contributed to the success of the TRIPs negotiations.

First, there was a clear recognition on the part of developing countries that the IP issue, if not addressed multilaterally, would not disappear. The choice was between addressing it multilaterally in the Uruguay Round, or bilaterally with major trading partners. Developing countries clearly preferred the multilateral approach, which offers protection against unilateral pressure and against unilateral determinations of what constitutes an appropriate standard, and whether it has been met. In reality, of course, many countries had to address the issue in both contexts, which created a complex negotiating dynamic. With agreement having been reached on TRIPs, it is now expected that there will be greater discipline in the use of unilateral trade actions in the area of IP. The new dispute-settlement rules embody this restraint on unilateral actions.

Second, the TRIPs agreement bears testimony to an important principle underlying the success of multilateral negotiations in general. Whenever the package of rewards is, *on balance,* positive for all participants, with enough advantages to offset the "concessions," agreement can be reached on difficult subjects which would be inconceivable in a negotiation centered on a single, or few issues. In a multi-issue negotiation, refusal to compromise on any one subject jeopardizes the whole in which all countries have a collective interest. In the case of TRIPs, it could be argued that some "concessions" were real — entailing a loss of efficiency and welfare — rather than mercantilist as in conventional trade liberalization. But, in return for making concessions in TRIPs, developing countries gained in areas of export interest to them such as textiles and clothing and agriculture. Even more important from their perspective, the successful conclusion of the Round and a strong and viable trading system will, in the long run, serve their interests well, since their growth prospects are intimately linked to an open trading system.

Third, it is undeniable that the winds of ideological change, particularly in developing countries, have blown away the earlier addiction to *dirigisme.* While it could be argued that free markets and open trade could coexist with weak IP regimes in certain sectors, the general perception remains that a strong regime of property rights is essential to a serious reform program, especially one aimed at attracting foreign investment and foreign technology. The vanes of ideological taste may veer again, but in this current phase of enchantment with open markets and open trade, strong IP protection is seen as a sine qua non of a move toward market-friendly economic policies.

Finally, as discussed in the previous section, TRIPs offered developing countries opportunities where they would gain as exporters of IP-related products. Some areas of potential long-term benefit include agriculture and genetic resources and other areas with possibly more immediate benefits including movies and sound recordings, computer software, and textile designs.

Conclusion

The TRIPs agreement will likely effect important changes in Asia. In several countries in the region, national IP regimes will have to be changed, with greater care devoted to ensuring that laws are implemented effectively. By establishing a functioning multilateral consensus, TRIPs provides a reprieve from, and hopefully a resolution of, the tension that had characterized previous unilateral efforts aimed at the IP regimes of several Asian countries.

TRIPs may not be a simple affair, producing uniformly malign or benign effects. It will present, instead, a palette of benefits, challenges, and opportunities. The major challenges will be in the patent area, particularly in some key sectors, where TRIPs could become a mere instrument of rent transfer away from Asian country consumers if the dynamic benefits are not forthcoming. But even here there may be strong mitigating factors: the transition provisions will delay any impacts until well into the twenty-first century; and enough policy instruments such as price controls, compulsory licensing, and competition policy, will remain at the disposal of countries to dilute any adverse impact.

On the other hand, TRIPs will also open up a number of opportunities. Higher IP protection could confer dynamic benefits, particularly in areas such as agriculture and software, where R&D potential is significant in Asian countries. These benefits could be maximized through an appropriate policy environment favoring R&D and the transfer of technology. In the area of genetic resources, Asian countries could advance the notion, based on efficiency rather than equity grounds, that an internationally recognized system of proprietary rights should be instituted for such resources.

TRIPs illustrates more vividly than any other area of the Uruguay Round negotiations the emergence of developing countries as equal partners in the multilateral trading system. Special and differential treatment has been shed in favor of equal obligations, with all the benefits that the latter confers. One manifestation of this equal status is that retaliation can now be a two-way street. Developing countries can threaten to withdraw IP protection in the event that industrialized countries do not implement their commitments to liberalize textiles and clothing and agriculture (for example, if the Multifiber Arrangement is not phased out on schedule).

TRIPs may not give grounds for a mindlessly cheerful Panglossian prognosis of being the best of all possible worlds. There is, however, room for cautious optimism for developing countries in their acceptance of TRIPs, based as much on the opportunities that TRIPs could provide, as on the sober and sobering evaluation that the alternatives (for example, dealing with IP bilaterally) would have been even worse. There is enough in this smorgasbord for all countries to chew upon, and hopefully, digest.

Annex

Table 1A. Salient Features of the TRIPs Agreement

1. **Coverage**	The TRIPs Agreement covers all the main categories of intellectual property rights, copyright and related rights, trademarks, geographical indications, industrial designs, patents, layout designs of integrated circuits, and undisclosed information.

2. **General Obligations**

a. National Treatment	The Agreement specifies national treatment which requires all members to treat nationals of other countries no less favorably than their own nationals on all matters concerning intellectual property rights, subject to certain exceptions.
b. Most-Favored Nation Treatment	The Agreement includes most-favored nation (MFN) treatment, which is an addition to international intellectual property agreements, and requires countries to treat nationals of any one member no less favorably than that of any other member. Unlike in GATT, MFN in the intellectual property sphere has limited significance; essentially, it is moot if the national treatment principle is respected. It becomes relevant if a country decides to give more favorable treatment to foreigners than to their own nationals; in such an event, MFN is necessary to prevent discrimination between foreigners.
c. Exhaustion/ Parallel Imports	The exhaustion principle relates to whether an IP owner can prevent imports of goods that have been put on the market in another country with the consent of the owner. An upholding of the exhaustion principle effectively prevents the IP owner from segmenting markets and behaving as a discriminating monopolist. The TRIPs agreement neither explicitly requires nor prevents countries from incorporating exhaustion in their national laws.

Table 1A. Salient Features of the TRIPs Agreement (cont'd.)

3. Minimum Standards

a. Copyright and
   Related Rights

Berne Convention	All members are required to comply with the substantive provisions of the Berne Convention, except for the obligation on moral rights, such as the rights of authors to claim authorship of their works and to object to any modification or derogatory action prejudicial to their honor or reputation.
Computer Programs	Computer programs and databases must be protected as literary works (for the normal period of "life of the author plus fifty years").
Rental Rights	Exclusive rental rights, such as rights accorded to IP owners to prevent unauthorized rentals of their works, for computer programs and sound recordings.
	Rental rights for cinematographic works if commercial rental has led to widespread copying.
Performers/ Broadcasting Organizations	Performers must be given the means to prevent any unauthorized use of their live performances, often referred to as bootlegging. Broadcasting organizations must have rights over the use that can be made of broadcast signals without their authorization; alternatively, owners of copyright in the subject matter of broadcasts must be able to prevent broadcasts without their authorization.
Sound Recordings	Duration of protection for record producers and performers extended from 20 to 50 years.
b. Trademarks	Service marks must be protected as service marks.
	Well-known marks must be protected even when not used in a country.
	Requirement that foreign trademarks should be used only with local trademarks must be eliminated.

345

Table 1A. Salient Features of the TRIPs Agreement (cont'd.)

c. Geographical Indications	All countries must provide the means to prevent the use of geographical names from misleading the public as to the true origin of the good, or which constitutes an act of unfair competition.
	In regard to wines and spirits, protection must be provided even where there is no threat of the public being misled as to the true origin of the good. Certain names, such as champagne and scotch that have become generic, can be grand-fathered, but the agreement provides for future negotiations to increase protection for such names.
d. Industrial Designs	Duration of protection must be ten years. Special provisions on textile designs.
e. Patents	
Scope of Protection (Pharmaceutical Products)	Patents must be available in all areas of technology, thereby disallowing the carve-out of pharmaceuticals and chemicals from patent protection. Inventions that threaten public order or morality need not be patented, provided the commercialization of such inventions must also be protected; but plants and animals and essentially biological processes for the production of plants and animals (excluding microorganisms and microbiological processes) can be exempted from patent protection. This whole area, currently clouded with legal uncertainty and subject to diverging national practices, will be reviewed by 1999.
Nondiscrimination/ Nonworking	TRIPs requires nondiscrimination in the grant of payments and the enjoyment of rights in relation to the field of technology, the place of invention, and whether patented products are imported or locally produced. Thus the discriminatory features of the first-to-invent system must be eliminated as must the grant of compulsory licenses on the ground that the patented product is not being produced locally.
Term of Protection	The duration of protection must not be less than 20 years from the date of filing of the patent application.

Table 1A. Salient Features of the TRIPs Agreement *(cont'd.)*

Compulsory Licensing	In principle, no restrictions are placed, but two stringent conditions must be satisfied: (i) it must be demonstrated that the patent holder has refused to make available a voluntary license on reasonable commercial terms and conditions; and (ii) the patent holder should be adequately compensated. These conditions can be waived if it can be shown that the patent holder's actions have resulted in an anticompetitive practice.
Plant Varieties/Seeds	Plant varieties, including seeds, must be protected through patents or alternative *(sui generis)* means.
f. Layout Designs of Integrated Circuits	Substantive provisions of the Washington Treaty must be respected. Scope of protection includes not only the protected chip, but also products incorporating it. Term of protection must be ten years. Compulsory licensing must be on the same terms as those specified for patents. An "innocent infringer" must be free from liability, but once one has received notice of infringement, one is liable to pay royalty on stock in hand or stock that was previously ordered.
g. Protection of Undisclosed Information and Test Area	Undisclosed information (or trade secrets) must be protected against acquisition, use, or disclosure in a manner contrary to honest commercial practices. To benefit from such protection, trade secrets must be secret, have commercial value, owing to such secrecy, and have been subject to reasonable steps to keep it secret.
	Test data provided by a company to obtain marketing approval for pharmaceutical and chemical products must be protected against unfair commercial use and disclosure.

Table 1A. Salient Features of the TRIPs Agreement *(cont'd.)*

---

h. Anticompetitive Practices in Contractual Licenses

The TRIPs Agreement recognizes that countries may specify in their domestic legislation the commercial licensing practices that constitute an abuse of intellectual property protection, and address these through remedies that must be consistent with the TRIPs Agreement.

Governments must cooperate with each other, including through the provision of information, in investigations of alleged abuse of intellectual property rights that has international dimensions.

4. Enforcement

a. General Obligations

Countries must provide effective means of action for any right holder, foreign or domestic, to secure the enforcement of his right, while at the same time preventing the abuse of the procedures. The general obligation is that procedures must be fair, equitable, and expeditious.

b. Responsibility

Responsibility of enforcement is essentially left to the private right holder.

c. Procedures

Procedures for civil judicial action are specified, including to ensure that there must be means to produce relevant evidence; that certain remedies must include injunctions, damages, and in some instances, forfeiture and disposal; that provisional measures must be available to prevent infringing activity and to preserve relevant evidence; and that judicial authorities must have the authority to adopt provisional measures *inaduita altera parte.*

d. Customs Cooperation

In regard to pirated and counterfeit goods, right holders must have the means to obtain cooperation of the customs authorities in preventing imports of such goods.

e. Criminal Procedures

Criminal procedures and penalties must be available in cases of willful trademark counterfeiting or copyright piracy on a commercial scale.

Table 1A. Salient Features of the TRIPs Agreement (cont'd.)

f. Safeguards	Safeguards against the abuse of enforcement measures are specified, including minimum requirements of evidence, prompt notification of affected parties, prompt right of review, and indemnification of adversely affected parties where subsequent innocence is established.
5. **Acquisition and Maintenance**	The general obligations are that procedures or formalities for obtaining intellectual property rights should be fair, reasonably expeditious, not unnecessarily complicated or costly, and generally sufficient to avoid impairment of the value of other commitments.
6. **Transitional Arrangements**	
a. All Countries	There is a one-year transitional period for all countries to apply the agreement.
b. Developing Countries/ Pharmaceutical Products	Developing countries and economies in transition can delay application of the agreement for another four years, except for the national treatment and MFN obligations. They are entitled to an additional five-year period for introducing product patents in areas of technology that were not protected at the date of application of the Agreement. However, this apparent ten (one + four + five)-year transition period has to be seen in conjunction with the provision (Article 70.8) that requires all pharmaceutical inventions made after the entry into force of WTO to be protected at the end of the ten-year transition period, which is in any case the approximate time that such inventions will be ready for commercial marketing. This is because inventions take an average of ten years to obtain regulatory approval. If such approval is obtained before a ten-year period, such inventions are required to be protected through an exclusive marketing right (Article 70.9).

Table 1A. Salient Features of the TRIPs Agreement *(cont'd.)*

c. Least-Developed Countries	Least-developed country members are entitled to a ten-year delay from the date of application of the agreement to comply with TRIPs obligations, except for national treatment and MFN, and can request a further delay. However, they too are covered by the requirement to protect all pharmaceutical inventions made after the entry into force of WTO.
d. Existing Subject Matter	As a general rule, all existing subject matter must be protected, while all matter in the public domain at the time of the entry into force of WTO need not be restored into protection.
7. **Dispute Settlement**	The new WTO dispute settlement procedures will apply to the TRIPs Agreement. Dispute settlement procedures will be faster than in GATT because of time limits at each stage of the process. There will be greater automaticity in the adoption of verdicts of dispute settlement panels and in their implementation because the scope for interested parties to block the process has been eliminated.
	There will also be scope for cross-retaliation, subject to certain conditions. A country could thus suspend benefits in the area of goods for violation of the TRIPs Agreement. All cross-retaliation will be subject to multilateral authorization and, if necessary, to binding arbitration.
8. **Other**	The Agreement calls upon developed country members to provide technical and financial assistance in favor of developing and least-developed country members on mutually agreed terms and conditions.

Acknowledgments

The author wishes to acknowledge the contribution, over many years, of Adrian Otten, whose intellectual property rights are being violated, but who cannot fairly be implicated in the final product. Thanks are also due to Parul for editorial assistance and for helping me finish this paper, and to Arvind Panagariya for helpful comments. The views expressed here are the author's own and do not necessarily reflect those of the International Monetary Fund.

Notes

[1] Unfair trade claims in other areas, such as antidumping, safeguards, and voluntary export restraints, were obliged to be less strident owing to the residual embarrassment that the outcomes being sought were still "protectionist." In IP, on the other hand, the proponents were seeking to "open" export markets for US industry.

[2] See Deardorff (1990) for a critique of the natural rights approach to IP protection.

[3] For the former, multilateral commitments that have been bound are more difficult to reverse than commitments that are offered, often reluctantly, under bilateral pressure. Also, unilateral enforcement mechanisms such as 301 rely to some extent on the government being willing to use up diplomatic capital, and possibly jeopardize bilateral relations to attempt to secure the economic interests of a narrow sectoral interest group. Under a multilateral agreement such enforcement action, through the dispute-settlement mechanism, would be a relatively nonconfrontational and routine exercise of mutually agreed procedures.

[4] These are patents, trademarks, copyright and related rights, geographical indications, layout designs of integrated circuits, industrial designs, and protection of undisclosed information (trade secrets).

[5] These are the Paris Convention for the Protection of Industrial Property, the Berne Convention for the Protection of Literary and Artistic Works, the Rome Convention (the International Convention for the Protection of Performers, Producers of Phonograms, and Broadcasting Organizations), and the Washington Treaty (the Treaty on Intellectual Property in Respect of Integrated Circuits).

[6] MFN started to assume importance in IP largely due to the success of bilateral initiatives. The most celebrated case was the agreement between the US and Korea, whereby the latter agreed to grant pipeline protection for past

pharmaceutical inventions made by US nationals. This kindled fears in Europe of discrimination by Korea against pharmaceutical inventions made by European companies, resurrecting a need for an MFN-type obligation. A similar possibility arose under the US-PRC IP agreement of 1992, which appeared to treat US inventions more favorably than European ones.

[7] Exhaustion refers to a situation when the owner of an IP right cannot present the import of a product into a country once it has been legitimately sold in another country. That is, IP owners' exclusive rights are "exhausted" after the first sale of the product. This opens up the possibility of parallel or gray market imports from low-price to high-price markets which will be considered legitimate in the importing country if its laws uphold the exhaustion principle. Exhaustion and parallel importation should not be confused with the situation of imports of products that are put on the market in another country illegitimately (without the consent of the IP owner). Such imports will constitute infringing activity in the importing country, regardless of the provisions on exhaustion, and hence impermissible.

[8] Copyright was an area that had as many, if not more, differences between the industrial countries than between industrial and developing countries. These differences derived from the different copyright traditions in the common law countries (for example, the US) and the civil law countries (for example, continental Europe). The US tradition places more emphasis on protecting the company that invests in and organizes the creation of the work. Thus, producers of films and sound recordings are regarded as authors in their own right, eligible for protection under the Berne Convention; in general, performers are not eligible for IPRs. In continental Europe, the emphasis is more on protecting the actual creators, authors, movie directors or performers, not only against the copying of their works, but also, to some extent, against the producers and publishers who produce or market their works. In general, producers of films and sound recordings are eligible for related rights rather than copyright protection because of not being considered authors.

[9] TRIPs also clarifies a provision of the Berne Convention by specifying that where the creator of a work is a corporation, the term of protection should not be less than 50 years.

[10] Of course, the other function of trademarks is to create more monopolistic market structures that yield advantages to the trademark holder in return for investments in quality enhancement and reputation (Shapiro, 1983; Grossman and Shapiro 1988a, 1988b). Trademarks might also serve to reduce search and information costs for the consumer because of the stake in reputation and quality that is created by allowing the association of goods with producers (Landes and Posner 1987).

[11] However, this apparently absolute commitment is qualified by an important exception, namely for names and terms that have become generic. To France and other *demandeurs*, such an exception was acceptable only if it were made clear that the TRIPs provisions did not legitimize a permanent "usurpation" of such

terms. To this end, a commitment was incorporated to negotiate in the future higher levels of protection for such terms (Article 24.1).

[12] This divide did not run along North-South lines.

[13] The TRIPs Agreement will affect three main, albeit overlapping, groups of industries: (i) *High technology* comprising pharmaceutical, chemical, and biotechnology industries (patent protection), other hi-tech industries (trade secrets protection); (ii) *Entertainment* comprising music (phonogram producers), motion pictures, and publishing industries (copyright protection); and (iii) *Luxury goods* comprising producers of luxury- branded products, for example, perfume, watches, and fashion clothing (trademark protection) and producers of alcoholic beverages, for example, champagne and scotch (protection of geographical indications). An important distinction between the hi-tech industries on the one hand and the entertainment and luxury industries on the other was that the former were especially keen on improving the standards of protection in national laws, while the latter place considerable emphasis on improving the mechanisms and procedures for the *enforcement* of rights already provided in national laws.

[14] The results are based on models described in Subramanian (1994).

[15] However, if one posits, more realistically, competition between patented therapeutic classes and allows governments to use compulsory licensing to regulate a post-TRIPs pharmaceutical market, the adverse effects shrink further in magnitude. In Subramanian (1994) this is modeled as a Bertrand duopoly in the pre- and post-patent situations, with one domestic and one foreign producer. The effect of the TRIPs Agreement is modeled as forcing an increase in the cost of the domestic producer which can be interpreted as the royalty that he would have to pay to the foreign patent holder for the use under compulsory licensing, of his patent. In the case of India, this model yields annual welfare losses of $220 million and price increases of between 2 percent and 3 percent, considerably less than the results shown in Table 5. Maskus and Konan (1994) calculate the economic impacts under other scenarios.

[16] The required reduction in marginal costs necessary to generate national welfare gains is sensitive inter alia to assumptions about market structure and elasticities of demand. The greater the elasticity of demand and the more imperfect the prepatent situation, the lower the cost reduction that creates national welfare gains. The figure quoted in the text is for a prepatent market characterized by a duopoly that yields to a monopoly after patent protection is introduced (as in Chin and Grossman 1990) and for an elasticity of -1. For details, see Subramanian (1994).

[17] That the use of such compulsory licensing by governments can reduce the adverse impacts was noted above. In such a case, the adverse price and welfare effects are considerably less than those obtained under scenarios III and IV in Table 5.

[18] According to a United Nations Development Programme (UNDP) (1994) study, about one quarter of global pharmaceutical sales of $130 billion in 1990 was based on products derived from medicinal plants found in developing countries.

Another study puts an estimate of $40 billion on the value of developing country germplasm (United Nations Environment Programme 1992).

[19] Several practical difficulties militate against instituting a proprietary system for genetic resources (Subramanian 1992). But one objection to such a system that stems from a legalistic perspective on IP is probably not valid. In the view of the legal community, only inventions that are "new," that is, not already found in nature, are eligible for IP protection. Patent laws all over the world reflect this view. However, the economic logic of an IP system rests on the fact that the results of human *effort* may be ex post appropriable, which dents the ex ante incentive to undertake that socially productive effort. This reasoning should apply equally to cases where the effort is directed at creating "new" knowledge as it does to preserving existing knowledge (in this case, genetic resources). Thus, the "new" versus "existing" distinction that is important for the legal perspective on IP, is not relevant to the efficiency case for a system of proprietary rights.

[20] An interesting proposal in this regard (UNDP 1994) suggests the establishment of a fund financed by levies on products that are presumed to be based on genetic resources found in developing countries. The inspiration for this proposal comes from the levy on blank cassettes in several European countries, where the cassettes are presumed to be used for recording copyrighted material. Monies from this levy are distributed to artists and authors on the basis of a specified formula.

References

Braga, C. A. P., 1995. "Trade-Related Intellectual Property Issues: The Uruguay Round and Its Economic Implications." Paper presented at the World Bank Conference on The Uruguay Round and the Developing Economies, 26-27 January, Washington, D. C.

Chin, J.C., and G.M. Grossman, 1990, "Intellectual Property Rights and North-South Trade." In R. W. Jones and A. O. Krueger, eds., *The Political Economy of International Trade: Essays in Honor of Robert Baldwin.* Cambridge, Massachusetts: Basil Blackwell.

Deardorff, A.V., 1990, "Should Patent Protection Be Extended to All Developing Countries?" *The World Economy* 13(4):497-508.

_____, 1992. "Welfare Effects of Global Patent Protection." *Economica* 59:35-51.

Diwan, I., and D. Rodrik, 1991. "Patents, Appropriate Technology and North-South Trade." *Journal of International Economics* 30(1-2):27-47.

Gadbaw, R.M., and T. Richards, 1988. *Intellectual Property Rights: Global Consensus, Global Conflict?* Boulder, Colorado: Westview Press.

GATT Secretariat, 1994. *Final Act Embodying the Results of the Uruguay Round of Multilateral Trade Negotiations.* Geneva: GATT.

Grossman, G.M., and C. Shapiro. 1988a. "Counterfeit-Product Trade." *American Economic Review* 78:59-75.

_____, 1988b. "Foreign Counterfeiting of Status Goods." *Quarterly Journal of Economics* 103:79-100.

Helpman, E., 1993. "Innovation, Imitation, and Intellectual Property Rights." *Econometrica* 61:1247-80.

International Intellectual Property Alliance, 1995. "1995 Special 301 Recommendations and Estimated Trade Losses Due to Piracy." Submitted to the United States Trade Representative, Washington, D.C.

Landes, W.M., and R. Posner, 1987. "Trademark Law: An Economic Perspective." *Journal of Law and Economics* 30:2.

Levin, R.C., A. K. Klevorick, R. R. Nelson, and S.G. Winter, 1987. "Appropriating the Returns from Industrial R&D." *Brookings Papers on Economic Activity* 3:783-820.

Mansfield, E., 1986. "Patents and Innovation: An Empirical Study." *Management Science* 32:173-81.

Mansfield, E. M. Schwartz, and S. Wagner, 1981. "Imitation Costs and Patents: An Empirical Study." *Economic Journal* 91:907-18.

Maskus, K. E., 1990. "Normative Concerns in the International Protection of Intellectual Property Rights." *The World Economy* 13:387-409.

Maskus, K. E., and D. Eby Konan, 1994. "Trade-Related Intellectual Property Rights: Issues and Exploratory Results." In A. Deardorff and R. Stern, eds., *Analytical and Nogotiating Issues in the Global Trading System.* Ann Arbor: University of Michigan.

Nogues, J., 1990. "Patents and Pharmaceutical Drugs: Understanding the Pressures on Developing Countries." *Journal of World Trade* 24(6):81-104.

Ogawa, N., 1994. "Protection of Intellectual Property Rights in Asian Countries." Paper presented at the APAA-FICPI Joint Seminar, Nigata, Japan.

Pray, C. E., and R. G. Echeverria, 1991. "Private-Sector Agricultural Research in Less-Developed Countries." In P. G. Pardey, J. Roseboom, and J. R. Anderson, eds., *Agricultural Research Policy: International Quantitative Perspectives.* United Kingdom: Cambridge University Press.

Rodrik, D., 1994. "Comments." In A. Deardorff and R. Stern, eds., *Analytical and Nogotiating Issues in the Uruguay Round.* Ann Arbor: University of Michigan.

Sedjo, R., 1992. "Property Rights, Genetic Resources, and Biotechnological Change." *Journal of Law and Economics* XXXV:199-213.

Shapiro, C., 1983. "Premiums for High Quality Products as Returns to Reputations." *Quarterly Journal of Economics* 81:359-94.

Siebeck, W. E., ed., 1990. *Strengthening Protection of Intellectual Property in Developing Countries: A Survey of the Literature.* Washington, D. C.: World Bank.

Subramanian, A., 1990. "TRIPs and the Paradigm of the GATT: A Tropical, Temperate View." *The World Economy* 13(4):509-21.

_____, 1992. "Genetic Resources, Biodiversity and Environmental Protection: An Analysis, and Proposals Toward a Solution." *Journal of World Trade* 26(5):105-09.

_____, 1994. "Putting Some Numbers on the TRIPs Pharmaceutical Debate." In *Integrating Two Systems of Innovation.* An independent study by the Rural Advancement Foundation International, New York.

United Nations Development Programme, 1994. "Conserving Indigenous Knowledge: Integrating Two Systems of Innovation." An independent study by the Rural Advancement Foundation International, New York.

United Nations Environment Programme, 1992. "Saving Our Planet: Challenges and Hopes." Kenya, Nairobi.

United States International Trade Commission, 1988. *Foreign Protection of Intellectual Property Rights and the Effect on U.S. Industry and Trade.* Washington, D.C.

Wattal, J., 1995. "Introducing Product Patents in the Indian Pharmaceutical Sector — Some Implications." New Delhi. Mimeographed.

357 - 61

Comments on "Trade-Related Intellectual Property Rights and Asian Developing Countries: An Analytical View"

by

Alan Deardorff

019
034
832

The chapter lays out remarkably clearly and completely the TRIPs Agreement. At the same time, it provides a thoughtful analysis of how it will affect Asian less-developed countries (LDCs), both in qualitative terms and, in some areas, in quantitative terms. The chapter should be of interest to all those wishing to learn how the TRIPs Agreement will impact developing countries.

This chapter raises several questions and brings to mind a couple of factors that might influence us in our final assessment of whether the TRIPs Agreement was a change for the better or for the worse, either from the world's point of view or from that of LDCs. As Dr. Subramanian notes, the net welfare effects of TRIPs are at best ambiguous, a point I have made myself (Deardoff 1990) in arguing for exemption of the poorest LDCs from the requirements of TRIPs. The biggest effect of international patent rights, in particular, is to transfer income from the poor nations to the rich. However, two considerations were absent from that analysis, one of which points toward a possible danger that the TRIPs Agreement poses to all countries, and a second that may indicate greater benefits to LDCs.

The following questions need to be addressed:

- The chapter refers occasionally, as the press has stated repeatedly throughout the last ten years, to the "losses" incurred by the owners of IP due to unauthorized copying and other forms of "piracy." I've always wondered how these "losses" are measured. If, as I suspect, they are the value of the pirated units at the IP holders' preferred retail price, then, of course, there are many reasons why this greatly overstates the actual economic loss to the IP holder. What have these "losses" been based on?

- In the estimates reported in Table 5 on the welfare effects of potential protection in pharmaceuticals, there are some that appear to represent the effects of moving to monopoly pricing in a market with elasticity of demand of -0.75. What is happening here? With inelastic demand, doesn't the monopolist raise prices without bound?

- The author notes that India and perhaps Pakistan may tend to gain from TRIPs on software, films, and sound recordings, because they are large exporters, it is suggested that Asia as a group may therefore gain in this area. But surely many other Asian LDCs are only importers here, and the gain to India would be small consolation. Also, I presume that it is *net* trade, not gross, that matters here; further, is India even a *net* exporter in these industries, or would it still be if its trade were to be liberalized?

- In India, there have been several mentions of what seems to be their biggest TRIPs concern: the patenting by western firms of traditional remedies derived from the tree known as neem. Indians are concerned, apparently, that TRIPs will deprive them of a remedy that they have had available long before western firms "discovered" it. Are their concerns warranted?

- As mentioned, the failure of TRIPs to prohibit "parallel" imports will mean that exporters will be unable to price-discriminate against LDC markets. Yet it is unclear to me why exporters would *want* to discriminate against LDCs. I would have thought the more usual case to be of LDC demand that would be more elastic than developed-country demand (at a given price) and therefore, that exporters would discriminate in their favor. Viewed in this light, is the failure to prohibit "exhaustion" really a triumph for LDCs? Why did they resist that exhaustion?

I now turn to a couple of broader issues where it occurs to me that developed countries may have more to lose, and LDCs more to gain, from TRIPs that I once supposed.

Pandora's Box

As noted in the chapter, the TRIPs Agreement extends WTO into areas quite unlike what it has dealt with before. First, TRIPs promotes protection in markets, not freedom in markets, albeit protection of a different sort than restrictions on trade. Second, TRIPs imposes discipline on domestic policies as GATT never had before: positive requirements to act, rather than negative prohibitions on behavior such as subsidies. Third, despite the cosmetic qualifier "trade-related" in the acronym for TRIPs, agreement really is an international undertaking to enforce certain "rights," something that GATT never attempted before. National treatment and most-favored nation were never right — they were just good items (and they have yet to be fully achieved even in what has been prospectively agreed upon in the Uruguay Round, contrary to the stated target of TRIPs).

My concern about this is that by opening up the WTO to issues like this — of rights in areas that are only loosely related to trade — the system becomes vulnerable to demands from all sorts of other constituencies to add them to WTO as well. This is not news. It is already happening in the areas of environment, labor standards, and competition policy. One of these issues has already been institutionalized in new working groups of WTO, and there is strong pressure from within the US at least, to include labor standards as well. Like the far-seeing proponents of intellectual property protection before them, these groups see the difficulty of securing meaningful international agreement in a single issue area alone, and they seek to harness the power of WTO to their objectives. With its potential for achieving trade-offs across issues, WTO, with all its faults and weaknesses, stands to be far more effective than any of the international institutions that have preceded it, a fact that is noted positively in the chapter. I merely note that these lessons have not been lost on interest groups of all sorts that until recently have been far removed from trade.

New Goods

My second concern has been stated repeatedly over the years by the advocates of TRIPs, but I have only recently given it serious thought, for several reasons. This is the contention that the absence of IP protection deprives LDCs of products that would be beneficial to them. I have normally thought of this as referring to new products of particular importance to the needs of LDCs, that will not be invented without a protected market there because there is not sufficient market for them elsewhere. This is, of course, a possibility, and it is one that Dr. Subramanian has addressed, noting several areas where IP protection in LDCs may be expected to induce research and development (R & D) there, to their benefit.

What struck me more recently, however, was the potential for even greater gain to LDCs, if IP protection affords them access to products that already exist in the developed world but have not yet penetrated LDC markets for fear of being undermined by local imitators. In a recent article on "New Goods," Paul Romer (1994) makes a compelling case that the gains from access to new goods are far greater than the conventional efficiency gains from trade liberalization. His argument is stated for tariffs, but to the extent that the absence of IP protection either precludes or makes more costly the entrance of new products to a market, his argument would apply here as well.

When I first heard this argument applied to IP, I found it implausible. It struck me that products that would be copied at all could be copied just as well at a distance from where they were actually produced. Only a sample of the good itself needs to move. This is surely true for a great many goods — indeed most of the ones that we think of as being widely copied in LDCs. But I now realize that it is not true of all goods. A great many more products are not available in LDCs, I suspect either because imitators need more than just the product, or because, without the products being available domestically, no potential imitator thinks of it as an opportunity.

My own admittedly limited experiences in poor countries suggests, in spite of rampant imitation, there are far fewer products available than in developed countries. Another bit of evidence may be found in the paper by Wattal (1995) cited in Dr. Subramanian's chapter. When I first read that there are small numbers of patentable drugs available in India, I did not believe it. But I now wonder if that report is not after all correct, and if most drugs really are not available in India. Now that I recognize from Romer's contribution how much more important the absence of goods in a market can be compared to the effects of a mere increase in their prices, this strikes me as an important question for further research. I conclude therefore with another question: Is it the case that large numbers of goods are unavailable in LDCs without IP protection, and how important will providing that protection be in making it possible for the producers of those goods to enter the markets? If this is a valid and quantitatively important consideration, then the TRIPs agreement could prove beneficial, not harmful, to even the poorest LDCs.

References

Deardoff, A. V., 1990. "Should Patent Production be Extended to All Developing Countries." *The World Economy* 13: 497-508.

Romer, P. R., 1994. "New Goods, Old Theories, and the Welfare Costs of Trade Restrictions." *Journal of Development Economics* 43:5-38.

Wattal, J., 1995. "Introducing the Product Patents in the Indian Pharmaceutical Sector — Some Implications." New Delhi. Mimeographed.

CHAPTER 10
TRADE REMEDIES AND LEGAL REMEDIES: ANTIDUMPING, SAFEGUARDS, AND DISPUTE SETTLEMENT AFTER THE URUGUAY ROUND

KENNETH W. ABBOTT
NORTHWESTERN UNIVERSITY SCHOOL OF LAW

Introduction

The grand conception underlying the General Agreement on Tariffs and Trade (GATT) entails a gradual move toward generally open trade in goods, with state intervention in international commerce both reduced and constrained. Highly distortive interventions like quotas are forbidden (Article XI). The transparency of tariffs is preferred over less transparent quantitative restraints and internal restrictions (Articles II, III, XI). Tariffs and most other permissible interventions are to be implemented on a nondiscriminatory basis (Article I). Tariffs are to be bound and negotiated downward on the basis of reciprocity (Articles II, XXVIII bis). And all of a nation's trade measures are to be implemented transparently (Article X).

At the same time, the General Agreement authorizes a variety of safeguard measures (SGMs), formal procedures by which governments may, in exceptional situations, suspend or withdraw GATT commitments affecting particular products and industries. Article XIX authorizes temporary interventions, Articles XXVIII and XXXV more permanent ones. Superficially, these measures appear at odds with the basic conception of GATT. Yet they have been widely seen as justifiable, because they allow governments to deal with the social and political tensions and the complex welfare calculations created by international trade.

In two narrow instances, GATT also authorizes governmental restrictions on imports to offset foreign practices that are seen as inappropriately distorting market competition and thus as "unfair." Especially important today, Article VI authorizes governments to impose special tariffs known as antidumping measures (ADMs) on imported goods that are, under highly technical criteria, priced inappropriately low. Similar measures are permitted in response to many foreign government subsidies.

By the time of the Uruguay Round, the grand conception of GATT had become increasingly skewed. With the success of trade liberalization, one would have expected formal SGMs like those authorized under Article XIX to play an increasingly important role. In fact, however, formal SGMs had become so rare as to be virtually irrelevant. Their role had to a large extent been usurped by various "gray-area measures," never satisfactorily dealt with in GATT jurisprudence, under which exports were "voluntarily" restrained by the exporting nation. These measures will be referred to as "voluntary restraint agreements" (VRAs). VRAs had become a significant burden on exports from the developing nations of Asia; when they achieved their full potential, as in the Multifiber Arrangement (MFA) and certain steel arrangements, they dominated international economic life in the affected sectors.

365

Just as striking was the rise of ADMs, seemingly a narrow, technical remedy, to prominence in international trade policy. In effect, ADMs had become the trade remedy of choice for import-competing firms and their governments in the West. Developing nations, especially in Asia, were frequent targets of ADMs and rightly saw ADMs as a significant threat to market access. At the same time, however, a number of developing countries became substantial users of ADMs, and others began to move rapidly to implement this form of market intervention.

Clearly, industries seeking protection, and governments willing to grant it, are often able to choose among two or more legal or political procedures to achieve their goals. There is, in short, a market in trade remedies. The measures offering the greatest procedural and substantive advantage, ADMs and VRAs, are utilized most often; others such as SGMs, are invoked less frequently. The market in trade remedies is highly significant for developing nations in Asia and elsewhere, as exporters, and thus as targets, and as importers. It is likely to be even more significant following the Uruguay Round, since the liberalization of textiles, agriculture, and other sectors will undoubtedly lead to new demands for protection.

The three trade remedies summarized here were all addressed in the Uruguay Round. The agreement on safeguards prohibits further use of VRAs and encourages resort to formal SGMs. At the same time, however, this agreement limits the potential restrictiveness of SGMs, weakening their appeal. Uruguay Round negotiators attempted to constrain the use of ADMs as well, but the demands of the United States (US) and the European Union (EU) blunted this effort. As a result, the relationship among the major trade remedies remains skewed in favor of ADMs. One can expect to see a continuing increase in the use of these measures as new demands for protection enter the system.

This chapter describes recent trends in the use of trade remedies, reviews the relevant policy issues, and analyzes the rules adopted in the Round. It also considers the future role of each trade remedy. Normatively, the chapter argues that growing reliance on ADMs by the West and the developing countries threatens the goals of liberalization, transparency, and nondiscrimination in the multilateral trading system. It argues that the use of ADMs in the West should be constrained and if possible rolled back; and that developing countries should be dissuaded from following in the steps of their Western trading partners, or at least similarly constrained. SGMs, especially as regulated after the Round, are a superior means of coping with the social, political, and economic strains of liberalization.

In Asia, the trade remedy laws are still in flux; it may yet be possible to constrain the adoption of excessive antidumping laws through persuasion.

In the West, unfortunately, the intellectual battle over the legitimacy of ADMs has probably been lost, at least in the political arena, and at least for the immediate future. To the extent persuasion is unsuccessful, the effort in the short run must be to constrain the use of ADMs and other trade remedies in line with the valuable if imperfect rules adopted in the Round. Given the power of protectionist demands, these rules are unlikely to be self-enforcing. To a lawyer, the natural response is litigation, in this case through the World Trade Organization (WTO).

The WTO dispute-settlement (DS) process is important to developing countries for many reasons beyond the enforcement of the new rules on ADMs and SGMs. It is the principal way in which all of the Uruguay Round commitments of concern to them, in agriculture, textiles, market access, and the like, can be enforced. Since the beginning of the Round, the DS system has been revolutionized, so that it now resembles a modern domestic legal system. Though it cannot solve all the problems of inequity in international life, such a system undoubtedly favors the less powerful, just as in domestic society. One can expect to see developing countries using the DS system more frequently than in the past, in spite of continuing practical obstacles.

The WTO DS will also be the principal way in which developing-country Uruguay Round commitments are enforced. The US has already begun a DS proceeding against the Republic of Korea (Korea) for its handling of ADMs; if other Asian countries begin to use these measures aggressively, they can expect to face similar litigation. WTO litigation may be a more frequent prospect for a broader reason as well: the Uruguay Round Understanding on Dispute Settlement (Understanding) prohibits the use of unilateral measures like US Section 301 in situations falling within any of the WTO agreements. A later section of this chapter reviews the innovations of the Understanding, with special reference to developing countries and the use of WTO procedures to discipline ADMs. The final section is a brief conclusion, which suggests that in the long run the power of reciprocity may combine with legal procedures to restrain the use of ADMs.

Antidumping Measures

Practice

ADMs have become the most frequently used trade remedy in Western countries. This is a significant change from earlier years: in 1958, scarcely more than three dozen antidumping orders were in effect in all

367

GATT member countries (Finger 1993:13-34). By 1990, Canada alone had over 100 orders in force; the US had nearly 200 (see Annex 1). Much of the increase was due to an "explosion" of antidumping proceedings during the 1980s (Clarida 1996:357, 359). Annex 1 traces the number of outstanding ADMs in the US over the last ten years: from 112 in 1985, to 151 in 1987, 198 in 1989, and 236 in 1992. ADMs were traditionally directed against capital-intensive cyclical products like steel.[1] Since the 1980s, though, they have been used against a wide range of products, from low- to high-technology (Clarida 1996:364, 372).

Until recently, only four to five nations, counting the European Community/EU as one, regularly used ADMs, and this small group still contains the principal users. As Annexes 1 and 2 demonstrate, the US, the European Community, Canada, and Australia have dominated the use of ADMs over the last ten years; New Zealand has also been a prominent user. Japan, unlike other leading industrialized countries, has used its antidumping law only a handful of times.

Developing countries, including those in Asia, have been frequent targets of Western ADMs (Anderson 1993:102; Messerlin 1988:163,165-6). Annex 1 highlights the Asian targets year by year. The People's Republic of China (PRC); Korea; Taipei,China; and Thailand have been most often subject to antidumping proceedings in all the principal user countries, but India, Malaysia, Indonesia, Philippines, and others are also frequent respondents. US ADMs against Asian developing countries have been especially common since 1985, constituting some 30 percent of the total.[2] The same nations have been prominent targets in recent EU antidumping practice (Nicolaides and Wijngaarden 1993:31, 34-5).

Use of ADMs by Asian developing countries, indeed by developing countries generally, has been a much different story. There were virtually no such proceedings until quite recently. As Annexes 1 and 2 demonstrate, however, while developing countries still initiate relatively few antidumping proceedings, the number is steadily growing. Mexico is by far the most active user of ADMs among developing countries, recently moving into the top five overall (Andere 1993); other Latin American countries have begun to follow suit. Within Asia, Korea has become the most consistent practitioner, though India has begun to appear in the data with some regularity. Singapore; Taipei,China; and Thailand have also been reported as imposing ADMs. A significant proportion of these measures has been imposed against other Asian developing countries.

Many developing countries have for years had provisions in their customs laws providing for antidumping proceedings (Messerlin

1988:166-7). Korea acted under such an early law in 1986, for example (see Annex). But developing countries in Asia and elsewhere have begun to "modernize" their laws and enact new ones, most often modeling them on the laws of the US and other frequent users. Thus, for example, Korea amended its law in 1988 on the US model (Krupp 1992:111). Some observers believe that most developing countries that become parties to the Uruguay Round ADM Code will adopt antidumping laws.

The use of ADMs by an Asian developing country has already had an effect on international trade law. The first case imposing duties under Korea's amended law, involving imports of polyacetal resin from the US and Japan, became something of a cause célèbre. In the West, the procedural and substantive deficiencies in the polyacetal resin decision, held to violate the prior GATT Anti-Dumping Code in a case brought by the US (BISD 1993:205), were seen as harbingers of future abuses by a new generation of ADM users. Partly in response to this concern, Western nations agreed to more stringent procedural rules in the ADM Code than they might otherwise have been willing to accept.[3]

Policy

ADMs have strong support among many industrial sectors in the Western developed nations, and within their governments. The US Congress has steadily strengthened its antidumping laws from 1921 to 1994, and the European Commission (1993:2.2-2.3) regularly asserts the importance of vigorous ADMs. Independent economists and trade policy analysts, however, are virtually unanimous in their opposition to ADMs, at least as currently utilized.

One common ground of opposition is that ADMs often contain what may be called "purely protectionist elements." The US, for example, has long determined the existence of international price discrimination (dumping) by comparing *individual* export prices with *average* home market prices. Even if sales are made in each market over an identical range of prices and at an identical weighted average price, this approach will inevitably show the lower-priced export sales to be dumped. Nothing in the rationales for ADMs requires such a substantively unjust calculation. Unfortunately, antidumping laws are a fruitful breeding ground for practices of this kind, as shown in the following subsection.

The present subsection summarizes the theoretical and policy debate over the validity of ADMs as such, leaving aside purely protectionist elements. Many volumes of sophisticated analysis have been devoted to this subject. This section is intended merely to demonstrate that scholars

369

operating from a variety of theoretical perspectives find ADMs to be generally inappropriate forms of government intervention.

National Welfare Policy

Economists analyze government policies like ADMs in terms of their effect on the welfare of a relevant community, typically the nation in question, other affected nations, or the world as a whole. The standard analysis of a tariff, for example, focuses on the tariff-imposing country. It calculates the reduction in consumer surplus, the increase in producer surplus, and the increase in government revenue, netting these gains and losses to demonstrate that the tariff will normally reduce national welfare.

Applying this analysis to international price discrimination, it is instructive to compare two cases (European Commission 1993:8). In the first, exporters sell abroad at higher prices than in their home market; because of market conditions, such as differing elasticities of demand, this pricing structure is optimal for the firms. In this case, it seems clear that the exporting country gains from price discrimination: its firms are more profitable and may employ more people, purchase more inputs, and so on, and its consumers do not have to pay higher prices. Importing countries are likely to lose by this type of price discrimination, because their consumers will be sending more wealth abroad.

In the second case, exporters sell abroad at lower prices than at home; in fact, they normally sell abroad at competitive prices and, because of market conditions in the home country, sell in the home market at super-competitive prices (European Commission 1993:7-8). Here the welfare effect on the exporting country is ambiguous. Firms profit by price discrimination, but local consumers must pay more. As Davey (1988) has pointed out, though, governments never prevent firms from pricing in this way, suggesting that the welfare effect is positive.

In the importing country, which benefits from lower prices, the welfare effect should also be positive. Domestic producers are likely to incur adjustment costs, and it is possible that these costs could outweigh the benefit to consumers. Over time, however, the benefits are likely to prevail: a US Congressional Budget Office (CBO) report concludes that the "importing country definitely gains from the price discrimination . . ." (1994). In addition, the foregoing analysis is static, simply comparing the welfare situations before and after dumping. As in the case of imports generally, price discrimination may also have valuable dynamic effects, spurring firms to innovate and reduce costs and providing a check on anticompetitive activity.[4]

These welfare conclusions may not, of course, apply in every case. The principal exception is predatory pricing, traditionally defined as selling below marginal cost (here, in the export market) for an extended period to drive out competitors, producing a monopoly market structure that will lead to a reduction in national welfare. Recent scholarship suggests that asymmetric information may make predatory pricing rational behavior for firms, even without the extensive and asymmetric access to capital required under traditional theory. Even so, however, firms are unlikely to pursue international predatory pricing strategies because of pervasive global competition (CBO Report 1994:5, 77-81).[5]

The broader point is that modern antidumping laws do not even permit an inquiry into national welfare. In most countries, dumping findings are automatic once the authorities establish price discrimination and determine that domestic producers have suffered "material" injury as a result. In effect, a reduction in national welfare is presumed whenever the relatively low threshold of material injury is met. The welfare benefits of low-priced imports are not considered, and consumers are typically not given any opportunity to argue against ADMs. In the US, the final decision on the imposition of SGMs is made by the President, who is institutionally responsible for the national welfare and is authorized to consider broader welfare effects. No such procedure, however, applies in decisions on ADMs.[6]

Competition Policy

Scholars of competition policy are also consistent critics of ADMs (Hoekman and Mavroidis 1996:27). Their criticism follows national welfare analysis, but from a somewhat different perspective. Competition law is designed to preserve the competitive quality of markets. Thus, predatory pricing, which destroys competition, is appropriately forbidden, but rationally competitive, efficient practices should be upheld. ADMs, in contrast, are designed to protect particular competitors, materially injured import-competing firms, even at the cost of reducing legitimate competition. In the US, the Antidumping Act of 1916 was based on competition policy. Plaintiffs had to prove that price discrimination was carried out "with the intent . . .of restraining or monopolizing . . . trade or commerce ...," or "with the intent of destroying or injuring an industry," an approximation of predatory pricing. With the passage of the Antidumping Act of 1921, however, the US antidumping law abandoned the preservation of competition rationale.

Competition scholars argue that most situations in which firms sell abroad at prices lower than in their home markets, or even below the full cost of production, are either fully consistent with market competition (for example, adjusting prices according to the elasticity of demand in particular markets, and reducing prices below full cost in times of declining demand) or positively procompetitive (using low prices to introduce new products, and pricing products with steep learning curves in relation to costs averaged over the entire product life cycle). Only predatory pricing threatens competition as such, and a competition law or an antidumping law focused on predatory pricing is sufficient to deal with that threat.

Unfair Market Conditions

ADMs are treated differently from most other trade barriers on the ground that dumping is an "unfair" practice; for example, there is a lower threshold of injury than with SGMs. As Cass and Boltuck (1996:351-3) have recently made clear, this kind of ethical rhetoric is quite different from an efficiency/welfare analysis, and it may lead to different results. The language of unfairness has become increasingly central to discourse on international economic policy, spreading from the classic "offensive" areas of dumping and subsidization to the "defensive" barriers to trade and investment addressed under US Section 301 (Abbott 1996:415) and more recently to divergences in national regulation in such areas as environmental protection and labor rights (Bhagwati and Hudec 1996).

The unfairness argument against nonpredatory dumping stems from two differences between the export market and the exporter's home market (Cass and Boltuck 1996; European Commission 1993). First, to charge a higher price at home, the exporter must have greater "market power" there, often as a result of a large market share in a concentrated market. Market power allows the exporter to earn returns higher than the competitive level at home, giving it the capital with which to finance or "subsidize" lower-price exports. Second, the home market must in some way be segregated, so that arbitrage, selling lower-price export goods back to the home market, is not possible. On both counts, the argument runs, "the foreign producer benefits from something that seems *wrong*, the restriction of competition in the home market" (Cass and Boltuck 1996:383).

There are, however, profound difficulties with this argument. First, the pricing policies followed by exporters when these two conditions exist are rational, private responses to the nature of the prevailing markets; they are not themselves unfair. The market power and market segregation must be the sources of any unfairness, and these could be due to perfectly innocent factors. Thus, market power could be due primarily to brand pref-erences in a market of differentiated products; market segregation could be due primarily to transportation costs or different national product stan-dards; and so on. Conditions like these are not at all uncommon.

Second, although the unfairness argument emphasizes cross-subsidies within firms, the existence of market power in a protected home market does not necessarily mean that an exporting firm will have greater wealth or access to resources than its competitors in the export market. The home market may, in fact, be quite small, and the petitioners far wealthier than the respondent firms.

Third, and most fundamentally, there are no accepted standards under which market conditions like these can be determined to be wrong. Even with a spreading free market consensus, there is no general agree-ment on the appropriate content of competition law, especially on issues like constraining market power. Successful capitalist economies have quite different views on these matters, and their views change over time. Simi-larly, even though liberalization is a basic thrust of the GATT/WTO sys-tem, the system does not demand any particular level of openness. Nations are not required to negotiate lower tariff rates, and even developed coun-tries may raise tariffs freely so long as they are willing to pay for the privi-lege. Numerous exceptions, including those available only to developing countries, authorize different levels of protection on independent norma-tive grounds.

The unfairness complaint against dumping resembles the reciproc-ity arguments leveled against "unfair" foreign trade practices under US Section 301 (Abbott 1996). Most commonly, US firms argue that foreign government measures or market conditions are unfair because they do not allow the same degree of access that firms from the foreign country have to the American market ("equal access reciprocity"). In a significant num-ber of 301 cases, and in recent demands for harmonization of labor and environmental laws, the normative claim is that an internal policy of a foreign government is, unfairly, more beneficial to local firms than the equivalent US program is to the US complainants ("equal production conditions reciprocity"). Both arguments are usually made on a sectoral or industry basis, and frequently ignore the existence of similar policies and offsetting advantages in the US.

The unfairness argument against dumping reflects very similar ideas. Here too, the argument is made sectorally, even firm-by-firm; here too, the existence of offsetting advantages such as superior access to capital, more beneficial national regulation, even subsidies, are ignored. As complaints of particular firms or industries, these arguments are perfectly complaints of particular firms or industries, these arguments are perfectly understandable. There is, however, no basis in international economic law for a requirement of equal access, much less equal production conditions between nations, and the latter rule, at least, would be quite unworkable (Abbott 1996). Production conditions reciprocity between sectors is even less legitimate. Sectoral conditions are rarely addressed in international economic law, and sectoral reciprocity has consistently been seen as an unworkable basis for national policy.[7]

Finally, whatever one might think of these fairness arguments, the fact remains that neither GATT, the ADM Code, nor any of the major national antidumping laws require any consideration of the underlying factors said to make price discrimination unfair. A case in which arbitrage is unprofitable because of transportation costs is treated exactly the same as one in which a foreign government blocks imports to protect a favored industry. A case in which small domestic firms are injured by the low export prices of a foreign monopolist is treated exactly the same as one in which American Telephone and Telegraph seeks relief from the low prices charged by small telephone manufacturers in Taipei,China (US International Trade Commission 1989:87).

Public Choice Theory

The theoretical perspectives discussed thus far take an optimistic view of government as an independent agent able to make decisions in the national interest, however that may be defined. Public choice theory, which applies economic theory to the behavior of political actors, takes a more pessimistic view. Public officials, not "government," are seen as the relevant actors, and these officials, like other individuals, act to maximize their own welfare. The standard view is that elected officials seek to maximize their chances of reelection. While judges and independent agency officials may have different incentives, political appointees are likely to be attuned to the incentives of their elected superiors.

In the public choice view, officials supply various forms of government largess, including ADMs and other forms of protection. Firms, industries, and other interests in society demand government actions of benefit to them, and are willing to pay in terms of political support, votes, contributions, and the like. Consumers also seek beneficial forms of government action, but tend to be systematically disadvantaged in political competition with concentrated, well-organized, and well-financed interest groups. The political market clears at an inefficiently high level of government intervention.

A corollary of the public choice vision is known ironically as the "theory of optimal obfuscation." The interest groups that demand government benefits, and the public officials that supply them, normally attempt to limit the visibility of their acts so as to minimize the chance of a negative political reaction. Private interests prefer such opaque approaches to the transparency of outright protection, or even formal SGMs, to protect their benefits; officials prefer them to avoid conflict among affected groups and the possible loss of political support.[8]

Public choice theory views ADMs in two different ways. The positive view holds that because ADMs are technical, mechanical remedies imposed through administrative procedures, they help equalize the political competition between import-competing firms and consumers: officials can avoid granting costly forms of protection by referring demanding groups to the antidumping authorities. The negative view, however, holds that ADMs fit perfectly with the theory of optimal obfuscation. Legislated quotas, presidentially imposed SGMs, and other visible forms of protection are likely to create political conflict. ADMs, in contrast, are so technical that few people even understand them; they are unlikely catalysts for political mobilization. Because they are implemented administratively, moreover, ADMs are less visible, and allow fewer opportunities for political opposition.

The negative public choice view helps explain the puzzle of antidumping laws: why they have been steadily strengthened, adopted by additional countries, and used at increasing rates even though economic theory suggests that they often reduce the welfare of the nations that use them. Public choice theory is an even stronger explanation for the appearance of purely protectionist elements amid the technical details of antidumping laws: these elements are clear examples of optimal obfuscation.

The suggestion that antidumping laws function to deflect demands for stronger forms of protection may also be, or once have been, true. In the principal user countries, however, the antidumping process appears to have been "captured" by import-competing domestic interests. Aside from the provisions of the laws themselves, the best evidence for capture is the success rates in antidumping cases. In the US from 1980 to 1992, for example, the antidumping authorities found dumping in over 90 percent of the cases filed, and the percentage rose during that period. Public choice and the theory of regulatory capture, bolstered by statistics like these, justify the most intense concern about the spread of antidumping laws and procedures modeled on those of the US.

Law

GATT authorizes the use of ADMs in Article VI, but provides little guidance as to the calculation of dumping, the determination of material injury, or the appropriate administrative procedures. The Tokyo Round Antidumping Code began to spell out the substantive determinations, but this agreement, like the companion Subsidies Code, made its greatest contribution by elaborating detailed procedural requirements. In general, the Uruguay Round simply tightened up this inherited procedural framework. Unfortunately, the Tokyo Round Code was not widely adopted, especially by developing countries. By 1990, only 35 nations had become parties.

The Uruguay Round ADM Code, to which all members of WTO must adhere, is the product of an unusual political process. Originally, ADMs were not on the agenda for the Round, but increasing concern about the use of these measures led to a decision to renegotiate the Tokyo Round Code. The Dunkel Draft of 1991 struck an uneasy balance in this area. It attempted to eliminate certain purely protectionist elements while making it easier for importing countries to use ADMs. The latter aspect was primarily the result of a common bargaining position by the US and the EU, which agreed to support each other's proposals on ADMs even though they disagreed on many other issues (Horlick 1993:5). In November 1993, near the end of the Round (US General Accounting Office 1994:73), the US returned to the negotiations, with EU support, to demand further relaxation of the Dunkel Draft; and it achieved most of its goals. The result remains a compromise, not a clear-cut reform.

In many countries, including the US, the provisions of the Code must be translated into domestic law. The US followed the Code in drafting its implementing legislation, but under pressure from affected domestic interests did so in a way that allows it to continue its previous methodologies in certain areas. In addition, the legislation added some new restrictive provisions. The EU, and doubtless other countries as well, modified the domestic law effect of the Code in similar ways.

The rest of this subsection summarizes the major innovations of the ADM Code, both restrictive and expansive (Palmeter 1995). It also analyzes some aspects of the US and EU implementing laws, both because these are significant to exporters in Asia and because they are object lessons in what to watch for in other countries, including one's own.

Restraining Purely Protectionist Elements

Price comparisons

The US, like the EU (Waer and Vermulst 1994:14), has for years compared the prices charged in *individual* export transactions with the *average* home market price in determining whether and to what extent dumping exists. As noted earlier, this methodology is almost guaranteed to find price discrimination even when none exists in an economic sense. The ADM Code adopts the general rule that a "fair comparison" between prices must be made. Section 2.4.2 specifically addresses the US practice, requiring that either average prices or transaction prices be compared, except in a few situations. This rule is a significant benefit to exporters. The US implementing statute[10] incorporates the rule, and the US has indicated that it will use average-to-average comparisons in most cases.

Looking more closely, however, one observes that Section. 2.4.2 requires equivalent price comparisons "during the investigation phase." This language has important implications for the US, where antidumping procedures are "retrospective." In the course of an investigation, the US antidumping authorities issue first a preliminary and then a final determination. If the authorities find dumping at either stage, they establish a specific dumping margin; liquidation of affected imports for customs purposes is suspended, and importers must post bond or otherwise provide for payment of duties equal to the dumping margin. Even a final determination, however, only establishes a *tentative* dumping margin. The *final* duties are set during an administrative review of the determination, a year or more later. At that time, the final duties are assessed retroactively. Importers either receive refunds or make additional payments, depending on the relationship between tentative and final duties (Horlick 1989:99,126-9).

Given this system, the US implementing legislation takes the Code at its word and requires equivalent price comparisons *only* "during the investigation phase," not when final duties are set during review.[11] This system may lead to fewer initial dumping findings, but it will produce more uncertainty and higher final duties once dumping has been found. There is some irony here, since administrative reviews are intended to be careful and objective, an opportunity to correct any injustices committed during the more hurried initial determination (Horlick 1989:128). This is a perfect example of a technical provision in which purely protectionist elements are easily buried.[12]

377

Calculating normal value with below cost sales

Section 2.2.1 of the ADM Code adopts the position of most ADM users that sales in the home market at prices less than the full per unit cost of production may be treated as "not being in the ordinary course of trade" (in the words of GATT Article VI) and disregarded in determining normal value. Exclusion of below-cost sales, of course, raises the normal value, leading to more frequent dumping findings and higher margins. Below-cost sales can be excluded only when made in "substantial quantities." The Code defines this phrase as 20 percent or more of total sales,[13] a cutoff that will require inclusion of more below-cost sales than the prior US "10-90-10" rule.[14] Below-cost sales are also considered to be made in substantial quantities, however, when the weighted average price of all home market sales is less than the total per unit cost, regardless of actual sales volumes. This rule should make it easier to find dumping when prices are lowered during recessions and other periods of slack demand.

An important restraint comes into effect at this point. When US authorities disregarded so many below-cost sales that home market prices were no longer a reliable indicator of price discrimination, they most often compared export prices with a statutory calculation known as "constructed value." Constructed value was based on the costs of production in the home market. By law, however, US authorities were required to add to the direct costs of labor and materials an amount for selling and general and administrative expenses ("overhead") equal to at least 10 percent of direct costs, even if actual overhead was lower. In addition, they were required to include an amount for profit equal to 8 percent of the total of direct costs plus overhead, even if actual profit was lower or, as in times of serious recession, nonexistent. Again, the result was to find dumping more frequently and to calculate higher dumping margins.

The ADM Code prohibits this kind of arbitrary calculation, requiring that overhead and profit be based on actual data.[15] The US implementing legislation conforms. Interestingly, however, the US statute includes what might be called a "countermeasure." Section 773(b)(1) of the statute drops the last part of the former "10-90-10" test, under which US authorities would look to constructed value whenever 90 percent or more of home market sales were disregarded as below cost. Under the new law, the US will utilize constructed value only when *all* home market sales are below cost; even if there are only a few above-cost sales in the ordinary course of trade, they will be used in calculating price discrimination. Under this policy, constructed value, now a more realistic figure, will be used less often. The danger is that a few aberrational above-cost sales may be unreliable bases for comparison, leading to unrealistic dumping margins.[16]

Standing

GATT Article VI provides that dumping is to be condemned only when it causes or threatens material injury to an "industry" in the importing country. When individual firms, trade associations, or other entities file antidumping petitions, they must in theory be acting "on behalf of" an industry. Yet if no objective determination of representation is made, the least-competitive firms can initiate antidumping proceedings, creating procedural burdens and uncertainty for importers, even if "the industry" is healthy. Until recently, US authorities simply presumed that petitioners were acting on behalf of an industry if they said they were. In 1990, however, this approach was held invalid in a GATT proceeding brought by Sweden.[17]

Section 5.4 of the ADM Code follows that decision, requiring an affirmative determination of representativeness. However, the standing test, while complex, is relatively lax. The petition must be "supported" (though not, apparently, joined) by producers (i) accounting for at least 25 percent of total production of the "like product;" and (ii) representing more than 50 percent of the production of those firms expressing a position, pro or con, on the petition. Under this test, a petition could satisfy the standing requirement with firms responsible for nearly half the industry's total production playing no role in the petition and expressing no position on it, and with firms responsible for almost a quarter of industry output actively opposed. Although a standing rule is desirable in principle, this weak test should have little impact on the use of ADMs in either the US or the EU.

Other Constraints

Sunset

Nations that were frequent targets of ADMs sought in the Uruguay Round a firm sunset provision, under which antidumping duties would automatically terminate after a certain period of time. The principal impetus was the practice of the US, where ADMs are typically in force for many years, longer than in other major user countries.[18] The ADM Code does include a sunset provision, but it is not the automatic cutoff proponents had hoped for. Under Section 11.3, ADMs are generally to be terminated five years after imposition, but they may be extended, apparently indefinitely, if the authorities determine that their expiration would be likely to lead to further dumping and material injury.[19] Section 11.3 puts virtually no constraints on this determination. The practical effect of the rule will thus depend on the facts of individual cases, the substantive rules of the Code and national law,[20] and the approach of national authorities.

De minimis rules

The US had for some time applied a de minimis rule under which it would not proceed against dumped imports if the dumping margin was very small. The cutoff point, however, was a dumping margin of less than .5 percent, low by any measure. Along with prevailing practices for determining injury and causation, it allowed antidumping proceedings to go forward with the attendant cost and uncertainty in cases where the degree of price discrimination had very limited economic effects.[21] Under the ADM Code, the de minimis level is raised to 2 percent of the export price; proceedings are to be terminated immediately if the dumping margin is found to be smaller.

The Code also adds a rule requiring immediate termination of proceedings if the volume of dumped imports from a particular country is "negligible." This will "normally" be the case when the dumped imports constitute less than 3 percent of total imports of the like product.[22] When several countries export small amounts of a product to a particular market, however, the importing country is entitled to cumulate them for purposes of the negligibility provision. If the dumped imports from all countries accounting individually for less than 3 percent of imports cumulatively account for more than 7 percent, none of the imports needs be regarded as negligible. It may be an unanticipated and perverse effect of this rule that complaining firms will name more small country exporters in their antidumping petitions in the hope of crossing the 7 percent threshold (Waer and Vermulst 1994:16).

Provisions Strengthening ADMs

Cumulation

When determining whether dumped imports have caused material injury to a domestic industry, both the US and the EU cumulate dumped imports from different firms and from different exporting countries. This practice has been neither explicitly recognized nor explicitly forbidden in GATT law. One of the major demands of the US in the Uruguay Round was that the ADM Code be changed to authorize cumulation.

Code Section 3.3, which the US regards as an important victory, authorizes cumulation of dumped imports for purposes of injury determination. But it also includes some constraining standards. First, only imports that are "simultaneously" the subject of antidumping proceedings may be cumulated. The US implementing legislation actually allows cumulation only of imports as to which antidumping petitions were filed on the same day. This timing is in the hands of complainants' lawyers, though, and petitions may be refiled to create simultaneity.[23] Second, imports may only be cumulated if their dumping margin is more than de minimis and their volume is more than negligible.[24] Finally, national authorities must make a formal determination that cumulation is appropriate given the conditions of competition in their market. These provisions will require some changes in US and EU laws, but they are unlikely to change significantly the practice in either country.[25]

Standard of review

When the US returned to the ADM negotiations in November 1993 to demand additional changes, the issue it pressed most strongly was the addition of an explicit standard for the review of national ADM determinations by WTO panels. Such a standard was included in Section17.6 of the Code. This is perhaps the most troubling aspect of the Code, for the new standard seeks to limit the institutional role of the recently strengthened WTO DS system, providing a layer of insulation for national ADM determinations. This issue will be addressed below in connection with DS procedures.

Unilateral Changes in National Antidumping Law

As already noted, both the US and the EU acted unilaterally to strengthen their antidumping procedures while implementing the Uruguay Round ADM Code. These unilateral reinforcements function as countermeasures, offsetting the constraints in the Code to maintain a similar overall level of protection. One example, the US amendment limiting resort to the revised constructed value calculation, has already been described. Two additional US enactments are of particular significance.

Constructed export price calculation

When goods are sold by a foreign exporter to an arm's length buyer in the US, the invoice price, properly adjusted, can be compared with "normal value," the exporter's home market price, to determine whether dumping has taken place. When goods are sold to a related party, or on terms involving unusual forms of compensation, however, the invoice price will be unreliable. In these circumstances, the US calculates what is now called a "constructed export price," typically by taking the invoice price in the first US sale of the imported goods to an unrelated buyer and deducting the costs associated with the intervening resales. These include such things as sales commissions, inland transportation, and additional processing costs.

The ADM Code authorizes construction of the export price, but Section 2.3 leaves the calculations almost completely to national discretion. Before the Uruguay Round, US authorities did not deduct any amount for profit on resale by related parties in the US. The theory was that the foreign exporter and the related US parties formed a single enterprise with a single overall profit. The implementing legislation, however, now provides that an allocation for profit attributable to US operations must be deducted in constructing an export price.[26] Actual profit figures for the related parties are, of course, unreliable. Thus, US profit is calculated by multiplying the total profit of the entire foreign enterprise by the ratio of covered US expenses to total enterprise expenses. The US argues that this procedure is "consistent" with the Code, and indeed it is, but it is still a unilateral amendment designed to strengthen US ADMs.

The profit deduction will increase the likelihood of dumping findings and the size of margins, particularly when home market sales are made directly rather than through related parties. More troubling, the US statute does not clearly provide for similar profit deductions in calculating *normal* value when home market sales are made through related parties, even though the Code requires "fair comparisons."[27] Finally, it is important to note that the new calculation will turn many investigations based on price comparisons into more burdensome investigations of production costs, especially when goods are processed in the US, since the expenses and profits of the foreign exporter must be determined to establish the profit allocation percentage (Palmeter 1995:55).

Circumvention

The US and the EU have both enacted provisions designed to deter "circumvention" of ADMs through two kinds of transactions: (i) shipping parts and components, rather than the finished products subject to ADMs, into the market for assembly there (known as the "screwdriver plant problem"); and (ii) shipping parts and components into third markets not subject to ADMs for assembly and export. This is a major issue for many Asian developing countries, whose exporters use such measures regularly in an ongoing chess game with ADM authorities. Earlier efforts by the EU to regulate screwdriver plants were disapproved in a GATT DS proceeding (European Commission 1990). The 1991 Dunkel Draft, reflecting that decision, included provisions authorizing and constraining both types of measures. The US regarded these rules as too restrictive, however, and "with the gleeful support of the European Union Commission" (Waer and Vermulst 1994:20) negotiated them out of the final text. Thus, no WTO rules govern anticircumvention measures.

The US implementing legislation modifies the previous anticircumvention rules. Under the prior rules, enacted in 1988, the principal criterion was whether the value added by US or third-country processing was "small." The new criterion is whether that process is "minor and insignificant."[28] These are very similar standards, but the factors considered in applying the new one are much broader. US authorities must now take into account the nature of the processing (mere assembly or something more) as well as its value, plus the level of investment, the nature of the production facilities, and the level of research and development in the US or third-country market. Firms without extensive foreign operations will more easily be found to have circumvented US ADMs.

The unilateral measures enacted by the EU Council are procedural. First, the EU amended its law to impose deadlines shorter than those mandated by the Code.[29] While deadlines can provide certainty to foreign respondents, the EU amendments were adopted in response to protectionist pressure, and may impose significant procedural burdens. The Council also modified its decision-making process in antidumping cases, moving from a qualified to a simple majority vote, making it more difficult for free-trade-oriented member states to oppose Commission recommendations for ADMs (Waer and Vermulst 1994:7-8).

Safeguard Measures

Practice

GATT Article XIX authorizes temporary SGMs, providing an explicit "escape clause" for nations whose industries suffer because of the liberalization of imports. These may be referred to as "formal" SGMs, since Article XIX requires national authorities to make formal findings that intervention is warranted under the standards set out in that Article. Significantly, Article XIX authorizes quantitative restraints on imports, even though the prohibition of quotas in most situations is a centerpiece of GATT. Article XIX was added at the insistence of the US, which included similar provisions in bilateral agreements under its Reciprocal Trade Agreements Program.

In spite of the Article XIX exception, GATT contracting parties, both developed and developing, have "rarely" used the formal SGMs that Article contemplates, and then only as a "last resort" (US General Accounting Office 1994:79). The latest edition of the GATT Analytical Index, for example, notes that there have only been some 150 notifications of SGMs since 1950, slightly more than three per year. Even in the US, an active user of trade remedies, and even after the Trade Act of 1974 made escape clause relief easier to obtain, only about three cases per year on average have been filed.[30] Of the developing countries in Asia, only Hong Kong and Korea have been the subject of a significant number of SGMs, and none has imposed Article XIX SGMs in significant numbers.

The principal reason for these surprising facts has been the availability of a number of alternate ways to shield industries from import competition. Many of these devices have, however, been limited in the Uruguay Round.

- Textiles have been subject to sweeping quota protection in developed countries under MFA. Under the Uruguay Round Agreement on Textiles and Clothing, however, MFA is to be phased out, subject to transitional SGMs. When this process is complete, Article XIX will again be relevant to this large sector of international commerce.

- Prior to the Uruguay Round, developing countries had bound relatively few tariffs, taking advantage of the GATT policy that equivalent concessions would not be demanded. They have therefore been able to increase ordinary tariff rates when greater protection was desired without regard to the normal constraints of GATT Article II. Developing countries did, however, bind a large number of tariffs in the Uruguay Round.

- Agriculture has been a unique situation, with numerous unbound tariffs and devices like the EU variable levy and the

GATT waiver for US agricultural programs providing protection without the need for SGMs. Again, however, the Uruguay Round introduced at least the beginnings of liberalization in this sector.

♦ Article XVIII: Sections A and C authorize developing countries to protect individual industries, though not necessarily in the same circumstances for which SGMs are intended.[31] These provisions have not been frequently used either, perhaps because of the relatively high level of GATT oversight they require.

♦ A number of developing countries have relied extensively on Article XVIII:B allowing intervention in international trade in cases of balance-of-payments (BOP) disequilibrium, as well as on the basic GATT BOP provisions, to support protective measures for less competitive industries. In 1983, for example, Korea notified GATT of 253 import quotas said to be justified by the BOP provisions; India notified 122. In the case of Korea, some BOP measures were maintained as long as 20 years. Many of these measures were inconsistent with the basic purpose of the BOP exceptions, which is to allow nations to control *overall* imports, not to protect specific industries. In 1989, the US challenged Korea's quotas on beef imports, said to be BOP measures. A GATT panel found the restrictions unjustified under Article XVIII:B, relying heavily on a finding by the International Monetary Fund Balance-of-Payment Committee to the same effect, and noting that Korea had made no move to phase out the restrictions as Article XVIII requires.[32] More generally, the Uruguay Round Understanding on Balance-of-Payments Measures restricts the BOP exceptions in a number of ways.

Two other alternatives to SGMs are especially relevant to this chapter. First, as already described, the use of ADMs has exploded even as formal SGMs have languished. Devices like the exclusion of home market sales below cost, protectionist methods of calculation, cumulation, and the weak material-injury test have made dumping, injury, and causation relatively easy to find, especially in the cyclical situations where SGMs are typically invoked. The success rate in antidumping cases has been startlingly high, at least in the US, much higher than for SGMs.

In addition, many industries and governments have preferred ADMs to SGMs because of procedural differences in the two remedies.

- ADMs, especially in their more technical aspects, are significantly less transparent than SGMs.

- Nations are not required to provide trade compensation to the countries affected by ADMs or to suffer retaliation by those countries, as is the case with Article XIX SGMs. This difference substantially reduces the political costs of imposing ADMs by eliminating opposition from the affected domestic industries.

- ADMs are selective in their application to exporting countries, while SGMs must be applied on a most-favored nation (MFN) basis. This allows for less extensive interference with international trade, but it also means that the political costs of imposing ADMs are significantly reduced, since fewer nations and fewer importers will object.

- At least until the ADM Code, there have been no restrictions on the duration of ADMs, whereas SGMs are intended to be limited to the time necessary for "adjustment."

- ADMs impose a higher procedural burden on respondent firms, in terms of the cost of providing the information demanded by the dumping authorities, the quantity and sensitivity of that information, and the uncertainty of the proceeding.

- In the US, Presidential approval is not required for ADMs.

For all these reasons, ADMs have become the preferred trade remedy in classic SGM situations as well as the narrow situations for which they were originally designed.

The second alternative is a different form of SGMs: VRAs, which in recent decades largely supplanted the formal procedures envisioned by Article XIX.[33] The popularity of such "gray-area measures" appears to have arisen largely because of characteristics similar to those of ADMs.

- VRAs are less transparent than formal SGMs.

- No trade compensation is required and no retaliation takes place because of the consensual nature of the arrangement.[34]

- VRAs are selective.

- There are no time limits.

In addition, VRAs are by their nature quantitative restraints, which give greater protection than increased tariffs. SGMs, in contrast, may well involve tariff increases, and ADMs are solely tariff remedies.

In the 1970s and 1980s, VRAs came to cover a substantial portion of all international trade. The US used VRAs frequently, the EU perhaps even more. As late as 1994, the EU maintained gray-area measures on some 40 products. Japan has been the most popular target, but Asian developing countries have also been subject to VRAs.

Policy

GATT Article XIX was based on a concern that negotiated liberalization of trade in particular products, coupled with economic developments not foreseen (and "paid for") at the time, might lead to import surges that could cause "serious injury" to domestic producers. In those cases, the government of the importing country should be able to invoke a temporary safety valve to prevent or remedy the injury, without establishing a link to any "unfair" practice. Exactly how long "temporary" protection should last was never made clear; nor was it made clear exactly what, if anything, the government or the affected industry should be required to do during the safeguard period.

One rationale for such a safety valve is that governmental actions to liberalize trade, while benefiting the nation as a whole, create short- and medium-term adjustment costs for particular economic sectors. It is just, and an appropriate function of government, the argument goes, to ease the burden on these sectors. Simply reversing the agreed liberalization would forfeit the common benefits. The government can best combine the common good with justice to the affected sectors by allowing them time to regain competitiveness, change product lines, or exit the industry in an orderly way. This rationale reflects a deeper principle: a product of its post-New Deal era, GATT rejected wholly free trade in favor of "embedded liberalism," accepting that governments must be permitted to intervene in markets, albeit with significant constraints, in pursuit of social peace and other social goals (Ruggie 1982).

Of course, the costs of many governmental acts fall on particular sectors, and there is no safety valve in most of those cases. Political realities, however, seemed to dictate the need for one in the case of international trade. A second rationale for an escape clause, then, was to help governments mute political opposition to liberalization by timely, limited interventions. Article XIX functioned as an insurance policy, assuring domestic industries ex ante that help was available if the costs of liberalization fell on them, so that they could support the program of negotiated liberalization.

A third rationale reflected the problem of adjustment costs. It was understood that trade liberalization would generally increase national economic welfare. The benefits to the nation could, however, be reduced or even eliminated in cases where the sectors adversely affected incurred large adjustment costs, due to imperfections in national labor or capital markets and the negative effects on families and communities. Appropriate interventions could actually increase national welfare. Needless to say, the three rationales were in most cases mutually supporting.

These arguments for SGMs are not without their weaknesses or their critics. For one thing, the link between a particular negotiated concession and a surge of imports causing injury has for many years been largely ignored, as has the notion that unanticipated market developments must have contributed to the import surge. These changes significantly weaken the first rationale described above. SGMs now respond simply to changes in markets, not particular government actions; yet it is not clear why international market shifts merit a unique response.

Economists also argue that government intervention to help firms adjust is often unnecessary. If such adjustments are feasible, private capital markets will finance them, at least in countries where those markets are well developed. Intervention may even be counterproductive. Governments may protect industries that should be allowed to disappear as often as they bolster potentially competitive sectors. When intervention is appropriate, moreover, direct subsidies, retraining programs, and the like are apt to be more efficient than temporary protection. In general, it is efficient to address a market failure with measures focused specifically on the problem; indirect measures introduce distortions of their own. Temporary protection is thus a second-best way to address problems in local labor or capital markets.

Public choice scholars advance a more cynical explanation for SGMs. Intervention in response to trade injury is simply another benefit that government officials can parcel out to rent-seeking interest groups when the demand becomes politically irresistible. In Alan Sykes' (1991: 255, 281-

2, 286-7) view, for example, Article XIX is a sophisticated international conspiracy among trade officials. It allows officials in importing countries to gain political benefits by intervening in markets, while limiting such intervention in a rough-and-ready way, through the requirements of increased imports and serious injury, to situations in which those benefits exceed the political costs to trade officials in affected exporting countries.

In spite of these problems, most analysts believe that the net effect of the SGM exception has been positive over time, and that there may well be reasonable political and social, if not always economic, reasons to justify temporary intervention. On the other hand, "adjustment assistance," or technical aid to firms, retraining, and relocation assistance for workers, even direct subsidies, will typically be more efficient, since these measures can be focused directly on the underlying market failures and tied to active efforts at adjustment. The costs of adjustment assistance are also more visible than the costs of protection, and if financed out of general revenues, more likely to be spread equitably over the population. That such measures are not more often used appears to be a case of optimal obfuscation.

Law

Except for the general language of Article XIX, there have been no multilateral legal standards governing the use of SGMs.[35] In the Uruguay Round, however, negotiators produced the first agreement on safeguards (SGM Code) in GATT history. Potentially, at least, this could be a significant turning point; one observer speaking from the perspective of developing countries calls it a "great achievement" (Rom 1994:5,17). The Code is quite brief, less than one third the length of the ADM Code. It avoids technical and procedural detail, and proceeds largely by laying down general rules.

From a practical perspective, the centerpiece of the SGM Code is Article 11. This article first provides that WTO member states may not take any "emergency action on imports of particular products as set forth in Article XIX" except in accordance with that Article and with the Code.[36] More specifically, Article 11 provides that member states "shall not seek, take or maintain any voluntary export restraints, orderly marketing arrangements, or any other similar measures on the export or the import side."[37] While it has long been understood that most VRAs imposed by exporting governments were violations of GATT Article XI, this striking provision also forbids importing governments from seeking VRAs. Existing VRAs are to be phased out over four years, an action that will undoubtedly lead to demands for offsetting protection in other forms.

The remainder of the Code constrains the use of formal SGMs.[38] Articles 2 and 4 reinforce the Article XIX requirement that importing-country authorities formally determine the existence of increased imports (absolute or relative), serious injury, and causation, and they spell out the meaning of those terms in some detail. Articles 3 and 4 seek to ensure procedural fairness and transparency, though without any detailed specification of procedures. Article 2:2 resolves the main stumbling block to agreement in the Tokyo Round by explicitly requiring that SGMs be imposed on an MFN basis.

Other articles of the Code deal with the terms of SGMs themselves, attempting to constrain them in line with their underlying rationales. Article 5, like GATT Article XIX, enunciates the principle that SGMs may only be applied to the extent necessary to prevent or remedy serious injury. The Code, however, adds a requirement that SGMs be used only to the extent necessary to facilitate adjustment. Rather than attempting to define these terms, Article 5 sets a quantitative parameter, requiring states to permit at least a minimum quantity of imports based on import levels in the last three representative years, except where a lower level can be justified.

Article 7:1 implements the same principle by limiting the duration of SGMs to four years, although this period may be extended for as many as four more years if the importing-country authorities determine that protection remains necessary and, in a surprising innovation, if there is evidence that the industry in question is actually adjusting. Article 7:4 further requires that SGMs be degressive, progressively liberalized at regular intervals, even during any extension period. For measures longer than three years, Article 7:4 requires a midterm review to determine if more rapid liberalization is appropriate. Article 7:5 and 6 limit the frequent reuse of SGMs to assist the same industry.[39]

Article XIX has always required some level of GATT involvement in the imposition of SGMs. Articles 12 and 13 of the Code, however, increase these institutional and procedural constraints by spelling out expanded obligations of notification and consultation, and by strengthening surveillance of SGMs through a WTO Safeguards Committee. Article 14 refers disputes over SGMs to the WTO DS procedures.

The SGM Code takes special account of developing-country interests.[40] First, in their role as exporters, Article 9:1 provides that developing-country exports will be exempt from SGMs so long as they constitute less than 3 percent of total imports of the product in question. As with the negligibility rule in the ADM Code, this exemption will not apply if the cumulated imports of all countries entitled to the exemption exceed a specified percentage. In this case, however, that level is 9 percent. The cumulation provision in the SGM Code should not create a perverse incentive to bring more small exporters into a safeguard proceeding, since all SGMs must be imposed on an MFN basis.

Second, in their role as users of SGMs, Article 9:2 authorizes the imposition of SGMs for as long as ten years, rather than the normal eight. This rule may be of little value in practice, however, as developing countries remain subject to the general MFN rule and the requirement to provide trade compensation, or suffer retaliation, after three years. As a result, the political and economic costs of lengthy SGMs may simply be too high (Rom 1994). Article 8:2 also permits developing countries to reuse SGMs more frequently; this could provide a way to minimize compensation.

Even though Article 11 requires the use of formal SGMs in a broad range of circumstances, the provisions of the Code described in this section limit the flexibility of these measures, make them more transparent, and increase their political costs, especially through the MFN requirement. One need not accept all the tenets of public choice theory to recognize that these provisions create incentives for industries and governments to seek alternative measures of protection.

The principal response of the Code is found in Article 8. The general provisions of this article actually exacerbate the problem, since they require governments imposing SGMs to negotiate trade compensation for affected exporting countries and, if no agreement can be reached, authorize those countries to suspend offsetting concessions. Article 8:3, however, contrary to the explicit terms of GATT Article XIX, eliminates the right of retaliation for the first three years an SGM is in effect, so long as it has been imposed in response to an absolute increase in imports and in accordance with the requirements of the Code. In the absence of a threat of retaliation, few importing countries will offer trade compensation. Thus, Article 8 of the Code seeks to reduce the political costs of SGMs, making them more attractive in comparison to alternative trade remedies.

How then, do SGMs under the Code compare with ADMs, the principal alternative for temporary protection? In general, as already noted, the ADM Code maintains much of the protectionist allure of ADMs. Even with a three-year exemption from compensation and retaliation, the SGM Code creates a fairly narrow and costly remedy, albeit one better suited to the basic rationale of adjustment. For developing countries, SGMs will undoubtedly be administratively easier to apply, and more consistent with current efforts to liberalize. Still, ADMs will be an attractive alternative. In the end, there may be some increase in the use of formal SGMs, but the basic balance between SGMs and ADMs seems unlikely to change significantly. If the industries now protected by VRAs, MFA, and other forms of protection limited in the Uruguay Round turn to ADMs rather than formal SGMs, there could be a substantial increase in the use of these measures.

It is also important to consider whether the prohibition on VRAs will stick. Gray-area measures, like ADMs, will continue to have their attractions, sometimes for exporting and importing countries alike. And there are structural reasons why VRAs may reappear, in spite of the clear prohibition in the SGM Code. VRAs were able to proliferate only because one group of natural complainants, the importing countries to which products were being denied, was the nations that had sought the measures in the first place, and because the other natural complainants, the exporting countries, were bought off by individual arrangements. A few complaints were raised by third countries to which exports were diverted, but most such countries simply negotiated their own VRAs. These underlying conditions have not been changed by the Code.

The Code relies on two institutional arrangements to police the prohibition on VRAs. First, under Article 14, it directs complaints about SGMs into the strengthened WTO DS procedures. Unfortunately, however, neither Article 14 nor the DS procedures themselves address the problem of the unwilling complainant.[41] Second, the Code establishes new procedures for notification, consultation, and surveillance. Article 12, however, appears not to require notification of a new VRA, or a request to establish one, presumably because such a requirement would admit the possibility that the rules of the Code might be disregarded.[42] And while Article 13 directs the Committee on Safeguards to monitor "the general implementation" of the Code and to "examine" VRAs and monitor their phaseout,[43] it has no actual enforcement power, not even the ability to initiate a DS proceeding. Preventing the reemergence of VRAs will depend almost wholly on the political will of the WTO member states.

Dispute Settlement

Practice

The GATT DS system has evolved steadily since the early 1970s, when some observers feared that the system might collapse out of disuse.[44] DS procedures were strengthened in 1979 (BISD 1980), 1989 (as a result of the Midterm Review of progress in the Uruguay Round),[45] and most recently in the Uruguay Round Understanding on Rules and Procedures Governing the Settlement of Disputes ("Understanding").

At the same time, the DS system has been used with increasing frequency. "Governments filed 115 legal complaints in the 1980s, of which 47 produced legal decisions by panels — more than in all the previous 30 years together. . . ." (Hudec 1993:14). Significantly, however, developing nations in Asia and elsewhere, have until recently been conspicuously absent from the DS process, most notably as complainants, but even as respondents.[46] During the entire decade of the 1980s, only five GATT complaints were initiated against Asian developing countries, and three of these concerned Korean beef quotas; only seven complaints were filed by any of those countries.[47] Asian developing countries have been involved in a few significant cases during the 1990s.[48] As Annex 3 demonstrates, developing-country involvement in the DS system appears to have increased markedly since the advent of WTO.

Policy

Traditionally, scholarly analysis and political debate concerning GATT DS have revolved around opposing views of the process, both descriptive and normative. The most influential of these dichotomies have been the distinctions between *legalism* and *pragmatism* and between *rule-oriented* and *power-oriented* diplomacy (Abbott 1992a,b).

As between the two poles of these parallel dichotomies, a more legalistic, rule-oriented DS system should in general be preferable for developing countries in Asia and elsewhere. As in domestic society, the existence of legal rules that restrain the self-interested actions of larger powers, coupled with an opportunity, in case those rules are violated, to obtain a fair hearing and a remedy from an independent, neutral third party, are bulwarks of political equality. If the alternative to a rule-based system is a power-based system, of course, it goes without saying that the former is more desirable for smaller, weaker nations. For the most part, developing countries have supported this view, though they have criticized elements of the GATT system.

GATT/WTO DS has moved fairly steadily toward a more legalistic system, even though many elements of a diplomatic approach remain.[49] It is perhaps surprising, then, that the system has been used so rarely by developing countries. A number of explanations can be suggested. Some relate to the nature of the system itself. For one thing, before the adoption of the Understanding, proceedings could be delayed, even blocked, by the respondent state. If DS proceedings did go forward, the ultimate sanction, although virtually never invoked, has been trade retaliation in an amount offsetting the effect of the violation; yet this sanction is virtually meaningless for a developing country acting against an economically powerful state.

Other explanations relate to the political realities surrounding the DS system. For example, while a rule-based system may benefit developing nations, it also imposes a burden, requiring trained personnel and resources to gather information and advance legal arguments. GATT has sponsored numerous training programs, but these have not been sufficient to overcome the problem, an example of a *political* market failure. What is more, powerful states may be able to deter use of the DS system. Developing nations may be reluctant to offend major trading partners even if they cannot exercise their superior power within the trade system itself.[50] Finally, the small number of DS proceedings initiated by developing countries may simply reflect the degree to which developed countries have used forms of protection, especially VRAs and MFA quotas, that are insulated from legal challenge.

These problems have been recognized within GATT, and some special provisions have been put in place to facilitate use of the DS system. A 1966 GATT decision, for example, adopted a special procedure for developing-country complainants, providing for mediation by the Director-General, the right to a DS panel, and time limits designed to prevent respondents from drawing out the process. Developing countries, however, have for at least 30 years sought changes in the DS process that reflect a different dichotomy, one that emphasizes the contrast between *global interests* and *national interests* (Abbott 1992a,b).

The prevailing GATT DS system is almost purely oriented to national interests. DS proceedings are initiated by the states affected by an alleged violation; proceedings are controlled by those states; claims are based on the damage incurred by them; remedies are aimed at restoring the balance of concessions between complainant and respondent states; and sanctions take the form of retaliation by affected states. The GATT panel is a passive third party; GATT itself takes no active role in DS proceedings except to encourage settlement of the dispute. The closest analogy is US civil litigation, though GATT DS is even more party-centered than many modern civil litigation systems. Several of the factors that discourage developing countries from using the system, such as the possibility of delay and blocking, the inadequacy of retaliation, the burden of initiating cases, and the fear of alienating the respondent, have been products of this horizontal, national-interests structure.

Beginning in the 1960s, developing countries sought reforms of the DS system that reflected global interests. Since violations of GATT rules were harmful to the common interests of the trading community, the institutions representing that community should help to enforce the rules. The 1966 Decision[51] was in fact a compromise between the national interests system and developing-country demands for a system in which the GATT Secretariat could initiate DS cases, at least when the affected states were unable to do so. Another proposal frequently advanced has been the possibility of collective sanctions when retaliation by the affected state alone would be ineffective in bringing about compliance with a GATT decision, a possibility consistent with the language of GATT Article XXIII.[52]

Even in the Uruguay Round, the global interests view was virtually ignored. WTO DS remains a horizontal, party-driven, national interests procedure. The Understanding does, however, strengthen this procedure to a remarkable degree, ameliorating several of the problems previously faced by developing countries. The DS system is now in a position to become the essential regulator of the rapidly expanding system of WTO rules.[53] In the areas discussed in this chapter, the DS system will play a central role in interpreting and applying the new limits on ADMs, SGMs, and VRAs, and will thus influence the choice among those remedies. The system will also help determine whether unilateral measures like US Section 301, in some ways a throwback to power relations, will continue to be a prominent part of the trade landscape.

Law

Consider first the effects of the Understanding on the potential for litigation *by* developing countries.[54] Since the DS system remains party-driven, a developing country that feels itself wronged by another nation's violation[55] of one of the Uruguay Round agreements[56] must initiate a proceeding[57] by request to the WTO Dispute-Settlement Body (DSB), the General Council. The Understanding provides that a state should, before beginning a case, "exercise its judgment" as to whether litigation would be "fruitful,"[58] but this injunction probably adds little to the political constraints a developing country would feel in any case. Either party to a dispute may request good offices, mediation or conciliation by the Director-General or another neutral party before adversary proceedings begin.[59]

Once a proceeding has been commenced, the complainant sets in motion a set of procedures that are remarkable, especially in light of past practice, for their automaticity.[60] At the outset, the complainant is automatically entitled to the creation of a DS panel, free of the threat of blocking by the respondent, unless formation of a panel is rejected by consensus of the DSB, including the complainant. What is more, the panel must be established by the second meeting of DSB at which the matter appears on the agenda, freeing the complainant from the threat of undue delay.[61] Other time limits apply to later stages of the proceeding. Though the details differ, it can be seen that many of the advantages of the 1966 Decision, such as the right to a panel, time limits, and the possibility of mediation, are now incorporated into the general DS procedures.

In one of the few reflections of a global interests perspective in the Understanding, the Secretariat, acting in an independent, neutral capacity, is required to propose nominees for the panel, and the parties are enjoined to accept its nominations unless there are "compelling reasons" to object. If the parties cannot agree on the makeup of the panel, the Secretariat may actually appoint its members, removing another occasion for delay.[62] The panel is instructed to "make an objective assessment of the matter before it," including both the facts and the law.[63] The panel is constituted with the well-established standard terms of reference that require it to examine the case "in light of the relevant provisions of" the applicable agreement, unless both parties agree on other terms.[64] The Understanding makes explicit for the first time that WTO agreements are to be interpreted in accordance with the rules of public international law, a provision that adds to the predictability of the process.[65]

If the panel finds that a violation has occurred, it is to "recommend" that the respondent state bring the offending measure into compliance.[66] The Understanding makes quite clear that the primary objective of a DS proceeding is to secure the removal of any offending measures; other sanctions are merely a means to this end.[67] The Understanding adds a new institutional element to the DS system by creating a standing Appellate Body, which is to hear party-filed appeals from panel decisions on issues of law and legal interpretation and can affirm, reverse, or modify panel decisions.[68] If the Appellate Body determines that a violation has occurred, it, too, is to recommend the removal of the offending measures.

Panel and Appellate Body decisions are advisory to DSB, which must approve them before they have formal effect. Like the creation of a panel, however, adoption of such decisions is automatic, unless there is a consensus against adoption.[69] At this point, the Understanding includes a significantly strengthened procedure for supervising the implementation of decisions.[70] The procedure turns on the establishment of a "reasonable period of time" for compliance; this period is proposed by the party subject to the decision, but it must be approved by the other party, DSB, or an arbitrator. During that period, implementation remains on the agenda of DSB. The party subject to the decision must report regularly, any member state can object to its implementation measures, and disputes over the adequacy or lawfulness of those measures may be referred to follow-up DS proceedings.

If a decision has not been complied with by the end of the "reasonable period," the complainant state may initiate negotiations for trade compensation. If no agreement is reached within the notably brief period of 20 days, the complainant may request DSB authorization to suspend an equivalent level of concessions; remarkably, approval for such retaliation is also automatic, again unless there exists a consensus against approval. Retaliation is, however, regarded as the "last resort," a temporary measure to encourage implementation. The Understanding generally limits retaliation to economic sectors related to the violation, though cross-sectoral sanctioning is possible.[71]

The openness of the new DS procedure, its automaticity, and its insulation from delay, blocking, and distortion by respondents mark it as closer to a modern domestic legal system than any previous version in the history of GATT. The power such a procedure gives complainants is matched with several provisions designed to ensure that DS decisions cannot easily be attacked by a losing respondent on grounds of unfairness. In addition to several guarantees of the neutrality of panels and the Appellate Body, which benefit both sides, provisions of this sort include efforts to encourage settlement throughout the procedure, the ability of the parties to comment on preliminary drafts of the panel's report, the new appellate procedure, and the allowance of a reasonable time for compliance (Abbott 1992b).

The foregoing description is based solely on the standard provisions of the Understanding. The Understanding, however, also includes a number of provisions designed specifically for cases brought by developing countries. As Palitha Kohona (1994:23) puts it, "the principle of special and differential treatment has been adhered to consistently" throughout the Understanding. First, Article 3:12 permits any developing country bringing a complaint against a developed country to invoke the relevant sections of the 1966 Decision in lieu of Articles 4 to 6 and 12 of the Understanding, concerned with consultations, good offices and mediation, establishment of panels, and panel procedure.[72] This may be a significant symbolic concession, but it seems unlikely to be significant in practice, both because the Decision itself has rarely been invoked and because the Understanding incorporates many of its benefits.[73]

Article 4:10 calls for special consideration of developing-country problems during consultations. If a dispute between a developing and developed country reaches the panel stage, the former is guaranteed, on request, the presence of at least one panelist from a developing country.[74]

In addition, while the Secretariat already supports states involved in DS proceedings to some extent, the Understanding requires it to make available to a developing-country party the assistance of a legal expert from the WTO technical cooperation services; the only constraint on this assistance is the need to maintain the overall neutrality of the Secretariat.[75] Finally, when a developing country is party to a DS proceeding, the panel must explicitly indicate in its report how it took account of any differential and more favorable treatment provisions in the applicable WTO agreements.[76]

Several provisions pertaining to the implementation of decisions take account of developing-country problems. One of these requires DSB to consider the possibility of additional measures to encourage implementation when the complainant is a developing country; another requires DSB to consider the impact of the measures complained of on the economy of the developing-country complainant, not simply the volume of trade affected by those measures, when deciding what additional actions should be taken.[77]

Between the general strengthening of the system and this range of special provisions, the WTO DS system should be a powerful tool for developing countries seeking to enforce the commitments made in the Uruguay Round. The data in Annex 3 suggest that developing countries have begun to recognize this potential. The obstacles that remain are largely practical. Even with assistance from the Secretariat, initiating and prosecuting a case will be burdensome for many developing countries, while the existence of disparate economic power may deter complaints against major trading nations; disparate power also continues to make the sanction of retaliation, more readily available than in the past, next to meaningless for many developing countries.

The same powerful, automatic procedures, including the provisions for retaliation, can and will be invoked *against* developing countries. There are, moreover, far fewer special provisions in the Understanding applicable to developing countries as respondents. Article 12:10 provides extra time for consultations and the preparation of legal arguments; and some of the provisions already discussed, such as the right to a panel member from a developing country, apply in this circumstance as well. The strongest provision is applicable only to *least*-developed countries. Article 24:1 requires all members to "exercise due restraint" in bringing cases against such countries and in seeking compensation and the authority to retaliate; it also requires that special attention be paid to their situation throughout the DS proceeding.

For developing countries concerned about challenges to their own policies and practices, the most important provision in the Understanding may be Article 23, "strengthening of the multilateral system." This article was carefully negotiated with the US, and was seen as a trade-off for the strengthening of the DS system. The trade-off is, quite simply, that the US and other countries will *use* the system put in place. The special focus of those insisting upon such a provision was the famous (or infamous) Section 301 procedure employed by the US with considerable effectiveness against a variety of countries, including India; Korea; Taipei,China; and Thailand.

Article 23 generally requires a state seeking redress of a violation of a WTO agreement, or of a nonviolation nullification or impairment, to utilize and abide by the rules of the WTO DS system as spelled out in the Understanding.[78] More specifically, it prohibits member states from determining the existence of a violation, or of nullification or impairment, except through the DS process. In addition, it prohibits states from making such determinations inconsistently with the final results of DS proceedings.[79]

Section 301 already requires that allegations of trade agreement violations be taken to the appropriate DS procedure, although it leaves US authorities some discretion to continue a proceeding in the face of a negative decision.[80] Many recent 301 proceedings, however, have not involved trade agreement violations; instead, they have concerned areas like intellectual property in which there were at the time no applicable trade agreements. Cases of this sort will undoubtedly continue, although the breadth of the Uruguay Round should reduce their ambit. In addition, the US will almost certainly initiate some 301 cases where the applicability of Article 23 will be disputed. Indeed, one such case has already arisen.

In May 1995, the US initiated procedures to impose trade sanctions against Japan under Section 301, following a determination that certain Japanese practices unreasonably restricted the access of US firms to the replacement auto parts market in Japan (Bureau of National Affairs 1995a). At the same time, the US announced its intention to begin a WTO DS proceeding against the entire Japanese auto and auto parts regime. Japan, for its part, initiated formal WTO consultations, the first step in the DS process. On June 28, hours before sanctions were due to take effect, the two countries reached a settlement based on "voluntary" "business forecasts" of increased purchases by Japanese auto companies that defused the dispute (Bureau of National Affairs 1995b).

The US argued that the practices it found unreasonable, especially discriminatory arrangements among private firms, were matters of competition law, not trade law. Since those practices were not covered by a trade agreement, the US actions did not run afoul of Article 23. Yet such practices, along with the regulatory context that makes them possible, *could* be characterized as trade agreement violations on some interpretations. More-over, they can easily be seen as "measures" or "situations" that nullify or impair agreed benefits or impede the attainment of the objectives of WTO, in the language of GATT Article XXIII, whether or not they are viola-tions.[81] Presumably the US would have advanced arguments like these at WTO. If any of these characterizations is accurate, however, the plain text of Article 23 prohibits unilateral action. These are complex issues. WTO cannot let any state determine the scope of Article 23 by the way it char-acterizes its own actions; yet the language of Article 23 is so broad that virtually any trade-related complaint could be brought within it. Ques-tions like these must be resolved before the effects of Article 23 are fully known.

A final DS issue of importance to this chapter concerns the special problems of disciplining SGMs and ADMs. The major difficulty in the area of SGMs is the failure of the Understanding to address the problem of the missing complainant in case states impose prohibited VRAs or similar gray-area measures. This problem illustrates the inadequacies of a purely na-tional-interests DS system. When the enforcement of community rules is entrusted solely to affected states, individualized arrangements based on side payments, such as the assignment of scarcity rents, or superior power can bypass the most elaborate DS system. This is an area where WTO may have to be strengthened, permitting the Secretariat to initiate DS pro-ceedings against VRAs or providing for more aggressive review and en-forcement by the SGM Committee.

The problem with ADMs is more complex. Article 1 of the Under-standing provides that the unified DS procedure applies to disputes arising under all the multilateral and plurilateral trade agreements listed in an Appendix, as well as the WTO Agreement itself. That procedure, how-ever, is made subject to certain inconsistent and additional DS rules in particular agreements. Several of those rules appear in the ADM Code. By far the most important is Article 17.6, which sets forth a unique "standard of review" for DS panels reviewing national ADMs, as demanded by the US in November 1993.

Under Article 17.6, a DS panel may review the facts determined by national ADM authorities, but its review must be limited to whether the authorities properly established those facts, an ambiguous phrase not oth-erwise defined, and whether their evaluation of the facts was "unbiased and objective." If these standards are met, the panel may not make differ-ent factual findings. The panel is also authorized to interpret the appli-cable provisions of the ADM Code. If the national authorities adopted a "permissible" interpretation of the Code, however, the panel must uphold it, even if the panel concludes that a different interpretation is preferable.

The portion of this provision dealing with factual determinations is similar to standards already applied by GATT panels.[82] But the standard of legal review and the role of the US in its inclusion are troubling. Unlike the rest of the Code, which establishes objective rules to govern ADMs, the standard of review attempts to carve out an area of national discretion. Unlike the Understanding, which creates a powerful DS procedure, the standard of review attempts to limit the authority of WTO DS institutions. The standard of review is based on a faulty analogy, to judicial review of administrative decisions within a national legal system (Palmeter 1995). It undercuts an important purpose of a global agreement by opening the door to inconsistent national practices. Finally, it sets a dangerous precedent by introducing a device that allows states to agree to strong rules in principle, while retaining the ability to dilute them in practice.[83]

Ironically, the effect of the restrictive standard of review will depend on the interpretation given to Article 17.6 within the WTO system, and this interpretation will not be constrained by the restrictive standard. To be sure, if panels and Appellate Body chambers hearing challenges to national ADMs implement the political intent behind Article 17.6, including the analogy to national administrative agency review, the language of the article can be read to limit severely the power of DS institutions. Yet Article. 17.6 can also be read more narrowly (Waer and Vermulst 1994:8-9).

Waer and Vermulst suggest that panels could, instead of requiring complainants to demonstrate that factual findings by national authorities were not made in an "unbiased and objective" manner, make their own evaluations of the findings, giving weight to the protective effect of the national measures, and reach an objective determination of bias or subjectivity.[84] Similarly, they suggest that panels could read particular Code provisions as unambiguous, capable of only one interpretation, so that any inconsistent national interpretation could be found improper. Normatively, they call for panels to "be alert to the dangers" of Article 17.6 and to "stand up to their responsibility" of ensuring a fair application of the ADM Code.

These arguments are appealing, but they entail certain problems. The lesser problem is that at least some of the proposed approaches involve unfortunate legal technique. For example, national courts routinely write opinions stating conclusively and conclusorily that statutory provisions admit only one interpretation, even though any observer with modest legal and linguistic skills can perceive that more than one is possible. This kind of judicial disingenuousness does nothing to increase respect for the law and legal institutions.

The more serious problem is that the kind of aggressive interpretation Waer and Vermulst propose could lead to a crisis in the WTO legal
system. Many commentators[85] have expressed concern that the openness
and automaticity of the new DS system may allow so-called "wrong cases,"
complaints that challenge politically entrenched programs of powerful
states, which might choose to ignore a DS decision or even withdraw from
WTO rather than abandon the programs, to enter the system and proceed to a conclusion, threatening to undercut the DS system itself. Aggressive interpretation of the sort suggested could produce even more
"wrong cases."

The 1994 agreement between the US Trade Representative and
Senator Bob Dole dramatizes this concern (Bhala 1996). The US Trade
Representative agreed to support legislation establishing a WTO Dispute-
Settlement Review Commission made up of federal judges. The Commission would review final WTO decisions adverse to the US to determine
whether the panel or the Appellate Body acted improperly. If the Commission made three affirmative decisions in a five-year period, any member of
Congress could initiate an expedited legislative procedure potentially leading to withdrawal from WTO. Failure to apply Article 17.6 is an explicit
basis for an affirmative decision. Although the proposed legislation had
not been adopted at the time this chapter was written, the WTO DS
institutions will almost certainly try to avoid kicking off the WTO era with
such a clear challenge to its most powerful member.

Conclusion

In areas of law, politics, and policy as complex as those reviewed
here, prediction is difficult. Yet a few things seem clear. First, the degree
of liberalization achieved in the Uruguay Round, and unilaterally, will put
great pressure on the market for trade remedies, as adversely affected
industries seek protection from imports. Second, the Uruguay Round agreements significantly modify the "competition" among trade remedies, especially by prohibiting gray-area measures, spelling out the terms of formal
SGMs, and prohibiting some egregious protectionist practices in antidumping regulation. Third, although this was apparently not the intent of the
negotiators (at least at the outset), the Round leaves ADMs at least
marginally more attractive to those seeking protection. Fourth, the strengthened DS system should play a growing role in the WTO system, and will
take on greater importance for developing countries, though even this
system has been skewed in favor of ADMs.

With these points in mind, let us return to the normative argument of the chapter, that the continued growth of ADMs undercuts the process of liberalization, reducing global and national economic welfare. The Introduction identified three possible approaches to restraining this growth: persuasion; international litigation; and the power of reciprocity. This chapter represents an effort at persuasion, and the discussion of WTO DS deals with the principal arena for litigation. The remainder of this section deals with the strategy of reciprocity.

In the long run, excessive use of ADMs can be constrained through strategic interaction. If antidumping laws spread throughout Asia, Latin America, and other regions, the US, the EU, and the other principal users will increasingly find their firms the targets of foreign ADM proceedings. Procedures and methods of calculation that were appealing when applied only to imports will become less attractive as others apply them to their exports. Developing countries that have only been targets of ADMs will find themselves with new bargaining chips, their own antidumping laws. In this prisoners' dilemma-like situation, there is the basis for a bargain on mutual restraint.

Robert Hudec has proposed a similar strategy in a related area, that of encouraging restraint in the use of US Section 301. In this setting, Hudec (1990:113,143-4) recommends that other countries apply parallel measures against the US to create the conditions of reciprocity that might lead to a negotiated agreement. For the reasons discussed earlier, one cannot in good conscience recommend the widespread adoption and application of antidumping laws. Still, if developing countries in Asia and elsewhere are intent on implementing such legislation, a more moderate strategy is worthy of consideration.

New antidumping laws must, of course, follow the ADM Code.[86] However, as already noted, the Code provides several areas of discretion, of which user countries have been quick to take advantage. Strategically, the wisest course for developing countries might be to mimic the laws of the US, the EU, and other users within these areas. This approach would have two benefits. First, if elements of the new laws were challenged as inconsistent with the Code, the same challenges would lie against the laws of those other countries. Litigation by one country would effectively liberalize the laws of many. Second, even if the new laws were not challenged or were upheld, the resulting symmetry would set the stage for negotiated liberalization. To repeat, the best result would be for Asian and other developing countries not to enact restrictive antidumping laws at all. If such laws are enacted, however, there may be significant benefits in a strategy of reciprocity.

Annex I

ANTIDUMPING MEASURES BY AND AGAINST ASIAN DEVELOPING COUNTRIES, 1984-1993

The following data are taken from country reports to the GATT Antidumping Committee, compiled in Committee reports published in the annual supplements to GATT, Basic Instruments and Selected Documents. As such, they may undercount the actual number of ADMs. Prior to the 1991/92 reporting year, European Community reports included only ADMs involving firms from countries signatory to the GATT Antidumping Code. The number of outstanding ADMs reported by the European Union in each year does not include outstanding measures maintained by individual member states.

The abbreviations for countries and customs territories used in this Annex, as in reports of the Antidumping Committee, are those adopted by the International Organization of Standardization. AR=Argentina; BD=Bangladesh; BR=Brazil; CN=People's Republic of China; DE=Federal Republic of Germany; FR=France; GB=Great Britain; HK=Hong Kong; ID=Indonesia; IN=India; JP=Japan; KR=Korea; MY=Malaysia; MX=Mexico; PH=Philippines; SG=Singapore; TH=Thailand; TW=Taipei,China; US=United States; n.a.=not available.

Numbers in parentheses indicate the number of products from a particular country subject to ADMs.

1 July 1984 to 30 June 1985

Reporting Country	Initiation		Provisional Measures		Definitive Duties		Outstanding Measures
	Total No.	Countries Involved	Total No.	Countries Involved	Total No.	Countries Involved	
Australia	63	CN KR(6) MY PH SG(2) TH(2) TW(6)	25	KR(3) MY PH SG TH(2) TW(2)	15	CN HK KR SG TW	167
Canada	35	HK(2) KR(3) TW	31	CN(2) HK(2) KR(2) TW	16	CN(2) HK(2) KR(2)	132
European Union	34		11		7	SG	146
United States	61	CN(2) HK IN KR(6)	37		13	CN KR	112

1 July 1985 to 30 June 1986

Reporting Country	Initiation		Provisional Measures		Definitive Duties		Outstanding Measures
	Total No.	Countries Involved	Total No.	Countries Involved	Total No.	Countries Involved	
Australia	54	CN HK KR(4) SG TH TW(4)	32	CN HK KR SG TW(4)	20	KR(2) PH SG TH TW(2)	171
Canada	27	CN KR(4) TW	23	CN KR(4) TW	25	CN KR(2) TW	152
European Union	23	KR	6		7		123
Korea[1]	3	JP(2) TW					
United States	63	CN(3) IN KR(3) PH SG TW(7)	43	CN(6) HK IN(2) KR(3) PH SG TH TW(5)	25	CN(3) HK IN(2) KR(3) TH TW(2)	122

[1] 1 January – 30 June 1986.

1 July 1986 to 30 June 1987

Reporting Country	Initiation		Provisional Measures		Definitive Duties		Outstanding Measures
	Total No.	Countries Involved	Total No.	Countries Involved	Total No.	Countries Involved	
Australia	40	CN(3) KR MY TW(5)	17	CN(2) TW(2) TH	3		109
Canada	24	KR MY SG TW	12	KR	8	KR(2) TW	150
European Union	17	KR SG	12		7		n/a
Korea	1	JP					n/a
United States	41	CN KR(3) SG TH TW(2)	55	CN KR(3) SG TW(4)	38	CN(3) KR(2) SG TW(4)	151

1 July 1987 – 30 June 1988

Country Reporting	Initiation		Provisional Measures		Definitive Duties		Outstanding Measures
	Total No.	Countries Involved	Total No.	Countries Involved	Total No.	Countries Involved	
Australia	20	CN HK(2) KR(3)	10	CN HK KR SG TW	5	CN MY	49
Canada	20	CN HK MY KR(2) SG TW	20	CN HK KR(2) MY(2) SG(2) TW(2)	18	CN HK KR MY(2) SG(2) TW(2)	159
European Union	30	HK(2) KR(7)	10	KR(2)	4		n/a
Mexico	2	MY	12	MY	2		n/a
New Zealand	4	CN MY TH	1	CN	1	CN	n/a
United States	31	CN HK MY SG TH TW	13		22	KR SG TH	167

1 July 1988 – 30 June 1989

Reporting Country	Initiation		Provisional Measures		Definitive Duties		Outstanding Measures
	Total No.	Countries Involved	Total No.	Countries Involved	Total No.	Countries Involved	
Australia	19	CN ID KR PH SG TH TW	9	KR	8	CN HK KR SG	19
Brazil	2	IN					n/a
Canada	14	KR TW(2)	13	TW(2)	4		143
European Union	29	KR(7) HK(6)	9	KR(2) HK	13	KR(2) HK	170
Korea			2	JP TW			n/a
Mexico[1]	12	MY TW	8	TW	3		n/a
New Zealand	8	MY TH					12
United States	25	KR(3) TW(5	36	CN HK KR MY	29	MY SG(2) TH TW(4)	198

[1] 1 July – 31 December 1988.

1 July 1989 – 30 June 1990

Reporting Country	Initiation		Provisional Measures		Definitive Duties		Outstanding Measures
	Total No.	Countries Involved	Total No.	Countries Involved	Total No.	Countries Involved	
Australia	23	CN KR(2)	10	KR(2) TH TW(2)			20
Canada	15	CN ID IN TW	7	CN TW	6	CN	103
European Union	15	IN(2) KR(4)	8	KR(3)	7	KR(3)	151
Korea	3	FR DE GB					n/a
Mexico	11	HK					n/a
New Zealand	1				1	TH	11
United States	24	CN(2) HK KR(3) TW(2)	20	CN HK KR(3) TW(3)	17	CN KR(3) TW(2)	196

1 July 1990 – 30 June 1991

Reporting Country	Initiation		Provisional Measures		Definitive Duties		Outstanding Measures
	Total No.	Countries Involved	Total No.	Countries Involved	Total No.	Countries Involved	
Australia	46	CN(3) KR(5) SG(2) TW	39	CN ID KR(3) PH SG(2) TH TW(2)	6	KR TW	20
Canada	12	IN PH TH(2) TW	12	ID IN(2) PH TH(2) TW	4	ID PH TH	71
European Union	15	IN(2) KR(2)	10	HK(2) IN KR(2)	9	KR	143
Korea	2	JP US					n/a
Mexico	13	HK IN	9	TW	5	TW	n/a
New Zealand	6	ID KR MY SG TH TW					n/a
United States	52	CN(9) HK IN KR SG TW(3) TH	30	IN KR TH TW(2)	17	CN(3) HK KR(2) TW	209

1 July 1991 – 30 June 1992

Reporting Country	Initiation		Provisional Measures		Definitive Duties		Outstanding Measures
	Total No.	Countries Involved	Total No.	Countries Involved	Total No.	Countries Involved	
Australia	76	CN(5) HK ID(3) IN(2) KR(5) MY(2) PH SG(2) TH(5) TW(5)	71	CN ID(2) IN KR(4) PH SG(3) TH(4) TW(3)	34	CN(3) ID KR(2) MY PH TW	44
Brazil	9	BD(2) IN(2)	8	BD(2) IN(2)			n/a
Canada	16	CN TW	9		11	IN TH TW(2)	71
European Union	23	CN(8) HK KR MY SG TW(3)	19	CN(2) ID IN KR TW	18	CN(6) HK ID IN(2) KR TH TW	157
India	5	AR BR KR MX US					n/a
Japan	3	CN					
Korea					2	JP US	n/a
Mexico	25	CN(4) HK KR(3) TW	29	CN(4) KR(3) TW	14	CN HK IN	24
New Zealand	13	CN(2) HK ID KR(4) TH TW(3)	13	CN(2) ID(2) KR(3) MY SG TH TW(3)	6	ID MY PH SG TW	14
United States	62	CN(3) IN(3) KR(5) MY SG TW(3)	37	BD CN(4) IN KR(2) TH TW(2)	15	BD CN(4) TW	236

1 July 1992 – 30 June 1993

Reporting Country	Initiation		Provisional Measures		Definitive Duties		Outstanding Measures
	Total No.	Countries Involved	Total No.	Countries Involved	Total No.	Countries Involved	
Australia	61	CN(3) ID(4) IN(3) KR(5) MY(3) SG(2) TH(5) TW(3)	21	CN HK IN(2) MY TH(2) TW(2)	24	CN(2) ID(2) IN KR(2) PH SG(2) TH(2)	64
Brazil[1]	4	CN KR TW	2		7	BD(2) CN IN(2)	n/a
Canada	37	CN KR TW	31	CN(2) KR TW(2)	12	CN TW	81
European Union	37	CN(4) HK KR(4) MY SG TH TW	17	CN(4) IN KR(3) SG	19	CN IN KR(3)	185
India	3	JP(2) KR	5	AR BR KR MX US			n/a
Japan					1	CN	2
Korea	7	CU(3) IN JP(2) TH	1	CN	2	CN TH	n/a
Mexico	24	CN(11) KR	32	CN(13) KR(3)	7	CN	26
New Zealand	4	IN			9	CN ID KR(2) TH TW(2)	24
United States	68	CN(3)	70	CN(4)	35	CN(3) IN(3) KR(5)	279

[1] Second half of 1992.

Annex II

THE SPREAD OF ANTIDUMPING MEASURES[1]

Antidumping Actions
1 July 1986 – 30 June 1987

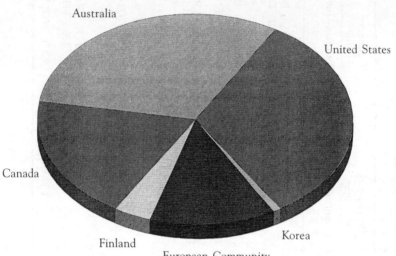

¹ The charts in Annex II show the total number of antidumping investigations initiated by members of the GATT/WTO Antidumping Code during three representative years, as reported to the Antidumping Committee. The data in the first two charts are taken from the annual reports of the Committee published in Basic Instruments and Selected Documents. The data in the third chart are taken from a preliminary summary of the Committee's report, *WTO Focus* (1995:10).

Because these data are based on country reports, the charts in Annex II probably undercount the actual number of ADMs. In regard to the 1994/95 data, the Committee notes that 34 notifications for the first half of the period, and 53 for the second half, had not been received; it is not clear how many of the delinquent countries initiated ADM investigations. As the Committee's comment suggests, however, one reason for the large increase in the number of countries reporting ADMs for 1994/95 may simply be an increase in the number of countries party to the WTO Code.

Antidumping Actions Initiated
1 July 1990 – 30 June 1991

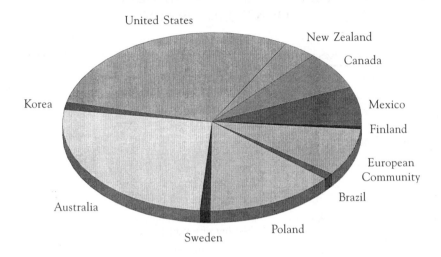

Antidumping Actions Initiated
1 July 1994 – 30 June 1995

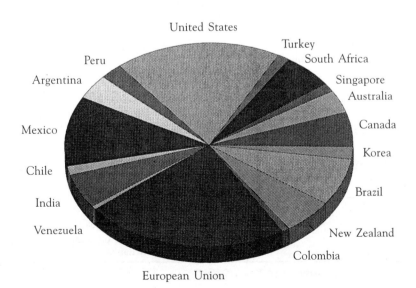

Annex III

WTO DISPUTES INVOLVING DEVELOPING COUNTRIES, 1995/1996

Complainant	Respondent	Subject	Panel Established
Singapore	Malaysia	Prohibition of imports of polythylene and polypropylene	
Venezuela	United States	Standards for reformulated and conventional gasoline	X
United States	Korea	Measures concerning the testing and inspection of agricultural products	
Brazil	United States	Standards for reformulated and conventional gasoline	X
United States	Korea	Measures concerning the shelf-life of products	
Peru	European Communities	Trade description of scallops	X
Chile	European Communities	Trade description of scallops	X
India	Poland	Import regime for automobiles	
Guatemala, Honduras, Mexico, United States	European Communities	Regime for the importation, sale, and distribution of bananas	
Thailand	European Communities	Duties on imports of rice	
Canada	Korea	Measures concerning bottled water	
Philippines	Brazil	Measures affecting desiccated coconut	X
Costa Rica	United States	Restrictions on imports of cotton and synthetic fiber underwear	X
Uruguay	European Communities	Implementation of the Uruguay Round commitments concerning rice	
Hong Kong	Turkey	Restrictions on imports of textile and clothing products	
Sri Lanka	Brazil	Countervailing duties on imports of desiccated coconut and coconut milk powder from Sri Lanka	

Source: WTO *Focus* (1995:6), WTO *Focus* (1996:3).

416

Notes

[1] Other products that might have been the subject of ADMs were dealt with in different ways, notably through VRAs.

[2] Thirty-six of 119 preliminary US dumping determinations on manufactured goods from 1979 to 1990 involved the Asian newly industrializing countries (Clarida 1996).

[3] Ironically, Korea had earlier pressed for similar rules (BISD 1993:121).

[4] There could also be negative dynamic effects. For example, dumping might force importing country firms out of industries that produce external benefits.

[5] An example is the case in 1986 of Matsushita v. Zenith Radio Corporation, volume 106 of the US Supreme Court Reports, page 1348. The relevant discussion is on pages 1357-8.

[6] Some scholars suggest that nations impose ADMs to promote particular industries, to encourage incoming investment, or to pressure foreign governments (Krupp 1992; Van Bael 1990). Such strategic uses could reflect calculations of national welfare. ADM decisions, however, are rarely made transparently or in a way that encourages objective welfare determinations.

[7] While the US is often criticized for its use of Section 301, executive branch officials have consistently opposed the more extreme demands for its use, arguing against sectoral approaches and against both equal access and production conditions reciprocity in favor of traditional international negotiations.

[8] For a clear presentation of the public choice approach, emphasizing the efforts of government officials to avoid political conflict, see Hayes (1981).

[9] The International Trade Commission, an independent agency, returned negative injury findings in a significantly larger percentage of cases, though still only in the range of 30 percent (CBO Report 1994:49-50).

[10] Tariff Act of 1930 Section 777A(d), 19 USC Section 1677f-1.

[11] Section 777A(d)(2). Home market prices will be averaged over one-month (rather than six-month) periods, however, making the comparison less distortive than prior practice.

[12] It is in dispute whether the "investigation phase" language was intended to permit the US interpretation (Palmeter 1995; Alan Holmer et al. 1995:483,491-4). In either case, the US approach is subject to challenge under the principle of "fair comparison," but it is not clear such a challenge would prevail.

[13] ADM Code 2.2.1, n.5.

[14] Under the "10-90-10" rule, US authorities would include below-cost sales in home market price if they accounted for less than 10 percent of all sales. If below-cost sales were more than 10 percent but less than 90 percent of home market sales, all below-cost sales would be excluded and the remaining sales would constitute home market price. If below-cost sales were more than 90 percent of home market sales, all such sales would be disregarded, and normal value would be determined by reference to sales to third countries or to constructed value.

417

[15] Code Section 2.2.2. The Section also specifies alternate calculations when costs and profit cannot be determined on this basis.

[16] In other contexts, the ADM Code avoids similar comparisons. Section 2.2, fn 2, provides that home market sales should only be used in determining normal value when they are large enough to "permit a proper comparison" with export prices. Generally, the Code provides that home market sales should be at least equal to 5 percent of exports to the state considering ADMs. In normal conditions, it is important to small countries that home market sales be used even if less than 5 percent (Waer and Vermulst 1994)

[17] See BISD (1990c) described in Robert Hudec (1993: 253-4, 572-3). The US blocked the panel report because it called for a refund of collected antidumping duties, but accepted the substantive holding.

[18] See Anderson (1993:103-4). This fact helps account for the steadily rising number of ADMs in effect in the US; see Annex I.

[19] See Trade Act of 1930 Section 751(c).

[20] In US law, the principal factors in determining the likelihood of further dumping are the volume of imports and the size of the dumping margin (Trade Act of 1930 Section 752(c)(1)). Thus, price comparison issues are relevant here as well.

[21] The dominant approach to the causation of injury in the 1980s was "bifurcated:" the authorities first asked if the domestic industry was in bad health, then asked if dumped imports made a material (that is, more than an immaterial) contribution to the industry's condition. A "unitary" approach, by contrast, would ask how much better off the industry would have been without the dumped imports (Cass and Boltuck 1996). Small price differences are more likely to lead to dumping findings under the former approach.

[22] ADM Code Section 5.8.

[23] Trade Act of 1930, Section 771(7)(G).

[24] This requirement apparently incorporates the standards discussed above.

[25] The Code does not address the US practice of cumulating dumped imports with subsidized imports for purposes of injury determinations.

[26] Trade Act of 1930, Section 772(d), (f).

[27] Trade Act of 1930, Section 773(a)(5).

[28] Trade Act of 1930, Section 781.

[29] Tellingly, the tighter deadlines are not applied to "sunset" reviews, which may lead to the removal of ADMs (Waer and Vermulst 1994: 5-7).

[30] Of these, nearly half have been rejected by the US International Trade Commission and nearly two thirds of the rest have been rejected or modified by the President (Jackson, Davey, and Sykes 1994).

[31] BISD (1979:209) apparently envisioned the use of these articles as quasi-SGMs, and eased the normal procedural requirements for that purpose.

[32] See BISD (1989). Korea has since disinvoked the BOP exceptions.

[33] Similarly, the US has pioneered the use of voluntary import expansion agreements in situations, especially involving Japan, where tariff reductions and other traditional measures appear not to produce the desired results.

[34] The exporting industry benefits from a VRA when it is allowed to extract the rents that flow from increased scarcity in the importing market. The same level of benefit may not accrue to the exporting country, however, since the industry may restrict production to comply with VRA, limiting employment and local expenditures.

[35] Tokyo Round negotiators could not reach agreement on SGMs. A number of later political statements calling for action on the issue failed to achieve concrete results.

[36] This provision could be interpreted quite narrowly by arguing that VRAs and other alternative SGMs are not the kinds of "emergency action . . . set forth in Article XIX" and thus are not subject to the Code. This interpretation would, however, make the provision meaningless. It was clearly intended to mean that situations in which increased imports cause or threaten serious injury to a domestic industry are to be addressed through SGMs consistent with the Code.

[37] Article 11:3 also prohibits governments from supporting equivalent measures by private enterprises.

[38] Unfortunately, the Code makes no effort to encourage the use of adjustment assistance.

[39] At least in the US, relatively few changes in domestic law were required to comply with the Code. The US introduced one significant unilateral change, reducing the time allowed for acting on requests for provisional relief in cases of alleged "critical circumstances" (Trade Act of 1974 Section 202[d]).

[40] BISD (1979), which made it easier to use GATT Article XVIII:A and C for safeguard purposes, may have been superseded legally by the SGM Code (Rom 1994:18-19).

[41] As discussed in the section on Dispute Settlement, a global interest conception of international DS might address this problem, but it is not reflected in the WTO DS system.

[42] Article 12:7 of the SGM Code requires notification only of VRAs in effect when the agreement comes into force, in connection with the phaseout requirement.

[43] From Article 13:1, textually, the latter provisions could well be interpreted as applying only to existing VRAs notified to WTO.

[44] This was the message of Robert Hudec (1975). Hudec (1993:13) characterizes the 1960s as "a period when GATT more or less suspended its legal system." Only one minor DS proceeding was instituted between mid-1963 and 1970.

[45] See Dispute Settlement, Midterm Review Agreements, 21 April 1989, GATT Doc. MTN.TNC/11, reprinted in GATT, News of the Uruguay Round, No. 27, 24 April 1989, at 24-31. Other less significant declarations on DS were also issued during the 1980s.

[46] Hudec's statistics indicate that developing countries have been respondents in 19 percent of the cases filed and complainants in only 13 percent (Hudec 1993:295). Many of these complaints did not lead to a final decision.

[47] The other two complaints were against India. The seven complaints were filed by India (4), Hong Kong (2) and Philippines (1) (Hudec 1993:296-7).

[48] For example, Thailand (BISD 1990a); US (BISD 1994); and Korea (BISD 1993). Thailand was one of several complainants.

[49] The diplomatic approach is reflected, for example, in the understanding of the system as one "governing the *settlement* of disputes" and in the continuing emphasis on settlement. See, for example, DS Understanding Articles 3:3, 3:4, 3:7 (italics added).

[50] Codifications of GATT DS practice have regularly enjoined states not to initiate proceedings in circumstances where they would not be "fruitful," probably referring to cases in which a powerful respondent would ignore a decision.

[51] Procedures Under Article XXIII, decision of 5 April 1966, GATT, BISD 14:18.

[52] Abbott (1992) also suggests other possible global interest reforms.

[53] DS Understanding Article 3:2.

[54] Many of the reforms included in the Understanding were anticipated in the DS document approved at the 1989 Midterm Review. For a more detailed review, based on the Midterm agreement and the 1990 Draft Final Act, see Abbott (1992b).

[55] Article 26 of the Understanding preserves the ability to initiate DS proceedings in cases of "non-violation nullification or impairment."

[56] The Understanding establishes a unified DS procedure; unlike the situation under the Tokyo Round arrangements, a single DS procedure governs all of the "covered agreements" listed in Appendix I to the WTO Agreement (see Article 1:1).

[57] Like GATT Articles XXII-XXIII, the Understanding requires an aggrieved party to exhaust bilateral consultations before initiating a proceeding (see Article 4:7).

[58] Understanding Article 3:7.

[59] Understanding Article 5. The parties may also agree to binding arbitration as an alternative to the normal procedure.

[60] The details of panel procedures are set forth in the Understanding, Article 12.

[61] Understanding Article 6.

[62] Understanding Article 8:6-7.

[63] Understanding Article 11.

[64] Understanding Article 7.

[65] Understanding Article 3:2.

[66] Understanding Article 19.

[67] Understanding Article 3:7.

[68] Members may also seek authoritative interpretations of agreements from WTO itself, which is explicitly given this power. Understanding Article 3:9.

[69] Understanding Article 16, 20. Adoption is also subject to a strict time limit.

[70] Understanding Article 21.

[71] Understanding Article 22.

[72] Article 3:12 provides for the extension of the time limit established in the Decision for the rendering of the panel's report.

[73] The Understanding (Article 24:2) includes special provisions for good offices, conciliation, and mediation in cases brought by least-developed countries.

[74] DS Understanding Article 8:10.

[75] DS Understanding Article 27:2

[76] DS Understanding Article 12:11.

[77] DS Understanding Article 21:2, :7, :8.

[78] DS Understanding Article 23:1.

[79] DS Understanding Article 23:2(a). Article 23 also requires states to follow the Understanding in setting the time allowed for compliance and the level of retaliation.

[80] Trade Act of 1974, Section 301(a)(1)-(2); 303.

[81] See GATT 1994 Article XXIII:1.

[82] See BISD (1993). (Panel should not substitute its judgment for that of national authorities on weight to be given facts, but should only determine if articulated factual findings reasonably support decision.)

[83] Indeed, the Final Act of the Uruguay Round provides that application of Article 17.6 will be reviewed after three years "with a view to considering the question of whether it is capable of general application." Final Act, Part III.

[84] A lesser option, not mentioned by Waer and Vermulst, would be to shift the burden of persuasion to the national authorities if the factual findings were not persuasive.

[85] Including the present author, see Abbott (1992b).

[86] See Agreement Establishing the WTO, Article XVI:4: "Each Member shall ensure the conformity of its laws, regulations and administrative procedures with its obligations as provided in the annexed Agreements."

References

Abbott, K. W., 1992a. "GATT as a Public Institution: The Uruguay Round and Beyond." *Brooklyn Journal of International Law* 18:31.

_____, 1992b. "The Uruguay Round and Dispute Resolution: Building a Private-Interests System of Justice." *Columbia Business Law Review* (111).

_____, 1996. "Defensive Unfairness: The Normative Structure of Section 301." In J. Bhagwati and R. Hudec, eds., *Fair Trade and Harmonization: Prerequisites for Free Trade?* Cambridge, Massachusetts: MIT Press.

Andere, E., 1993. "The Mexican Antidumping Regime." *Journal of World Trade Law* 27(2):5-36.

Anderson, K., 1993. "Antidumping Laws in the United States: Use and Welfare Consequences." *Journal of World Trade Law* 27(2):99-117.

Basic Instruments and Selected Documents (BISD), 1979. "Decision on Safeguard Action for Development Purposes." 26:209.

_____, 1980. "Understanding Regarding Notification, Consultation, Dispute Settlement and Surveillance." 26:210.

_____, 1989. "Republic of Korea—Restrictions on Imports of Beef." 36:268.

_____, 1990a. "Thailand — Restrictions on Importation of and Internal Taxes on Cigarettes." 37:200.

_____, 1990b. "United States — Antidumping Duties on Stainless Seamless Pipes and Tubes from Sweden."

_____, 1993. "Korea — Anti-Dumping Duties on Imports of Polyacetal Resins from the United States." 40:205.

_____, 1994. "United States — Measures Affecting the Importation, Internal Sale and Use of Tobacco." 12 August.

Bhagwati, J., and R. Hudec, eds., 1996. *Fair Trade and Harmonization: Prerequisites for Free Trade?* Cambridge, Massachusetts: MIT Press.

Bhala, R., 1996. "Description of Dole Agreement and Letter from USTR Michael Kantor to Senator Bob Dole." *International Trade Law* (23 November):174.

Bureau of National Affairs, 1995a. *International Trade Reporter* 12:848.

_____, 1995b. *International Trade Reporter* 12:1132.

Cass, R., and R. Boltuck, 1996. "Antidumping and Countervailing Duty Law: The Mirage of Equitable International Competition." In J. Bhagwati and R. Hudec, eds., *Fair Trade and Harmonization: Prerequisites for Free Trade?* Cambridge, Massachusetts: MIT Press.

Clarida, R., 1996. "Dumping: In Theory, in Policy, and in Practice." In J. Bhagwati and R. Hudec, eds., *Fair Trade and Harmonization: Prerequisites for Free Trade?* Cambridge, Massachusetts: MIT Press.

Congress of the United States, Congressional Budget Office (CBO), 1994. "How the GATT Affects US Antidumping and Countervailing-Duty Policy." 8.

Davey, W. J., 1988. "Antidumping Laws: A Time for Restriction." Fordham Corporate Law Institute (8-1).

European Community Commission, 1993. "Eleventh Annual Report on the Community; Anti-Dumping and Anti-Subsidy Activities."

Finger, J. M., 1993. "The Origins and Evolution of Antidumping Regulation." In *Antidumping: How It Works and Who Gets Hurt.* Ann Arbor, Michigan: University of Michigan Press.

GATT Secretariat, 1994. *Final Act Embodying the Results of the Uruguay Round of Multilateral Trade Negotiations.* Geneva: GATT.

Hayes, M., 1981. *Lobbyists and Legislators: A Theory of the Political Process.* New Brunswick, New Jersey: Rutgers University Press.

Hoekman, B., and P. Mavroidis, 1996. "Dumping, Antidumping and Antitrust." *Journal of World Trade Law* 30:6-27.

Horlick, Gary 1989. "The United States Antidumping System." In J. Jackson and E. Vermulst, eds., *Antidumping Law and Practice: A Comparative Study.*

_____, 1993. "How the GATT Became Protectionist: An Analysis of the Uruguay Round Draft Final Antidumping Code." *Journal of World Trade Law* 27(5):5-17.

Holmer, A., et al., 1995. "Enacted and Rejected Amendments to the Antidumping Law: In Implementation or Contravention of the Antidumping Agreement?" *International Lawyer* 29(2):483-511.

Hudec, R., 1975. *The GATT Legal System and World Trade Diplomacy.*

_____, 1990. "Thinking About the New Section 301: Beyond Good and Evil." In J. Bhagwati and H. Patrick, eds., *Aggressive Unilateralism: America's 301 Trade Policy and the World Trading System. Studies in International Trade Policy.* Ann Arbor: University of Michigan Press.

_____, 1993. *Enforcing International Trade Law: The Evolution of the Modern GATT Legal System.*

Jackson, J. H., W. J. Davey, and A. Sykes, 1994. *International Economic Relations* 610. 3rd ed.

Kohona, P., 1994. "Dispute Resolution Under the World Trade Organization." *Journal of World Trade Law* 28(2):23-47.

Krupp, C., 1992. "A Shot Across the Bow: South Korea's First Test of Its Antidumping Law." *Journal of World Trade Law* 26(3):111-124.

Messerlin, P., 1988. "The Developing Countries and The Uruguay Round Negotiations on The Antidumping Code." In D. C. Dicke and E. U. Petersmann, eds., *Foreign Trade in the Present and a New International Economic Order. Progress and Undercurrents in Public International Law Series.* Vol. 4. University Press in cooperation with the International Law Association's Committee on Legal Aspects of a New International Economic Order, Fribourg, Switzerland.

Nicolaides, P., and R. van Wijngaarden, 1993. "Reform of Anti-Dumping Regulations: The Case of the EC." *Journal of World Trade Law* 27(3):31-53.

Palmeter, D., 1995. "United States Implementation of the Uruguay Round Antidumping Code." *Journal of World Trade Law* 29(3):39-82.

Rom, M., 1994. "Some Early Reflections on the Uruguay Round Agreement as Seen from the Viewpoint of a Developing Country." *Journal of World Trade Law* 28(6):5-30.

424

Ruggie, J. G., 1982. "International Regimes, Transactions and Change: Embedded Liberalism in the Postwar Economic Order." *International Organization* 36:379.

Sykes, A., 1991. "Protectionism as a 'Safeguard': A Positive Analysis of the GATT 'Escape Clause' with Normative Speculations." *University of Chicago Law Review* 58:255.

United States General Accounting Office, 1994. *The General Agreement on Tariffs and Trade: Uruguay Round Final Act Should Produce Overall US Economic Gains* 2.

Van Bael, I., 1990. "EEC Anti-Dumping Law and Procedure Revisited." *Journal of World Trade Law* 24(2):5-23.

Waer, P., and E. Vermulst, 1994. "EC Anti-Dumping Law and Practice after the Uruguay Round: A New Lease on Life?" *Journal of World Trade Law* 28(2):5-21.

425 - 51

Comments on "Trade Remedies and Legal Remedies: Antidumping, Safeguards, and Dispute Settlement After the Uruguay Round"

by

David Palmeter

P rofessor Abbott insightfully explores a paradox of the Uruguay Round: the degree of trade liberalization achieved in the Round will increase the pressure for trade remedies, foremost among them antidumping, to a lesser extent safeguards. Implementation of these remedies will detract from the liberalization achieved in the Round. Tempering the imposition of trade remedies, however, will be a greatly improved dispute-settlement mechanism, one of the Round's most significant achievements.

Antidumping

Professor Abbott correctly argues that growing reliance on antidumping "threatens the goals of liberalization, transparency, and nondiscrimination in the multilateral trading system." He argues, too, that "the intellectual battle over the legitimacy of [antidumping] has probably been lost, at least in the political arena, and at least for the immediate future." Here I disagree mildly, but I share his concern. I would argue that the intellectual battle is still under way, and that the political battle may have been lost for now, but the political war is not over.

When antidumping regimes effectively were legitimized by the Tokyo Round Antidumping Code, there was little if any protest from liberal trade policy circles. Antidumping was considered a technical sideshow, a minor price to pay for the benefits of the Tokyo Round. By the late 1980s, that had begun to change. Economists — prominent among them, Jagdish Bhagwati, Michael Finger, Brian Hindley, and Patrick Messerlin — published devastating critiques of the antidumping regimes of the US and the European Community, as the EU was then called. We are now at the point where only Flat Earth Economists seriously defend antidumping.

But the case against antidumping, like the case for free trade generally, simply has not been made to a public captivated by the intuitive appeal of mercantilism. Too many people still think imports are the price we pay for exports, that access to our market is a benefit we confer on deserving countries, at a cost to ourselves. The intellectual case has been made in seminar rooms, but it has not been made in many living rooms — and certainly not on the evening news. It has to be made there.

A case in point is the recent North American Free Trade Agreement (NAFTA) debate. An opponent of NAFTA would appear on a television talk show and assert that the pact would cost jobs. A supporter would deny this, and assert that it would create jobs. "No-it-won't-yes-it-will" ad infinitum while the stumped moderator was unable to ask, why should NAFTA have any net impact on jobs at all?

Didn't we moderators, journalists, and lawyers and other noneconomists learn in Econ 1A about wine from Portugal and cloth from Britain, and didn't we learn, too, that there should be no job loss or job creation, but simply job change as each country increasingly specialized in the products in which it had a comparative advantage? And isn't the policy problem the fact that not all wine makers have the ability to become weavers, that the specific individuals who lose their jobs to import competition will not necessarily be the same individuals who get better jobs through export opportunities? And isn't the tough question for the politicians how to take care of the inevitable losers while at the same time taking advantage of the benefits of expanded trade?

Where was any of this in the debate? What journalist or television moderator ever put these questions to the politicians and interest group advocates for both sides? Few, if any, because few, if any, ever grasped the point.

If it is not easy to educate generalists about trade at this basic level, it is all but impossible to educate them about antidumping. The subject is highly complex and technical — it operates, in Abbott's words, under the "theory of optimal obfuscation." Virtually all of the policy justification for antidumping centers on predation, but predation is no part of the World Trade Organization's Antidumping Code, or is it part of any of the many national laws that implement that Code (see Palmeter 1996).

The spread of antidumping regimes to many countries in recent years raises the specter that these regimes will be captured not only by import-competing interests, but also by the antidumping bureaucracies they create. In the US, for example, we have six members of the International Trade Commission, their personal staff, a general counsel's office, an investigations office, an economic office, an accounting office, and an industries office; we also have the International Trade Administration of the Department of Commerce with an assistant secretary, deputy assistant secretaries, assistant deputy assistant secretaries, a chief counsel with many assistants, and dozens of analysts who do the hands-on case work. Other enforcers of antidumping laws are developing comparable bureaucracies. At the World Trade Organization (WTO) there is a Rules Division whose size, scope, and importance would be greatly reduced if antidumping were abolished. And, of course, there are the congressional committees and staff who work on antidumping, as well as the multitude of lawyers, economists, accountants, computer programmers, and consultants who work on antidumping proceedings.

If antidumping goes away, a lot of jobs will go away — so antidumping will go away only over the dead bodies of many who hold those jobs. It is not likely to happen soon because any future WTO antidumping negotiations will be conducted by these same antidumping bureaucrats. The only way this kind of power can be overcome is through what Jagdish Bhagwati (1988:85) calls the "Dracula Effect" — shedding light on it. And that will require making the case to those who are not in the choir: to the public, through the media.

427

Safeguards

One of the leading characters in Joseph Heller's satirical war novel, *Catch 22*, is named Major-Major. Reminiscent of *Catch 22*, the Safeguard — or "Escape Clause" — of the 1962 Trade Expansion Act contained a Major-Major test. While the legal Major-Major test did not operate in the insane way that *Catch 22* operated, it had much the same results.[1] To qualify for import relief, an industry had to show that it was experiencing serious injury that was caused in "major" part by increased imports. This was the first "major." Next, it had to show that the increase in imports itself was caused in "major" part by past tariff concessions. This was the second "major."

Most industries did not qualify, the "major" stumbling block being the second "major," the so-called "link to concessions." For those industries that did qualify, there was the further problem of compensation or retaliation. Any relief granted in the form of import restrictions required compensation to the affected trading partners who otherwise might retaliate against exports. It was fairly easy to mobilize the likely "contributors" of compensation and the potential targets of retaliation against the granting of import relief at their expense.

Import-competing industries, therefore, increasingly looked for other forms of protection. They found antidumping. Perhaps the Uruguay Round's more lenient Safeguards Agreement will lead to the diminution of antidumping. The compensation problem, for example, is greatly reduced. Nevertheless, there is reason to be skeptical. Antidumping remains more attractive than safeguards to most industries seeking protection. To make safeguards more attractive than antidumping would be folly. The only option is to make antidumping less attractive.

Dispute Settlement

The movement of the General Agreement on Tariffs and Trade (GATT)/ WTO dispute settlement toward a rule-based rather than a power-based system has been widely hailed, and rightly so. But this means increased legal complexity, and as Abbott observes, "while a rule-based system may benefit developing nations, it also imposes a burden, requiring trained personnel and resources to gather information and advance legal arguments."

Few, if any developing countries, or even smaller developed countries, have their own trained and experienced international trade lawyers. The US and the EU, on the other hand, maintain a large stable of them, in Geneva as well as in Washington and Brussels. For this reason, it is disturbing that a WTO dispute-settlement panel in late 1996 excluded lawyers for a developing country after the US and others objected that they were not permanent government officials.

The practical effect of this policy is to deprive smaller countries and developing countries of legal representation of their choice in panel proceedings. To confine legal representation to permanent government officials in practice is to reserve that advantage only for those governments that can afford them, or whose volume of litigation makes the investment worthwhile.

There are no apparent legal grounds for excluding the lawyers. The Dispute-Settlement Understanding (DSU) is silent on the subject, as are all of the other WTO agreements. This suggests that the issue is not one of WTO law, but of the national law of the Member, as in the case in the International Court of Justice. Indeed, authority to attend meetings of an international organization normally is a matter of credentials, and credentials are granted by member states, not by the organization. To put the matter in some perspective, if private lawyers can represent governments before the International Court of Justice why not before WTO panels?

DSU rightly is described as an enormous step forward in the rule of law in international affairs. While its scope is narrow, encompassing only the limited spheres of international relations covered by WTO, its jurisdiction is compulsory, something unprecedented in international law. It is a significant step forward, but a limited one, and should not be oversold.

For example, the dispute-settlement process does not make litigants whole. The preferred solution simply is removal of the offending measure; there are no damages for trade lost during the process. Moreover, the ultimate legal sanction of the process — retaliation — greatly disadvantages smaller countries, as the Netherlands discovered in the 1950s in the only instance of GATT-authorized retaliation. The Netherlands ultimately did not retaliate because there was nothing it could do against the US that would not hurt the Netherlands more.

There is also a lesson here, however, that goes back to the need to educate the public about the benefits of trade. The experience of the Netherlands in trying to find a product of the US against which it could retaliate without more cost to itself than to the US, makes concrete the point that imports are the benefit from trade, not the cost, while exports are the cost, not the benefit. This is why the only real sanction of the system is the value that the parties — especially the large parties — place on it. The integrity of the system depends more on voluntary compliance than on enforceable sanctions — something that is true of any system of law.

When Members value the system enough to comply with adverse reports of WTO panels or its new Appellated Body, however, headlines and politicians sometimes shout that GATT and now WTO threaten to "invalidate" laws, or "order" governments to do something. As this is not the case, it is important to be precise about just what goes on in dispute settlement and its aftermath.

When a WTO Member takes domestic action that is, in the view of another Member, inconsistent with its WTO obligations, the WTO itself limits the response of the complaining member. WTO Members have agreed not to take retaliatory action until (1) a party of disinterested observers — a panel — has examined the matter and ruled in its favor; (2) its report has been affirmed by the Appellate Body, or not appealed; and (3) the report of the panel or the Appellate Body finding in its favor has been adopted by the Dispute-Settlement Body.

This is the heart of the effective commitment to WTO dispute settlement. Defendants — those accused of acting in a manner inconsistent with their WTO obligations — do not really agree to anything other than to participate in the process. Complainants are the ones who agree to be limited, and that limitation is to go through the process before acting. They have agreed to stay their retaliatory hand and to conform to the controls the trade community imposes on unilateral retribution.

If we had the non-WTO world that Patrick Buchanan and Ralph Nader would seem to prefer, things would be very different. Whenever one country was aggrieved by another's exercise of its sovereign rights to, say, impose a discriminatory environmental regulation, the aggrieved party immediately could exercise its equally sovereign right to take retaliatory action, and, if the original actor thought this unjustified, it could counter-retaliate. This system was tried before, particularly in the 1930s, and was found wanting.

An additional important point is that panels do not "invalidate" national legislation, nor do they "order" Members to take particular action. What they do is determine whether a Member has broken an agreement, whether it has kept its word. In the first case to go through the panel and appellate process, for example, both the panel and the Appellate Body found that the US had acted in a manner inconsistent with its commitment not to treat imports less favorably than domestic merchandise, except in the limited instances contemplated by Article XX. They therefore *recommended* that the US be *requested* by DSB to conform its regulations to its commitments.[2] Recommending that a request be made is a far cry from "invalidating" or "ordering" anything. Moreover, if the request is denied, the complaining party simply is entitled to take the action it could have taken initially in the absence of WTO.

Conclusion

Professor Abbott's chapter deals with two of the most significant public misunderstandings concerning WTO: antidumping and dispute settlement. The facts are very different from the highly inaccurate references that are made on the nightly news and in most of the print media. The trade community has a huge educational task before it — getting the message of Abbott's chapter out to the world.

Notes

[1] For those who haven't read the World War II novel, "Catch 22" resulted from the requirement that airmen could be relieved from flying further combat missions only if they were diagnosed as crazy, but before they could be diagnosed as crazy, they had to ask to be grounded — which proved they were sane.

[2] United States - Standards for Reformulated and Conventional Gasoline, WT /DS2/R (29 January 1996); AB -1996-1, WT/DS2/AB/R (29 April 1996).

References

Bhagwati, J., 1988. *Protectionism.* Cambridge, Massachusetts: MIT Press.

Palmeter, D., 1996. "A Commentary on the WTO Antidumping Code." *Journal of World Trade* 4:43.

Standards for Reformulated and Conventional Gasoline, 1996. WT/DS2/R and AB-1996-1, WT/Ds2/AB/R.

PART 3

URUGUAY ROUND: AREAS OF FUTURE ACTION

CHAPTER 11
WORLD AGRICULTURAL TRADE AFTER THE URUGUAY ROUND: DISARRAY FOREVER?

AMMAR SIAMWALLA
THAILAND DEVELOPMENT RESEARCH INSTITUTE FOUNDATION

I n his classic political tract that inveighed against agricultural protectionism in industrial countries, D. Gale Johnson (1973:250-1) wrote:

> It is a common failing of man that he so often believes that his problems are unique in history. ...The problems that we believe confront agriculture today are the same problems that have concerned policymakers since at least the fifteenth century.
>
> Nor are the solutions that we have discovered in any way unique. The recent pattern of substantial protection of agricultural production in most countries is not new in the history of the modern world. It is, in fact, an old story; anything approximating free trade has been the exception in the annals of history.

Despite this expression of profound pessimism, and at times coming close to confirming it, governments engaged for eight years in long and painful negotiations to cut down on agricultural protectionism worldwide. These negotiations have borne fruits as the Agreement on Agriculture, considered by many to be a key outcome of the Uruguay Round.

This chapter attempts to examine the fruit of these negotiations, and to evaluate whether the burden of history that underlay Johnson's pessimism still is with us. The chapter has only two parts: one is a review of what was actually agreed; and the other examines the various models which attempt to measure the impact of the agreement.

What Was Agreed

Agriculture in the General Agreement on Tariffs and Trade 1947

To appreciate what the Uruguay Round has achieved, we need to look back to the situation as it was before the Round was launched. The General Agreement on Tariffs and Trade (GATT), as it was then (henceforth GATT 1947[1]), exempted agriculture from the key disciplines that apply to trade and trade policies for industrial goods. In particular, two crucial exceptions were made in Articles XI and XVI.

Article XI (General Elimination of Quantitative Restrictions) imposed a general prohibition on quantitative restrictions on trade, but paragraph 2(c) allowed import restrictions on any agriculture or fisheries products. This exception was hedged with the caveat that the import restrictions "shall not be such as to reduce the total of imports relative to the total of domestic production, as compared with what might reasonably be expected to rule between the two in the absence of restrictions." Not content with even these exceptions, the United States (US), the main protagonist for free trade in the immediate postwar period, obtained a waiver from this clause, to be free to pursue its dairy, sugar, and peanuts policies. In any case, the caveat of requiring an import level to be maintained was ignored by other countries for most of the period, and the European Community for example, was able to move through a highly protectionist regime, from importing cereals to exporting them, from importing sugar to exporting it.

The second exception was in Article XVI (Subsidies). In paragraph 4, there was a clear statement that as from 1 January 1958, "contracting parties shall cease to grant either directly or indirectly any form of subsidy on the export of any product *other than a primary product*" (italics added). There was a caveat that "such subsidy shall not be applied in a manner which results in that contracting party having more than an equitable share of world export trade in that product." Again, what constituted an equitable share of the world export trade was the subject of a number of disquisitions by various bodies of GATT (Sathirathai and Siamwalla 1987:595-618). In the end, this caveat did not prevent the European Union (EU) from including itself into the export market for sugar, and indeed becoming the largest sugar exporter.

Whatever the intent of the framers of GATT 1947, these exceptions[2] had the effect of removing agricultural trade from any discipline that usually applied to trade in manufactured goods. The escalating protection given by developed countries to their agriculture sector was a natural consequence.

Broad Outline of the New Agreement on Agriculture

GATT 1994 regularizes these exceptions and then tries to bind them. Under the new agreement, the World Trade Organization (WTO) members may continue with a form of quantitative restrictions on imports and may still subsidize exports, but they are made to commit themselves on how stringently and extensively they will use these trade-distorting instruments. These bindings are then expected to decline over time.

Regularizing rather than eliminating a highly distorted and interventionist system that has characterized postwar agricultural trade implies, of course, that the ideal of a free and efficient system of agricultural trade and production remains a distant dream (or nightmare, depending on one's point of view).[3] As we shall see below, some of the exceptional trade restrictive measures are now going to be not only accepted, but will be a standard feature involving an extensive system of interventions. Further, there is a strong likelihood that these will be highly opaque in their applications. Such interventions can only generate large economic rents which will help entrench the new regularized system.

Roughly speaking, the regularization of quantitative restrictions on imports such as the Article XI exception, introduces the concept of "market access" to GATT. Direct export subsidies at the border, such as the Article XVI exception, receives a special treatment in the new Agreement. In addition, the Agreement also regulates domestic support given to both exportables and importables. Both the issues of export subsidies and domestic support tackle the Article XVI exception. We shall examine each of these three topics in turn.

Because the various conditions apply differentially between developed and developing countries, in what follows, we shall indicate in the general text the requirements for the developed countries, with the special dispensation given to developing countries in parentheses immediately after. A third category, the least-developed countries, is exempt from reduction commitments, although not from the binding commitments.

Market Access and Tariffication

The Agreement on Agriculture requires all Members to introduce tariff quotas on all agricultural imports that are currently subject to quantitative restrictions. In a tariff quota, there are two tiers of tariffs that are levied on a given product. A lower tariff rate is to be set for a certain quantity, called the minimum access commitment for that item. The quantity is set at a level equal to 3 (2) percent of consumption rising over the six- (ten-) year period to 5 (3.33) percent. The quota allocation is supposed to be on a nondiscriminatory basis, although the present allocation of sugar quotas given to the Lome Convention countries by the EU, and to another set of countries by the US in its sugar program may be continued.

Beyond this minimum access, all Members are expected to convert all the restrictive measures[4] to bound tariffs, which would apply to the extra quota import. All other quantitative restrictions are to be discontinued.

The rates for this extra quota amount must be one of the following:

- ◆ where the rates were already bound, then the preexisting rates would be new bound rates;

◆ where the rates were not bound, but where the imports were not subject to any restrictions other than ordinary customs duties, then the duty rates ruling on 1 September 1986 were to be the new bound rates; developing countries have "the flexibility to offer ceiling bindings" (Modalities, paragraph 14, the Agreement on Agriculture); and

◆ where quantitative restrictions are applied, then the tariff equivalents of these restrictions for the years 1986 to 1988 are to be computed, and these rates are to be bound rates; developing countries have the same privilege as in the second case.

The tariff rates are then bound and members commit themselves to a cut in these bound rates of 36 (24) percent on a simple average across tariff lines, with a minimum reduction of 15 (10) percent for each tariff line, over the period 1995 to 2000 (1995 to 2004). Every item defined as agricultural must have a bound tariff. In this respect (and only in this respect), the discipline on agriculture has exceeded that in industry where it is not required that every tariff line must have a bound rate.

There is one important exception to this tariffication. This is the "rice clause" (Annex 5 to the Agreement on Agriculture), so-called because it was designed specifically to placate Japanese and Korean fears of unmanaged rice imports.[5] This clause allowed some commodities in some countries to be subject to "special treatment." A country seeking special treatment for a product (designated "ST-Annex 5" in the Schedules) need not allow any extra quota imports; in other words, it need not tariffy this product. In exchange, the country concerned must allow a market access of 4 (1) percent in 1995 rising to 8 (4) percent in 2000 (2004).

Export Subsidies

The term "export subsidies" is defined to include an outlay of budget for the following:

◆ the provision of subsidies and payments in kind that are contingent on export performance;

◆ the sale by the government of its stocks at prices below the comparable price for domestic products;

- payments to exporters of any proceeds that arise as a result of government action;

- subsidies on marketing costs, including internal transport and freight charges; developing countries are exempt from making any reduction commitments on these up to 2004; and

- subsidies on agricultural products contingent on their incorporation in exported products.

Note the absence from the list of export credits or credit guarantees. These are to be subject to further negotiations.

Members then make commitments to reduce export subsidies in two dimensions. The *quantities* for which export subsidies are paid are to be reduced by 21 (14) percent from the average levels prevailing in 1986 to 1990. This will be done over the period 1995 to 2000 (1995 to 2004). The *budgetary outlays* on these subsidies will be reduced by 36 (24) percent from the same base levels over the same implementation period. Note that the outlay commitments are in *nominal* terms and not in real terms.

Subsidies that are granted within the terms of these commitments may be countervailed upon determination of injury to the domestic producers.

Domestic Support

The key elements that go into the definition of domestic support for which reduction commitments are to be made are as follows:

- market price support, in other words, any policy measure which would enable producers to receive a price higher than the prevailing world price, including activities that involve transfers from consumers; and

- for developed countries, any subsidies that are given to inputs; developing countries are exempt from reduction commitments on input subsidies that are provided to "low-income or resource-poor producers."

There is in addition, a lengthy treatment of exemptions from what would constitute domestic support. We shall return to this problem in the next section.

The domestic support for agriculture is to be calculated for the base period of 1986 to 1988 and totaled for all agricultural commodities to obtain a figure called Total Aggregate Measure of Support (Total AMS). Each Member then has to make a commitment to reduce this figure by 20 percent by the year 2000 (2004). Again, this figure requires a nominal decline; the real decline would, of course, be much larger. If AMS is less than 5 (10) percent of the value of production, then no reduction commitments need to be made.

Domestic support granted within the terms of these commitments may not be countervailed.

Reduction in Tariffs and Tariff Escalation

Usually overlooked in the discussion of the results of the Uruguay Round are the straightforward reductions in tariffs for those items for which there are no other nontariff barriers, particularly for tropical products in which governments of developed countries do not have to contend with domestic farm lobbies. On average, all nontariff barriers are to be removed and tariffs on tropical products were cut by an average of 43 percent, with tariffs on spices, flowers, and plants reduced by 52 percent, and on tropical fruits and nuts by 37 percent (Duncan, Robertson, and Yang 1995:3-111). Compare this to the average (weighted by imports from developing countries) tariff cuts in industrial goods of 37 percent (GATT Secretariat 1994).

Generally tariffs on these items were low compared with other agricultural products, but higher than for industrial goods. More importantly, the tariffs on these items tend to show an escalation at higher stages of production for which processing industries exist in developed countries (Valdes and Zietz 1980). The tariff cuts have reduced both the tariff levels and the escalation, as is shown in Table 1.

Fine Prints and Loopholes

The broad principles outlined above are the major gains achieved by the Uruguay Round. But agreement on these was only arrived at after strenuous negotiations. Inevitably, during the negotiations, compromises were struck among the various parties, particularly in the crucial final negotiations between the US and the EU in 1992 and 1993. These compromises undermined some of these principles substantially, indeed, according to some (Hathaway and Ingco 1995), and left untouched the extent of much of the protection being given to agriculture in both developed and

Table 1. Changes in Tariff Escalation on Products Imported by Developed
Economies from Developing Economies
($ million and percent)

Production Category/ Stage of Processing	Imports	Share of Each Stage	Tariff Pre-Uruguay Round	Post-Uruguay Round	Absolute Reduction
Canada					
Hides, skins, and leather					
Raw	1	0.3	0.0	0.0	0.0
Semimanufactured	67	35.3	9.9	6.5	3.4
Finished products	122	64.4	19.7	12.2	7.5
Total	189	100.0	16.2	10.2	6.0
Rubber					
Raw	54	46.9	0.0	0.0	0.0
Semimanufactured	2	2.1	11.0	7.2	3.8
Finished products	59	51.0	12.0	7.2	4.8
Total	116	100.0	6.3	3.8	2.5
Jute					
Fibers	0	—	n/a	n/a	—
Yarns	0	—	9.0	9.0	6.0
Fabrics	0	—	10.7	10.7	4.9
Total	0	—	10.0	10.0	5.3
Tobacco					
Not manufactured	0	25.8	7.7	4.9	2.8
Manufactured	1	74.2	25.5	16.3	9.2
Total	1	100.0	20.9	13.4	7.5
European Union					
Hides, skins, and leather					
Raw	237	12.6	0.0	0.0	0.0
Semimanufactured	1,062	56.3	4.2	3.6	0.6
Finished products	586	31.1	7.5	5.2	2.3
Total	1,886	100.0	4.7	3.7	1.0
Rubber					
Raw	975	77.4	0.0	0.0	0.0
Semimanufactured	24	1.9	5.1	2.8	2.3
Finished products	261	20.7	5.4	3.2	2.2
Total	1,260	100.0	1.2	0.7	0.5
Jute					
Fibers	15	11.2	0.0	0.0	0.0
Yarns	65	50.0	5.3	0.0	5.3
Fabrics	50	38.8	9.0	4.0	5.0
Total	130	100.0	6.1	1.6	4.5
Tobacco					
Not manufactured	433	92.3	20.2	16.2	4.0
Manufactured	36	7.7	51.4	25.8	25.6
Total	469	100.0	22.6	16.9	5.7

Table 1. Changes in Tariff Escalation on Products Imported by Developed
Economies from Developing Economies *(cont'd.)*
($ million and percent)

Production Category/ Stage of Processing	Imports	Share of Each Stage	Tariff Pre-Uruguay Round	Post-Uruguay Round	Absolute Reduction
Japan					
Hides, skins, and leather					
Raw	50	5.6	0.3	0.1	0.2
Semimanufactured	93	10.4	10.5	6.2	4.3
Finished products	744	84.0	15.4	13.9	1.5
Total	886	100.0	14.0	12.3	1.7
Rubber					
Raw	821	87.1	0.0	0.0	0.0
Semimanufactured	14	1.5	4.9	0.1	4.8
Finished products	108	11.4	3.3	0.1	3.2
Total	943	100.0	0.5	0.0	0.5
Jute					
Fibers	3	9.3	0.0	0.0	0.0
Yarns	7	23.8	10.0	0.0	10.0
Fabrics	20	66.9	20.0	10.0	10.0
Total	30	100.0	15.8	6.7	9.1
Tobacco					
Not manufactured	110	93.4	0.0	0.0	0.0
Manufactured	8	6.6	20.4	17.3	3.1
Total	118	100.0	1.3	1.1	0.2
United States					
Hides, skins, and leather					
Raw	19	2.7	0.0	0.0	0.0
Semimanufactured	358	48.3	3.8	2.9	0.9
Finished products	355	48.4	6.1	5.2	0.9
Total	732	100.0	4.8	4.0	0.8
Rubber					
Raw	975	66.8	0.0	0.0	0.0
Semimanufactured	33	2.3	3.4	1.4	2.0
Finished products	453	31.0	3.9	2.5	1.4
Total	1,461	100.0	1.3	0.8	0.5
Jute					
Fibers	1	2.0	0.0	0.0	0.0
Yarns	5	10.1	3.7	0.0	3.7
Fabrics	48	87.9	0.0	0.0	0.0
Total	54	100.0	0.4	0.0	0.4
Tobacco					
Not manufactured	380	98.3	10.5	7.1	3.4
Manufactured	6	1.7	8.1	3.7	4.4
Total	387	100.0	10.5	7.0	3.5

developing countries. There are many areas where the principles of liberalization are undermined. In the following we shall focus on six areas: the aggregation issue, the weakening of the definition of domestic support, the choice of the base period, "dirty" tariffication, the special safeguards, and the use of state enterprises.

The Aggregation Issue

Perhaps the most glaring loopholes are in the way the cuts are aggregated across tariff lines. The following summarizes the aggregation procedures used for the three key elements of the Agreement:

Market access	At the four-digit level within the Harmonized Commodity Description and Coding System (HS)
Cuts in import tariffs	Simple unweighted average cuts of 36 (24) percent, but the cut must be at least 15 (10) percent for each four-digit tariff line
Cuts in export subsidies	22 groups of products were specially drawn up, and the reduction commitments are made for each of these groups
Cuts in domestic support	The commitments are for agricultural support as a whole, not for each item

Of these, the worst problems arise in the case of the cuts in import tariffs. The outcome would inevitably be that the cuts in tariffs on products imported in significant quantities will be closer to the 15 (10) percent level than the 36 (24) percent level. The total constraints on domestic support rather than a product-specific constraint implies that governments can systematically bias their support to favor products which are largely exported such as rice in the US, and thus undermine the requirements to cut their direct export subsidies.

Domestic Payments to Producers

The new Agreement attempts to make a distinction between what constitutes a trade-distorting support of agriculture from the more general support of agriculture and rural development (the "green box"). Two criteria

445

are given for nontrade-distorting support: it must be paid out of the government budget and not levied from consumers; and it must not have the effects of providing a price support to the producers.

Consequently, Annex 2 of the Agreement lists activities such as agricultural research, extension, pest and disease control, inspection, and so on, as items that do not count as domestic support. Capital expenditures on irrigation and other production and marketing infrastructure are included in the list, *but not recurrent expenditures or preferential user charges*. Developing countries may provide subsidies for these recurrent expenditures if they are provided to "low-income or resource-poor producers." Currently, there is little discussion of whether the standard practice of Asian developing countries of providing cheap fertilizers and water to all farmers would be exempted or not, as it is a moot point whether Asian farmers are "low-income or resource-poor."

The most significant exemptions, however, are in the area of direct payments to producers, and these exemptions were built-in largely to accommodate the deficiency payments programs in the US and the compensation payments in the EU. These allow various forms of payments to agricultural producers. To qualify for these exemptions, the key element is that the payments should not be related to the volume of production in the current year, or to any other period after the base year.

The idea behind such "decoupled" income support is that the payments made by the government no longer provide incentives for farmers to produce more, and are therefore no longer trade distorting. In principle, such payments would be received by the factors of production specific to agricultural production. In particular, the farmers themselves would benefit. If the payments prevent farmers from exiting the industry, then they are trade distorting.

Choice of the Base Period

The Uruguay Round was launched at the end of 1984, at the time when agriculture was probably going through its most wrenching period in postwar history, considerable spare capacity having been built up in the aftermath of the world food crisis of the early 1970s. Prices remained low throughout the mid-1980s (see Figure 1). As a result, export subsidies and protective tariffs were at their highest levels then, particularly in the EU. By the time the Round came to an end in 1994, prices had edged up somewhat. The use of the base years 1986 to 1988 for the calculation of tariff equivalents and for AMS, therefore, had the impact of making the starting base of protection quite high, indeed in many cases as high as or higher than the level of protection current in 1994 (Hathaway and Ingco 1995).

Figure 1. Nominal and Real Price Trends of Some Agricultural Commodities 1970-1995

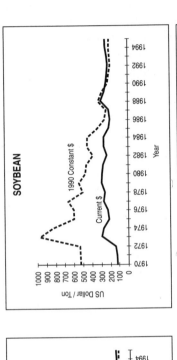

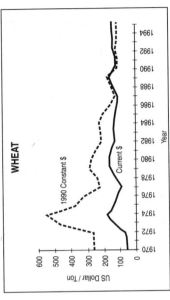

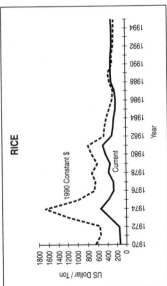

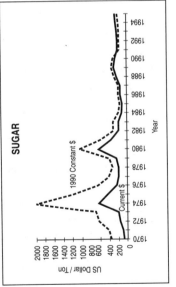

Source: World Bank "Price Prospects for Major Primary Commodities, 1990-2005 Volume II Agricultural Products, Fertilizers, Tropical Timber.

For export subsidies, the base date was stretched to cover a longer period 1986 to 1990. But these years are not sufficient to meet the needs of the two major trading partners, namely the US and the EU. The use of 1991 and 1992 as base years was allowed as an option for the commitment in the initial year, although by 2000 (2004), the target reductions of 21 (14) percent by quantity and 36 (24) percent by outlay must be made relative to the 1986 to 1990 period.

"Dirty" Tariffication

Not content with these various stratagems, the US and the EU, particularly the latter, engaged in no small amount of "dirty" tariffication, although in this they were joined by most developing countries as well. Table 2, drawn from Hathaway and Ingco (1995), gives a comparison of the bound tariffs as they appear in the Schedules and independently computed tariff equivalents based on 1986 to1988 data. It can be seen that most countries (Japan being a notable exception) tend to set up their tariff rates at levels much higher than those that prevailed in the base year.

Special Safeguards

The commodity markets are notorious for their instability. Hence, it is natural to expect participants in the Uruguay Round to wish for some safeguards measures. The measures that were built into the Agreement on Agriculture allowed safeguards measures to be invoked if either or both of the following conditions hold.

- If the *quantity* imported exceeds a certain trigger level, then an additional duty may be imposed, not exceeding one third of the scheduled tariff. The trigger level is defined as follows. First, a base trigger level is defined to be equal to 125, 110, or 105 percent of the minimum access level in cases where the minimum access levels are respectively equal to 10, 20, and 30, or greater than 30 percent of the 1986 to 1988 level of domestic consumption. With this definition of the base trigger level, then the actual trigger level that may allow the deployment of the safeguards is set equal to the sum of the tonnage implied by the base trigger percentages and any decline in the consumption in the two most recent consecutive years for which data are available. Once this trigger level is reached, an additional duty not exceeding one third of the customs duty prevailing in that year may be levied.

♦ If the import *price* falls below the trigger price defined as the average ruling in 1986 to 1988, then a variable schedule of allowable additional duty (which is progressive with respect to the price shortfall) is set out in the Agreement.

No domestic injury test is required to invoke this safeguards measure.

The first point about these safeguards measures is that they are an addition to what should already be adequate protection that countries have against import surges or price declines. Recall that the new import regime will be mostly a form of tariff quotas, with a two-tier tariff system, the second tier being considerably higher than the first. Considering the amount of "dirty" tarrifications that has been built into the Schedules, it is not clear why additional safeguards are needed.

Further, if the justification for these safeguards is the instability characteristic of markets for agricultural products, then the Agreement has treated importers and exporters asymmetrically. Additional duties are allowed for importers, but not additional subsidies for exporters. This essentially allows importers to shift the burden of instability to the exporters. Against this, it also needs to be said that under the previous regime, when both sides could engage in any degree of import restrictions or export subsidization they wished, importer attempts to shift the burden of instability away increased the volatility of the world markets enormously. We shall return to this issue when discussing the impact.

State Enterprises

The continuation of quantitative restrictions in the market access commitments (in the form of tariff quotas) will generate quota rents. The Agreement on Agriculture is silent on the method by which quotas are to be allocated, although, significantly, it specifically prohibits "non-tariff measures maintained through state-trading enterprises" for imports at the higher bound tariff rates (fn 1 to Article 4 [2]).

This allows a government to subvert the market access commitments substantially. A simple way by which its commitments may be subverted is to authorize a state enterprise to be the sole importer for the quota amount. At least two countries in Asia (Philippines and Thailand) have revived their near-moribund state enterprises and have given them these monopoly rights. Other countries, for example India, Indonesia, and Japan

Table 2. Comparison of Estimated Ad-Valorem Tariff Equivalent, 1986 to 1988 and Tariffs Declared in Country Schedules*
(percent)

Country	Rice Estimate 1986-1988	Rice Uruguay Round Base	Wheat Estimate 1986-1988	Wheat Uruguay Round Base	Coarse Grains Estimate 1986-1988	Coarse Grains Uruguay Round Base	Sugar Estimate 1986-1988	Sugar Uruguay Round Base	Pork Estimate 1986-1988	Pork Uruguay Round Base	Poultry Estimate 1986-1988	Poultry Uruguay Round Base
Industrial Countries												
Australia	13.5	0.0	0.7	0.0	0.0	0.4	11.8	52.4	0.0	0.0	0.0	0.0
Canada	n/a	0.9	30.0	57.7	39.0	34.7	39.0	34.7	0.0	0.0	19.0	226
United States	1.0	5.0	20.0	6.0	4.0	8.0	131.0	197.0	0.0	0.0	15.0	7
European Union	153.0	360.5	103.0	155.6	133.0	134.4	234.0	297.0	40.0	51.7	51.0	44.5
Japan	500.0	n/a[1]	651.0	239.6	679.0	233.1	184.0	126.1	99.0	87.3	13.0	14
New Zealand	0.0	0.0	0.0	0.0	0.0	7.2	0.0	2.9	1.7	20.0	100.7	28.5
Austria	0.0	0.0	188.0	400.0	108.0	241.0	183.0	178.0	72.0	178.0	41.0	38
Finland	n/a	10.0	239.0	352.0	342.0	204.0	265.0	493.0	227.0	320.0	206.6	264
Norway	n/a	454.0	266.0	495.0	361.0	394.0	0.0	n/a	255.0	428.0	614.0	379
Switzerland	0.0	67.0	245.0	179.0	226.0	242.0	277.0	273.0	157.0	227.0	585.0	767
Turkey	n/a	50.0	36.0	200.0	35.0	200.0	12.0	150.0	n/a	250.0	11.5	30
Developing Countries												
Mexico	6.8	50.0	-1.0	74.0	73.0	174.0	-57.7	173.0	n/a	50.0	n/a	217.67
Colombia	4.0	210.0	20.0	138.0	14.0	221.0	25.3	130.0	n/a	120.0	n/a	126
Venezuela	174.9	135.0	n/a	130.0	293.0	123.0	47.0	100.0	n/a	53.0	n/a	150
Thailand	1.0	58.0	n/a	64.0	n/a	81.0	n/a	104.0	n/a	60.0	n/a	60
South Africa	n/a	5.0	10.3	74.5	47.8	68.0	98.0	124.0	n/a	50.0	30.0	116.7
Indonesia	8.8	180[2]	n/a	30.0	6.0	70[2]	87.0	110[2]	n/a	70.0	n/a	70
Republic of Korea	213.8	n/a[1]	n/a	10.9	421.3	450.0	n/a	23.7	38.7	33.3	2.2	26.3
Mexico	6.8	50.0	-1.0	74.0	73.0	174.0	-57.7	173.0	n/a	50.0	n/a	217.67
Morocco	n/a	233.5	14.0	224.0	8.0	150.0	53.3	221.0	n/a	45.0	n/a	132.5
Czech Republic	14.0	70.0	-38.0	16.0	-8.0	20.0	14.0	70.0	15.0	46.0	n/a	36

Note: n/a = Not available.

[1] Delayed Tariffication.

[2] Ceiling Binding.

* Selected commodities where tarrification was applied and are subject to safeguards.

Source: Hathaway and Ingco (1995).

have always had their state enterprises dealing with imports of key commodities on an exclusive basis.

The current discipline on state enterprises in Article XVII of GATT 1947 is extremely weak. There is a requirement of notification of items for which the imports are to be handled by a state enterprise and a requirement that in its trading activities, it act in a "manner consistent with the general principles of non-discriminatory treatment." The lack of realism in that requirement seems now to have been recognized, for in the Understanding on the Interpretation of Article XVII of GATT 1994, the following "working definition" of a state trading enterprise is offered:

> Government and non-governmental enterprises, including marketing boards, which have granted exclusive or special rights or privileges, including statutory or constitutional powers, *in the exercise of which they influence through their purchase the level or direction of imports or exports* (italics added).

A working party has been set up to review the notifications and counter-notifications by Members who have reasons to question other Members' notifications. It is not clear how the results of the work of this party will be used.

Sanitary and Phyto-Sanitary Measures

The Agreement on the Application of Sanitary and Phyto-Sanitary (SPS) Measures is separate from but related to the Agreement on Agriculture. Its role is to make more precise the General Exceptions in Article XX of GATT 1947, which allowed measures against trade that are "necessary to protect human, animal or plant life or health."

Inasmuch as agricultural commodities are biological products, that many of them are consumed by people, and that they generate hazards to human, animal, and plant life, and health, SPS measures are a standard part of international trade. The application of these measures can, however, be subject to a great deal of dispute. The imposition of multilateral discipline on a Member's freedom to impose SPS measures is to prevent the Member from using them as disguised protective devices or as a means to discriminate among different sources of supply. This was stated in the first lines of Article XX of GATT 1947. Although there may appear to be simple tests to find out whether the SPS measures are being thus deployed (for example whether the measures are being equally applied to domestic and imported products), there are also many borderline cases. Thus, it appears reasonable to apply more stringent tests on tropical fruit because of its higher pest infestation, but the stringency may be increased in a temperate country to provide protection to the domestic fruit producers. Another case would be certain inputs or technology such as bovine somatotropine, a growth hormone derived by biotechnical means given to cattle, may be deemed to give another country a competitive edge, and therefore measures may be introduced that prohibit imports (as well as domestic products) that use those inputs or technology, thereby protecting domestic producers who employ different methods.

The new Agreement on SPS measures is a considerable advance on the old Article XX, all the more surprising because writing rules on procedural matters, in an area beset with much scientific uncertainty and political sensitivity, is inherently difficult. What the Agreement achieved was to introduce certain principles: the requirement of transparency, the priority of international standards, the concept of equivalence, and the requirement to assess risks.

- ◆ *The Requirement of Transparency.* The Agreement goes into considerable detail, devoting an entire Annex to spell out the requirements that SPS measures followed by an importing country be transparent, requiring a Notification if the standards followed depart from international standards. It devotes still another Annex to the control, inspection, and approval procedures to ensure that such measures are promptly attended to, a critical consideration for trade in perishable products.

- ◆ *The Priority of International Standards.* Article 3 of the SPS Agreement states that, in general, exporters who conform to international standards such as the Codex Alimentarius on food safety, are deemed to have met the SPS standards. Where importing countries have more stringent standards, they have to be based on scientific evidence and be based on systematic risk assessment (see below).

- ◆ *The Concept of Equivalence.* Article 4 states that the test of a particular SPS measure adopted by an exporting country is whether it meets the objective of providing the importing country's appropriate level of sanitary and phyto-sanitary protection, and not on testing procedures to be followed.

- *Risk Assessment.* Aside from the injunction to base risk assessment on scientific evidence, Article 5 goes into considerable detail on the considerations that should guide risk assessment for the sanitary and phyto-sanitary standards. For example, in setting up appropriate measures to protect animal or plant life or health, concerns are economic factors, such as the potential damage in terms of loss of production arising from the entry, establishment, or spread of a pest or a disease, and the relative cost-effectiveness of alternative approaches to limiting risks.

Calculations of Impact

The impact of a reform laid out in the Agreement on Agriculture can be measured from two perspectives: global and national.

From a global perspective, the reforms that will be carried out by each country can be expected to have an impact on the import demand function or the export supply function for each commodity of each trading nation with the rest of the world. The technical explanation is that the reforms will affect the price wedge that currently separates the world price and the domestic price(s) facing the producers and consumers of a commodity. Any change in this price wedge will shift that country's import demand function or the export supply demand function of that commodity. These changes are then aggregated across all the trading countries, and the effects on prices then calculated. Obviously, these calculations require extensive databases of volumes and prices of commodities produced and consumed in each country and for each commodity, and for the various behavioral parameters, such as supply and demand elasticities. Most important and most delicate of all, the various government measures, which are sometimes quite complex, have to be specified, both before and after the liberalization. How thoroughly these measures are specified in the model will have an impact on the results.

Thus Whalley and Wigle (1990:371-90) demonstrated that the proper specification of an acreage restriction program may have sufficient impact as to reverse the sign of the predicted consequence.[6] Most models summarize all policy measures into a producer-subsidy equivalent (PSE) and a consumer-subsidy equivalent (CSE) for each commodity, and assume that this leads to a parallel (or parallel in logarithm if the PSE and CSE are ad valorem) shift in the demand and supply curves. When a liberalization is simulated, it is assumed that there is a similar shift. Clearly, where quantitative controls are in effect, the shift is not necessarily parallel, and this is a central thrust of the critique by Whalley and Wigle.

General equilibrium models, which obviously are even more data-intensive, incorporate the loop from changes in prices and quantities supplied and demanded back to income (and therefore to demand again), and from output demand and supply changes to factor demands and supplies, and then to income distribution, and again back to demand. Because these income effects are included, the results from general-equilibrium models are potentially more accurate. Unfortunately, there is a price to be paid for such accuracies. Because of the data requirements, the specification of government policies and the level of aggregation are in general somewhat cruder than is the case with partial-equilibrium models. Further, the fuller specification of the model puts a major demand on the number of parameter estimates, most of which are missing even in the most intensively researched economies such as that of the US (Gardner 1989:361-71).

From a national perspective, if the trading country is a relatively small one, changes in the world prices that occur as a result of the Agreement can be taken as given from the global models. The impact of these price changes on the economy, for example, on national welfare, on producer's welfare, or on "consumer's" welfare, and on the government budget, can all be calculated once domestic policy adjustments are specified. In almost all instances, the qualitative impact and at least the order of magnitude of the quantitative impact of the changes can then readily be assessed. Ideally, what the country in question intends to do should be incorporated in both the global and national models, so that there is no inconsistency between the global and national perspectives. However, most global models cannot, in the nature of things, be as refined as some national policy analysts would like, and therefore the compromise of fine-tuning the national models using the price prediction is perhaps a practicable way out, *as long as the country in question is a small player in the world market,* and as long as the errors in the global model are not systematic and can therefore be assumed to be subject to the law of large numbers. The key linkage between the global and national models is then the vector of world market prices.

This chapter will focus on the global impact of the Agreement on Agriculture on world prices. In assessing this impact, it is important to bear in mind that there are other changes impinging on the global markets concurrently with the reform process, such as technical change in agriculture and in incomes, and so on.[7] Contrary to public opinion, during this century, agriculture has been technologically one of the more dynamic sectors in the world economy, both in developed countries and in developing countries, particularly in Asia during the last three decades. Primarily as a consequence of this dynamism plus the effects of Engel's law, real agriculture prices, particularly real food prices, have trended downwards for most of this century, except for occasional blips such as during the early and mid-1970s. As will be presently discussed, the price change arising from these other changes is sometimes considerably more than that arising from the reforms. In assessing the impact of the Agreement on Agriculture, all of the models discussed below attempt to filter out the effects of these other changes, with varying degrees of sophistication.

Effects on Prices: Based on Assumed Degrees of Liberalization

While the Uruguay Round of negotiations were going on, many studies were conducted that tried to assess the impact of trade liberalization. The assumptions that were necessarily made in these studies have in most cases been overtaken by the actual results of the Round. It may therefore appear that the results of these studies have been rendered totally obsolete. However, they do give some necessary insights into the effects of the protectionism that existed prior to the Round. Table 3, summarizes what these studies show to be the impact of various assumed liberalization scenarios.

The range of estimates in Table 3 is very large. That, in fact, is the first conclusion that strikes one from looking at the table. Partly that is to be expected, as the shocks that are introduced into the models are different. What is disturbing is the fact that even when the shocks are similar, the results can vary a great deal. Thus, compare the effects of full liberalization in the Organisation for Economic Co-operation and Development (OECD) countries in Zietz and Valdes (Number 1 in Table 3) against the results from similar exercises in Frohberg, Fischer, and Parikh (Number 2) and the United Nations Conference on Trade and Development (UNCTAD) (Number 3). In the case of rice, the most important agricultural industry in Asia, even the signs obtained from different models are not the same. The main reason for these widely divergent results is, of course, because the specifications in the models are different. In particular, by and large, partial-equilibrium models tend to result in smaller impacts than general-equilibrium models (with UNCTAD as a striking exception[8]). This makes comparisons of substantive results across models difficult.

Nonetheless, if we pass over for the time being the question of the magnitudes of the impacts across different models and confine ourselves to comparing results within the same models, we can ease out from the results shown in Table 3 some worthwhile conclusions regarding the effects

Table 3. Effects of Assumed Liberalization Scenarios on Selected Commodity Prices
(percent change over base run)

Study and Assumption	Model Type	Effect as of	Commodity						
			Rice	Coarse Grains	Wheat	Soybeans	Sugar	Dairy Products	Chicken
1. Zietz and Valdes (1990)	Partial Equilibrium	1985 to 2000							
50% reduction of CSEs and PSEs in industrialized countries			0.9	-0.7	2.0	-1.5	7.6	n/a	n/a
100% reduction of CSEs and PSEs in industrialized countries			1.7	-2.8	3.5	-4.0	15.0	n/a	n/a
100% reduction of CSEs and PSEs in developing countries			-21.8	-20.9	-13.6	-11.5	-12.1	n/a	n/a
100% reduction of CSEs and PSEs in all countries			-21.1	-24.4	-11.7	-15.9	0.8	n/a	n/a
2. Frohberg, Fischer, and Parikh (1990)	General Equilibrium	2000							
Complete liberalization of agriculture in OECD countries			21.0	11.0	18.0	13.0[3]	n/a	n/a	n/a
3. UNCTAD (1990)	Partial Equilibrium	No date							
20% reduction in producer support price			18.3	4.8[1]	7.5	0.0	10.6	n/a	n/a
Export subsidy elimination			8.5	0.1[1]	12.2	0.0	0.9	n/a	n/a
10% import increase			2.2	3.9[1]	1.1	2.5	4.3	n/a	n/a
Complete liberalization			42.6	15.1[1]	20.4	3.6	26.5	n/a	n/a

Table 3. Effects of Assumed Liberalization Scenarios on Selected Commodity Prices *(cont'd.)*

Study and Assumption	Model Type	Effect as of	Commodity						
			Rice	Coarse Grains	Wheat	Soybeans	Sugar	Dairy Products	Chicken
4. Tyers and Anderson (1992)	Partial Equilibrium	2000							
Tariffication at 1991 levels and 50% reduction of tariffs in OECD			4.1	-4.3	2.6	n/a	12.3	39.7	3.2[2]
5. Goldin, Knudsen, and van der Mensbrugghe (1993)	General Equilibrium	2002							
30% reduction in tariff equivalents for agriculture only			-1.9	3.6	5.9	n/a	10.2	7.2	1.0[2]
30% reduction in tariff equivalents for agriculture and nonagriculture			-5.0	1.5	3.5	n/a	8.0	5.1	-1.2[2]
6. Rosegrant, Agcaoili-Sombilla, and Nicostrato Perez (1995)	Partial Equilibrium	2020							
Full liberalization of agricultural markets			5.4	3.6	-3.0	0.0	n/a	n/a	4.8

Note: n/a = Not available.
  [1] maize prices
  [2] nonruminant meat prices
  [3] protein feed

Sources: Original publications listed in the References.

of the various strands of interventions that go to make up for a worldwide disarray in agriculture policy-making.

First, the Zietz and Valdes study (Number 1 in Table 3) indicates that developed countries have been protecting their agriculture, a well enough known fact. The study also indicates that the developing countries have been disprotecting their agriculture, and indeed the degree of their disprotection has been quite extensive, so that its influence over the world prices has tended to dominate the protection given by the developed countries, because of the greater role of developing countries in world agricultural production and trade. Removal of the developing countries' distortions, either by themselves or in conjunction with the removal of distortions in the developed countries, will substantially reduce world prices for most agricultural commodities. The general direction of this finding, although not its magnitude, is corroborated by other studies (whose analyses are not reported in Table 3), for example, Tyers and Anderson (1992:216 ff.) and Moreddu, Parris, and Huff (1990:115-57).

A caveat is necessary to that broad conclusion, however. Most of these studies were based on data from the early to mid-1980s. The wave of liberalization since then has induced a curtailment of the developing countries' disprotection policies. Thus, the Economic and Social Commission for Asia and the Pacific (1995) found that almost all regions provide production subsidies to their agriculture.

Nonetheless, during the Uruguay Round negotiations, the perception that developing countries disprotect their agriculture was present. This has an interesting implication. Traditionally, GATT has had an asymmetric influence on a government's trade policy. Protective measures are subject to disciplines, whereas disprotective measures are not, even though the latter are potentially as harmful to global and national welfare as the former. Restrictions of import are both more widely practiced and are more strictly disciplined than are restrictions on exports.[9] Similarly, subsidies on exports of goods are considered more worthy of discipline than are subsidies on imports. Interestingly, to the extent that there was outside pressure, the developing countries' dismantling of the various disprotective measures was largely the consequence more of the World Bank's and International Monetary Fund's activities than of GATT's.

In the final analysis, it is because of the basic symmetry in GATT's treatment of protection versus disprotection that there was widespread assumption that "liberalization" of agricultural trade would mean reduction of positive PSEs only, and therefore that this would lead to an increased price for agricultural goods. This sparked fears among the developing countries themselves, particularly the food importers among them, to the point where a special (although toothless) Decision on Measures Concerning the Possible Negative Effects of the Reform Programme on Least-Developed and Net Food-Importing Developing Countries was inserted into the package of agreements.[10]

A second conclusion that can be drawn concerns the interaction between liberalization of the agriculture sector and of the other sectors in the economy. Because the new WTO Agreement covers many sectors simultaneously, we need to look at how liberalization in the other sectors affects agriculture. The study by Goldin, Knudsen, and van der Mensbrugghe (Number 5 in Table 3) indicates that liberalization of all sectors would lead to slightly smaller price changes than if the liberalization was in the agriculture sector alone. This is to be expected. Remember that prices shown in Table 3 are relative prices. Removal of protection in the two sectors would individually increase prices of the sectors that are liberalized, and therefore, if both sectors are liberalized simultaneously, the effect on the ratios of the prices will be less. In addition, even though more incomes are increased as a result of the liberalization, there is also more competition for the incremental consumption dollar of purchasing power thus generated, so that the pressure on agriculture prices would be dampened.

Among the commodities, and if we ignore rice as being fraught with greater uncertainty in these models, then sugar appears to be most strongly influenced by the liberalization — this is our third and final conclusion from Table 3. This is mostly due to the fact that the degree of protection of sugar is high in almost all OECD countries. An earlier Valdes and Zietz (1980) study which had a very wide commodity coverage also indicated that the two commodities subject to the highest protection in these countries are sugar and beef.

However, the case of sugar also illustrates the weakness of the various models used to predict the consequences of the Uruguay Round, including those summarized in Table 3. The method of protection for sugar in the two largest OECD markets, namely the US and the EU, involves quantitative restrictions on imports with the import quotas allocated to individual countries so that the latter can issue the export licenses. This method of quota allocation implies that the quota rent would be captured by the exporting countries. How the exporting countries in turn allocate these quota rents would, of course, affect their production. None of the models examined this problem with the thoroughness that is required.

Jabara and Valdes (1993) examine the problem specific to the sugar sector in greater detail, but still do not fully take into account quantitative restrictions of production in developing countries as a result of the quantitative restrictions on imports in OECD countries. They are subsumed under PSEs. The model yields the results reported in Table 4 below.

**Table 4. Effects of Developed and Developing Countries' Policies
on World Sugar Price, 2002**
(percent over base run)

10 percent reduction in US PSEs and CSEs	0.2
50 percent reduction in US PSEs and CSEs	0.9
US PSEs and CSEs reduced to zero	1.8
OECD PSEs and CSEs reduced to zero	14.0
Global liberalization by all countries	-1.6

Source: Jabara and Valdes, 1993:154.

As can be seen, the effects of developing countries' policies (a great deal of them in response to the quota system in OECD countries) are quite dramatic, causing sugar prices to drop relative to the base run, rather than rise. This result is a consequence of the fact that developing countries are lower-cost sugar producers. Currently their production is suppressed, mostly to give room for the higher-cost developed country producers. Further, among developing countries, there are also differences in costs. The current quota allocation system, neither in the US nor in the EU, makes any attempt to minimize the cost of production. A liberalization of the sugar regime would therefore have led to reallocation among the developing countries.

Effects on Prices: Based on the Actual Results of the Round

Five extant analyses exist that take account of the impact of the actual outcome of the Uruguay Round on the prices of commodities.[11] The results of four of these studies are reproduced in Table 5.

The first of these studies (Brandao and Martin 1993:313-43) examines, not the Reform as finally signed in Marrakesh, but the Dankel Draft written by the then Secretary-General of GATT at the end of 1992. It is based on a general-equilibrium model called RUNS, incidentally, the same

Table 5. Effects of Actual Results of the Uruguay Round on Selected Commodity Prices
(percent increase over base run)

Commodity	Brandao and Martin	Vansetti, et al.	FAO	Duncan, Robertson, and Yang		
Partial/General Equilibrium	General	Partial Income	Partial with Effect	General	General	General
Group of Countries Assumed to be Liberalizing	All	All	All	Industrial	All	All
Sectors Liberalizing	Agriculture	Agriculture	All	Agriculture	Agriculture	All
Rice	4.2	7	8	6.9	7.8	8.1
Wheat	6.3	6	7	10.4	10.5	10.0
Maize	4.4[1]	6	4	n/a	n/a	n/a
Millet/Sorghum	n/a	n/a	5	n/a	n/a	n/a
Other Grains[2]	n/a	6[4]	7	6.8	7.0	7.1
Sugar	10.2	3	n/a	n/a	n/a	n/a
Fats and Oils	4.5[3]	6[5]	4	n/a	n/a	n/a
Oilmeal Proteins	n/a	1[6]	0	n/a	n/a	n/a
Nongrain Crops	n/a	n/a	n/a	3.4	3.9	4.4
Milk and Dairy Products	4.5	10[7]	8	12.8	13.1	12.8

Note: n/a = Not available.

[1] Coarse Grains.
[2] "Other Grains" in the FAO study means other than the four listed. In the Duncan, Robertson, and Yang study it means other than wheat and rice.
[3] Oilseeds.
[4] Coarse Grains and other maize.
[5] Oilseeds other than soybeans.
[6] Soybeans.
[7] Milk powder only.
Sources: Vanzetti et al. (1994); Brandao and Martin (1993); FAO (1995); and Duncan, Robertson, and Yang (1995).

as was used by Goldin, Knudsen, and van der Mensburgghe. They made the forecast for the year 2002, expecting that by then all the changes in the Dunkel Draft will have been implemented.

The second study also uses the partial-equilibrium multicommodity SWOPSIM model developed by the US Department of Agriculture to work out the results, not of the Agreement of Agriculture as signed in Marrakesh, but of the Dunkel Draft, as well as the results of the Blair House accord.[12] Since the Dunkel Draft as modified by the Blair House accord became the Agreement on Agriculture, the study in effect predicts the impact of the Agreement.

The third study, from the Food and Agriculture Organization (FAO) (1995:257-87), is based on a partial-equilibrium model with an ad hoc adjustment for the income effect arising out of the gains from the entire Marrakesh Agreement.[13] An interesting point that they made in this context is the small size of the income effect. The estimate they use in their calculations is the study by Goldin, Knudsen, and van der Mensbrugghe (1990), which obtained an increase in welfare of $213 billion by 2000 which is less than a single year's growth in income.

The fourth study, from the National Centre for Development Studies of the Australian National University (Duncan, Robertson, and Yang 1995:3-111), is based on a general-equilibrium model. They constructed five different scenarios, from which three are reported in Table 5, to examine the relative contribution of the distortions in the different sectors and in industrial versus developing countries. They did not state explicitly for which year the impact is calculated, but from their comments, it appears that they are calculating the impact upon the completion of the Uruguay Round liberalization, which would mean 1999 for the first of their simulations shown in Table 5, and 2003 for the remaining simulations.

A weakness of these studies is that they calculated the degree of protection accorded by the various relevant policy instruments themselves, and then lopped off the percentage cuts as agreed in the Round. None of them employed the Schedules of actual level of tariffs and subsidy commitments submitted by WTO Members. The phenomenon of "dirty" tariffication as described earlier in this chapter is not tackled. Therefore, the results reported in Table 5 should be looked at as upper bounds of the impact of the Agreement on Agriculture.

The most striking feature in Table 5 is that all simulations result in price increases. This faithfully reflects the fact that the liberalization agreed to reduce only the protection accorded to agriculture, not the disprotection imposed on it. More significantly, the three studies, although employing different methods or models came up with miraculously similar results, as far as the impact of the Round on prices is concerned. Except for sugar (for which the results still yield a large range) and dairy products, the range of price changes will be less than 10 percent. For rice and wheat, the price changes are of the order of 4 to 10 percent. This is what we take to be the current consensus view.

Are these increases "large?" We have already remarked that these estimates should be regarded as upper bounds on the actual impact. Also, the reform process will be phased in over a period of ten years and, therefore, the price increases reported in Table 5 will also take place gradually. This will lead to a small incremental change from year to year during this period. The order of magnitude of this change is about the same as the secular decline in the prices of most food items over the last century. Historians in the twenty-first century will be able to observe at best an arresting of that secular decline in the last decade of this century. But they will have to sift out this finding from the fluctuations in the market, which is considerably larger than these gradual increases.

Effects on Price Stability

A frequent criticism of the agriculture trading regime before the Marrakesh Agreement is the adverse effects that it has on the stability of world market prices of most agricultural commodities, particularly on food items. Many countries, pursuing price stability in their own home markets, "export" the price stability abroad. Many policy instruments were (and still are) deployed. The most well-known, because they are the most transparent, are the variable import levy and the variable export restitution in the EU. But many state trading monopolies also vary their imports in response to domestic production shortfalls, and not in response to world price movements. This affects the world markets similarly to the variable import levy or variable export subsidy.

Calculations of how such domestic price insulation policies increase world price instability were made by Tyers and Anderson (1992:225ff.). Their conclusions are quite striking. They compare the price instability as it existed in their base period 1980 to 1982, against the case where governments intervene only by having fixed ad valorem tariffs and export taxes and subsidies. They show that if this form of trade intervention replaces the existing regime only in industrial countries, then the price instability is reduced by a quarter. And if developing countries, particularly the larger countries in Asia, also do the same, the instability would be reduced much further, so that the weighted coefficient of variation in world food prices is less than one third of what it was. For rice, the coefficient of variation will be reduced from 38 percent to 9 percent, and for sugar, from 36 percent to 7 percent. Indeed, if every country adopts the fixed ad valorem trade barrier, the coefficient variation on food prices in many developing countries would become less than what they can manage under the current regime.

Would the Agreement on Agriculture bring greater stability to world markets? We have already described above the safeguards provisions. This will allow the insulation policies to continue, but they are not subject to some disciplines, even though the leeway that Member countries have obtained through the "dirty" tariffication means that the disciplines will be fairly slack. Furthermore, insulation through variable export subsidies will no longer be possible, although countries can continue to insulate through variable export taxes. On the whole, therefore, we should be able to expect, at best, a slight reduction in world price fluctuations.

Relocation of Agricultural Production

Changes in world prices, together with the partial dismantling of trade barriers as specified in the Agreement on Agriculture, can be expected to relocate agricultural production away from countries that have been heavily protectionist (mostly in Europe, Japan, and some of the newly industrializing economies in East Asia) to countries which are less so (mostly the land-surplus OECD countries and some developing countries).

The relocation may be taking place against a backdrop of a fall in world production of many commodities, as producers receive on a net basis less than what they would have gotten without the Agreement. In the aggregate, agricultural production is expected to be so little affected by the Agreement as to be barely perceptible (FAO 1995:268), but for individual commodities there will be important changes. The focus of protection, particularly among OECD countries, has been in cereals, and in these, there may well be falls in production. If general equilibrium effects are included in the analysis, then in some of the industrializing Asian economies, the liberalization of the textiles and clothing sector at the end of ten years may draw sufficient resources away from the agriculture sector, so that its production may fall.

Table 6 shows the changes in agricultural production that have been calculated by Duncan, Robertson, and Yang (1995:69), which are reflected in the above observations. Except for agriculturally insignificant economies (such as Singapore and Hong Kong), the changes in production of most commodities are of the order of magnitude of less than 10 percent,

Table 6. Effects of the Uruguay Round Agricultural Trade Liberalization on Production
(percent change over base run)

Commodity	North America European Union	Australia	Japan	Republic of Korea	Indonesia	Malaysia	Philippines	Singapore	Thailand	PRC	Hong Kong	Latin America	Sub-Saharan Africa	South Asia	Rest of World
Rice	-5.6	6.4	0.0	-1.0	0.2	-3.3	-1.1	5.8	-0.1	-0.	21.9	-1.3	-0.2	-0.3	0.3
Wheat	-2.9	7.2	-46.0	19.3	1.9	-10.1	-8.5	6.3	12.5	0.9	7.7	4.9	8.1	-0.1	8.7
Other Grain	-0.6	11.6	-51.9	-38.0	-1.3	-4.8	-5.4	7.7	1.6	0.1	5.9	1.0	1.1	-0.5	-0.1
Nongrain	-5.8	6.8	-11.6	-13.4	-2.1	0.2	0.6	4.2	6.4	3.3	15.4	5.4	7.4	2.8	0.8
Wool	-7.9	-4.8	19.1	-3.4	56.2	-14.5	-11.7	16.4	-8.5	-10.2	-1.5	-1.2	-3.2	-7.1	-0.1
Other Livestock	-1.5	8.2	-3.3	-7.7	1.4	-0.8	-1.4	2.6	0.3	1.8	1.1	1.3	-0.4	0.9	2.6
Forestry	1.0	0.9	-0.1	-6.9	-5.4	-18.9	-2.8	2.0	-4.9	-2.7	49.4	-0.5	-1.2	-1.4	0.5
Fishery	1.4	6.7	-1.3	-0.9	-5.7	-5.9	-3.7	-2.1	-3.6	-4.4	-4.8	1.7	0.2	-2.3	2.6
Processed Rice	0.1	5.9	0.1	-0.6	0.1	-5.2	-1.1	5.0	-0.2	-0.4	-10.7	-1.3	-0.5	-0.7	0.1
Milk	-1.2	6.3	-1.6	-1.1	0.1	-0.4	-0.7	8.8	1.5	-0.3	8.5	1.7	1.5	-0.9	2.0
Milk Products	-2.3	16.6	-7.0	-3.9	15.6	2.5	-1.3	25.5	0.4	-1.6	16.2	1.9	5.4	-5.1	6.7
Other Food	-0.1	-0.3	1.4	7.0	-0.5	-10.3	-6.3	2.5	-2.1	-3.6	2.8	0.6	-1.4	-2.0	-0.3
Beverages and Tobacco	0.8	-0.6	-0.8	-4.4	-1.1	-2.9	-7.5	27.9	-2.0	-3.4	6.6	0.2	1.1	-1.1	-0.2
Minerals	1.0	3.7	-1.7	-4.5	-14.4	-24.0	-14.2	-2.6	-14.8	-6.2	-6.5	-0.3	-0.3	-8.4	1.2
Textiles and Clothing	-20.0	-9.5	-2.2	49.5	158.0	697.4	115.7	53.9	24.7	27.8	13.9	-2.4	-11.9	22.9	-9.7
Other Manufacturing	0.5	-4.8	0.8	-0.3	-8.0	-18.4	-2.2	-0.2	-2.7	-6.4	11.1	-1.6	-3.3	-4.2	-0.1
Services	0.4	0.1	0.2	-0.1	0.6	-0.9	-1.5	-0.8	-0.8	-0.1	-3.2	0.0	-0.5	-0.7	0.0

Source: Duncan, Robertson, and Yang, 1995 (A13).

with the fall in production of cereals less than 5 percent (again, excepting insignificant cases such as wheat in Japan and Thailand).

Changes in Food Consumption

Because the point of trade reform is to enhance people's welfare by promoting their consumption of goods and services, and because there is widespread hunger and poverty in the world, from an equity point of view, how the Uruguay Round would affect the food consumption of the poor should be critically important. One would suppose that the central feature of most quantitative studies of the impact of the Uruguay Round would concentrate on how the fruits of the Round would impact on the poor's food consumption.

Unfortunately, in contrast to reams of predictions on how the Round will affect various countries' imports and exports of agricultural goods, there is very little prediction on how food consumption (even at the aggregative national level, let alone among the poor) will be affected by the Round. The one study which paid attention to this problem (FAO 1995:269) shows a crude picture. Per capita food consumption in low-income food-deficient countries (in all regions) is predicted to increase by 18 percent between the average of 1987 to 1989 and 2000, with one region (the Near East) and a few Asian countries expected to undergo a decline (Bangladesh, Bhutan, Mongolia, and Nepal). Against this secular trend, the effect of the Uruguay Round is barely perceptible. A few countries (India) and regions (Africa and the Near East) will experience a very slight adverse effect of 1 to 2 percent, with Indonesia and the Philippines experiencing a gain from the Uruguay Round.

Which Countries Gained, Which Lost, and by How Much?

In the ideal world of a simple general-equilibrium model, any external shock to a trading system will affect the countries' welfare in two ways: by causing a terms-of-trade shift and by increasing or decreasing the efficiency with which a country uses its resources to produce goods and services. Where imperfections exist pervasively as in this case, there are second-best effects also at work. For example, consider a country which has been heavily protecting its agriculture with all the other sectors being unprotected, and let there be an exogenous shift in the international prices favoring agriculture. That country would then pour more of its resources into agriculture by pulling them away from the unprotected sectors. This shift in resources would subtract from the national welfare (Stoekel, Vincent, and Cuthbertson 1989). In addition to these static gains, many studies also model endogenous efficiency gains, which of course tend to boost the favorable effects of the liberalization.

The Uruguay Round will not administer simply a point shock into the trading system. It is an across-the-board reform which affects many other sectors as well. For developing countries, a most important outcome of the Round is the dismantling of its textiles and garments. At the same time, however, they have been enjoying considerable quota rents under the Multifiber Arrangement. The disappearance of these rents will dent considerably the welfare gains some of them would have enjoyed from both the agricultural liberalization and the limitation on their protection of the industrial sector.

Table 7 shows side by side the effects of the Uruguay Round on the (static) welfare of the various countries, as calculated by Brandao and Martin (1993:313-43) for the agriculture sector liberalization (according to the Dunkel Draft) only, and by Duncan, Robertson, and Yang (1995:3-111) for the across-the-board reform as signed in Marrakesh. There are disturbing anomalies in these results, such as the prediction that partial liberalization in Brandao and Martin appears to increase welfare by more than the across-the-board one in the other study.

The most important conclusion to be drawn is that the major beneficiaries of the Round, whether we look at only agriculture or across-the-board liberalization, are the developed countries. Within Asia, it is Japan and the Republic of Korea that top the list in welfare gains. This is a robust result, and is only to be expected since, as far as agriculture is concerned, they have by far the most distortive set of interventions. Besides being richer, each time they impose a given percentage of distortion, it would be in dollar terms more expensive. Even though the developing countries also have distortive policies in agriculture, many of them are beyond the scope of agreements, and the least developed among them are not subject to many of the disciplines.

The role of agriculture in the Round is assessed also in a study by Francois, McDonald, and Nordstrom (1994). They explicitly model separate efforts of the various reforms in the Uruguay Round. They found that the most important effect worldwide is the dismantling of industrial nontariff barriers, among which the textiles and clothing quotas are by far the most important. In this respect, again, the developed countries are the gainers and the developing countries the losers. Next in importance is agriculture. Here everyone gains, although the developed countries again gain more than the developing countries.

For a Martian (particularly a Martian economist), this is a paradoxical result, because those countries that gained the most have been the most

467

Table 7. Welfare Effects of Trade Liberalization

Agricultural Liberalization Only (Dunkel Draft)		Across-the-Board Liberalization (Uruguay Round)	
Low-Income Asia	585	Australia	807
PRC	893	Japan	31,333
India	2,555	Republic of Korea	3,644
Upper-Income Asia	9,556	Indonesia	2,302
Indonesia	7	Malaysia	2,864
Africa	-217	Philippines	304
Nigeria	93	Singapore	-245
South Africa	111	Thailand	-1,192
Maghreb	-123	PRC	2,448
Mediterranean	-975	Hong Kong	418
Middle East Oil Export	207	Latin America	-211
Latin America	3,843	Sub-Saharan Africa	-535
Brazil	2,057	South Asia	-556
Mexico	1,199	Rest of the World	-6,257
Total Developing	**19,791**		
		Subtotal: ESCAP* region	**42,128**
Eastern Europe	2,202		
Commonwealth of Independent States	3,557	**Subtotal: Developing**	**2,974**
Total non-OECD	**25,550**	**Total World**	**84,124**
United States	11,443	* Economic and Social Commission for Asia and the Pacific	
Canada	2,327		
Australasia	2,145		
Japan	13,197	*Source:* Duncan, Robertson, and Yang, 1995.	
European Community	26,382		
European Free Trade Area	7,810		
Total OECD	**63,304**		
Total World	**88,854**		

Source: Brandao and Martin, 1993.

reluctant to agree to reform. They have to be dragged kicking and screaming to enjoy these welfare gains. Further, their reluctance has (at least as far as the US and EU are concerned) given them more of a bargaining leverage to extract other gains. No doubt, some of those "gains" are as illusory as what they have considered losses, when they agree to relax their agricultural protection. No doubt, also, some of the "losses" from which developing countries thought they "suffered," such as the reduction of industrial trade barriers, are just as illusory.

For these paradoxes to be resolved, a political-economic approach is called for. Such a model (which is beyond the scope of this chapter) would have to specify more correctly the objective functions of the governments, none of which maximizes the social welfare function as is normally assumed by economists.[14]

Conclusions

The discussion above seems to point to different conclusions. An examination of the legal texts with their fine prints and loopholes, calls for a healthy dose of skepticism. The results of the models that predict the outcome of the Round seem, on the other hand, to show significant (although not large) positive results for developing as well as for developed countries. Not reported in this chapter is the opposite fear that the Agreement on Agriculture will work against the interests of the developing countries (Panchamukhi, Dhar, and Mohanty 1995:181-255).

By and large, given the inability of many of the models to incorporate the devilishly devious special arrangements (as well as just plain crude tactics such as "dirty" tariffication), skepticism should win the day. However, we should not let the best be the enemy of the better, but measure what was achieved against what was there previously. By that yardstick, then, some real progress has been made.

- ◆ Both developed and developing countries bind *all tariffs*, except for very few items under Special Treatment (Annex 5), which is for very few countries. This puts agriculture ahead of industry.[15] True, some of the bound tariffs are astronomically high, but over the decades, negotiations can bring them down.

- ◆ Export subsidies for agricultural goods are now finally subject to disciplines. True, the present subsidies are not going to be quickly reduced, but the basis has been laid for future reductions.

- ◆ SPS measures can now be subject to some discipline, the effectiveness of which will depend very much on dispute-settlement procedures.

Note that the emphasis is on the fact that there are now some rules that govern agricultural trade, even though the actual level of protection currently permitted under the rules is still extremely high.

These observations lead to the central conclusion that the significant impact of the Round will be quite delayed and stretched out over the decades rather than years. It is hard to see how any impact can even be observed during the remaining years of this century, given all the noise that afflicts the world commodity markets.

The question then arises as to whether major trading partners, in particular, the US and EU, will have the political will to continue trade liberalization at the same rate as has been observed for industrial goods in the three decades after the Second World War. Judging from their current behavior, there are grounds for pessimism.

Many developing countries are now keener to have a more open trading regime for themselves, particularly in Latin America. Will this newly found enthusiasm be sufficient to thrust the world community toward an open regime for agriculture? The developing countries are expected to be undergoing rapid industrialization, and will therefore be experiencing severe social strains in the countryside, not unlike those experienced by the developed countries in their past. Such strains will fuel domestic pressures for protection.

It may well be that Johnson's (1973) pessimism as to agricultural free trade being a rare phenomenon may turn out to be right after all. The best that could be hoped for is that we have frozen the degree of protection that currently is in place, and are preventing it from rising further.

Annex

A NOTE ON THE LEGAL TEXTS[16]

Technically, the main text of what was signed in Marrakesh was the Marrakesh Agreement Establishing the World Trade Organization, but this text concerns itself with institutional matters regarding that organization (decision making, financing, amendments, and the like). For our purposes it is worth pointing out that the Charter puts an end to the practice introduced in the Tokyo Round of having various Codes, which allowed individual Contracting Parties to opt out of certain agreements (to the cognoscenti this practice came to be know as "GATT a la carte"). From now on, every Agreement entered in at Marrakesh will be for all Members.

As Annex 1A to this there is a General Agreement on Tariffs and Trade 1994 (known in other texts as GATT 1994). Within the same annex are the two documents discussed extensively in this chapter: the Agreement on Agriculture and the Agreement on Sanitary and Phyto-Sanitary Measures.

Attached to and considered as part of GATT 1994 are the Schedules whereby every WTO Member specified exactly the extent of its commitments for each tariff line. The way these commitments were to be calculated is set out in a key document that is *not* part of the legal texts, namely the Modalities for the Establishment of Specific Binding Commitments under the Reform Programme, issued by the Negotiating Group on Market Access (MTN.GNG/MA/W/24). This document spells out the principles of the commitments, and can be regarded as a sort of instruction manual for the Members to calculate the exact level of commitments they will make in the Schedules. Once the Schedules are notified, and no counter notification made by other Members, then those are what is committed, regardless of whether they conform to the spirit of the letter of the Modalities, which then become legally moribund.

Notes

[1] Despite the date, the term refers to the Agreement, including all the changes that were made in the various rounds prior to Uruguay.

[2] There was a third exception, in Article VI, which exempts a subsidy given for the exports of a primary commodity for which the intent was to stabilize domestic prices.

[3] Admittedly, Article 20 of the Agreement on Agriculture does not hold out the hope that over the long term there should be a progressive reduction in protection and support for agriculture.

[4] "These measures include quantitative import restrictions, variable import levies, minimum import prices, discretionary import licensing, nontariff measures maintained through state-reading enterprises, voluntary export restraints, and similar border measures other than ordinary customs duties, whether or not the measures are maintained under country-specific derogations from the provisions of GATT 1947" (Agreement of Agriculture, Article 4, footnote 1).

[5] Aside from Japan and Korea, the Philippines has also invoked this special treatment for rice. Israel has invoked it for pigmeat, cheese, and milk powder (Tangermann 1994).

[6] The authors went further and argued against the use of producer subsidy equivalents or similar aggregate measures of support as tools for negotiations and agreement.

[7] Valdes and Zietz (1995) make the same point in greater detail.

[8] A possible reason for the rather high response shown from the UNCTAD study is that it is more of a partial equilibrium model than even other partial equilibrium models, such as Zietz and Valdes, in that it assumes zero cross-price elasticities throughout the model, so that the adjustment to any change in protection has to be borne entirely by each individual market.

[9] Article 12 of the Agreement on Agriculture (Disciplines on Export Prohibitions and Restrictions) merely to "give due consideration to the effects...on importing Members' food security," and to notify the Committee on Agriculture "as far in advance as is practicable." Developing countries are exempt from the provisions of this article, except if they are a net food exporter of the foodstuff concerned. Note also that this article is applicable only to foodstuffs, and uncharacteristically, the scope of term is not anywhere defined in the text of the Agreement.

[10] For an analysis of how this particular confluence of policies among developed and developing countries would shape negotiations, see Siamwalla (1989).

[11] One publication was published by the US Department of Agriculture in March 1994 (USDA 1994), in the immediate aftermath of the Round, based partly on the models and on the department analysts' judgments. Since the derivation of the results is not documented, we shall ignore it in the rest of this chapter.

[12] When the Dunkel Draft was proposed as the basis for an agreement, the EU remained dissatisfied. Eventually, the US and the EU met to iron out the remaining differences, and came up with an agreement that (i) reduced the volume of subsidized exports from 24 percent in the Dunkel Draft to 21; (ii) allowed aggregation of commodities for minimum access requirements; (iii) allowed aggregation across the entire sector for the domestic subsidies; (iv) exempted from domestic subsidy reduction the EU compensation payments and the US deficiency payments; and (v) created the cease-fire clause that makes a number of measures nonactionable (Hathaway and Ingco 1995).

[13] An interesting point that they made in this context is the small size of the income effect. The estimate they use in their calculations is the study by Goldin, Knudsen, and van der Mensbrugghe (1993), who obtained an increase in welfare of $213 billion by 2000 which is less than a single year's growth in income.

[14] Siamwalla (1989) is one such attempt.

[15] As a percentage of tariff lines, developed countries now have bound tariffs for 99 percent among industrial goods against 78 percent before the Uruguay Round, and now they have almost 100 percent of tariff lines among agricultural goods (the main exception being Japanese rice) as against 58 before. Developing countries now have 73 percent of the tariff lines in industrial goods bound as against 21 percent before, while the figures for agricultural goods have been leapfrogged to nearly 100 percent from 17 percent (GATT Secretariat 1994).

[16] Except for the last paragraph, this appendix is drawn mostly from Jackson (1994:131-51).

References

Brandao, A. S. P., and W. J. Martin, 1993. "Implications of Agricultural Trade Liberalization for the Developing Countries." *Agricultural Economics* 8.

Duncan, R., D. Robertson, and Y. Z. Yang, 1995. "Analysis of the Benefits and Challenges Facing Asia-Pacific Agricultural Exporting Countries in the Post-Uruguay Round Period." In *Benefits and Challenges Facing Asia-Pacific Agricultural Trading Countries in the Uruguay Round Period. Studies in Trade and Investment 11.* United Nations Economic and Social Commission for Asia and the Pacific, New York.

Food and Agriculture Organization (FAO), 1995. "Implications for Food Security in the Asia and Pacific Region." In *Benefits and Challenges Facing Asia-Pacific Agricultural Trading Countries in the Post-Uruguay*

Round Period. Studies in Trade and Investment 11. United Nations Economic and Social Commission for Asia and the Pacific, New York.

Francois, J. F., B. McDonald, and H. Nordstrom, 1994. "The Uruguay Round: A General Equilibrium Assessment." Mimeographed.

Frohberg, K., G. Fischer, and K. S. Parikh, 1990. "Would Developing Countries Benefit from Agricultural Trade Liberalization in OECD Countries?" In I. Goldin and O. Knudsen, eds., *Agricultural Trade Liberalization: Implications for Developing Countries.* Organisation for Economic Co-operation and Development and the World Bank, Paris and Washington, D.C.

GATT Secretariat, 1994. "Market Access for Goods and Services: Overview of the Results." In the series *The Results of the Uruguay Round of Multilateral Trade Negotiations.* Mimeographed.

Gardner, B., 1989. "Recent Studies on Agricultural Trade Liberalization." In A. Maunder and A. Valdes, eds., *Agriculture and Governments in an Interdependent World: Proceedings of the Twentieth International Conference of Agricultural Economics.* Dartmouth, Aldershot, UK.

Goldin, I., O. Knudsen, and D. van der Mensbrugghe, 1993. *Trade Liberalisation: Global Economic Implications.* Organisation for Economic Co-operation and Development and the World Bank, Paris and Washington, D.C.

Hathaway, D. E., and M. D. Ingco, 1995. "Agricultural Liberalization and the Uruguay Round." Paper presented at the World Bank Conference on The Uruguay Round and the Developing Economies, 26-27 January, Washington, D.C.

Jabara, C., and A. Valdes, 1993. "World Sugar Policies and Developing Countries." In S. Marks and K. E. Maskus, eds., *The Economics and Politics of World Sugar Policies.* Ann Arbor, Michigan: The University of Michigan Press.

Jackson, J. H., 1994. "Managing the Trading System: The World Trade Organization and the Post-Uruguay Round GATT Agenda." In P. B. Kenen, ed., *Managing the World Economy: Fifty Years after Bretton Wood.* Washington, D.C.: Institute for International Economics.

Johnson, D. G., 1973. *World Agriculture in Disarray*. London: Trade Policy Research Center.

Moreddu, C., K. Parris, and B. Huff, 1990. "Agricultural Policies in Developing Countries and Agricultural Trade." In I. Goldin and O. Knudsen, eds., *Agricultural Trade Liberalization: Implications for Developing Countries*. OECD and the World Bank, Paris and Washington, D.C.

Panchamukhi, V. R., B. Dhar, and S. K. Mohanty, 1995. "Analysis of the Challenges Arising from the Agriculture-Related Agreements of the Uruguay Round." In *Benefits and Challenges Facing Asia-Pacific Agriculture Trading Countries in the Post-Uruguay Round Period. Studies in Trade and Investment 11*. United Nations Economic and Social Commission for Asia and the Pacific, New York.

Siamwalla, A., 1989. "Agriculture, the Uruguay Round and Developing Countries." In A. Maunder and A. Valdes, eds., *Agriculture and Governments in an Interdependent World: Proceedings of the Twentieth International Conference of Agricultural Economics*. Dartmouth, Aldershot, UK.

Stoeckel, A. B., D. Vincent, and S. Cuthbertson, eds., *Macroeconomic Consequences of Farm Support Policies*. Durham: Duke University Press.

Sathirathai, S., and A. Siamwalla, 1987. "GATT Law, Agriculture Trade, and Developing Countries." *World Bank Economic Review* 1(4): 595-618.

Tangermann, S., 1994. "An Assessment of the Uruguay Round Agreement on Agriculture." Paper prepared for the Directorate of Food, Agriculture and Fisheries and the Trade Directorate of OECD. Mimeographed.

Tyers, R., and K. Anderson, 1992. *Disarray in World Food Markets: A Quantitative Assessment*. Cambridge, U.K.:Cambridge University Press.

United States Department of Agriculture (USDA), 1994. *Effects of the Uruguay Round Agreement on US Agricultural Commodities*. USDA, Economic Research Service, Washington, D.C.

Valdes, A., and J. Zietz, 1980. Agricultural Protection in OECD Countries: Its Cost to Less-Developed Countries. Research Report 21. International Food Policy Research Institute, Washington, D.C.

_____, 1995. "Distortions in World Food Markets in the Wake of the GATT: Evidence and Policy Implications." *World Development* 23(6):913-26.

Vanzetti, D., N. Andrews, S. Hester, and B.S. Fisher, 1994. "U.S.-E.C. Agricultural Trade Relations and the Uruguay Round: A Cairns Group Perspective." In G. Anania, C.A. Carter, and A. F. McCalla, eds., *Agricultural Trade Conflicts and GATT: New Dimensions in North-American-European Agricultural Trade Relations*. Boulder: Westview.

Whalley, J., and R. Wigle, 1990. "Terms of Trade Effects, Agricultural Trade Liberalization and Developing Countries." In I. Goldin and O. Knudsen, eds., *Agricultural Trade Liberalization: Implications for Developing Countries*. OECD and the World Bank, Paris and Washington, D.C.

Zietz, J., and A.Valdes, 1990. "International Interactions in Food and Agricultural Policies: Effects of Alternative Policies." In I. Goldin and O. Knudsen, *Agricultural Trade Liberalization: Implications for Developing Countries*. OECD and the World Bank, Paris and Washington, D.C.

4 77 - 80

F13
5l3
Ql7
5l9

Comments on "World Agricultural Trade After the Uruguay Round: Disarray Forever?"

(global)

by

T. N. Srinivasan

I enjoyed reading Siamwalla's chapter. Both of its two parts, one a review of the main features of the Uruguay Round agreement with respect to agriculture, and the other a critical assessment of model-based projection of the possible impact of the agreement, are informative and insightful. The history of agriculture in the global trading system, since the General Agreement on Tariffs and Trade (GATT) was concluded in 1947 until the conclusion of the Uruguay Round, is nothing short of scandalous. Although GATT rules as originally drafted were meant to apply to trade in all commodities, things worked out differently. As a GATT (1979:7) report pointed out, "Agriculture has been virtually excluded from the broad sweep of trade liberalization and insulated from the normal disciplines of market forces and international competition...." While subsidies for manufactured exports were prohibited in GATT, subsidies for agriculture were legal as long as they did not result in the subsidizing country getting "more than an equitable share of world trade," an obviously nonoperational and meaningless criterion. Quantitative restrictions were again banned on manufactured imports except for economically nonsensical balance-of-payments reasons (an exception which, alas, is still permitted under the rules of the newly established World Trade Organization [WTO], but were allowed in the case of imports of agricultural products for various reasons including "enforcement of domestic production or marketing restriction measures" and to "remove a temporary surplus," and so on. It is no wonder that agricultural trade became very distorted with heavy involvement of governments in managing it. From sugar quotas, peanut quotas, and the noxious and notorious Common Agriculture Policy (of the European Community) in the developed countries, to marketing boards, import quotas, export tariffs, multiple exchange rates, and so on in developing countries, almost every conceivable form of intervention was the outcome.

Until the end of the 1960s, agricultural trade was conducted by either completely bypassing GATT rules or obtaining exemptions and waivers from their applications. The Kennedy Round (1963 to 1967) of multilateral trade negotiations did not accomplish much on agricultural trade primarily because of the conflict between efficient agricultural producers, such as the US which wanted liberalization of trade, and the less efficient European Community which preferred to manage agricultural trade through commodity agreements to protect its agriculture and raise farm incomes. During the Tokyo Round there was some progress with liberalization of trade in a number of products and an agreement was reached on dairy products and bovine meat. There was a compromise on subsidies, though its application to agriculture was rather general. In sum, until the Uruguay Round, agricultural trade was largely outside the GATT framework. (For a history of agriculture in GATT, see Hathaway 1987.)

Has the Uruguay Round (UR) agreement brought about a significant change in the scandalous situation? Certainly not, if by significant change one means instituting a rule-based system of free and efficient system of agricultural trade. Siamwalla is correct in suggesting that the UR agreement simply regularizes, binds, and brings some discipline to the exercise of exceptions from GATT rules that countries were practicing in their agricultural trade. This is certainly a step toward bringing trade in all goods and services under a common set of rules. But, beyond that, in terms of reducing pre-UR barriers to trade in agriculture, the UR agreement, on balance, achieved very little.

The most significant regularization is the requirement that all non-tariff border measures be replaced by tariffs that initially provide the same level of protection and bound. Tariffs resulting from this "tariffication" process and other agricultural tariffs are to be reduced over a period of six (ten) years by an average of 36 percent (24 percent) in the case of developed (developing) countries, with minimum reductions required under each tariff line. The tariffication is subject to the maintenance of existing market access opportunities. Siamwalla rightly draws attention to the fact that in actual implementation, the process of tariffication has resulted in tariff bindings that are much above the prevailing average levels in many cases. Two countries, Japan and Korea, have even succeeded in negotiating a delay in tariffication of their very high barriers to rice imports. Even countries that have no import-competing production, such as Norway in rice or, in fact, export, such as Thailand in rice again, have chosen to set egregiously high tariff bounds (a tariff of 454 percent and 48 percent, respectively by Norway and Thailand in rice; see Siamwalla's Table 2). Also, given the agreed tariff cut of 36 percent which is to apply on a simple average of four-digit tariff lines with a cut of at least 15 percent on each line, it is very likely, as Siamwalla points out, that the specified average will be achieved by cutting tariffs a lot on nonsensitive items while sticking to the 15 percent floor on sensitive items. He is again on solid ground in drawing attention to the possibility that in implementing the tariff-quota arrangements with respect to minimum market access commitments, governments could subvert them by authorizing a state enterprise to be the sole importer for the quota amount.

While Siamwalla is right in highlighting the weaknesses of most models in assessing the likely impact of the Uruguay Round liberalization, he does not adequately acknowledge their strengths. After all, the UR agreement is a complex one and involves global reductions in several trade barriers at different speeds over several years. Simplifying them, sometimes drastically, for modeling purposes is unavoidable. However, there simply is no meaningful alternative to a multi-country general-equilibrium model for evaluating the likely combined effect of simultaneous changes in several barriers in more than one country. It is true that the sizes, and even signs, of simulated effects can vary depending on alternative modeling assumptions, from those relating to commodity aggregation to treatment of the degree of product differentiation across sectors and countries, not to mention possible alternative numerical specification of several parameters for which econometrically estimated values are unavailable. Such variation is seen in the results reported by Siamwalla. Yet, across models, a robust conclusion seems to emerge, viz. that the global welfare effects of agricultural trade liberalization of the UR agreement is likely to be extremely modest, and few countries are likely to gain or lose significant welfare. As is to be expected, in contrast to welfare effects, the world price effects are larger in size, particularly in commodities like rice where only a small part of output is internationally traded, or sugar where the pre-UR market is heavily distorted.

Siamwalla refers to a study based on data for the early to mid-1980s that indicated that the removal of distortions in developing countries, either unilaterally or in conjunction with the removal of distortions in developed countries, would substantially reduce the world prices of most agricultural commodities. The reason for this is the influence of extensive disprotection in developing countries, which together have a greater role in a world agricultural production and trade, tended to dominate that of protection in developed countries. As Siamwalla suggests, many developing countries have since considerably reduced their agricultural disprotection at the urging of the World Bank and the International Monetary Fund, even prior to the UR agreement. I would add that a significant component of disprotection, according to Krueger et al. (1988), was indirect arising from protection of industries that supplied agricultural inputs and from exchange rate overvaluation in developing countries. With macroeconomic stabilization and reduction in industrial protection following the UR agreement, disprotection should further decrease. Siamwalla is critical of GATT for being concerned exclusively with protection and not with disprotection. Such a concern is not unreasonable if disprotection in any sector is largely a consequence of protection elsewhere. Thus, to the extent agricultural disprotection is largely due to protection of industry, GATT's efforts in reducing industrial protection should reduce agricultural disprotection as well.

Finally, Siamwalla draws attention to one of the less frequently noted, but nonetheless important effects, of the policies of insulation of domestic agricultural markets in increasing the volatility of world market prices. Whether the UR agreement significantly affects insulation policies is, as he rightly emphasizes, somewhat doubtful. Although tariffication and re-duction of variable export subsidies should reduce insulation, there are three factors that suggest otherwise. First, since tariffs have been bound at very high levels, significant fluctuations in tariff below the bound levels are possible. Second, could safeguard provisions be invoked if imports surge? Third, variable export taxes are allowed. Let me conclude by endorsing Siamwalla's summary assessment of the UR agreement on agriculture: "The best that could be hoped for is that we have frozen the degree of protection that currently is in place, and are preventing it from rising further."

References

GATT, 1979. *Report on Multilateral Trade Negotiations*. Geneva: GATT Secretariat.

Hathaway, D., 1987. *Agriculture and the GATT: Rewriting the Rules*. Washington, D.C.: Institute for International Economics.

Krueger, A. O., M. Schiff, and A. Valdes, 1988. "Agricultural Incentives in Developing Countries: Measuring the Effect of Sectoral and Economy-wide Policies." *World Bank Economic Review* 2(2): 225-38.

CHAPTER 12

IMPACT OF THE URUGUAY ROUND ON ASIA: TRADE IN SERVICES AND TRADE-RELATED INVESTMENT MEASURES

PATRICK LOW
WORLD TRADE ORGANIZATION

The inclusion of trade in services and trade-related investment measures (TRIMs) under the umbrella of the World Trade Organization (WTO) has brought a vast new sphere of economic activity within the purview of the multilateral trading system. The attempt to address these issues was a bold and complicated initiative, and in some areas the resulting provisions are incomplete. Several aspects of the services agreement seem almost experimental, because negotiators had to deal with economic relationships never previously addressed in a multilateral context, and with novel determinants of the conditions of market access. As the services agreement starts to operate, clarification will be needed about what certain provisions actually mean, and different approaches to some aspects of the rules may be required. A program of negotiations has continued since the completion of the Uruguay Round in 1994, and governments are already committed to subsequent rounds of multilateral negotiations aimed at further liberalization. The first such round is due to commence no later than the year 2000.

The services negotiations in the Uruguay Round probably achieved limited trade liberalization. In fact, the absence of satisfactory data makes all statements on this point speculative. But the negotiations did define certain basic principles intended to apply to all international service transactions; they created a framework of rules; they specified a guaranteed level of market access in those areas where commitments were scheduled; and they established a basis for future multilateral rule making and trade liberalization.

Two particular features of services activities that distinguish them from production and trade in goods deserve mention at the outset, as these help to explain what made the negotiation and final shape of the General Agreement on Trade in Services (GATS) so different from the General Agreement on Tariffs and Trade (GATT). First, production and consumption of a service may occur simultaneously, because no possibility exists of storing certain services produced now for consumption later. Hair-cutting and shoe-shining are obvious examples of this class of service. In such cases, a transaction requires that the producer and the consumer must be in one location. For other services, such as construction, arm's length supply is impossible because the service is not transportable. A physical presence is therefore necessary. This implies that if a government grants market access rights to foreign suppliers in relation to nonstorable or nontransportable services, it may have to accept either that foreign enterprises can establish a commercial presence in its territory, or that the services suppliers in question may enter its territory on a temporary basis.[1]

The delivery of many services is not so intrinsically restricted, and arms-length delivery across frontiers is feasible, although not necessarily desirable from the point of view of the supplier and the consumer.[2] Thus, even where establishment or temporary presence is not essential to an exchange, a preference may exist for the physical presence of the producer in the territory of the consumer, or vice versa. On the other hand, modern information technology[3] has greatly increased the scope for arm's length delivery. The essential point here is that either through force of circumstance, or because of the nature of an activity, trade in services cannot be promoted without a willingness on the part of governments to contemplate multiple modes of delivery, involving the movement across national jurisdictions of the services themselves, or of producers, or of consumers. As discussed below, these realities are reflected in GATS.

The second important distinguishing feature of services activities is that they tend to be subject to a greater degree of regulatory supervision than are physical goods. In part, this reflects concerns about consumer protection, or in the case of financial services, prudential issues. Since fraud, sharp practice, and substandard output may be difficult or impossible to detect and prevent before the damage is done, governments feel obliged to control supply ex ante rather than output on an ex post basis. Another consideration is that some services sectors, like banking, have economy-wide externalities, such that regulation erring on the side of caution is considered necessary to avoid the widespread damage that would be caused by specific sectoral failures. Moreover, in making the comparison with goods, it should be borne in mind that GATS covers services suppliers as in the case of production, as well as services, whereas in GATT only products are covered.

On the other hand, heavy regulation may also reflect protectionist policy, where for one reason or another, governments are unwilling to countenance foreign competition. Either way, the relative intensity of regulation in many services industries contributes to the complexities of promoting trade liberalization. The focus of negotiations on trade in services will tend to be upon sectors, although there is undoubtedly room to do more by way of developing principles applicable to all services trade, regardless of the degree of sector-specific liberalization that governments are willing to countenance. Given the greater necessity of regulation from a consumer protection perspective in the sphere of services, progress in trade liberalization should not be judged merely by reference to the pace and degree of deregulation. Conversely, deregulation does not always mean the same as liberalization. For example, a large country can easily deregulate a services activity without inviting foreign competition. The role of regulation loomed large in the Uruguay Round negotiations, and an implicit tension exists between some elements in the GATS general framework and the specifics of scheduled sectoral access commitments.

A final point worth making at the outset concerns the severe dearth of information available to policymakers and analysts about service transactions. For the most part, governments have not collected data on international services transactions in a systematic fashion, save in a highly aggregated and not always internationally comparable form in the balance-of-payments accounts. As Richard Cooper puts it, "we are wallowing in ignorance when it comes to international transactions and services" (Cooper 1988). Attempts are being made by the Organisation for Economic Cooperation and Development (OECD), Eurostat, and the International Monetary Fund to improve the standard of data collection in services (World Bank 1995), but these efforts will take several years to bear fruit. Moreover, problems will still arise because of a growing range of intrafirm electronic services transactions that are not recorded in conventional balance-of-payments statistics. A further limitation of data on services transactions is that so-called "establishment" trade, the sales of foreign-owned enterprises in the host country, is not recorded under existing statistical methodologies.[4] Finally, as Jagdish Bhagwati (1984) pointed out over ten years ago, services statistics will be influenced by economic structure. For example, where a manufacturing firm maintains in-house advertising services, advertising will be recorded as goods production; but a manufacturer who buys in advertising from an agency triggers a transaction that will be recorded in national output statistics as advertising services. Specialization that leads to out-sourcing of service inputs into manufacturing is referred to as "splintering."

What of the second subject covered in this chapter, that of TRIMs? If the Uruguay Round outcome in services is less than some governments had hoped for, it nevertheless looks impressive against the modesty of the TRIMs results. Despite the efforts of some countries at the beginning of the Uruguay Round to take GATT into the field of investment, all that emerged was a reiteration of the applicability to certain TRIMs of GATT provisions on national treatment and quantitative import and export restrictions. Indeed, some would argue that this was a retrograde result, since the agreement also established grace periods within which governments could bring GATT-illegal measures into conformity. Of greater interest in the TRIMs field, however, was the remit to examine within five years whether the TRIMs agreement should be complemented with provisions on investment and competition policy. As discussed later in this chapter, the prospect of a broad based, horizontal approach to multilateral rules on investment carries intriguing implications for GATS, where governments have already accepted investment disciplines through their commitments on access through market presence.

Services in the World Economy

Advances in transport and information technologies have contributed to a dramatic expansion of trade in services. A myriad of international transactions, which in earlier times would have been impossible or prohibitively expensive, have now become commonplace because of the ease with which people can move and communicate electronically across frontiers. Growing interlinkages among national economies are dramatically changing the way in which business is done and economic transactions are carried out.[5] Services transactions play a large part in this story, both in relation to increased trade in services and growing service-related investment.

Another notable feature of the international economy is the shifting balance of economic power reflected in relative economic growth rates. The clear front-runner in the growth stakes is East Asia, with South Asia somewhat behind, but still among the leaders in global terms. According to World Bank data (see Table 1), the economies of East Asian developing countries grew at an annual average rate of about 8 percent for the last decade and a half. South Asia's rate over this period was around 5 percent. These rates compare with a global average of around 3 percent, and a developing-country average of somewhat less than that. In effect, Asian economic growth rates have been significantly ahead of world averages for at least 30 years. The picture for trade growth is similar, with the world average at a little over 6 percent from 1981 to 1993, and the South Asian rate at over 10 percent for the same period.

Behind these figures is the reality that many Asian economies are rapidly modernizing. Their production structures and patterns of specialization increasingly resemble those of industrial economies, with the implication that services activities are also likely to grow in importance. The Uruguay Round negotiations on services addressed issues of considerable interest to most Asian economies. A major determinant of competitiveness, especially in the context of a highly integrated world economy, is access to efficient and low-priced producer services, such as telecommunications and financial services. Governments that protect high-cost domestic services input industries inevitably place many other producers at a disadvantage. This consideration makes the continuing work pro-

Table 1. World Growth Summary
(Annual Percentage Change in Real GDP)

Region	1966-1973	1974-1980	1981-1990	1991-1993	1994
World	5.1	3.4	3.2	1.2	2.8
High-Income Countries	4.8	3.0	3.2	1.3	3.0
OECD	4.8	2.9	3.1	1.2	2.9
Non-OECD	8.4	7.0	5.0	6.2	5.8
All Developing Countries	6.9	5.0	3.2	0.8	2.0
East Asia	7.9	6.8	7.6	8.7	9.3
South Asia	3.7	4.0	5.7	3.2	4.7
Sub-Saharan Africa	4.7	3.4	1.7	0.6	2.2
Latin America and Caribbean	6.4	4.8	1.7	3.2	3.9
Middle East and North Africa	8.5	4.7	0.2	3.4	0.3
Europe and Central Asia	7.0	4.9	2.9	-9.4	-7.5
Memo Items: Growth of Trade					
World			6.1	6.7	
All Developing Countries			2.4	3.5	
East Asia			9.9	11.8	

Source: World Bank Stars Database.

gram on services under WTO potentially important to many countries, including in Asia.

Table 2 demonstrates how trade in services has grown faster than merchandise trade over the last decade or more. While services exports accounted for about 16 percent of world exports in 1980, the share had risen to almost 21 percent 12 years later. Annual average growth in services exports was 8.1 percent from 1980 to 1992, compared with 5.2 percent for merchandise exports. Some of this extra growth may reflect changes in production structures and relationships, rather than increases in output. This is the point about "splintering" noted earlier.

Table 3 lists the world's leading exporters and importers of traded commercial services in 1993. According to these data, the largest Asian exporter is Hong Kong, placing eleventh. People's Republic of China (PRC); Republic of Korea (Korea); Malaysia; Philippines; Singapore; Taipei,China;

Table 2. World Exports of Merchandise and Commercial Services,
1980 to 1992
($ billion and percentage)

	Value		Share in Total Trade		Average Annual Change
	1980	1992	1980	1992	1980-92
Merchandise	2,037	3,731	84.5	79.5	5.2
Commercial Services	375	960	15.5	20.5	8.1
Total	2,412	4,691	100.0	100.0	5.7

Sources: International Monetary Fund Balance-of-Payments Statistics (see text), supplemented with national sources for Hong Kong and Taipei,China.

and Thailand also figure among the world's 30 largest exporters. On the import side, Taipei,China is the tenth largest buyer of traded commercial services, and PRC, Hong Kong, Indonesia, Korea, Malaysia, Singapore, and Thailand are also among the top 30. The 30 countries listed for both exports and imports account for over 85 percent of world trade.

Table 4 attempts a sectoral breakdown of commercial services exports in 1980 and 1992. The share of transport services exports in total services exports fell from 37 percent to 26 percent over this period, with other private services and income taking up most of the slack. These data illustrate how poor the data base is, even on traded services. Over the next few years, however, an increasing number of countries will begin to report on the basis of the International Monetary Fund's new and more detailed balance-of-payments accounts.

Table 5 presents some interesting figures on trade shares in commercial services between 1980 and 1992. It is somewhat surprising to note that despite Asia's impressive overall income and trade growth performance, its share of services trade growth has increased modestly, from 14 percent to 17 percent from 1980 to 1992. By contrast, the North American share jumped from 12 percent to 19 percent over this period. Both the Asian and the North American increases were mostly at the expense of Western Europe, whose share fell by some six percentage points, but from a significantly larger base.

Part of the explanation for the relatively low gains in services trade shares of Asia is that foreign direct investment (FDI) growth was stronger during this period than in many other regions (see below), suggesting that to the extent FDI was in services industries, this mode of services supply was favored in Asia over cross-border supply. Another part of the explanation is that Asian export dynamism is still to be found predominantly in manufactured exports, and not in the export of services. Table 6 breaks down services by sector and compares the sectoral composition of traded services in Asia with the rest of the world. Transport services appear relatively more important for Asia, with travel and other private services and income being less so.

As already noted, FDI has played a major role in the globalization of the world economy. Table 7 shows that FDI growth dramatically outpaced income and trade growth between 1986 and 1993, and Asia's share of this increase in FDI was far larger than that of any other region. For Asian countries, FDI has been as much or more important as a source of technology transfer and know-how and organizational/managerial skill development, as it has been a source of financial resources. Unfortunately, data that disaggregate investment by sector are not available on a systematic basis, so it is impossible to say how much of the rapid investment expansion that has occurred in Asia has involved services industries. It is reasonable to assume, however, that services-related investments are a significant part of the story.

The General Agreement on Trade in Services

GATS is a cautious agreement,[6] in that it provides signatories with ample scope to condition their multilateral commitments. Only some of the provisions of the GATS framework agreement relate to the universe of trade in services, as defined under the agreement, while others are restricted to those services activities subject to scheduled commitments. Several provisions clearly reflect the pervasiveness of regulations in many services sectors and the intent to prevent the protectionist abuse of such regulations. The specific schedules indicate which services sectors each signatory has been willing to subject to nongeneral obligations under GATS. The schedules also provide for qualifications to the national treatment and market access commitments that otherwise apply to sectoral commitments. Finally, a series of annexes and decisions elaborate on commitments and exceptions with respect to different rules and sectors, and also establish a work program, including further sectoral negotiations.

Certain definitions are required before addressing these various aspects of GATS. The scope of the agreement, the definition of trade in services, and sectoral coverage are laid out in Part I of GATS. Trade in services is defined in Article I in terms of four modes of supply. The first

Table 3. Leading Exporters and Importers in World Trade in Commercial Services, 1993
($ billion and percent)

Rank	EXPORTERS	Value	Share	Annual Change	Rank	IMPORTERS	Value	Share	Annual Change
1	United States	167.5	16.4	4	1	United States	113.4	11.5	8
2	France	100.8	9.9	-2	2	Germany	111.9	11.3	-3
3	Germany	61.8	6.1	-8	3	Japan	100.7	10.2	3
4	Italy	59.0	5.8	-8	4	France	83.3	8.4	-1
5	United Kingdom	53.5	5.2	-5	5	Italy	58.8	5.9	-16
6	Japan	53.2	5.2	7	6	United Kingdom	44.4	4.5	-5
7	Netherlands	37.0	3.6	1	7	Netherlands	35.9	3.6	-2
8	Belgium-Luxembourg	36.7	3.6	2	8	Belgium-Luxembourg	32.3	3.3	-3
9	Spain	31.7	3.1	12	9	Canada	27.1	2.7	1
10	Austria	29.7	2.9	-1	10	Taipei,China	21.3	2.2	11
11	Hong Kong	28.9	2.8	16	11	Austria	21.1	2.1	6
12	Singapore	20.8	2.0	11	12	Spain	19.3	1.9	-13
13	Switzerland	19.7	1.9	0	13	Switzerland	16.8	1.7	-6
14	Canada	16.7	1.6	3	14	Korea, Republic of	16.5	1.7	13
15	Korea, Republic of	15.4	1.5	20	15	Hong Kong	16.0	1.6	9

Table 3. Leading Exporters and Importers in World Trade in Commercial Services, 1993 *(cont'd.)*
($ billion and percent)

Rank	EXPORTERS	Value	Share	Annual Change	Rank	IMPORTERS	Value	Share	Annual Change
16	Mexico	14.3	1.4	6	16	Saudi Arabia	13.9	1.4	-8
17	Taipei,China	13.8	1.4	29	17	Norway	13.9	1.4	-6
18	Denmark	12.8	1.3	-14	18	Sweden	13.6	1.4	-30
19	Norway	12.6	1.2	-6	19	Australia	13.1	1.3	-5
20	Sweden	12.6	1.2	-21	20	Thailand	11.8	1.2	20
21	Thailand	11.2	1.1	17	21	PRC	11.6	1.2	26
22	PRC	10.9	1.1	21	22	Singapore	11.5	1.2	14
23	Australia	10.9	1.1	3	23	Mexico	-11.2	1.1	-3
24	Turkey	9.4	0.9	13	24	Denmark	10.0	1.0	-7
25	Greece	8.5	0.8	-4	25	Indonesia	8.8	0.8	11
26	Egypt	7.4	0.7	1	26	Brazil	8.7	0.9	36
27	Philippines	6.9	0.7	2	27	Malaysia	8.3	0.8	8
28	Portugal	6.8	0.7	19	28	Israel	7.2	0.7	12
29	Israel	6.2	0.6	5	29	Finland	6.4	0.6	-15
30	Malaysia	5.9	0.6	7	30	Portugal	5.5	0.6	20
	Total of above	883.0	86.5	-		Total of above	874.4	88.3	-
	World	1,020.0	100.0	1		World	990.0	100.0	0

Source: WTO Secretariat.

Table 4. Composition of Commercial Services Exports in 1980 and 1992
($ billion and percent)

	Value		Share in Exports of Commercial Services		Average Annual Change
	1980	1992	1980	1992	1980-1992
Transportation	140	253	37	26	5.0
• Shipment	63	105	17	11	4.3
• Passenger Transport	19	54	5	6	9.3
• Other Transportation	59	94	16	10	4.0
Travel	99	285	26	30	9.2
Other Private Services and Income	135	423	36	44	10.0
Commercial Services	375	960	100	100	8.1

Sources: International Monetary Fund Balance-of-Payments Statistics (see text), complemented with national sources for Hong Kong and Taipei,China.

mode involves the cross-border (arm's length or long-distance) supply of a service from one jurisdiction to another. This mode of delivery is analogous to international trade in goods in that a product crosses a frontier. Many different kinds of electronic information flow occur across national borders. The second mode of supply involves consumption abroad, including the movement of consumers to the jurisdiction of suppliers.[7] Tourism is a good example of this mode, involving the movement of (mobile) tourists to (immobile) tourist facilities in another country. The third mode of supply is through the commercial presence of a supplier in the jurisdiction of consumers. This is the investment mode, which caused so much difficulty in the early stages of the services negotiations. Developing countries argued that commitments on services transactions under this mode of supply were tantamount to a surrogate obligation on FDI, and they expressed unwillingness to tie in their investment regimes in this manner. Finally, the fourth mode entails the movement of natural persons from one jurisdiction to another. This is the mode under which the sensitive issue of the movement of labor is addressed. The fourth mode relates both to independent services suppliers and to employees of juridical persons supplying services.

The conceptual approach underlying these modes was first developed in the academic literature (Sampson and Snape 1985) as a heuristic

Table 5. Trade in Commercial Services for Selected Regions and Countries, 1980 and 1992
($ billion and percent)

	1980		1992		Average
	Value	Share	Value	Share	Annual Change
World	375.0	100.0	960.0	100.0	8.1
North America	43.6	11.6	179.7	18.7	12.5
• Canada	7.1	1.9	16.5	1.7	7.3
• United States	36.5	9.7	163.2	17.0	13.3
Latin America	19.5	5.2	38.8	4.0	5.9
Western Europe	226.7	60.4	522.9	54.5	7.2
• France	43.0	11.5	103.1	10.7	7.6
• Germany	30.4	8.1	67.1	7.0	6.8
• Italy	21.2	5.7	62.8	6.5	9.5
• United Kingdom	34.3	9.1	56.1	5.8	4.2
Africa	13.7	3.7	23.0	2.4	4.4
Middle East	12.9	3.4	17.2	1.8	2.5
Asia	52.7	14.0	164.2	17.1	9.9
• Australia	4.1	1.1	10.6	1.1	8.3
• PRC[1]	2.6	0.7	9.1	0.9	13.6
• Taipei,China	2.1	0.6	10.6	1.1	14.3
• Hong Kong	4.4	1.2	18.4	1.9	12.7
• Japan	18.9	5.0	49.6	5.2	8.4
• Korea, Republic of	4.5	1.2	12.8	1.3	9.1
• Singapore	6.0	1.6	18.2	1.9	9.7
• Thailand	1.7	0.5	9.0	0.9	14.7

[1] As data for 1980 were not available, data for 1982 were used.

Sources: International Monetary Fund Balance-of-Payments Statistics (see text), complemented with national sources for Hong Kong and Taipei,China.

Table 6. Sectoral Composition of Commercial Services Exports,
1982 to 1992
($ million and percent)

	Share in Commercial Services in 1992		Average Annual Growth Rate, 1982-1992	
	World	Asia	World	Asia
Transportation	26.3	34.2	6.6	6.8
• Shipment	10.9	15.2	5.9	6.5
• Passenger	5.6	4.6	11.0	13.2
• Other Transport	9.8	14.4	5.5	5.7
Travel	29.7	25.6	11.8	13.6
Other Private Services and Income	44.0	40.3	10.9	11.6
Commercial Services	100	100	9.8	10.0

Sources: International Monetary Fund Balance-of-Payments Statistics (see text), complemented with national sources for Hong Kong and Taipei,China.

device to explain the nature of international transactions in services. Differentiation by modes of supply later formed the basis on which governments defined market access commitments under GATS, permitting a choice to be made from among alternative modes. The use of modal distinctions is a reflection of the manner in which liberalization is defined under the agreement, and the possibility of applying different policy regimes to different modes of supply is a potential source of economic distortion. DeAnne Julius (1994) has discussed such asymmetry in terms of the notion of "modal neutrality," arguing that the absence of neutrality or symmetry imposes limitations on the reach of liberalization. Despite early reservations about commercial presence, a tendency to encourage this mode is discernible in the schedules of commitments (see below). In some cases, this may be because countries have attempted to use GATS as an instrument for encouraging foreign direct investment. In others, it reflects the desire to avoid "regulatory competition" between different jurisdictions. Furthermore, where regulatory control is considered important, as in prudential controls in banking, for example, governments find it easier to impose and enforce regulations in their own territories. The extent to which the absence of modal neutrality under GATS is the source of distortion is an empirical question well beyond the scope of this chapter.

Table 7. FDI Inflows in Developing Countries and Other Indicators, 1986 to 1993

Item	Developing Countries					World
	Total	Africa[1]	Latin America and Caribbean	Western Asia[2]	South, East, and Southeast Asia	World
Growth Rate of Foreign Direct Investment Inflows						
1986-1990 (average)	21.0	7.4	15.7	21.4	35.9	32.6
1991	24.3	18.3	73.6	-1.9	4.9	-21.3
1992	18.7	12.5	-2.6	-50.0	36.5	-6.0
1993	57.0	--	--	--	--	23.0
Growth Rate of Gross Domestic Product[3]						
1986-1990 (average)	4.7	2.5	2.0	3.4	7.1	3.6
1991	4.5	1.6	3.3	2.4	6.1	0.6
1992	5.8	0.4	2.5	7.8	7.8	1.7
1993[4]	6.1	1.6	3.4	3.4	8.7	2.2
Export Growth Rate[5]						
1986-1990 (average)	11.4	3.7	5.0	7.6	13.1	6.1
1991	8.1	1.9	4.7	3.1	11.9	2.4
1992	9.5	2.1	8.5	8.4	11.2	4.6
1993	9.4	0.1	4.1	6.9	12.7	3.0

[1] Egypt and Libyan Arab Jamahiriya are included in Western Asia, except for the item on FDI.
[2] Includes Cyprus, Malta, and Turkey, except for the item on FDI.
[3] Data in this table are not weighted averages.
[4] Projection by the International Monetary Fund.
[5] Volume of merchandise exports.

Source: United Nations Conference on Trade and Development, 1994.

A second feature of the definition of services covered by GATS is the exclusion of services supplied in the exercise of governmental authority. The definition of a service supplied in the exercise of governmental authority in Article 1.3(c) is "any service which is supplied neither on a commercial basis, nor in competition with one or more services suppliers." The intention of this provision is to permit governments to exclude basic infrastructure and social services which they supply their populations on an exclusive basis from the purview of the agreement.

GATS is based on the most-favored nation (MFN) principle (Article II), designed to prevent Members from discriminating against their trading partners. To attain final agreement on the MFN principle, and to avoid the wholesale exclusion of sectors from GATS coverage, limited exemptions to MFN are permitted under the Agreement. The MFN exemption provisions reflected the concern of some larger countries that by granting MFN access to their markets, they would be losing the opportunity to exchange their relatively open access for further liberalization in other markets. In other words, these countries were arguing that "free riding" would occur in the absence of an effective instrument to ensure reciprocity. The issue was raised most explicitly in the telecommunications and financial services negotiations. Some 70 countries have taken MFN exemptions, affecting most significantly the audiovisual, financial, basic telecommunications, and transport services sectors. The MFN exemption in the financial services sectors was suspended pending the outcome of the post-Uruguay Round negotiations in this sector. MFN provisions do not apply to basic telecommunications and maritime services (except where specific scheduled commitments have been undertaken) pending completion of negotiations in these areas. Audiovisual MFN exemptions reflect European concerns about the cultural reach of United States (US) entertainment products, and are justified by the Europeans in terms of arguments about defending the national heritage. The European Union (EU) not only exercised its right to insist on an MFN exclusion, but also failed to make any specific commitments in this sector. A number of European and other countries apply quantitative restrictions to foreign entertainment products. The sector nevertheless remains subject to negotiation in the future.

A fundamental feature of GATS is the principle of progressive liberalization. It reflects the reality that governments were neither willing nor able simply to open up their services markets to international competition from one day to the next. Progressive liberalization implies a gradual approach, and the structure of GATS accommodates such gradualism. A question to consider, however, is whether GATS does indeed offer a vehicle for achieving trade liberalization, or whether its structure is such as to allow governments to support a putatively market opening instrument while in practice holding off liberalization into the indefinite future. In other words, has a proper balance been struck between gradualism and the gradual attainment of ever-higher levels of liberalization?

In considering this question, it is useful to examine certain structural features of GATS which, it could be argued, are important in determining the pace of liberalization. Four issues in particular suggest themselves. First, there is the question of the scope of application of the provisions of GATS. Under the existing structure, few obligations in GATS apply unless a sector and the associated modes of delivery have been made subject to specific commitments in the schedule of a Member. The MFN principle in Article II and the transparency commitments in Article III are the main general obligations of the agreement. In addition, the obligation to establish appropriate judicial, arbitral, and administrative complaint procedures (Article VI:2) is of a general nature, as are certain provisions dealing with recognition of qualifications (Article VII), monopolies and exclusive suppliers (Article VIII), and business practices (Article IX). The main gaps in general application, which have the effect of reducing the reach of GATS, are those relating to domestic regulation and national treatment. National treatment is discussed later in the chapter.

On the question of domestic regulation, it is important to bear in mind that for reasons already referred to, services activities tend to be regulation-intensive. That is to say, governments feel the need to protect consumer and other interests via regulation to a greater degree than is the case with production and trade in goods. Moreover, it should be remembered that in contrast to GATT, GATS deals with investment as well as trade, and this also explains why regulatory regimes are more important determinants of market access under GATS than GATT. In any event, to the extent that the disciplines on regulations laid out in Article VI do not apply to unscheduled activities and sectors, the disciplinary impact of GATS is correspondingly limited. Paragraph 4 of Article VI calls for a work program whose objective would be to ensure that measures relating to technical standards, licensing requirements, and qualification requirements do not constitute unnecessary barriers to trade in services. There is no reason why such a work program should develop disciplines that apply only to scheduled sectors, and this might provide an opportunity for extending GATS disciplines to all services covered by GATS.

The second structural issue relates to the difference between a "positive" list and a "negative" list approach to scheduling specific commitments under GATS. A positive list approach to sectoral coverage requires that Members list the sectors in which they are willing to undertake commitments, and any sector or activity not so listed in a Member's schedule is not subject to specific commitments. GATS has adopted a positive list approach to scheduling sectors. A negative list approach, by contrast, requires that Members list those sectors or activities in respect of which they are unwilling to assume commitments, leaving all other sectors covered by implication.

Three arguments are advanced as to why a negative list approach may foster greater liberalization than a positive list approach. First, it is argued that with a negative list greater transparency is assured. Given that all governments know what services are included in the established sectoral nomenclature under GATS, the validity of the transparency argument would seem to depend on whether adequate transparency provisions per se are in place, rather than upon the choice of means to indicate sectoral coverage. The second argument is that by forcing governments to list sectors in which they are unwilling to accept commitments, a greater proliberalization dynamic will be created, as long lists might cause embarrassment. It is not altogether clear, however, why governments should be more embarrassed by long negative lists than short positive ones. The third argument is probably the most powerful in favor of a negative list approach. It is that with a negative list, new sectors would automatically be covered by GATS disciplines, unless explicit action were taken to exclude them. As technology moves fast in many services sectors, this is a significant consideration, and may help explain the reluctance of governments to adopt a negative list approach.

The third structural argument concerns the manner in which market access limitations are expressed in Article XVI. As explained in Annex I, the market access limitations that Members are entitled to impose in sectors subject to specific scheduling commitments are laid out under items (a) to (f) in Article XVI. If none of these limitations is inscribed, the scheduled sector or activity concerned is free of any market access limitations. This is, in effect, a negative list approach to scheduling access limitations. Items (a) to (d) of Article XVI are expressed in terms of quantitative market access limitations: the number of suppliers, the value of transactions or assets, the number of operations or quantity of output, or the number of natural persons that may be employed.[8] The question to be considered is whether it would be more appropriate to express these limitations in terms of price measures rather than quantitative limitations. Access limitations could be imposed on foreign suppliers through fiscal measures, and perhaps even subjected to periodic negotiations aimed at reducing such limitations. If this approach were adopted, governments may then want to consider whether the framework agreement contained enough provisions for applying quantitative restraints on services trade under particular circumstances. A structural change of this nature would almost certainly imply a greater degree of liberalization than the existing arrangements. It is questionable, however, whether governments would be willing, in the foreseeable future, to move in this direction.

The final structural argument referred to above concerns the role played by the national treatment commitment under GATS. In contrast to GATT, national treatment under GATS is not a general principle. Rather, it is a matter for negotiation. National treatment applies to scheduled commitments unless an explicit indication is given to the contrary. This makes national treatment into a negotiating chip. One reason why governments may have been unwilling to see national treatment play the same role in GATS as in GATT, or the role that MFN plays in GATS as a general principle, is that under the commercial presence and movement of natural persons modes in GATS (Mode 3 and 4), full national treatment is equivalent to free trade; it would guarantee unlimited investment rights for foreign services suppliers. While governments were willing to guarantee this treatment in some sectors where they made scheduled commitments unencumbered by national treatment limitations, it is difficult to imagine the circumstances in which governments would have been willing to do this across the board.

An intermediate approach to using the national treatment rule as a more effective instrument of liberalization would be to impose limitations on the nature of permissible departures from national treatment. At present, any kind of departure is permitted, provided the limitation is entered in the schedule against the relevant sectoral commitment.[9] The nature of departures from national treatment could be defined, with an emphasis on price-based measures, and these measures could also be subject to progressive reductions in the context of negotiations aimed at greater liberalization. Once again, it is an open question whether governments would be willing to embark on a structural change of this nature.

Without any alterations to the structure of GATS of the kind discussed above, what are the prospects for continuing liberalization, as foreseen in Article XIX of the agreement (see Annex I)? Clearly, considerable scope exists for increasing the level of obligations accepted by governments without undertaking these kinds of adjustments. Action could be taken on several fronts. First, governments could reduce and eventually eliminate all exemptions to the MFN principle. A presumption already exists in GATS that this ought to occur over time. Second, governments could include more sectors and activities in their schedules of specific commitments. Third, they could reduce and eliminate the market access and national treatment limitations that they have inscribed in their schedules. Fourth, governments could eliminate the gap that is sometimes maintained between the actual policies they apply in practice and the level of commitments they undertake in GATS. By aligning GATS commitments with policies actually in place, governments would be providing greater market security and ultimately a more liberal trading environment. The degree to which Members have bound their policies through specific commitments is the subject of the next section.

Schedules of Specific Commitments

Explanations are provided in the Annex of the manner in which specific commitments are scheduled under GATS, and how these commitments might be conditioned in respect of market access and national treatment. This section takes a brief look at the extent and nature of commitments undertaken by different countries and groups of countries. As noted at the beginning of this chapter, any analysis of GATS or trade in services more generally, suffers from an acute shortage of reliable data. In the case of specific commitments, no statistical base exists from which to estimate the value in trade or welfare terms of what countries have bound. The only alternative is to undertake a frequency count of commitments. This is similar to what analysts often do in the case of quantitative trade restrictions, although in that case, frequency ratios are usually expressed in terms of trade flows. For what follows, it has only been possible to make frequency counts of commitments made against the population of all possible commitments. Such a procedure ignores the relative importance of different services activities, and takes no account of the implications of market access and national treatment limitations inscribed in the schedules.[10]

Table 8 provides an overview of the coverage of specific commitments. According to these figures, developed countries on average made commitments on 64 percent of all services activities, while the comparable figures for transition and developing economies were 52 percent and 16 percent. It is important to note that these averages conceal significant variance among countries within the groupings. This is especially true of the developing countries, of whom a number made commitments more far-reaching than suggested by the average. For various reasons, commitments were more sparse in the audiovisual sector, basic telecommunications, and transportation. When these are excluded from the reckoning, the shares increase to 82 percent for industrial economies, 66 percent for transitional economies, and 19 percent for developing economies.

Table 8. Commitments on Services Activities by Country Group

	Percentage of 149 Services Activities	Percentage of 149 Activities excluding transportation and audiovisual, postal, courier, and basic telecommunications
Developed Economies	64	82
Transition Economies	52	66
Developing Economies	16	19

Note: The total number of activities is the number of sectors listed in GATT document MTN.GNS/W/120.
Source: Altinger and Enders, 1995.

Table 9 pursues the coverage question further by indicating numerical ranges for each country within which commitments were made. Thus, only five participants made more than 100 commitments out of the population of 149 possible sectoral commitments: Austria, the EU, Japan, Switzerland, and the US. At the other extreme, 28 countries made less than ten commitments.

Table 10 uses a slightly different approach to counting sectoral coverage. Each of the four modes of delivery are counted as a possible commitment, so the total number of possible commitments rose to 620.[11] This difference did not have an appreciable effect on the coverage ratios, although the country categorizations help to illustrate the point made earlier about high variance in these ratios among developing countries. While high-income countries, which include Korea and Mexico, recorded an average coverage ratio of some 53 percent, the comparable figure for large developing countries was 30 percent. Asian countries among the large developing-country group include PRC,[12] India, Indonesia, Malaysia, Pakistan, the Philippines, and Thailand. The lowest coverage ratio among this group was for Pakistan at 17 percent and the highest was for Thailand at 42 percent.

Table 10 is also useful in providing an idea of the degree to which market access and national treatment limitations accompanied specific commitments. The picture is one of pervasive limitations, and this is an important indicator of the scope that exists for further liberalization of trade in services. Looking at the country group average aggregates, the high-income group scheduled a good number of services without limitations on one or other of market access (56 percent) or national treatment

Table 9. Number of Commitments on Services Activities of
GATS Participants

More than 100	Austria, European Union, Japan, Switzerland, United States
Between 81 and 100	Australia, Canada, Czech Republic, Hungary, Iceland, Norway, Slovak Republic, Sweden
Between 71 and 80	Finland, Hong Kong, Republic of Korea, Liechtenstein, New Zealand, South Africa, Thailand, Turkey
Between 61 and 70	Dominican Republic, Malaysia, Mexico
Between 51 and 60	Argentina, Poland, Singapore, Venezuela
Between 41 and 50	Brazil, Colombia, Israel, Kuwait, Morocco, Nicaragua, Philippines, Romania
Between 31 and 40	Chile, Cuba, Ghana, India, Jamaica, Pakistan
Between 21 and 30	Aruba, Brunei Darussalam, Egypt, El Salvador, Kenya, Macao, Netherlands Antilles, Nigeria, Peru, Senegal, Uruguay
Between 11 and 20	Antigua and Barbuda, Benin, Costa Rica, Gabon, Guatemala, Guyana, Honduras, Ivory Coast, Mauritius, Mozambique, Trinidad and Tobago, Tunisia, Zambia, Zimbabwe
Between 1 and 10	Algeria, Bahrain, Bangladesh, Barbados, Belize, Bolivia, Burkina Faso, Cameroon, Congo, Cyprus, Dominica, Fiji, Grenada, Indonesia, Madagascar, Malta, Mozambique, Myanmar, Namibia, New Caledonia, Niger, Saint Lucia, Sri Lanka, St. Vincent and the Grenadines, Suriname, Swaziland, Tanzania, Uganda

Note: The total number of activities is the number of sectors listed in GATT document MTN.GNS/W/120.

Source: Altinger and Enders, 1995.

(65 percent), but far *fewer* with limitations on neither market access nor national treatment. The share for no limitations on either market access or national treatment reported for high-income countries in Table 10 is 28 percent, but this is the share in respect of all possible sectors that could have been scheduled, and not only of the sectors that actually were

scheduled (as is the case in the separate market access and national treatment columns in the table). A similar pattern is discernible for the large developing countries, where the share of commitments, free either of market access or of national treatment limitations in relation to all possible commitments was only 10 percent. The figure for all other countries was only a little over 6 percent.

Finally, Table 11 lists all the sectors in which commitments were made and indicates the number of commitments made by different country groupings. The two sectors with the most commitments are financial services and tourism. Basic telecommunications and transport services appear to be the least-well represented in the schedules. Since the numbers reported for each country grouping are not normalized by the number of countries in each group, national income, or any other variable, comparisons among the groups have limited meaning.

The Trade in Services Work Program

The post-Uruguay Round work program took up several issues on which agreement proved impossible within the time frame of the negotiations. In some areas, the program was a "rescue" operation, designed to prevent the withdrawal of market access offers or the adoption of a discriminatory approach at the sectoral level. In other cases, participants simply wished to make further progress. This section will briefly discuss the sectoral elements of the work program, leaving aside activities relating to government procurement, safeguards, subsidies, and domestic regulation (see the Annex).

Movement of Natural Persons

The Annex on Movement of Natural Persons Supplying Services Under the Agreement establishes that GATS applies both to independent natural persons supplying services, and natural persons employed by a services supplier. The Annex makes it clear that GATS disciplines do not apply in respect of job seekers, or to any policies regarding citizenship, residence, or employment on a permanent basis. Questions relating to immigration are thus distinguished from questions of market access. Moreover, the Annex recognizes the right of signatories to apply policies relating to the granting of visas in a discriminatory fashion. Much of the discussion on this mode of service supply was framed in terms of the "temporary" presence of natural persons, although the definition of the mode

Table 10. Specific Sectoral Commitments

Countries	Total Number of Commitments	Share of Commitments in Relation to All Sectors (Percent)	Share of Commitments with No Market Access (MA) Limitations (Percent)	Share of Commitments with No National Treatment (NT) Limitations (Percent)	Share of Commitments Without MA or NT Limitations in Relation to All Sectors (Percent)
High-Income Countries		53.3	56.4	65.1	28.0
Large Developing Countries		29.6	36.7	49.3	10.0
All Other Countries		15.1	47.3	60.4	6.4
High-Income Countries					
Australia	360	58.1	61.7	71.4	35.3
Austria	412	66.5	68.7	69.7	43.2
Canada	352	56.8	52.8	62.5	29.0
European Union	392	63.2	43.1	59.4	26.3
Finland	328	52.9	61.6	96.7	32.1
Hong Kong	200	32.3	45.0	20.5	5.0
Japan	408	65.8	56.4	48.8	25.0
Korea, Republic of	311	50.2	43.1	60.1	21.5
Mexico	252	40.7	31.4	49.2	12.6
New Zealand	276	44.5	68.2	65.9	26.8
Norway	360	58.1	58.3	65.8	32.9
Singapore	232	37.4	50.9	65.5	18.6
Sweden	320	51.6	67.2	67.8	33.4
Switzerland	400	64.5	61.8	62.8	38.9
Turkey	276	44.5	60.9	77.2	24.8
United States	384	61.9	63.5	84.4	35.2

Table 10. Specific Sectoral Commitments *(cont'd.)*

	Total Number of Commitments	Share of Commitments in Relation to (percent)	Share of Commitments with No Market Access (MA) (percent)	Share of Commitments with No National Treatment (NT) (percent)	Share of Commitments Without MA or NT Limitations in Relation to (percent)
Less-Developed Countries					
Argentina	208	33.6	65.4	65.4	21.9
Brazil	156	25.2	12.2	17.3	2.7
Chile	140	22.6	25.7	34.3	5.8
China, People's Republic of	196	31.6	21.4	27.6	6.0
Colombia	164	26.5	37.8	37.8	10.0
India	132	21.3	7.6	23.5	1.6
Indonesia	140	22.6	30.0	21.4	4.5
Israel	180	29.0	50.0	50.6	14.4
Malaysia	256	41.3	39.1	64.9	14.5
Pakistan	108	17.4	27.8	35.2	4.8
Philippines	160	25.8	63.8	90.0	14.7
Poland	212	34.2	37.3	77.4	12.7
South Africa	288	46.5	52.1	63.2	24.0
Thailand	260	41.9	22.7	50.8	9.4
Venezuela	156	25.2	34.0	34.0	8.6

[1] The total number of commitments is counted as the number of services activities multiplied by the number of modes in respect of which commitments have been made. This means that the maximum number of possible commitments is 620 (155 activities times 4 modes of supply).

[2] Less-developed countries are classified as those with GDP of $40 billion which do not fall into the high-income group.

Source: Hoekman, 1995.

Table 11. Commitments in Services Activities by Major Country Group
(Number of countries)

Service Activity	Developed Country	Less-Developed Country	Transition	Total
I. BUSINESS SERVICES				
A. Professional Services				
1. Legal	25	19	4	48
2. Accounting, Auditing and Bookkeeping	25	26	4	55
3. Taxation	22	12	3	40
4. Architectural	25	21	3	49
5. Engineering	25	27	4	56
6. Integrated Engineering	24	11	3	38
7. Urban Planning and Landscape Architecture	23	11	3	37
8. Medical and Dental	18	15	4	37
9. Veterinary	21	3	3	27
10. Midwives, Nurses, Physiotherapists and Paramedical Personnel	17	2	1	20
11. Other	14	3	0	17
B. Computer and Related Services				
1. Consultancy Services Related to the Installation of Computer Hardware	24	27	4	55
2. Software Implementation	24	27	4	55
3. Data Processing	24	27	4	55
4. Database	23	21	4	48
5. Other	23	7	2	32
C. Research and Development				
1. R&D on Natural Sciences	3	11	1	15
2. R&D on Social Sciences and Humanities	22	12	3	37
3. Interdisciplinary R&D	4	9	1	14
D. Real Estate Services				
1. Owned or Leased Property	22	2	0	24
2. On a Fee or Contract Basis	23	3	0	26
E. Rental/Leasing without Operators				
1. Ships	22	5	3	30
2. Aircraft	22	4	1	27
3. Other Transport Equipment	25	10	3	38
4. Other Machinery and Equipment	24	7	1	32
5. Other	4	2	1	7

Table 11. Commitments in Services Activities by Major Country Group
(cont'd.)

Service Activity	Developed Country	Less-Developed Country	Transition	Total
F. Other Business Services				
1. Advertising Services	23	16	4	43
2. Market Research and Public Opinion Polling	24	14	3	41
3. Management Consulting	24	25	4	53
4. Related to Management Consulting	24	8	2	34
5. Technical Testing and Analysis	21	13	1	35
6. Incidental to Agriculture, Hunting, and Forestry	24	11	4	39
7. Incidental to Fishing	21	9	1	31
8. Incidental to Mining	21	11	2	34
9. Incidental to Manufacturing	6	5	1	12
10. Incidental to Energy Distribution	2	1	1	4
11. Placement and Supply of Personnel	20	4	1	25
12. Investigation and Security	20	1	1	22
13. Related Scientific and Technical Consulting Services	12	5	3	20
14. Maintenance and Repair on Equipment[1]	23	11	3	37
15. Building, Cleaning Services	25	6	3	34
16. Photographic Services	23	5	4	32
17. Packaging Services	20	4	3	27
18. Printing, Publishing	21	3	5	29
19. Convention Services	22	7	0	29
20. Other	19	11	1	31
II. COMMUNICATIONS SERVICES				
A. Postal Services	0	3	0	3
B. Courier Services	4	15	3	22
C. Telecommunications Services				
1. Voice Telephone Services	0	10	0	10
2. Packet-Switched Data Transmission Services	2	9	0	11
3. Circuit-Switched Data Transmission Services	2	10	0	12
4. Telex Services	1	6	0	7
5. Telegraph Services	0	6	0	6
6. Facsimile Services	1	8	2	11
7. Private Leased Circuit Services	1	7	0	8
8. Electronic Mail	25	19	4	48
9. Voice Mail	25	17	4	46
10. On-line Information and Data Base Retrieval	25	21	4	50
11. Electronic Data Interchange (EDI)	25	14	4	43

Table 11. Commitments in Services Activities by Major Country Group
(cont'd.)

Service Activity	Developed Country	Less-Developed Country	Transition	Total
12. Enhanced/Value-Added Facsimile Services, (including store and forward, store and retrieve)	9	16	4	29
13. Code and Protocol Conversion	25	12	4	41
14. On-line Information and/or Data Processing (including transaction processing)	9	16	4	29
15. Other	4	15	2	21
D. Audiovisual Services				
1. Motion Picture and Videotape Production and Distribution Services	3	10	0	13
2. Motion Picture Projection Services	3	3	0	6
3. Radio and Television Services	2	1	0	3
4. Radio and Television Services	2	4	0	6
5. Sound Recording	2	2	0	4
6. Other	2	2	0	4
E. Other	0	6	0	6
III. CONSTRUCTION AND RELATED ENGINEERING SERVICES				
A. General Construction Work for Buildings	24	22	3	49
B. General Construction Work for Civil Engineering	24	21	3	48
C. Installation and Assembly Work	23	19	3	45
D. Building Completion and Finishing Work	23	13	3	39
E. Other	20	13	3	36
IV. DISTRIBUTION SERVICES				
A. Commission Agents' Services	23	4	0	27
B. Wholesale Trade Services	25	8	4	37
C. Retailing Services	25	9	4	38
D. Franchising	23	5	3	31
E. Other	14	0	0	14
V. EDUCATIONAL SERVICES				
A. Primary Education Services	18	4	4	26
B. Secondary Education Services	19	6	3	28
C. Higher Education Services	18	3	4	25
D. Adult Education	18	1	4	23

Table 11. Commitments in Services Activities by Major Country Group
(cont'd.)

	Service Activity	Developed Country	Less-Developed Country	Transition	Total
E.	Other Education Services	3	4	2	9
VI.	**ENVIRONMENTAL SERVICES**				
A.	Sewage Services	23	6	2	31
B.	Refuse Disposal Services	24	6	3	33
C.	Sanitation and Similar Services	23	5	3	31
D.	Other	23	6	1	30
VII.	**FINANCIAL SERVICES**				
A.	All Insurance and Insurance-Related Services				
	1. Life, Accident, and Health Insurance Services	24	38	4	66
	2. Nonlife Insurance Services	25	37	4	66
	3. Reinsurance and Retrocession	25	41	4	70
	4. Services Auxiliary to Insurance (including brokering and agency services)	24	36	4	64
B.	Banking and Other Financial Services (excluding insurance)				
	1. Acceptance of Deposits and Other Repayable Funds from the Public	24	35	4	63
	2. Lending of All Types (including, inter alia, consumer credit, mortgage credit, factoring and financing of commercial transactions)	23	35	4	62
	3. Financial Leasing	24	22	2	48
	4. All Payment and Money Transmission Services	24	25	3	52
	5. Guarantees and Commitments	23	24	4	51
	6. Trading for Own Account or for Account of Customers, whether on an Exchange, in an Over-the-Counter Market or Otherwise the following:				
	a. Money Market Instruments	23	21	3	47
	b. Foreign Exchange	24	23	3	50
	c. Derivative Products (including, but not limited to, futures and options)	24	11	1	36

Table 11. Commitments in Services Activities by Major Country Group
(cont'd.)

Service Activity	Developed Country	Less-Developed Country	Transition	Total
d. Exchange Rate and Interest Rate Instruments, (including products such as swaps, forward-rate agreements, and so on)	23	15	3	41
e. Transferable Securities	22	20	3	45
f. Other Negotiable Instruments and Financial Assets (including bullion)	24	15	0	39
7. Participation in Issues of All Kinds of Securities[2]	23	27	4	54
8. Money Brokering	24	13	0	37
9. Asset Management[3]	23	23	2	48
10. Settlement and Clearing Services for Financial Assets (including securities, derivative products, and other negotiable instruments)	23	13	3	39
11. Advisory and Other Auxiliary Financial Services[4]	23	28	2	53
12. Provision and Transfer of Financial Information, and Financial Data Processing and Related Software by Providers of Other Financial Services	23	20	2	45
C. Other	1	10	0	11
VIII. HEALTH-RELATED AND SOCIAL SERVICES (other than those listed under professional services)				
A. Hospital Services	15	15	2	32
B. Other Human Health Services	2	4	1	7
C. Social Services	13	1	1	15
IX. TOURISM AND TRAVEL-RELATED SERVICES				
A. Hotel and Restaurants (including catering)	25	69	4	98
B. Travel Agencies and Tour Operators Services	25	53	4	82
C. Tourist Guide Services	24	24	2	50
D. Other	1	12	0	13

Table 11. Commitments in Services Activities by Major Country Group
(cont'd.)

Service Activity	Developed Country	Less-Developed Country	Transition	Total
X. RECREATIONAL, CULTURAL, AND SPORTING SERVICES				
A. Entertainment Services (other than audiovisual)	17	16	1	34
B. News Agency Services	22	1	0	23
C. Libraries, Archives, Museums and Other Cultural Services	5	4	0	9
D. Sporting and Other Recreational Services	20	15	1	36
E. Other	2	2	0	4
XI. TRANSPORT SERVICES				
A. Maritime Transport Services				
1. Passenger Transportation	3	16	0	19
2. Freight Transportation	3	22	0	25
3. Rental of Vessels with Crew	14	6	0	20
4. Maintenance and Repair of Vessels	1	8	1	10
5. Pushing and Towing Services	1	3	0	4
6. Supporting Services for Maritime Transport	1	6	0	7
B. Internal Waterways Transport				
1. Passenger Transportation	1	4	2	7
2. Freight Transportation	1	1	2	4
3. Rental of Vessels with Crew	13	0	2	15
4. Maintenance and Repair of Vessels	1	0	3	4
5. Pushing and Towing Services	2	0	2	4
6. Support for Internal Waterway Transport	2	2	2	6
C. Air Transport Services				
1. Passenger Transportation	0	3	1	4
2. Maintenance and Repair of Aircraft	20	13	4	37
3. Supporting Services for Air Transport	19	14	2	35
D. Space Transport	2	0	0	2
E. Rail Transport Services				
1. Passenger Transportation	4	4	1	9
2. Freight Transportation	4	5	1	10
3. Pushing and Towing Services	3	2	0	5
4. Maintenance and Repair of Rail Transport Equipment	19	4	3	26

Table 11. Commitments in Services Activities by Major Country Group
(cont'd.)

Service Activity	Developed Country	Less-Developed Country	Transition	Total
5. Supporting Services for Rail Transport	2	3	0	5
F. Road Transport Services				
1. Passenger Transportation	23	9	0	32
2. Freight Transportation	22	14	0	36
3. Rental of Commercial Vehicles with Operator	18	2	0	20
4. Maintenance and Repair of Road Transport Equipment	22	4	3	29
5. Supporting Services for Road Transport	2	2	0	4
G. Pipeline Transport				
1. Transportation of Fuels	2	0	1	3
2. Transportation of Other Goods	3	1	0	4
H. Services Auxiliary to All Modes of Transport				
1. Cargo-Handling Services	3	11	0	14
2. Storage and Warehouse Services	21	13	0	35
3. Freight Transport Agency Services	21	9	0	30
4. Other	19	8	0	27
I. Other Transport Services	14	6	0	20

[1] Not including maritime vessels, aircraft, or other transport equipment.

[2] Including underwriting and placement as agent (whether publicly or privately) and provision of services related to such issues.

[3] Such as cash or portfolio management, all forms of collective investment management, pension fund management, custodial depository, and trust services.

[4] On all the activities listed in Article 1B or MTN-TNC/W/50, including credit reference and analysis, investment and portfolio research and advice, advice on acquisitions and on corporate restructuring and strategy.

Source: Altinger and Enders, 1995.

in Article I makes no reference to this temporal dimension. On the other hand, the explicit exclusion in the Annex of citizenship, residence, and employment on a permanent basis makes it clear that any commitments under this mode are for temporary presence. Moreover, in the schedules of specific commitments, time limits may be specified, sometimes with provision for extensions.

The ministerial Decision on Negotiations on Movement of Natural Persons taken at the end of the Uruguay Round was a reflection of the paucity and narrowness of commitments undertaken, and the determination of India, supported by some other developing countries, to seek improvements in these commitments. The work of the negotiating group was to be completed within six months of entry into force of GATS, 30 June 1995. However, the negotiations were not completed until the end of July 1995, in parallel with those on financial services (see below). Most countries made commitments on the movement of natural persons, but nearly all of them were narrow, limited to intracorporate transferees,[13] and then only to personnel at the managerial level. A few schedules, notably those of Canada and the US, also contained limited commitments in respect of independent professional services suppliers. India and others would have wished to see more scope for the movement of independent professional service suppliers, rather than those linked explicitly to an enterprise. Some countries would also like to see a relaxation of the limitations relating to skill levels. But movement of labor is a sensitive issue for all governments, and it is noteworthy that even those countries pressing for better access for different categories of natural persons are unwilling to offer much themselves. The post-Uruguay Round negotiations on movement of natural persons brought very little by way of improvements in the schedules of offers, again reflecting the unwillingness of governments to forego control over what is universally seen as a sensitive policy area. Only six countries, Australia, Canada, the EU, India, Norway, and Switzerland, made improvements in their schedules of commitments during the extended negotiations. It may be noted that at the end of these negotiations, a Committee on Specific Commitments was established with the mandate to oversee the implementation of the commitments. The Committee's mandate is wider than that, however, and it will become increasingly involved in considering technical questions relating to GATS schedules. The Committee has already begun to examine problems relating to the use of a highly aggregated sectoral classification system in the Uruguay Round.

Trade in Financial Services

Financial services is the largest of the sectors on which negotiations are taking place, involving substantial economic interests among the major trading countries. Financial services are defined in an Annex to GATS to include insurance and insurance-related services, and banking and other financial services.[14] As well as defining sectoral coverage in terms of specific activities, the Annex on Financial Services excludes from GATS coverage

central banks and monetary authorities, activities forming part of a statutory system of social security or public retirement plan, and activities of
public entities guaranteed by or using governmental financial resources.
The Annex also contains what is commonly referred to as the "prudential
carve-out" for financial services. A recurrent theme in the negotiations
was that governments must retain sufficient flexibility to act unilaterally
in defense of national interests. The prudential provisions are wide ranging,
permitting governments to take measures "for prudential reasons, including for the protection of investors, depositors, policyholders or persons to
whom a fiduciary duty is owed by a financial service supplier, or to ensure
the integrity and stability of the financial system."[15]

Toward the end of the Uruguay Round, it became clear that some
countries, in particular the US, were dissatisfied with the level of specific
commitments offered in the negotiations. Japan and other Asian countries
were among those whose intended commitment levels were the focus of
this attention. To try to force improved offers, the US threatened to adopt
a two-tier approach to the negotiations, such that the most favorable access
offered to foreign financial services suppliers in the US would be reserved
for countries judged to have attained an acceptable level of reciprocal
openness. This departure from MFN treatment would have required the
US to take an Article II exemption, leaving little or nothing to be scheduled as specific commitments. If the US did not make GATS commitments
in financial services, nor would many other countries. The EU would have
received the most favorable treatment on offer from the US, but had strong
reservations about the US approach, in large part because non-MFN access would not carry the same contractual guarantee as MFN access bound
under GATS. This reluctance on the part of the EU made it more difficult
for the US to follow through with its two-tier approach.

In the end, participants agreed to prolong the negotiations. Thus,
the Second Annex on Financial Services entitled signatories to improve,
modify, or withdraw all or part of their specific commitments on financial
services, and to take MFN exemptions during a 60-day period ending six
months after WTO entered into force (30 June 1995).[16] A ministerial
Decision on Financial Services established that pending a six-month
period during which negotiations on trade in financial services were to
continue, any MFN exemptions already inscribed under Article II
provisions were to be suspended. Negotiations did not wait for the entry
into force of WTO, but continued immediately after the Marrakesh
meeting in April 1994. Two bilateral agreements were reached between
the US and Japan, one on insurance and the other on banking and
securities.

Shortly before the negotiating deadline of 30 June 1995, the US announced that it was not satisfied with the improved level of offers resulting from the prolonged financial services negotiations. The US therefore indicated its intention to retain its original MFN exemption, and also to extend it to cover insurance. Fearful that this decision would produce a "domino" effect with all governments reducing their financial services offers to a minimum, the EU managed to secure agreement that the negotiations would be prolonged for a further month, until the end of July. Efforts to persuade the US to reconsider its position during this period were to no avail. Nevertheless, some 30 countries continued to negotiate, and agreement was reached among them to maintain the best offers that had been made in the negotiations. A package of improvements, judged by some to be quite significant, was thus preserved, despite the fact that the US had reverted to its position immediately prior to the completion of the Uruguay Round. However, largely because of the US stance, this arrangement was to remain in place only until the beginning of November 1997, when a further 60-day period would come into effect, during which Members will be free once again to make any adjustments they wish to their scheduled commitments and MFN exemption lists with respect to financial services. It is to be expected that this arrangement will lead to further negotiations in this sector during the course of 1997.

A special feature of the financial services negotiations during the Uruguay Round was the establishment of the Understanding on Commitments in Financial Services. The Understanding, drawn up largely at the behest of the US, attempted to define in some detail a broad based set of commitments that would apply to the sector. These commitments were to supplement those made in Members' schedules established under Part III of GATS, and would be applied on an MFN basis. The Understanding spells out a range of commitments involving each mode of supply that could have been scheduled in the normal way, but achieves a greater level of precision and uniformity than was considered attainable under regular scheduling.

More significantly, the Understanding also involves particular undertakings not provided for in GATS, such as MFN and national treatment in procurement, and a best-endeavors commitment to eliminate or reduce the scope of monopoly rights. Another feature of the Understanding is the standstill commitment, under which adherents refrain from taking any new measures that would not conform with the provisions of the Understanding. This is conceptually close to scheduled commitments under Part III of GATS, although the standstill applies to measures actually in force, whereas the schedules may bind levels of lesser commitment that do not reflect actual policies. Few countries have agreed so far to abide by the Understanding,[17] preferring the mainstream approach to making commitments. It is interesting to note, however, that the Understanding reflected the misgivings of at least one party to GATS as to the adequacy of normal scheduling techniques and of the framework disciplines in defining market access commitments. Similar initiatives may well emerge from negotiations in other sectors.

Whether existing scheduling techniques are adequate to express sector-specific commitments is a disputed point. The determinants of market access may be too idiosyncratic, and the ways of frustrating general commitments on market access or national treatment too numerous, for the detailed specification of obligations to be altogether avoided. The risk, of course, is that forays into sector-specific detail may lead to nonliberalizing outcomes. In other words, specificity may be the ingredient that allows departures from generally applicable rules or principles, rather than a vehicle for ensuring that such rules and principles do apply. A principle broadly followed in the formulation of annexes during the Uruguay Round was that these should elaborate and explain commitments undertaken in the framework or schedules, and not add to or detract from them. As long as annexes and the sector-specificity associated with them remain essentially interpretative and explanatory or illustrative, they can serve the useful purpose of providing clarity in areas where signatories might otherwise have resorted to litigation at some later date.

Basic Telecommunications

Telecommunications is another large and important sector subject to continuing negotiation under the post-WTO work program on trade in services. Like financial services, telecommunications is a basic industry whose products are a major input into many other sectors of the economy. The negative competitive consequences of poor or highly priced telecommunications and financial services are pervasive in a modern economy. In addition to normal scheduling, an Annex on Telecommunications was negotiated in the Uruguay Round to clarify the coverage of commitments and to guarantee certain basic access rights.[18] This was similar to the Annex on Financial Services, except that the latter was concerned primarily with the prudential carve-out and the question of sectoral coverage, while the Telecommunications Annex concentrates more on defining the access rights of signatories, and is also applicable to all GATS signatories. The Annex on Telecommunications reflects the fact that adequate access to telecommunications networks is a sine qua non for supplying a range of other services, and that restrictions on such access could easily nullify undertakings in other sectors. The main purpose of the Annex, therefore, is to ensure ready, nondiscriminatory access to public telecommunications, transport networks, and services. The Annex also includes provisions on transparency and technical cooperation.

As with financial services, negotiations in basic telecommunications were prolonged beyond the end of the Uruguay Round, against a background of the risk that major participants would schedule limited commitments and seek reciprocity-based exchanges of market access on a discriminatory basis. It became clear before the end of the negotiations that significant liberalization was unattainable within the time frame of the Round. While a few countries such as the US, the United Kingdom, Australia, New Zealand, Sweden, Chile, and Mexico had already opened their telecommunications sectors, or were in the process of doing so, others, most notably the EU were still deciding what to do.

A worldwide trend toward liberalization in the telecommunications sector is clearly discernible. Two main factors account for this trend. First, globalization of economic activity has increased the importance of telecommunications as a production input, making firms much more sensitive to competitive disadvantages arising from poor or costly services. This has mobilized powerful private sector constituencies in many countries that are pushing governments to liberalize and to eliminate or dilute telecommunications monopolies. Secondly, new technologies are outwitting the regulators. A good example of this is the growth of call-back services in voice telephony. These services allow customers in one country to originate their long distance calls in another country and pay the lower tariffs of the latter country. Savings to consumers from such services reflect price differentials among telecommunications service suppliers in different countries, and can amount to more than 50 percent.

At the end of the Uruguay Round, governments felt that negotiations on basic telecommunications could not be completed rapidly, and the Decision on Negotiations on Basic Telecommunications set 30 April 1996 as the date by which the negotiations should be completed. The negotiations were voluntary, in the sense that not all countries are committed to participate. The ministerial decision on the negotiations established that no basic telecommunications sector should be excluded a priori from the negotiations, and also that participants should not take any measures whose effect would be to improve a negotiating position and provide greater negotiating leverage. The Annex on Negotiations on Basic Telecommunications provided that the MFN provisions of GATS (Article II and the Annex on Article II Exemptions) will not become operative in the telecommunications sector until after the completion of the negotiations. The MFN provision does remain operative, however, wherever signatories have made specific commitments in their schedules.

In addition to the efforts of governments to develop or improve schedules of specific commitments, the negotiations have concentrated on establishing a set of common regulatory principles. These principles are primarily concerned with interconnection obligations and competition safeguards relating to the handling of commercially necessary and commercially sensitive information. They apply to major suppliers with market power. The regulatory principles were developed in realization of the fact that dominant and often recently privatized suppliers would be in a position to frustrate the market access commitments made by governments. The inclusion of regulatory principles in the negotiations was a new departure for the GATT/WTO system, touching directly for the first time on the behavior of firms.

It proved impossible to complete the telecommunications negotiations by the prescribed deadline of 30 April 1996. Difficulties had arisen primarily in relation to the question of how satellite services were to be treated and concern over the possibility that as a result of the application of the commitments made in the negotiations on an MFN basis, countries that had not liberalized their markets would be able to establish a commercial presence in liberalized markets and behave in an anticompetitive manner in those markets (one-way accounting rate bypass). Governments failed to agree on licensing criteria that would address this latter problem. In addition, the US indicated its dissatisfaction with the overall quality of the market access offers of certain countries and the absence of any offer at all from other countries.

In the end, governments agreed to freeze the offers that had been made, and provided for a one-month period ending on 15 February 1997, during which they would be at liberty to improve or remove these offers and define their final positions with respect to MFN exemptions. Some 34 governments have frozen offers on the table. From the Asian region these include Hong Kong, India, Japan, Korea, Pakistan, Philippines, Singapore, and Thailand. Thirty participants in the negotiations subscribed to the regulatory principles mentioned above.

Maritime Transport Services

Despite the efforts of negotiators, it became obvious toward the end of 1993 that it would be impossible to reach a broad based agreement on maritime services. A decision was therefore taken to prolong the negotiations until 30 June 1996. A number of countries have traditionally maintained restrictive shipping regimes. The US, for example, maintains a pervasive cargo reservation system and prohibits foreign participation in cabotage.[19] Liner conferences have played a prominent role in EU shipping arrangements in various parts of the world. By contrast, the Nordic countries, some EU nations, a number of Asian countries, and others maintain relatively open maritime regimes. When maritime services were initially placed on the negotiating table, the US opposed the move, seeking the explicit exclusion of the sector from GATS coverage.

As the negotiations progressed, the maritime discussions were broken into international shipping, auxiliary services, and access to and use of ports services. At this point, the position of the US softened, and its conditional offer in the negotiations included commitments on auxiliary services and access to and use of ports services. Nevertheless, this offer was not sufficient to deter the EU and Japan from withdrawing significant parts of their conditional offers prior to the completion of the Uruguay Round. Several other countries did the same, although some 30 countries retained their scheduled commitments. The direction that the maritime negotiations take will depend largely on how far the US is able to go in liberalizing its shipping sector. A factor that could favor liberalization in the future is pressure in the US to reduce subsidies on shipping.

The Annex on Negotiations on Maritime Transport Services is similar to the telecommunications annex in that it suspended all MFN provisions pending the termination of negotiations, except where specific commitments had been made. The Maritime Annex also allowed improvements, modifications, or withdrawals of specific commitments in the light of the results of the negotiations. The Decision on Negotiations on Maritime Transport Services set out the terms of the maritime negotiations, including their termination date of 30 June 1996 and the stipulation that participants must not take measures that would improve their negotiating position and leverage during the negotiations. Some 42 governments participated in the negotiations, including Hong Kong, Indonesia, Korea, Malaysia, the Philippines, Singapore, and Thailand. A further 16 countries were observers.

Despite considerable efforts, it proved impossible to complete the negotiations by the 30 June 1996 deadline. A major factor was the decision of the US not to improve its market access offer. In the face of the prospect that the US would take a broad based MFN exemption in respect of maritime transport services, governments agreed to suspend the negotiations and resume them on the basis of existing or improved offers in the context of the comprehensive services negotiations already mandated to begin no later than the year 2000. In the meantime, governments are committed not to apply measures affecting trade in maritime transport services in such a manner as to improve their negotiating leverage. Twenty-four governments made improved market access offers in the context of the extended negotiations. Among Asian countries were India, Indonesia, Japan, and Korea. Other Asian countries, including Singapore, had already made significant commitments in this sector in the context of the Uruguay Round.

The difficulties encountered in securing significant and timely results in the post-Uruguay Round sectoral negotiations on the movement of natural persons, financial services, basic telecommunications, and maritime services are illustrative of the fact that governments are hard-pressed to conduct negotiations at the sectoral level. This is because such negotiations do not offer the same prospect of trade-offs among different sectors and interests that are possible in a broad based negotiating round. In this situation, it is harder for governments to offset domestic producer interests hostile to liberalization with proliberalization interests. In addition, in single-sector negotiations, governments are more likely to succumb to the mercantilist temptation of identifying their interests exclusively in terms of imports or exports, rather than in terms of the benefits of trade liberalization more broadly defined.

Trade-Related Investment Measures in the Uruguay Round

TRIMs was one of the so-called "new" issues that found its way, along with trade-related intellectual property rights (TRIPs) and trade in services, onto the Uruguay Round negotiating agenda. Unlike TRIPs and services, however, little that was new emerged from the TRIMs exercise, except a mandate to look at the issue again later. Some industrial countries, most notably the US, had pressed for a far-reaching mandate to negotiate about investment in the broad sense. Many developing countries were unwilling to engage in such an exercise at that time. They believed that it would challenge a basic tenet of their development policy, which saw the careful management of investment flows as indispensable to appropriate, balanced growth.

Investment policy, involving a mix of controls and incentives, has traditionally been used by many countries as a tool for promoting specific objectives, such as technology transfer, industrialization, regional development, and export expansion (Maskus and Eby 1990). Some of these objectives, like regional development, have also been pursued through investment incentives in industrial countries. The emphasis of the Uruguay Round TRIMs exercise, however, was mostly on trade-related investment conditionality. The subsidy aspect of investment policy was addressed in the Agreement on Subsidies and Countervailing Measures, where regional subsidies are defined as nonactionable, provided they are granted in the context of an overall regional development program,[20] are nonspecific to an enterprise or industry, and do not result in serious adverse effects to the industry of another party.

Moreover, the ability to condition and control investment flows has traditionally been considered necessary to avoid monopolistic abuses by transnational corporations. Seen from this perspective, multilateral efforts to liberalize investment threatened to weaken the ability of countries to pursue active development policies. Under certain conditions, a welfare case can be made for TRIMs (Balasubramanyam 1991), although it is frequently argued that alternative, less interventionist policy approaches are preferable to dealing with problems that TRIMs are designed to remedy, especially if such problems can be shown to flow from other government interventions.

Opposition to a broad based negotiation on investment in the Uruguay Round was strong enough, given the disposition of interests and priorities in other areas (especially TRIPs and services for the US), for agreement to be reached on a narrow negotiating mandate for TRIMs (Low and Subramanian 1995).[21] The Punta del Este negotiating mandate simply called for an examination of the operation of GATT articles related to the trade-restrictive and distorting effects of investment measures, following which "negotiations should elaborate, as appropriate, further provisions that may be necessary to avoid such adverse effects on trade." The use of the phrase "as appropriate," along with the conditional tense, left open the possibility that governments might agree to nothing at all.

In the end, the Uruguay Round TRIMs agreement only reaffirmed existing GATT rules on national treatment (Article III) and on the prohibition of quantitative restrictions (Article XI). An illustrative list of TRIMs identified two measures as being inconsistent with GATT's national treatment provisions and three as constituting illegal quantitative restrictions. The first category included local content requirements and trade balancing requirements. TRIMs identified as quantitative restrictions included trade balancing requirements (also Article III-inconsistent), foreign exchange balancing requirements, and domestic sales requirements.[22] The agreement requires that WTO-inconsistent TRIMs must be phased out, and that no new WTO-inconsistent TRIMs are to be introduced during the phaseout period.[23] Industrial countries must complete the phaseout within two years, developing countries within five years, and least-developed countries within seven years. These transition periods may be extended for developing and least-developed countries under certain circumstances. All TRIMs subject to the phaseout requirement had to be notified to WTO within 90 days of the agreement's entry into force.

Only some 19 countries have notified TRIMs subject to phase-out commitments since WTO entered into force. The Asian countries among them are India, Malaysia, Pakistan, Philippines, and Thailand. The GATT's Trade Policy Review Mechanism reports have identified Bangladesh, India, Indonesia, Korea, Malaysia, Philippines, and Thailand as countries which maintain one particular kind of TRIM — local content requirements (Low and Subramanian 1995). A number of the notifications of WTO-inconsistent TRIMs were made after the 90-day deadline established for this purpose, and more may be made. A potential source of difficulty for countries that have not notified their WTO-inconsistent TRIMs is that their trading partners may decide that a failure to do so on time would be grounds for denying the countries concerned their right to the phaseout period. This would establish a requirement for immediate elimination of WTO-inconsistent measures. Another potential source of difficulty is that the provisions of the TRIMs agreement are unlikely to offer sufficient guidance in all cases as to whether particular measures are inconsistent.

Investment Issues in a Broader Setting

While the TRIMs discussions continued in Geneva during the latter half of the 1980s, within the narrow confines of the agreed negotiating mandate, significant changes were taking place in the world economy and in the attitudes of policymakers. The role of FDI as an instrument for promoting growth and development was being reappraised. In some ways, these developments left the TRIMs discussions behind. But the commitment in the TRIMs agreement to consider within five years whether further provisions should be negotiated on investment and competition policy is clearly a reflection of new attitudes toward FDI.

Whether as a consequence or a contributing factor, the explosion of FDI from the mid-1980s onward provided the backdrop against which new attitudes and policy stances were developing. While investment inflows averaged $50 billion per annum in the 1981 to 1985 period, they more than tripled to $155 billion per annum from 1986 to 1990 (Low and Subramanian 1995). As Table 7 shows, Asian countries were among the preferred FDI destinations during the latter period, and this trend appears to have continued into the 1990s. Moreover, FDI growth has been spread across many sectors (Julius 1994).

Several factors explain why many governments that used to show an inclination toward rationing and conditioning the entry of FDI into their markets now go to some lengths to encourage these flows. Trade liberalization, and market-oriented policy reform more generally, has replaced an earlier emphasis on the role of government involvement in resource allocation decisions. Governments have become less confident that they are better placed than markets to deliver economic prosperity. Outward-oriented trade policies have emphasized the need to compete on world markets on the basis of productive efficiency, which in turn calls for new investment in modern plant and continual upgrading of human skills. Modern technology, especially in transport and communications, has given a fillip to globalized production structures, blurring the old distinctions between trade and investment as alternative means of securing access to markets (Organisation for Economic Co-operation and Development [OECD] 1995).

Governments have lost some of their earlier distrust of transnational corporations, and the fear that uncontrolled, they would act in ways contrary to the national economic interest. This is partly because of the realization that these corporations will have to compete with each other if they do not operate behind government-granted market-entry barriers. In other words, many of the markets in which they operate are contestable (Graham 1995). It is also because of a growing appreciation of transnational corporations as purveyors of skills and modern technology.

How, if at all, does all this translate into intergovernmental agreements on investment policy? Some pointers are already discernible from various regional integration initiatives with investment provisions. The North American Free Trade Agreement, for example, contains a comprehensive investment agreement based on MFN, national treatment and a negative list of exceptions. The Asia-Pacific Economic Cooperation (APEC) forum has drawn up a set of nonbinding investment principles. The nonbinding principles cover transparency issues, nondiscrimination, national treatment, incentives, performance requirements, expropriation and compensation, repatriation and convertibility, settlement of disputes, temporary entry of technical and managerial personnel, avoidance of double taxation, investor behavior, and barriers to capital exports. The fact that adherence to the principles remains voluntary will reduce the influence that the principles exert on government policy, but the initiative represents a first step in the direction of international commitments on investment policies for the countries concerned.

OECD has worked for many years on investment issues, and has established Codes of Liberalization and a National Treatment Instrument. Beginning in 1991, OECD has been working on a multilateral agreement on investment (MAI).[24] The proposal establishes a two-year time frame for completing negotiations. It seeks to set a "high standard" of liberalization covering both the establishment and postestablishment phase of investment, to provide full protection for investment, and to create effective dispute settlement and enforcement arrangements. An MAI would be legally binding, and would adopt MFN and national treatment as generally applicable basic principles. Exceptions to the principles would be made explicit through a negative list of exceptions, upon which future negotiations would take place. Because OECD has selective membership, arrangements would be made to permit nonmembers to participate in some so far unspecified manner in the negotiations. The issue of where an MAI would stand in relation to existing WTO arrangements such as GATS, TRIMs, and TRIPS also has to be addressed. The GATS approach to national treatment will not meld in a straightforward manner with an investment agreement that takes national treatment as a principle from which departures are only possible through inscription on a negative list. Moreover, it is probable that some non-OECD governments will have misgivings about participation in an exercise in which they may see themselves as less-than-full negotiating partners.

Whatever the short-term outcome of efforts in APEC, OECD, and elsewhere to establish international rules on investment, the interest of governments in doing so is unlikely to wane in the foreseeable future. Among the reasons that can be cited to justify attempts to draw up multilateral investment rules are that domestic reforms can be "locked in" through international commitments, that such commitments will provide greater predictability and security for foreign investors, and that governments can cooperate to avoid wasteful competition through investment incentive packages. Although the details of possible investment agreements are not discussed here,[25] there are many issues on which governments may disagree. This makes it important for governments to define clearly their priorities.

Conclusions

The foregoing discussion has attempted to explain what the Uruguay Round achieved in the areas of services and trade-related investment measures, and to gauge the significance of these endeavors for Asian countries. As a first multilateral attempt to establish disciplines and a framework for liberalization, GATS made some headway, but has left a considerable amount to be done. By restricting the applicability of many rules only to those sectors or activities subject to specific commitments, the coverage of GATS disciplines is limited by the propensity of governments to schedule commitments. Of the two options to improve upon this situation, making more of the rules generally applicable or expanding the coverage of sectoral commitments, it is the latter approach that is more likely to achieve progress, although there is doubtless also a role for the former.

More careful analysis than has been possible here would be required to determine the degree of liberalization achieved through the framework and the specific commitments. What is more certain is that commitments under GATS have created a benchmark that guarantees defined levels of market access, and against which future liberalization can be undertaken. The "double exit" possibilities offered by selective scheduling (combined with relatively few rules of general application) together with market access and national treatment limitations in schedules will become less permissive as sectoral coverage expands. But there is also scope for enhancing liberalization through the imposition of more stringent rules on the nature of limitations on market access and national treatment, especially if the role of price-based over quantity-based limitations were to be emphasized.

An acute dearth of trade and output data for services restricts analysis of the significance and reach of GATS. An effort was made, however, to provide some indication of the sectoral coverage of scheduled commitments. More work is required to evaluate the relative importance of specific commitments, the gaps in specific commitments, and the importance of market access and national treatment limitations where specific commitments have been made. Some attention was paid to the continuing negotiations on the movement of natural persons, trade in financial services, telecommunications, and maritime transport. It was argued that access to efficient and competitively priced (factor and nonfactor) producer services was a key ingredient of competitive success across a wide range of economic activities. Thus, even if countries do not have any immediate export interests in the sectors concerned, they nevertheless have an important stake in open access arrangements.

It was shown that the TRIMs negotiations in the Uruguay Round were narrowly based and achieved little more than to reiterate the relevance of GATT rules on national treatment and the use of quantitative restrictions, and establish a timetable for the elimination of nonconforming TRIMs. On the other hand, the mandate in the TRIMs agreement to give further consideration to investment and competition policy corresponds to an evolving interest among a number of governments in establishing new international rules on the subject. Some work has already been done in the context of regional agreements. The case for an open international investment regime is very similar to that for an open trade regime, and much the same arguments apply when considering the merits of establishing international rules in the area. It is becoming more urgent for governments to evaluate where their interests lie in this matter.

Annex

MAIN PROVISIONS OF THE GENERAL AGREEMENT ON TRADE AND SERVICES

Scope and Definition

As noted previously, Part I (Article I) of GATS establishes the scope of the agreement, defines trade in services, and specifies sectoral coverage. Article I states that the agreement applies to measures taken by central, regional, or local governments and authorities, and nongovernmental bodies in the exercise of powers delegated by central, regional, or local government authorities. GATS excludes services supplied in the exercise of governmental authority, and these are defined as services which are not supplied on an economical basis or in competition with one or more services suppliers.

Trade in services is defined in terms of four modes of supply. Mode 1 involves cross-border supply of services, and is recognizable as equivalent in principle to cross-border flows of goods. Mode 2 concerns consumption abroad. Consumption abroad is straightforward where consumers actually travel to the territory of another party to the agreement and consume services there, such as tourism. Slightly less straightforward is the case where consumption abroad occurs without the consumer actually traveling to the territory of the supplier of the service. There are cases where, at the margin, it is difficult to tell whether the consumption taking place is in effect a Mode 1 or a Mode 2 transaction. Mode 3 involves the commercial presence of the supplier in the territory of the consumer. This is sometimes referred to as the investment mode, and the trade covered under this mode is referred to as establishment trade. Finally, Mode 4 relates to the temporary movement of natural persons. Natural persons may either be employees of services suppliers, or independent services suppliers in their own right.

General Obligations and Disciplines

Part II of GATS contains general obligations and disciplines, although some of the provisions in Part II only apply in relation to specific commitments made in the schedules. Article II spells out the MFN principle, which is intended to apply to all services activities. It requires that signatories accord services and services suppliers of any signatory treatment no less favorable than that accorded to any other service or services supplier of any other country. Unfortunately, negotiators could not agree in the Uruguay Round to give MFN treatment to all signatories in all sectors, and the Annex on Article II exemptions permitted signatories to schedule exemptions from MFN treatment. However, these exemptions could only be taken at the time of entry into force of the agreement,[26] and would be reviewed after five years. Although no firm commitment exists on the elimination of MFN exemptions, it is stated in the Annex that "in principle," exemptions should be eliminated within ten years. If no exemptions of this kind had been permitted, it is highly probable that entire sectors would have simply been removed from the purview of GATS.[27]

Most MFN reservations, with the notable exception of audiovisual, are expressed in terms of more favorable treatment for particular suppliers in the context of regional arrangements. It may be that these will disappear if the signatories concerned develop their regional agreements to the point where they qualify as MFN departures covered by the regional economic integration provisions of Article V. This is the only other provision in GATS that permits MFN departures. Article V is modeled closely on Article XXIV of GATT, in insisting upon substantial sectoral coverage, the absence of an a priori exclusion of any mode of supply, the elimination of substantially all discrimination among the parties, and the maintenance of all barriers to the trade of third parties at levels no more restrictive than those existing prior to the establishment of the regional agreement. The provisions apply to all services, not just those sectors subject to specific commitments. Article V envisages lesser disciplines for regional agreements involving developing countries, such that greater flexibility would be granted in relation to the interpretation of the provision requiring removal of substantially all discrimination among the parties in the covered sectors. Where a regional integration agreement exclusively involves developing countries, signatories may also apply more favorable treatment to nationally owned or controlled enterprises, notwithstanding the requirement that foreign firms located and undertaking business in the preferential area should be granted the same treatment as national firms.

Signatories involved in regional integration agreements are required to notify them to the Council on Trade in Services, and subsequently to notify any modifications in an agreement. The Council may decide to establish a working party to examine a notified agreement. No experience has yet been accumulated on the interpretation of these provisions. Judging from GATT experience with Article XXIV, and attempts to determine whether customs unions or free trade areas comply with the relevant provisions,[28] Article V will be a source of some difficulty in the first instance, not least because it will be even harder to attain precision in services than in goods.

Article III of GATS contains important transparency provisions. These require signatories to publish all relevant measures of general application affecting trade in services, as well as any international agreements pertaining to or affecting trade in services. Signatories are also required to notify all new or modified laws, regulations, and administrative guidelines affecting scheduled commitments at least once a year, and to supply information relevant to commitments under GATS to other signatories upon request. In fulfillment of the latter obligation, signatories must establish enquiry points within two years.[29] Signatories are entitled to cross-notify any measures of other signatories that they consider relevant to the agreement. Article III (bis) concerns the protection of confidential information.

In addition to the developing-country provisions found in other parts of GATS, Article IV entreats all Members to undertake specific commitments beneficial to developing countries, to strengthen the domestic supply capacity, efficiency, and competitiveness of developing-country services supply. Among measures that might be adopted to achieve these objectives are liberalization of market access in sectors and supply modes of interest to developing countries, and better access to technology, distribution channels, and information networks. Developed countries, and to the extent possible, developing countries are also to establish contact points to facilitate access by developing countries to information on commercial and technical aspects of the supply of services, registration, recognition, and obtaining professional qualifications, and the availability of services technology. Special mention is made of the least-developed countries, both in respect of the support they require in strengthening their services supply capacity, and constraints on their ability to accept specific commitments, which arise from their special economic situation and their development, trade, and financial needs.

The content of Article IV and the way it is worded reflects a long-standing debate in GATT on the nature and extent of developing country rights and obligations in the trading system. A particular point worth noting is that all countries, and not just the developed countries, are expected to help developing countries in the manner specified. This point was never so clearly established in GATT.[30] Second, all commitments under GATS Article IV, except that relating to the establishment of contact points by industrial countries, are of a best-endeavors variety. It is, therefore, doubtful that legally enforceable obligations to undertake positive action have been created under Article IV. Third, no provision has been made for preferences in trade in services, as they exist in the goods sphere through such arrangements as the Generalized System of Preferences. Nor have developing countries been given legal cover for preferences among themselves, as they have in trade in goods under the 1979 Enabling Clause.[31]

Article XIX, dealing with the negotiation of specific commitments (see below) also has provisions specific to developing countries. These state that the process of liberalization of trade in services shall take place with due respect for national policy objectives and the level of development of individual Members, both overall and in individual sectors. Developing countries are to be accorded greater flexibility for opening fewer sectors, liberalizing fewer types of transactions, progressively extending market access in line with their development situation, and when making access to their markets available to foreign suppliers, attaching to such access conditions aimed at achieving the development objectives spelled out in Article IV.

Article VI addresses domestic regulation as this affects trade in services. Signatories are required to ensure that regulations of general application are administered in a reasonable, objective, and impartial manner. The formulation of this commitment in Article IV.1 makes it clear that the obligation is extended only to sectors subject to specific commitments.[32] But Paragraph 2, requiring the establishment of judicial, arbitral, or administrative procedures to ensure that services suppliers can secure remedies for any inappropriate or GATS-inconsistent use of domestic regulations, applies to all services trade covered by the agreement. In cases where no specific commitments exist, however, it appears that recourse would be limited only to general obligations contained in the agreement, most notably those of MFN and transparency.

Article VI also calls for a work program to develop necessary disciplines to ensure that standards and licensing procedures do not constitute unnecessary barriers to trade in services, that they are based on objective and transparent criteria, and that they are no more burdensome than necessary to ensure the quality of a service. Pending the establishment of these disciplines, signatories are to ensure that any technical standards, licensing, or qualification requirements arising in respect of sectors subject to specific commitments neither create barriers to trade nor involve procedures of any kind that could not have been reasonably expected when specific commitments were made.

Article VII focuses on qualification regulations and criteria required to authorize, license, or certify services suppliers. Signatories should not define or apply standards or criteria relating to recognition in a manner that constitutes discrimination or a disguised restriction on trade. Members may recognize education, experience, and qualifications as criteria for licensing or certification, either through harmonization, prior agreement on recognition mutual or otherwise, or autonomously. Any recognition agreements should allow for other signatories to negotiate comparable arrangements. Wherever appropriate, signatories are encouraged to base recognition on multilaterally agreed criteria, and to work toward developing common international standards and criteria for recognition and licensing of relevant services, trades, and professions. Members are required to notify their existing arrangements for recognition, any new arrangements or modifications to existing ones, and participation in any negotiations on recognition. These provisions reflect the tension between universal recognition, which would amount to nondiscrimination in its purest sense, and the desire of governments to maintain a selective approach to recognition on account of concerns about differences in the level of professional standards and qualifications in various countries. The objective of Article VII is to preserve the rights of governments to be selective in matters of recognition, but to ensure that this selectivity is equitable and therefore nondiscriminatory in terms of objective standards. These commitments apply to the universe of services covered by GATS.

Article VIII deals with monopoly suppliers of services. Signatories must not allow monopoly services suppliers to conduct operations in a manner that undermines the MFN obligation or any specific commitments in the schedules. In addition, where a monopoly supplier competes in the supply of a service outside the scope of its monopoly rights, but in a sector which is subject to a specific commitment, the supplier must not take advantage of its monopoly position in a manner inconsistent with the latter commitment. It is noteworthy that whereas GATT's state trading disciplines do not cover national treatment,[33] the GATS provision does so in respect of scheduled commitments, unless an explicit limitation on national treatment has been inscribed in a Member's schedule. Article VIII also permits a Member to request information on the operations of a monopoly supplier in another Member's jurisdiction upon suspicion that the latter is acting inconsistently with Article VIII. One limitation of the present formulation of Article VIII is that it applies only to monopolies or exclusive services suppliers, and not to entities with dominant market positions but less-than-full monopoly power.

Article IX of GATS has no parallel in GATT, and represents the first time that private sector business practices have been explicitly addressed in a multilateral context.[34] In recognition of the fact that certain business practices of services suppliers might frustrate competition and thereby restrict trade, signatories agree to consult on the possible elimination of such measures. This is not a strong obligation, since the only firm commitment is to provide information and consult. Nevertheless, the inclusion of Article IX does raise the prospect that firmer rules, including on substantive aspects of competition policy, may be taken up for consideration at a later date. Along with Article VIII, it also steers the rules in the direction of a competition policy approach to dealing with alleged anticompetitive behavior, and away from an antidumping approach. This is at least in part attributable to the fact that GATS covers investment as well as cross-border trade.

Article X consists of a negotiating mandate on emergency safeguard measures, reflecting the inability of negotiators to agree upon appropriate rules. A safeguard provision would allow a signatory to withdraw benefits contingent upon some occurrence or development adversely affecting domestic production. The absence of safeguard measures at the outset would have presented governments with greater difficulty had they not been given scope through other means to avoid the application of GATS disciplines in sensitive areas.[35] On the other hand, some might argue that safeguard provisions are now required to allow governments to extend their specific commitments into new areas. Article X provides three years in which to negotiate appropriate provisions. The mandate indicates the negotiations on emergency safeguard measures will be based on the principle of nondiscrimination. An interim arrangement is foreseen, pending agreement on safeguards, whereby signatories have slightly more flexibility to modify their scheduled commitments than provided for by Article XXI (see below).

Article XI of GATS is designed to prevent trade in services from being frustrated through restrictions on capital flows or on the means of payment for services. The provisions recognize that current and capital account transactions might be affected if the Article XII balance-of-payments provisions are invoked (see below). Any action under Article XI must be consistent with Members' rights and obligations under the Articles of the International Monetary Fund, and any capital account restrictions must be consistent with a Member's specific commitments, except under Article XII or at the request of the Fund. It may also be noted that a footnote to Article XVI of GATS (see below) requires that any capital flows consequent upon a market access commitment must be permitted to occur.

Article XII allows signatories to adopt or maintain restrictions on trade in services, notwithstanding prior specific commitments, in circumstances of serious balance-of-payments and external financial difficulties. Any restrictions taken must be nondiscriminatory, consistent with the Articles of Agreement of the International Monetary Fund, no more restrictive than necessary to remedy the balance-of-payments problem, of temporary duration, and should avoid unnecessary damage to the commercial, economic, and financial interests of other Members. When determining the incidence of restrictions, signatories are permitted to give priority to services whose supply is more essential to economic and development programs, but restrictions should not be applied so as to afford protection to particular industries.

Article XIII deals with government procurement, which is defined as the purchase of services for governmental purposes and not with a view to commercial resale or use in the supply of services for commercial sale. Procurement is exempted from market access and national treatment provisions (Articles XVI and XVII), as well as from the MFN rule in Article II. This exemption in GATS is similar to what is found in GATT, although in the latter case the exemption applies to national treatment but not the MFN principle. Article XIII of GATS calls for negotiations on government procurement within two years. The existing government procurement agreement under WTO, which was first negotiated in the Tokyo Round (1973 to 1979), is one of the few agreements with membership restricted to less than the full complement of WTO signatories.[36] But the existing agreement covers both goods and services, so the question arises as to how this agreement would relate to any provisions on procurement developed under GATS.

Article XIV and Article XIV (bis) spell out the general and security exceptions of the agreement, and are modeled closely on the equivalent GATT provisions (Articles XX and XXI). These provisions deal with such public interest matters as health, safety, public order, and national security. Areas where GATS provisions place additional emphasis are the protection of privacy in handling personal data, departures from national treatment aimed at ensuring equality of direct tax treatment between domestic and foreign services and services suppliers, and departures from MFN to accommodate differences among signatories arising from existing double taxation agreements. On the other hand, GATT provisions contain a number of items specific to goods which are not repeated such as commodity agreements and natural resource management.

Article XV concerns subsidies, but contains no substantive provisions, reflecting the difficulties faced by negotiators in the Uruguay Round in deciding how subsidies on services activities should be treated. The article contains general GATT-like language recognizing that subsidies may distort trade, but also that they may play an important role in development. Negotiations are called for with a view to establishing subsidy disciplines and examining the case for countervailing remedies. Unlike the negotiations foreseen for safeguards and government procurement, no time frame is set for these negotiations. Pending their outcome, signatories are entitled to request consultations when they consider that adverse effects result from the subsidies of other parties, and such requests are to be accorded sympathetic consideration.

Specific Commitments under the Framework Agreement

Articles XVI, XVII, and XVIII are the core of the agreement as far as specific commitments are concerned. Article XVI deals with market access, which is defined in a very specific manner. Having established that signatories will accord services and services suppliers treatment at least as favorable as that provided for in the schedules, the Article goes on to define six types of market access restrictions that will not be adopted in respect of sectors where market access commitments are undertaken *unless* there is a specification to the contrary in the schedule of specific commitments. In other words, disciplines on market access impediments will apply to scheduled commitments unless a reservation is registered to the contrary. The six impediments or limitations on access are defined as (i) limitations on the number of suppliers; (ii) limitations on the total value of services transactions or assets; (iii) limitations on the total number of services operations or on the total quantity of services output; (iv) limitations on the total number of natural persons that may be employed; (v) measures which restrict or require specific types of legal entity or joint venture; and (vi) limitations on the participation of foreign capital. Article XVI limitations are exhaustive, in the sense that these are the only limitations on market access that Members are permitted to inscribe in their schedules. In practice, this means that certain measures, such as taxation, which could limit market access, are not covered by the Agreement.

Article XVII contains the national treatment provision of the agreement. The approach here is very similar to that of market access, with national treatment applicable only to scheduled commitments, and only then if reservations are not made to the contrary. National treatment is defined in the traditional GATT manner, as treatment no less favorable than that accorded to domestic homologues, in this case services and services suppliers. Article XVII recognizes, however, that the attainment of national treatment may require formally equivalent treatment, or may involve treatment that is not formally equivalent. Thus, Article XVII deals with both de jure and de facto national treatment. As with market access, the greatest number of sectoral commitments subject to national treatment limitations is associated with the commercial presence and movement of natural persons modes of delivery. A significant difference between national treatment in GATT and in GATS is that in the former case, national treatment is established as a principle to be applied across the board,[37] whereas in the latter case, national treatment has been given negotiating currency. It is something to be granted, denied, or qualified, depending on the sector and signatory concerned.

Article XVIII offers the possibility for signatories to negotiate additional commitments not dealt with under the market access and national treatment provisions of Article XVI and Article XVII. These commitments could apply to such matters as qualifications, standards and licensing, and would be inscribed in Members' schedules. Limited use was made of this option in the Uruguay Round negotiations. In the case of telecommunications, however, the additional commitments column has been used by Members subscribing to the regulatory principles. The most important aspect of Article XVIII measures is that they must express commitments favoring more open access, and not additional market barriers.

Progressive Liberalization

Article XIX of GATS establishes a continuing program of future negotiations, the first of which is to begin five years after the entry into force of GATS. Explicit provision for rounds of negotiations is a novel feature of the agreement, with no precedent in GATT. It reflects recognition by governments of the scope that exists for extending the coverage and quality of specific commitments. Article XX deals with the schedules of specific commitments. The tabulation reproduced in Table 12 illustrates the structure of GATS schedules of specific commitments. The purpose of the horizontal section is to avoid repetition, and it contains market access and national treatment limitations that apply to all scheduled sectors. Limitations on market access and national treatment, as well as additional commitments, must be recorded in respect of each of the four modes of supply for every sector entered on the schedule. Entries showing "none" in the market access and national treatment columns mean that no limitations are imposed. The entry "unbound" indicates the complete absence of a market access or national treatment commitment, and would appear in a schedule only if a commitment had been accepted in at least one of the four modes of supply. Partial limitations on market access or national treatment are described against the relevant mode of supply.

Article XX also envisages that commitments may be phased in over time, and this would also be reflected in the schedule of commitments. If both market access and national treatment limitations apply to the same commitment— that is, if an Article XVI measure is applied in a discriminatory fashion as between domestic and foreign services or services suppliers— both restrictions are to appear as a limitation under Article

Table 1A. Example of GATS Schedule of Commitments

Services Activity	Mode of Supply	Limitation on Market Access	Limitation on National Treatment
Part I: Horizontal Commitments			
All Sectors	1. Cross-border	None	None
	2. Consumption abroad	None	None
	3. Commercial presence	None	Subsidies for research and development
	4. Temporary presence of natural persons	Unbound except for intracorporate transferees of executives and senior managers for initial stay of four years; extensions of stays subject to economic needs test	Unbound, except as indicated in market access column
Part II: Sector-specific Commitments			
Accounting Services	1. Cross-border	None	None
	2. Consumption abroad	None	None
	3. Commercial presence	Only natural persons may be registered as auditors	At least one equity partner in a firm must be a permanent resident
	4. Temporary presence of natural persons	Unbound, except as provided in the horizontal section	Unbound, except as provided in the horizontal section
Electronic Data Interchange	1. Cross-border	None	None
	2. Consumption abroad	None	None
	3. Commercial presence	None	None
	4. Temporary presence of natural persons	Unbound, except as provided in the horizontal section	Unbound, except as provided in the horizontal section

XVI and the qualification to national treatment will not appear separately as an Article XVII limitation.

Article XXI sets out procedures for withdrawing or modifying commitments in the schedules. Modifications require renegotiation, and cannot be entertained for three years after the entry into force of a commitment. Exceptions to this time frame were established for the sectoral negotiations in financial services and maritime transport services. A further exception is permitted under the Article X safeguard provisions, where, if good cause is shown, the three-year period can be reduced to one year pending the establishment of safeguard provisions. The negotiations on schedule modifications are designed to compensate affected parties for any withdrawal of benefits. All compensatory adjustments to schedules must be applied on an MFN basis. If agreement on appropriate compensation is not reached, affected parties may go to arbitration. If the modifying party does not implement the findings of arbitration, affected parties are entitled to withdraw equivalent benefits from the modifying Member.

Institutional and Final Provisions

The dispute-settlement provisions of GATS, contained in Article XXII and Article XXIII, rely on the centralized dispute-settlement apparatus of WTO. Article XXII provides for consultation, both bilaterally and through the Council for Trade in Services or the Dispute-Settlement Body. Disputes arising under double taxation agreements are excluded from GATS dispute settlement. Article XXIII establishes the right of signatories to use the mechanisms of the WTO Dispute-Settlement Understanding. Other institutional provisions of GATS concern the establishment of the Council for Trade in Services (Article XXIV), technical cooperation (Article XXV), and relationships with other international organizations (Article XXVI).

Finally, Part VI of GATS contains two articles, one dealing with the denial of benefits and the other with definitions. Article XXVII states that the agreement does not apply to services found to originate in the territory of a non-Member, or where the agreement is not applied between the parties concerned. Article XXVIII contains definitions of terms used in the agreement. These definitions are important to an understanding of the reach of GATS. The definition of "supply," for example, refers to production, distribution, marketing, sale, and delivery of a service. This means that a commercial presence commitment relates to the terms and conditions upon which a services supplier can locate in the host country and upon which operations are carried out. A juridical person is deemed to be "owned" by a Member if more than 50 percent of the equity is owned by persons of that Member, and "controlled" by persons of a Member if such persons have power to name a majority of its directors or otherwise legally to direct its actions. One implication of these definitions is that foreign investors in services industries who fall below the thresholds would not be covered by the agreement.

Annexes, Decisions, and Understanding

Eight annexes appended to GATS, eight related decisions, and an understanding are key elements of the overall services package emerging from the Uruguay Round. The annexes form an integral part of GATS, and relate to MFN exemptions, the movement of natural persons, air transport services, financial services, maritime services, and telecommunications. The sectoral annexes combine several objectives, including restrictions on coverage of the agreement,[38] clearer definition of services activities to which the agreement applies, elaboration of commitments on specific elements of market access, and the establishment of programs of negotiations.

The ministerial decisions, or so-called Related Instruments, are more varied in subject matter. On the sectoral plane, decisions prescribe negotiations on movement of natural persons, financial services, maritime transport services, basic telecommunications services, and professional services. There is also an Understanding on Commitments in Financial Services. The Decision on Professional Services calls for work on professional services, starting with accountancy, but also refers to the work program on professional qualifications, technical standards, and licensing mandated in Article VI (see above). A decision on institutional arrangements establishes the right for the Council on Trade in Services to set up subsidiary bodies to carry out its work, and defines a number of responsibilities falling upon any sectoral committees that may be established. Another decision deals with certain dispute-settlement procedures, such as the establishment of a roster of panelists.

The Decision on Trade in Services and the Environment acknowledges the possibility that environmental protection measures might conflict with GATS provisions, and then goes on to note that the general exceptions in Article XIV may be sufficient to deal with this eventuality. The active part of the decision calls for the WTO Committee on Trade and Environment to determine whether Article XIV is indeed adequate, and also to examine the relevance of intergovernmental environment agreements and their relationship to GATS. The results of this exercise were made a part of the report to the biennial meeting of ministers, held in Singapore toward the end of 1996. The Decision reflects the disquiet of environmental interest groups at the prospect that trade liberalization in services may cause damage to the environment. The references in the Decision to Article XIV indicate the response from a trade policy perspective to these concerns, namely that adequate safeguards against this eventuality already exist in GATS. The sectors most likely to attract attention in this discussion are transportation and tourism.

Notes

[1] Some internationally traded services, such as unrecorded telephone conversations, may also involve instantaneous production and consumption, but in this case the transaction takes place across a frontier and is therefore similar to cross-border exchanges of goods.

[2] Where repeated transactions are required, such as in after-sales services, a continuing local presence is obviously more desirable than long-distance supply.

[3] Information technology is a general term covering computer and communications technology used to generate, process, analyze, and transmit information (World Bank, 1995).

[4] The implied allocation of locally generated output as domestic sales or foreign trade on the basis of the ownership of the equity responsible for production appears to have limited economic relevance. Yet under GATS, governments have assumed obligations in respect of production attributable to foreign equity.

[5] For recent discussions of globalization, see World Bank (1995), Oman (1994), and Julius (1990).

[6] Relatively few analyses exist of GATS. See Hoekman (1995), Hoekman and Sauvé (1994), Altinger and Enders (1995), Sauvé (1994), and Snape (1994).

[7] Both a services supplier and a services consumer could, of course, move to a third jurisdiction. Under GATS, this would be treated as two separate transactions from the point of view of the host country.

[8] Items (e) and (f) refer to restrictions on types of legal entity and participation of foreign capital.

[9] As with Article XVI (market access) limitations entered in the schedules, this is a negative list and not a positive list approach.

[10] Hoekman (1995) also attempted to weight specific commitments according to whether or not they were associated with market access or national treatment limitations. This may help, but the procedure cannot assure that commitments will be appropriately weighted in terms of their relative worth. More far-reaching commitments with limitations may receive a lower weight than minor, but unlimited commitments that are worth far less.

[11] Hoekman (1995) counted 155 sectors, compared with the 149 identified by Altinger and Enders (1995). These different numbers reflect the manner in which the sectoral classification developed for the negotiations has been interpreted, and the differences appear in the tables. The attempt to standardize the sectoral nomenclature used in the Uruguay Round was only partially successful because of excessive aggregation. In practice, countries departed from the nomenclature in certain circumstances, and even introduced entirely new sectoral descriptions. Members recognize the need to address this problem in the context of future negotiations.

[12] PRC has been included in the Table 9 data even though PRC is not a WTO Member and has no commitments under GATS. The commitments recorded for PRC were the result of incomplete accession negotiations, and the precise content of PRC's schedule of specific commitments may be different from this initial schedule when PRC eventually joins WTO.

[13] Some commitments also refer to the sales representatives of services enterprises.

[14] Insurance services include direct insurance (life and nonlife), reinsurance and retrocession, insurance intermediation (including brokerage and agency), and auxiliary services relating to insurance (including consultancy, actuarial, risk assessment, and claim settlement services). Banking and other financial services include acceptance of deposits from the public; lending; financial leasing; payment and money transmission services; guarantees and commitments; trading in financial instruments (money market instruments, foreign exchange, derivatives, exchange rate and interest rate instruments, transferable securities, and other negotiable instruments and financial assets); securities trading; money brokering; asset management; settlement and clearing services for financial assets; provision and transfer of financial information and data processing; and advisory, intermediation, and other auxiliary financial services.

[15] Paragraph 3(a) of the Annex on Financial Services.

[16] Some 76 countries made specific commitments on financial services, and many of them, including the EU, left these commitments in their schedules pending the outcome of the negotiations.

[17] Participants willing to do so included the Quad: the US, the EU, Canada, and Japan, and a few other industrial countries.

[18] It should be noted that the access rights spelled out in the Annex on Telecommunications are already established in a more generic manner in Article XXVIII of GATS, where "measures by Members affecting trade in services" are defined to include "access to and use of, in connection with the supply of a service, services which are required . . . to be offered to the public generally."

[19] The Jones Act requires that US coastal trade should be conducted by US-owned, US-built and US-operated vessels.

[20] The Agreement spells out specific criteria relating to income and unemployment levels to determine whether a region is to be considered disadvantaged.

[21] It is noteworthy that some industrial countries, such as Australia, also had misgivings about multilateral efforts to influence national investment policies.

[22] Other TRIMs identified in the Uruguay Round discussions, but not mentioned in the illustrative list annexed to the TRIMs agreement, include manufacturing requirements, export performance requirements, product mandating requirements, manufacturing limitations, technology transfer requirements, licensing requirements, remittance restrictions, and local equity requirements. The TRIMs agreement would have needed to go further than reiterating the established interpretations of GATT Article III and Article XI to cover most of these measures. A notable omission of the TRIMs agreement, however, was its silence on export performance requirements which are analogous to local requirements on the import side, and strongly resemble export subsidies, which are prohibited on manufactured goods under WTO.

[23] It is provided, however, that existing TRIMs may be imposed on new enterprises during the phaseout period if this is considered necessary in order not to place existing enterprises subject to the same measures at a disadvantage.

[24] Until recently, the OECD initiative was referred to as MIA (multilateral investment agreement), but the US objected that this acronym also applied to persons "missing in action."

[25] See Low (1995) for such a discussion.

[26] Any subsequent withdrawal of MFN treatment, except in the framework of an economic integration agreement (see discussion of Article V), requires a waiver under Article IX of the Marrakesh Agreement establishing the World Trade Organization.

[27] As it is, some air transport services were excluded from GATS coverage.

[28] Rarely have GATT members been able to agree that a customs union or a free trade area conforms with the provisions of Article XXIV, largely because the concept of "substantially all" and the notion of full elimination of all trade barriers have not been given sufficient precision to squeeze out competing interpretations of the required standards for compliance (Low 1993). Article V of GATS attempts to provide some specificity to the notion of "substantial sectoral coverage" by requiring that regional integration agreements should not provide for the a priori exclusion of any services sector or mode of supply.

[29] Developing countries may have flexibility in relation to the time limit for establishing enquiry points.

[30] The relevant GATT texts were Part IV of the General Agreement and the 1979 Enabling Clause. Between them these texts contained a best-endeavors clause entreating developed countries to encourage developing country trade growth, recognition of the principle of nonreciprocity, an expression of the notion of graduation, and permanent legal cover for trade preferences in favor of developing countries.

[31] A preferential element would, however, be permitted under GATS Article V.3, but only in the broader context of a regional economic integration agreement.

[32] In addition, Paragraph 3 requires that where authorization is required for the supply of a service on which a specific commitment has been made, the decision on such authorization must be promptly made, and any information must also be provided upon request as to the status of an application.

[33] This point has been the subject of some debate, but significant elements of GATT jurisprudence point in the direction of excluding national treatment from GATT Article XVII requirement that state trading enterprises act solely in accordance with commercial considerations (Article XVII.1(b) of GATT 1994).

[34] The Havana Charter contained provisions on restrictive business practices, but these died along with the stillborn International Trade Organization (Jackson 1969).

[35] Scope for restricting the application of GATS to particular activities or disciplines resides in the choice of whether to accept market access commitments in respect of particular sectors and subsectors, or particular modes of supply, and whether to impose limitations on market access or national treatment in respect of scheduled commitments.

[36] This is one of the so-called plurilateral agreements, for which membership is optional and must be separately negotiated. The other plurilateral agreements are the Agreement on Trade in Civil Aircraft, the International Dairy Agreement, and the International Bovine Meat Agreement.

[37] Exceptions to national treatment under GATT exist in respect of subsidies and government procurement.

[38] The two Annexes which specify restrictions on the coverage of GATS are those on financial services and air transport services. The one on financial services will be discussed below in relation to the financial services work program. On air transport, however, where no work program was initiated, it may be noted that the purpose of the Annex is to exclude traffic rights and services directly related to the exercise of traffic rights, from the purview of the agreement. GATS is to cover only aircraft repair and maintenance services, selling and marketing of air transport services, and computer reservation systems. The coverage question is to be reviewed at least every five years.

References

Altinger, L., and A. Enders, 1995. "The Scope and Depth of GATS Commitments." Mimeographed.

Balasubramanyam, V. N., 1991. "Putting TRIMs to Good Use." *World Development* 19:1215-24.

Bhagwati, J., 1984. "Splintering and Disembodiment of Services and Developing Nations." *The World Economy* 7:133-44.

Cooper, R., 1988. "Survey of Issues and Review." In L. V. Castle and C. Findlay, eds., *Pacific Trade in Services*. Sydney: Allen and Unwin.

Graham, E. M., 1995. "Competition Policy and the New Trade Agenda." In *New Dimensions of Market Access in a Globalizing World Economy*. Paris: OECD.

Hoekman, B., 1995. "Tentative First Steps: An Assessment of the Uruguay Round Agreement on Services." Paper presented at the World Bank Conference on The Uruguay Round and the Developing Countries, 26-27 January, Washington, D.C.

Hoekman, B., and P. Sauvé, 1994. Liberalizing Trade in Services. Discussion Paper No. 243. World Bank, Washington, D.C.

Jackson, J. H., 1969. *World Trade and the Law of GATT*. Charlottesville: The Michie Company.

Julius, D., 1990. *Global Companies and Public Policy: The Growing Challenge of Direct Investment*. London: Pinter.

_____, 1994. "International Direct Investment: Strengthening the Policy Regime." Paper presented at the IIE Conference on Managing the World Economy of the Future: Lessons from the First Fifty Years After Bretton Woods.

Low, P., 1993. *Trading Free: U.S. Trade Policy and the GATT*. New York: The Twentieth Century Fund Press.

_____, 1995. "Market Access through Market Presence: A Look at the Issues." In *New Dimensions of Market Access in a Globalizing World Economy*. Paris: OECD.

Low, P., and A. Subramanian, 1995. "TRIMs in the Uruguay Round: An Unfinished Business?" Paper presented at the World Bank Conference on The Uruguay Round and the Developing Countries, 26-27 January, Washington, D.C.

Maskus, E., and D. R. Eby, 1990. "Developing New Rules and Disciplines on Trade-Related Investment Measures." *The World Economy* 13:523-39.

Organisation for Economic Co-operation and Development (OECD), 1995. *New Dimensions of Market Access in a Globalizing World Economy.* Paris: OECD.

Oman, C., 1994. *Globalization and Regionalization: The Challenge for Developing Countries.* Paris: OECD Development Centre.

Sampson, G., and R. H. Snape, 1985. "Identifying the Issues in Trade in Services." *The World Economy* 8(2):171-81.

Sauvé, P., 1994. "The General Agreement on Trade in Services: Much Ado About What?" Mimeographed.

Snape, R., 1994. "Services in the Uruguay Round." In *The New World Trading System: Readings.* Paris: OECD.

United Nations Conference on Trade and Development, 1994. *World Investment Report.*

World Bank, 1995. *Global Economic Prospects.* Washington, D.C.: World Bank.

544-47

Comments on "Impact of the Uruguay Round on Asia: Trade in Services and Trade-Related Investment Measures"

by

Richard H. Snape

Patrick Low's chapter gives an excellent description and analysis of the General Agreement on Trade in Services (GATS) and Trade-Related Investment Measures (TRIMs). Like him I shall focus mainly on GATS. I agree with his general assessment, though some of my emphases may be a little different.

But first I should make the point that in talking about the implications of the Uruguay Round agreements for Asia, the primary consideration is the implications for the global trading system, of which Asia is a part. For an unhealthy global system and the associated lack of growth of international trade and income that will accompany this will harm all countries. And generally, Asian countries would be harmed more by a less healthy system than they would gain by any country or industry protection which they may secure as part of (and as contributing to) that less healthy system. Thus, I suggest that in looking at the implications of GATS and TRIMs (and the other Uruguay Round agreements) for Asia, the main concern for Asian countries should be how to foster that system, and not how to protect specific industries or secure special benefits, for the former is what will bring them the greatest and lasting benefit. But, of course, lobbies generally support specific industries rather than the system as a whole.

So, how does GATS rate as a liberalizing international agreement? As Patrick has said, though it has achieved something, and there has been much learning, one must judge it to be well short of the General Agreement on Tariffs and Trade (GATT) in terms of a liberalizing trade agreement. But then services are much more complicated, and the "trade in services agreement" waters are relatively uncharted as compared with the "trade in goods agreement" waters, not just in the 1980s and 1990s, but also as compared with the "trade in goods agreement" waters at the time of GATT's birth in 1947.

GATS is an extraordinarily ambitious agreement. In one sense it is a more general agreement than GATT for it covers all modes of delivery or services, including investment. In contrast, GATT still has little to say regarding foreign investment, even though foreign investment in the production of goods for the supply of a market may often be an alternative to exporting to that market, and the decision to do one or the other will be influenced by the size of trade and investment barriers. For some services there is a choice between cross-border trade and foreign investment; for other services a foreign presence may be necessary to supply the market. GATS addresses both the trade and investment "modes of delivery" and thus has the potential for preventing distortions between the two forms of delivery for particular services which can occur when only one mode of delivery is addressed. But that has remained a potential, for not only have the scheduled commitments been modest, little attention has been given to securing consistency among the commitments relating to the different modes of delivery for particular services.

Incidentally, the different approaches to investment by GATT and GATS have created problems for the Trade Policy Review Mechanism of the World Trade Organization (WTO). That part of a country review which relates to GATT does not look at investment regulations; that part which related to GATS does.

As Patrick mentions, the taxonomy of forms of services trade was set out originally in an article by Sampson and Snape (1985). Setting out this taxonomy did not mean that the authors necessarily thought it would be a good idea to have one agreement covering all the modes of delivery. Indeed Snape (1988:85) argued that "it would seem appropriate to keep the negotiations that relate to those forms of services trade that involve the international movement of people or capital quite separate from negotiations for other services, and to separate the negotiations for labor from those for capital." This separation could still occur, for if negotiations regarding international investment proceed on a wider front, involving both goods and services investment — as foreshadowed in TRIMs — then the sections of GATS relating to investment (and the scheduled commitments) may have to be revisited and probably amended.

While in regard to the modes of delivery, GATS is more general than GATT 1947 or GATT 1994, and certainly in terms of inaugural membership it is much more general than GATT 1947; in some other regards it is markedly less general. The lack of generality arises from the predominantly positive rather than negative list approach with regard to inclusion of sectors and trade measures. The difference of treatment centers on the national treatment provisions of the two agreements and the "market access" provisions of GATS.

In GATT, national treatment does not mean free trade. Rather, it amounts to all forms of trade barriers other than tariffs being prescribed (though some can be used in exceptional circumstances). GATT applies to all goods, though some goods have been extracted from coverage, in particular in agriculture and clothing and textiles. Thus, there is a negative list approach to all goods and to all barriers other than tariffs. Tariff bindings are negotiated on specific goods, so that only tariffs are dealt with on a positive list basis.

This contrasts sharply with the GATS approach, as has been detailed by Patrick. For goods it was easy to identify a form of barrier — the tariff — that is relatively nondistorting, which can be measured easily, is transparent, and which is amenable to negotiation and cross-product trade-offs. It was a bold and important move by the framers of GATT to ban (subject to exceptions) all other forms of barrier. But as Patrick points out, many of the policy measures which affect services trade are highly product-specific, are regulatory, and hence, affect prices in indirect manners, and often could not be converted into "tariff equivalents."

A dozen years ago, Jan Tumlir said regarding goods trade, "As long as the sectoral view dominates the trade policy of the major trading countries, only a progressive tightening of the existing systems of industrial protection can be expected, a development that can only multiply economic difficulties for the countries concerned and opportunities for conflict among them" (Tumlir 1982:33). Developments in agriculture and the Multifiber Arrangement support this view. And yet, in services the negotiations are almost entirely on a sector-by-sector approach. The sector-specific approach induces "total" rather then first-differences reciprocity, discourages cross-product or cross-sector trade-offs, and focuses the attention of vested interests. We need, I think, to address the sector and mode specificity problems and reduce them.

There was very little enthusiasm, if any, for the tariffication — even where it is possible — of the barriers to services trade. One negative list manner which could have reduced the specificity and which could have been adopted is the prescription of all barriers to trade, unless they are scheduled. This is the path of NAFTA (in contrast to the earlier US-Canada Trade Agreement) and the Closer Economic Relations Agreement between Australia and New Zealand. It has been suggested that lessons learned in the negotiation of GATS led to the switch to negative listing in NAFTA. But this approach may be too bold for a multilateral agreement.

Another less bold but essentially negative list approach is to permit one or two specified forms of barrier that cross many or all service sectors, and perhaps one which is specific to each sector, and then proscribe all others. The legitimized barriers would then parallel tariffs under GATT and would be the focus for subsequent negotiations.

Perhaps the best hope for change will arise if an international investment agreement is negotiated. As mentioned above, GATS could then be revisited and reformulated as an agreement which is less general with respect to potential mode coverage, but more general with respect to actual commitments.

References

Sampson, G., and R. H. Snape, 1985. "Identifying the Issues in Trade in Services." *The World Economy* 8(2):171-81.

Snape, R. H., 1988. "Prospects for Liberalising Services Trade." In L. V. Castle and C.Findlay, eds., *Pacific Trade in Services.* Sydney: Allen and Unwin.

Tumlir, J., 1982. "International Economic Order: Can the Trend Be Reversed?" *The World Economy* 5(1):31-43.

AUTHOR INDEX

Abbot, K. W., 372–374, 393, 394, 397, 420, 421
Alam, A., 221
Altinger, L., 501, 502, 512, 539, 540
Andere, E., 368
Anderson, K., 89, 241, 253, 368, 418, 457, 458, 463
Arase, D., 118
Ariff, M., 147
Asian Development Bank, 5, 40, 179, 246, 253

Bagwell, K., 106
Balasubramanyam, V. N., 521
Baldwin, R., 109, 157
Banks, G., 89
Barro, R. J., 182
Basic Instruments and Selected Documents (BISD), 369, 392, 417–421
Beghin, J., 237, 241
Bergsten, C. F., 106, 112
Bertola, G., 162
Bhagwati, J., 6, 40, 49, 53, 59, 70, 75–77, 97, 106, 108, 111, 117–119, 186, 210–215, 221, 222, 239, 372, 427, 485
Bhala, R., 402
Bliss, C., 117
Boltuck, R., 372, 418
Bond, E., 106, 114, 120
Borjas, G. J., 180
Bradford, C., Jr., 119
Braga, C., 86, 251, 307
Brandao, A. S. P., 460, 461, 467, 468

Brecher, R. A., 146
Brown, D., 103, 111, 113, 120, 209, 210, 221
Bureau of National Affairs, 399
Business News Advisory, 237

Cable, V., 280
Calvo, G. A., 148
Canonero, G., 40, 97, 102, 103
Cass, R., 372, 418
Cecchini, P., 90
Chakwin, N., 119
Charnovitz, S., 205, 221
Chaudhry, S. A., 276, 295
Chichilnisky, G., 233
Chinn, J. C., 328, 333, 353
Chinn, M. D., 152, 154, 162
Claessens, S., 149
Clarida, R., 368, 417
Cline, W. R., 279
Collingsworth, T., 213, 221
Congress of the United States, Congressional Budget Office (CBO), 370, 371, 417, 418
Cooper, R., 485
Copeland, B. R., 234, 250
Corden, W. M., 160
Cox, D., 86
Cuchan, P., 149
Cuthbertson, S., 466
Cyrus, T. 119

Dahejia, V., 214
Davenport, M., 8, 90
Davey, W. J., 370, 418
de la Torre, A., 117
de Melo, J., 40, 110, 117, 294

de Rosa, D., 40, 83, 102, 103, 119
Deardorff, A., 103, 111, 113, 120,
    209, 210, 221, 328, 351, 357
Dehejia, V., 75
Dhar, B., 469
Dhar, S., 115, 118
Diaz-Alejandro, C. F., 146
Dicke, H., 118
Dimaranan, B., 284, 300, 301
Diwan, I., 328
Dornbusch, R., 118
Duncan, R., 442, 461-62, 464-65

Easterly, W., 118
Eby, D. R., 520
Echeverria, R. G., 334
Edwards, S., 119
Eliott, K. A., 222
Encarnation, D., 118
Enders, A., 501, 502, 512, 539,
    540
Esty, D. C., 253
Ethier, W. J., 187
European Community Commission,
    369, 370, 372, 383
Evans, P., 246

Faini, R., 294
Feder, G., 119
Fernandez, R., 111
Fields, G., 16, 174, 215–218
Fieleke, N., 117
Financial Times, 133
Findlay, R., 106, 189
Finger, J. M., 368
Fischer, B., 159
Fischer, G., 455, 456
Fong, P., 189
Food and Agriculture Organization
    (FAO), 244, 461. 462, 464,
    466

Francois, J. F., 301, 467
Francois, M., 290, 292
Frankel, J., 94, 111, 112, 114,
    117–120, 139, 152, 154, 162
Freeman, G. P., 184, 185, 199
Frohbert, K., 455, 456
Froot, K., 105
Fry, M. J., 146

Gadbaw, R. M., 333
Gardner, B., 454
General Agreement on Tariffs and
    Trade, (GATT), 35, 287, 294,
    307, 395, 477, 478
Glick, R., 153, 159
Goldin I., 457, 459, 462, 473
Golub, S. S., 152
Gooptu, S., 149
Goto, J., 167
Gould, T. W., 213, 221
Graham, E. M., 523
Greenaway, D., 89
Greenpeace, 250
Greenway, D., 195
Grossman, G., 105, 107, 109, 328,
    333, 352, 353
Gundlach, E., 89, 90

Haaland, J. I., 89
Hafbauer, G., 222
Hamada, K., 167
Hamid, J., 276, 295
Hamilton, B., 180
Hamilton, C., 118, 276
Harris, R., 86
Harrison, G. W., 284
Harvey, P. J., 213, 221
Hathaway, D. E., 442, 446, 448,
    450, 473
Haveman, J., 105
Hayes, M., 417

Helpman, E., 105, 107, 109, 180, 328
Hertel, T., 284, 300, 301
Hettige, H., 241, 261
Hewison, G., 238
Hiemenz, U., 89, 90
Hirayama, K., 159, 162
Hoekman, B., 371, 505, 539, 540
Holmer, A., 417
Horlick, G., 376, 377
Hudec, R., 75, 221, 372, 393, 403, 418, 419, 420, 427
Hufbauer, G., 7, 8, 88, 117
Huff, B., 458
Hutton, E., 295

Ingco, M. D., 36, 38, 442, 446, 448, 450, 473
Ingram, J., 167
Intal, P., Jr., 233, 241, 251
International Finance Corporation (IFC), 149
International Intellectual Property Alliance, 321
International Monetary Fund (IMF), 5, 40, 94
International Textiles and Clothing Bureau (ITCB), 273

Jabara, C., 459, 460
Jackson, J. H., 418, 473, 542
Jackson, T., 83
Jaggi, G., 83
Johnson, D. G., 437
Julius, D., 494, 523, 539

Kahler, M., 112, 117, 118, 120
Kawaguchi, O., 145
Kelly, M., 117
Khan, M., 147, 150
Khanna, Sri Ram, 276

Kim, J. I., 195
Kirmani, N., 275
Klevorick, A. K., 330, 333
Knudsen, O., 457, 459, 462, 473
Koekoek, A., 89
Kohona, P., 397
Konan, D. E., 329, 353
Kosters, M., 75
Kreinin, M., 7, 8, 86, 87, 89–91
Kremer, M., 118
Kreuger, A., 77, 87, 107, 108, 117
Krishna, K., 283
Krishna, P., 107, 109
Krueger, A. O., 479
Krugman, P., 92, 105, 106, 111, 120, 155, 156, 162, 179, 180
Krupp, C., 369, 417
Kumar, K., 276
Kuyvenhoven, A., 89
Kwan, C. H., 118

Landes, W. M., 352
Langhammer, R., 89, 90, 118
Lau, L., 195
Lawrence, R., 75, 110, 214
Leiderman, L., 148
Levin, R. C., 330, 333
Levinson, A., 40, 75, 76
Levy, P., 109, 112
Lewis, J., 40, 103
Lim, L., 189
Lineman, H., 118
Lopez, R., 235
Low, P., 160, 293, 541, 521, 522
Lucas, R. E., Jr., 155, 156, 162, 233, 234, 241, 261
Lutz, M., 107

MacAleese, D., 90
Mahathir bin Mohammed, 214
Mamingi, N., 149

Mansfield, E., 330, 333, 334, 336
Markusen, J. R., 187
Martin, P., 261
Martin, W., 103, 284, 300, 301, 460, 461, 467, 468
Maskus, E., 520
Maskus, K. E., 328, 329, 353
Matthews, A., 90
Mayer, T., 275
McCleery, R., 8, 87
McDonald B., 301, 467
McKinnon, R., 167
Mensbrugghe van der, D., 457, 459, 462, 473
Messerlin, P., 368
Mo, J., 199
Mohanty, S. K., 469
Mokre, M. E., 276
Molajani, P., 275
Molle, W., 90
Montiel, P. J., 139, 151, 153
Moreddu, C., 458
Moreno, R., 153, 159
Mori, H. 176
Mundell, R., 167, 187

Nagaoka, S., 107
Nelson, R. R., 330, 333
Nicolaides, P., 368
Nogues, J., 311
Noland, M., 86
Nordstrom, H., 290, 292, 301, 467
Norman, V. D., 89
Nunnenkamp, P., 89, 90

Obstfeld, M., 179
Ogawa, N., 314, 318
Oman, C., 539
Organisation for Economic Co-operation and Development

(OECD), 53, 216, 235, 275, 294, 485, 423, 523, 524
Oye, K., 112

Page, S., 8, 90, 118
Palmeter, D., 376, 382, 417, 427
Panagariya, A., 8, 9, 19, 40, 41, 83, 103, 106-108, 110, 111, 115, 117–119
Panchamukhi, V. R., 469
Parikh, K. S., 455, 456
Parris, K., 458
Pearce, D., 89
Perroni, C., 108
Petri, P., 103, 119
Plummer, M., 7, 8, 86, 90, 91
Posner, R., 352
Pray, C. E., 334
Primo, A., 86
Pritchett, L., 118

Quibria, M. G., 19, 179, 195
Quintos, P., 233, 241, 251

Radetzki, M., 234
Rao, N., 19
Razin, A., 187
Reinhart, C., 148
Reisen, H., 159
Repetto, R., 237
Reuters, 236, 244, 245, 252, 253
Rhee, Y. W., 280
Richards, T., 333
Riedel, J., 157
Robertson, D., 442, 461, 462, 464, 465
Robinson, S., 40, 103
Rodrik, D., 110, 111, 117, 119, 309, 328
Roland-Holst, D., 237, 241
Rom, M., 389, 391, 419

Romer, D., 119
Romer, P., 156, 162, 360
Ruggie, J. G., 388
Rutherford, T. F., 284

Sachs, J., 75
Sadka, E., 187
Safadi, R., 8, 86
Sala-i-Martin, X., 119, 182, 186, 187
Sampson, G., 492, 546
Sathirathai, S., 438
Sauve, P., 539
Saxonhouse, G., 114, 117, 120
Schatz, H., 75
Schiff, M., 188
Schott, J. J., 7, 8, 41, 88, 117, 222
Schwartz, M., 330
Scott, M. F. G., 156
Sedjo, R., 341
Shah, N., 175–177
Shapiro, C., 181, 352
Siamwalla, A., 438, 472
Siebeck, W. E., 328
Siebert, H., 237
Simon, J., 184
Sinclair, P., 106
Slaughter, M. J., 214
Snape, R. H., 492, 539, 546
Solow, R., 181
Srinivasan, T. N., 40, 76, 97, 102, 103, 195, 210, 215, 219, 239
Staiger, R., 106
Steil, B., 221
Stein, E., 94, 113, 114, 118–120
Stern, R., 103, 111, 113, 120, 209, 210, 221
Stiglitz, J., 181
Stoeckl, A., 89, 466
Subramanian, A., 160, 329, 341, 353, 354, 521, 522

Summers, L., 92, 111, 118
Sung, Y. W., 147
Sykes, A., 388, 418
Syropoulos, C. 106, 114, 120

Taiwan Statistical Data Book, 162
Takacs, W., 294
Tan, L. H., 283
Tang, M., 118
Tangermann, S., 472
Tarr, D. G., 284
Taylor, M. S., 234
Textile Asia, 276
Tho, N. S., 147
Thurow, L., 118
Tobey, J. A., 237
Trela, I., 19, 271, 276, 278, 281–285, 294, 301
Tsay, C., 177
Tumlir, J. 547
Tyers, R., 457, 458, 463

United Nations (UN), 142
United Nations Conference on Trade and Development (UNCTAD), 248, 271, 275, 279, 495
United Nations Development Programme (UNDP), 353, 354
United Nations Environment Programme, 354
United Nations Industrial Development Organization, 288, 289
United Nations International Trade Commission, 322
United States Department of Agriculture (USDA), 472
United States General Accounting Office, 376, 384
United States International Trade Commission (USITC), 276

Valdes, A., 442, 455, 456, 459, 460, 458, 472
van Bael, I., 417
van der Mensbrugghe, 237, 241
Vanzetti, D., 461
Vaughan, S., 236
Verbiest, J. P., 118
Vermulst, E., 377, 383, 401, 418
Vincent, D., 466
Vines, D., 106

Waer, P., 377, 383, 401, 418
Wagner, S., 330
Walsh, J., 246
Wang, Z., 40, 103, 118
Washington Post, 134
Wattal, J., 333, 360
Wei, S. J., 94, 111, 112, 114, 117, 118, 120
Whalley, J., 19, 108, 180, 276, 281–285, 295, 301, 453
Wheeler, D., 241, 261
Wigle, R., 453

Wijngaarden van, R., 368
Wilson, J., 40, 75
Winter, S. G., 330, 333
Winters, L. A., 111, 118
Wong, K. Y., 187
Wonnacott, P., 107
Woo, W. T., 159, 162
Wood, A., 75
World Bank, 141, 143, 144, 147, 148, 150, 151, 161, 485, 539
World Trade Organization (WTO), 117

Yanagishima, K., 103, 284, 300, 301
Yang, Y. Z., 442, 461, 462, 464, 465
Yeats, A., 8, 86, 293
Yoffie, D., 105
Young, A., 189, 195

Zietz, J., 442, 455, 456, 459, 458, 472
Zimmerman, K. F., 181–184

SUBJECT INDEX

Ad-valorem tariff equivalents, 450 (table)
Agreement on Agriculture, 35-9, 437, 438-51, 469
  base period, 446, 448
  economic impact of, 38-9
  impact of, 453-5, 460-9, 478-9
  safeguard measures, 448-9
Agreement on the Application of Sanitary and Phyto-Sanitary Measures, 451-3
Agreement on the Trade-Related Aspects of Intellectual Property Rights, see TRIPs Agreement
Agriculture, 24, 35, 244, 334, 338, 384-5, 477-8
  commodities, 447 (table)
  exempted from GATT, 437-8
  production, relocation of, 464-6
  protectionism, 437
  see also Agreement on Agriculture
Air transport services, 542n38
Antidumping, 25-6, 426-7
  weakness of dispute system in, 32
  see also Antidumping measures
Antidumping measures (ADMs), 366, 367-83, 402-3
  alternative to formal SGMs, 385
  by and against Asian developing countries, 404-13 (table)

Code, 26-7, 376-83, 427
  economic effects of, 27
  policy debate on, 369-75
  SGMs, compared with, 391-2
  spread of, 414-15 (charts)
  use of, 367-9
Apparel, see Textiles and apparel
Asia-Pacific Economic Cooperation forum (APEC), 6, 73-4, 84, 98, 112, 134, 523
Association of Southeast Asian Nations (ASEAN), 7, 83, 132-3

Banking services, 509-10 (table), 540n14
Berne Convention, 345 (table)
Bond flows, 149-50, 151 (table)
Business services, 506-07 (table)

Capital
  contribution to growth, 155-7
  flows, 139-42, 143 (table), 151, 159
  see also Portfolio capital, Private capital
Capital market integration, 150
  Asia, 139-61, 166-9
  precondition for currency union, 167-8
  stability and, 158, 159-60
Chemicals, see Pharmaceuticals
Child labor, 64-5, 214-15
People's Republic of China (PRC)
  impact of MFA elimination on, 286

Chinese language
    as factor in gravity model, 96
Clothing, *see* Textiles and apparel
Communications services, 507-08
    (table)
Competition policy, 68-9, 371-2
Computer software, 339, 345
    (table)
Construction services, 508 (table)
Convention on the Rights of the
    Child, 63, 76n17
Copyright, 352 n8
    protection of, 312, 313
        (table), 315-16, 345 (table)
    see also Piracy
Cultural services, 511 (table)
Currency union
    preconditions for, 167-8

Deforestation, 244
Dispute settlement, 30-3, 428-30
    GATT system, 392-5
    procedures, 324, 350 (table)
    provisions under GATS, 537
    WTO system, 367, 395-402
    see also Uruguay Round
        Understanding on Rules and
        Procedures Governing the
        Settlement of Disputes
Distribution services, 508 (table)
Domestic support, 37, 441-2, 445

East Asian Economic Caucus
    (EAEC), 7
Econometric models, *see* Gravity
    model
Economic growth rates, 486, 487
    (table)
Educational services, 508-9 (table)
Environment
    agreements, 238, 240

controls, contrary effect of,
    259-60
developing Asia, impact of,
    243-4
product life cycle, impact of,
    235-6
protection, in context of
    sustainable development,
    258
services, 509 (table)
trade, effect of, 233-5
trade liberalization, effect of,
    241-3
Environmental policies, 236-7
    factors contributing to
        adoption of, 260-2
    trade, links between,
        231-2
Environmental standards, 10, 12,
    54-62, 237-8
    extension to low standard
        countries, 58-60
    "race to the bottom" theory,
        57
European Community, 83
European Union, 83
    antidumping law, 383
    Asia, effect on, 89-91
    social charter on workers'
        rights, 205-06, 207, 221 n1
Exhaustion, 340, 344 (table), 352
    n7, 359
Export, 4-6, 40 n1
    commercial services, 488
        (table), 490-1 (table), 492
        (table), 494 (table)
    constituencies, 111-12
    environmentally sensitive,
        247, 248 (table)
    merchandise, 488 (table)
    subsidies, 440-1, 445, 469

Films, 339
Financial services, 509-10 (table),
513-16, 542 n38
Food consumption, 466
Foreign direct investment (FDI),
142, 144-7, 160, 161 n2,
201, 488, 489
growth of, 522-3
impact of NAFTA on, 8
inflows, 495 (table)
intellectual property
protection, effects of , 335-6
(table)
Japan and, 168-9
portfolio investment,
compared with, 157, 166-7
Free trade
free trade areas and, 131
labor standards and, 210
Free trade areas, 70-4, 105
of the Americas, effects of
enlarged, 88-9
APEC-wide, 9
business support for,
an exemption of sectors in,
107
exploitation of rules of origin
by, 107
geographically proximate,
118n18
misunderstandings, 119 n26
obstacle to multilateralism,
108-9

General Agreement on Tariffs and
Trade (GATT), xvii, 35, 49,
68, 106, 132, 471, 477-8
agriculture exempted under,
437-8
dispute settlement system,
392-5

GATS, compared with, 483-4,
546
limited application of labor
standards, 207
safeguard measures
authorized by, 365, 383-4
state trading enterprises, 451
General Agreement on Trade in
Services (GATS), 33-5, 489,
492, 494, 496-7, 525, 538-9
application of provisions, 497
compared with GATT, 483-4,
546
definitions, 527, 537-8
general obligations and
disciplines, 527-34
market access limitations,
498-9
role of national treatment
commitment, 499
schedules of specific
commitments in, 34, 497-8,
500-03, 504-12 (table),
525, 534-7
scope, 527
trade liberalizing agreement,
545
Genetic resources, 340-1, 354n19
and n20
Geographical indications
protection of, 314 (table),
319, 346 (table)
Gold-collar workers, 226
Gravity model, 92-4, 97, 115
trade, 99-100 (table)
Gross capital flows, 151
Gross domestic product, 244
Gross national product (GNP)
factor in gravity model, 93
FDI as percentage of, 142,
144 (table)

relationship with real wages, 216, 217 (table)
Gross trade flows, 151

Havana Charter, 542 n34
Health-related services, 510 (table)
Hong Kong
    labor market, 189-90
    migrant workers, 177

Immigration
    Hong Kong, 189-90
    external effects, 180
    policies, 184-5, 199
    unemployment and, 181, 182-4
Importers, 490-01 (table)
Income, see Per capita income
Income growth
    as factor in environmental quality, 244-5
Industrial design, 314 (table)
Insurance services, 509 (table), 540n14
Integrated circuits, 313 (table), 316, 347 (table)
Intellectual property
    Conventions, Asian membership of, 315 (table)
    protection, access to products consequent on, 360-1
    protection, inadequate enforcement of, 321-2
    see also TRIPs Agreement
Interest rates differentials, 152-4
International Convention for the Protection of New Varieties of Plants (UPOV), 312, 337, 338
International Labour Organisation (ILO), 3

conventions on labor standards, 207
Investment, 156-7
    see also Foreign direct investment, Trade-related investment measures

Japan
    migrant workers, 176
Jones Act, The (US), 540 n19

Korea
    migrant workers, 176-7

Labor market
    flexibility, 188-92, 194
    integration, 173-94
    measurement of, 173
Labor movement
    Asia, 173
    changes in pattern, 199
    economic efficiency and, 179-81
    future demand in Asia, 178-9
    linked to capital flows, 201
    long-term growth and, 181-2
    restrictions, 184-7, 192
    unemployment and, 182-4
    within Asia, 174-7
    see also Migrant workers
Labor rights
    enforcement, 219
    labor standards, distinguished from, 218
Labor standards, 3, 10, 14-15, 54, 62-8, 224-7
    arguments for rise in, 211-15
    definition of, 207
    economics, 207-10
    labor rights, 218

international harmonization, 209

mechanisms for raising, 215-17

perception of, in developing countries, 193

social clause for, 62, 65, 66

trade policy, 205-06, 214

Labor unions, 64, 65, 181, 215

Languages

common, as factor in gravity model, 93

Law of one price, 139, 152-4

Licensing, 320, 348 (table)

compulsory, 24, 340, 347 (table)

Malaysian migrant workers, 177

Marakesh Agreement Establishing the World Trade Organisation, 471

Maritime transport services, 518-20

Market access, 34, 49, 445, 483, 498-9, 501-03, 504-05 (table), 534-5

Matsushita v Zenith Radio Corporation (1986), 417 n5

MERCOSUR, 40 n4, 70, 83, 120 n34

Mexico, 87, 88

Migrant workers, 191-2

demand for, 195 n4

national composition, 175-6

Most-favored nation (MFN), 311, 344 (table), 496

exemptions, 514, 515, 528, 541 n26

Multifiber Arrangement (MFA), 16, 193

effects on Asian economies of elimination, 281-8, 289

long-term effect of elimination, 275-81

phaseout of, 17-18, 19-20, 267-93, 298-302

Multilateral trade liberalization

implications of regional trading arrangements for, 105-17

support for FTAs an obstacle to, 108-09

Natural persons

movement of, 503, 512-13

Natural resources, 232

Net capital flows, 140-1, 143 (table)

North American Free Trade Area (NAFTA), 6, 8, 71, 112, 523

Asia, effect on, 86-8

debate on, 131

negotiations, 205

North-south attitudes, 49-52

Openness to trade, 115-16

Organisation of Economic and Cooperative Development (OECD), 524

Parallel imports, 340, 344 (table), 352 n7, 358

Patents, 311-12, 313 (table), 356-7 (table)

Per capita income, 155, 194n1, 245

Pharmaceuticals, 23-4

impact of TRIPs provisions, 326-7, 330-4, 349 (table)

patent protection for, 311

Phyto-sanitary measures, 451-3
Piracy, 321 (table), 358
Plant varieties, 312, 337-8, 347 (table)
Plurilateral agreements, 542 n36
Pollution, 233, 234, 245
    global, 60-1
    national, 11-12
    transnational, 13
Population, 243
Portfolio capital, 117 n5, 147-9, 157, 158
Portfolio investment
    compared with FDI, 157, 166-7
Preferential trading areas, 7, 120 n29
    see also Free trade areas
Price
    Agreement on Agriculture, effects of, 460-3
    controls, 339-40
    discrimination, 370-2
    trade liberalization, effect of, 455-60
    stability, 463-4
Private capital, 142
Product
    diversification, 280
    life cycle impact on environment, 235-6
    standards, 237
Production
    elimination of MFA, effects of, 284-6
Property rights, 233, 244
Public choice, 374-5

Quality upgrading, 279-80
Quotas, 17, 18
    allocation under MFA, 281

growth rates for textiles and clothing, 270, 271 (table), 273
MFA, export tax equivalents of, 301 (table)
offsetting effects of, 279-80
restrictiveness and utilization of, 277-9

Recreational services, 511 (table)
Regional trading arrangements, 83, 131, 250-1
    implications for multilateral trade liberalization, 105-17
Regionalism, 6-10
Rent transfers
    termination between textile importing and exporting countries, 276
Research and development, 328-30, 333-4, 338
Rules of origin
    exploitation by FTAs, 107

Safeguard measures (SGM), 18, 40 n12, 270, 272, 298-9, 428, 448-9
    alternatives to, 384-6
    Code, 28-9, 389-92
    compared with ADMs, 391
    exceptions to trade liberalization, 387-9
    under GATT, 365, 383
Sanitary measures, 451-3
Services and service industry, 483-5
    see also General Agreement on Trade in Services, Trade in services
Singapore, 190-2

Social clause
in WTO, 62, 65, 66
Social services, 510 (table)
South Asian Association for
Regional Cooperation
(SAARC), 83, 102-03
South Asian Preferential Trading
Area (SAPTA), 7
Sporting services, 511 (table)
Standards
see Environmental standards,
Labor standards, Product
standards
State enterprises, 449, 451
Stock markets, 148, 149 (table)
Subsidies, 36-7, 41n15, 440-1,
445
"Sullivan Principles", 58, 215
Sustainable development, 258

Taipei,China
direct investment, 142, 147,
168
migrant workers, 177
Tariffs, 384, 439-40, 442, 445,
448, 469, 478-9
agricultural commodities, 36,
38
changes in tariff escalation,
443-4 (table)
estimated ad-valorem
equivalents, compared with,
450 (table)
preferences, 133
reductions, 290, 294 n7
Technology, 320
transfer, 329-30, 335-6 (table)
Telecommunications, 516-18
Terms-of-trade
labor standards, effect on, 209

Test data, 314 (table), 319-20, 347
(table)
Textiles and apparel, 16-17, 384
restraint on world trade in,
267
see also Multifiber
Arrangement, Uruguay
Round Agreement on
Textiles and Clothing
Tourist services, 510 (table)
Trade
Asian, key indicators of, 5
(table)
elimination of MFA, effects
of, 284-6
environment, in relation to
233-5
growth in, as factor in
environmental quality,
245-50
sanctions, 13, 253 n6
secrets, 319-20, 347 (table)
strategies for Asian countries,
100-04
substitute for labor mobility,
187-8
unions, see Labor unions
world, sub-periods in, 195 n3
Trade blocs, 10, 103, 104,
113-14
effect on non-members, 85
in Asia, 9, 84, 91-2, 94-8
"incentive to protect",
105-07
see also Free trade areas
Trade in services, 486-9, 490-2
(tables), 493-4 (tables)
post-Uruguay Round work
program, 503, 512-20
see also GATS

Trade liberalization
environmental effects, 241-3
temporary exceptions to,
387-8
welfare effects of, 468 (table)
Trade policies, 15-16, 20, 24-5
environmental consequences
of, 239
instruments of, 25
linked with labor standards,
205-06, 214
links between environment
and, 231-2, 239, 251
misappropriation of, as
environmental policy, 259
Trade related investment measures
(TRIMs), 485, 520-2, 525-6,
541 n22
Trade remedies, see Antidumping
measures, Safeguard
measures, Voluntary restraint
agreements
Trademarks, 314 (table), 319, 345
(table), 352 n10
Transport services, 511-12 (table),
518-20
Travel-related services, 510 (table)
TRIPs Agreement, 20-1, 311, 344-
50 (table)
application of dispute
procedures to, 324, 350
(table)
Asia, impact on 312-25,
342-3
economic impact of, 23-4,
325, 328-36, 338-9
enforcement provisions, 22,
321-4, 348-9 (table)
factors in success, 341-2
origins, 307-09
significance, 309-10, 359-60

transitional arrangements,
325, 349 (table)
Undisclosed information, 314
(table), 319-20, 347 (table)
Unemployment
immigration and, 181, 182-4
"Unfair" competition, 54, 56, 62,
372-4
Unilateral liberalization, 100, 101,
119 n20
United States
antidumping legislation, 376,
377-8, 382
labor standards in, 63-4
Unskilled labor, 52-3
Uruguay Round, xvii, 307, 437
agreements, implications for
Asia, 301-02, 544-5
effects on market access for
Asian economies, 290-3
enforcement, 367
Final Act, 421 n83
Uruguay Round Agreement, 3, 16
Uruguay Round Agreement on
Textiles and Clothing, 17,
268-75, 294 n3, 299-300
Uruguay Round Understanding
on Rules and Procedures
Governing the Settlement of
Disputes (Understanding), 30-
3, 367, 392, 429

Video cassettes, 339
Voluntary restraint agreements
(VRAs), 365, 386-7, 392

Wages, 15, 182, 216
apparel industries, 289 (table)
Singapore, 190-1
unskilled, 52, 53, 213-4
Waste imports, 247, 250 (table)

Welfare
    elimination of MFA, 282-4
    labor standards, impact of,
        208
    national, 370-1
    trade liberalization, effects of,
        468 (table)
World economy
    attitudes to integration, 50-4
    services in, 486-9
World Intellectual Property
    Organization (WIPO), 308
World Trade Organization, xvii,
        359, 471
    dispute settlement system,
        367, 395-402
    disputes involving developing
        countries, 416 (table)
    forum for environmental
        issues, 243
    social clause, 62, 65, 66